Existentialism and the Philosophical Tradition

Existentialism and the Philosophical Tradition

DIANE BARSOUM RAYMOND
Simmons College

PRENTICE HALL, Englewood Cliffs, New Jersey 07632

Library of Congress Cataloging-in-Publication Data

Existentialism and the philosophical tradition / [compiled by] Diane
  Barsoum Raymond.
      p.   cm.
    Includes bibliographical references and index.
    ISBN 0-13-295775-2
    1. Existentialism.   I. Raymond, Diane Christine
  B819.E86 1990
  142'.78--dc20   90-33746
                                                         CIP

Editorial/production supervision and
   interior design: Patricia V. Amoroso
Cover design: Marianne Frasco
Prepress buyer: Herb Klein
Manufacturing buyer: David Dickey

Printed in the United States of America

10 9 8 7 6 5 4 3

ISBN 0-13-295775-2

PRENTICE-HALL INTERNATIONAL (UK) LIMITED, London
PRENTICE-HALL OF AUSTRALIA PTY. LIMITED, Sydney
PRENTICE-HALL CANADA INC., Toronto
PRENTICE-HALL HISPANOAMERICANA, S.A., Mexico
PRENTICE-HALL OF INDIA PRIVATE LIMITED, New Delhi
PRENTICE-HALL OF JAPAN, INC., Tokyo
SIMON & SCHUSTER ASIA PTE. LTD., Singapore
EDITORA PRENTICE-HALL DO BRASIL, LTDA., Rio de Janeiro

To my daughter Katherine,
whose love of learning is an inspiration to me

It is not necessary at all—not even desirable—that you should argue in my favor; on the contrary, a dose of curiosity, as in the presence of a foreign plant, with an ironic resistance, would seem to me an incomparably more intelligent attitude.

FRIEDRICH NIETZSCHE

Contents

5   FREEDOM AND RESPONSIBILITY   *292*

6   THE OTHER AND THE BODY   *368*

7   EXISTENTIALISM AND THE MORAL LIFE   *440*

Preface

Today, the philosophy of existentialism lacks the notoriety it once had in this country and abroad. Particularly since the deaths of Sartre and de Beauvoir, existentialism has lost popularity. However, it is still worthy of serious attention. Indeed, it is taught in most undergraduate philosophy curricula. And undergraduate students continue to be excited and engaged by the issues central to existentialist philosophy: anxiety and alienation, meaning, freedom, intersubjectivity, and authenticity.

This text is a result of my fifteen years of teaching undergraduate philosophy, including existentialism. During that time, I experimented with a variety of teaching approaches. Some semesters I used all primary texts; other semesters I used a number of different anthologies, at times supplementing them with a primary text or two or a work of fiction, such as *The Plague* by Camus. I was never completely satisfied with any approach. The primary text approach suffered from a number of shortcomings. Students often complained about the long period of time committed to one person's work, and I was keenly aware of the number of important existentialist thinkers who had to be omitted because of time constraints and the expense of additional books. Yet I found the available anthologies almost useless pedagogically. Students were both unimpressed and confused by the short selections and the unexplained leaps from one thinker to another. In addition, there was little or no introductory material to ground the student in the philosophical history so essential to understanding existentialism.

I hope that *Existentialism and the Philosophical Tradition* overcomes these difficulties. In the introduction to each chapter I provide the history of the philosophical issue under consideration. With this basis the student new to philosophy will be familiar with some of the more important philosophical approaches to these themes. Others, who have had previous philosophy courses, can reacquaint themselves with the background material. In this way, all students will better appreciate both the complexities of the issues and the uniqueness of existentialism's approach to them.

Further, I have included reading selections that are representative of the thinker and are of sufficient length to provide a feeling for stylistic nuance and a basis for understanding the writer's philosophical position. Many of the readings I have chosen—for example, Kierkegaard's *Fear and Trembling*—are considered classics of existentialism; others, such as Heidegger's "What Is Metaphysics?" and the excerpt from Jaspers, are less well known. There is sufficient breadth here that students will become aware of the divergences within existentialist philosophy. In addition, the fictional selections provide another, perhaps more compelling, approach to the theoretical materials.

A cursory glance at the Contents reveals that this text is organized thematically rather than historically. Having found that students respond with greater interest to such an approach, I focus on the key themes of existentialism, including alienation, freedom, interpersonal relationships, and ethics. The chapter on existentialism and theism (featuring lengthy selections from Kierkegaard) considers an issue that most existentialism anthologies ignore or trivialize. The chapter on intersubjectivity contrasts differing existentialist views on this issue and includes an important discussion of a feminist perspective on " the other." The final chapter explores the question of whether the notion of an existentialist ethic makes sense. But despite this thematic approach, this text can be adapted to a number of different pedagogical approaches, including more historical ones.

There is enough material in this text for a full semester's work, and it is intended to serve as a primary text for undergraduate courses in existentialism. Some instructors, however, may wish to supplement this text with other readings. I suggest the following, all of which appear in inexpensive paperback editions: *No Exit, Nausea,* and *The Flies* by Sartre; *The Misunderstanding, Caligula,* and *The Stranger* by Camus (I often begin the semester with *The Stranger* before students have read anything else); and *A Very Easy Death,* by de Beauvoir. I refer to these works in chapter introductions, and having students read them will obviously make the references more meaningful. In addition, each chapter ends with a list of suggested readings for those students who want to explore topics in greater depth.

It would be impossible to recognize all those whose helpful suggestions improved this collection, but I want to single out the following people for special thanks: Elisabeth Angus, Rose Barsoum, Michael Hoffman, Chip Hughes, Linda Singer, and Hugh Wilder. I thank our department secretary, Cathy Clunie, who made time in her already frantic schedule for this book. I would also like to acknowledge the reviewers of this text: Hugh Wilder of The College of Charleston, Charleston, South Carolina; Winston A. Wilkinson of Michigan State University, East Lansing, Michigan; and W. Michael Hoffman of Bentley College, Waltham, Massachusetts. Though I did not make all the changes they urged, their comments were enormously helpful. Finally, my work on this volume was greatly facilitated by the staff at Prentice Hall; in particular, Pattie Amoroso provided just the right combination of nudging, encouragement, and support.

Existentialism and the Philosophical Tradition

Introduction:
What Is Existentialism?

This is the age when man has become fully and thoroughly problematic to himself.
Max Scheler

Jean-Paul Sartre once complained that the word *existentialism* was "so loosely applied to so many things that it no longer means anything at all." (*Existentialism*, p. 15) What began as a serious philosophy soon became a fad, so that the label was applied not only to self-professed representatives of the philosophy itself but also to others more remotely connected to it in style or content. Few philosophers have called themselves existentialists, and some, like Kierkegaard and Nietzsche, predate the use of the term. To what does *existentialism* refer?

Some of the difficulty in defining existentialism results from characteristics of the philosophy itself. For example, most existentialists deny that reality can be neatly summarized into a system, and so they reject all-inclusive views like Hegel's. This does not mean that existentialists are unsystematic, but rather that they tend to emphasize the richness of human experience rather than construct a tidy theoretical framework. As Gabriel Marcel has put it: "Whatever its ultimate meaning, the universe into which we have been thrown cannot satisfy our reason — let us have the courage to admit it once and for all." (*The Philosophy of Existentialism*, p. 124) Reality cannot ever be summed up, demonstrated through a series of deductive arguments. And the more one tries to synthesize the richness of experience, the more individual experiences drop out, leaving a series of platitudes, lifeless and bland and unfaithful to reality. But their repudiation of schematic thinking makes classification of existentialist philosophers extremely problematic.

Philosophers have traditionally defined *Homo sapiens* as the rational animal. Existentialists, however, have refused to privilege the intellect, seeking instead to provide accounts of a variety of human experiences, including will and emotion. Many have preferred poetry and fiction to capture such experiences without imprisoning them in philosophical categories and systems. Existentialism does not ignore rationality, but it is suspicious of the sort of mystique of reason to which so many earlier philosophers have succumbed. Traditional philosophers have tended to assume that "true" philosophy is grounded in the intellect, which is capable of understanding the workings of the universe and our place in it. But existentialist thinkers have asserted the validity of nonintellectual modes of experience and the responsibility of philosophy to re-cover and explore these new categories. As Spanish philosopher Miguel de Unamuno points out, we philosophize not with reason only, but with the entire body and soul. "Philosophy is a product of the humanity of each philosopher." (*The Tragic Sense of Life*, p. 28)

Finally, there is great diversity among existential thinkers themselves. Some, for example, hold that God exists, whereas others do not. Some are more optimistic than others about the meaningfulness of human existence. Some emphasize freedom, others absurdity, and still others the world of the interpersonal. Those who deal with similar topics often treat them in quite different ways. For these reasons, it has been suggested that existentialism be thought of not as a philosophy but rather as a style of philosophizing. Certainly, the writers we will be exploring here do not form a school in the usual sense that, say, Thomism or Stoicism or Utilitarianism does. Some philosophers have even suggested that no self-respecting existentialist would ever accept the label *existentialist*, for that would be to agree to limit oneself unnecessarily.

Some critics, noting the divergent perspectives that characterize existentialism, have dismissed that view as unphilosophical, unsystematic, or idiosyncratic. How can philosophy not be systematic? How can philosophers write poetry? Others more sympathetic to existentialism have responded to this charge by accepting it and valorizing it; that is, they argue that it is precisely this antisystematic character of existentialism that recommends it to us. Such a character offers, they claim, a refreshing breath of air from smothering, rigid, conventional philosophy. This text, however, rejects the view that existentialism is un- or even antisystematic. Granted, there are differences within existentialism. Not all of what existentialists claim can be true (e.g., God exists and God does not exist). Existentialism rejects systematic philosophy if what that term refers to is any view that claims to capture the world of human existence with tidy formulae that ultimately erase all difference. But the major existentialist thinkers we will discuss — Camus, de Beauvoir, Heidegger, Kierkegaard, Merleau-Ponty, Nietzsche, and Sartre — are all systematic thinkers though they all reject the possibility of a fixed, complete system. One should not, then, let the unconventional methods of expression that existentialists employ — autobiography, aphorism, drama, poetry, narrative — prevent one from looking for the vision around which those writings are organized. Many of the major existentialist thinkers, as we shall see, present complex networks of concepts, employ technical terms, classify phenomena, and provide arguments in defense of their positions. And even though these writings do not always agree, existentialism itself is characterized by several general themes, which we outline in this introduction.

This text attempts to make sense of existentialist philosophy. It is not organized in any straightforwardly chronological sense (though chapters 3 and 4 on Kierkegaard and Nietzsche are more clearly historical than others). Rather, its focus is a thematic one, exploring some of the major topics that recur in the writings of existentialists. No one book (or even several) can capture all of this rich and multidimensional philosophy; certainly no one chapter of a text can do that. But this introduction, like succeeding chapters, looks at a contrasting philosophical approach in the history of philosophy. This strategy may afford a better sense of what distinguishes existentialism from other philosophical systems.

PLATO AND THE BEGINNINGS
OF WESTERN PHILOSOPHY

It has been said that all philosophy is nothing but a footnote to Plato. Though this statement is exaggerated, there is no doubt that the philosophical system of Plato — its metaphysics, epistemology, politics, ethics, and even aesthetics — sets a tone for much of the future of philosophy; in particular Plato raised a series of questions that succeeding philosophers have struggled, in their varied ways, to answer.

Before Socrates and Plato, there were Greek philosophers — fragments of whose views we now possess — who began to raise questions about the nature of the world and our place in that cosmos. In particular, these pre-Socratics developed cosmologies that attempted to explain the workings of the universe. Further, as early metaphysicians, they sought to discover the essential "what-ness" of the material world. Some said it was fire, others water, still others atoms that formed building blocks of all that was. Some were dualists, maintaining that the world was, for example, essentially light and dark; others defended a unitary explanation.

It was the pre-Socratic Heraclitus who coined the statement, "You cannot step twice into the same river." All, he maintained, is flux; like the river whose waters are always flowing past, the world and our knowledge of it are in constant change. It is a small step from this claim to that of

Heraclitus' student Cratylus, who insisted that it was not possible to step into the same river even *once*. Thus, all is relative and temporary.

The pre-Socratic Protagoras connected this view of the nature of the world to the realm of the individual perceiver. "Man is the measure of all things: of things that are, that they are; of things that are not, that they are not." (Fragment 1) Protagoras argued that our perception of the world tells us what is true about the world. Thus, there is no higher order to knowledge, no authority on matters of truth. Each person's perception counts as being true.

The vehemence with which Plato challenged these views may surprise many of us. Indeed, statements like those of Heraclitus and Protagoras are almost truisms today. We are all too aware of flux: We have seen science move from Newtonian physics to Einstein's theory of relativity to Heisenberg's uncertainty principle; we have studied far more cultures than Plato knew existed, and we speak disparagingly of the ethnocentrism of individuals who judge other cultures based on their own cultural values; we marvel even at how aesthetic standards change from one time period to another, from one social grouping to the next. We have seen abandoned much that once was held to be incontrovertibly true. We are comfortable with statements such as, "It may be right for you, but not for me," and "We have no right to impose our moral judgments on others," and even "Nothing is certain." Such relativism seems unthreatening. For Plato, however, it would mean the end of philosophy, and his system is devoted to the search for certain and universal knowledge.

The term *philosophy* comes from two Greek words: *philos* (love of) and *sophia* (wisdom). The true philosopher, Plato claimed, is a seeker after truth without regard for consequences. The search for truth is incompatible with desire for material comforts, even absorption in family concerns. As Socrates, Plato's teacher, described his mission: "For I spend all my time going about trying to persuade you, young and old, to make your first and chief concern not for your bodies nor for your possessions, but for the highest welfare of your souls." (*Apology* 30b) But how does one know when one has found truth?

Plato believed that the world of the everyday cannot provide a basis for knowledge. Like the Skeptics, who argued that knowledge is impossible (some even went so far as to refuse to utter assertions!), Plato maintained that knowledge must be universal, immutable, and eternal. Our sense perception, in contrast, is notoriously inaccurate and deceptive. Think of simple optical illusions, or a mirage in the desert, or even judgments about time and distance. We are frequently mistaken about what is real — the straight stick looks bent when we place it in water, the magician's tricks lead us to believe over and over in what is not real, and our perception of food and drink changes when we have a fever. The body, for Plato, is a distraction from the truth, and the true philosopher in pursuit of wisdom despises the body. In searching for the real nature of things, one must cut oneself off from the senses, for they are unclear and inaccurate. According to Plato,

> [T]he body provides us with innumerable distractions in the pursuit of our necessary sustenance, and any diseases which attack us hinder our quest for reality. Besides, the body fills us with loves and desires and fears and all sorts of fancies and a great deal of nonsense, with the result that we literally never get an opportunity to think at all about anything. Wars and revolutions and battles are due simply and solely to the body and its desires. All wars are undertaken for the acquisition of wealth, and the reason why we have to acquire wealth is the body, because we are slaves in its service. That is why, on all these accounts, we have so little time for philosophy. Worst of all, if we do obtain any leisure from the body's claims and turn to some line of inquiry, the body intrudes once more into our investigation, interrupting, disturbing, distracting, and preventing us from getting a glimpse of the truth.
>
> *Phaedo, 66b–d*

Though we cannot escape the body, it is possible for us to achieve a harmony that enables us to pursue wisdom. Such wisdom, Plato says, cannot be based on sense perception alone, for the world we perceive is one of constant change. If everything changes, deteriorates, and dies, what can we know? If, as Protagoras claimed, "man is the measure of all things" epistemological and ethical, then there might be a different truth for each of us; but this would mean that *nothing* is false, in which case perhaps there is nothing that is true. Indeed, why do we need teachers if "each of us is himself the measure of his own wisdom"? (Plato, *Theaetetus*, 161de)

Finally, Plato explained not only how we can know in a world of change and error, but also how we learn the basic elements of that knowledge, that is, *concepts.* A concept tells us what is the essence of some idea, the essential "what-ness" of beings in the world, whether they are tables or persons or trees or straight lines. Yet it seems clear that we have never had an experience of a concept, for concepts are not subjects of sense perception but are ideas. From what, then, do we derive these ideas? However many trees we have seen, each is unique: Our concept of a tree is neither a summary of all the trees we have seen, nor is it one unique tree we have picked out from all the trees we have observed. Even more confounding is that we have never even had the experience of, say, certain mathematical concepts like a perfect straight line. Yet we do know what is a tree, and we do understand the concept of a straight line.

For Plato, there can be only one solution to these puzzles: Since he was not willing to abandon philosophy, then knowledge must be possible. But true knowledge can only be of the eternal and unchanging. Since everything material constantly changes and inevitably deteriorates and dies or changes into some other form, knowledge cannot be knowledge of this world. The material world, said Plato, is not the real world, but rather a shadow world. Reality lies in the world of the Forms, which contains in it perfect versions of what our concepts refer to. There is a perfect tree, perfect straight line, perfect color blue, and perfect goodness, the highest of all the forms. And we judge lines, trees, people, colors, and so forth by how closely they mirror ("participate in," as some translations put Plato's phrase) the perfect form that resides in this other world. In the *Republic*, Plato's treatise on politics and justice, Socrates tells a story meant to explain by analogy his theory of the forms. This story, now referred to as the analogy of the cave, relates a parable wherein cave dwellers with their legs and necks "fettered from childhood" mistakenly confuse the shadow cast by objects and peoples from above with real objects.

All of us, according to Plato, are like those cave dwellers. Our world is like the cave where we see shadows on the wall and mistake them for reality (see *Republic*, VII, 514–517). And those — the philoso-phers — who *have* seen the light are taunted, even punished, by the cave dwellers who refuse to emerge from the shadows. "And if it were possible to lay hands on and kill the man who tried to release them and lead them up, would they not kill him?" (*Republic*, 517a)

For Plato, it is no wonder that the journey into truth changes a person irrevocably. The ordinary concerns of everyday life seem insig-nificant in comparison with the light of truth.

> [D]o not be surprised that those who have attained to this height are not willing to occupy themselves with the affairs of men, but their souls ever feel the upward urge and the yearning for that sojourn above. For this, I take it, is likely if in this point too the likeness of our image holds.
>
> *Republic, 517d*

How, though, can one know in any real sense, if we are so caught up in the everyday and divorced from this perfect world? What is the con-nection between this world and that one? Plato's theory of reality does not automatically solve the problem of knowledge until he provides us with a theory of knowledge that gives us access to the world of forms. The answer for Plato lies in the transmigration of souls: reincarnation. It is only after we die that we catch glimpses of this other world, so that when we are once again embodied we come into the world with knowledge. Some of us who have died and been reborn many times have had more opportunity to attend to these perfect models, and so we may be wiser. But regardless, Socrates believed that a true teacher does not impart new information to a student but rather acts as a "midwife" to help the student give birth to his or her own ideas.

It is not difficult to find criticisms of this theory of knowledge. Beginning with Aristotle almost immediately after Plato, there were devastating challenges to the Platonic system. Our purpose here is not to enumerate those criticisms or the competing proposals. It is, rather, to emphasize that (1) the Platonic system is a coherent one whose pieces fit together like an intricate jigsaw puzzle; (2) the Platonic system provides an alternative to the aforementioned problem of relativism; and (3) the Platonic system had profound repercussions for the history of philosophy. Let's look at some of those repercussions in the context of our exploration of existentialism.

The Platonic system has several important implications. In particular, Plato's idealism leads to a number of dualisms. For one, there is the dualism of mind and body in which body imprisons mind (or soul). This dichotomy between the mental and the physical is grounded in the belief that the physical is the basis of error and temptation. The body houses the soul, yet it is the source of great suffering and pain. The life of intellectual contemplation — the life of the philosopher — is the ideal. Sense perception, whose origin is the material body, cannot be trusted to reveal knowledge. In addition, the material world is not the real world, for matter changes, deteriorates, and dies. The rational and the true cannot be part of that world of shadows. Rather, the world of forms provides the metaphysical basis for our understanding of the material world. Through it, we know the essence of all that is. Reason becomes the vehicle by which we know truth; all other aspects of human experience are inferior. Thus, the world of Plato is a static one in which what is truly real is rational, unchanging, and complete. Our proper function in life is to use our faculty of reason to discover this world.

Plato's impact on the future of philosophy is undeniable. Systematic thinkers, however much they disagreed with the specifics of Plato's arguments, tended to accept many of his presuppositions. For one, the body tends to be held in contempt; even nonreligious philosophers tend to view the physical body as the vehicle for sin, whether it be moral or intellectual. In addition, the methodology of most philosophies has been based on the elevation of rationality and deductive thinking. Indeed, many philosophers, such as Descartes and Spinoza, used mathematics as the paradigm for speculative thinking. Further, philosophers tend to be suspicious of sense perception, viewing it as notoriously untrustworthy. The senses do not provide us with certainty, with what is truly real, that is, the unchanging. Finally, philosophers continue to struggle with the question of essence. Can we ever really know the essential "what-ness" of some thing in the world? How do we bridge the gap between our perception of what is and the reality of what is? For many philosophers, we cannot. Thus, for Berkeley, we get *esse est percipi* — to be is to be perceived — that the existence of an external world depends on our (or God's) perception of it. This sort of thinking culminates in the metaphysics of Kant, who maintained that we cannot reach the *noumenal* world, the world of the real, but must instead be satisfied with the *phenomenal* appearances of things, knowing that they are grounded in a deeper, noumenal reality. (See chapter 2, pages 93–95, for a more detailed analysis of the modern period and existentialist philosophy.)

How has existentialism broken with this tradition? For existentialists, existence — that something is — precedes essence — what it is. This implies a rejection of other-worldly essences or realities behind appearances. Instead, existentialists in general repudiate the notion that existence is somehow less real than essence, though they may disagree on what they mean by existence. The word *exist* has its origin in Latin, and it literally means "stand out." Though today we think of *existence* as fairly passive — think of the phrase "mere existence" — the word is in fact quite a dynamic one. It is that more dynamic connotation that existentialists want to recover. For existentialists, we are immersed in the concreteness of existence. Humans exist always in-situation, with the world given to us rich and independent of our will. Existence, then, is primary. And, for existentialists, we create meaning. Thus, no essences exist separate from human reality. This reversal of the Platonic world gives existentialism some specific characteristics that distinguish it from more traditional philosophy.

DESPAIR

Suffering is the origin of consciousness.
Dostoyevsky

[Life] is a tale
Told by an idiot, full of sound and fury,
Signifying nothing.
Shakespeare

Any view that essence precedes existence, however contemptuous of existence it might be, will tend toward a certain optimism. That optimism is grounded in the belief that there is a solid foundation of meaning outside of us, waiting to be discovered by us. Though humans are doubtless fallible and so may miss the bull's-eye, there is no question in these views that the bull's-eye exists. Claims to knowledge, descriptions of reality, and judgments about conduct, then, can all be judged against these standards of objectivity, these essences. And, at the very least, we can trust the law of contradiction that differing judgments cannot all be true.

But, for existentialists, if existence precedes essence, then we carry the burden of being meaning makers. We have no absolutely trustworthy guide to or guarantee of meaning. This uncertainty may lead to despair, a uniquely human capacity. We are conscious of our limitations, of our potential, of our future, and conscious that our future will end someday. This capacity to experience despair is a burden we bear, but it is also what makes us great. According to Pascal, whom some describe as the first existentialist,

> The greatness of man is great in that he knows himself to be miserable. A tree does not know itself to be miserable. It is then being miserable to know oneself to be miserable; but it is also being great to know that one is miserable.
>
> *Pascal,* Pensees, *no. 397*

Existentialist thinkers rebel against the Platonic picture of reality as perfect and unchanging. Rather, human existence is always in process and dynamic; and the experience of despair reminds us that there are no guarantees. In a story by Dostoyevsky, the Underground Man declares that, though consciousness is our greatest plague, we are not likely to trade it for anything else. But it is that suffering of self-awareness to which existentialist thinkers are drawn; indeed, just as suffering is the origin of human consciousness, so one might say that suffering is the beginning point for existential philosophy.

Few philosophers have thought such topics either worthy of or amenable to philosophical analysis. While critics have accused existentialism of being overly attentive to negativities, one might wonder why so few of us — laypeople as well as philosophers — explore the possibilities inherent in the negative. If "everything significant is disquieting" (Goethe), then we should not let our discomfort keep us from investigating this aspect of human experience. Mere techniques — whether they be in the form of programs for building nuclear weapons or manuals for having more satisfying sexual relationships — do not guarantee happiness or personal fulfillment.

Particularly in the modern age, one can no longer assume that progress is inevitable or even that answers are possible. The very science that was once thought to promise profound security and material comfort now seems a threat to that very security. We face possible annihilation from nuclear war or slow death from the pollutants in our atmosphere. We feel small and insignificant, wedged between the minute particles revealed by the microscope and the awesome expanses of the galaxies beyond us. We live longer, but we are bored by the comfortable lives we lead. Pascal wrote about similar feelings in the early days of developing modern science:

> When I see the blindness and the wretchedness of man, when I regard the whole silent universe, and man without light, left to himself, and, as it were, lost in this corner of the universe, without knowing who has put him there, what he has come to do, what will become of him at death, and incapable of all knowledge, I become terrified, like a man who should be carried in his sleep to a dreadful desert island, and should awake without knowing where he is, and without means of escape.
>
>   Pensees, *no. 194*

Why are we here? Why must we suffer? Perhaps every generation has asked these questions, but there may be no generation for whom these questions are more urgent than our own. Chapter 1 explores these questions in greater depth.

TEMPORALITY AND FINITUDE

> *We do not rest satisfied with the present. We anticipate the future as too slow in coming, as if in order to hasten its course; or we recall the past, to stop its too rapid flight. So imprudent are we that we wander in the times which are not ours, and do not think of the only one which belongs to us; and so idle are we that we dream of those times which are no more, and thoughtlessly overlook that which alone exists. For the present is generally painful to us. We conceal it from our sight, because it troubles us; and if it be delightful to us, we regret to see it pass away. We try to sustain it by the future, and think of arranging matters which are not in our power, for a time which we have no certainty of reaching.*
>
> *Let each one examine his thoughts, and he will find them all occupied with the past and the future. We scarcely ever think of the present; and if we think of it, it is only to take light from it to arrange the future. The present is never our end. The past and the present are our means; the future alone is our end. So we never live, but we hope to live; and, as we are always preparing to be happy, it is inevitable we should never be so.*
>
>   Pascal, *Pensees*, no. 172

The world of forms admits of no change. It is a timeless and eternal world of perfection without beginning or end. But, for existentialists, the importance of time (temporality) cannot be overstated. And our awareness of time is inextricably connected to our awareness that our time will inevitably end in death.

Human beings are in time and space in a way that is very different from the ways in which inanimate objects and even nonhuman animals are in time and space. This is the essence of the human being as a self-conscious being, separate from the world of objects. Though I am in the room like this chair on which I sit and the pen with which I write, the reality of the chair and the pen is that they are objects that can be nothing other than what they are. In contrast, I am a subject, not an object, and the essence of subjectivity is that I am always beyond myself, both spatially and temporally. Thus, I am in the present (like the chair and the pen), but I am not limited to the present: My mind may wander, as I think about and imagine places I've been or would like to go, wonder if I should put gas in my car, or stop what I am doing and doubt the worth of this whole enterprise. The chair is uncomfortable, and I get up and move around. I dream, anticipate, worry, remember, and question. I live in many different temporal and spatial modes at one time. I am, that is to say, a reflective being who is not limited to my concreteness.

We are not our pasts, since the past has already occurred; yet we are not the future, which has not yet occurred. Who are we? What is the present? Regardless of the answer, it is clear that we resist easy descriptions; we cannot be tied down. There is no resting place from which we might understand being. Yet we search for this finality, which ironically comes only with death. We endow everything around us with a certain significance beyond our mere objective reality. We are always beyond ourselves in time and space, and we organize the objects around us by "going beyond the pure present and explaining it by the future." (Sartre, *Search for a Method*, p. 152) In a sense, then, we are, as Protagoras claimed, the "measure of all things."

Philosophers tend to discount the importance of change. And, since time is inextricably connected to change, traditional philosophers have sought out worlds which are timeless, beyond change. This approach has important implications both for our understanding of reality and our analyses of what matters. Traditional metaphysics has searched for ideas beyond time, ideas that do not succumb to the effects of temporal change. This usually means that what is most common, ordinary, and everyday becomes unreal; and the real — however we ultimately define it — is transcendent, that is, other-worldly. More concretely, phenomena like birth, aging, and death — what some maintain are the most important facts about us — are relegated to the world of the unreal. Death as an inescapably human reality is replaced with philosophical musings over the possibility of life after death, where souls exist but do not change or ever die. For existentialism, however, to be human is to be grounded in temporality, and temporality is a ceaseless reminder of our own finitude. How we interpret the reality of death is a matter of some disagreement for existentialists. Chapter 1 (pp. 47–54) explores these differing perspectives in more detail.

CONCRETENESS OF EXPERIENCE

Gray is all theory; green is life's glowing tree.
    Goethe

Camus in *The Stranger* powerfully describes the concreteness of human experience, a concreteness that defies easy categories and tidy systems. Take, for example, the following passage:

> Marie taught me a new game. The idea was, while one swam, to suck in the spray off the waves and, when one's mouth was full of foam, to lie on one's back and spout it out against the sky. It made a sort of frothy haze that melted into the air or fell back in a warm shower on one's cheeks. But very soon my mouth was smarting with all the salt I'd drawn in; then Marie came up and hugged me in the water, and pressed her mouth to mine. Her tongue cooled my lips, and we let the waves roll us about for a minute or two before swimming back to the beach. (p. 43)

This passage contains no word of more than two syllables, and yet it conjures up powerful images. And when, at the conclusion of *The Stranger*, a priest comes to the prison to assure Meursault of the existence of an afterlife, Meursault angrily rejects him, claiming, "none of his certainties was worth one strand of a woman's hair." (p. 151)

Just as traditional philosophers have tended to subsume individuals within systems of one sort or another, so has much of philosophy ignored the richness and diversity of concrete experience in favor of universal generalization. Philosophers have, for example, generally ignored or disparaged the realms of sense perception and emotion as too changeable, too subjective, and linked to the body. Such views tend to two positions: either they exclude certain groups (like women) or styles of thinking, since generalizations cannot tolerate any differences not easily subsumed under them; or they are contemptuous of such differences, assigning them to the realm of the irrational. Why analyze that which is incoherent and untrustworthy?

It is not only existentialists who have criticized such approaches. Feminist philosophers have argued that such approaches ignore the experiences of half our population, and Marx claimed that they are ahistorical. Political philosophers and anthropologists have pointed to the dangers inherent in an ethnocentrism that reduces all experience to that of Western, usually white male, society. For existentialists, the dichotomy between feeling and intellect has served as the basis for a paradigm that must be challenged. Existentialists reject systems that erase individuals for the sake of a bland oneness. Such systems fail to capture the richness of concrete experience, and they ignore or trivialize those experiences that do not fit. As the Underground Man states:

> I will admit that reason is a good thing. No argument about that. But reason is only reason, and it only satisfies man's rational requirements. Desire, on the other hand, is the manifestation of life itself — of all life — and it encompasses everything from reason down to scratching oneself. And although, when we're guided by our desires, life may often turn into a messy affair, it's still life and not a series of square roots.
>
> *Dostoyevsky, Notes from Underground, p. 112*

Many people "love abstract reasoning and neat systematization so much that they think nothing of distorting the truth, closing their eyes and ears to contrary evidence to preserve their logical constructions." (Dostoyevsky, pp. 108–9) But a science of humanity or a mathematics of experience, existentialists would argue, is unattainable, and the very attempt is pernicious. It makes, as Nietzsche put it, a "tyrant of reason."

> When one finds it necessary to create a tyrant out of reason, as Socrates did, there is no small danger that something else wishes to play the tyrant. Reason was then discovered as a savior; neither Socrates nor his 'patients' were at liberty to be rational or not, as they pleased; it was de rigeur, it had become a last shift. The fanaticism with which the whole of Greek thought plunges into reason, betrays a critical condition of things; there was danger, there were only two alternatives: either perish or else be ABSURDLY RATIONAL. The moral bias of Greek philosophy from Plato onward is the outcome of a pathological condition; as is also its appreciation of dialectics. Reason = virtue = happiness, simply means: we must imitate Socrates, and confront the dark passions permanently with the light of day — the light of reason. We must at all costs be clever, precise, clear: all yielding to the instincts, to the unconscious, leads DOWNWARD.
>
> *Twilight of the Idols, p. 15*

For existentialists, the darkness is part of the truth and so must be sought after. Life is not always a series of clean, deductive arguments, reasoned from premise to conclusion, inevitably leading to progress and light. We cannot escape its darkness by, as Nietzsche says, "waging war against it," and should be distrustful of any "truths" that "give rise to contentment." (*Will to Power*, no. 537) To acknowledge the richness and variety of human experience is perforce to embrace its tragedy as well as its joy. Existentialists do not deny the seductive power of systems. But they insist on the value of ambiguity and the inevitability of uncertainty.

FREEDOM AND CONTINGENCY

Men are bits of paper, whirled by the cold wind.
   T. S. Eliot

*When I consider the brief span of my life, swallowed up in the eternity
before and after, the little space which I fill, and even can see, engulfed in
the infinite immensity of spaces of which I am ignorant, and which know
me not, I am frightened, and am astonished at being here rather than there;
for there is no reason why here rather than there, now rather than then.*
   Pascal, *Pensees*, no. 205

The concept of freedom is fundamental to existentialism. In fact, it
may be the thread that ties together all of the characteristics outlined in
this introduction. Existentialists reject views that maintain that we are
mere products of our conditioning. At the same time, though, they reject
the naive optimism of views that claim that we are essentially free and
that this freedom is an unmitigated blessing for our species. On the
contrary, for existentialists, as we are free, we cannot be sure what — if
anything — we can count on. Even if God exists, we have the freedom to
believe or not to believe, the choice about how to live our lives. We are
thrown into the world, without anchor, without lifeline, with no predetermined meanings and no set values. As we are free to create meaning, so
we are free to create ourselves. And we bear the full responsibility for that
creation.

In *Nausea*, one of Sartre's earliest and most well-known works, the
protagonist Roquentin comes face to face with the "obscene nakedness"
of raw existence when he looks at the roots of a large chestnut tree:

And then all of a sudden, there it was, clear as day: existence had suddenly
unveiled itself. It had lost the harmless look of an abstract category: it was
the very paste of things, this root was kneaded into existence. Or rather the
root, the park gates, the bench, the sparse grass, all that had vanished: the
diversity of things, their individuality, were only an appearance, a veneer.
This veneer had melted, leaving soft, monstrous masses, all in disorder — naked, in a frightful, obscene nakedness.[1]

Here reality appears to Roquentin in its rawest form. He realizes that
everything is contingent, superfluous, without any essential meaning;
thus, anything can just as well not exist as exist.

---

[1] Jean-Paul Sartre, *Nausea*, Translated by Lloyd Alexander, p. 127. Copyright © 1964
by New Directions Publishing Corporation. All rights reserved.

I understood the Nausea, I possessed it. . . . The essential thing is contingency. I mean that one cannot define existence as necessity. To exist is simply *to be there;* those who exist let themselves be encountered, but you can never deduce anything from them. I believe there are people who have understood this. Only they tried to overcome this contingency by inventing a necessary, causal being. But no necessary being can explain existence: contingency is not a delusion, a probability which can be dissipated; it is the absolute, consequently, the perfect free gift. All is free, this park, this city and myself. when you realize this, it turns your heart upside down and everything begins to float, as the other evening at the "Railwaymen's Rendezvous": here is Nausea; here there is what those bastards — the ones on the Coteau Vert and others — try to hide from themselves with their idea of their rights. But what a poor lie: no one has any rights; they are entirely free, like other men, they cannot succeed in not feeling superfluous. And in themselves, secretly, they are *superfluous,* that is to say, amorphous, vague, and sad.[2]

But Roquentin cannot resist applying these observations to his own existence, as he realizes that we are all "without reason."

And I — soft, weak, obscene, digesting, juggling with dismal thoughts — I, too, was *in the way.* Fortunately, I didn't feel it, although I realized it, but I was uncomfortable because I was afraid of feeling it (even now I am afraid — afraid that it might catch me behind my head and lift me up like a wave). I dreamed vaguely of killing myself to wipe out at least one of these superfluous lives. But even my death would have been *in the way. In the way,* my corpse, my blood on these stones, between these plants, at the back of this smiling garden. And the decomposed flesh would have been *in the way* in the earth which would receive my bones, at last, cleaned, stripped, peeled, proper and clean as teeth, it would have been *in the way:* I was *in the way* for eternity.[3]

Chapter 5 looks at existentialist analyses of freedom and contingency.

AUTHENTICITY AND THE INDIVIDUAL

[I]t seems to me that the meaning of a person's life consists in proving to himself every minute that he's a person and not a piano key.
Dostoyevsky, *Notes from Underground,* p. 115

---

[2] Ibid., p. 131.
[3] Ibid., p. 128.

We are accustomed to hearing in news reports all sorts of numbers: hundreds die in an airplane crash, thousands of children are abused, millions are starving throughout the world, and so forth. As a result, we may become numb to the realities of each individual's life experiences. Such an attitude is not simply the result of the influence of the popular media. Philosophers have developed theories with little attention to the differences of experience from one individual to another; indeed, it seems that such differences are subsumed under or erased by ethical principles and metaphysical systems. The notions that "everyone should . . ." or "all reality is . . ." ignore the individual, leaving little of the real lives of those who constitute the "everyone." In reading the works of Aquinas or Kant or Hegel, one has little sense of human beings as flesh-and-blood creatures who eat, sleep, breathe, catch the flu, feel angry, make love, have children, experience boredom, and finally (and perhaps most importantly) die.

In contrast, existentialists are more suspicious of groups, for groups emphasize a conformity which ultimately effaces differences among individuals. Heidegger, for example, writes disparagingly of the "masse-mensch" or "mass person" who hides in the safety of the "we" or the "they," seeking refuge in sameness and mediocrity. In a group we feel that we are just like everybody else, and we surrender to the safety of the unanimous. The Spanish philosopher Ortega y Gasset has referred to this as a preoccupation with becoming unpreoccupied, that is, a desire to free oneself from the burden of one's own existence by throwing that weight onto the collective group. But this is not possible, for no group, not even the entire species, can take over the burden of one person's existence. And in the futile attempt to hide in the group, we instead get lost in lies and cowardice. We engage in idle talk rather than real dialogue to lose ourselves in the "they" which, as Heidegger says, is really "nothing definite." (*Being and Time*, p. 164) We let the "they" set standards to which we can then compare ourselves. This enables us to escape from our own responsibilities for our thoughts and actions. Heidegger says we are "disburdened" by how easy the "they" makes it all for us:

> Yet because the "they" presents every judgment and decision as its own, it deprives the particular [person] of its answerability. The "they" can, as it were, manage to have 'them' constantly invoking it. It can be answerable for everything most easily, because it is not someone who needs to vouch for anything. It 'was' always the "they" who did it, and yet it can be said that it has been 'no one.' In the human being's everydayness the agency through which most things come about is one of which we must say that "it was no one."
>
> *Being and Time, p. 165*

The "they" is characterized by its averageness, which tends toward a "levelling down." (*Being and Time*, p. 165) The "they" is the public and "by publicness everything gets obscured, and what has thus been covered up gets passed off as something familiar and accessible to everyone." (*Being and Time*, p. 165) The they, then, can never really get to the heart of the matter, can never really be *genuine*.

Kierkegaard too (see chapter 2) has nothing but contempt for those who lose themselves in sayings like "the race" or "our age." While he recognizes that it is easy to trivialize one "mere" particular human being, Kierkegaard insists that for this reason it requires courage to insist on individual significance. The notion of the public is a myth:

> A public is everything and nothing, the most dangerous of all powers and the most insignificant: one can speak of a whole nation in the name of the public and still the public will be less than a single real man, however unimportant. The qualification 'public' is produced by the deceptive juggling of an age of reflection, which makes it appear flattering to the individual who in this way can arrogate to himself this monster, in comparison with which concrete realities seem poor. The public is the fairy story of an age of understanding, which in imagination makes the individual into something even greater than a king above his people; but the public is also a gruesome abstraction. . . .
>
> *Kierkegaard, The Present Age, pp. 63–64*

Nietzsche (see chapter 3), like Kierkegaard, recognizes the power of the social. Indeed, he notes, our very consciousness is mediated by social reality. This reality provides the symbols that enable us to generalize and provide the basis for communication. Thus, our consciousness of ourselves is developed as part of our "herd nature." "Consequently, given the best will in the world to understand ourselves as individually as possible, 'to know ourselves,' each of us will always succeed in becoming conscious only of what is not individual but 'average.'" (Nietzsche, *Gay Science*, p. 299) This is clearly a paradoxical position, for it means that to know ourselves *qua* individuals we must use that consciousness which has been created as a function of communal relations. Nietzsche continues, "Our thoughts themselves are continually governed by the character of consciousness — by the 'genius of the species' that commands it — and translated back into the perspective of the herd. Fundamentally, all our actions are altogether incomparably personal, unique, and infinitely individual. . . . But as soon as we translate them into consciousness, *they no longer seem to be*. (p. 299) The result is that:

> Whatever becomes conscious *becomes* by the same token shallow, thin, relatively stupid, general, sign, herd signal; a becoming conscious involves

a great and thorough corruption, falsification, reduction to superficialities, and generalization.

Gay Science, pp. 299–300

Much of existential fiction deals with the individual's confrontation with law or society or custom. Meursault in Camus's *The Stranger* realizes ultimately that he is sentenced to die not because he has killed but because he has violated social norms: He smoked cigarettes and drank café au lait as he sat vigil beside his mother's coffin. Sartre's dramatization in *The Flies* of the original Greek story of Orestes reveals a character who — unlike the other citizens of the city-state of Argos — is willing to battle anything (including Zeus himself) that prevents him from asserting his own individuality. Existentialism, then, deals less with abstractions and more with the individuals who, alone and unprotected, face the world and in so doing create themselves.

Existentialism's elevation of the individual and accompanying critique of groups provokes a number of profound oppositions. The philosophy and the literature of existentialism reveal certain antagonisms that may be inherent in this view: between individual and society, between self-consciousness and consciousness of the other, and between a personal value framework and the norms of one's group. Chapter 6 explores the tension in existentialist thought between the individual and others, and chapter 7 considers whether an authentic existential ethic is possible.

CONCLUSION

No single text can provide a complete picture of existentialism, for it covers several centuries and a broad range of authors. But this text, through its original sources and introductory selections, provides a basis for beginning the study of existential philosophy. Included here are representative works both from philosophers commonly regarded as existentialists as well as others whose status is somewhat more controversial. This approach is not meant to suggest any rankings of these writers; nor are all existentialist views fully or even equally represented here. Further, reading edited selections is not preferable to reading complete works. Nevertheless, these selections are of sufficient length to provide a feeling for these writers' styles, methodologies, and viewpoints; it is not meant, though, to substitute for reading the complete versions of such works. Indeed, you may discover that these readings whet your appetite for certain authors and that you seek out more of their writings. To aid in this process, at the end of each chapter is a list of recommended readings on the topics discussed in that chapter. Finally, many existentialists have relied on fiction and poetry to convey some of their views; existentialism is a philosophy which, for reasons we discuss in detail later, may be best expressed in fiction, not in theoretical system building. For this reason, chapters may refer to works of fiction to highlight key concepts.

This text's emphasis is on the themes that play a major role in existential philosophy. This approach provides a more solid basis for exploring these themes than an arbitrary arrangement dependent on dates. In addition, each chapter introduction offers a context for the particular philosophical issue under discussion and grounds that discussion in a philosophical tradition. The development of existentialism as a more or less systematic approach to philosophy was not a fluke or an intellectual aberration; rather, existentialism evolved in part as a response to social and historical circumstances and in part as an outright repudiation of a particular method of approaching philosophical questions. Chapter introductions ground this new philosophy in that historical and intellectual tradition.

Thus, this text illuminates not only what existentialism *is,* but also what it *is not,* not only how existentialism approaches philosophical problems, but also how that approach is radically different from others in the past. This strategy is not meant to favor existentialism or any other competing view; rather, its purpose is to create a basis for distinguishing the relative merits of these competing philosophies.

Existentialists do not seek students in the usual sense of that word; most would rather be ignored than be blindly accepted or deemed sacred scripture. Nietzsche once wrote that "one repays a teacher badly by remaining only a student," and all of us, as students, can benefit if we heed his words. Existentialism is one part of the journey that we call the history of philosophy. This text is one step in beginning that journey.

QUESTIONS

1. Consider the major characteristics of existentialism outlined in this chapter. Are there currently writers you might now label "existential"? Poets? Songwriters? Choose a contemporary song or poem that you think fits the characteristics of existential philosophy and defend your selection of it from this perspective.

2. At the end of *The Stranger,* Meursault realizes that the universe is indifferent, but that it is also benign. What might this mean? Do you agree?

3. How does Sartre's story "The Wall" (see pp. 22–36) illustrate these existential themes?

4. Is the development of one's own personal identity incompatible with membership in a group? Discuss the dynamic relationship between

individuals and groups. Do you agree with most existentialists that one is antithetical to the other?

REFERENCES

CAMUS, ALBERT. *The Plague.* Translated by Stuart Gilbert. New York: The Modern Library, 1948.

——. *The Stranger.* Translated by Stuart Gilbert. New York: Vintage Books, 1954.

DOSTOYEVSKY, FYODOR. *Notes from Underground.* Translated by Andrew R. MacAndrew. New York: New American Library, 1961, pp. 90–203.

HEIDEGGER, MARTIN. *Being and Time.* Translated by John Macquarrie and Edward Robinson. New York: Harper and Row, 1962.

HOLDERLIN, FRIEDRICH. *Poems.* Translated by Michael Hamburger. New York: Pantheon Books, 1952.

KIERKEGAARD, SOREN. *The Present Age.* Translated by Alexander Dru. New York: Harper Torchbooks, 1962.

MARCEL, GABRIEL. *The Philosophy of Existentialism.* Tranlated by Manya Harari. New York: Philosophical Library, 1973.

NIETZSCHE, FRIEDRICH. *Twilight of the Idols.* Translated by Anthony M. Ludovici. New York: Russell & Russell, Inc., 1964.

——. *The Will to Power.* Translated by Walter Kaufmann and R. J. Hollingdale. New York: Vintage, 1968.

ORTEGA Y GASSET, JOSÉ. *The Revolt of the Masses.* New York: W. W. Norton & Co., 1957.

PASCAL, BLAISE. *Pensees.* Translated by W. F. Trotter. New York: Modern Library, 1941.

PLATO. *The Apology.* Translated by Hugh Tredennick. In *The Collected Dialogues of Plato.* Edited by Edith Hamilton and Huntington Cairns. New York: Pantheon Books, 1961, pp. 3–26.

——. *The Phaedo.* Translated by Hugh Tredennick. In Hamilton and Cairns, pp. 40–98.

——. *The Protagoras.* Translated by W. K. C. Guthrie. In Hamilton and Cairns, pp. 308–52.

——. *The Republic.* Translated by Paul Shorey. In Hamilton and Cairns, pp. 575–844.

——. *The Theaetetus.* Translated by F. M. Cornford. In Hamilton and Cairns, pp. 845–919.

PROTAGORAS. "Fragments." In *The Presocratics*. Edited by Philip Wheelwright. New York: The Odyssey Press, Inc., 1966, pp. 239–48.

SARTRE, JEAN-PAUL. *Existentialism* (or *Existentialism Is a Humanism*). Translated by Bernard Frechtman. New York: Philosophical Library, 1947.

——. *The Flies*. Translated by Stuart Gilbert. In *No Exit and Three Other Plays*. New York: Vintage Books, 1946.

——. *Nausea*. Translated by Lloyd Alexander. New York: New Directions Publishing Corporation. 1964.

——. *Search for a Method*. Translated by Hazel Barnes. New York: Knopf, 1963.

TOLSTOY, LEO. *The Death of Ivan Ilyich*. Translated by Margaret Wettlin. In *Six Short Masterpieces by Tolstoy*. New York: Dell Publishing Co., 1963.

UNAMUNO, MIGUEL DE. *The Tragic Sense of Life*. Translated by J. E. Crawford Flitch. New York: Dover Publications, 1954.

JEAN-PAUL SARTRE

This powerful short story by Sartre intermingles many of the characteristic themes of existentialism discussed in this introduction.

The Wall

They pushed us into a big white room and I began to blink because the light hurt my eyes. Then I saw a table and four men behind the table, civilians, looking over the papers. They had bunched another group of prisoners in the back and we had to cross the whole room to join them. There were several I knew and some others who must have been foreigners. The two in front of me were blond with round skulls; they looked alike. I suppose they were French. The smaller one kept hitching up his pants; nerves.

It lasted about three hours; I was dizzy and my head was empty; but the room was well heated and I found that pleasant enough: for the past 24 hours we hadn't stopped shivering. The guards brought the prisoners up to the table, one after the other. The four men asked each one his name and occupation. Most of the time they didn't go any further — or they would simply ask a question here and there: "Did you have anything to do with the sabotage of munitions?" Or "Where were you the morning of the 9th and what were you doing?" They didn't listen to the answers or at least didn't seem to. They were quiet for a moment and then looking straight in front of them began to write. They asked Tom if it were true he was in the International Brigade; Tom couldn't tell them otherwise because of the papers they found in his coat. They didn't ask Juan anything but they wrote for a long time after he told them his name.

"My brother José is the anarchist," Juan said, "you know he isn't here any more. I don't belong to any party, I never had anything to do with politics."

They didn't answer. Juan went on, "I haven't done anything. I don't want to pay for somebody else."

His lips trembled. A guard shut him up and took him away. It was my turn.

"Your name is Pablo Ibbieta?"
"Yes."

The man looked at the papers and asked me, "Where's Ramon Gris?"

"I don't know."

"You hid him in your house from the 6th to the 19th."

"No."

They wrote for a minute and then the guards took me out. In the corridor Tom and Juan were waiting between two guards. We started walking. Tom asked one of the guards, "So?"

"So what?" the guard said.

"Was that the cross-examination or the sentence?"

"Sentence," the guard said.

"What are they going to do with us?"

The guard answered dryly, "Sentence will be read in your cell."

As a matter of fact, our cell was one of the hospital cellars. It was terrifically cold there because of the drafts. We shivered all night and it wasn't much better during the day. I had spent the previous five days in a cell in a monastery, a sort of hole in the wall that must have dated from the middle ages: since there were a lot of prisoners and not much room, they locked us up anywhere. I didn't miss my cell; I hadn't suffered too much from the cold but I was alone; after a long time it gets irritating. In the cellar I had company. Juan hardly ever spoke: he was afraid and he was too young to have anything to say. But Tom was a good talker and he knew Spanish well.

There was a bench in the cellar and four mats. When they took us back we sat and waited in silence. After a long moment, Tom said, "We're screwed."

"I think so too," I said, "but I don't think they'll do anything to the kid."

"They don't have a thing against him," said Tom. "He's the brother of a militiaman and that's all."

I looked at Juan: he didn't seem to hear. Tom went on, "You know what they do in Saragossa? They lay the men down on the road and run over them with trucks. A Moroccan deserter told us that. They said it was to save ammunition."

"It doesn't save gas," I said.

I was annoyed at Tom: he shouldn't have said that.

"Then there's officers walking along the road," he went on, "supervising it all. They stick their hands in their pockets and smoke cigarettes. You think they finish off the guys? Hell no. They let them scream. Sometimes for an hour. The Moroccan said he damned near puked the first time."

"I don't believe they'll do that here," I said. "Unless they're really short on ammunition."

Day was coming in through four airholes and a round opening, they had made in the ceiling on the left, and you could see the sky through it. Through this hole, usually closed by a trap, they unloaded coal into the cellar. Just below the hole there was a big pile of coal dust; it had been used to heat the hospital but since the beginning of the war the patients were evacuated and the coal stayed there, unused; sometimes it even got rained on because they had forgotten to close the trap.

Tom began to shiver. "Good Jesus Christ, I'm cold," he said. "Here it goes again."

He got up and began to do exercises. At each movement his shirt opened on his chest, white and hairy. He lay on his back, raised his legs in the air and bicycled. I saw his great rump trembling. Tom was husky but he had too much fat. I thought how rifle bullets or the sharp points of bayonets would soon be sunk into this mass of tender flesh as in a lump of butter. It wouldn't have made me feel like that if he'd been thin.

I wasn't exactly cold, but I couldn't feel my arms and shoulders any more. Sometimes I had the impression I was missing something and began to look around for my coat and then suddenly remembered they hadn't given me a coat. It was rather uncomfortable. They took our clothes and gave them to their soldiers leaving us only our shirts — and those canvas pants that hospital patients wear in the middle of summer. After a while Tom got up and sat next to me, breathing heavily.

"Warmer?"

"Good Christ, no. But I'm out of wind."

Around eight o'clock in the evening a major came in with two *falangistas*. He had a sheet of paper in his hand. He asked the guard, "What are the names of those three?"

"Steinbock, Ibbieta and Mirbal," the guard said.

The major put on his eyeglasses and scanned the list: "Steinbock . . . Steinbock . . . oh yes . . . you are sentenced to death. You will be shot tomorrow morning." He went on looking. "The other two as well."

"That's not possible," Juan said. "Not me."

The major looked at him amazed. "What's your name?"

"Juan Mirbal," he said.

"Well, your name is there," said the major. "You're sentenced."

"I didn't do anything," Juan said.

The major shrugged his shoulders and turned to Tom and me.

"You're Basque?"

"Nobody is Basque."

He looked annoyed. "They told me there were three Basques. I'm not going to waste my time running after them. Then naturally you don't want a priest?"

We didn't even answer.

He said, "A Belgian doctor is coming shortly. He is authorized to spend the night with you." He made a military salute and left.

"What did I tell you," Tom said. "We get it."

"Yes," I said, "it's a rotten deal for the kid."

I said that to be decent but I didn't like the kid. His face was too thin and fear and suffering had disfigured it, twisting all his features. Three days before he was a smart sort of kid, not too bad; but now he looked like an old fairy and I thought how he'd never be young again, even if they were to let him go. It wouldn't have been too hard to have a little pity for him but pity disgusts me, or rather it horrifies me. He hadn't said anything more but he had turned grey; his face and hands were both grey. He sat down again and looked at the ground with round eyes. Tom was good hearted, he wanted to take his arm, but the kid tore himself away violently and made a face.

"Let him alone," I said in a low voice, "you can see he's going to blubber."

Tom obeyed regretfully; he would have liked to comfort the kid, it would have passed his time and he wouldn't have been tempted to think about himself. But it annoyed me: I'd never thought about death because I never had any reason to, but now the reason was here and there was nothing to do but think about it.

Tom began to talk. "So you think you've knocked guys off, do you?" he asked me. I didn't answer. He began explaining to me that he had knocked off six since the beginning of August; he didn't realize the situation and I could tell he didn't *want* to realize it. I hadn't quite realized it myself, I wondered if it hurt much, I thought of bullets, I imagined their burning hail through my body. All that was beside the real question; but I was calm: we had all night to understand. After a while Tom stopped talking and I watched him out of the corner of my eye; I saw he too had turned grey and he looked rotten; I told myself "Now it starts." It was almost dark, a dim glow filtered through the airholes and the pile of coal and made a big stain beneath the spot of sky; I could already see a star through the hole in the ceiling: the night would be pure and icy.

The door opened and two guards came in, followed by a blond man in a tan uniform. He saluted us. "I am the doctor," he said. "I have authorization to help you in these trying hours."

He had an agreeable and distinguished voice. I said, "What do you want here?"

"I am at your disposal. I shall do all I can to make your last moments less difficult."

"What did you come here for? There are others, the hospital's full of them."

"I was sent here," he answered with a vague look. "Ah! Would you like to smoke?" he added hurriedly, "I have cigarettes and even cigars."

He offered us English cigarettes and *puros*, but we refused. I looked him in the eyes and he seemed irritated. I said to him, "You aren't here on an errand of mercy. Besides, I know you. I saw you with the fascists in the barracks yard the day I was arrested."

I was going to continue, but something surprising suddenly happened to me; the presence of this doctor no longer interested me. Generally when I'm on somebody I don't let go. But the desire to talk left me completely; I shrugged and turned my eyes away. A little later I raised my head; he was watching me curiously. The guards were sitting on a mat. Pedro, the tall thin one, was twiddling his thumbs, the other shook his head from time to time to keep from falling asleep.

"Do you want a light?" Pedro suddenly asked the doctor. The other nodded "Yes": I think he was about as smart as a log, but he surely wasn't bad. Looking in his cold blue eyes it seemed to me that his only sin was lack of imagination. Pedro went out and came back with an oil lamp which he set on the corner of the bench. It gave a bad light but it was better than nothing: they had left us in the dark the night before. For a long time I watched the circle of light the lamp made on the ceiling. I was fascinated. Then suddenly I woke up, the circle of light disappeared and I felt myself crushed under an enormous weight. It was not the thought of death, or fear; it was nameless. My cheeks burned and my head ached.

I shook myself and looked at my two friends. Tom had hidden his face in his hands. I could only see the fat white nape of his neck. Little Juan was the worst, his mouth was open and his nostrils trembled. The doctor went to him and put his hand on his shoulder to comfort him: but his eyes stayed cold. Then I saw the Belgian's hand drop stealthily along Juan's arm, down to the wrist. Juan paid no attention. The Belgian took his wrist between three fingers, distractedly, the same time drawing back a little and turning his back to me. But I leaned backward and saw him take a watch from his pocket and look at it for a moment, never letting go of the wrist. After a minute he let the hand fall inert and went and leaned his back against the wall, then, as if he suddenly remembered something very important which had to be jotted down on the spot, he took a notebook from his pocket and wrote a few lines. "Bastard," I thought angrily, "let him come and take my pulse. I'll shove my fist in his rotten face."

He didn't come but I felt him watching me. I raised my head and returned his look. Impersonally, he said to me, "Doesn't it seem cold to you here?" He looked cold, he was blue.

"I'm not cold," I told him.

He never took his hard eyes off me. Suddenly I understood and my hands went to my face: I was drenched in sweat. In this cellar, in the midst of winter, in the midst of drafts, I was sweating. I ran my hands through my hair, gummed together with perspiration; at the same time I saw my shirt was damp and sticking to my skin: I had been dripping for an hour and hadn't felt it. But that swine of a Belgian hadn't missed a thing; he had seen the drops rolling down my cheeks and thought: this is the manifestation of an almost pathological state of terror; and he had felt normal and proud of being alive because he was cold. I wanted to stand up and smash his face but no sooner had I made the slightest gesture than my rage and shame were wiped out; I fell back on the bench with indifference.

I satisfied myself by rubbing my neck with my handkerchief because now I felt the sweat dropping from my hair onto my neck and it was unpleasant. I soon gave up rubbing, it was useless; my handkerchief was already soaked and I was still sweating. My buttocks were sweating too and my damp trousers were glued to the bench.

Suddenly Juan spoke. "You're a doctor?"

"Yes," the Belgian said.

"Does it hurt . . . very long?"

"Huh? When . . . ? Oh, no," the Belgian said paternally. "Not at all. It's over quickly." He acted as though he were calming a cash customer.

"But I . . . they told me . . . sometimes they have to fire twice."

"Sometimes," the Belgian said, nodding. "It may happen that the first volley reaches no vital organs."

"Then they have to reload their rifles and aim all over again?" He thought for a moment and then added hoarsely, "That takes time!"

He had a terrible fear of suffering, it was all he thought about: it was his age. I never thought much about it and it wasn't fear of suffering that made me sweat.

I got up and walked to the pile of coal dust. Tom jumped up and threw me a hateful look: I had annoyed him because my shoes squeaked. I wondered if my face looked as frightened as his: I saw he was sweating too. The sky was superb, no light filtered into the dark corner and I had only to raise my head to see the Big Dipper. But it wasn't like it had been: the night before I could see a great piece of sky from my monastery cell and each hour of the day brought me a different memory. Morning, when the sky was a hard, light blue, I thought of beaches on the Atlantic; at noon I saw the sun and I remembered a bar in Seville where I drank *manzanilla* and ate olives and anchovies; afternoons I was in the shade and I thought of the deep shadow which spreads over half a bull-ring leaving the other half shimmering in sunlight; it was really hard to see the whole world reflected in the sky like that. But now I could watch the sky as much as I pleased, it no longer evoked anything in me. I liked that better. I came back and sat near Tom. A long moment passed.

Tom began speaking in a low voice. He had to talk, without that he wouldn't have been able to recognize himself in his own mind. I thought he was talking to me but he wasn't looking at me. He was undoubtedly afraid to see me as I was, grey and sweating: we were alike and worse than mirrors of each other. He watched the Belgian, the living.

"Do you understand?" he said. "I don't understand."

I began to speak in a low voice too. I watched the Belgian. "Why? What's the matter?"

"Something is going to happen to us that I can't understand."

There was a strange smell about Tom. It seemed to me I was more sensitive than usual to odors. I grinned. "You'll understand in a while."

"It isn't clear," he said obstinately. "I want to be brave but first I have to know. . . . Listen, they're going to take us into the courtyard. Good. They're going to stand up in front of us. How many?"

"I don't know. Five or eight. Not more."

"All right. There'll be eight. Someone'll holler 'aim!' and I'll see eight rifles looking at me. I'll think how I'd like to get inside the wall, I'll push against it with my back . . . with every ounce of strength I have, but the wall will stay, like in a nightmare. I can imagine all that. If you only knew how well I can imagine it."

"All right, all right!" I said, "I can imagine it too."

"It must hurt like hell. You know, they aim at the eyes and mouth to disfigure you," he added mechanically. "I can feel the wounds already; I've had pains in my head and in my neck for the past hour. Not real pains. Worse. This is what I'm going to feel tomorrow morning. And then what?"

I well understood what he meant but I didn't want to act as if I did. I had pains too, pains in my body like a crowd of tiny scars. I couldn't get used to it. But I was like him, I attached no importance to it. "After," I said, "you'll be pushing up daisies."

He began to talk to himself: he never stopped watching the Belgian. The Belgian didn't seem to be listening. I knew what he had come to do; he wasn't interested in what we thought; he came to watch our bodies dying in agony while yet alive.

"It's like a nightmare," Tom was saying. "You want to think something, you always have the impression that it's all right, that you're going to understand and then it slips, it escapes you and fades away. I tell myself there will be nothing afterwards. But I don't understand what it means. Sometimes I almost can . . . and then it fades away and I start thinking about the pains again, bullets, explosions. I'm a materialist, I swear it to you; I'm not going crazy. But something's the matter. I see my corpse; that's not hard but *I'm* the one who sees it, with *my* eyes. I've got to think . . . think that I won't see anything any more and the world will go on for the others. We aren't made to think that, Pablo. Believe me: I've already stayed up a whole night waiting for something. But this isn't the same: this will creep up behind us, Pablo, and we won't be able to prepare for it."

"Shut up," I said. "Do you want me to call a priest?"

He didn't answer. I had already noticed he had the tendency to act like a prophet and call me Pablo, speaking in a toneless voice. I didn't like that: but it seems all the Irish are that way. I had the vague impression he smelled of urine. Fundamentally, I hadn't much sympathy for Tom and I didn't see why, under the pretext of dying together, I should have any more. It would have been different with some others. With Ramon Gris, for example. But I felt alone between Tom and Juan. I liked that better, anyhow: with Ramon I might have been more deeply moved. But I was terribly hard just then and I wanted to stay hard.

He kept chewing his words, with something like distraction. He certainly talked to keep himself from thinking. He smelled of urine like an old prostate case. Naturally, I agreed with him, I could have said everything he said: it isn't *natural* to die. And since I was going to die, nothing seemed natural to me, not this pile of coal dust, or the bench, or Pedro's ugly face. Only it didn't please me to think the same things as Tom. And I knew that, all through the night, every five minutes, we would keep on thinking things at the same time. I looked at him sideways and for the first time he seemed strange to me: he wore death on his face. My pride was wounded: for the past 24 hours I had lived next to Tom, I had listened to him, I had spoken to him and I knew we had nothing in common. And now we looked as much alike as twin brothers, simply because we were going to die together. Tom took my hand without looking at me.

"Pablo, I wonder . . . I wonder if it's really true that everything ends."

I took my hand away and said, "Look between your feet, you pig."

There was a big puddle between his feet and drops fell from his pants-leg.

"What is it ?" he asked, frightened.

"You're pissing in your pants," I told him.

"It isn't true," he said furiously. "I'm not pissing. I don't feel anything."

The Belgian approached us. He asked with false solicitude, "Do you feel ill?"

Tom did not answer. The Belgian looked at the puddle and said nothing.

"I don't know what it is," Tom said ferociously. "But I'm not afraid. I swear I'm not not afraid."

The Belgian did not answer. Tom got up and went to piss in a corner. He came back buttoning his fly, and sat down without a word. The Belgian was taking notes.

All three of us watched him because he was alive. He had the motions of a living human being, the cares of a living human being; he shivered in the cellar the way the living are supposed to shiver; he had an obedient, well-fed body. The rest of us hardly felt ours — not in the same way anyhow. I wanted to feel my pants between my legs but I didn't dare; I watched the Belgian, balancing on his legs, master of his muscles, someone who could think about tomorrow. There we were, three bloodless shadows; we watched him and we sucked his life like vampires.

Finally he went over to little Juan. Did he want to feel his neck for some professional motive or was he obeying an impulse of charity? If he was acting by charity it was the only time during the whole night.

He caressed Juan's head and neck. The kid let himself be handled, his eyes never leaving him, then suddenly, he seized the hand and looked at it strangely. He held the Belgian's hand between his own two hands and there was nothing pleasant about them, two grey pincers gripping this fat and reddish hand. I suspected what was going to happen and Tom must have suspected it too: but the Belgian didn't see a thing, he smiled paternally. After a moment the kid brought the fat red hand to his mouth and tried to bite it. The Belgian pulled away quickly and stumbled back against the wall. For a second he looked at us with horror, he must have suddenly understood that we were not men like him. I began to laugh and one of the guards jumped up. The other was asleep, his wide-open eyes were blank.

I felt relaxed and over-excited at the same time. I didn't want to think any more about what would happen at dawn, at death. It made no sense. I only found words or emptiness. But as soon as I tried to think of anything else I saw rifle barrels pointing at me. Perhaps I lived through my execution twenty times; once I even thought it was for good: I must have slept a minute. They were dragging me to the wall and I was struggling; I was asking for mercy. I woke up with a start and looked at the Belgian: I was afraid I might have cried out in my sleep. But he was stroking his moustache, he hadn't noticed anything. If I had wanted to, I think I could have slept a while; I had been awake for 48 hours. I was at the end of my rope. But I didn't want to lose two hours of life: they would come to wake me up at dawn, I would follow them, stupefied with sleep and I would have croaked without so much as an "Oof!"; I didn't want that, I didn't want to die like an animal, I wanted to understand. Then I was afraid of having nightmares. I got up, walked back and forth, and, to change my ideas, I began to think about my past life. A crowd of memories came back to me pell-mell. There were good and bad ones — or at least I called them that *before*. There were faces and incidents. I saw the face of a little *novillero* who was gored in Valencia during the *Feria*, the face of one of my uncles, the face of Ramon Gris. I remembered my whole life: how I was out of work for three months in 1926, how I almost starved to death. I remembered a night I spent on a bench in Granada: I hadn't eaten for three days. I was angry, I didn't want to die. That made me smile. How madly I ran after happiness, after women, after liberty. Why? I wanted to free Spain, I admired Pi y Margall, I joined the anarchist movement, I spoke in public meetings: I took everything as seriously as if I were immortal.

At that moment I felt that I had my whole life in front of me and I thought, "It's a damned lie." It was worth nothing because it was finished. I wondered how I'd been able to walk, to laugh with the girls: I wouldn't have moved so much as my little finger if I had only imagined I would die like this. My life was in front of me, shut, closed, like a bag and yet everything inside of it was unfinished. For an instant I tried to judge it. I wanted to tell myself, this is a beautiful life. But I couldn't pass judgment on it; it was only a sketch; I had spent my time counterfeiting eternity, I had understood nothing. I missed nothing: there were so many things I could have missed, the taste of *manzanilla* or the baths I took in summer in a little creek near Cadiz; but death had disenchanted everything.

The Belgian suddenly had a bright idea. "My friends," he told us, "I will undertake — if the military administration will allow it — to send a message for you, a souvenir to those who love you. . . ."

Tom mumbled, "I don't have anybody."

I said nothing. Tom waited an instant then looked at me with curiosity. "You don't have anything to say to Concha?"

"No."

I hated this tender complicity: it was my own fault, I had talked about Concha the night before, I should have controlled myself. I was with her for a year. Last night I would have given an arm to see her again for five minutes. That was why I talked about her, it was stronger than I was. Now I had no more desire to see her, I had nothing more to say to her. I would not even have wanted to hold her in my arms: my body filled me with horror because it was grey and sweating — and I wasn't sure that her body didn't fill me with horror. Concha would cry when she found out I was dead, she would have no taste for life for months afterward. But I was still the one who was going to die. I thought of her soft, beautiful eyes. When she looked at me something passed from her to me. But I knew it was over: if she looked at me *now* the look would stay in her eyes, it wouldn't reach me. I was alone.

Tom was alone too but not in the same way. Sitting cross-legged, he had begun to stare at the bench with a sort of smile, he looked amazed. He put out his hand and touched the wood cautiously as if he were afraid of breaking something, then drew back his hand quickly and shuddered. If I had been Tom I wouldn't have amused myself by touching the bench; this was some more Irish nonsense, but I too found that objects had a funny look: they were more obliterated, less dense than usual. It was enough for me to look at the bench, the lamp, the pile of coal dust, to feel that I was going to die. Naturally I couldn't think clearly about my death but I saw it everywhere, on things, in the way things fell back and kept their distance, discreetly, as people who speak quietly at the bedside of a dying man. It was *his* death which Tom had just touched on the bench.

In the state I was in, if someone had come and told me I could go home quietly, that they would leave me my life whole, it would have left me cold: several hours or several years of waiting is all the same when you have lost the illusion of being eternal. I clung to nothing, in a way I was calm. But it was a horrible calm — because of my body; my body, I saw with its eyes, I heard with its ears, but it was no longer me; it sweated and trembled by itself and I didn't recognize it any more. I had to touch it and look at it to find out what was happening, as if it were the body of someone else. At times I could still feel it, I felt sinkings, and fallings, as when you're in a plane taking a nose dive, or I felt my heart beating. But that didn't reassure me. Everything that came from my body was all cockeyed. Most of the time it was quiet and I felt no more than a sort of weight, a filthy presence against me; I had the impression of being tied to an enormous vermin. Once I felt my pants and I felt they were damp; I didn't know whether it was sweat or urine, but I went to piss on the coal pile as a precaution.

The Belgian took out his watch, looked at it. He said, "It is three-thirty."

Bastard! He must have done it on purpose. Tom jumped; he hadn't noticed time was running out; night surrounded us like a shapeless, somber mass, I couldn't even remember that it had begun.

Little Juan began to cry. He wrung his hands, pleaded, "I don't want to die. I don't want to die."

He ran across the whole cellar waving his arms in the air then fell sobbing on one of the mats. Tom watched him with mournful eyes, without the slightest desire to console him. Because it wasn't worth the trouble: the kid made more noise than we did, but he was less touched: he was like a sick man who defends himself against illness by fever. It's much more serious when there isn't any fever.

He wept: I could clearly see he was pitying himself; he wasn't thinking about death. For one second, one single second, I wanted to weep myself, to weep with pity for myself. But the opposite happened: I glanced at the kid, I saw his thin sobbing shoulders and felt inhuman: I could pity neither the others nor myself. I said to myself, "I want to die cleanly."

Tom had gotten up, he placed himself just under the round opening and began to watch for daylight. I was determined to die cleanly and I only thought of that. But ever since the doctor told us the time, I felt time flying, flowing away drop by drop.

It was still dark when I heard Tom's voice: "Do you hear them?"
Men were marching in the courtyard.

"Yes."

"What the hell are they doing? They can't shoot in the dark."

After a while we heard no more. I said to Tom, "It's day."

Pedro got up, yawning, and came to blow out the lamp. He said to his buddy, "Cold as hell."

The cellar was all grey. We heard shots in the distance.

"It's starting," I told Tom. "They must do it in the court in the rear."

Tom asked the doctor for a cigarette. I didn't want one; I didn't want cigarettes or alcohol. From that moment on they didn't stop firing.

"Do you realize what's happening?" Tom said.

He wanted to add something but kept quiet, watching the door. The door opened and a lieutenant came in with four soldiers. Tom dropped his cigarette.

"Steinbock?"

Tom didn't answer. Pedro pointed him out.

"Juan Mirbal?"

"On the mat."

"Get up," the lieutenant said.

Juan did not move. Two soldiers took him under the arms and set him on his feet. But he fell as soon as they released him.

The soldiers hesitated.

"He's not the first sick one," said the lieutenant. "You two carry him; they'll fix it up down there."

He turned to Tom. "Let's go."

Tom went out between two soldiers. Two others followed, carrying the kid by the armpits. He hadn't fainted; his eyes were wide open and tears ran down his cheeks. When I wanted to go out the lieutenant stopped me.

"You Ibbieta?"

"Yes."

"You wait here; they'll come for you later."

They left. The Belgian and the two jailers left too, I was alone. I did not understand what was happening to me but I would have liked it better if they had gotten it over with right away. I heard shots at almost regular intervals; I shook with each one of them. I wanted to scream and tear out my hair. But I gritted my teeth and pushed my hands in my pockets because I wanted to stay clean.

After an hour they came to get me and led me to the first floor, to a small room that smelt of cigars and where the heat was stifling. There were two officers sitting smoking in the armchairs, papers on their knees.

"You're Ibbieta?"

"Yes."

"Where is Ramon Gris?"

"I don't know."

The one questioning me was short and fat. His eyes were hard behind his glasses. He said to me, "Come here."

I went to him. He got up and took my arms, staring at me with a look that should have pushed me into the earth. At the same time he pinched my biceps with all his might. It wasn't to hurt me, it was only a game: he wanted to dominate me. He also thought he had to blow his stinking breath square in my face. We stayed for a moment like that, and I almost felt like laughing. It takes a lot to intimidate a man who is going to die; it didn't work. He pushed me back violently and sat down again. He said, "It's his life against yours. You can have yours if you tell us where he is."

These men dolled up with their riding crops and boots were still going to die. A little later than I, but not too much. They busied themselves looking for names in their crumpled papers, they ran after other men to imprison or suppress them; they had opinions on the future of Spain and on other subjects. Their little activities seemed shocking and burlesqued to me; I couldn't put myself in their place, I thought they were insane. The little man was still looking at me, whipping his boots with the riding crop. All his gestures were calculated to give him the look of a live and ferocious beast.

"So? You understand?"

"I don't know where Gris is," I answered. "I thought he was in Madrid."

The other officer raised his pale hand indolently. This indolence was also calculated. I saw through all their little schemes and I was stupefied to find there were men who amused themselves that way.

"You have a quarter of an hour to think it over," he said slowly. "Take him to the laundry, bring him back in fifteen minutes. If he still refuses he will be executed on the spot."

They knew what they were doing: I had passed the night in waiting; then they had made me wait an hour in the cellar while they shot Tom and Juan and now they were locking me up in the laundry; they must have prepared their game the night before. They told themselves that nerves eventually wear out and they hoped to get me that way.

They were badly mistaken. In the laundry I sat on a stool because I felt very weak and I began to think. But not about their proposition. Of course I knew where Gris was; he was hiding with his cousins, four kilometers from the city. I also knew that I would not reveal his hiding place unless they tortured me (but they didn't seem to be thinking about that). All that was perfectly regulated, definite and in no way interested me. Only I would have liked to understand the reasons for my conduct. I would rather die than give up Gris. Why? I didn't like Ramon Gris any more. My friendship for him had died a little while before dawn at the same time as my love for Concha, at the same time as my desire to live. Undoubtedly I thought highly of him: he was tough. But it was not for this reason that I consented to die in his place; his life had no more value than mine; no life had value. They were going to slap a man up against a wall and shoot at him till he died, whether it was I or Gris or somebody else made no difference. I knew he was more useful than I to the cause of Spain but I thought to hell with Spain and anarchy; nothing was important. Yet I was there, I could save my skin and give up Gris and I refused to do it. I found that somehow comic; it was obstinacy. I thought, "I must be stubborn!" And a droll sort of gaiety spread over me.

They came for me and brought me back to the two officers. A rat ran out from under my feet and that amused me. I turned to one of the *falangistas* and said, "Did you see the rat?"

He didn't answer. He was very sober, he took himself seriously. I wanted to laugh but I held myself back because I was afraid that once I got started I wouldn't be able to stop. The *falangista* had a moustache. I said to him again, "You ought to shave off your moustache, idiot." I thought it funny that he would let the hairs of his living being invade his face. He kicked me without great conviction and I kept quiet.

"Well," said the fat officer, "have you thought about it?"

I looked at them with curiosity, as insects of a very rare species. I told them, "I know where he is. He is hidden in the cemetery. In a vault or in the gravediggers' shack."

It was a farce. I wanted to see them stand up, buckle their belts and give orders busily.

They jumped to their feet. "Let's go. Molés, go get fifteen men from Lieutenant Lopez. You," the fat man said, "I'll let you off if you're telling the truth, but it'll cost you plenty if you're making monkeys out of us."

They left in a great clatter and I waited peacefully under the guard of *falangistas*. From time to time I smiled, thinking about the spectacle they would make. I felt stunned and malicious. I imagined them lifting up tombstones, opening the doors of the vaults one by one. I represented this situation to myself as if I had been someone else: this prisoner obstinately playing the hero, these grim *falangistas* with their moustaches and their men in uniform running among the graves; it was irresistibly funny. After half an hour the little fat man came back alone. I thought he had come to give the orders to execute me. The others must have stayed in the cemetery.

The officer looked at me. He didn't look at all sheepish. "Take him into the big courtyard with the others," he said. "After the military operations a regular court will decide what happens to him."

"Then they're not . . . not going to shoot me . . . ?"

"Not now, anyway. What happens afterwards is none of my business."

I still didn't understand. I asked, "But why . . . ?"

He shrugged his shoulders without answering and the soldiers took me away. In the big courtyard there were about a hundred prisoners, women, children and a few old men. I began walking around the central grass-plot, I was stupefied. At noon they let us eat in the mess hall. Two or three people questioned me. I must have known them, but I didn't answer: I didn't even know where I was.

Around evening they pushed about ten new prisoners into the court. I recognized Garcia, the baker. He said, "What damned luck you have! I didn't think I'd see you alive."

"They sentenced me to death," I said, "and then they changed their minds. I don't know why."

"They arrested me at two o'clock," Garcia said.

"Why?" Garcia had nothing to do with politics.

"I don't know," he said. "They arrest everybody who doesn't think the way they do. He lowered his voice. "They got Gris."

I began to tremble. "When?"

"This morning. He messed it up. He left his cousin's on Tuesday because they had an argument. There were plenty of people to hide him but he didn't want to owe anything to anybody. He said, 'I'd go and hide in Ibbieta's place, but they got him, so I'll go hide in the cemetery.'"

"In the cemetery?"

"Yes. What a fool. Of course they went by there this morning, that was sure to happen. They found him in the gravediggers' shack. He shot them and they got him."

"In the cemetery!"

Everything began to spin and I found myself sitting on the ground: I laughed so hard I cried.

chapter 1

Existentialism and the Search for Meaning

There is something which, for lack of a better name, we will call the tragic sense of life, which carries with it a whole conception of life itself and of the universe, a whole philosophy more or less formulated, more or less conscious . . . (I)t is useless to speak of . . . people who are healthy and people who are not healthy. Apart from the fact that there is no normal standard of health, nobody has proved that the human being is necessarily cheerful by nature. . . .

Unamuno, pp. 17–18

It has dawned on you that a man needn't have done anything for him to die.

Camus, *Caligula*, Act II, p. 24

INTRODUCTION

Suffering is a spiritual thing. It is the most immediate revelation of consciousness, and it may be that our body was given us simply in order that suffering might be enabled to manifest itself. . . . The child first cries at birth when the air, entering into its lungs and limiting it, seems to say: "you have to breathe me in order that you may live!"

Unamuno, p. 211

Feelings of despair are not uncommon in human experience. When we fail to win the hoped-for scholarship, when we suffer through a long illness, when a loved one dies — experiences like these are part and parcel of the human condition, and no one wonders why we feel despair when they occur. Nevertheless, most people assume that such despair lasts for an "appropriate" period of time. Further, we usually think of despair as being in reference to some event, something we can pinpoint in time and space. So popular advice urges us to move on, not to dwell on the painful. Psychiatrists regularly treat clients whose despair is identified as pathological because it lacks a specifiable object or is excessively morbid or excessively protracted.

But what if there is another sort of despair, a kind of existential despair, which no therapy can ameliorate? Like it or not, human existence is full of suffering, and the world does not do our bidding. What good are all of our scientific achievements when we still wonder what meaning there is to our lives? The Spanish philosopher Miguel de Unamuno, quoted at the beginning of this chapter, writes of suffering as spiritual, not physical. Even the newborn, in order to breathe its first breath, must cry.

Camus, in *The Myth of Sisyphus*, maintains that the greatest philosophical problem is the problem of suicide. Our tendency is to view suicide as aberrant behavior motivated by some sort of pathology. We wonder about the state of mind of anyone who could do such a thing. But Camus frames the issue very differently: The question for him is not why anyone would take his or her own life, but rather why anyone *wouldn't*. This is really a question about existential meaning.

This deeply felt insecurity such as we have described here is not necessarily tied to any object or event. It is not, then, a phobia like a fear of heights. Though it might occur when we have suffered a loss, it can also thrust itself on us during moments of great happiness. Or it can happen during our regular humdrum routine. As Camus writes in *The Myth of Sisyphus*,

> Rising, streetcar, four hours in the office or the factory, meal, streetcar, four hours of work, meal, sleep, and Monday Tuesday Wednesday Thursday Friday and Saturday according to the same rhythm — this path is easily followed most of the time. But one day the 'why' arises and everything begins in that weariness tinged with amazement. (p. 10)

Questions about the *why*, even though we struggle to avoid them, demand our attention.

We can despair of reality in virtually the same way that we might despair of a person. Reality can disappoint us, let us down. The universe, existentialists repeatedly tell us, is indifferent to us, and this realization is terrifying. Even with advanced technology, we cannot control Being. Indeed, with today's technology, we may be deluded into thinking that we have control while instead we have become reduced (like machines) to our functions; these functions, however, cannot save us. Thus, we search for some meaning, or we hide and pretend that the problem does not exist.

PERSPECTIVES ON DESPAIR

Though existentialist thinkers make despair the beginning point of philosophy, there are differing viewpoints on the significance of this ontological reality. In fact, generally speaking, one might roughly sketch out three perspectives — existential theism, existential nihilism, and existential revolt — on the meaning of human existence.

Existential theism holds that anxiety is fundamental to the human condition, for it exposes how unsatisfying the world of the conditional is. Money, power, fame, beauty — these may provide us with some temporary pleasure, but the pleasure is fleeting at best. The contingent cannot provide genuine satisfaction, for its existence is always insecure. This insecurity cannot help but reveal itself at key moments in our lives. Philosopher Karl Jaspers (1883–1969), for example, writes of the *grenzsituation* — the boundary situation — in which one's everyday being is shattered. Such ruptures may be brought on by illness or guilt or despair, but they are unavoidable. In this process we are confronted with a reality far greater than ourselves, when despair and forlornness eat away at the certainties that once offered us comfort.

These insights, for theists Jaspers, Paul Tillich (1886–1965), and Gabriel Marcel (1889–1973), point to the possibility of salvation. As Marcel writes, "the only genuine hope is hope in what does not depend on ourselves." (p. 32) Through *Transcendence*, to use Jaspers's term, we move beyond our own finite nature to that which is not conditional. Without some ground in an Absolute, there cannot be any meaning. Whether we call that Absolute the *Unconditional* (Tillich's term) or the Transcendent or God, this source of meaning is the reason why our despair is not in vain. Our suffering, though constituitive of human existence, is meaningful. Life requires faith, what Tillich calls the "courage to be." This courage to be is essential in the face of meaninglessness and anxiety over our inevitable death. Tillich writes: "Courage always includes risk, it is always threatened by nonbeing, whether the risk of losing oneself and becoming a thing within the whole of things or of losing one's world in an empty self-relatedness." (*The Courage to Be*, p. 155) And that we choose to live signals our possession of this courage, no matter what else we may claim constitutes our reason for being.

According to this particular version of existentialism, there is nothing concrete or contingent that can address our anxiety over nonbeing. We can seek power or money, but there is the ever-present possibility that we will lose that power or money and the certainty that others exist with more of each than we have. Or we can, as Tillich puts it, "build a narrow castle of certitude which can be defended and is defended with the utmost tenacity." (*The Courage to Be,* p. 76) That is, we cling tenaciously to a firm moral code, ignoring the ambiguity between good and evil, the merits of competing positions, and the anxiety over our own imperfections. Such rigid dogmatism masks the fear of nonbeing, which haunts all of us.

For existential theists, a life limited to contingency would be meaningless. Such a life becomes either an avoidance of anxiety through the endless pursuit of material comforts, or a pathological obsession with despair whose only logical end is suicide. But are these our only alternatives? For theists, a life of faith provides a way out of this hopeless bind. Such a life requires courage of a particular sort, for it is not a courage which confronts any particular object or situation, such as the courage of a soldier in battle or the courage of a woman in childbirth. Rather, it is courage in the face of the "anxiety of a finite being about the threat of non-being." It is a courage that "belongs to existence itself." (Tillich, 1952, p. 39) This stance presupposes that there is something greater than one's own power or even the power of one's world. This is what enables us to transcend the anxiety of nonbeing by taking it upon ourselves. This capacity makes humans the most truly alive of all beings, as we can transcend any given situation to create *beyond* ourselves.

Thus, for theistic existentialists, "every courage to be has an open or hidden religious root." (Tillich, 1952, p. 156) And the faith that permits courage, though it offers no guarantees of salvation or eternal life or even the existence of an Unconditional, is the only way one can "say Yes to being" (p. 189) and not give in to despair. "Courage as the universal and essential self-affirmation of one's being is an ontological concept. The courage to be is the ethical act in which human beings affirm their own being "in spite of those elements of . . . existence which conflict with . . . essential self-affirmation." (p. 3) Chapter 2 explores in greater depth this view, which we call existential theism.

There are other thinkers in the existentialist tradition who agree with the basic premise that the world of the contingent is without meaning. But unlike the theistic view just described, proponents of this position defend some version of nihilism, that is, the view that nothing has value or meaning in a world of contingency. The term *nihilism* was probably first coined in Russia in the second quarter of the nineteenth century and popularized in Russian novelist Ivan Turgenev's *Fathers and Sons.* Bazarov, the novel's central character, identifies with nihilism and calls it one of the "most advanced ideas" of the time. One frequently quoted statement of the nihilist position is: "Here is the ultimatum of our camp: what can be smashed should be smashed; what will stand the blow is good; what will fly into smithereens is rubbish; at any rate, hit out right and left — there will and can be no harm from it." (Yarmolinsky, p. 720)

Nihilism is not an organized body of thought, and literary and philosophical expressions of nihilism take many different forms. But in general, nihilists accept the premise that nothing is of value in a contingent world and reject the possibility of anything beyond that contingent world. The nihilist's only comfort (if such a term can be applied to this view) is that he or she is no longer a victim of any illusions. Life, the nihilist argues, is not made for happiness; life may be silly or insignificant or boring or a cruel farce, but it is without any sort of purpose. The absurdity of human suffering and the inevitability of death make all projects meaningless and all searches futile. The nihilist may end up in hedonism or a ceaseless quest for power or even suicide. Ironically, though a nihilist might commit suicide, that act too is without meaning. (pp. 176–77 explore Nietzsche's analysis of nihilism.)

Finally, there are those existentialists who argue that our projects and our freedom are all that we have and that these provide meaning for human existence. Though this meaning is contingent and subjective, it is all that we have and it must be enough. There is nothing beyond us, no Absolute, no eternal life; anything more, however, would overwhelm us. We struggle, like Sisyphus, even knowing that we will all die, knowing that no project is ever truly complete. Camus refers to this as our "revolt," and in *The Myth of Sisyphus* he imagines Sisyphus, though condemned eternally to roll a rock up a hill without ever getting it over the top, to be happy.

This perspective is not dismissive of theism and nihilism. Rather, representatives of this view understand the anger of the nihilist over the world's purposelessness, while they adopt the courage of the theist who refuses to give in to despair. Like the nihilist, these existentialists reject absolutes; unlike the nihilist, they believe in the possibility of happiness. "In the darkest depths of our nihilism, I have sought only for the means to transcend nihilism," said Camus in an interview. (Cruikshank, p. 3) In *Resistance, Rebellion, and Death* he wrote, "I continue to believe that the world has no ultimate meaning. But I know that something in it has meaning and that is man, because he is the only creature to insist on having one." (p. 14) The world may defy all our attempts to make sense of it, for the world is absurd and reason is feeble by comparison. But this does not mean that it is a world without meaning. The point is not to resign ourselves to suicide or to hedonism or even to hope for some afterlife. The point is to revolt.

> The absurd man thus catches sight of a burning and frigid, transparent and limited universe in which nothing is possible but everything is given, and beyond which all is collapse and nothingness. He can then decide to accept such a universe and draw from it his strength, his refusal to hope, and the unyielding evidence of a life without consolation.
>
> *Myth of Sisyphus, p. 44*

In a sense, our happiness *is* our revolt.

At the powerful conclusion of the novel *The Plague*, Camus describes the feelings of Dr. Rieux, who has struggled throughout the plague's siege only to see many of his friends die and to find himself exhausted and yet transformed. Rieux exemplifies what Camus has in mind when he writes of "heroism without God." (*Notebooks*, p. 15) This heroism is our rebellion against death, though we know we are outmatched by the competition. As Rieux tells his dying friend Tarrou, "To become a saint, you need to live. So fight away!" (see p. 75 in this text) Rieux has watched his fellow human beings fight this natural force, and he "bears witness" to the heroism of those who lived and those who died. Are the "knowledge and memories" (see p. 79) with which we are left enough? Unlike the others who celebrate the eventual victory over the plague, Rieux knows that such victories are at best only temporary ones:

Tarrou, the men and the woman Rieux had loved and lost — all alike, dead or guilty, were forgotten. Yes, the old fellow had been right; these people were 'just the same as ever.' But this was at once their strength and their innocence, and it was on this level, beyond all grief, that Rieux could feel himself at one with them. And it was in the midst of shouts rolling against the terrace wall in massive waves that waxed in volume and duration, while cataracts of colored fire fell thicker through the darkness, that Dr. Rieux resolved to compile this chronicle, so that he should not be one of those who hold their peace but should bear witness in favor of those plague-stricken people; so that some memorial of the injustice and outrage done them might endure; and to state quite simply what we learn in a time of pestilence: that there are more things to admire in men than to despise.

None the less, he knew that the tale he had to tell could not be one of a final victory. It could be only the record of what had had to be done, and what assuredly would have to be done again in the never ending fight against terror and its relentless onslaughts, despite their personal afflications, by all who, while unable to be saints but refusing to bow down to pestilences, strive their utmost to be healers.

And, indeed, as he listened to the cries of joy rising from the town, Rieux remembered that such joy is always imperiled. He knew what those jubilant crowds did not know but could have learned from books: that the plague bacillus never dies or disappears for good; that it can lie dormant for years and years in furniture and linen-chests; that it bides its time in bedrooms, cellars, trunks, and bookshelves; and that perhaps the day would come when, for the bane and the enlightening of men, it would rouse up its rats again and send them forth to die in a happy city.[1]

[1] From *The Plague* by Albert Camus, translated by Stuart Gilbert. Copyright © 1958 by Alfred A. Knopf Inc. Reprinted by permission of Alfred A. Knopf Inc.

Given these perspectives on despair, let us examine more carefully some of the specific concepts related to the existentialist interpretation of meaning.

ALIENATION AND MEANING

The term *alienation* has a long history of varied meanings. It derives from the Latin word *alienus,* which means foreign or strange or belonging to another. The term connotes feelings of estrangement or detachment from self and from others. The word also has an obscure meaning in the law, referring to the transfer of property to another person or — as in lawsuits for alienation of affection — the transfer even of one's feelings to another person. *Alienation* was also used to refer to insanity; at one time an alienist was one who treated persons with mental disorders.

Today, the term *alienation* has been used to refer to a wide variety of psychological and social disorders, including conditions that are based on supposedly objective circumstances and those that are based on subjective states of being. Growing numbers of writers have referred to the crisis of the modern age as one of alienation, maintaining that there are specific concrete differences between our age and others that would account for the phenomenon of alienation. Some, for example, focus on the tedium of work where workers are nothing but expendable cogs in a vast machine. Others address modern technology, which threatens to dehumanize us and to manipulate our feelings. Still others charge that our commodity orientation, which equates material comforts with personal happiness, has diverted us from issues of real importance. What is it that these expressions of alienation have in common?

The way one defines alienation has important implications for how one sees the problem and the possibilities for its solution. If one assumes that alienation is the result of certain objective conditions, then it follows that one can eradicate it, that it is either a form of psychopathology or a result of certain oppressive material circumstances. For example, according to traditional Marxism, one can end alienation by transforming the structure of society to one that is classless and where work is meaningful. Religious spokespeople might argue that present-day alienation is the result of a profound loss of faith and an absence of social norms; hence, the solution is a return to spirituality and moral community. Radical individualists might urge us to reject the pressures of the masses and proclaim our own unique individuality, whatever form that might take.

Each view differs in its diagnosis and its prescription, yet each assumes that the source of alienation is outside us and that there is some solution to the problem. But suppose that alienation is no pathology but rather an inescapable by-product of the human condition. Perhaps every age has its own particular anxiety. Perhaps we are all — for no other reason but that we are human — alienated. Perhaps the "normally alienated" person fails to get noticed because he or she is no different from anyone else. Indeed, perhaps those who claim to suffer no feelings of alienation are the sickest among us! Each age, then, may have its own particular expression of alienation which varies depending on the concrete circumstances of the time; but the search for the good old days before alienation is a futile one. Suppose, then, that to be human is inevitably to feel separate from nature, separate from others, even separate from oneself.

Heidegger retells an ancient fable to illustrate what it means to be human:

> Once when 'Care' was crossing a river, she saw some clay; she thoughtfully took up a piece and began to shape it. While she was meditating on what she had made, Jupiter came by. 'Care' asked him to give it spirit, and this he gladly granted. But when she wanted her name to be bestowed upon it, he forbade this, and demanded that it be given his name instead. While 'Care' and Jupiter were disputing, Earth arose and desired that her own name be conferred on the creature, since she had furnished it with part of her body. They asked Saturn to be their arbiter, and he made the following decision, which seemed a just one: 'Since you, Jupiter, have given its spirit, you shall receive that spirit at its death; and since you, Earth, have given its body, you shall receive its body. But since 'Care' first shaped this creature, she shall possess it as long as it lives. And because there is now a dispute among you as to its name, let it be called 'homo,' for it is made out of humus (earth).
>
> *Being and Time, p. 242*

For Heidegger, the human being is a being essentially full of care. Here *care* has a double meaning: It signifies concern and commitment but it also signifies a kind of anxiousness. And this caring may be unique to the human being. For it is the human being alone who is capable of experiencing the ontological, that is, the only being for whom Being is at issue. Through our capacity for care, we can project ourselves into a future that is all possibility. (See chapter 4, pp. 241–45, for a longer analysis of Heidegger's notion of care.)

If this is true, then we are also the only beings capable of experiencing alienation. For alienation is a kind of rupture, a splitting in which one feels not at home. But isn't this experience a function of that self-consciousness that is unique to humans? As Camus observes:

> If I were a tree among trees, a cat among animals, this problem would not arise, for I should belong to this world. I should *be* this world to which I am now opposed by my whole consciousness and my whole insistence upon familiarity.
>
> *The Myth of Sisyphus, p. 38*

But humans can never *be* the world and remain inevitably severed from it. Anything else would make us objects rather than subjects.

ALIENATION OF SELF

In Robert Louis Stevenson's novel *The Strange Case of Dr. Jekyll and Mr. Hyde,* a scientist is transformed into an evil counterpart as a result of testing a serum he has created. Stevenson makes clear, however, that this evil is not at all alien to Jekyll but is rather another expression of his own self, as real albeit repressed. And each of us is really two beings, not one, engaged in a struggle for control. As Dr. Jekyll realized,

> With every day, and from both sides of my intelligence, the moral and the intellectual, I thus drew steadily nearer to that truth, by whose partial discovery I have been doomed to such a dreadful shipwreck: that man is not truly one, but truly two. (p. 383)

However terrifying is this transformation, Dr. Jekyll cannot help but admire Hyde's spiritedness unbounded by conventional morality. Indeed, at first, he feels no repugnance toward him, "but rather a leap of welcome. This too was myself. It seemed natural and human." (pp. 387–88).

What does it mean for a self to be at war with itself? Logical identity corresponds to the logical propositions $A = A$ and A is not *not-A.* So, in logical terms, the question makes no sense. But humans are obviously not logical propositions. Humans, as self-conscious animals, have the capacity to doubt and question our own identities. Though we may long for some fixed identity, this search is futile, for we are endlessly in process. Personality in the sense of a fixed, static entity is, then, a myth. At times we may try to compensate for this by identifying ourselves with some physical characteristic, such as beauty, or some attribute, such as wealth. But what happens when beauty fades or we discover that there are others even wealthier? Conversely, we may identify with some negative characteristics and decide that our destiny is determined by the possession of this feature: "If only I weren't so short . . ."

There is an obvious paradox in the notion of alienation from self. If the self is a whole, continuous and identifiable, how is it possible for that self to be alienated from itself? Does this make it two selves? Descartes, for example, (see chapter 4, pp. 232–35) maintained that the self is the mind (or soul) and that the soul is itself indivisible, eternal, and unchanging. If this is so (and much of traditional philosophy has viewed the self in this way), then alienation either makes no sense or is attached to some part of the person other than the soul. Does the experience of alienation make one into two selves? Or why not speak of a split or severed or incomplete self? But the concept of self-alienation implies more than a simple split of one self into two distinct parts. Rather, the self, when alienated, is still a whole self where one part of the self feels alien to the self as a whole. One might see alienation as a severance of oneself from one's possibilities, with one part of the self laying claim to represent the self as a whole. But then who is this "real" self?

ALIENATION FROM NATURE

The comtemporary philosopher William Barrett has described our present state as one of "homelessness." We are, unlike all other living creatures, without a natural home. We are alone in the world without moorings and without obvious purpose.

Modern science since the 1500s has irrevocably changed our relationship to nature; as the natural world is increasingly demystified, we come to view natural objects as merely instrumental. Where once the world was seen as full of meaning and purpose, our vision of today's world is a product of the scientific revolution and the mechanistic principles on which it is based. Instead of asking about reasons and purposes in nature, we hypothesize about causes and effects.

Yet it would be overly simplistic to attribute our alienation from nature to the development of modern science. Doing so suggests that this is a fairly recent phenomenon in human history. Instead, one could argue that this sense of separation from nature is a fundamental aspect of the Judeo-Christian tradition. We might think in this context, for example, of the story of creation in Genesis: "And God said, let us make man in our image, after our likeness: and let them have dominion over the fish of the sea, and over the fowl of the air, and over the cattle, and over all the earth, and over every creeping thing that creepeth upon the earth." (Gen. 1:26) Here nature is clearly ordered in a hierarchical fashion. Indeed, God gives Adam the power to name all the animals. "And out of the ground the Lord God formed every beast of the field, and every fowl of the air, and brought *them* unto Adam to see what he would call them: and whatsoever Adam called every living creature, that *was* the name thereof." (Gen. 2:19) Such a power — the power of naming — gives us control over the thing named. But this power has its cost as well, for it severs us from those over whom we have control. Throughout the Judeo-Christian tradition, it is human beings alone who are created in God's image. Whether understood literally or allegorically, this narrative makes clear our status as forever in between, wedged between the kingdom of God and the nonhuman natural order. Once again, we appear not to fit. Our potential to share in God's goodness is merely the other side of our potential to fall from grace.

ALIENATION FROM OTHERS

It would appear that as humans we all share the same plight, the same burden of self-consciousness and awareness of separation, and that common burden should lead us to a sense of community with others. Yet we often feel alone and isolated. We wonder whether others think and feel as we do. The prospect of a world of selves exactly identical to each other is a terrifying one, but how can we bridge the gap that does exist between ourselves and others?

Once again our self-consciousness makes us aware not only of the self *as* self, but of the self as different from others. Though we are all members of the species Homo sapiens, we appear to be radically different from all other species. Whereas all salmon or porcupine or tigers share the same being, humans seem to be as different as we are alike. We speak different languages, have different cultures, espouse different values, and construct different realities. And we war with each other when those differences become intolerable.

Some maintain that consciousness is what makes us human. But this world of consciousness is inescapably our own. How do we know that others possess it in the same way that we do? We observe people's behavior, notice actions similar to our own; but can we be sure that others' feelings are the same as ours? When someone says "ouch," does it mean the same as when another says it? We cannot see inside someone's soul or consciousness. Perhaps others are no more than sophisticated automata with all the trappings of human beings. Can we know that there are other minds like our own?

This sense of isolation is not disconnected from the existential experience of estrangement from others. At a time when we are feeling the effects of increasing "massification," we may be more and more disconnected from others. We feel anonymous, barely known to our closest neighbors. Yet, even in our most intimate relationships, can we ever experience anything but estrangement? Are we not in some fundamental sense horribly severed from each other, each locked in his or her own private world?

ABSURDITY AND DEATH

Anguish is that which makes consciousness return upon itself. He who knows no anguish knows what he does and what he thinks, but he does not truly know that he does it and that he thinks it. . . . For it is only anguish, it is only the passionate longing never to die, that makes a human spirit master of itself.

Unamuno, p. 212

I don't mind dying. I just don't want to be there when it happens.
Woody Allen

There's nothing like insecurity for stimulating the brain.
Camus, *Caligula,* Act IV, p. 58

In Camus's play *Caligula,* Emperor Caligula sums up the human condition: "men die; and they are not happy." (Act I, p. 8) This statement conjoins two ideas central to existentialism: the significance of death and the despair of being human.

We have repeatedly returned to the uniquely human capacity for self-consciousness as the source of paradox and conflict. If suffering is the origin of consciousness, then human suffering must be very different from nonhuman suffering. There is also the particularly human suffering of knowing that we all suffer and ultimately die. We want to understand suffering, yet we cannot. We want to be immortal, yet we know we must die. Isn't all of it absurd?

Philosopher Thomas Nagel has suggested that absurdity is a result of our ability to "step back" and examine the world around us. "In ordinary life a situation is absurd when it includes a conspicuous discrepancy between pretension or aspiration and reality." (p. 13) One could easily imagine particular events that are absurd — your pants fall down as you are being knighted, a conquering hero trips on a banana peel. But is there something about human existence per se that is absurd?

In Franz Kafka's novel *The Trial,* Joseph K. is an ordinary citizen who is arrested one day. "Someone must have been telling lies about Joseph K., for without having done anything wrong he was arrested one fine morning." (p. 3) Even to the day he is executed, the nature of Joseph K.'s crime is completely unclear. He is the absurd person, completely ordinary and yet condemned to die. Reason is unable to help us sort this out, for it is by its very nature irrational.

Absurdity is relational; it lies in the confrontation between humans and the world. Thus, it is neither in us nor in the world. Roquentin, Sartre's protagonist in *Nausea* (see pp. 14–15), realizes the absurdity in the world. The human mind cannot digest it all, for reality is *de trop,* too much.

> The word absurdity is coming to life under my pen; a little while ago, in the garden, I couldn't find it, but neither was I looking for it, I didn't need it: I thought without words, *on* things, *with* things. Absurdity was not an idea in my head, or the sound of a voice, only this long serpent dead at my feet, this wooden serpent. Serpent or claw or root or vulture's talon, what difference does it make. And without formulating anything clearly, I understood that I had found the key to Existence, the key to my Nauseas, to my own life. In

fact, all that I could grasp beyond that returns to this fundamental absurdity. Absurdity: another word; I struggle against words; down there I touched the thing. But I wanted to fix the absolute character of this absurdity here. A movement, an event in the tiny coloured world of men is only relatively absurd: by relation to the accompanying circumstances. A madman's ravings, for example, are absurd in relation to the situation in which he finds himself, but not in relation to the delirium. But a little while ago I made an experiment with the absolute or the absurd. This root — there was nothing in relation to which it was absurd. Oh, how can I put it in words? Absurd: in relation to the stones, the tufts of yellow grass, the dry mud, the tree, the sky, the green benches. Absurd, irreducible; nothing — not even a profound, secret upheaval of nature — could explain it.[2]

The world of rationality and explanation is not the existing world. This world of rationality is the world of circles and triangles, not an absurd world. A circle, Roquentin explains, "is clearly explained by the rotation of a straight segment around one of its extremities." (p. 129) But circles do not exist. Roquentin sees the root, he understands its function; but that only allows one "to understand generally that it was a root, but not *that one* at all." (p. 129) What is real confounds us, and what is most confounding is the reality of our own death.

We all can acknowledge that there was a time when we did not exist, though our memories become more and more blurred as we try to remember further back in time. Similarly, we can grant that there will come a time when we cease to exist. But our beginnings have dates, times, and places attached to them; our endings do not. So death is inevitable, yet unpredictable and unfathomable. "The world's all wrong" Caligula remarks (Act I, p. 15), and death in particular puts everything into question. Caligula is the absurd hero who wants three equally impossible things: happiness, the moon, and eternal life. As a result, he becomes a tyrant whose abuses of power can only lead to his own death. But he does not regret this:

> (W)hat's the use to me of a firm hand, what use is the amazing power that's mine, if I can't have the sun set in the east, if I can't reduce the sum of suffering and make an end of death? (Act I, p. 16)

Ironically, Caligula, however cruel he is, is referred to as an "idealist"; others — the "realists" — come to terms with the truth of human despair and death "without much trouble." (Act I, p. 9) But isn't this another example of inauthenticity, of the extent to which we are willing to deceive ourselves in order to avoid the confrontation with absurdity?

---

[2] Jean-Paul Sartre, *Nausea*, translated by Lloyd Alexander, p. 129. Copyright © 1964 by New Directions Publishing Corporation. All rights reserved.

Philosophers are not so different from anyone else in their general aversion to thinking about human finitude. What could be more horrifying and less understandable than the prospect of our own nonexistence? Even in the sixteenth century, Pascal understood how inauthentically we deal with the inevitability of death: "Diversion: As men are not able to fight against death, misery, ignorance, they have taken it into their heads, in order to be happy, not to think of them at all." (*Pensees*, no. 168) Or: "Despite these miseries, man wishes to be happy, and only wishes to be happy, and cannot wish not to be so. But how will he set about it? To be happy he would have to make himself immortal; but, not being able to do so, it has occurred to him to prevent himself from thinking of death." (*Pensees*, no. 169) Pascal describes with a graphic metaphor the pain of the human condition:

> Let us imagine a number of people in chains, and all condemned to death, where some are killed each day in the sight of the others, and those who remain see the fate in that of their fellows, and wait their turn, looking at each other, sorrowfully and without hope. That is an image of the human condition.
>
> Pensees, *no. 199*

In a classic novel by Leo Tolstoy, *The Death of Ivan Ilyich*, Ivan Ilyich is an ordinary person with a terminal illness. Here he expresses the dread and the disbelief surrounding the idea of his own mortality:

> All his life he had regarded the syllogism he had learned while studying Kiesewetter's *Logics:* 'Caius is a man, men are mortal, and therefore Caius is mortal,' as being true only in respect to Caius, not to himself. Caius was a man, a man in the abstract sense, and so the syllogism applied to him; but Ivan Ilyich was not Caius, and not a man in the abstract sense; he had always been quite, quite different from all other men. He had been little Vanya to his mama and papa, to his brothers Mitya and Volodya, to the coachman and the nursemaid and to his toys, and to Katya; Vanya, who had lived through all the joys and sorrows and ecstasies of childhood, boyhood, and youth. Had Caius ever known the leathery smell of a football that Vanya had loved so dearly? Had Caius ever kissed his mother's hand with such feeling, or so loved the rustle of her silk shirts? Had Caius ever made a row over the buns at school? Or ever been so in love? Or presided so brilliantly over a court session?
>
> Caius was indeed mortal, and it was only right and proper that he should die, but he, Vanya, Ivan Ilyich, with all his thoughts and feelings — it was quite a different matter with him. And it could not be right and proper that he should die. The thought was too horrifying.[3]

[3] Leo Tolstoy, *The Death of Ivan Ilyich*, translated by Margaret Wettlin, 1963, pp. 258–59. Reprinted by permission of Dell Publishing Co.

What is especially distressing for Ivan is his contemporaries' denial of the fact of his dying: the doctor who urges more medicine on him and then flees, the friends who hide in the language of the "everyday," the wife who continues to be absorbed in household affairs:

> At work, Ivan Ilyich noticed, or at least thought he noticed, a strange attitude toward him: at times he felt that his colleagues were stealing glances at him as at one who was about to vacate a post; at other times his friends would chaff him amiably about his fancied illness, as if that fearful, that horrible, that unheard-of something that was growing inside him and gnawing at his vitals night and day, irresistibly dragging him off somewhere, was a highly appropriate subject for a joke. He became especially irritated by Schwartz, whose liveliness, playfulness, and quality of being always *comme il faut* reminded Ivan Ilyich of himself ten years earlier.[4]

Each of us is like Ivan. Each of us feels unique and special. Perhaps no one of us can understand in any real way the idea of death in any sense other than the sterile syllogisms we learn in logic class or the inauthentic ways we speak of death to one another. Even the most sophisticated empirical works — whether they be studies like those of sociologist Emile Durkheim on suicide or physician Elisabeth Kübler-Ross's explorations of the five stages of the dying process, or anthropological reports on death rituals in varied cultures — can at best only approach death from the outside. This sort of conventional knowledge may be helpful in some ways, but can never provide us with an understanding of death. As Kierkegaard (see chapter 2) writes:

> For example, the problem of what it means to die: I know concerning this what people in general know about it; I know I shall die if I take a dose of sulphuric acid, and also if I drown myself, or go to sleep in an atmosphere of coal gas, and so forth. I know that Napoleon always went about with poison ready at hand, and that Juliet in Shakespeare poisoned herself. I know that the Stoics regarded suicide as a courageous deed, and that others consider it a cowardly act. I know that the tragic hero dies in the fifth act of the drama, and that his death has an infinite significance in pathos, but that when a bartender dies death does not have this significance. . . . I know further what the clergy are accustomed to say on this subject, and I am familiar with the general run of themes treated at funerals. . . . Nevertheless, in spite of this almost extraordinary knowledge or facility in knowledge, I can by no means regard death as something I have understood.
>
> Concluding Unscientific Postscript, *p. 156*

What is the connection between death and human meaning? Does death provide a basis for meaning or destroy any possibility of it? It is

[4] Ibid., p. 252.

often death which stirs us to reassess life. When a loved one or family member dies, when we hear or read of some particularly tragic death, we cannot help but seek some explanation. In *Caligula* Cherea explains that death is not so terrible, but "what's intolerable is to see one's life being drained of meaning, to be told there's no reason for existing. [One] can't live without some reason for living." (Act II, p. 21) But this point does not address the question of how the inevitability of death affects meaning. How can there be any meaning at all if we must die?

In the excerpt from *Being and Time* (pp. 58–72), Heidegger makes Being-toward-death constituitive of Dasein's nature. But Heidegger shifts the focus away from death as termination to an understanding of one's own being as being-toward-death. We are temporal beings, and Care (*Sorge*) constitutes the everyday being of Dasein; thus, animals are "carefree," for they live in the "now." Unlike animals, we must live with the anxiety that we might end at any moment. This anxiety is not simple fear or individual weakness; rather, it "belongs to Dasein 'universally.'" Death is for Dasein a "possibility-of-Being" (p. 59), but unlike other possibilities, "death is the possibility of no-longer-being-able-to-be-there." Death is always on the horizon and is "not to be outstripped." Anxiety is Dasein's recognition that "death is the possibility of the absolute impossibility of Dasein." (p. 59) Thus, "Being-towards-death is essentially anxiety." (p. 60)

The "everyday" or "inauthentic" attitude toward death is flight and avoidance. The "they" tries to conceal Dasein's Being-toward-Death with "tranquillization" about death, by speaking of death as already-occurred rather than as potential. We send sympathy cards that never mention death. We speak of "passing on" or "passing away"; we hide our dying in institutions like hospitals and nursing homes.

"One dies, they say, but not right away." (*Being and Time*, p. 5) This inauthentic mode treats death as a fact — "'only' empirical" (p. 65) — but not an existential reality. Ivan Ilyich's friends exemplify this attitude. Yet Heidegger is not recommending the sort of morbid fascination with death one sometimes sees in individuals who, for example, never miss a funeral of even the most distant acquaintance. Such behavior — though death-obsessed — is more like a fear of living than real death awareness. For Heidegger, authentic being-toward-death is not a brooding about death. Rather, authentic being-toward-death requires that we stop behaving as though we were immortal and realize that death is a reality not to be "outstripped." It requires that we make death our "ownmost possibility" in what Heidegger calls "freedom towards death."

Death plays a key role in many of the works of existential fiction. In Camus's *The Stranger*, Meursault is radically transformed when he directly confronts his own inevitable death. Unwilling to accept the priest's assurance of heavenly salvation, he replies that though he may have wished for an afterlife, that wish is no more important than "wishing to be rich, or to swim very fast, or to have a better-shaped mouth. It was in the same order of things." (p. 150) Meursault does not desire a spiritual existence, but only the time to remember his life on earth and that he had been happy. Our recognition of death can, he tells us, be liberating, can put us "on the brink of freedom, ready to start life all over again." (p. 154) And that he is about to be executed matters very little, since "this business of dying had to be got through, inevitably." (p. 143)

Meursault's sentiments are not unlike those expressed in these lines of the Russian poet Nikolai Berdyaev (1874–1949): "Meaning is linked with ending. And if there were no end, if in our world there was no evil and endlessness of life, there would be no meaning to life whatever . . ." (lines 13–17, "If There Were No Death in the World")

Thus, for Berdyaev, the meaning of life is linked inextricably with the meaning of death. To live forever would be to deprive life of any meaning, for it would make all of our projects and concerns trivial. Indeed, the possession of immortal life would enable us quite literally to procrastinate forever. Or, as the poet Holderlin (1770–1843) wrote: "Once I lived like the gods, and more is not needed." (lines 14–15, "To the Parcae")

Existentialists closer to the nihilist tradition view death as preferable to life, which is full of despair and frustration. Death is not what makes life meaningful, for life has no meaning, but it is a final liberation from the torture of human existence. "Not to be born is best when all is reckoned, but once one has seen the light the next best thing, by far, is to go back where he came from, quickly as he can," wrote Sophocles (ca. 495–406 B.C.) in his play *Oedipus at Colonus*. (lines 1388–1391) This view is consistent with the claim that suicide is morally permissible; indeed, one might argue that this view makes suicide morally obligatory. "The gods," wrote one suicide, "pity them, unlike us cannot kill themselves."

For others, particularly Sartre and de Beauvoir, death is inherently absurd and unnatural. One cannot wait for one's death, yet one knows that it is coming. To be conscious, human, is to be openness, nothingness. We continue to search, however, for finality. This finality never comes except with death. Yet this is absurd, for in death we become objects rather than subjects. A dead body can be manipulated by others concretely in, for example, funeral arrangements and abstractly in the ways in which people remember the dead person. Sartre rejects Heidegger's analysis of death as possibility; rather, for Sartre, death is the destruction of possibilities.

For atheistic existentialists like de Beauvoir, Sartre, and Camus, this life is all that we have. The prospect of some sort of life after death is not likely from a logical point of view and also not particularly appealing existentially. Can we imagine ourselves without a physical body? Would we be a set of disembodied memories? Could we see without eyes, hear without ears? Could we have projects and concerns? Thus, not only may we be unable to imagine on any real level the extinction of self, so also do thoughts of a possible afterlife fail to reassure us. Anxiety in the face of death is not, then, a result of a failure of faith or a failure of nerve. Indeed, even existentialist theists spend very little time on the question of personal immortality. For example, Tillich writes: "Even if the so-called arguments for the 'immortality of the soul' had argumentative power (which they do not have) they would not convince existentially. For existentially everybody is aware of the complete loss of self which biological extinction implies." (*The Courage to Be*, p. 42)

How can we make any sense of all this? Simone de Beauvoir considers some of these issues in *A Very Easy Death*, a work that chronicles her mother's death from cancer:

> 'He is certainly of an age to die.' The sadness of the old; their banishment: most of them do not think that this age has yet come for them. I too made use of this cliche, and that when I was referring to my mother. I did not understand that one might sincerely weep for a relative, a grandfather aged seventy and more. If I met a woman of fifty overcome with sadness because she had just lost her mother, I thought her neurotic: we are all mortal, at eighty you are quite old enough to be one of the dead. . . .

> But it is not true. You do not die from being born, nor from having lived, nor from old age. You die from *something*. The knowledge that because of her age my mother's life must soon come to an end did not lessen the horrible surprise: she had sarcoma. Cancer, thrombosis, pneumonia: it is as violent and unforeseen as an engine stopping in the middle of the sky. My mother encouraged one to be optimistic when, crippled with arthritis and dying, she asserted the infinite value of each instant; but her vain tenaciousness also ripped and tore the reassuring curtain of everyday triviality. There is no such thing as a natural death: nothing that happens to a man is ever natural, since his presence calls the world into question. All men must die: but for every man his death is an accident and, even if he knows it and consents to it, an unjustifiable violation. (pp. 105–6)

CONCLUSION

Psychiatrist Viktor Frankl (see also chapter 5, p. 306 and the excerpt, pp. 344–52) has coined the term *noogenic neurosis* to refer to the loss of existential meaning which he thinks is a product of the present age. Certain neuroses, he believes, may be inescapably connected to the human condition. If such is the case, then we need not spend our money and time on psychoanalysis, behavior modification, group therapy, or any of the myriad strategies offered us for overcoming neurosis.

This chapter has explored some of the competing perspectives on the subject of existential meaning: theism, which maintains that contingency cannot provide meaning for existence and so demands a foundation in the Unconditional; nihilism, which rejects *all* absolutes and so concludes that life is meaningless; and those who defend resistance as the basis for meaning in a world without absolutes. Succeeding chapters will explore these views in more depth.

Jean-Paul Sartre tells of a dignified Parisian lady who, at a social event, let slip a vulgar word. Abashed, she apologized to her hosts, adding, "I suppose I must be becoming an existentialist." Like the woman in this story, many associate existentialism with a focus on the vulgar or the grotesque or the absurd. Indeed, critics have accused existentialism of an almost pathological obsession with the dark side of human existence. Existentialists might respond that authenticity requires that we not turn away from that which is most disquieting. Some existentialists have even described that view as one of optimism, for it frees humans from God's rules and the dictates of conventional morality. Regardless of which side one takes, there is no doubt that existentialism's approach to this issue distinguishes it from traditional philosophical views.

QUESTIONS FOR CONSIDERATION

1. What does it mean to refer — as Heidegger does — to death as a possibility? Based on the reading (pp. 58–72), what is authentic being-toward-death? Does this concept make sense? Why or why not?

2. How is the concept of alienation different — if at all — from religious notions of sin?

3. Toward which of the three perspectives on meaning discussed in this chapter are you most sympathetic? Defend your preference.

4. Is human existence absurd? What does this mean? Is death absurd? Why or why not?

5. If one could prove that there is no afterlife, what changes (if any) would you make in your life? Why?

6. Suppose we *do* live forever after physical death as immortal souls. How — if at all — would that affect our earthly existence?

7. How is death portrayed in popular media? Give some examples of what you think are authentic and inauthentic approaches.

8. Can you think of popular examples (books, stories, television shows,

etc.) which seem representative of any of the three existential views on despair? Discuss your choices.

REFERENCES

BARRETT, WILLIAM. *Irrational Man*. Garden City, N. Y.: Doubleday, 1958.

CAMUS, ALBERT. *Caligula*. Translated by Stuart Gilbert. In *Caligula and Three Other Plays*. New York: Vintage Books, 1958.

——. *The Myth of Sisyphus*. Translated by Justin O'Brien. New York: Vintage Books, 1955.

——. *Notebooks 1942–1951*. Translated by Justin O'Brien. New York: Oxford University Press, 1950.

——. *The Plague*. Translated by Stuart Gilbert. New York: Vintage Books, 1954.

——. *Resistance, Rebellion and Death*. Translated by Justin O'Brien. New York: Alfred A. Knopf, 1961.

——. *The Stranger*. Translated by Stuart Gilbert. New York: Vintage Books, 1946.

CRUIKSHANK, JOHN. *Albert Camus and the Literature of Revolt*. New York: Oxford University Press, 1950.

DURKHEIM, EMILE. *Suicide: A Study in Sociology*. New York: Free Press, 1951.

FEUER, LEWIS. "*What is Alienation? The Career of a Concept.*" *New Politics* 1 (1962): 116–34.

FRANKL, VIKTOR E. *Psychotherapy and Existentialism*. New York: Simon & Schuster, 1967.

FROMM, ERICH. *Marx's Concept of Man*. New York: Frederick Ungar Publishing Co., 1961.

GLICKSBERG, CHARLES I. *The Literature of Nihilism*. Lewisburg, Pa.: Bucknell University Press, 1975.

HEIDEGGER, MARTIN. *Being and Time*. Translated by John Macquarrie and Edward Robinson. New York: Harper & Row, 1962.

HESSE, HERMANN. *Steppenwolf*. New York: Holt, Rinehart and Winston, 1957.

JASPERS, KARL. *The Way to Wisdom*. Translated by Ralph Manheim. New Haven, Conn.: Yale University Press, 1951.

JOSEPHSON, ERIC AND MARY, eds. *Man Alone: Alienation in Modern Society*. New York: Dell Publishing, 1962.

KAFKA, FRANZ. *The Trial*. Translated by Willa and Edwin Muir. New York: Alfred A. Knopf, 1948.

KIERKEGAARD, SOREN. *Concluding Unscientific Postscript.* Translated by David F. Swenson and Walter Lowrie. Princeton, N. J.: Princeton University Press, 1941.

KÜBLER-ROSS, ELISABETH. *On Death and Dying.* New York: Macmillan, 1969.

LYND, HELEN W. "Alienation: Man's Fate and Man's Hope." *American Journal of Psychoanalysis* 21 (1961): 166–72.

MARCEL, GABRIEL. *The Philosophy of Existentialism.* Translated by Manya Harari. New York: Philosophical Library, 1973.

NAGEL, THOMAS. "The Absurd." In *Mortal Questions,* edited by Thomas Nagel, pp. 11–23. Cambridge: Cambridge University Press, 1979.

PASCAL, BLAISE. *Pensees.* Translated by W. F. Trotter. New York: Modern Library, 1941.

SARTRE, JEAN-PAUL. *Nausea.* Translated by Lloyd Alexander. New York: New Directions Publishing, 1964.

SCHACHTEL, ERNEST. "On Alienated Concepts of Identity." *American Journal of Psychoanalysis* 21 (1961): 120–31.

SEEMAN, MELVIN. "On the Meaning of Alienation." *American Sociological Review* 24 (1959): 783–91.

SOPHOCLES. *Oedipus at Colonus.* Translated by Robert Fagles. New York: Viking, 1979.

STEVENSON, ROBERT LOUIS. *The Strange Case of Dr. Jekyll and Mr. Hyde.* New York: Charles Scribner's Sons, 1904.

TILLICH, PAUL. *The Courage to Be.* New Haven, Conn.: Yale University Press, 1952.

——. *The Dynamics of Faith.* New York: Harper Colophon, 1957.

——. What Is Religion? Translated by James Luther Adams. New York: Harper Torchbooks. 1969.

TOLSTOY, LEO. *The Death of Ivan Ilyich.* Translated by Margaret Wettlin. In *Six Short Masterpieces by Tolstoy.* New York: Dell Publishing Co., 1963.

UNAMUNO, MIGUEL DE. *The Tragic Sense of Life.* Translated by J. E. Crawford Flitch. New York: Dover Publications, 1954.

WEISS, FREDERICK A. "Self-Alienation: Dynamics and Therapy." *American Journal of Psychoanalysis* 21 (1961): 207–18.

MARTIN HEIDEGGER

Martin Heidegger (1889–1976) grew up in Baden in southwest Germany. Though we know relatively little about his early life, we know that at one time he entered a Jesuit seminary, intending to become a priest. He was educated at the University of Freiburg and taught there and at the University of Marburg. There he knew Jaspers, Max Scheler, and Tillich. He was originally a student in theology but eventually dedicated himself entirely to philosophy. He was recalled to Freiburg when the philosopher Edmund Husserl (see pp. 236–38) retired in 1928 and became rector of the university in 1933, shortly after the Nazis came to power in Germany. He was for a time an ardent supporter of the Nazi regime, but his enthusiasm later declined and he resigned as rector in 1935. He continued to lecture until he retired, at which time he withdrew more and more from public life. He spent his last days secluded at his home on a mountaintop in the Black Forest.

In this excerpt from Being and Time, *one of Heidegger's most well-known works, Heidegger analyzes the nature of human existence (Dasein) as Being-toward-Death.*

Being-Towards-Death

50. PRELIMINARY SKETCH OF THE EXISTENTIAL-ONTOLOGICAL STRUCTURE OF DEATH

From our considerations of totality, end, and that which is still outstanding, there has emerged the necessity of Interpreting the phenomenon of death as Being-towards-the-end, and of doing so in terms of Dasein's basic state. Only so can it be made plain to what extent Being-a-whole, as constituted by Being towards-the-end, is possible in Dasein itself in conformity with the structure of its Being. We have seen that care is the basic state of Dasein. The ontological signification of the expression "care" has been expressed in the 'definition': "ahead-of-itself-Being-already-in (the world) as Being-alongside entities which we encounter (within-the-world)". In this are expressed the fundamental characteristics of Dasein's Being: existence, in the "ahead-of-itself"; facticity, in the "Being-already-in"; falling, in the "Being-alongside". If indeed death belongs in a distinctive sense to the Being of Dasein, then death (or Being-towards-the-end) must be defined in terms of these characteristics.

From Martin Heidegger, *Being and Time*, translated by John Macquarrie and Edward Robinson, pp. 250–67. Copyright © 1962 by SCM Press Ltd. Reprinted by permission of Harper & Row Publishers, Inc. Footnotes deleted.

We must, in the first instance, make plain in a preliminary sketch how Dasein's existence, facticity, and falling reveal themselves in the phenomenon of death.

The Interpretation in which the "not-yet — and with it even the uttermost "not-yet", the end of Dasein — was taken in the sense of something still outstanding, has been rejected as inappropriate in that it included the ontological perversion of making Dasein something present-at-hand. Being-at-an-end implies existentially Being-towards-the-end. The uttermost "not yet" has the character of something *towards which* Dasein *comports itself*. The end is impending [steht . . . bevor] for Dasein. Death is not something not yet present-at-hand, nor is it that which is ultimately still outstanding but which has been reduced to a minimum. *Death is something that stands before us — something impending.*

However, there is much that can impend for Dasein as Being-in-the-world. The character of impendence is not distinctive of death. On the contrary, this Interpretation could even lead us to suppose that death must be understood in the sense of some impending event encountered environmentally. For instance, a storm, the remodelling of the house, or the arrival of a friend, may be impending; and these are entities which are respectively present-at-hand, ready-to-hand, and there-with-us. The death which impends does not have this kind of Being.

But there may also be impending for Dasein a journey, for instance, or a disputation with Others, or the forgoing of something of a kind which Dasein itself can be — its own possibilities of Being, which are based on its Being with Others.

Death is a possibility-of-Being which Dasein itself has to take over in every case. With death, Dasein stands before itself in its ownmost potentiality-for-Being. This is a possibility in which the issue is nothing less than Dasein's Being-in-the-world. Its death is the possibility of no-longer being-able-to-be-there. If Dasein stands before itself as this possibility, it has been *fully* assigned to its ownmost potentiality-for-Being. When it stands before itself in this way, all its relations to any other Dasein have been undone. This ownmost non-relational possibility is at the same time the uttermost one.

As potentiality-for-Being, Dasein cannot outstrip the possibility of death. Death is the possibility of the absolute impossibility of Dasein. Thus death reveals itself as that *possibility which is one's ownmost, which is non-relational, and which is not to be outstripped [unüberholbare].* As such, death is something *distinctively* impending. Its existential possibility is based on the fact that Dasein is essentially disclosed to itself, and disclosed, indeed, as ahead-of-itself. This item in the structure of care has its most primordial concretion in Being-towards-death. As a phenomonon, Being-towards-the-end becomes plainer as Being towards that distinctive possibility of Dasein which we have characterized.

This ownmost possibility, however, non-relational and not to be outstripped, is not one which Dasein procures for itself subsequently and occasionally in the course of its Being. On the contrary, if Dasein exists, it has already been *thrown* into this possibility. Dasein does not, proximally and for the most part, have any explicit or even any theoretical knowledge of the fact that it has been delivered over to its death, and that death thus belongs to Being-in-the-world. Throwness into death reveals itself to Dasein in a more primordial and impressive manner in that state-of-mind which we have called "anxiety". Anxiety in the face of death is anxiety 'in the face of' that potentiality-for-Being which is one's ownmost, non-relational, and not to be outstripped. That in the face of which one has anxiety is Being-in-the-world itself. That about which one has this anxiety is simply Dasein's potentiality-for-Being. Anxiety in the face of death must not be confused with fear in the face of one's demise. This anxiety is not an accidental or random mood of 'weakness' in some individual; but, as a basic state-of-mind of Dasein, it amounts to the disclosedness of the fact that Dasein exists as thrown Being *towards* its end. Thus the existential conception of "dying" is made clear as thrown Being towards its ownmost potentiality-for-Being, which is non-relational and not to be outstripped. Precision is gained by distinguishing this from pure disappearance, and also from merely perishing, and finally from the 'Experiencing' of a demise.

Being-towards-the-end does not first arise through some attitude which occasionally emerges, nor does it arise as such an attitude; it belongs essentially to Dasein's throwness, which reveals itself in a state-of-mind (mood) in one way or another. The factical 'knowledge' or 'ignorance' which prevails in any Dasein as to its ownmost Being-towards-the-end, is only the expression of the existentiell possibility that there are different ways of maintaining oneself in this Being. Factically, there are many who, proximally and for the most part, do not know about death; but this must not be passed off as a ground for proving that Being-towards-death does not belong to Dasein 'universally'. It only proves that proximally and for the most part Dasein covers up its ownmost Being-towards-death, fleeing *in the face* of it. Factically, Dasein is dying as long as it exists, but proximally and for the most part, it does so by way of *falling*. For factical existing is not only generally and without further differentiation a thrown potentiality-for-Being-in-the-world, but it has always likewise been absorbed in the 'world' of its concern. In this falling Being-alongside, fleeing from uncanniness announces itself; and this means now, a fleeing in the face of one's ownmost Being-towards-death. Existence, facticity, and falling characterize Being-towards-the-end, and are therefore constitutive for the existential conception of death. *As regards its ontological possibility, dying is grounded in care.*

But if Being-towards-death belongs primordially and essentially to Dasein's Being, then it must also be exhibitable in everydayness, even if proximally in a way which is inauthentic. And if Being-towards-the-end should afford the existential possibility of an existentiell Being-a-whole for Dasein, then this would give phenomenal confirmation for the thesis that "care" is the ontological term for the totality of Dasein's structural whole. If, however, we are to provide a full phenomenal justification for this principle, a *preliminary sketch* of the connection between Being-towards-death and care is not sufficient. We must be able to see this connection above all in that *concretion* which lies closest to Dasein — its everydayness.

51. BEING-TOWARDS-DEATH AND THE EVERYDAYNESS OF DASEIN

In setting forth average everyday Being-towards-death, we must take our orientation from those structures of everydayness at which we have earlier arrived. In Being-towards-death, Dasein comports itself *towards itself* as a distinctive potentiality-for-Being. But the Self of everydayness is the "they". The "they" is constituted by the way things have been publicly interpreted, which expresses itself in idle talk. Idle talk must accordingly make manifest the way in which everyday Dasein interprets for itself its Being-towards-death. The foundation of any interpretation is an act of understanding, which is always accompanied by a state-of-mind, or, in other words, which has a mood. So we must ask how Being-towards-death is disclosed by the kind of understanding which, with its state-of-mind, lurks in the idle talk of the "they". How does the "they" comport itself understandingly towards that ownmost possibility of Dasein, which is non-relational and is not to be outstripped? What state-of-mind discloses to the "they" that it has been delivered over to death, and in what way?

In the publicness with which we are with one another in our everyday manner, death is 'known' as a mishap which is constantly occurring — as a 'case of death'. Someone or other 'dies', be he neighbour or stranger. . . .

People who are no acquaintances of ours are 'dying' daily and hourly. 'Death' is encountered as a well-known event occurring within-the-world. As such it remains in the inconspicuousness characteristic of what is encountered in an everyday fashion. The "they" has already stowed away [gesichert] an interpretation for this event. It talks of it in a 'fugitive' manner, either expressly or else in a way which is mostly inhibited, as if to say, "One of these days one will die too, in the end; but right now it has nothing to do with us."

The analysis of the phrase 'one dies' reveals unambiguously the kind of Being which belongs to everyday Being-towards-death. In such a way of talking, death is understood as an indefinite something which, above all, must duly arrive from somewhere or other, but which is prox-imally *not yet present-at-hand* for oneself, and is therefore no threat. The expression 'one dies' spreads abroad the opinion that what gets reached, as it were, by death, is the "they". In Dasein's public way of interpreting, it is said that 'one dies', because everyone else and oneself can talk himself into saying that "in no case is it I myself", for this "one" is *the "nobody"*. 'Dying' is levelled off to an occurrence which reaches Dasein, to be sure, but belongs to nobody in particular. If idle talk is always ambiguous, so is this manner of talking about death. Dying, which is essentially mine in such a way that no one can be my representative, is perverted into an event of public occurrence which the "they" encoun-ters. In the way of talking which we have characterized, death is spoken of as a 'case' which is constantly occurring. Death gets passed off as always something 'actual'; its character as a possibility gets concealed, and so are the other two items that belong to it — the fact that it is nonrelational and that it is not to be outstripped. By such ambiguity, Dasein puts itself in the position of losing itself in the "they" as regards a distinctive potentiality-for-Being which belongs to Dasein's ownmost Self. The "they" gives its approval, and aggravates the *temptation* to cover up from oneself one's ownmost Being-towards-death. This evasive concealment in the face of death dominates everydayness so stubbornly that, in Being with one another, the 'neighbours' often still keep talking the 'dying person' into the belief that he will escape death and soon return to the tranquillized everydayness of the world of his concern. Such 'solicitude' is meant to 'console' him. It insists upon bringing him back into Dasein, while in addition it helps him to keep his ownmost non-relational possibility-of-Being completely concealed. In this manner the "they" provides [besorgt] a *constant tranquillization about death*. At bottom, however, this is a tranquillization not only for him who is 'dying' but just as much for those who 'console' him. And even in the case of a demise, the public is still not to have its own tranquillity upset by such an event, or be disturbed in the carefreeness with which it concerns itself. Indeed the dying of Others is seen often enough as a social inconve-nience, if not even a downright tactlessness, against which the public is to be guarded.

But along with this tranquillization, which forces Dasein away from its death, the "they" at the same time puts itself in the right and makes itself respectable by tacitly regulating the way in which *one* has to com-port oneself towards death. It is already a matter of public acceptance that 'thinking about death' is a cowardly fear, a sign of insecurity on the part of Dasein, and a sombre way of fleeing from the world. *The "they" does not permit us the courage for anxiety in the face of death*. The dominance of the manner in which things have been publicly interpreted by the "they", has already decided what state-of-mind is to determine our attitude towards death. In anxiety in the face of death, Dasein is brought face to face with itself as delivered over to that possibility which is not to be outstripped. The "they" concerns itself with transforming this anxiety into fear in the face of an oncoming event. In addition, the anxiety which has been made ambiguous as fear, is passed off as a weakness with which no self-assured Dasein may have any acquaintance. What is 'fitting' [Was sich . . . "gehört"] according to the unuttered decree of the "they", is indifferent tranquillity as to the 'fact' that one dies. The cultivation of such a 'superior' indifference *alienates* Dasein from its ownmost non-relational potentiality-for-Being.

But temptation, tranquillization, and alienation are distinguishing marks of the kind of Being called *"falling"*. As falling, everyday Being-towards-death is a constant *fleeing in the face of death*. Being-*towards-the-end* has the mode of *evasion in the face of it* — giving new explanations for it, understanding it inauthentically, and concealing it. Factically one's own Dasein is always dying already; that is to say, it is in a Being-towards-its-end. And it hides this Fact from itself by recoining "death" as just a "case of death" in Others — an everyday occurrence which, if need be, gives us the assurance still more plainly that 'oneself' is still 'living'. But in thus falling and fleeing *in the face of* death, Dasein's everydayness attests that the very "they" itself already has the definite character of *Being-towards-death,* even when it is not explicitly engaged in 'thinking about death'. *Even in average everydayness, this own-most potentiality-for-Being, which is non-relational and not to be out-stripped, is constantly an issue for Dasein. This is the case when its concern is merely in the mode of an untroubled indifference* **towards** *the uttermost possibility of existence.*

In setting forth everyday Being-towards-death, however, we are at the same time enjoined to try to secure a full existential conception of Being-towards-the-end, by a more penetrating Interpretation in which falling Being-towards-death is taken as an evasion *in the face of death. That in the face of which one flees* has been made visible in a way which is phenomenally adequate. Against this it must be possible to project phenomenologically the way in which evasive Dasein itself understands its death.

52. EVERYDAY BEING-TOWARDS-THE-END, AND THE FULL EXISTENTIAL CONCEPTION OF DEATH

In our preliminary existential sketch, Being-towards-the-end has been defined as Being towards one's ownmost potentiality-for-Being, which is non-relational and is not to be outstripped. Being towards this possibility, as a Being which exists, is brought face to face with the absolute impossibility of existence. Beyond this seemingly empty characterization of Being-towards-death, there has been revealed the concretion of this Being in the mode of everydayness. In accordance with the tendency to falling, which is essential to everydayness, Being-towards-death has turned out to be an evasion in the face of death — an evasion which conceals. While our investigation has hitherto passed from a formal sketch of the ontological structure of death to the concrete analysis of everyday Being-towards-the-end, the direction is now to be reversed, and we shall arrive at the full existential conception of death by rounding out our Interpretation of everyday Being-towards-the-end.

In explicating everyday Being-towards-death we have clung to the idle talk of the "they" to the effect that "one dies too, sometime, but not right away." All that we have Interpreted thus far is the 'one dies' as such. In the 'sometime, but not right away', everydayness concedes something like a *certainty* of death. Nobody doubts that one dies. On the other hand, this 'not doubting' need not imply that kind of Being-certain which corresponds to the way death — in the sense of the distinctive possibility characterized above — enters into Dasein. Everydayness confines itself to conceding the 'certainty' of death in this ambiguous manner just in order to weaken that certainty by covering up dying still more and to alleviate its own thrownness into death.

By its very meaning, this evasive concealment in the face of death can *not* be *authentically* 'certain' of death, and yet it *is* certain of it. What are we to say about the 'certainty of death'?

To be certain of any entity means to *hold* it for true as something true. But "truth" signifies the uncoveredness of some entity, and all uncoveredness is grounded ontologically in the most primordial truth, the disclosedness of Dasein. As an entity which is both disclosed and disclosing, and one which uncovers, Dasein is essentially 'in the truth'. *But certainty is grounded in the truth, or belongs to it equiprimordially.* The expression 'certainty', like the term 'truth', has a double signification. Primordially "truth" means the same as "Being-disclosive", as a way in which Dasein behaves. From this comes the derivative signification: "the uncoveredness of entities". Correspondingly, "certainty", in its primordial signification, is tantamount to "Being-certain", as a kind of Being which belongs to Dasein. However, in a derivative signification, any entity of which Dasein can be certain will also get called something 'certain'.

One mode of certainty is *conviction*. In conviction, Dasein lets the testimony of the thing itself which has been uncovered (the true thing itself) be the sole determinant for its Being towards that thing understandingly. Holding something for true is adequate as a way of maintaining oneself in the truth, if it is grounded in the uncovered entity itself, and if, as Being towards the entity so uncovered, it has become transparent to itself as regards its appropriateness to that entity. In any arbitrary fiction or in merely having some 'view' ["Ansicht"] about an entity, this sort of thing is lacking.

The adequacy of holding-for-true is measured according to the truth-claim to which it belongs. Such a claim gets its justification from the kind of Being of the entity to be disclosed, and from the direction of the disclosure. The kind of truth, and along with it, the certainty, varies with the way entities differ, and accords with the guiding tendency and extent of the disclosure. Our present considerations will be restricted to an analysis of Being-certain with regard to death; and this Being-certain will in the end present us with a distinctive *certainty of Dasein.*

For the most part, everyday Dasein covers up the ownmost possibility of its Being — that possibility which is non-relational and not to be outstripped. This factical tendency to cover up confirms our thesis that Dasein, as factical, is in the 'untruth'. Therefore the certainty which belongs to such a covering-up of Being-towards-death must be an inappropriate way of holding-for-true, and not, for instance, an uncertainty in the sense of a doubting. In inappropriate certainty, that of which one is certain is held covered up. If 'one' understands death as an event which one encounters in one's environment, then the certainty which is related to such events does not pertain to Being-towards-the-end.

They say, "It is certain that 'Death' is coming." *They* say it, and the "they" overlooks the fact that in order to be able to be certain of death, Dasein itself must in every case be certain of its ownmost non-relational potentiality-for-Being. They say, "Death is certain"; and in saying so, they implant in Dasein the illusion that it is *itself* certain of its death. And what is the ground of everyday Being-certain? Manifestly, it is not just mutual persuasion. Yet the 'dying' of Others is something that one experiences daily. Death is an undeniable 'fact of experience'.

The way in which everyday Being-towards-death understands the certainty which is thus grounded, betrays itself when it tries to 'think' about death, even when it does so with critical foresight — that is to say, in an appropriate manner. So far as one knows, all men 'die'. Death is probable in the highest degree for every man, yet it is not 'unconditionally' certain. Taken strictly, a certainty which is 'only' *empirical* may be attributed to death. Such certainty necessarily falls short of the highest certainty, the apodictic, which we reach in certain domains of theoretical knowledge.

In this 'critical' determination of the certainty of death, and of its impendence, what is manifested in the first instance is, once again, a failure to recognize Dasein's kind of Being and the Being-towards-death which belongs to Dasein — a failure that is characteristic of everydayness. *The fact that demise, as an event which occurs, is 'only' empiri-*

cally certain, is in no way decisive as to the certainty of death. Cases of death may be the factical occasion for Dasein's first paying attention to death at all. So long, however, as Dasein remains in the empirical certainty which we have mentioned, death, in the way that it 'is', is something of which Dasein can by no means become certain. Even though, in the publicness of the "they", Dasein seems to 'talk' only of this 'empirical' certainty of death, *nevertheless at bottom* Dasein does *not* exclusively or primarily stick to those cases of death which merely occur. *In evading its death,* even everyday Being-towards-the-end is indeed certain of its death in another way than it might itself like to have true on purely theoretical considerations. This 'other way' is what everydayness for the most part veils from itself. Everydayness does not dare to let itself become transparent in such a manner. We have already characterized the every-day state-of-mind which consists in an air of superiority with regard to the certain 'fact' of death — a superiority which is 'anxiously' concerned while seemingly free from anxiety. In this state-of-mind, everydayness acknowledges a 'higher' certainty than one which is only empirical. One *knows* about the certainty of death, and yet 'is' not authentically certain of one's own. The falling everydayness of Dasein is acquainted with death's certainty, and yet evades *Being*-certain. But in the light of what it evades, this very evasion attests phenomenally that death must be conceived as one's ownmost possibility, non-relational, not to be outstripped, and — above all — certain.

One says, "Death certainly comes, but not right away". With this 'but . . .', the "they" denies that death is certain. 'Not right away' is not a purely negative assertion, but a way in which the "they" interprets itself. With this interpretation, the "they" refers itself to that which is proximally accessible to Dasein and amenable to its concern. Everydayness forces its way into the urgency of concern, and divests itself of the fetters of a weary 'inactive thinking about death'. Death is deferred to 'sometime later', and this is done by invoking the so-called 'general opinion' ["allegmeine Ermessen"]. Thus the "they" covers up what is peculiar in death's certainty — *that it is possible at any moment.* Along with the certainty of death goes the *indefiniteness* of its "when". Everyday Being-towards-death evades this indefiniteness by conferring definiteness upon it. But such a procedure cannot signify calculating when the demise is due to arrive. In the face of definiteness such as this, Dasein would sooner flee. Everyday concern makes definite for itself the indefiniteness of certain death by interposing before it those urgencies and possibilities which can be taken in at a glance, and which belong to the everyday matters that are closest to us.

But when this indefiniteness has been covered up, the certainty has been covered up too. Thus death's ownmost character as a possibility gets veiled — a possibility which is certain and at the same time indefinite — that is to say, possible at any moment. . . .

53. EXISTENTIAL PROJECTION OF AN
AUTHENTIC BEING-TOWARDS-DEATH

Factically, Dasein maintains itself proximally and for the most part in an inauthentic Being-towards-death. How is the ontological possibility of an *authentic* Being-towards-death to be characterized 'Objectively', if, in the end, Dasein never comports itself authentically towards its end, or if, in accordance with its very meaning, this authentic Being must remain hidden from the Others? Is it not a fanciful undertaking, to project the existential possibility of so questionable an existentiell potentiality-for-Being? What is needed, if such a projection is to go beyond a merely fictitious arbitrary construction? Does Dasein itself give us any instructions for carrying it out? And can any grounds for its phenomenal legitimacy be taken from Dasein itself? Can our analysis of Dasein up to this point give us any prescriptions for the ontological task we have now set ourselves, so that what we have before us may be kept on a road of which we can be sure?

The existential conception of death has been established; and therewith we have also established what it is that an authentic Being-towards-the-end should be able to comport itself towards. We have also characterized inauthentic Being-towards-death, and thus we have prescribed in a negative way [prohibitiv] how it is possible for authentic Being-towards-death *not* to be. It is with these positive and prohibitive instructions that from it, or *give a new explanation* for it to accord with the common sense of the "they". In our existential projection of an authentic Being-towards-death, therefore, we must set forth those items in such a Being which are constitutive for it as an understanding of death — and as such an understanding in the sense of Being towards this possibility without either fleeing it or covering it up.

In the first instance, we must characterize Being-towards-death as a *Being towards a possibility* — indeed, towards, a distinctive possibility of Dasein itself. "Being towards" a possibility — that is to say, towards something possible — may signify "Being out for" something possible, as in concerning ourselves with its actualization. Such possibilities are constantly encountered in the field of what is ready-to-hand and present-at-hand — what is attainable, controllable, practicable, and the like. In concernfully Being out for something possible, there is a tendency to *annihilate the possibility* of the possible by making it available to us. But the concernful actualization of equipment which is ready-to-hand (as in producing it, getting it ready, readjusting it, and so on) is always merely relative, since even that which has been actualized is still characterized in terms of some involvements — indeed this is precisely what characterizes its Being. Even though actualized, it remains, as actual, something possible for doing something; it is characterized by an "in-order-to". What our analysis is to make plain is simply how Being out for something concernfully, comports itself towards the possible: it does so not by the theoretico-thematical consideration of the possible as possible, and by having regard for its possibility as such, but rather by looking *circumspectively away* from the possible and looking at that for which it is possible. . . .

Manifestly Being-towards-death, which is now in question, cannot have the character of concernfully Being out to get itself actualized. For one thing, death as possible is not something possible which is ready-to-hand or present-at-hand, but a possibility of *Dasein's* Being. So to concern oneself with actualizing what is thus possible would have to signify, "bringing about one's demise". But if this were done, Dasein would deprive itself of the very ground for an existing Being-towards-death.

Thus, if by "Being towards death" we do not have in view an 'actualizing' of death, neither can we mean "dwelling upon the end in its possibility". This is the way one comports oneself when one 'thinks about death', pondering over when and how this possibility may perhaps be actualized. Of course such brooding over death does not fully take away from it its character as a possibility. Indeed, it always gets brooded over as something that is coming; but in such brooding we weaken it by calculating how we are to have it at our disposal. As something possible, it is to show as little as possible of its possibility. On the other hand, if Being-towards-death has to disclose understandingly the possibility which we have characterized, and if it is to disclose it *as a possibility*, then in such Being-towards-death this possibility must not be weakened: it must be understood *as a possibility*, it must be cultivated *as a possibility*, and we must *put up with* it *as a possibility*, in the way we comport ourselves towards it.

However, Dasein comports itself towards something possible in its possibility by *expecting it* [im *Erwarten*]. Anyone who is intent on something possible, may encounter it unimpeded and undiminished in its 'whether it comes or does not, or whether it comes after all'. But with this phenomenon of expecting, has not our analysis reached the same kind of Being towards the possible to which we have already called attention in our description of "Being out for something" concernfully? To expect something possible is always to understand it and to 'have' it with regard to whether and when and how it will be actually present-at-hand. Expecting is not just an occasional looking-away from the possible to its possible actualization, but is essentially a *waiting for that actualization* [ein *Warten auf diese*]. Even in expecting, one leaps away from the possible and gets a foothold in the actual. It is for its actuality that what is expected is expected. By the very nature of expecting, the possible is drawn into the actual, arising out of the actual and returning to it.

But Being towards this possibility, as Being-towards-death, is so to comport ourselves towards *death* that in this Being, and for it, death reveals itself *as a possibility*. Our terminology for such Being towards this possibility is *"anticipation" of this possibility*. But in this way of behaving does there not lurk a coming-close to the possible, and when one is close to the possible, does not its actualization emerge? In this kind of coming close, however, one does not tend towards concernfully making available something actual; but as one comes closer understandingly, the possibility of the possible just becomes 'greater'. *The closest closeness which one may have in Being towards death as a possibility, is as far as possible from anything actual.* The more unveiledly this possibility gets understood, the more purely does the understanding penetrate into it *as the possibility of the impossibility of any existence at all*. Death, as possibility, gives Dasein nothing to be 'actualized', nothing which Dasein, as actual, could itself *be*. It is the possibility of the impossibility of every way of comporting oneself towards anything, of every way of existing. In the anticipation of this possibility it becomes 'greater and greater'; that is to say, the possibility reveals itself to be such that it knows no measure at all, no more or less, but signifies the possibility of the measureless impossibility of existence. In accordance with its essence, this possibility offers no support for becoming intent on something, 'picturing' to oneself the actuality which is possible, and so forgetting its possibility. Being-towards-death, as anticipation of possibility, is what first *makes* this possibility *possible,* and sets it free as possibility.

Being-towards-death is the anticipation of a potentiality-for-Being of that entity whose kind of Being is anticipation itself. In the anticipatory revealing of this potentiality-for-Being, Dasein discloses itself to itself as regards its uttermost possibility. But to project itself on its ownmost potentiality-for-Being means to be able to understand itself in the Being of the entity so revealed — namely, to exist. Anticipation turns out to be the possibility of understanding one's *ownmost* and uttermost potentiality-for-Being — that is to say, the possibility of *authentic existence*. The ontological constitution of such existence must be made visible by setting forth the concrete structure of anticipation of death. How are we to delimit this structure phenomenally? Manifestly, we must do so by determining those characteristics which must belong to an anticipatory disclosure so that it can become the pure understanding of that ownmost possibility which is non-relational and not to be outstripped — which is certain and, as such, indefinite. It must be noted that understanding does not primarily mean just gazing at a meaning, but rather understanding oneself in that potentiality-for-Being which reveals itself in projection.

Death is Dasein's *ownmost* possibility. Being towards this possibility discloses to Dasein its *ownmost* potentiality-for-Being, in which its very Being is the issue. Here it can become manifest to Dasein that in this distinctive possibility of its own self, it has been wrenched away from the "they". This means that in anticipation any Dasein can have wrenched itself away from the "they" already. But when one understands that this is something which Dasein 'can' have done, this only reveals its factical lostness in the everydayness of the they-self.

The ownmost possibility is *non-relational*. Anticipation allows Dasein to understand that that potentiality-for-being in which its own-most Being is an issue, must be taken over by Dasein alone. Death does not just 'belong' to one's own Dasein in an undifferentiated way; death *lays claim* to it as an *individual* Dasein. The non-relational character of death, as understood in anticipation, individualizes Dasein down to it-self. This individualizing is a way in which the 'there' is disclosed for existence. It makes manifest that all Being-alongside the things with which we concern ourselves, and all Being-with Others, will fail us when our ownmost potentiality-for-Being is the issue. Dasein can be *authentically itself* only if it makes this possible for itself of its own accord. But if concern and solicitude fail us, this does not signify at all that these ways of Dasein have been cut off from its authentically Being-its-Self. As structures essential to Dasein's constitution, these have a share in conditioning the possibility of any existence whatsoever. Dasein is authentically itself only to the extent that, *as* concernful Being-alongside and solicitous Being-with, it projects itself upon its ownmost potentiality-for-Being rather than upon the possibility of the they-self. The entity which anticipates its non-relational possibility, is thus forced by that very anticipation into the possibility of taking over from itself its ownmost Being, and doing so of its own accord.

The ownmost, non-relational possibility is *not to be outstripped*. Being towards this possibility enables Dasein to understand that giving itself up impends for it as the uttermost possibility of its existence. Anticipation, however, unlike inauthentic Being-towards-death, does not evade the fact that death is not to be outstripped; instead, anticipation frees itself *for* accepting this. When, by anticipation, one becomes free *for* one's own death, one is liberated from one's lostness in those possibilities which may accidentally thrust themselves upon one; and one is liberated in such a way that for the first time one can authentically understand and choose among the factical possibilities lying ahead of that possibility which is not to be outstripped. Anticipation discloses to existence that its uttermost possibility lies in giving itself up, and thus it shatters all one's tenaciousness to whatever existence one has reached. In anticipation, Dasein guards itself against falling back behind itself, or behind the potentiality-for-Being which it has understood. It guards itself against 'becoming too old for its victories' (Nietzsche). Free for its own-most possibilities, which are determined by the *end* and so are understood as *finite [endliche]*, Dasein dispels the danger that it may, by its own finite understanding of existence, fail to recognize that it is getting outstripped by the existence-possibilities of Others, or rather that it may explain these possibilities wrongly and force them back upon its own, so that it may divest itself of its ownmost factical existence. As the non-relational possibility, death individualizes — but only in such a manner that, as the possibility which is not to be outstripped, it makes Dasein, as Being-with, have some understanding of the potentiality-for-Being of Others. Since anticipation of the possibility which is not to be outstripped discloses also all the possibilities which lie ahead of that possibility, this anticipation includes the possibility of taking the *whole* of Dasein in advance [Vorwegnehmens] in an existentiell manner; that is to say, it includes the possibility of existing as a *whole potentiality-for-Being.*

The ownmost, non-relational possibility, which is not to be outstripped, is *certain.* The way *to be* certain of it is determined by the kind of truth which corresponds to it (disclosedness). The certain possibility of death, however, discloses Dasein as a possibility, but does so only in such a way that, in anticipating this possibility, Dasein *makes* this possibility *possible* for itself as its ownmost potentiality-for-Being. The possibility is disclosed because it is made possible in anticipation. To maintain oneself in this truth — that is, to be certain of what has been disclosed — demands all the more that one should anticipate. We cannot compute the certainty of death by ascertaining how many cases of death we encounter. This certainty is by no means of the kind which maintains itself in the truth of the present-at-hand. When something present-at-hand has been uncovered, it is encountered most purely if we just look at the entity and let it be encountered in itself. Dasein must first have lost itself in the factual circumstances [Sachverhalte] (this can be one of care's own tasks and possibilities) if it is to obtain the pure objectivity — that is to say, the indifference — of apodictic evidence. If Being-certain in relation to death does not have this character, this does not mean that it is of a lower grade, but that *it does not belong at all to the graded order of the kinds of evidence we can have about the present-at-hand.*

Holding death for true (death *is* just one's own) shows another kind of certainty, and is more primordial than any certainty which relates to entities encountered within-the-world, or to formal objects; for it is certain of Being-in-the-world. As such, holding death for true does not demand just *one* definite kind of behaviour in Dasein, but demands Dasein itself in the full authenticity of its existence. In anticipation Dasein can first make certain of its ownmost Being in its totality — a totality which is not to be outstripped. Therefore the evidential character which belongs to the immediate givenness of Experiences, of the "I", or of consciousness, must necessarily lag behind the certainty which anticipation includes. Yet this is not because the way in which these are grasped would not be a rigorous one, but because in principle such a way of grasping them cannot hold *for true* (disclosed) something which at bottom it insists upon 'having there' as true: namely, Dasein itself, which I myself *am*, and which, as a potentiality-for-Being, I can be authentically only by anticipation.

The ownmost possibility, which is non-relational, not to be outstripped, and certain, is *indefinite* as regards its certainty. How does anticipation disclose this characteristic of Dasein's distinctive possibility? How does the anticipatory understanding project itself upon a potentiality-for-Being which is certain and which is constantly possible in such a way that the "when" in which the utter impossibility of existence becomes possible remains constantly indefinite? In anticipating [zum] the indefinite certainty of death, Dasein opens itself to a constant *threat* arising out of its own "there". In this very threat Being-towards-the-end must maintain itself. So little can it tone this down that it must rather cultivate the indefiniteness of the certainty. How is it existentially possible for this constant threat to be genuinely disclosed? All understanding is accompanied by a state-of-mind. Dasein's mood brings it face to face with the thrownness of its 'that it is there'. *But the state-of-mind which can hold open the utter and constant threat to itself arising from Dasein's ownmost individualized Being, is anxiety.* In this state-of-mind, Dasein finds itself *face to face* with the "nothing" of the possible impossibility of its existence. Anxiety is anxious *about* the potentiality-for-Being of the entity so destined [des so bestimmten Seienden], and in this way it discloses the uttermost possibility. Anticipation utterly individualizes Dasein, and allows it, in this individualization of itself, to become certain of the totality of its potentiality-for-Being. For this reason, anxiety as a basic state-of-mind belongs to such a self-understanding of Dasein on the basis of Dasein itself. Being-towards-death is essentially anxiety. This is attested unmistakably, though 'only' indirectly, by Being-towards-death as we have described it, when it perverts anxiety into cowardly fear and, in surmounting this fear, only makes known its own cowardliness in the face of anxiety.

We may now summarize our characterization of authentic Being-towards-death as we have projected it existentially: *anticipation reveals to Dasein its lostness in the they-self, and brings it face to face with the possibility of being itself, primarily unsupported by concernful solicitude, but of being itself, rather, in an impassioned* **freedom towards death** — *a freedom which has been released from the Illusions of the "they", and which is factical, certain of itself, and anxious.* . . .

ALBERT CAMUS

For Camus, there is no sun without shadow, yet "it is essential to know the night."
(The Myth of Sisyphus, *p. 91) Absurdity and happiness are but two sides of the same*
coin — we can feed our greatness on the "bread of indifference," which is the
universe. The revolt that is human existence is what gives life its value. The following
excerpt from The Plague *describes the last stage of a dying process as related by Dr.*
Rieux, who struggles against the havoc the plague wreaks. We all must die, that is
clear. But for Camus we must also resist; we must never resign ourselves to the
absurd; we must die unreconciled. This powerful excerpt makes clear what Camus
means when he states, "there is no finer sight than that of the intelligence at grips
with a reality that transcends it." (The Myth of Sisyphus, *p. 41) We must each wage*
this struggle alone, but it is the struggle which "restores majesty to that life." (p. 41)
Thus, the following excerpt is only in part about dying; it is foremost about what it
means to be a human alive in a world that is absurd and without hope.

The Plague

PART V

When next day, a few days before the date fixed for the opening of the
gates, Dr. Rieux came home at noon, he was wondering if the telegram he
was expecting had arrived. Though his days were no less strenuous than
at the height of the epidemic, the prospect of imminent release had
obliterated his fatigue. Hope had returned and with it a new zest for life.
No man can live on the stretch all the time, with his energy and willpower
strained to the breaking-point, and it is a joy to be able to relax at last and
loosen nerves and muscles that were braced for the struggle. If the telegram, too, that he awaited brought good news, Rieux would be able to
make a fresh start. Indeed, he had a feeling that everyone in those days
was making a fresh start.

He walked past the concierge's room in the hall. The new man, old
Michel's successor, his face pressed to the window looking on the hall,
gave him a smile. As he went up the stairs, the man's face, pale with
exhaustion and privation, but smiling, hovered before his eyes.

Yes, he'd make a fresh start, once the period of "abstractions" was
over, and with any luck — He was opening the door with these thoughts

in his mind when he saw his mother coming down the hall to meet him. M. Tarrou, she told him, wasn't well. He had risen at the usual time, but did not feel up to going out and had returned to bed. Mme Rieux felt worried about him.

"Quite likely it's nothing serious," her son said.

Tarrou was lying on his back, his heavy head deeply indenting the pillow, the coverlet bulging above his massive chest. His head was aching and his temperature up. The symptoms weren't very definite, he told Rieux, but they might well be those of plague.

After examining him Rieux said: "No, there's nothing definite as yet."

But Tarrou also suffered from a raging thirst, and in the hallway the doctor told his mother that it might be plague.

"Oh!" she exclaimed. "Surely that's not possible, not now!" And after a moment added: "Let's keep him here, Bernard."

Rieux pondered. "Strictly speaking, I've no right to do that," he said doubtfully. "Still, the gates will be opened quite soon. If you weren't here, I think I'd take it on myself."

"Bernard, let him stay, and let me stay too. You know, I've just had another inoculation."

The doctor pointed out that Tarrou, too, had had inoculations, though it was possible, tired as he was, he'd overlooked the last one or omitted to take the necessary precautions.

Rieux was going to the surgery as he spoke, and when he returned to the bedroom Tarrou noticed that he had a box of the big ampoules containing the serum.

"Ah, so it *is* that," he said.

"Not necessarily; but we mustn't run any risks."

Without replying Tarrou extended his arm and submitted to the prolonged injections he himself had so often administered to others.

"We'll judge better this evening." Rieux looked Tarrou in the eyes.

"But what about isolating me, Rieux?"

"It's by no means certain that you have plague."

Tarrou smiled with an effort.

"Well, it's the first time I've known you do the injection without ordering the patient off to the isolation ward."

Rieux looked away.

"You'll be better here. My mother and I will look after you."

Tarrou said nothing and the doctor, who was putting away the ampoules in the box, waited for him to speak before looking round. But still Tarrou said nothing, and finally Rieux went up to the bed. The sick man was gazing at him steadily, and though his face was drawn, the gray eyes were calm. Rieux smiled down on him.

"Now try to sleep. I'll be back soon."

As he was going out he heard Tarrou calling, and turned back. Tarrou's manner had an odd effect, as though he were at once trying to keep back what he had to say and forcing himself to say it.

"Rieux," he said at last, "you must tell me the whole truth. I count on that."

"I promise it."

Tarrou's heavy face relaxed in a brief smile.

"Thanks. I don't want to die, and I shall put up a fight. But if I lose the match, I want to make a good end of it."

Bending forward, Rieux pressed his shoulder.

"No. To become a saint, you need to live. So fight away!"

In the course of that day the weather, which after being very cold had grown slightly milder, broke in a series of violent hailstorms followed by rain. At sunset the sky cleared a little, and it was bitterly cold again. Rieux came home in the evening. His overcoat still on, he entered his friend's bedroom. Tarrou did not seem to have moved, but his set lips, drained white by fever, told of the effort he he was keeping up.

"Well?" Rieux asked.

Tarrou raised his broad shoulders a little out of the bedclothes.

"Well," he said, "I'm losing the match."

The doctor bent over him. Ganglia had formed under the burning skin and there was a rumbling in his chest, like the sound of a hidden forge. The strange thing was that Tarrou showed symptoms of both varieties of plague at once.

Rieux straightened up and said the serum hadn't yet had time to take effect. An uprush of fever in his throat drowned the few words that Tarrou tried to utter.

After dinner Rieux and his mother took up their posts at the sick man's bedside. The night began with a struggle, and Rieux knew that this grim wrestling with the angel of plague was to last until dawn. In this struggle Tarrou's robust shoulders and chest were not his greatest assets; rather, the blood that had spurted under Rieux's needle and, in this blood, that something more vital than the soul, which no human skill can bring to light. The doctor's task could be only to watch his friend's struggle. As to what he was about to do, the stimulants to inject, the abscesses to stimulate — many months' repeated failures had taught him to appreciate such expedients at their true value. Indeed, the only way in which he might help was to provide opportunities for the beneficence of chance, which too often stays dormant unless roused to action. Luck was an ally he could not dispense with. For Rieux was confronted by an aspect of the plague that baffled him. Yet again it was doing all it could to confound the tactics used against it; it launched attacks in unexpected places and retreated from those where it seemed definitely lodged. Once more it was out to darken counsel.

Tarrou struggled without moving. Not once in the course of the night did he counter the enemy's attacks by restless agitation; only with all his stolid bulk, with silence, did he carry on the fight. Nor did he even try to speak, thus intimating, after his fashion, that he could no longer let his attention stray. Rieux could follow the vicissitudes of the struggle only in his friend's eyes, now open and now shut; in the eyelids, now more closely welded to the eyeball, now distended; and in his gaze fixed on some object in the room or brought back to the doctor and his mother. And each time it met the doctor's gaze, with a great effort Tarrou smiled.

At one moment there came a sound of hurrying footsteps in the street. They were in flight before a distant throbbing which gradually approached until the street was loud with the clamor of the downpour; another rain-squall was sweeping the town, mingled presently with hail-stones that clattered on the sidewalk. Window awnings were flapping wildly. Rieux, whose attention had been diverted momentarily by the noises of the squall, looked again across the shadows at Tarrou's face, on which fell the light of a small bedside lamp. His mother was knitting, raising her eyes now and then from her work to gaze at the sick man. The doctor had done everything that could be done. When the squall had passed, the silence in the room grew denser, filled only by the silent turmoil of the unseen battle. His nerves overwrought by sleeplessness, the doctor fancied he could hear, on the edge of the silence, that faint eerie sibilance which had haunted his ears ever since the beginning of the epidemic. He made a sign to his mother, indicating she should go to bed. She shook her head, and her eyes grew brighter; then she examined carefully, at her needle-tips, a stitch of which she was unsure. Rieux got up, gave the sick man a drink, and sat down again.

Footsteps rang on the pavement, nearing, then receding; people were taking advantage of the lull to hurry home. For the first time the doctor realized that this night, without the clang of ambulances and full of belated wayfarers, was just like a night of the past — a plague-free night. It was as if the pestilence, hounded away by cold, the street-lamps, and the crowd, had fled from the depths of the town and taken shelter in this warm room and was launching its last offensive at Tarrou's inert body. No longer did it thresh the air above the houses with its flail. But it was whistling softly in the stagnant air of the sickroom, and this it was that Rieux had been hearing since the long vigil began. And now it was for him to wait and watch until that strange sound ceased here too, and here as well the plague confessed defeat.

A little before dawn Rieux leaned toward his mother and whispered:

"You'd better have some rest now, as you'll have to relieve me at eight. Mind you take your drops before going to bed."

Mme Rieux rose, folded her knitting, and went to the bedside. Tarrou had had his eyes shut for some time. Sweat had plastered his hair on his stubborn forehead. Mme Rieux sighed, and he opened his eyes. He saw the gentle face bent over him and, athwart the surge of fever, that steadfast smile took form again. But at once the eyes closed. Left to himself, Rieux moved into the chair his mother had just left. The street was silent and no sound came from the sleeping town. The chill of daybreak was beginning to make itself felt.

The doctor dozed off, but very soon an early cart rattling down the street awaked him. Shivering a little, he looked at Tarrou and saw that a lull had come; he, too, was sleeping. The iron-shod wheels rumbled away into the distance. Darkness still was pressing on the windowpanes. When the doctor came beside the bed, Tarrou gazed at him with expressionless eyes, like a man still on the frontier of sleep.

"You slept, didn't you?" Rieux asked.

"Yes."

"Breathing better?"

"A bit. Does that mean anything?"

Rieux kept silent for some moments; then he said:

"No, Tarrou, it doesn't mean anything. You know as well as I that there's often a remission in the morning."

"Thanks." Tarrou nodded his approval. "Always tell me the exact truth."

Rieux was sitting on the side of the bed. Beside him he could feel the sick man's legs, stiff and hard as the limbs of an effigy on a tomb. Tarrou was breathing with more difficulty.

"The fever'll come back, won't it, Rieux?" he gasped.

"Yes. But at noon we shall know where we stand."

Tarrou shut his eyes; he seemed to be mustering up his strength. There was a look of utter weariness on his face. He was waiting for the fever to rise and already it was stirring somewhat in the depths of his being. When he opened his eyes, his gaze was misted. It brightened only when he saw Rieux bending over him, a tumbler in his hand.

"Drink."

Tarrou drank, then slowly lowered his head on to the pillow.

"It's a long business," he murmured.

Rieux clasped his arm, but Tarrou, whose head was averted, showed no reaction. Then suddenly, as if some inner dike had given way without warning, the fever surged back, dyeing his cheeks and forehead. Tarrou's eyes came back to the doctor, who, bending again, gave him a look of affectionate encouragement. Tarrou tried to shape a smile, but it could not force its way through the set jaws and lips welded by dry saliva. In the rigid face only the eyes lived still, glowing with courage.

At seven Mme Rieux returned to the bedroom. The doctor went to the surgery to ring up the hospital and arrange for a substitute. He also decided to postpone his consultations; then lay down for some moments on the surgery couch. Five minutes later he went back to the bedroom. Tarrou's face was turned toward Mme Rieux, who was sitting close beside the bed, her hands folded on her lap; in the dim light of the room she seemed no more than a darker patch of shadow. Tarrou was gazing at her so intently that, putting a finger to her lips, Mme Rieux rose and switched off the bedside lamp. Behind the curtains the light was growing, and presently, when the sick man's face grew visible, Mme Rieux could see his eyes still intent on her. Bending above the bed, she smoothed out the bolster and, as she straightened up, laid her hand for a moment on his moist tangled hair. Then she heard a muffled voice, which seemed to come from very far away, murmur: "Thank you," and that all was well now. By the time she was back in her chair Tarrou had shut his eyes, and, despite the sealed mouth, a faint smile seemed to hover on the wasted face.

At noon the fever reached its climax. A visceral cough racked the sick man's body and he now was spitting blood. The ganglia had ceased swelling, but they were still there, like lumps of iron embedded in the joints. Rieux decided that lancing them was impracticable. Now and then, in the intervals between bouts of fever and coughing fits, Tarrou still gazed at his friends. But soon his eyes opened less and less often and the glow that shone out from the ravaged face in the brief moments of recognition grew steadily fainter. The storm, lashing his body into convulsive movement, lit it up with ever rarer flashes, and in the heart of the tempest he was slowly drifting, derelict. And now Rieux had before him only a masklike face, inert, from which the smile had gone forever. This human form, his friend's, lacerated by the spear-thrusts of the plague, consumed by searing, superhuman fires, buffeted by all the raging winds of heaven, was foundering under his eyes in the dark flood of the pestilence, and he could do nothing to avert the wreck. He could only stand, unavailing, on the shore, empty-handed and sick at heart, unarmed and helpless yet again under the onset of calamity. And thus, when the end came, the tears that blinded Rieux's eyes were tears of impotence; and he did not see Tarrou roll over, face to the wall, and die with a short, hollow groan as if somewhere within him an essential chord had snapped.

The next night was not one of struggle but of silence. In the tranquil death-chamber, beside the dead body now in everyday clothing — here, too, Rieux felt it brooding, that elemental peace which, when he was sitting many nights before on the terrace high above the plague, had followed the brief foray at the gates. Then, already, it had brought to his mind the silence brooding over the beds in which he had let men die. There as here it was the same solemn pause, the lull that follows battle; it was the silence of defeat. But the silence now enveloping his dead friend, so dense, so much akin to the nocturnal silence of the streets and of the town set free at last, made Rieux cruelly aware that this defeat was final, the last disastrous battle that ends a war and makes peace itself an ill beyond all remedy. The doctor could not tell if Tarrou had found peace, now that all was over, but for himself he had a feeling that no peace was possible to him henceforth, any more than there can be an armistice for a mother bereaved of her son or for a man who buries his friend.

The night was cold again, with frosty stars sparkling in a clear, wintry sky. And in the dimly lit room they felt the cold pressing itself to the windowpanes and heard the long, silvery suspiration of a polar night. Mme Rieux sat near the bed in her usual attitude, her right side lit up by the bedside lamp. In the center of the room, outside the little zone of light, Rieux sat, waiting. Now and then thoughts of his wife waylaid him, but he brushed them aside each time.

When the night began, the heels of passers-by had rung briskly in the frozen air.

"Have you attended to everything?" Mme Rieux had asked.

"Yes, I've telephoned."

Then they had resumed their silent vigil. From time to time Mme Rieux stole a glance at her son, and whenever he caught her doing this, he smiled. Out in the street the usual night-time sounds bridged the long silences. A good many cars were on the road again, though officially this was not yet permitted; they sped past with a long hiss of tires on the pavement, receded, and returned. Voices, distant calls, silence again, a clatter of horse hoofs, the squeal of streetcars rounding a curve, vague murmurs — then once more the quiet breathing of the night.

"Bernard?"

"Yes?"

"Not too tired?"

"No."

At that moment he knew what his mother was thinking, and that she loved him. But he knew, too, that to love someone means relatively little; or, rather, that love is never strong enough to find the words befitting it. Thus he and his mother would always love each other silently. And one day she — or he — would die, without ever, all their lives long, having gone farther than this by way of making their affection known. Thus, too, he had lived at Tarrou's side, and Tarrou had died this evening without their friendship's having had time to enter fully into the life of either. Tarrou had "lost the match," as he put it. But what had he, Rieux, won? No more than the experience of having known plague and remembering it, of having known friendship and remembering it, of knowing affection and being destined one day to remember it. So all a man could win in the conflict between plague and life was knowledge and memories. But Tarrou, perhaps, would have called that winning the match.

Another car passed, and Mme Rieux stirred slightly. Rieux smiled toward her. She assured him she wasn't tired and immediately added:

"You must go and have a good long rest in the mountains, over there."

"Yes, Mother."

Certainly he'd take a rest "over there." It, too, would be a pretext for memory. But if that was what it meant, winning the match — how hard it must be to live only with what one knows and what one remembers, cut off from what one hopes for! It was thus, most probably, that Tarrou had lived, and he realized the bleak sterility of a life without illusions. There can be no peace without hope, and Tarrou, denying as he did the right to condemn anyone whomsoever — though he knew well that no one can help condemning and it befalls even the victim sometimes to turn execu-tioner — Tarrou had lived a life riddled with contradictions and had never known hope's solace. Did that explain his aspiration toward saint-liness, his quest of peace by service in the cause of others? Actually Rieux had no idea of the answer to that question, and it matterd little. The only picture of Tarrou he would always have would be the picture of a man who firmly gripped the steering-wheel of his car when driving, or else the picture of that stalwart body, now lying motionless. Knowing meant that: a living warmth, and a picture of death.

That, no doubt, explains Dr. Rieux's composure on receiving next morning the news of his wife's death. He was in the surgery. His mother came in, almost running, and handed him a telegram; then went back to the hall to give the telegraph-boy a tip. When she returned, her son was holding the telegram open in his hand. She looked at him, but his eyes were resolutely fixed on the window; it was flooded with the effulgence of the morning sun rising above the harbor.

"Bernard," she said gently.

The doctor turned and looked at her almost as if she were a stranger.

"The telegram?"

"Yes," he said, "that's it. A week ago."

Mme Rieux turned her face toward the window. Rieux kept silent for a while. Then he told his mother not to cry, he'd been expecting it, but it was hard all the same. And he knew, in saying this, that this suffering was nothing new. For many months, and for the last two days, it was the self-same suffering going on and on.

LORRIE MOORE

This short story, by contemporary writer Lorrie Moore, chronicles the last stages of one woman's dying in a way that mirrors the previous analysis by Heidegger.

Go Like This

> *If an elephant missteps and dies in an open place, the herd will not leave him there . . .*
>
> — Lewis Thomas, *The Lives of a Cell*

I have written before. Three children's books: *William, William Takes a Trip, More William.* Perhaps you've heard of them. In the first, William gets a duck, builds it a house with a doorbell. In the second, William goes to Wildwood and has a good time. In the third, William finds a wildebeest in his closet. It messes up his room. Life is tough all around.

I was planning a fourth book, but I didn't know finally what William should do. So instead, I am writing of rational suicide — no oxymoron there. I eschew all contradictions, inconsistencies, all stripes with plaids. I write as a purist, a lover of skim milk, a woman who knows which pieces of furniture look right together in the living room. A month ago I was told I have cancer. It was not the clean, confined sort I might have hoped for, suspended neatly in my breast with its slippery little convolutions turned tortuously inward on itself, hardened, wizened to a small extractable walnut. Or even two. It had spread through my body like a clumsy uninvited guest who is obese and eats too much, still finding, filling rooms. I tried therapy for three weeks, wearing scarves, hiding hair-brushes. I turned up the stereo when rushing into the bathroom to be sick. Blaine heard my retching above the Mozart only twice. Mommyouall-right? Her voice had a way of drifting through the door, a small, misplaced melody that had lost its way, ending up in a room full of plumbing and decaying flesh, cavorting innocently with the false lilac aerosol and the mean stench of bile and undigested foods. Okay, honey, I'm okay. Hell, I'm okay.

*   *   *

Dr. Torbein said that many women go like this for months and improve. Live many years after. Go Christmas shopping, have birthday cakes, all those simple pleasures, now you certainly would like that wouldn't you, Elizabeth?

I am not a skinny child with charge cards, I said. You can't honestly expect me to like this. And please: don't call me Elizabeth.

He was taken aback, vaguely annoyed. Ad lib unpleasantries, my, my. He did not have lines for this. He took off his glasses, no, perhaps you'd call them spectacles, and stared at me over his clipboard, the glare one gives a fractious child who is not going to get ice cream. This is not going to be easy, he informed me. (No maple walnut.) But women have survived much greater damage than you have suffered, much worse odds, worse pain than this.

Well, waddaya know, I cheered heartily. Bully for them.

Now Elizabeth, he scolded. He started to raise a finger, then changed his mind. Go like this, he said instead, demonstrating that I should lift my arm as high as possible over my head so he could examine tissue, feel for further lumps of something. He began to whistle "Clementine."

Ouch! I shrieked. He stopped whistling.

Dreadful sorry, he murmured, trying to probe more gently.

I try not to look at my chest. It is ravaged, paved over, mowed down by the train tracks and parking lots of the Surgical Way. I know there are absences, as if the hollows were the surreptitious marks of a child's spoon in tomorrow night's dessert. The place where I thought my soul was located when I was five is no longer there.

I haven't worn falsies since junior high, I smiled and told the doctor, my future spreading before me, a van Ruisdael cemetery. Thank god I don't have to take gym like y'know wadda mean, doc?

* * *

Joanie, Joanie, my friend with the webbed toes, why do I make Dr. Torbein so uncomfortable, don't you think he'd be used to this by now, he must get it all the time, even if he doesn't get it *all* all the time, you know what I mean? (Joanie smiles and looks at her feet a lot.) I mean, he's got his glasses so far down here, see, that he has to tuck two of his chins back into the recesses of his throat in order to read The Clipboard, which seems to grow out of his gut like some visceral suburbia, and unless we are speaking of the ferrous content of blood, he is utterly ill at ease with irony and gets twitches, like this, see? (Horrid, feeble humor.)

Joanie groans and rolls her eyeballs like Howdy Doody. Jesusmaryandjoseph, Liz, she sighs. (Only Catholics can say that.) You're really getting silly.

Even wit deteriorates, I say, my eye running fast out of twinkles.

* * *

I have decided on Bastille Day. It is a choice of symbol and expedience. Elliott will have time enough before he begins teaching again in the fall.

Blaine will not go to camp this year and can spend some time with Elliot's folks upstate. As it will be unbearably hot, I'm sure, I will tell everyone to wear light clothes. No black, no ties, no hats, no coats. The dead are cruel to inflict that misery in July. Open-toed shoes and parasols de rigueur, I will tell everyone. (Ditto: pastels, seersucker, flasks and vials of Scotch, cocaine.) They should require little prompting. They're enlightened. They've seen others go like this before. They read the papers, see the movies, watch the television broadcasts. They know how it's done. They know what for. It's existential. It's Hemingway. It's familiar. They know what to do.

When I told Elliott of my suicide we were in the kitchen bitching at each other about the grease in the oven. Funny, I had planned on telling him a little differently than No one has fucking cleaned this shithole in weeks Elliott I have something to tell you. It wasn't exactly Edna Millay.

I have lain. In bed. So many nights. Thinking of how it would be when I told him. And plotting, ruminating, remembering the ways our bodies used to love each other, touch, waltz. Now my body stands in the corner of the gym by the foul lines and extra crepe paper and doesn't get asked to dance at all. Blighted, beaten, defeated friend. I rock it, hold it like a sick child; alone, my body and I, we weep for the missing parts. I never question Elliott's reluctance to have sex with me. It is not the same body to him, with his simple, boyish perceptions of the physical. It's okay, I say, but I look at the curve of his bones, the freckled skin of his back, something wildly magical still, something precious. I always think he's the first one to drop off to sleep at night, but I have often awoken in the morning to find the hand lotion bottle on the floor by his side of the bed, so I know it's not always so. It's like some rude poem of my stupidity, of this space grown between us. (Oh, Elliot, I am so sorry.) I return the lotion to the bathroom sometimes only to discover it by the bed again the next morning. I never hear him. (Elliot, is there nothing I can do? Is there nothing?)

He looked a little white, standing there by the oven. He took my hand, kissed it, held it between his, patted it. Let's think about it for a day or two or whatever. Then we'll discuss it further.
Then we'll discuss it further, I repeated.
Yes, he said.
Yes, I said.

But we didn't. Not really. Oh, it drifted piecemeal into subsequent dialogues like a body tossed out to sea and washed days later back into shore, a shoe there, a finger here, a breast-bone in weed tide-bumping against the sand. But we never truly discussed it, never truly. Instead, allusions, suggestions, clues, silent but palpable, crawled out of the night ocean, as in a science fiction movie: black and slow they moved in and arranged themselves around the apartment like precocious, breathing houseplants, like scavengers.

I heard Elliott last night. He thought I was asleep, but I could see his motions under the covers and the tense drop of his jaw. I thought of Ivan Ilych who, dying, left his overweight wife in the master bedroom (with the knickknacks?) to sleep alone in a small room next to the study.

Darkness. The late spring sky has strangely emptied. The moon rummages down in the alleyway like somebody's forgotten aunt.

* * *

I have invited our closest friends over tonight, seated them around the living room, and told them that I wanted to die, that I had calculated how much Seconal was required. They are a cool intellectual lot. They do not gasp and murmur among themselves. I say I have chosen suicide as the most rational and humane alternative to my cancer, an act not so much of self-sacrifice as of beauty, of sparing. I wanted their support.

You have obviously thought this out, says Myrna, the poet whom I have loved since childhood for the burlap, asthma-rasp of her voice, making decisions of a lifetime with the speed of deli orders. She can dismiss lovers, choose upholstery, sign on dotted lines, and fly to Olbia faster than anyone I know. She is finality with a hard obsidian edge. We are dealing, she continues, with a mind, as Williams put it, like a bed all made up. You have our love and our support, Liz.

I look around and try to smile gratefully as Myrna seems to speak for everyone, even without conferring. A miracle, that woman. There appears to be no dissent.

I say, Well now, and sip my Scotch and think of my bed in the next room strangled in the twists of sheets and blankets, edges dragging on the floor. I am not afraid of death, I decide to add. I am afraid of what going on like this will do to me and to my daughter and to my husband.

Elliott, arranged next to me on the sofa, looks at his fingers, which tip to tip form a sort of steeple between his knees.

I am getting into the swing of it. I tell them the cancer is poisoning at least three lives and that I refuse to be its accomplice. This is not a deranged act, I explain. Most of them have known for quite a while my belief that intelligent suicide is almost always preferable to the stupid lingering of a graceless death.

There is silence, grand as Versailles. It seems respectful.

Shennan, Algonquin princess with black braids and sad eyes, stands and says in the oratory deadpan of sixth-grade book reports: I think I can speak for Liz when I say that suicide can be, often is, the most definitive statement one can make about one's life, to say that it's yours and that you are not going to let it wither away like something decaying in a refrigerator drawer. As it is Liz's life to do with as she pleases, so it is her death. As long as Liz and I have known one another, I think we have both realized that she would probably be a suicide. It is no inchoate fancy. It is Liz's long-held vision, a way of meeting one's death squarely, maturely. It is an assertion of life, of self.

(Ah, Shennan dear, yes, but didn't I always say that seventy-one would be better than forty-two, in love as I am with prime numbers, those curious virginal devils, and they could always say, ah, yes, she died in her prime — even at seventy-one — good god I'm really getting awful, Joanie, what did I tell you, babe?)

Shennan finishes by saying it is the culmination of a life philosophy, the triumph of the artist over the mortal, physical world.

It will possibly be the most creative act Liz has ever accomplished, adds my husband. I mean, it could be viewed that way.

He swallows with some difficulty, his wonderful Adam's apple gliding up and down his throat, a tiny flesh elevator. I think of the warm beers, unfinished books, the buttonless sweaters, and the miscarriages upstairs. I wonder if he could be right.

I think it is beautiful she is doing this for me, Elliott adds as a further announcement. He squeezes my shoulder. I look for tears in his eyes and think I spot the shiny edge of one, like a contact lens.

Well now, I say.

Now we all get up and cry and eat brie and wheat thins. Joanie steps toward me with her husband, William. Until now no one has mentioned God.

I fear for you, Liz. She is crying. I hold her. Why didn't you tell me this before? she murmurs. Oh, Liz, I fear hell for you. What are you doing?

William doesn't bullshit: It's crap, Liz. There's no such thing as an aesthetic suicide. You're not going to be able to stand back afterward and say by jove what a damn good job I did of it. You'll make the *Post*, Liz, not the Whitney. This all smacks of some perverse crypto-Catholic martyrdom of yours. It's deluded. It's a power play.

(I can clear my throat louder than anyone I know.)

I appreciate your candor, William.

You know, he continues, a roomful of people, it sounds beautiful, but it's fishy. Something's not right underneath.

Joanie the star of catechism class: We love you, Liz. God loves you, please —

I understand, I interrupt, if you cannot help me do it.

Help you *do* it? they chorus, horrified. They leave early, forgetting their umbrellas. The room is reeling.

Frank Scherman Franck pulls at his cowlick, sips Cherry Heering. His cowlick bounces back up again, something vaguely lewd. You are a marvel, Liz, he coos. It's a brave and awesome thing you are doing. I never thought you'd actually go through with it, but here you are . . .

(Cherry Heering, Hairy Cherring.) Do you believe in God, Frank Scherman Franck? I ask.

Well, long story, he begins. We have a kind of mutual agreement: I won't believe in him and he won't believe in me. That way no one gets hurt.

Sometimes I still believe in God, Frank Scherman Franck, I say, but then that belief flies away from me like a child on a swing, back and forth, back and forth, and I do not really say this. (Cow lick, lick cow.) I notice William has returned for his umbrella. He stops Elliott in the foyer, says something urgent, something red. I can hear Elliott's reply: If I saw or felt any ambivalence I would, William, but there's no ambivalence. She's sure. She's strong. She knows what she's doing. I have to believe in her.

Excuse me, I say to Frank as I run off to hide temporarily in the bathroom. I lock the door behind me and bury my face in Elliott's bathrobe hanging on the inside hook like a sheepish animal. Hug. Clutch. Press. Cry. I could get lost in it, this vast white country of terrycloth, the terrain of it against my face, Elliott's familiar soapy smells inextricable, filling, spinning my head. I turn around and sink back against the door, against the robe. I do not look in the mirror. This place is a mausoleum of pills and ceramic and fluorescent lights blinking on and off so quickly you think they're on all the time, those clever devils. But we know better don't we. This is where the dead belong, with the dying belonging to the dead belonging to no one. This is not supposed to go like this. I am getting drunk. I think we were supposed to sit around rather politely, perhaps even woodenly, and discuss this thing, cool as iced tea, a parlor of painters and poets like the Paris salons, like television, and we would all agree (my reasoning flawless) that my life ultimately meant my death as well and that is was a right both civil and humane to take whatever actions my free will so determined yadada yadada, and they would pronounce me a genius and not steal the best lines and they would weep just the right amount that anyone should weep for Bastille Day and no one would fucking mention God or hell and when I stepped out of the bathroom I would not see Shennan eyeing Elliott's ass as the two of them stand alone in the kitchen, one slicing cheese, the other arranging crackers, nor would I have to suffer the aphasic stupidity of the articulate (therefore unforgivable) who when offered the topaz necklace of a dying woman do not know what to say (and Myrna, this is not Myrna, Myrna is a poet who flies to Olbia, dismisses lovers, sculpts in words, her poems like the finest diamonds in the finest Fabergés of the finest Czar, not faltering, defeated by topaz). I do not like to watch Myrna grope; she doesn't do it well.

I am something putrid. I wonder if I smell, decaying from the inside out like fruit, yet able to walk among them like the dead among the living, like Christ, for a while, only for a while, until things begin to show, until things become uncomfortable. I return to the living room, grin weakly, stand among my friends. I am something incorrect: a hair in the cottage cheese. Something uncouth: a fart in the elevator.

*   *   *

Go like this; my husband pushes my head between my knees.

Ugh, what a night, I say, huh.

Ssshhhh. Be quiet. This increases the oxygen to the cortex. You know you're not supposed to drink like that.

I inhale four times with the drama of the first amphibian. How am I doing so far?

The sun is up, depressing me like the mindless smile of a cheer-leader. My face is the big bluish-white of white elephants.

The phone rings.

It is Olga, her quiet Slavic cheekbones pale and calming even through the wires, her voice a learned English breathiness affected in the style of too much late night Joan Fontaine. She is sorry, she says, for not having spoken much to me last night. She felt a little bewildered both by my announcement and by the reaction of the others. It was, she says, as if they had already known before and had nothing but clinically prepared affirmations for me, convinced as always of Liz's sound-mindedness.

Well, the dissent left early, I say, and forgot its umbrella.

I, too, am dissenting, she says slowly, like Jane Eyre. Don't the others know what you still have to offer, in terms of your writing, in terms of your daughter?

Olga, I despise people propping my pillows.

Olga is getting cheeky: Perhaps the time has come for you to learn to need people, Liz. And to be patient. You haven't earned your death yet. You want the orgasm without the foreplay.

Look, Olga, at this point I'd take what I could get. Don't get too sexual on me, okay, sweetie? (I can feel myself starting to get mean, my tone invidious.)

Please, Liz. I'm trying to tell you what your sister might have told you. I mean, I couldn't let last night just sit there like that, Shennan standing there like an Indian priestess celebrating death in this fraudu-lent guise of a philosophy, and Myrna — well, Myrna will be Myrna.

(And sometimes not, I think. God, I'm not in the mood for this. Olga, dear, go back to the moors.)

I care so much for you, Liz, she continues. (Oh, Rochester, take her the fuck away.) It's just that . . . it's like you and your death, you're facing each other like loners from a singles bar who have scarcely spoken. You haven't really kissed or touched and yet are about to plunge into bed together.

(Sex again. Jane Eyre, indeed.)

Honestly, Olga. All this erotica on a Sunday. Has Richard returned for free piano lessons or something? (I am cruel; a schoolmaster with a switch and a stool.) I really must see what Blaine is shouting about; she's downstairs and has been calling to me for a while now. It may be one of her turtles or something.

Liz, look. I don't want to go like this. Let's have lunch soon.

(We make plans to make plans.)

I think about what William should do.

* * *

Elliott and I have weekly philharmonic seats. I am in bed this Friday, not feeling up to it.

Go ahead, I say. Take Blaine. Take Shennan.

Liz, he drawls, a mild reprimand. He sits at the bed's edge, zooted, smelling of Danish soap, and I think of Ivan Ilych's wife, off to the theater while her husband's kidneys floated in his eyes like cataracts, his legs propped up on the footboard by the manservant — ah, where are the manservants?

Elliott, look at how I'm feeling today. I can't go like this. Please, go ahead without me.

You feel pretty bad, huh, he says, looking at his watch at the same time. He gives me the old honey I'll bring you home a treat, like I'm a fucking retard or something whose nights can be relieved of their hellish sameness with gifts of Colorforms and Sky Bars.

Enjoy, enjoy, you asshole, I do not chirp.

* * *

It is already July. The fireflies will soon be out. My death flashes across my afternoon like a nun in white, hurrying, evanescing, apparitional as the rise of heat off boulevards, the parched white of sails across cement, around the corner, fleeing the sun. I have not yet seen the face, it is hooded, perhaps wrapped, but I know the flow, the cloth of her, moving always in diagonals, in waves toward me, then footlessly away again.

* * *

We told Blaine tonight. We had decided to do it together. We were in the living room

You're going to die, she said, aren't you? before I had a chance to say, Now you're young and probably don't understand. She has developed a habit of tucking her hair nervously behind her ears when she does not want to cry. She is prophetic. Tuck, tuck.

Yes. And we told her why. And I got a chance, after all, to say you're young and probably don't understand, and she got a chance to look at me with that scrambled gaze of contempt and hurt that only fourth-graders know, and then to close her eyes like an angel and fall into my arms, sobbing, and I sobbed too into that hair tucked behind those ears and I cursed God for this day and Blaine of course wanted to know who would take her to clarinet class.

Tuck, tuck. She laid her head in my lap like a leaky egg. We stayed like that for an hour. I whispered little things to her, smoothing back her hair, about how much I loved her, how patient she would have to be, how strong. At nine-thirty she went silently to her room and lay in bed, swollen-eyed, facing the wall like a spurned and dying lover.

*　*　*

I realize now what it is that William should do. When the badass wildebeest comes out of the closet and messes up his room, William should blow a trumpet and make the wildebeest cease and desist. He should put his foot down and say, Enough of this darned nonsense, silly wildebeest: Let's get this room picked up! I am practically certain that wildebeests listen to trumpets.

I would tell this to Elliott, but the wildebeest was in the third book. And I finished that long ago.

No. I must think of something else.

*　*　*

Oh God, it's not supposed to go like this. There I was like Jesus, sure as a blazing rooster, on Palm Sunday riding tall, dauntless as Barbra Streisand, now suddenly on Thursday shoved up against the softer edges of my skin and even Jesus, look, he's crying and whimpering and heaving so, Christ, he pees in his pants, please god, I mean God, don't let me go like this but let me stay right in this garden next to the plastic flamingoes and let me croon the blues till I am crazy with them.

*　*　*

Elliott has a way of walking in just before dinner and kissing me as if for a publicity shot.

What do we have out there waiting in the wings, Elliott, fucking Happy Rockefeller? Channel 6 News? Hey, baby, I'm not dead yet; I'm writing, I'm hungry: let's make love, baby, let's do it on the terrace, high and cool, sugar, hey how about the terrace Elliott babydoll, waddaya say?

And if he does not stride angrily from the room, he stays, fumbles insincerely, makes me weep. He has no taste for necrophilia, and I sigh and crave the white of his shoulders under my chin, his breath on my neck, the plum smoothness of him in my hands. And I want it still for me here now as I lie in the blue-black of this aloneness thirsting for love more than I ever thought I could

*　*　*

Even at midnight the city groans in the heat. We have had no rain for quite a while. The traffic sounds below ride the night air in waves of trigonometry, the cosine of a siren, the tangent of a sigh, a system, an axis, a logic to this chaos, yes.

*　*　*

Tomorrow's Bastille Day, Elliott, and I want what I've written for the fourth William book changed. So far William thinks he forgot his umbrella and wanders all over the city looking for it, misfortune following him like an odious dog, until after he is splashed by a truck and nearly hit by a cab, he goes home only to realize he never forgot his umbrella at all. I want that changed. I want him to have all kinds of wonderful, picaresque adventures so that it doesn't even matter if he has lost his umbrella or not. Can you change that for me? Can you think of some wonderful adventures for me? Maybe he meets up with cowboys and a few Indians and has a cookout with music and barbecue beans.

Or meets a pretty little Indian girl and gets married, suggests Elliott, an asshole sometimes, I swear. He doesn't even realize, I guess.

My turn: Yeah, and scalps her and wins hero-of-the-day badge. I guess I'll just have to entrust it all to you, Elliott.

Don't worry, he says, gingerly stroking my hair, which I picture now like the last pieces of thread around a spool.

I really would like to finish it myself, but tomorrow is Bastille Day.

Yes, says Elliott.

* * *

Joanie, hon, Joanie with the webbed toes, I know it's late, no, no, don't feel you have to come over, no please don't, Elliott's here, it's fine. I just wanted to say I love you and don't feel sad for me please . . . you know I feel pretty good and these pills, well, they're here in a little saucer staring at me, listen, I'm going to let you go back to bed now and well you know how I've always felt about you Joan and if there is an afterlife . . . yeah well maybe *I'm* not going to heaven, okay . . . what . . . do you think I'm silly? I mean if it wouldn't scare you, maybe I'll try to get in touch, if you wouldn't mind, yes, and please keep an eye out for Blaine for me, Joan, would you, god she's so young and I only just told her about menstruation this past spring and she seemed so interested but then only said, So does that mean all twins look alike? so I know there will be other things she will want to know, you know, and she loves you, Joan, she really does. And be good to Olga for me, I have been so unkind, and remind your husband I've immortalized him, ha! yeah . . . can you believe it, dear rigid soul, and Joanie, take care of yourself and say prayers for me and for Blaine and for Elliott who did cry this morning for the first helpless time, how I do love him, Joan, despite everything

everything I can see from the round eye of this empty saucer, faintly making out a patch of droughted trees and a string of wildebeests, one by one, like the sheep of a child's insomnia, throwing in the towel, circling, lying down in the sun silently to decompose, in spite of themselves, god, there's no music, no trumpet here, it is fast, and there's no sound at all, just this white heat of July going on and on, going on like this

chapter 2

Existentialism and Theism: Kierkegaard's Contribution to Existentialism

The Son of God died; it is by all means to be believed, because it is absurd. And He was buried and rose again; the fact is certain because it is impossible.

Tertullian (150 A.D.–225)

To stand on one leg and prove God's existence is a very different thing from going on one's knees and thanking Him.

Kierkegaard, *Journals*, 1841, p. 68

Luther had 95 theses. I have only one — that Christianity has not been made a reality.

Kierkegaard, *Attack*, X, p. 32 (Jan. 26, 1855)

INTRODUCTION

Søren Kierkegaard (1813–1855) viewed himself a modern-day Socrates, a gadfly stinging at the most powerful institutions of his time, including Christianity and the philosophy of Hegel. His philosophy was essentially a personal one, and Kierkegaard himself was introverted and introspective. Indeed, he once remarked that the only inscription he wanted for his tombstone was, "That Individual." In an age that he viewed as secure and passionless, he sought a return to concrete existence, subjectivity, and paradox.

The enormous body of writing Kierkegaard left us — twenty-four volumes translated in English — were produced in only fourteen years. These writings, as is evident in the excerpts at the end of this chapter, do not lend themselves to facile generalizations. Kierkegaard's thought is itself ambiguous, his method almost always indirect and frequently ironic. He used the dash more frequently than any other writer, and his storytelling leaves great room for interpretation. Further, he often hid his own identity in pseudonyms, arguing that this strategy gave his works independence:

> So in the pseudonymous work there is not a single word that is mine, I have no opinion about these works except as a reader, not the remotest private relation to them, since such a thing is impossible in the case of a doubly reflected communication.
>
> *Concluding Unscientific Postscript, p. 551*

All his books, he said, came "without authority," and he went to great lengths to develop what he terms the art of "indirect communication." He knew that he was misunderstood, and even wrote that "people understand me so little that they do not even understand when I complain of being misunderstood." (*Journals*, 1836, p. 50)

At times Kierkegaard is probably guilty of deliberate obfuscation. In fact, he frequently warns his reader to expect a challenge and to pay attention: How could we expect anything else from one "in the service of something true"? (*Attack Upon Christendom*, p. 96) In his journal Kierkegaard tells the story of a hunting dog ill-treated and misunderstood. There can be no doubt who is the hunting dog:

> Imagine a big, well-trained hunting dog. He accompanies his master on a visit to a family where, as all too often in our time, there is a whole assembly of ill-behaved youths. Their eyes hardly light upon the hound before they begin to maltreat it in every kind of way. The hound, which was well-trained, as these youths were not, fixes his eye on his master to ascertain from his expression what he expects him to do. And he understands the glance to mean that he is to put up with all the ill-treatment, accept it indeed as though it were sheer kindness conferred upon him. Thereupon the youths of course became still more rough, and finally they agreed that it must be a prodigiously stupid dog which puts up with everything.
>
> The dog meanwhile is concerned only about one thing, what the master's glance commands him to do. And, lo, that glance is suddenly altered; it signifies — and the hound understands it at once — use your strength. That instant with a single leap he has seized the biggest lout and thrown him to the ground — and now no one stops him, except the master's glance, and the same instant he is as he was a moment before. — Just so with me.
>
> *Journals, X12 A 423*

Like the hunting dog in this parable, Kierkegaard too serves only one master, God; and, even if no one understands his work, his master understands and provides the strength to meet the challenge.

Though the term *existentialism* was not yet coined in Kierkegaard's day, there can be no doubt that the label is a fitting one. In this section we explore some of the more basic aspects of Kierkegaard's views that link him to existentialist thought. In particular, we focus on four key concerns: his view of dread and the possibility of salvation; his critique of traditional Christianity and his own perspective on theism; his analysis of truth as subjectivity; and his structural framework for personal development.

Hegel's influence on nineteenth-century thinkers in general, and Kierkegaard in particular, is undeniable. "All the great philosophical ideas of the past century — the philosophies of Marx and Nietzsche [see chapter 3], phenomenology, German existentialism, and psychoanalysis — had their beginnings in Hegel; it was he who started the attempt to explore the irrational and integrate it into an expanded reason, which remains the task of our century." (Merleau-Ponty, p. 63) Though we do not have enough space here to do justice to the philosophy of Hegel, it is essential to look at some of the aspects of Hegel's philosophy against which Kierkegaard rebels.

For Hegel, there is a faith in the ultimate harmony of things, and a belief that all of human existence can be enclosed within a system. The goal of philosophy is to synthesize all knowing, to seek out the unity that exists at the core of human consciousness. This search for synthesis is "the true form in which truth exists" and is the only real scientific system. (Hegel, *Phenomenology*, p. 14) But by science Hegel does not refer to the "dead, fixed" propositions of the natural sciences. Rather, he saw his task as the exposition of a systematic history of the development of consciousness, through a method termed *dialectic*.

The word *dialectic* now has many meanings in philosophy. The term may have originated with Zeno in the fifth century B.C. to refer to the refutation of hypotheses by drawing out the absurdities of their consequences. (This later came to mean any argument used to win a debate, whether it was a strong one or one that was merely persuasive.) At times (e.g., during the Middle Ages), the term *dialectic* was used interchangeably with *logic*.

In the *Critique of Pure Reason,* Kant's "transcendental dialectic" (see also chapter 4, 235–36) was concerned with exposing the illusion of transcendental judgments, that is, judgments that attempted to go beyond the limits of experience. Kant's method unfolds the contradictions of pure reason by setting metaphysically provable but mutually contradictory propositions over against each other. His "antinomies of pure reason" contain four sets of thesis and antithesis statements; but he did not call their resolution a synthesis, as Hegel later did in his dialectical approach.

Hegel presented his doctrines in what tended to be a triadic form as a process that arrived at a higher truth through contradiction. This "passing over into the opposite" was not, according to Hegel, a contradiction as in formal logic but rather a process that led by necessity to a further phase of development. The task of dialectical thinking, he said, was to change "fixed and fast" concepts into "fluid" ones where truth and falsity are bound together; in this process, Hegel believed, we can move beyond the finite to what he termed Absolute Idea (*Geist*). Hegel's *Phenomenology of Spirit* follows *Geist* through a series of changes in consciousness to its culmination in absolute knowledge. In each successive stage *Geist* preserves, negates, and surpasses particular determinations, and it recognizes that each stage is a necessary expression of its essence. In absolute knowledge, there are no longer any divisions. As Hegel notes in his *Reason in History*, the presupposition of the philosophy of world history is "that the ideal accomplishes itself, that only what accords with the idea has actuality." (p. 256)

Like Plato (see pp. 3–8), Hegel makes the transcendence of temporal existence a necessary condition for knowledge. Such knowledge is timeless, eternal, and absolute. Hegel's optimism regarding the possibility of such knowledge exposes his attachment to the intellectual tradition of the Age of Enlightenment. This Age was marked by a powerful belief in reason and inevitable progress. For Hegel, rationality and progress are united, and world history is proof of that progress.

But for Hegel, all development is dialectical, that is, the negative always appears with the positive. Indeed, Hegel believed that just before the last stage of the absolute idea, the negative appears at its strongest. We find, for example, in the *The Phenomenology of Spirit*, the chapter "Self-Alienated Spirit" just before "Spirit that Is Certain of Itself." Hegel, then, does not ignore the negative, but his optimism pervades his work. For Hegel, "what is rational is real and what is real is rational." "The time has come," he wrote in the preface to his *Phenomenology*, "for the elevation of philosophy to a science." But for Kierkegaard, science can never enclose all of concrete existence in a system.

> System and finality correspond to one another, but existence is precisely the opposite of finality. It may be seen, from a purely abstract point of view, that system and existence are incapable of being thought together; because in order to think existence at all, systematic thought must think it as abrogated, and hence as not existing. Existence separates, and holds the various moments of existence discretely apart; the systematic thought consists of the finality which brings them together.
>
> *Concluding Unscientific Postscript, p. 107*

Further, Kierkegaard maintained, the philosophical system builder must abstract himself or herself from that system; given the nature of the system, such detachment is impossible.

> In relation to their systems most systematizers are like a man who builds an enormous castle and lives in a shack close by; they do not live in their own enormous systematic buildings. But spiritually that is a decisive objection. Spiritually speaking a man's thought must be the building in which he lives — otherwise everything is topsy-turvy.
>
> *Journals, 1846, p. 98*

Systems like Hegel's are too grandiose, drawing our attention away from the humbler concerns of the finite knower, of "that individual." In Hegel's "world historical absent-mindedness," he has forgotten what it means to exist as a human being. According to Kierkegaard,

> Being an individual man is a thing that has been abolished, and every speculative philosopher confuses himself with humanity at large; whereby he becomes something infinitely great, and at the same time nothing at all.
>
> *Concluding Unscientific Postscript, p. 113*

For Kierkegaard, Hegel's system, in trying to assimilate the varied aspects of existence, collapses all difference. But according to Kierkegaard, either difference is real and no reconciliation is possible or reconciliation is possible but otherness is erased. We must not, Kierkegaard cautions us, allow our theory to make us forget existence, any more than we would allow a restaurant's menu to make us forget the actual food we consume. Too many people "reach their conclusions about life like schoolboys; they cheat their master by copying the answer out of a book without having worked out the sum for themselves." (*Journals,* January 17, 1873, p. 53)

Like those schoolboys, many philosophers treat existence as if it were a category to be studied and analyzed, poked at and probed. And like those schoolboys, they fail to realize that the answers must come from within, through *living*. For Kierkegaard, the concept of existence is not general or remote, but concrete and rich. I begin with "I am," with, as Kierkegaard says, "my own little I." This is not the sterile speculative "I" of some disembodied mind, but rather the personal and passionate "I" of concrete, everyday existence. We encounter this self, according to Kierkegaard, not in detached thought but in our involvement in living, particularly in choice. Our essential task is to exist as finite, particular individuals; it is, he tells us, "the task of becoming subjective."

For Kierkegaard, life — though philosophers tell us it must be understood backwards — must be lived forwards. If this is true, then perhaps "life can never be understood in time simply because at no particular moment can I find the necessary resting-place from which to understand it — backwards." (*Journals,* 1843, p. 89)

DREAD AND THE POSSIBILITY OF SALVATION

Kierkegaard (like Hegel's other major critic, Marx) lacked the optimism of the Enlightenment and saw the world as falling apart and humanity in a state of disintegration. He wrote in his journals of the "total bankruptcy" and decline of spirit that Europe was facing in his day. Where Hegel through his dialectic insisted that the negative was also positive, for Kierkegaard the reverse is true.

Freedom itself, which most philosophers have taken to constitute the decisive difference between Homo sapiens and beasts, is the source of great anxiety. We must live our lives with no guarantee of their meaning, but with responsibility for their results. This recognition of choice leads to an awareness of our own freedom and the power to create truth. And, as we acknowledge our freedom, so too must we recognize what Kierkegaard calls the "heaviest of all categories," possibility. For Kierkegaard, this is not the glib possibility of usual concerns: for example, tonight I may go to a movie or read a book or visit a friend. Rather it is the realization that we may do *anything,* that everything is possible, that nothing is necessary. Such an awareness, if one has any spirit at all, leads to an experience of dread.

Humans, Kierkegaard tells us, are the only beings capable of experiencing dread. "Whosoever has learned to be anxious in the right way has learned the ultimate." (*The Concept of Anxiety,* p. 155) If we were angels or beasts, we would not be able to experience this ontological anxiety. And for Kierkegaard, our greatness is measured by the intensity of our experience of dread; "the more profoundly he is in anxiety, the greater is the man." (p. 155) This anxiety, though, is not over any external object but rather comes from subjectivity. "Anxiety is freedom's possibility, and only such anxiety is through faith absolutely educative, because it consumes all finite ends and discovers all their deceptiveness." (p. 155) The goal, then, is neither to ignore anxiety nor to be consumed by it. In this "educative" experience is the possibility of salvation through the infinite. According to Kierkegaard, "Whoever is educated by anxiety is educated by possibility, and only he who is educated by possibility is educated according to his infinitude. Therefore possibility is the weightiest of all categories." (*The Concept of Anxiety,* p. 155)

No doubt this was at least in part an autobiographical report, for Kierkegaard himself confesses in his *Journals* that he spent much of his life in anguish over personal decisions he made and possibilities he foreclosed. Further, Kierkegaard argued, reason does not provide solutions, though it may deceive us temporarily. Indeed, Kierkegaard tells us, there was a time in his life — when he was "without hope" — that he grabbed at the "considerable powers of the mind" and clung desperately to the powers of the intellect. (*Journals,* p. 40) Tolstoy's description of the anguish he went through in sorting out these questions (see pp. 151–61) is not dissimilar.

Like Kierkegaard and Tolstoy, all of us struggle to create strategies to run from despair. Some of us hide in the intellect. Others, after glimpsing dread, may seek comfort in material pleasures, or we may try to deny our actual freedom. We reach for, as the Grand Inquisitor reminds us (see chapter 5, pp. 221–30), the "bread" rather than the "mystery." Apparently, Kierkegaard tried all of these strategies, but found none truly consoling.

> I have looked in vain for an anchorage in the boundless sea of pleasure and in the depth of understanding. . . . I have tasted the fruit of the tree of knowledge, and often delighted in its taste. But the pleasure did not outlast the moment and left no profound mark upon me.
>
> *Journals, pp. 45–46*

But one must know oneself before one can find peace, and neither reason nor pleasure can reveal that self.

"The ordinary view of despair" (see p. 132) that Kierkegaard criticizes assumes that each individual is the best judge of whether he or she is in despair. But, for Kierkegaard, most of us are in despair whether or not we know it. Just as one can have cancer without one's awareness, so one can suffer from a "sickness of the spirit" (p. 133) while believing that one is at peace. To be human is to be "always in a critical condition." (p. 133) This despair is not over any particular external object, though awareness of despair may be provoked by a loss like death or the end of a relationship. These losses are all contingent, whereas dread and despair are "related to the eternal." (p. 133) This despair, then, is over ourselves.

If the experience of dread is actually edifying, then anyone who is destroyed by dread has not understood it fully. Freedom is by its nature full of possibilities, and, for Kierkegaard, the possibility of personal salvation lies hidden in the experience of dread. Indeed, the worst possible fate is for one to be so deceived by the joys of life (or even its sorrows) that those experiences — their maintenance or their avoidance — become one's only preoccupation. Those masses of people who succeed in holding dread at bay are life's greatest losers. In *Fear and Trembling* (see pp. 110–24), Kierkegaard mourns for those individuals. Rich or poor, man or woman, lucky or unlucky, famous or unknown, kind or cruel — all this makes no difference: "for thee, all is lost, eternity knows thee not, it never knew thee, or (even more dreadful) it knows thee as thou are known, it puts thee under arrest by thyself in despair." (see p. 136) Dread, then, opens rather than closes a door for us; those who lack courage to pass through the door are forever trapped in the world of the finite. More specifically, only through our confrontation with dread do we find faith.

KIERKEGAARD AND THEISM

Kierkegaard sought to make things as difficult as he could, for to see things as they really are can never be simple. All he sought, he said, was simple honesty (see p. 139); it was, he believed, a quality lacking in his own time. In particular, his criticisms of the public and its hypocrisy are not unlike those of later existentialists:

> . . . the larger the crowd, the more probable that that which it praises is folly, and the more improbable that it is truth, and the most improbable of all that it is any eternal truth. For in eternity crowds simply do not exist. The truth is not such that it at once pleases the frivolous crowd — and at bottom it never does.
>
> *Purity, p. 191*

Kierkegaard, believing himself to be "a spy in the service of God," rejects the institutionalization of Christianity. He is not out to improve or modify Christianity. In fact, he compares the Christianity of his own day to a hospital where the patients are dying like flies because the whole building is full of poison. The whole building, then, must be toppled and a new structure erected. In an age where everyone is Christian, no one is Christian. According to Kierkegaard, "the present age" had missed the essentially paradoxical and passionate individualism of true Christianity. In a sense, it is easier to become a Christian when one is not Christian than when one is: In a state of "Christendom" we take for granted that all of us are Christian and fail to think about what it means to be one.

For Kierkegaard, there is an inverse relationship between Christianity and number; the myth that there is a "Christian state" is a dangerous one. In fact, the Christianity of the New Testament no longer exists.

> Christianity stands in a different relation to number: one single true Christian is enough to justify the assertion that Christianity exists. In fact, Christianity is inversely proportionate to number; for the concept "Christian" is a polemical concept, one can only be a Christian in contrast or contrastedly. So it is also in the New Testament: to God's desire to be loved, which essentially is a relationship of contrast or opposition in order to raise love to a higher power, corresponds the fact that the Christian who loves God in contrast and opposition to other men has to suffer from their hate and persecution. As soon as the opposition is taken away, the thing of being a Christian is twaddle — as it is in "Christendom," which has slyly done away with Christianity by the affirmation that we are all Christians.
>
> *Attack Upon "Christendom," p. 127*

As the excerpts at the end of this chapter make clear, Kierkegaard saw Christianity as an essentially individual experience. The myth that everybody is Christian is more dangerous than outright rebellion against God. (See, for example, p. 141.) According to Kierkegaard, Christianity had suffered the worst of all possible fates: It had become a "philosophy," a tidy system free of doubt and free of anguish, assuring its practitioners that they are guaranteed an afterlife at no expense to themselves. (See p. 140.) What is forgotten is the anguish and suffering of early Christians, the willingness to be "salt and to be sacrificed." (p. 137) Today, instead, Christianity has become the "enjoyment of life, tranquillized . . . by the assurance that the thing about eternity is settled." (*Attack*, p. 35) Christianity, like Hegelianism, has come to glorify reason and to defend itself on rational grounds. To defend Christianity, though, thought Kierkegaard, is to become a "second Judas."

Theists have for centuries struggled to use reason to prove the existence of an omnipotent, omniscient, omnibenevolent Being. Anselm (1033–1109), for example, maintained that we can deduce God's existence from our intellectual understanding that God is perfect, a "Being than which none greater can be conceived." (p. 26) To exist is better than not to exist, so, he argued, God *must* exist. Thomas Aquinas (1255?–1274) used rational arguments to defend the existence of God. Through our perception of God's effects and our knowledge of certain causal relationships, we can derive God's existence. He explicitly rejects views that claim one must believe simply on faith:

> The fact that God exists and similar truths about him that are knowable by strict reasoning are not articles of faith but preambles to them. Just as grace presupposes nature, and perfection presupposes the capacity for perfection, so faith presupposes natural knowledge. Yet nothing stops any man from accepting as an article of faith something that can be scientifically known and proven, although perhaps not by him.
>
> *Summa Theologica, I, q. 2, a. 2*

This position is consistent with what we might term "rational theism," the view that God exists and His existence can be proven. Indeed, Aquinas argues for the "five ways" to prove God's existence. These arguments focus on the concepts of change, causation, necessary being, gradation, and order. One example illustrates Aquinas's methodology.

The argument from causation (now referred to as the "cosmological" argument) adduces the existence of God from our observation of a succession of causes and the impossibility of an event's either being uncaused or causing itself:

> In the sensible world we find causes in an order or succession; we never see, nor could we, anything causing itself, for then it would have to pre-exist itself, and this is impossible. Any such succession of causes must begin

somewhere, for in it a primary cause influences an intermediate, and the intermediate a last (whether the intermediate be one or many). Now, if you eliminate a cause, you also eliminate its effects, so that you cannot have a last cause or an intermediate one without having a first cause. Without an origin to the series of causes, and hence no primary cause, no intermediate causes would function and therefore no last effect, but the facts seem to contradict this. We must therefore suppose a First Cause, which all call 'God.'

Summa Theologica, I, q. 2, a. 3

This argument and others like it suffer from two kinds of failings, one logical and the other existential. From a logical perspective, there appears to be no necessary reason why we must accept these conclusions. For instance, why can there not be an infinite sequence of causes and effects? Further, why is it that God does not need a cause? These sorts of arguments may persuade those predisposed to theism but do not rationally compel belief.

Kierkegaard attacks these proofs on spiritual as well as logical grounds. He argues that any "proof" must presuppose the very Being whose existence it is attempting to demonstrate. "If God does not exist it would of course be impossible to prove it; and if he does exist it would be folly to attempt it." (*Philosophical Fragments*, p. 49) In the same way, to try to prove the existence of Napoleon from his deeds must presuppose that Napoleon already exists. Kierkegaard argues that we may only reason *from* existence (that is, once we have that which exists), but that we cannot use reason to arrive at existence. God as the Unknown is beyond the limit of human reason.

There is also good spiritual reason to abandon attempts to prove God's existence. For Kierkegaard, any proof would undermine the existential significance of faith. Faith requires that we *not* know for certain that God exists and that instead we *choose* to believe, or, as Kierkegaard puts it, make a "leap of faith." That leap takes us over a chasm — a paradox — that reason simply cannot bridge. And, for Kierkegaard, there really is no freedom without choosing God:

The most tremendous thing which has been granted to [us] is: the choice, freedom. And if you desire to save it and preserve it there is only one way: in the very same second unconditionally and in complete resignation to give it back to God, and yourself with it. If the sight of what is granted to you tempts you, and if you give way to the temptation and look with egoistic desire upon the freedom of choice, then you lose your freedom. And your punishment is: to go on in a kind of confusion priding yourself on having — freedom of choice, but woe upon you, that is your judgment: You have freedom of choice, you say, and still you have not chosen God. Then you will grow ill, freedom of choice will become your *idee fixe*, till at last you will be like the rich man who imagines that he is poor, and will die of want: you sigh that you have lost your freedom of choice — and your fault is only that you do not grieve deeply enough or you would find it again.

Journals, 1850, p. 189

In Exodus 3:14, God tells Moses no more than *"I am that I am."* For a person of faith, no more is necessary. Without faith, no words would be sufficient. In "fear and trembling" we choose God. Rational proofs are only necessary when faith has lost its passion. They deny the concrete personal relationship one can have with God and make of God a mere abstraction. Though rational theists may rest more easily at night, they lack what for Kierkegaard is the anguish of genuine faith. This is what Pascal referred to as the "true fear" of faith as opposed to the "false fear" of doubt. Faith does not provide guarantees. According to Kierkegaard,

> Becoming a Christian is then the most fearful decision of a man's life, a struggle through to attain faith against despair and offense, the twin Cerberuses that guard the entrance to a Christian life. This most terrible of all tests in human life, where eternity is the examiner, cannot possibly have been solved by a child of fourteen days, even if it has ever so many certificates from the parish clerk as to its having been baptized.
>
> *Concluding Unscientific Postscript, p. 333*

Christianity is not, then, a "doctrine" one adopts simply as a matter of course. It is far better to blaspheme than to settle for easy answers: "So rather let us mock God, out and out, as has been done before in the world — this is always preferable to the disparaging air of importance with which one would prove God's existence." (*Concluding Unscientific Postscript*, p. 485) To prove the existence of one who is present is an affront, not, as some would claim, a "pious undertaking." To attempt to prove God is to permit the possibility that God does not exist. Like that of a king, God's existence demands obedience alone:

> The existence of a king, or his presence, is commonly acknowledged by an appropriate expression of subjection and submission — what if in his sublime presence one were to prove that he existed? Is that the way to prove it? No, that would be making a fool of him; for one proves his presence by an expression of submission, which may assume various forms according to the customs of the country — and thus it is also one proves God's existence by worship . . . not by proofs. . . . [A]n omnipresent being can only by a thinker's pious blundering be brought to this ridiculous embarrassment.
>
> *Concluding Unscientific Postscript, p. 485*

The excerpt at the end of this chapter from twentieth-century existential theist Karl Jaspers represents a similar approach to the existence of God. (See pp. 143–50.)

TRUTH AND SUBJECTIVITY

For Kierkegaard, the "task of becoming subjective" is part of a lifelong process of reflection and faith. It is not the subjectivity of selfishness or eccentricity, but is rather genuine "inwardness" involving commitment, passion, and decision. For many philosophers, truth is universality. But, for Kierkegaard, truth is always in relation to a particular individual. The commitment to something "objective," in contrast, does not individuate one. "Subjectivity," however, "culminates in passion, Christianity is the [absolute] paradox, paradox and passion are a mutual fit." (*Concluding Unscientific Postscript*, p. 206)

For Kierkegaard, the question what Christianity is is neither speculative nor objective; rather, Christianity's truth is essentially subjective and paradoxical. This may be nonrational, but it is not irrational. "Christianity is spirit, spirit is inwardness, inwardness is subjectivity, subjectivity is essentially passion, and in its maximum an infinite, personal, passionate interest in one's eternal happiness." (*Concluding Unscientific Postscript*, p. 33) Indeed, much of Kierkegaard's critique of the "present age" is that it is without passion, and that Western thought has lost its sense of inwardness.

> Subjectively, what it is to become a Christian is defined thus: the decision lies in the subject. The appropriation is the paradoxical inwardness which is specifically different from all other inwardness. The thing of being a Christian is not determined by the *what* of Christianity but by the *how* of the Christian. This *how* can only correspond with one thing, the absolute paradox. There is therefore no vague talk to the effect that being a Christian is to accept, and to accept, and to accept quite differently, to appropriate, to believe, to appropriate by faith quite differently (all of them purely rhetorical and fictitious definitions); but *to believe* is specifically different from all other appropriation and inwardness. *Faith is the objective uncertainty along with the repulsion of the absurd held fast in the passion of inwardness, which precisely is inwardness potentiated to the highest degree.* This formula fits only the believer, no one else, not a lover, not an enthusiast, not a thinker, but simply and solely the believer who is related to the absolute paradox.
>
> *Concluding Unscientific Postscript, p. 540, emphasis added*

Kierkegaard's use of dialectic, like Socrates' and unlike Hegel's, reveals untruths, partial truths, and contradictions in existence. In exposing absurdity and ignorance, he makes subjective becoming the basis for truth. For Kierkegaard, truth is never fixed and static, removed from its object. Indeed, he tells us that Christianity does not even exist in any "objective" sense. (*Concluding Unscientific Postscript*, p. 116) A subjective thinker must possess imagination, passion, and feeling. Passion, for Kierkegaard, is "first and last," for "it is impossible to think about existence in existence without passion." (p. 124) And, without passion, the thinker is "mediocre."Kierkegaard's approach does not end up in the glorious synthesis of a Hegelian dialectic. Indeed, he drives the contradictions even more deeply into the final analysis. The further one delves to find truth, the greater are the paradoxes. "Existence involves a tremendous contradiction, from which the subjective thinker does not have to abstract, though he can if he will, but in which it is his business to remain." (p. 124)

Kierkegaard's real concern in religion is the question of relatedness between God and the individual. This relatedness is essentially based on action, on choice. And that choice involves great risk and uncertainty. There are no proofs beforehand; rather, one's life is the proof that one believes. "Without risk faith is an impossibility." (*Journals*, 1850, p. 185) And, ultimately, we end up in deeper paradox. Though, for example, Kierkegaard admires Abraham more than any other, he tells us that he does not understand him at all. Johannes Climacus, the pseudonymous author of *Fear and Trembling*, concludes that he is not really a Christian, as he is "taken up with the thought how difficult it must be" to be one.

Like Kierkegaard, twentieth-century theologian Paul Tillich maintains that "the pole of individualization expresses itself in the religious experience as a personal encounter with God." (*The Courage to Be*, p. 160) Twentieth-century theist Martin Buber expands this idea:

> The description of God as a Person is indispensable for everyone who like myself means by "God" not a principle (although mystics like Eckhart sometimes identify him with 'Being') and like myself means by "God" not an idea (although philosophers like Plato at times could hold that he was this): but who rather means by "God", as I do, him who — whatever else he may be — enters into a direct relationship with us in creative, revealing and redeeming acts, and thus makes it possible for us to enter into a direct relation with him. This ground and meaning of our existence constitutes a mutuality, arising again and again, such as can subsist only between persons. The concept of personal being is indeed completely incapable of declaring what God's essential being is, but it is both permitted and necessary to say that God is also a person.
>
> *I and Thou, p. 135*

Similarly, for Kierkegaard, being a Christian is essentially about how one *is*, not what one thinks. Though the world may admire hypocrisy, God despises nothing more. It is thus by our actions that we define ourselves.

STAGES ON LIFE'S WAY

Kierkegaard did not intend his three stages of human development in a normative sense, but rather as an elucidation of a process by which we make choices and come to define ourselves. Like Hegel's dialectic, Kierkegaard's framework revolves around a triadic division of the aesthetic stage, the ethical stage, and the religious stage. And, like Hegel, Kierkegaard treats these three stages as a progression, though he explicitly denies any interest in prescribing conduct. But unlike Hegel's synthesis, which includes thesis and antithesis, Kierkegaard's last stage — the religious — is a radical departure from the two previous stages.

The first stage, Kierkegaard tells us, is the *aesthetic,* which glories in feelings, in particular pleasures. This need not be the pleasure of crass hedonism, for it includes the intellectual pleasures of "high culture" and even philosophical speculation. This stage represents a flight from boredom and despair, a flight from oneself. There is nothing inherently wrong with such a posture, but it is ultimately doomed to collapse in despair. The flight from boredom, because it must find ever more intense pleasures, leads back to boredom. Or, as Pascal wrote, "the only thing which consoles us for our miseries is diversion, and yet this is the greatest of our miseries." (*Pensees,* no. 171) Kierkegaard may have been writing from personal experience, for he tells us in his *Journals:* "I have just returned from a party of which I was the life and soul; wit poured from my lips, everyone laughed and admired me — but I went away — and the dash should be as long as the earth's orbit — — — and wanted to shoot myself." Thus, the aesthetic stage of life is built on despair.

The aesthetic stage may lead to the *ethical* stage, which is a period bound by notions of duty and obedience to rules (see, e.g., p. 116). This, for Kierkegaard, is best represented by the judge or the family person who lives for duty and adheres to impartiality. This is the stage of Kant's universal categorical imperative, where we hold that "everyone should do *x*" and we lose ourselves in the Moral Law. This is the stage of Abraham (Genesis 20 — 22) as husband of Sarah and father of Isaac, as family man. In marriage and family we become temporal beings. Kierkegaard himself rejected his great love Regine rather than be limited to this temporality. The best thing a woman can do for a man is to be unfaithful to him, Kierkegaard wrote. "A positive relationship to a woman reduces a man to finiteness in the greatest conceivable degree." (*Stages,* p. 73) In the ethical stage, one is no longer living a life of despair.

> Every esthetical view of life is despair, it was said. This was attributed to the fact that it was built upon what may be and may not be. Such is not the case with the ethical view of life, for it builds life upon what essentially belongs

to being. The esthetical, it was said, is that in a man whereby he immediately is the man he is; the ethical is that whereby a man becomes what he becomes. By this I do not intend to say that the man who lives esthetically does not develop but he develops by necessity not by freedom; no metamorphosis takes place in him, no infinite movement where he reaches the point from whence he becomes what he becomes.

Either/Or, Volume II, p. 191

The final stage is what Kierkegaard calls the *religious* or the *teleological*. This stage is eminently paradoxical, for in it the individual becomes "higher than the universal." Kierkegaard uses the story of Abraham and Isaac (see pp. 112–24) to illustrate such a "teleological suspension of the ethical." As a knight of faith, Abraham stands alone, without recourse to politics or ethical theory or even religion. Indeed, he cannot even speak of his anguish, for in language is the universal; "he speaks no human language." (p. 124) This is the person who lives in anguish, who can never be sure of his or her choice.

He must comprehend that no one can understand him, and must have the constancy to put up with it that human language has for him naught but curses, and the human heart has for his sufferings only the feeling that he is guilty. And he must not harden himself against this, for that very same moment he is unjustified. He must feel how misunderstanding tortures him, just as the ascetic felt every instant the prick of the penitential shirt he wore next to his skin.

Stages, p. 175

The spiritual passion of the knight of faith can never be generalized into ethical norms, for it is inexplicable, unjustified, and unique to the individual. Indeed, Kierkegaard calls it "appalling." (p. 115) The true knight of faith is a witness, never a teacher, and so must rely on himself or herself alone (see p. 123).

Kierkegaard's last stage returns us to his critique of "Christendom." The true Christian, the true knight of faith, is essentially alone and essentially single-minded. Thus, the notion of a "Christian nation" is a contradiction. God does not have any interest in "the crowd"; "He desires the individual." (*Purity*, p. 185) It does not matter to God whether one is high- or low-born or how many accomplishments one had in one's lifetime; what matters instead is whether one followed one's faith. One must, then, continue to "will one thing" despite ridicule and despite pressure. Though one might be forsaken by the multitudes and one's voice ignored, one will find comfort and be heard in eternity. Each individual is completely responsible for whatever judgments he or she makes.

And in eternity, you will not be asked inquisitively and professionally, as though by a newspaper reporter, whether there were many that had the same — wrong opinion. You will be asked only whether you have held it, whether you have spoiled your soul by joining in this frivolous and thoughtless judging, because the others, because the many judged thoughtlessly.

Purity, p. 190

For Kierkegaard, this stage is a painful one; "to exist as the individual is the most terrible thing of all." (*Fear and Trembling*, p. 11) Yet "the degree of one's faith is proved only by the degree of one's willingness to suffer for one's faith." (*Attack Upon "Christendom,"* p. 271) One should not assume that God always shares our moral judgments or that God would never contravene our consciences; if that were the case, then God would be a mere redundancy. For Kierkegaard, if God is to make a moral difference, we must acknowledge that He may go against reason and still must be obeyed. The knight of faith knows that no sacrifice is too hard if God requires it. This faith is the greatest passion of which we are capable. There is certainly enough to occupy us even if we do not reach this stage; such a life would "by no means be wasted," but "it never is comparable to the life of those who sense and grasped the highest." (*Fear and Trembling*, p. 131) Finally, though one does not go any further than this stage, it is hardly a stagnant existence: rather, "my whole life is in this." (p. 131)

Hence, for Kierkegaard, truth is ultimately inextricably linked to our experience. The question of faith is a "how," not a "what" question. The subjective thinker prescribes for no one but himself or herself, and is willing to risk uncertainty.

But the above definition of truth is an equivalent expression for faith. Without risk there is no faith. Faith is precisely the contradiction between the infinite passion of the individual's inwardness and the objective uncertainty. If I am capable of grasping God objectively, I do not believe, but precisely because I cannot do this I must believe. If I wish to preserve myself in faith I must constantly be intent upon holding fast the objective uncertainty, so as to remain out upon the deep, over seventy thousand fathoms of water, still preserving my faith.

Concluding Unscientific Postscript, p. 182

And "subjectivity culminates in passion, Christianity is the paradox, paradox and passion are a mutual fit, and the paradox is altogether suited to one whose situation is to be in the extremity of existence." (*Concluding Unscientific Postscript*, p. 206.) Contemporary intuitive theists, like Gabriel Marcel, Karl Jaspers, Paul Tillich, and Martin Buber, take up similar concerns. Like Kierkegaard, they reject rational proofs for the existence of God and focus instead on the meaning of faith and spirituality. Like Kierkegaard, they view belief in God as essentially a way of being and not about dogma and doctrine. The excerpt from Karl Jaspers's book *The Way to Wisdom* (see pp. 143–50), provides a sense of how contemporary thinkers influenced by Kierkegaard frame their concerns.

CONCLUSION

This brief introduction to Kierkegaard's philosophy cannot begin to touch the complexity of his thought and his intensely personal approach. One must be humble in approaching Kierkegaard, for he is fond of paradox and contradiction, and he insists that he is not a systematic thinker. He once remarked that he was more afraid of his friends than his enemies, so one must be suspicious of even sympathetic treatments. If Kierkegaard's goal is ultimately to offend, have we betrayed him if we fail to be offended? It would not, however, be overly confident to insist that Kierkegaard's view is essentially about the *how* of living, not the why or the what; and that his life reflected better than anything else that approach. The following excerpt from his *Journals* shows how important the connection between belief and action is for Kierkegaard:

> . . . What I really lack is to be clear in my mind *what I am to do, not* what I am to know, except insofar as a certain understanding must precede every action. The thing is to understand myself, to see what God really wishes *me* to do; the thing is to find a truth which is true *for me*, to find *the idea for which I can live and die.* What would be the use of discovering so-called objective truth, of working through all the systems of philosophy and of being able, if required, to review them all and show up the inconsistencies within each system; what good would it do me to be able to develop a theory of the state and combine all the details into a single whole, and so construct a world in which I did not live, but only held up to the view of others; what good would it do me to be able to explain the meaning of Christianity if it had *no* deeper significance *for me and for my life;* what good would it do me if truth stood before me, cold and naked, not caring whether I recognized her or not, and producing in me a shudder of fear rather than a trusting devotion? I certainly do not deny that I still recognize an *imperative of understanding* and that through it one can work upon men, *but it must be taken up into my life,* and *that* is what I now recognize as the most important thing. . . .
>
> *Journals, 1835, p. 44*

QUESTIONS FOR CONSIDERATION

1. Can one meaningfully be both an existentialist and a theist? Consider this question in conjunction with the characteristics of existentialism outlined in the introduction to this text (pp. 1–19).

2. Theist Karl Jaspers has maintained that the philosophy of Kierkegaard (and perhaps by analogy others as well) is not a theory that we can agree with or refute but is rather a view of life to which each of us can respond. What do you think about this claim? Can one refute a view like Kierkegaard's? If so, how? If not, what implications follow?

3. What does Kierkegaard's view of Christianity do to other religions (e.g., Judaism)? Why do such implications follow?

4. Given Kierkegaard's perspective, how might one distinguish the conduct of a true Christian from one who is simply mad? Relate your answer to the story of Abraham and Isaac (see *Genesis*, chapters 20 — 22).

5. Kierkegaard draws a close connection between Christianity and the concept of sacrifice. Is your view of Christianity similar or different? If different, in what ways is it different?

6. Is Kierkegaard right that the aesthetic stage is one of futility? Does there have to be some stage beyond this one?

7. Are community and the religious life compatible? Why or why not? Discuss Kierkegaard's answer to this question as well as your own.

REFERENCES

ANSELM. "The Ontological Argument." In *The Existence of God,* edited by John Hick. New York: Macmillan, 1964, pp. 23–30.

AQUINAS, THOMAS. *Summa Theologica.* In *Basic Writings of Saint Thomas Aquinas,* edited by Anton C. Pegis. New York: Random House, 1945.

BUBER, MARTIN. *I and Thou.* Translated by Walter Kaufmann. New York: Charles Scribner's Sons, 1970.

HEGEL, G. W. F. *Phenomenology of Spirit.* Translated by A. V. Miller. Oxford: Oxford University Press, 1977.

——. *Reason in History.* Translated by Robert S. Hartman. Indianapolis, Indiana: Bobbs-Merrill, 1977.

HEISS, ROBERT. *Hegel, Kierkegaard, Marx: Three Great Philosophers Whose Ideas Changed the Course of Civilization.* Translated by E. B. Garside. New York: Delta Books, 1965.

The Holy Bible (King James Version). New York: American Bible Society, 1986.

HOOK, SIDNEY. "What is Dialectic?" *Journal of Philosophy* 26 (1929): 85–99, 113–23.

JASPERS, KARL. *Way to Wisdom.* New Haven, Conn.: Yale University Press, 1951.

KANT, IMMANUEL. *Critique of Pure Reason.* Edited by Norman K. Smith. New York: St Martin's, 1969.

KAUFMANN, WALTER. *Hegel: A Reinterpretation.* Garden City, N. Y.: Doubleday Anchor, 1966.

KIERKEGAARD, SØREN. *Attack upon "Christendom."* Translated by Walter Lowrie. Boston: Beacon Press, 1966.

——. *The Concept of Anxiety.* Translated by Reidar Thomte. Princeton, N. J.: Princeton University Press, 1980.

——. *Concluding Unscientific Postscript.* Translated by David Swenson and Walter Lowrie. Princeton, N. J.: Princeton University Press, 1941.

——. *Either/Or.* 2 Vols. Vol. I translated by D. F. Swenson and L. M. Swenson. Vol. II. translated by W. Lowrie. Princeton, N. J.: Princeton University Press, 1941 (I), 1944 (II).

——. *Fear and Trembling* and *The Sickness unto Death.* Translated by Walter Lowrie. Princeton, N. J.: Princeton University Press, 1941.

——. *The Journals of Kierkegaard.* Translated by Alexander Dru. New York: Harper Torchbooks, 1959.

——. *Philosophical Fragments.* Translated by David Swenson; revised translation by Howard Hong. Princeton, N. J.: Princeton University Press, 1961.

——. *Purity of Heart Is to Will One Thing.* Translated by Douglas V. Steeree. New York: Harper & Row, 1938.

——. *Stages on Life's Way.* Translated by Walter Lowrie. New York: Schocken Books, 1967.

——. *Works of Love.* Translated by Howard and Edna Hong. New York: Harper & Row, 1962.

MERLEAU-PONTY, MAURICE. *Sense and Non-Sense.* Translated by H. C. Dreyfus and P. A. Dreyfus. Evanston, Ill.: Northwestern University Press, 1964.

PASCAL, BLAISE, *Pensees.* Translated by W. F. Trotter. New York: Modern Library, 1941.

POPPER, K. R. "What Is Dialectic?" *Mind* 49 (1940):403–26.

SCHACHT, RICHARD. *Hegel and After: Studies in Continental Philosophy between Kant and Sartre.* Pittsburgh: University of Pittsburgh Press, 1975.

STACE, W. T. *The Philosophy of Hegel: A Systematic Exposition.* New York: Dover Publications, Inc., 1955.

TILLICH, PAUL. *The Courage to Be.* New Haven, Conn.: Yale University Press, 1952.

——. *The Dynamics of Faith.* New York: Harper & Row, 1957.

——. *What Is Religion?* New York: Harper & Row, 1969.

SØREN KIERKEGAARD

Kierkegaard referred to Fear and Trembling *(1843) and* The Sickness unto Death *(1849) as his "most perfect works," and* Fear and Trembling *as sufficient to guarantee his reputation: "Oh, when I am dead, then* Fear and Trembling *alone will be enough to give me the name of an immortal author." (Journals, p. 89) Both works are written pseudonomously — Fear and Trembling by Johannes de Silentio and The Sickness unto Death by Anti-Climacus. In Fear and Trembling there is none of the irony of Kierkegaard's earlier works. Here the religious theme so central to Kierkegaard's life fully appears as he addresses the "problemata" emerging from the Biblical story of Abraham's sacrifice of Isaac. Though his earlier work* Either/Or *provides the study of the aesthetic and the ethical life,* Fear and Trembling *gives us the religious stage — with Abraham the knight of faith willing to leave behind the realm of the ethical in order to affirm his private relationship with God.* Fear and Trembling *may have been Kierkegaard's indirect message to his fiancee Regine Olsen, comparing his own sacrifice of marriage and family with that of Abraham. Like the pseudonymous Johannes de Silentio, Kierkegaard is "bound to silence" regarding his reasons for breaking off his engagement to Regine.*

The subheading of The Sickness unto Death *reads "a Christian Psychological Exposition for Edification and Awakening," and this work does indeed explore the psychology of the human being, that being who alone is capable of experiencing dread. But it is in this work that Kierkegaard not only proposes a diagnosis but also suggests the prescription: faith. He concludes: "By relating itself to its own self and by willing to be itself, the self is grounded transparently in the Power which constituted it." (p. 262) Thus, it is only through faith that one can transform dread into the creative and paradoxical act of salvation.*

Fear and Trembling

PROBLEM I

Is There Such a Thing as a Teleological Suspension of the Ethical?

The ethical as such is the universal, and as the universal it applies to everyone, which may be expressed from another point of view by saying that it applies every instant. It reposes immanently in itself, it has nothing without itself which is its *telos*, but is itself *telos* for everything outside it,

Soren Kierkegaard, *Fear and Trembling* and *The Sickness Unto Death*, translated with Introductions and Notes by Walter Lowrie. Copyright 1941, 1954, © renewed 1982 by Princeton University Press. Excerpts, pp. 65–129 and 147–161, reprinted with permission of Princeton University Press.

and when this has been incorporated by the ethical it can go no further. Conceived immediately as physical and psychical, the particular individual is the individual who has his *telos* in the universal, and his ethical task is to express himself constantly in it, to abolish his particularity in order to become the universal. As soon as the individual would assert himself in his particularity over against the universal he sins, and only by recognizing this can he again reconcile himself with the universal. Whenever the individual after he has entered the universal feels an impulse to assert himself as the particular, he is in temptation (*Anfechtung*), and he can labor himself out of this only by penitently abandoning himself as the particular in the universal. If this be the highest thing that can be said of man and of his existence, then the ethical has the same character as man's eternal blessedness, which to all eternity and at every instant is his *telos*, since it would be a contradiction to say that this might be abandoned (i.e. teleologically suspended), inasmuch as this is no sooner suspended than it is forfeited, whereas in other cases what is suspended is not forfeited but is preserved precisely in that higher thing which is its *telos*. . . .

For faith is this paradox, that the particular is higher than the universal — yet in such a way, be it observed, that the movement repeats itself, and that consequently the individual, after having been in the universal, now as the particular isolates himself as higher than the universal. If this be not faith, then Abraham is lost, then faith has never existed in the world . . . because it has always existed. For if the ethical (i.e. the moral) is the highest thing, and if nothing incommensurable remains in man in any other way but as the evil (i.e. the particular which has to be expressed in the universal), then one needs no other categories besides those which the Greeks possessed or which by consistent thinking can be derived from them. This fact Hegel ought not to have concealed, for after all he was acquainted with Greek thought.

One not infrequently hears it said by men who for lack of losing themselves in studies are absorbed in phrases that a light shines upon the Christian world whereas a darkness broods over paganism. This utterance has always seemed strange to me, inasmuch as every profound thinker and every serious artist is even in our day rejuvenated by the eternal youth of the Greek race. Such an utterance may be explained by the consideration that people do not know what they ought to say but only that they must say something. It is quite right for one to say that paganism did not possess faith, but if with this one is to have said something, one must be a little clearer about what one understands by faith, since otherwise one falls back into such phrases. To explain the whole of existence and faith along with it, without having a conception of what faith is, is easy, and that man does not make the poorest calculation in life who reckons upon admiration when he possesses such an explantion; for, as Boileau says, *"un sot trouve toujours un plus sot qui l'admire."*[1]

Faith is precisely this paradox, that the individual as the particular is higher than the universal, is justified over against it, is not subordinate but superior — yet in such a way, be it observed, that it is the particular individual who, after he has been subordinated as the particular to the universal, now through the universal becomes the individual who as the particular is superior to the universal, for the fact that the individual as the particular stands in an absolute relation to the absolute. This position cannot be mediated, for all mediation comes about precisely by virtue of the universal; it is and remains to all eternity a paradox, inaccessible to thought. And yet faith is this paradox — or else (these are the logical deductions which I would beg the reader to have in mente at every point, though it would be too prolix for me to reiterate them on every occasion) — or else there never has been faith . . . precisely because it always has been. In other words, Abraham is lost.

That for the particular individual this paradox may easily be mistaken for a temptation (*Anfechtung*) is indeed true, but one ought not for this reason to conceal it. That the whole constitution of many persons may be such that this paradox repels them is indeed true, but one ought not for this reason to make faith something different in order to be able to possess it, but ought rather to admit that one does not possess it, whereas those who possess faith should take care to set up certain criteria so that one might distinguish the paradox from a temptation (*Anfechtung*).

Now the story of Abraham contains such a teleological suspension of the ethical. There have not been lacking clever pates and profound investigators who have found analogies to it. Their wisdom is derived from the pretty proposition that at bottom everything is the same. If one will look a little more closely, I have not much doubt that in the whole world one will not find a single analogy (except a later instance which proves nothing), if it stands fast that Abraham is the representative of faith, and that faith is normally expressed in him whose life is not merely the most paradoxical that can be thought but so paradoxical that it cannot be thought at all. He acts by virtue of the absurd, for it is precisely absurd that he as the particular is higher than the universal. This paradox cannot be mediated; for as soon as he begins to do this he has to admit that he was in temptation (*Anfechtung*), and if such was the case, he never gets to the point of sacrificing Isaac, or, if he has sacrificed Isaac, he must turn back repentantly to the universal. By virtue of the absurd he gets Isaac again. Abraham is therefore at no instant a tragic hero but something quite different, either a murderer or a believer. The middle term which saves

---

[1] "A fool will always find another fool who admires him."

the tragic hero, Abraham has not. Hence it is that I can understand the tragic hero but cannot understand Abraham, though in a certain crazy sense I admire him more than all other men.

Abraham's relation to Isaac, ethically speaking, is quite simply expressed by saying that a father shall love his son more dearly than himself. Yet within its own compass the ethical has various gradations. Let us see whether in this story there is to be found any higher expression for the ethical such as would ethically explain his conduct, ethically justify him in suspending the ethical obligation toward his son, without in this search going beyond the teleology of the ethical.

When an undertaking in which a whole nation is concerned is hindered,[2] when such an enterprise is brought to a standstill by the disfavor of heaven, when the angry deity sends a calm which mocks all efforts, when the seer performs his heavy task and proclaims that the deity demands a young maiden as a sacrifice — then will the father heroically make the sacrifice. He will magnanimously conceal his pain, even though he might wish that he were "the lowly man who dares to weep," not the king who must act royally. And though solitary pain forces its way into his breast, he has only three confidants among the people, yet soon the whole nation will be cognizant of his pain, but also cognizant of his exploit, that for the welfare of the whole he was willing to sacrifice her, his daughter, the lovely young maiden. O charming bosom! O beautiful cheeks! O bright golden hair! And the daughter will affect him by her tears, and the father will turn his face away, but the hero will raise the knife. — When the report of this reaches the ancestral home, then will the beautiful maidens of Greece blush with enthusiasm, and if the daughter was betrothed, her true love will not be angry but be proud of sharing in the father's deed, because the maiden belonged to him more feelingly than to the father. . . .

If, on the other hand, while a favorable wind bore the fleet on with swelling sails to its goal, Agamemnon had sent that messenger who fetched Iphigenia in order to be sacrificed; if Jephtha, without being bound by any vow which decided the fate of the nation, has said to his daughter. "Bewail now thy virginity for the space of two months, for I will sacrifice thee"; if Brutus had had a righteous son and yet would have ordered the lictors to execute him — who would have understood them? If these three men had replied to the query why they did it by saying, "It is a trial in which we are tested," would people have understood them better?

When Agamemnon, Jephtha, Brutus at the decisive moment heroically overcome their pain, have heroically lost the beloved and have

[2] i.e., the Trojan War

merely to accomplish the outward sacrifice, then there never will be a noble soul in the world who will not shed tears of compassion for their pain and of admiration for their exploit. If, on the other hand, these three men at the decisive moment were to adjoin to their heroic conduct this little word, "But for all that it will not come to pass," who then would understand them? If as an explanation they added, "This we believe by virtue of the absurd," who would understand them better? For who would not easily understand that it was absurd, but who would understand that one could then believe it?

The difference between the tragic hero and Abraham is clearly evident. *The tragic hero still remains within the ethical.* He lets one expression of the ethical find its *telos* in a higher expression of the ethical; the ethical relation between father and son, or daughter and father, he reduces to a sentiment which has its dialectic in its relation to the idea of morality. Here there can be no question of a teleological suspension of the ethical itself.

With Abraham the situation was different. By his act he overstepped the ethical entirely and possessed a higher *telos* outside of it, in relation to which he suspended the former. For I should very much like to know how one would bring Abraham's act into relation with the universal, and whether it is possible to discover any connection whatever between what Abraham did and the universal . . . except the fact that he transgressed it. It was not for the sake of saving a people, not to maintain the idea of the state, that Abraham did this, and not in order to reconcile angry deities. If there could be a question of the deity being angry, he was angry only with Abraham, and Abraham's whole action stands in no relation to the universal, is a purely private undertaking. Therefore, whereas the tragic hero is great by reason of his moral virtue, Abraham is great by reason of a purely personal virtue. In Abraham's life there is no higher expression for the ethical than this, that the father shall love his son. Of the ethical in the sense of morality there can be no question in this instance. In so far as the universal was present, it was indeed cryptically present in Isaac, hidden as it were in Isaac's loins, and must therefore cry out with Isaac's mouth, "Do it not! Thou art bringing everything to naught."

Why then did Abraham do it? For God's sake, and (in complete identity with this) for his own sake. He did it for God's sake because God required this proof of his faith; for his own sake he did it in order that he might furnish the proof. The unity of these two points of view is perfectly expressed by the word which has always been used to characterize this situation: it is a trial, a temptation (*Fristelse*). A temptation — but what does that mean? What ordinarily tempts a man is that which would keep him from doing his duty, but in this case the temptation is itself the ethical . . . which would keep him from doing God's will. But what then is duty? Duty is precisely the expression for God's will.

Here is evident the necessity of a new category if one would understand Abraham. Such a relationship to the deity paganism did not know. The tragic hero does not enter into any private relationship with the deity, but for him the ethical is the divine, hence the paradox implied in his situation can be mediated in the universal.

Abraham cannot be mediated, and the same thing can be expressed also by saying that he cannot talk. So soon as I talk I express the universal, and if I do not do so, no one can understand me. Therefore if Abraham would express himself in terms of the universal, he must say that his situation is a temptation (*Anfechtung*), for he has no higher expression for that universal which stands above the universal which he transgresses.

Therefore, though Abraham arouses my admiration, he at the same time appalls me. He who denies himself and sacrifices himself for duty gives up the finite in order to grasp the infinite, and that man is secure enough. The tragic hero gives up the certain for the still more certain, and the eye of the beholder rests upon him confidently. But he who gives up the universal in order to grasp something still higher which is not the universal — what is he doing? Is it possible that this can be anything else but a temptation (*Anfechtung*)? And if it be possible . . . but the individual was mistaken — what can save him? He suffers all the pain of the tragic hero, he brings naught his joy in the world, he renounces everything . . . and perhaps at the same instant debars himself from the sublime joy which to him was so precious that he would purchase it at any price. Him the beholder cannot understand nor let his eye rest confidently upon him. Perhaps it is not possible to do what the believer proposes, since it is indeed unthinkable. Or if it could be done, but if the individual had misunderstood the deity — what can save him? The tragic hero has need of tears and claims them, and where is the envious eye which would be so barren that it could not weep with Agamemnon; but where is the man with a soul so bewildered that he would have the presumption to weep for Abraham? The tragic hero accomplishes his act at a definite instant in time, but in the course of time he does something not less significant, he visits the man whose soul is beset with sorrow, whose breast for stifled sobs cannot draw breath, whose thoughts pregnant with tears weigh heavily upon him, to him he makes his appearance, dissolves the sorcery of sorrow, loosens his corslet, coaxes forth his tears by the fact that in his sufferings the sufferer forgets his own. One cannot weep over Abraham. One approaches him with a *horror religiosus*, as Israel approached Mount Sinai. — . . .

But now when the ethical is thus teleologically suspended, how does the individual exist in whom it is suspended? He exists as the particular in opposition to the universal. Does he then sin? For this is the form of sin, as seen in the idea. Just as the infant, though it does not sin, because it is not as such yet conscious of its existence, yet its existence is sin, as seen in the idea, and the ethical makes its demands upon it every instant. If one denies that this form can be repeated [in the adult] in such a way that it is not sin, then the sentence of condemnation is pronounced upon Abraham. How then did Abraham exist? He believed. This is the paradox which keeps him upon the sheer edge and which he cannot make clear to any other man, for the paradox is that he as the individual puts himself in an absolute relation to the absolute. Is he justified in doing this? His justification is once more the paradox; for if he is justified, it is not by virtue of anything universal, but by virtue of being the particular individual. . . .

The story of Abraham contains therefore a teleological suspension of the ethical. As the individual he became higher than the universal. This is the paradox which does not permit of mediation. It is just as inexplicable how he got into it as it is inexplicable how he remained in it. If such is not the position of Abraham, then he is not even a tragic hero but a murderer. To want to continue to call him the father of faith, to talk of this to people who do not concern themselves with anything but words, is thoughtless. A man can become a tragic hero by his own powers — but not a knight of faith. When a man enters upon the way, in a certain sense the hard way of the tragic hero, many will be able to give him counsel; to him who follows the narrow way of faith no one can give counsel, him no one can understand. Faith is a miracle, and yet no man is excluded from it; for that in which all human life is unified is passion, and faith is a passion.

PROBLEM II

Is There Such a Thing as an Absolute Duty Toward God?

The ethical is the universal, and as such it is again the divine. One has therefore a right to say that fundamentally every duty is a duty toward God; but if one cannot say more, then one affirms at the same time that properly I have no duty toward God. Duty becomes duty by being referred to God, but in duty itself I do not come into relation with God. Thus it is a duty to love one's neighbor, but in performing this duty I do not come into relation with God but with the neighbor whom I love. If I say then in this connection that it is my duty to love God, I am really uttering only a tautology, inasmuch as "God" is in this instance used in an entirely abstract sense as the divine, i.e. the universal, i.e. duty. So the whole existence of the human race is rounded off completely like a sphere, and the ethical is at once its limit and its content. God becomes an invisible vanishing point, a powerless thought, His power being only in the ethical which is the content of existence. If in any way it might occur to any man to want to love God in any other sense than that here indicated, he is romantic, he loves a phantom which, if it had merely the power of being able to speak, would say to him, "I do not require your love. Stay where you belong." If in any way it might occur to a man to want to love God otherwise, this love would be open to suspicion, like that of which Rousseau speaks, referring to people who love the Kaffirs instead of their neighbors.

So in case what has been expounded here is correct, in case there is no incommensurability in a human life, and what there is of the incommensurable is only such by an accident from which no consequences can be drawn, in so far as existence is regarded in terms of the idea, Hegel is right; but he is not right in talking about faith or in allowing Abraham to be regarded as the father of it; for by the latter he has pronounced judgment both upon Abraham and upon faith. In the Hegelian philosophy *das Äussere (die Entäusserung)* is higher than *das Innere*. This is frequently illustrated by an example. The child is *das Innere*, the man *das Äussere*. Hence it is that the child is defined by the outward, and conversely, the man, as *das Aussere*, is defined precisely by *das Innere*. Faith, on the contrary, is the paradox that inwardness is higher than outwardness — or, to recall an expression used above, the uneven number is higher than the even.

In the ethical way of regarding life it is therefore the task of the individual to divest himself of the inward determinants and express them in an outward way. Whenever he shrinks from this, whenever he is inclined to persist in or to slip back again into the inward determinants of feeling, mood, etc., he sins, he is in a temptation (*Anfechtung*). The paradox of faith is this, that there is an inwardness which is incommensurable for the outward, an inwardness, be it observed, which is not identical with the first but is a new inwardness. This must not be overlooked. Modern philosophy has permitted itself without further ado to substitute in place of "faith" the immediate. When one does that it is ridiculous to deny that faith has existed in all ages. In that way faith comes into rather simple company along with feeling, mood, idiosyncrasy, vapors, etc. To this extent philosophy may be right in saying that one ought not to stop there. But there is nothing to justify philosophy in using this phrase with regard to faith. Before faith there goes a movement of infinity, and only then, *necopinate*, by virtue of the absurd,[3] faith enters upon the scene. This I can well understand without maintaining on that account that I have faith. If faith is nothing but what philosophy makes it out to be, then Socrates already went further, much further, whereas the contrary is true, that he never reached it. In an intellectual respect he made the movement of infinity. His ignorance is infinite resignation. This task in itself is a

---

[3] unexpected

match for human powers, even though people in our time disdain it; but only after it is done, only when the individual has evacuated himself in the infinite, only then is the point attained where faith can break forth.

The paradox of faith is this, that the individual is higher than the universal, that the individual (to recall a dogmatic distinction now rather seldom heard) determines his relation to the universal by his relation to the absolute, not his relation to the absolute by his relation to the universal. The paradox can also be expressed by saying that there is an absolute duty toward God; for in this relationship of duty the individual as an individual stands related absolutely to the absolute. So when in this connection it is said that it is a duty to love God, something different is said from that in the foregoing; for if this duty is absolute, the ethical is reduced to a position of relativity. From this, however, it does not follow that the ethical is to be abolished, but it acquires an entirely different expression, the paradoxical expression — that, for example, love to God may cause the knight of faith to give his love to his neighbor the opposite expression to that which, ethically speaking, is required by duty.

If such is not the case, then faith has no proper place in existence, then faith is a temptation (*Anfechtung*), and Abraham is lost, since he gave in to it.

This paradox does not permit of mediation, for it is founded precisely upon the fact that the individual is only the individual. As soon as this individual [who is aware of a direct command from God] wishes to express his absolute duty in [terms of] the universal [i.e. the ethical, and] is sure of his duty in that [i.e. the universal or ethical precept], he recognizes that he is in temptation [i.e. a trial of faith], and, if in fact he resists [the direct indication of God's will], he ends by not fulfilling the absolute duty so called [i.e. what here has been called the absolute duty]; and, if he doesn't do this, [i.e. doesn't put up a resistance to the direct intimation of God's will], he sins, even though *realiter* his deed were that which it was his absolute duty to do. So what should Abraham do? If he would say to another person, "Isaac I love more dearly than everything in the world, and hence it is so hard for me to sacrifice him"; then surely the other would have shaken his head and said, "Why will you sacrifice him then?" — or if the other had been a sly fellow, he surely would have seen through Abraham and perceived that he was making a show of feelings which were in strident contradiction to his act.

In the story of Abraham we find such a paradox. His relation to Isaac, ethically expressed, is this, that the father should love the son. This ethical relation is reduced to a relative position in contrast with the absolute relation to God. To the question, "Why?" Abraham has no answer except that it is a trial, a temptation (*Fristelse*) — terms which, as was remarked above, express the unity of the two points of view: that it is for God's sake and for his own sake. In common usage these two ways of regarding the matter are mutually exclusive. Thus when we see a man do something which does not comport with the universal, we say that he scarcely can be doing it for God's sake, and by that we imply that he does it for his own sake. The paradox of faith has lost the intermediate term, i.e. the universal. On the one side it has the expression for the extremest egoism (doing the dreadful thing it does for one's own sake); on the other side the expression for the most absolute self-sacrifice (doing it for God's sake). Faith itself cannot be mediated into the universal, for it would thereby be destroyed. Faith is this paradox, and the individual absolutely cannot make himself intelligible to anybody. People imagine maybe that the individual can make himself intelligible to another individual in the same case. Such a notion would be unthinkable if in our time people did not in so many ways seek to creep slyly into greatness. The one knight of faith can render no aid to the other. Either the individual becomes a knight of faith by assuming the burden of the paradox, or he never becomes one. In these regions partnership is unthinkable. Every more precise explication of what is to be understood by Isaac the individual can give only to himself. And even if one were able, generally speaking, to define ever so precisely what should be intended by Isaac (which moreover would be the most ludicrous self-contradiction, i.e. that the particular individual who definitely stands outside the universal is subsumed under universal catagories precisely when he has to act as the individual who stands outside the universal), the individual nevertheless will never be able to assure himself by the aid of others that this application is appropriate, but he can do so only by himself as the individual. Hence even if a man were cowardly and paltry enough to wish to become a knight of faith on the responsibility of an outsider, he will never become one; for only the individual becomes a knight of faith as the particular individual, and this is the greatness of this knighthood, as I can well understand without entering the order, since I lack courage; but this is also its terror, as I can comprehend even better.

In Luke 14:26, as everybody knows, there is a striking doctrine taught about the absolute duty toward God: "If any man cometh unto me and hateth not his own father and mother and wife and children and brethren and sisters, yea, and his own life also, he cannot be my disciple." This is a hard saying, who can bear to hear it? For this reason it is heard very seldom. This silence, however, is only an evasion which is of no avail. . . .

But how hate them? I will not recall here the human distinction between loving and hating — not because I have much to object to in it (for after all it is passionate), but because it is egoistic and is not in place here. However, if I regard the problem as a paradox, then I understand it, that is, I understand it in such a way as one can understand a paradox. The absolute duty may cause one to do what ethics would forbid, but by no means can it cause the knight of faith to cease to love. This is shown by Abraham. The instant he is ready to sacrifice Isaac the ethical expression for what he does is this: he hates Isaac. But if he really hates Isaac, he can be sure that God does not require this, for Cain and Abraham are not identical. Isaac he must love with his whole soul; when God requires Isaac he must love him if possible even more dearly, and only on this condition can he *sacrifice* him; for in fact it is this love for Isaac which, by its paradoxical opposition to his love for God, makes his act a sacrifice. But the distress and dread in this paradox is that, humanly speaking, he is entirely unable to make himself intelligible. Only at the moment when his act is in absolute contradiction to his feeling is his act a sacrifice, but the reality of his act is the factor by which he belongs to the universal, and in that aspect he is and remains a murderer.

Moreover, the passage in Luke must be understood in such a way as to make it clearly evident that the knight of faith has no higher expression of the universal (i.e. the ethical) by which he can save himself. Thus, for example, if we suppose that the Church requires such a sacrifice of one of its members, we have in this case only a tragic hero. For the idea of the Church is not qualitatively different from that of the State, in so far as the individual comes into it by a simple mediation, and in so far as the individual comes into the paradox he does not reach the idea of the Church; he does not come out of the paradox, but in it he must find either his blessedness or his perdition. Such an ecclesiastical hero expresses in his act the universal, and there will be no one in the Church — not even his father and mother etc. — who fails to understand him. On the other hand, he is not a knight of faith, and he has also a different answer from that of Abraham: he does not say that it is a trial or a temptation in which he is tested.

People commonly refrain from quoting such a text as this in Luke. They are afraid of giving men a free rein, are afraid that the worst will happen as soon as the individual takes it into his head to comport himself as the individual. Moreover, they think that to exist as the individual is the easiest thing of all, and that therefore people have to be compelled to become the universal. I cannot share either this fear or this opinion, and both for the same reason. He who has learned that to exist as the individual is the most terrible thing of all will not be fearful of saying that it is great, but then too he will say this in such a way that his words will scarcely be a snare for the bewildered man, but rather will help him into the universal, even though his words do to some extent make room for the great. The man who does not dare to mention such texts will not dare to mention Abraham either, and his notion that it is easy enough to exist as the individual implies a very suspicious admission with regard to himself; for he who has a real respect for himself and concern for his soul is convinced that the man who lives under his own supervision, alone in the whole world, lives more strictly and more secluded than a maiden in her lady's bower. That there may be some who need compulsion, some who, if they were free-footed, would riot in selfish pleasures like unruly beasts, is doubtless true; but a man must prove precisely that he is not of this number by the fact that he knows how to speak with dread and trembling; and out of reverence for the great one is bound to speak, lest it be forgotten for fear of the ill effect, which surely will fail to eventuate when a man talks in such a way that one knows it for the great, knows its terror — and apart from the terror one does not know the great at all.

Let us consider a little more closely the distress and dread in the paradox of faith. The tragic hero renounces himself in order to express the universal, the knight of faith renounces the universal in order to become the individual. As has been said, everything depends upon how one is placed. He who believes that it is easy enough to be the individual can always be sure that he is not a knight of faith, for vagabonds and roving geniuses are not men of faith. The knight of faith knows, on the other hand, that it is glorious to belong to the universal. He knows that it is beautiful and salutary to be the individual who translates himself into the universal, who edits as it were a pure and elegant edition of himself, as free from errors as possible and which eveyone can read. He knows that it is refreshing to become intelligible to oneself in the universal so that he understands it and so that every individual who understands him under-stands through him in turn the universal, and both rejoice in the security of the universal. He knows that it is beautiful to be born as the individual who has the universal as his home, his friendly abiding-place, which at once welcomes him with open arms when he would tarry in it. But he knows also that higher than this there winds a solitary path, narrow and steep; he knows that it is terrible to be born outside the universal, to walk without meeting a single traveller. He knows very well where he is and how he is related to men. Humanly speaking, he is crazy and cannot make himself intelligible to anyone. And yet it is the mildest expression, to say that he is crazy. If he is not supposed to be that, then he is a hypocrite, and the higher he climbs on this path, the more dreadful a hypocrite he is.

The knight of faith knows that to give up oneself for the universal inspires enthusiasm, and that it requires courage, but he also knows that security is to be found in this, precisely because it is for the universal. He knows that it is glorious to be understood by every noble mind, so glo-rious that the beholder is ennobled by it, and he feels as if he were bound: he could wish it were this task that had been allotted to him. Thus Abraham could surely have wished now and then that the task were to love Isaac as becomes a father, in a way intelligible to all, memorable throughout all ages; he could wish that the task were to sacrifice Isaac for the universal, that he might incite the fathers to illustrious deeds — and he is almost terrified by the thought that for him such wishes are only temptations and must be dealt with as such, for he knows that it is a solitary path he treads and that he accomplishes nothing for the universal but only himself is tried and examined. Or what did Abraham accomplish for the universal? Let me speak humanly about it, quite humanly. He spent seventy years in getting a son of his old age. What other men get quickly enough and enjoy for a long time he spent seventy years in accomplishing. And why? Because he was tried and put to the test. Is not that crazy? But Abraham believed, and Sarah wavered and got him to take Hagar as a concubine — but therefore he also had to drive her away. He gets Isaac, then he has to be tried again. He knew that it is glorious to express the universal, glorious to live with Isaac. But this is not the task. He knew that it is a kingly thing to sacrifice such a son for the universal, he himself would have found repose in that, and all would have reposed in the commendation of his deed, as a vowel reposes in its consonant, but that is not the task — he is tried. . . .

This is the terrible thing. He who does not see it can always be sure that he is no knight of faith, but he who sees it will not deny that even the most tried of tragic heroes walks with a dancing step compared with the knight of faith, who comes slowly creeping forward. And if he has perceived this and assured himself that he has not courage to understand it, he will at least have a presentiment of the marvellous glory this knight attains in the fact that he becomes God's intimate acquaintance, the Lord's friend, and (to speak quite humanly) that he says "Thou" to God in heaven, whereas even the tragic hero only addresses Him in the third person.

The tragic hero is soon ready and has soon finished the fight, he makes the infinite movement and then is secure in the universal. The knight of faith, on the other hand, is kept sleepless, for he is constantly tried, and every instant there is the possibility of being able to return repentantly to the universal, and this possibility can just as well be a temptation as the truth. He can derive evidence from no man which it is, for with that query he is outside the paradox. . . .

Whether the individual is in temptation (*Anfechtung*) or is a knight of faith only the individual can decide. Nevertheless it is possible to construct from the paradox several criteria which he too can understand who is not within the paradox. The true knight of faith is always absolute isolation, the false knight is sectarian. This sectarianism is an attempt to leap away from the narrow path of the paradox and become a tragic hero at a cheap price. The tragic hero expresses the universal and sacrifices himself for it. The sectarian punchinello, instead of that, has a private theatre, i.e. several good friends and comrades who represent the universal just about as well as the beadles in *The Golden Snuffbox*[4] represent

---

[4] persons appointed to witness legal proceedings

justice. The knight of faith, on the contrary, is the paradox, is the individual, absolutely nothing but the individual, without connections or pretensions. This is the terrible thing which the sectarian manikin cannot endure. For instead of learning from this terror that he is not capable of performing the great deed and then plainly admitting it (an act which I cannot but approve, because it is what I do) the manikin thinks that by uniting with several other manikins he will be able to do it. But that is quite out of the question. In the world of spirit no swindling is tolerated. A dozen sectaries join arms with one another, they know nothing whatever of the lonely temptations which await the knight of faith and which he dares not shun precisely because it would be still more dreadful if he were to press forward presumptuously. The sectaries deafen one another by their noise and racket, hold the dread off by their shrieks, and such a hallooing company of sportsmen think they are storming heaven and think they are on the same path as the knight of faith who in the solitude of the universe never hears any human voice but walks alone with his dreadful responsibility.

The knight of faith is obliged to rely upon himself alone, he feels the pain of not being able to make himself intelligible to others, but he feels no vain desire to guide others. The pain is his assurance that he is in the right way, this vain desire he does not know, he is too serious for that. The false knight of faith readily betrays himself by this proficiency in guiding which he has acquired in an instant. He does not comprehend what it is all about, that if another individual is to take the same path, he must become entirely in the same way the individual and have no need of any man's guidance, least of all the guidance of a man who would obtrude himself. At this point men leap aside, they cannot bear the martyrdom of being uncomprehended, and instead of this they choose conveniently enough the worldly admiration of their proficiency. The true knight of faith is a witness, never a teacher, and therein lies his deep humanity, which is worth a good deal more than this silly participation in others' weal and woe which is honored by the name of sympathy, whereas in fact it is nothing but vanity.

The tragic hero does not know the terrible responsibility of solitude. In the next place he has the comfort that he can weep and lament with Clytemnestra and Iphigenia — and tears and cries are assuaging, but unutterable sighs are torture. Agamemnon can quickly collect his soul into the certainty that he will act, and then he still has time to comfort and exhort. This Abraham is unable to do. When his heart is moved, when his words would contain a blessed comfort for the whole world, he does not dare to offer comfort, for would not Sarah, would not Eleazar, would not Isaac say, "Why wilt thou do it? Thou canst refrain"? And if in his distress he would give vent to his feelings and would embrace all his dear ones before taking the final step, this might perhaps bring about the dreadful consequence that Sarah, that Eleazar, that Isaac would be offended in him and would believe he was a hypocrite. He is unable to speak, he speaks no human language. Though he himself understood all the tongues of the world, though his loved ones also understood them, he nevertheless cannot speak — he speaks a divine language . . . he "speaks with tongues."

This distress I can well understand, I can admire Abraham, I am not afraid that anyone might be tempted by this narrative light-heartedly to want to be the individual, but I admit also that I have not the courage for it, and that I renounce gladly any prospect of getting further — if only it were possible that in any way, however late, I might get so far. Every instant Abraham is able to break off, he can repent the whole thing as a temptation (*Anfechtung*), then he can speak, then all could understand him — but then he is no longer Abraham. . . .

Here again it appears that one may have an understanding of Abraham, but can understand him only in the same way as one understands the paradox. For my part I can in a way understand Abraham, but at the same time I apprehend that I have not the courage to speak, and still less to act as he did — but by this I do not by any means intend to say that what he did was insignificant, for on the contrary it is the one only marvel.

And what did the contemporary age think of the tragic hero? They thought that he was great, and they admired him. And that honorable assembly of nobles, the jury which every generation impanels to pass judgment upon the foregoing generation, passed the same judgment upon him. But as for Abraham there was no one who could understand him. And yet think what he attained! He remained true to his love. But he who loves God has no need of tears, no need of admiration, in his love he forgets his suffering, yea, so completely has he forgotten it that afterwards there would not even be the least inkling of his pain if God Himself did not recall it, for God sees in secret and knows the distress and counts the tears and forgets nothing.

The Sickness unto Death

I. THAT DESPAIR IS THE SICKNESS UNTO DEATH

A. Despair Is a Sickness in the Spirit, in the Self, and So It May Assume a Triple Form: in Despair at Not Being Conscious of Having a Self (Despair Improperly So Called); in Despair at Not Willing to Be Oneself.

Man is spirit. But what is spirit? Spirit is the self. But what is the self? The self is a relation which relates itself to its own self, or it is that in the relation [which accounts for it] that the relation relates itself to its own self; the self is not the relation but [consists in the fact] that the relation relates itself to its own self. Man is a synthesis of the infinite and the finite, of the temporal and the eternal, of freedom and necessity, in short it is a synthesis. A synthesis is a relation between two factors. So regarded, man is not yet a self.

In the relation between two, the relation is the third term as a negative unity, and the two relate themselves to the relation, and in the relation to the relation; such a relation is that between soul and body, when man is regarded as soul. If on the contrary the relation relates itself to its own self, the relation is then the positive third term, and this is the self.

Such a relation which relates itself to its own self (that is to say, a self) must either have constituted itself or have been constituted by another.

If this relation which relates itself to its own self is constituted by another, the relation doubtless is the third term, but this relation (the third term) is in turn a relation relating itself to that which constituted the whole relation.

Such a derived, constituted, relation is the human self, a relation which relates itself to its own self, and in relating itself to its own self relates itself to another. Hence it is that there can be two forms of despair properly so called. If the human self had constituted itself, there could be a question only of one form, that of not willing to be one's own self, of willing to get rid of oneself, but there would be no question of despairingly willing to be oneself. This formula [i.e. that the self is constituted by

Søren Kierkegaard, *Fear and Trembling* and *The Sickness Unto Death*, translated with Introductions and Notes by Walter Lowrie. Copyright 1941, 1954, © renewed 1982 by Princeton University Press. Excerpts, pp. 65–129 and 147–161, reprinted with permission of Princeton University Press.

another] is the expression for the total dependence of the relation (the self namely), the expression for the fact that the self cannot of itself attain and remain in equilibrium and rest by itself, but only by relating itself to that Power which constituted the whole relation. Indeed, so far is it from being true that this second form of despair (despair at willing to be one's own self) denotes only a particular kind of despair, that on the contrary all despair can in the last analysis be reduced to this. If a man in despair is as he thinks conscious of his despair, does not talk about it meaninglessly as of something which befell him (pretty much as when a man who suffers from vertigo talks with nervous self-deception about a weight upon his head or about its being like something falling upon him, etc., this weight and this pressure being in fact not something external but an inverse reflection from an inward experience), and if by himself and by himself only he would abolish the despair, then by all the labor he expends he is only laboring himself deeper into a deeper despair. The disrelationship of despair is not a simple disrelationship but a disrelationship in a relation which relates itself to its own self and is constituted by another, so that the disrelationship in that self-relation reflects itself infinitely in the relation to the Power which constituted it.

This then is the formula which describes the condition of the self when despair is completely eradicated: by relating itself to its own self and by willing to be itself the self is grounded transparently in the Power which posited it.

B. Possibility and Actuality of Despair

Is despair an advantage or a drawback? Regarded in a purely dialectical way it is both. If one were to stick to the abstract notion of despair, without thinking of any concrete despairer, one might say that it is an immense advantage. The possibility of this sickness is man's advantage over the beast, and this advantage distinguishes him far more essentially than the erect posture, for it implies the infinite erectness or loftiness of being spirit. The possibility of this sickness is man's advantage over the beast; to be sharply observant of this sickness constitutes the Christian's advantage over the natural man; to be healed of this sickness is the Christian's bliss.

So then it is an infinite advantage to be able to despair; and yet it is not only the greatest misfortune and misery to be in despair; no, it is perdition. Ordinarily there is no such relation between possibility and actuality; if it is an advantage to be able to be this or that, it is a still greater advantage to be such a thing. That is to say, being is related to the ability to be as an ascent. In the case of despair, on the contrary, being is related to the ability to be as a fall. Infinite as is the advantage of the possibility, just so great is the measure of the fall. So in the case of despair the ascent consists in not being in despair. Yet this statement is open to misunderstanding. The thing of not being in despair is not like not being lame, blind, etc. In case the not being in despair means neither more nor less than not being this, then it is precisely to be it. The thing of not being in despair must mean the annihilation of the possibility of being this; if it is to be true that a man is not in despair, one must annihilate the possibility every instant. Such is not ordinarily the relation between possibility and actuality. Although thinkers say that actuality is the annihilated possibility, yet this is not entirely true; it is the fulfilled, the effective possibility. Here, on the contrary, the actuality (not being in despair), which in its very form is a negation, is the impotent, annihilated possibility; ordinarily, actuality in comparison with possibility is a confirmation, here it is a negation.

Despair is the disrelationship in a relation which relates itself to itself. But the synthesis is not the disrelationship, it is merely the possibility, or, in the synthesis is latent the possibility of the disrelationship. If the synthesis were the disrelationship, there would be no such thing as despair, for despair would then be something inherent in human nature as such, that is, it would not be despair, it would be something that befell a man, something he suffered passively, like an illness into which a man falls, or like death which is the lot of all. No, this thing of despairing is inherent in man himself; but if he were not a synthesis, he could not despair, neither could he despair if the synthesis were not originally from God's hand in the right relationship.

Whence then comes despair? From the relation wherein the synthesis relates itself to itself, in that God who made man a relationship lets this go as it were out of His hand, that is, in the fact that the relation relates itself to itself. And herein, in the fact that the relation is spirit, is the self, consists the responsibility under which all despair lies, and so lies every instant it exists, however much and however ingeniously the despairer, deceiving himself and others, may talk of his despair as a misfortune which has befallen him, with a confusion of things different, as in the case of vertigo aforementioned, with which, though it is qualitatively different, despair has much in common, since vertigo is under the rubric soul what despair is under the rubric spirit, and is pregnant with analogies to despair.

So when the disrelationship — that is, despair — has set in, does it follow as a matter of course that it continues? No, it does not follow as a matter of course; if the disrelationship continues, it does not follow as a consequence of the disrelation but as a consequence of the relation which relates itself to itself. That is to say, every time the disrelation expresses itself, and every instant it exists, it is to the relation one must revert. Observe that we speak of a man contracting a disease, maybe through carelessness. Then the illness sets in, and from that instant it affirms itself and is now an *actuality,* the origin of which recedes more and more into the *past.* It would be cruel and inhuman if one were to continue to say incessantly, "This instant thou, the sick man, art contracting this disease"; that is, if every instant one were to resolve the actuality of the disease into its possibility. It is true that he did contract the disease, but this he did only once; the continuance of the disease is a simple consequence of the fact that he once contracted it, its progress is not to be referred every instant to him as the cause; he contracted it, but one cannot say that he is *contracting* it. Not so with despair: every actual instant of despair is to be referred back to possibility, every instant the man in despair is *contracting* it, it is constantly in the present tense, nothing comes to pass here as a consequence of a bygone actuality superseded; at every actual instant of despair the despairer bears as his responsibility all the foregoing experience in possibility as a present. This comes from the fact that despair is a qualification of spirit, that it is related to the eternal in man. But the eternal he cannot get rid of, no, not to all eternity; he cannot cast it from him once for all, nothing is more impossible; every instant he does not possess it he must have cast it or be casting it from him — but it comes back, every instant he is in despair he contracts despair. For despair is not a result of the disrelationship but of the relation which relates itself to itself. And the relation to himself a man cannot get rid of, any more than he can get rid of himself, which moreover is one and the same thing, since the self is the relationship to oneself.

C. Despair Is "The Sickness unto Death."

The concept of the sickness unto death must be understood, however, in a peculiar sense. Literally it means a sickness the end and outcome of which is death. Thus one speaks of a mortal sickness as synonymous with a sickness unto death. In this sense despair cannot be called the sickness unto death. But in the Christian understanding of it death itself is a transition unto life. In view of this, there is from the Christian standpoint no earthly, bodily sickness unto death. For death is doubtless the last phase of the sickness, but death is not the last thing. If in the strictest sense we are to speak of a sickness unto death, it must be one in which the last thing is death, and death the last thing. And this precisely is despair.

Yet in another and still more definite sense despair is the sickness unto death. It is indeed very far from being true that, literally understood, one dies of this sickness, or that this sickness ends with bodily death. On the contrary, the torment of despair is precisely this, not to be able to die. So it has much in common with the situation of the moribund when he lies and struggles with death, and cannot die. So to be sick *unto* death is, not to be able to die — yet not as though there were hope of life; no, the hopelessness in this case is that even the last hope, death, is not available. When death is the greatest danger, one hopes for life; but when one becomes acquainted with an even more dreadful danger, one hopes for death. So when the danger is so great that death has become one's hope, despair is the disconsolateness of not being able to die.

It is in this last sense that despair is the sickness unto death, this agonizing contradiction, this sickness in the self, everlastingly to die, to die and yet not to die, to die the death. For dying means that it is all over, but dying the death means to live to experience death; and if for a single instant this experience is possible, it is tantamount to experiencing it forever. If one might die of despair as one dies of a sickness, then the eternal in him, the self, must be capable of dying in the same sense that the body dies of sickness. But this is an impossibility; the dying of despair transforms itself constantly into a living. The despairing man cannot die; no more than "the dagger can slay thoughts" can despair consume the eternal thing, the self, which is the ground of despair, whose worm dieth not, and whose fire is not quenched. Yet despair is precisely *self-consuming*, but it is an impotent self-consumption which is not able to do what it wills; and this impotence is a new form of self-consumption, in which again, however, the despairer is not able to do what he wills, namely, to consume himself. This is despair raised to a higher potency, or it is the law for the potentiation. This is the hot incitement, or the cold fire in despair, the gnawing canker whose movement is constantly inward, deeper and deeper, in impotent self-consumption. The fact that despair does not consume him is so far from being any comfort to the despairing man that it is precisely the opposite, this comfort is precisely the torment, it is precisely this that keeps the gnawing pain alive and keeps life in the pain. This precisely is the reason why he despairs — not to say despaired — because he cannot consume himself, cannot get rid of himself, cannot become nothing. This is the potentiated formula for despair, the rising of the fever in the sickness of the self.

A despairing man is in despair over *something*. So it seems for an instant, but only for an instant; that same instant the true despair manifests itself, or despair manifests itself in its true character. For in the fact that he despaired of *something*, he really despaired of himself, and now would be rid of himself. Thus when the ambitious man whose watchword was "Either Caesar or nothing" does not become Caesar, he is in despair thereat. But this signifies something else, namely, that precisely because he did not become Caesar he now cannot endure to be himself. So properly he is not in despair over the fact that he did not become Caesar, but he is in despair over himself for the fact that he did not become Caesar. This self which, had he become Caesar, would have been to him a sheer delight (though in another sense equally in despair), this self is now absolutely intolerable to him. In a profounder sense it is not the fact that he did not become Caesar which is intolerable to him, but the self which did not become Caesar is the thing that is intolerable; or, more correctly, what is intolerable to him is that he cannot get rid of himself. If he had become Caesar he would have been rid of himself in desperation, but now that he did not become Caesar he cannot in desperation get rid of himself. Essentially he is equally in despair in either case, for he does not possess himself, he is not himself. By becoming Caesar he would not after all have become himself but have got rid of himself, and by not becoming Caesar he falls into despair over the fact that he cannot get rid of himself. Hence it is a superficial view (which presumably has never seen a person in despair, not even one's own self) when it is said of a man in despair, "He is consuming himself." For precisely this it is he despairs of, and to his torment it is precisely this he cannot do, since by despair fire has entered into something that cannot burn, or cannot burn up, that is, into the self.

So to despair over something is not yet properly despair. It is the beginning, or it is as when the physician says of a sickness that it has not yet declared itself. The next step is the declared despair, despair over oneself. A young girl is in despair over love, and so she despairs over her lover, because he died, or because he was unfaithful to her. This is not a declared despair; no, she is in despair over herself. This self of hers, which, if it had become "his" beloved, she would have been rid of in the most blissful way, or would have lost, this self is now a torment to her when it has to be a self without "him"; this self which would have been to her her riches (though in another sense equally in despair) has now become to her a loathsome void, since "he" is dead, or it has become to her an abhorrence, since it reminds her of the fact that she was betrayed. Try it now, say to such a girl, "Thou art consuming thyself," and thou shalt hear her reply, "Oh, no, the torment is precisely this, that I cannot do it."

To despair over oneself, in despair to will to be rid of oneself, is the formula for all despair, and hence the second form of despair (in despair at willing to be oneself) can be followed back to the first (in despair at not willing to be oneself), just as in the foregoing we resolved the first into the second. A despairing man wants despairingly to be himself. But if he despairingly wants to be himself, he will not want to get rid of himself. Yes, so it seems; but if one inspects more closely, one perceives that after all the contradiction is the same. That self which he despairingly wills to be is a self which he is not (for to will to be that self which one truly is, is indeed the opposite of despair); what he really wills is to tear his self away from the Power which constituted it. But notwithstanding all his despair, this he is unable to do, notwithstanding all the efforts of despair, that Power is the stronger, and it compels him to be the self he does not will to be. But for all that he wills to be rid of himself, to be rid of the self which he is, in order to be the self he himself has chanced to choose. To be *self* as he wills to be would be his delight (though in another sense it would be equally in despair), but to be compelled to be *self* as he does not will to be is his torment, namely, that he cannot get rid of himself.

Socrates proved the immortality of the soul from the fact that the sickness of the soul (sin) does not consume it as sickness of the body consumes the body. So also we can demonstrate the eternal in man from the fact that despair cannot consume his self, that this precisely is the torment of contradiction in despair. If there were nothing eternal in a man, he could not despair; but if despair could consume his self, there would still be no despair.

Thus it is that despair, this sickness in the self, is the sickness unto death. The despairing man is mortally ill. In an entirely different sense than can appropriately be said of any disease, we may say that the sickness has attacked the noblest part; and yet the man cannot die. Death is not the last phase of the sickness, but death is continually the last. To be delivered from this sickness by death is an impossibility, for the sickness and its torment . . . and death consist in not being able to die.

This is the situation in despair. And however thoroughly it eludes the attention of the despairer, and however thoroughly the despairer may succeed (as in the case of that kind of despair which is characterized by unawareness of being in despair) in losing himself entirely, and losing himself in such a way that it is not noticed in the least — eternity nevertheless will make it manifest that his situation was despair, and it will so nail him to himself that the torment nevertheless remains that he cannot get rid of himself, and it becomes manifest that he was deluded in thinking that he succeeded. And thus it is eternity must act, because to have a self, to be a self, is the greatest concession made to man, but at the same time it is eternity's demand upon him.

II. THE UNIVERSALITY
OF THIS SICKNESS (DESPAIR)

Just as the physician might say that there lives perhaps not one single man who is in perfect health, so one might say perhaps that there lives not one single man who after all is not to some extent in despair, in whose inmost parts there does not dwell a disquietude, a perturbation, a discord, an anxious dread of an unknown something, or of a something he does not even dare to make acquaintance with, dread of a possibility of life, or dread of himself, so that, after all, as physicians speak of a man going about with a disease in him, this man is going about and carrying a sickness of the spirit, which only rarely and in glimpses, by and with a dread which to him is inexplicable, gives evidence of its presence within.

At any rate there has lived no one and there lives no one outside of Christendom who is not in despair, and no one in Christendom, unless he be a true Christian, and if he is not quite like that, he is somewhat in despair after all.

This view will doubtless seem to many a paradox, an exaggeration, and a gloomy and depressing view at that. Yet it is nothing of the sort. It is not gloomy; on the contrary, it seeks to throw light upon a subject which ordinarily is left in obscurity. It is not depressing; on the contrary it is uplifting, since it views every man in the aspect of the highest demand made upon him, that he be spirit. Nor is it a paradox; on the contrary, it is a fundamental apprehension consistently carried through, and hence it is no exaggeration.

On the other hand, the ordinary view of despair remains content with appearances, and so it is a superficial view, that is, no view at all. It assumes that every man must know by himself better than anyone else whether he is in despair or not. So whoever says that he is in despair is regarded as being in despair, but whoever thinks he is not in despair is not so regarded. Consequently despair becomes a rather rare phenomenon, whereas in fact it is quite universal. It is not a rare exception that one is in despair; no, the rare, the very rare exception is that one is not in despair.

But the vulgar view has a very poor understanding of despair. Among other things (to mention only one which, if rightly understood, would bring thousands, yea, millions under this category), it completely overlooks the fact that one form of despair is precisely this of not being in despair, that is, not being aware of it. The vulgar view is exposed, though in a much deeper sense, to the same fallacy it sometimes falls into when it would determine whether a man is sick or not. In a much deeper sense, I say, for the vulgar view has a far more inadequate notion of spirit than of sickness and health — and without understanding spirit it is impossible to understand despair. It is ordinarily assumed that a man is well when he does not himself say that he is sick, and still more confidently when he says that he is well. The physician on the other hand regards sickness differently. And why? Because he has a definite and well thought out conception of what it is to be in sound health, and by this he tests the man's condition. The physician knows that just as there is sickness which is only imaginary, so also there is such a thing as fictitious health. In the latter case, therefore, the physician first employs medicines to cause the disease to become manifest. Generally the physician, just because he is a physician, i.e. the competent man, has no unconditional faith in a person's own assertion about the state of his health. If it were true that what every man says about the state of his health (as to whether he is sick or well, where he suffers, etc.) were absolutely to be relied upon, it would be an illusion to be a physician. For a physician does not merely have to prescribe medicines, but first and foremost he has to be acquainted with sickness, and so first and foremost to know whether a supposedly sick man really is sick, or whether a supposedly well man is not really sick. So it is also with the physician of souls when dealing with despair. He knows what despair is, he is acquainted with it, and hence he is not satisfied with a man's assertion that he is in despair or that he is not. For it must be observed that in a certain sense not even all who say they are in despair always are so. One may affect despair, and one may make a mistake and confuse despair with all sorts of transitory dejection or grief which pass away without coming to the point of despair. However, the physician of souls does, it is true, regard these states also as forms of despair. He perceives very well that this is affectation — but precisely this affectation is despair. He perceives very well that this dejection etc. does not mean much — but precisely this fact, that it does not mean much, is despair.

Furthermore, the vulgar view overlooks the fact that, as compared with sickness, despair is much more dialectical than what is commonly called sickness, because it is a sickness of the spirit. And this dialectical quality, rightly understood, again brings thousands under the category of despair. For in case at a given moment a physician is convinced that this or that person is in good health and at a later moment becomes sick — the physician may be right in affirming that the person was well then, and at a later moment became sick. With despair it is different. As soon as despair manifests itself in a person, it is manifest that the person was in despair. For this reason one cannot at a given moment decide anything about a person who is not saved by the fact that he has been in despair. For in case the condition comes about which brings him to despair, it is at that same moment manifest that he has been in despair throughout the whole of his previous life. On the other hand, one is by no means justified in saying, when a man has a fever, that he has had a fever throughout his whole life. But despair is a phenomenon of the spirit, is related to the eternal, and therefore has something of the eternal in its dialectic.

Not only is despair far more dialectical than an illness, but all its symptoms are dialectical, and for this reason the superficial view is so readily deceived in determining whether despair is present or not. For not to be in despair may mean to be in despair, and it may also mean to be delivered from being in despair. A sense of security and tranquillity may mean that one is in despair, precisely this security, this tranquillity, may be despair; and it may mean that one has overcome despair and gained peace. In this respect despair is unlike bodily sickness; for not to be sick cannot possibly mean to be sick; but not to be despairing may mean precisely to be despairing. It is not true of despair, as it is of bodily sickness, that the feeling of indisposition is the sickness. By no means. The feeling of indisposition is again dialectical. Never to have been sensible of this indisposition is precisely to be in despair.

This points to the fact, and has its ground therein, that man, regarded as spirit, is always in a critical condition — and if one is to talk of despair, one must conceive of man as spirit. In relation to sickness we talk of a crisis, but not in relation to health. And why not? Because bodily health is an "immediate" qualification, and only becomes dialectical in sickness, when one can speak of the crisis. But spiritually, or when man is regarded as spirit, both health and sickness are critical. There is no such thing as "immediate" health of the spirit.

So long as one does not regard man as spirit (in which case we cannot talk about despair) but only as a synthesis of soul and body, health is an "immediate" determinant, and only the sickness of soul or body is a dialectical determinant. But despair is expressed precisely by the fact that a person is unaware of being characterized as spirit. Even that which, humanly speaking, is the most beautiful and lovable thing of all, a feminine youthfulness which is sheer peace and harmony and joy — even that is despair. For this indeed is happiness, but happiness is not a characteristic of spirit, and in the remote depths, in the most inward parts, in the hidden recesses of happiness, there dwells also the anxious dread which is despair; it would be only too glad to be allowed to remain therein, for the dearest and most attractive dwelling-place of despair is in the very heart of immediate happiness. All immediacy, in spite of its illusory peace and tranquillity, is dread, and hence, quite consistently, it is dread of nothing; one cannot make immediacy so anxious by the most horrifying description of the most dreadful something, as by a crafty, apparently casual half word about an unknown peril which is thrown out with the surely calculated aim of reflection; yea, one can put immediacy most in dread by slyly imputing to it knowledge of the matter referred to. For immediacy doubtless does not know; but never does reflection catch its prey so surely as when it makes its snare out of nothing, and never is reflection so thoroughly itself as when it is . . . nothing. There is need of an eminent reflection, or rather of a great faith, to support a reflection based upon nothing, i.e. an infinite reflection. So even the most beautiful and lovable thing of all, a feminine youthfulness which is sheer peace and harmony and joy, is nevertheless despair, is happiness. Hardly will one have the good hap to get through life on the strength of this immediacy. And if this happiness has the hap to get through, it would be of little help for it is despair. Despair, just because it is wholly dialectical, is in fact the sickness of which it holds that it is the greatest misfortune not to have had it — the true good hap to get it, although it is the most dangerous sickness of all, if one does not wish to be healed of it. In other cases one can only speak of the good fortune of being healed of a sickness, sickness itself being misfortune.

Therefore it is as far as possible from being true that the vulgar view is right in assuming that despair is a rarity; on the contrary, it is quite universal. It is as far as possible from being true that the vulgar view is right in assuming that everyone who does not think or feel that he is in despair is not so at all, and that only he is in despair who says that he is.

On the contrary, one who without affectation says that he is in despair is after all a little bit nearer, a dialectical step nearer to being cured than all those who are not regarded and do not regard themselves as being in despair. But precisely this is the common situation (as the physician of souls will doubtless concede), that the majority of men live without being thoroughly conscious that they are spiritual beings — and to this is referable all the security, contentment with life, etc., etc., which precisely is despair. Those, on the other hand, who say that they are in despair are generally such as have a nature so much more profound that they must become conscious of themselves as spirit, or such as by the hard vicissitudes of life and its dreadful decisions have been helped to become conscious of themselves as spirit — either one or the other, for rare is the man who truly is free from despair.

Ah, so much is said about human want and misery — I seek to understand it, I have also had some acquaintance with it at close range; so much is said about wasted lives — but only that man's life is wasted who lived on, so deceived by the joys of life or by its sorrows that he never became eternally and decisively conscious of himself as spirit, as self, or (what is the same thing) never became aware and in the deepest sense received an impression of the fact that there is a God, and that he, he himself, his self, exists before this God, which gain of infinity is never attained except through despair. And, oh, this misery, that so many live on and are defrauded of this most blessed of all thoughts; this misery, that people employ themselves about everything else, or, as for the masses of men, that people employ them about everything else, utilize them to generate the power for the theater of life, but never remind them of their blessedness; that they heap them in a mass and defraud them, instead of splitting them apart so that they might gain the highest thing, the only thing worth living for, and enough to live in for an eternity — it seems to me that I could weep for an eternity over the fact that such misery exists! And, oh, to my thinking this is one expression the more of the dreadfulness of this most dreadful sickness and misery, namely, its hiddenness — not only that he who suffers from it may wish to hide it and may be able to do so, to the effect that it can so dwell in a man that no one, no one whatever discovers it; no, rather that it can be so hidden in a man that he himself does not know it! And, oh, when the hour-glass has run out, the hour-glass of time, when the noise of worldliness is silenced, and the restless or the ineffectual busyness comes to an end, when everything is still about thee as it is in eternity — whether thou wast man or woman, rich or poor, dependent or independent, fortunate or unfortunate, whether thou didst bear the splendor of the crown in a lofty station, or didst bear only the labor and heat of the day in an inconspicuous lot; whether thy name shall be remembered as long as the world stands (and so was remembered as long as the world stood), or without a name thou didst cohere as nameless with the countless multitude; whether the glory which surrounded thee surpassed all human description, or the judgment passed upon thee was the most severe and dishonoring human judgment can pass — eternity asks of thee and of every individual among these million millions only one question, whether thou hast lived in despair or not, whether thou wast in despair in such a way that thou didst not know thou wast in despair, or in such a way that thou didst hiddenly carry this sickness in thine inward parts as thy gnawing secret, carry it under thy heart as the fruit of a sinful love, or in such a way that thou, a horror to others, didst rave in despair. And if so, if thou hast lived in despair (whether for the rest thou didst win or lose), then for thee all is lost, eternity knows thee not, it never knew thee, or (even more dreadful) it knows thee as thou art known, it puts thee under arrest by thyself in despair.

Kierkegaard's Attack upon "Christendom" *(1855) was written as a series of pamphlets and is primarily an attack on the "massification of Christianity." For Kierkegaard, "Christendom" was an illusion that kept one from seeing Christianity in the only way in which it is meaningful: from the point of view of the individual. Written at the very end of his life and almost the last of Kierkegaard's writings to be translated into English, this work seeks to make inwardness the focus of the teachings of Christianity. Here Kierkegaard warns his readers that since he is "in the service of something true" they should expect a challenge and pay careful attention. Indeed, he believed it was his duty to see that his readers expended great effort in order to counteract all the falsifications and misrepresentations of popular religious thinking.*

Attack upon "Christendom"

IX. THE *FATHERLAND*, MONDAY, MARCH 26, 1855

The Religious Situation

January 1855.   S. Kierkegaard.

The religious situation in our country is: Christianity (that is, the Christianity of the New Testament — and everything else is not Christianity, least of all by calling itself such), Christianity does not exist — as almost anyone must be able to see as well as I.

We have, if you will, a complete crew of bishops, deans, and priests; learned men, eminently learned, talented, gifted, humanly well-meaning; they all declaim — doing it well, very well, eminently well, or tolerably well, or badly — but not one of them is in the character of the Christianity of the New Testament. But if such is the case, the existence of this Christian crew is so far from being, Christianly considered, advantageous to Christianity that it is far rather a peril, because it is so infinitely likely to give rise to a false impression and the false inference that when we have such a complete crew we must of course have Christianity, too. A geographer, for example, when he has assured himself of the existence of this crew, would think that he was thoroughly justified in putting into his geography the statement that the Christian religion prevails in the land.

We have what one might call a complete inventory of churches, bells, organs, benches, alms-boxes, foot-warmers, tables, hearses, etc. But when Christianity does not exist, the existence of this inventory, so far from being, Christianly considered, an advantage, is far rather a peril, because it is so infinitely likely to give to a false impression and the false inference that when we have such a complete Christian inventory we must of course have Christianity, too. A statistician, for example, when he had assured himself of the existence of this Christian inventory, would think that he was thoroughly justified in putting into his statistics the statement that the Christian religion is the prevailing one in the land.

We are what is called a "Christian" nation — but in such a sense that not a single one of us is in the character of the Christianity of the New Testament, any more than I am, who again and again have repeated, and do now repeat, that I am only a poet. The illusion of a Christian nation is due doubtless to the power which number exercises over the imagination. I have not the least doubt that every single individual in the nation will be honest enough with God and with himself to say in solitary conversation, "If I must be candid, I do not deny that I am not a Christian in the New Testament sense; if I must be honest, I do not deny that my life cannot be called an effort in the direction of what the New Testament calls Christianity, in the direction of denying myself, renouncing the world, dying from it, etc.; rather the earthly and the temporal become more and more important to me with every year I live." I have not the least doubt that everyone will, with respect to ten of his acquaintances, let us say, be able to hold fast to the view that they are not Christians in the New Testament sense, and that their lives are not even an effort in the direction of becoming such. . . . It is said that [an innkeeper] sold his beer by the bottle for a cent less than he paid for it; and when a certain man said to him, "How does that balance the account? That means to spend money," he replied, "No, my friend, it's the big number that does it" — big number, that also in our time is the almighty power. When one has laughed at this story, one would do well to take to heart the lesson which warns against the power which number exercises over the imagination. For there can be no doubt that this innkeeper knew very well that one bottle of beer which he sold for 3 cents meant a loss of 1 cent when it cost him 4 cents. Also with regard to ten bottles the innkeeper will be able to hold fast that it is a loss. But 100,000 bottles! Here the big number stirs the imagination, the round number runs away with it, and the innkeeper becomes dazed — it's a profit, says he, for the big number does it. So also with the calculation which arrives at a Christian nation by adding up units which are not Christian, getting the result by means of the notion that the big number does it. For true Christianity this is the most dangerous of all illusions, and at the same time it is of all illusions precisely the one to which every man is prone; for number (the high number, when it gets up to 100,000, into the millions) tallies precisely with the imagination. But Christianly of course the calculation is wrong, and a Christian nation composed of units which honestly admit that they are not Christians, *item* honestly admit that their life cannot in any sense be called an effort in the direction of what the New Testament understands by Christianity — such a Christian nation is an impossibility. On the other hand, a knave could not wish to find a better hiding-place than behind such phrases as "the nation is Christian," "the people are making a Christian endeavor," since it is almost as difficult to come to close quarters with such phrases as it would be if one were to say, "N. N. is a Christian, N. N. is engaged in Christian endeavor."

But inasmuch as Christianity is spirit, the sobriety of spirit, the honesty of eternity, there is of course nothing which to its detective eye is so suspicious as are all fantastic entities: Christian states, Christian lands, a Christian people, and (how marvelous!) a Christian world. And even if there were something true in this talk about Christian peoples and states — but, mind you, only when all mediating definitions, all divergencies from the Christianity of the New Testament, are honestly and honorably pointed out and kept in evidence — yet it is certain that at this point a monstrous criminal offense has been perpetrated, yea, everything this world has hitherto seen in the way of criminal affairs is a mere bagatelle in comparison with this crime, which has been carried on from generation to generation throughout long ages, eluding human justice, but has not yet got beyond the arm of divine justice.

This is the religious situation. And to obviate if possible a waste of time I will at once anticipate a turn which one will perhaps give the matter. Let me explain by means of another case. If there were living in the land a poet who in view of the ideal of what it is to love talked in this fashion: "Alas, I must myself admit that I cannot truly be said to be in love; neither will I play the hypocrite and say that I am endeavoring more and more in this direction, for the truth unfortunately is that things are rather going backward with me. Moreover, my observation convinces me that in the whole land there is not a single person who can be said to be truly in love" — then the inhabitants of the land could reply to him, and in a certain degree with justice: "Yes, my good poet, that may be true enough with your ideals; but we are content, we find ourselves happy with what we call being in love, and that settles it." But such can never be the case with Christianity. The New Testament indeed settles what Christianity is, leaving it to eternity to pass judgment upon us. In fact the priest is bound by an oath upon the New Testament — so it is not possible to regard that as Christianity which men like best and prefer to call Christianity. As soon as we assume that we may venture to give the matter this turn, Christianity is *eo ipso* done away with, and the priest's oath . . . but here I break off, I do not wish to draw the inference before they constrain me further to do so, and even then I do not wish to do it. But if we do not dare to give the matter this turn, there are only two ways open to us: either (as I propose) honestly and honorably to make an admission as to how we are related to the Christianity of the New Testament; or to perform artful tricks to conceal the true situation, tricks to conjure up the vain semblance that Christianity is the prevailing religion in the land. . . .

XII. ARTICLES IN THE *FATHERLAND*, MARCH 31, 1855

What Do I Want?

March 1855.   S. Kierkegaard.

Quite simply: I want honesty. I am not, as well-intentioned people represent (for I can pay no attention to the interpretations of me that are advanced by exasperation and rage and impotence and twaddle), I am not a Christian severity as opposed to a Christian leniency.

By no means. I am neither leniency nor severity: I am . . . a human honesty.

The leniency which is the common Christianity in the land I want to place alongside of the New Testament in order to see how these two are related to one another.

Then, if it appears, if I or another can prove, that it can be maintained face to face with the New Testament, then with the greatest joy I will agree to it.

But one thing I will not do, not for anything in the world. I will not by suppression, or by performing tricks, try to produce the impression that the ordinary Christianity in the land and the Christianity of the New Testament are alike.

Behold, this it is I do not want. And why not? Well, because I want honesty. Or, if you wish me to talk in another way — well then, it is because I believe that, if possibly even the very extremest softening down of Christianity may hold good in the judgment of eternity, it is impossible that it should hold good when even artful tricks are employed to gloss over the difference between the Christianity of the New Testament and this softened form. What I mean is this: If a man is known for his graciousness — very well then, let me venture to ask him to forgive me all my debt; but even though his grace were divine grace, this is too much to ask, if I will not even be truthful about how great the debt is.

And this in my opinion is the falsification of which official Christianity is guilty: it does not frankly and unreservedly make known the Christian requirement — perhaps because it is afraid people would shudder to see at what a distance from it we are living, without being able to claim that in the remotest way our life might be called an effort* in the direction of fulfilling the requirement. Or (merely to take one example of what is everywhere present in the New Testament): when Christ requires us to save our life eternally (and that surely is what we propose to attain as Christians) and to hate our own life in this world, is there then a single one among us whose life in the remotest degree could be called even the weakest effort in this direction? And perhaps there are thousands of "Christians" in the land who are not so much as aware of this requirement. So then we "Christians" are living, and are loving our life, just in the ordinary human sense. If then by "grace" God will nevertheless regard us as Christians, one thing at least must be required: that we, being precisely aware of the requirement, have a true conception of how infinitely great is the grace that is showed us. "Grace" cannot possibly stretch so far, one thing it must never be used for, it must never be used to suppress or to diminish the requirement; for in that case "grace" would turn Christianity upside down. — Or, to take an example of another kind: A teacher is paid, let us say, several thousand. If then we suppress the Christian standard and apply the ordinary human rule, that it is a matter of course a man should receive a wage for his labor, a wage sufficient to support a family, and a considerable wage to enable him to enjoy the consideration due to a government official — then a few thousand a year is certainly not much. On the other hand, as soon as the Christian requirement of poverty is brought to bear, family is a luxury, and several thousand is very high pay. I do not say this in order to deprive such an official of a single shilling, if I were able to; on the contrary, if he desired it, and I were able, he might well have double as many thousands: but I say that the suppression of the Christian requirement changes the point of view for all his wages. Honesty to Christianity demands that one call to mind the Christian requirement of poverty, which is not a capricious whim of Christianity, but is because only in poverty can it be truly served,

* footnote deleted

and the more thousands a teacher of Christianity has by way of wages, the less he can serve Christianity. On the other hand, it is not honest to suppress the requirement or to perform artful tricks to produce the impression that this sort of business career is simply the Christianity of the New Testament. No — let us take money, but for God's sake not the next thing: let us not wish to gloss over the Christian requirement, so that by suppression or by falsification we may bring about an appearance of decorum which is in the very highest degree demoralizing and is a sly death-blow to Christianity.

Therefore I want honesty; but till now the Established Church has not been willing of its own accord to go in for that sort of honesty, and neither has it been willing to let itself be influenced by me. That does not make me, however, a leniency or a severity; no, I am and remain quite simply a human honesty.

Let me go to the utmost extreme in order, if possible, to make people understand what I want.

I want honesty. If that is what the human race or this generation wants, if it will honorably, honestly, openly, frankly, directly rebel against Christianity, if it will say to God, "We can but we will not subject ourselves to this power" — but note that this must be done honorably, honestly, openly, frankly, directly — very well then, strange as it may seem, I am with them; for honesty is what I want, and wherever there is honesty I can take part. An honest rebellion against Christianity can only be made when a man honestly confesses what Christianity is, and how he himself is related to it.

If this is what they want, if they are honest, open, candid, as it is seemly for a man to be when he talks with his God, which therefore everyone is if he respects himself and does not so deeply despise himself that he would be insincere in the face of God — well then, if we honestly, candidly, frankly, completely admit to God how it really stands with us men, that the human race in the course of time has taken the liberty of softening and softening Christianity until at last we have contrived to make it exactly the opposite of what it is in the New Testament — and that now, if the thing is possible, we should be so much pleased if this might be Christianity. If that is what they want, then I am with them.

But one thing I will not do; no, not for anything in the world: I will not, though it were merely with the last quarter of the last joint of my little finger, I will not take part in what is known as official Christianity, which by suppression and by artifice gives the impression of being the Christianity of the New Testament; and upon my knees I thank my God that He has compassionately prevented me from becoming too far embroiled in it.*

* footnote deleted

If then official Christianity in this country takes occasion from what is said here to employ power against me, I am ready; for I want honesty.

For this honesty I am ready to take the risk. On the other hand, I do not say that it is for Christianity I take the risk. Just suppose the case, suppose that quite literally I were to become a sacrifice: I would not even in that case be a sacrifice for Christianity, but because I wanted honesty.

But although I dare not say' that I make a venture for the sake of Christianity, I am fully and blessedly convinced that this venture of mine is well-pleasing to God, has His consent. Yea, this I know, that it has His consent that in a world of Christians, where millions upon millions call themselves Christians, there is one man who says, "I dare not call myself a Christian, but I want honesty, and I will venture into the end." . . .

KARL JASPERS

Karl Jaspers (1883–1969), though his degree was in medicine, is considered by some historians of philosophy to have written the first existential work of the twentieth century, Psychologie der Weltanschauungen *(1919). His views were profoundly influenced by the writings of Nietzsche and Kierkegaard, from whom he took the idea of the importance of contingency. In the essay that follows, Jaspers makes clear not only how his theism is different from traditional views, but also how great is his debt to the work of Kierkegaard.*

The Idea of God

Our western idea of God springs from two historical roots: the Bible and Greek philosophy.

When Jeremiah saw the ruin of everything for which he had worked all his life, when his country and his people were lost, when in Egypt the last remnants of his people turned aside from their faith in Yahweh and offered sacrifices to Isis, and when his disciple Baruch despaired, "I fainted in my sighing, and I find no rest," Jeremiah answered, "Behold, that which I have built will I break down, and that which I have planted I will pluck up, even this whole land. And seekest thou great things for thyself? Seek them not."

In such a situation these words mean: It is enough that God is. Do not ask whether there is immortality; the question of whether God forgives is no longer important. Man no longer matters, his defiance as well as his concern for his own beatitude and eternity is extinguished. It is also impossible that the world should have a purpose susceptible of fulfilment, that it should endure in any form; for everything has been created out of nothing by God and is in His hand. When everything is lost, but one thing remains: God is. If a life in this world, even with faith in God's guidance, has failed, this overpowering reality still remains: God is. If man fully renounces himself and his aims, this reality can be manifested to him as the only reality. But it does not manifest itself in advance, it does not manifest itself abstractly, but descends into the existence of the world, and only here manifests itself at the limit. Jeremiah's words are hard words. They are no longer bound up with any will to historical efficacy in the world, though such a will has preceded them throughout a

From Karl Jaspers, *The Way to Wisdom,* translated by Ralph Manheim (New Haven, Conn.: Yale University Press, 1951), Chapter IV, "The Idea of God," pp. 39–51. © Yale University Press. Reprinted by permission of Yale University Press.

lifetime and ultimately, through total failure, made them possible. They are simple words, free from imaginative flight, and they contain unfathomable truth, precisely because they are without finite content or any fixation in the world.

The Greek philosophers expressed a similar thought in different terms.

At about 500 B.C. Xenophanes proclaimed: There is only one God, resembling mortals neither in his aspect nor in his thoughts. Plato conceived of the godhead — he called it the Good — as the source of all knowledge. Not only is the knowable known in the light of the godhead; it also derives its being from the godhead which excels being both in rank and power.

The Greek philosophers understood that the many gods were decreed merely by custom, whereas in nature there was only one God; that God is not seen with our eyes, that he resembles no one and can be recognized in no image.

God is conceived as cosmic reason or cosmic law, or as fate and providence, or as demiurge.

But this God of the Greek thinkers is a God originating in thought, not the living God of Jeremiah. In essence the two coincide. From this twofold root Western theology and philosophy have, in infinite modulations, reflected that God is and pondered on what He is.

The philosophers of our day seem to evade the question of whether God exists. They do not say that He exists nor do they deny His existence. But anyone engaging in philosophical thought must answer for his opinions. If a philosopher doubts, he must say why, else he cannot progress beyond the sceptical philosophy which asserts nothing at all, which affirms nothing and denies nothing. Or, limiting himself to determinate object knowledge, that is to scientific cognition, he ceases to philosophize, saying: It is best not to talk of what we do not know.

The question of God is discussed on the basis of conflicting propositions which we shall examine.

The theological proposition is: We can know of God only because He revealed Himself to certain men from the prophets to Jesus. Without revelation God can have no reality for man. God is accessible not through thought but through faith and obedience.

But long before and far outside the world of biblical revelation there was certainty as to the reality of the godhead. And within the world of the Christian West many men have derived certainty of God without the guarantee of revelation.

There is an old philosophical proposition opposed to this theological doctrine: We know of God because His existence can be proved. The proofs for the existence of God form an impressive document.

But if the proofs for the existence of God are construed as scientifically compelling proofs such as we find in mathematics or the empirical sciences, they are false. In this light Kant radically confuted them.

Then came the reverse proposition: Since all proofs of the existence of God can be refuted, there is no God.

This inference is false. For the nonexistence of God can be proved no more than his existence. The proofs and their confutations show us only that a proved God would be no God but merely a thing in the world.

The truth, as against all supposed proofs and refutations of the existence of God, seems to be this: The so-called proofs of the existence of God are fundamentally no proofs at all, but methods of achieving certainty through thought. All the proofs of the existence of God and their variants that have been devised through the centuries differ essentially from scientific proofs. They are attempts to express the experience of man's ascent to God in terms of thought. There are roads of thought by which we come to limits at which the consciousness of God suddenly becomes a natural presence.

Let us consider a few examples:

The oldest of proofs is the cosmological proof. From the existence of the cosmos (the Greek name for universe) we infer that God exists; from the world process, in which everything is effect, we infer a last cause; from motion the source of all motion; from the accident of the particular the necessity of the whole.

If by this syllogism we mean to infer the existence of one thing from the existence of another thing, as we do for example in inferring from the existence of the side of the moon which faces us the existence of the other side which we never see, it is inapplicable. In this manner we can only infer the existence of things in the world from the existence of other things. The world as a whole is not an object, because we are always in it and we never confront the world as a whole. Hence we cannot, from the existence of the world as a whole, infer the existence of something other than the world.

But this notion takes on a new meaning when it is no longer regarded as a proof. Then metaphorically, in the form of an inference, it expresses awareness of the mystery inherent in the existence of the world and of ourselves in it. If we venture the thought that there might be nothing, and ask with Schelling: Why is there something and not nothing? we find that our certainty of existence is such that though we cannot determine the reason for it we are led by it to the Comprehensive, which by this very essence is and cannot not be, and through which everything else is.

True, men have looked on the world as eternal and said that it existed out of itself and hence was identical with God. But this is not possible:

Everything in the world which is beautiful, appropriate, ordered, and embodies a certain perfection — the vast abundance of things that fill us with emotion in our immediate contemplation of nature — all this cannot be apprehended through any fully knowable worldly thing, through matter, for example. The design of organic life, the beauty of nature in all its forms, the order of the universe in general become increasingly mysterious as our knowledge advances.

But if from all this we infer that God, the benevolent creator, exists, we must call to mind all that is ugly, disordered, base in the world. And this gives rise to fundamental attitudes for which the world is alien, frightening, terrible, and it seems as plausible to infer the existence of the devil as of God. The mystery of transcendence is not thereby solved but merely grows deeper.

But what clinches the matter is the imperfectibility of the world. The world is not finished, but in continuous change; our knowledge of the world cannot be completed, the world cannot be apprehended through itself.

Far from proving the existence of God, these so-called proofs mislead us into placing God within the real world, or second cosmos, which is as it were ascertained at the limits of the cosmos. Thus they obscure the idea of God.

But they move us deeply when, leading through the concrete phenomena of the cosmos, they confront Nothingness and imperfectibility. For then they seem to admonish us not to content ourselves with the world as the sole meaning of our life in the world.

Again and again it is brought home to us that God is not an object of knowledge, of compelling evidence. He cannot be experienced by the senses. He is invisible, He cannot be seen but only believed in.

But whence comes this faith? Its source is not in the limits of worldly experience but in the freedom of man. The man who attains true awareness of his freedom gains certainty of God. Freedom and God are inseparable. Why?

This I know: in my freedom I am not through myself, but am given to myself, for I can fail myself and I cannot force my freedom. Where I am authentically myself, I am certain that I am not through myself. The highest freedom is experienced in freedom from the world, and this freedom is a profound bond with transcendence.

We also call man's freedom his existence. My certainty of God has the force of my existence. I can have certainty of Him not as a content of science but as presence for existence.

If certainty of freedom encompasses certainty of God's existence, there must be a connection between the negation of freedom and the negation of God. If I do not experience the miracle of selfhood, I need no relation to God, I am content with the empirical existence of nature, many gods, demons.

There is, on the other hand, a connection between the belief that there can be freedom without God and the deification of man. This is an illusory, arbitrary freedom, in which man's will is taken to be absolute and independent. I rely in the force of my will and in a defiant acceptance of death. But this delusion that I am through myself alone turns freedom into perplexity and emptiness. A savage drive for self-assertion turns to a despair, in which Kierkegaard's "desperate will to be oneself" and "desperate will not to be oneself" become one.

God exists for me in the degree to which I in freedom authentically become myself. He does not exist as a scientific content but only as openness to existence.

But the illumination of our existence as freedom does not prove the existence of God; it merely points, one might say, to the area in which certainty of his existence is possible.

The thought that strives for compelling certainty cannot realize its aim in any proof of God's existence. But the failure of thought does not result in nothingness. It points to that which resolves into an inexhaustible, forever-questioning, Comprehensive consciousness of God.

God never becomes a tangible object in the world — and this means that man must not abandon his freedom to the tangibilities, authorities, powers of the world; that he bears responsibility for himself, and must not evade this responsibility by renouncing freedom ostensibly for the sake of freedom. He must owe his decision and the road he chooses to himself. Kant has said that God's unfathomable wisdom is as admirable in what it gives us as in what it denies us. For if God's wisdom in its majesty were always before our eyes, if it were an absolute authority, speaking unequivocally in the world, we should be puppets of its will. But God in his wisdom wanted us to be free.

Instead of the knowledge of God, which is unattainable, we gain through philosophy a Comprehensive consciousness of God.

"God is." The essential in this proposition is the reality to which it points. We do not encompass this reality in thinking the proposition; merely to think it leaves us empty. For it means nothing to the understanding and to sensory experience. We apprehend its meaning only as we transcend, as we pass beyond the world of objects and through it discover authentic reality. Hence the climax and goal of our life is the point at which we ascertain authentic reality, that is, God.

This reality is accessible to existence through the orientation toward God that lies at its source. Hence faith in God, springing as it does from the source, resists any mediation. This faith is not laid down in any definite articles of faith applicable to all men or in any historical reality which mediates between man and God and is the same for all men. The individual, always in his own historicity, stands rather in an immediate, independent relation to God that requires no intermediary.

This historicity, which can be communicated and described, is in this form not absolute truth for all, and yet in its source it is absolutely true.

God is reality, absolute, and cannot be encompassed by any of the historical manifestations through which He speaks to men. If He is, man as an individual must be able to apprehend Him directly.

The reality of God and the immediacy of our historical relation to God exclude any universally compelling knowledge of God; therefore what matters is not our knowledge of God but our attitude towards God. From time immemorial God has been conceived in empirical forms, including a personification after the image of man. And yet every such conception is at the same time in the nature of a veil. God is not what we may see with our eyes.

Our true attitude toward God has found its profoundest expression in a few biblical injunctions:

Thou shalt not make unto thee any graven image or likeness. This meant, to begin with, that because God is invisible man must not worship Him in statues, idols, effigies. Gaining in depth, this tangible prohibition developed into the idea that God is not only invisible but also inconceivable, unthinkable. No symbol or metaphor can describe Him and none may take His place. All metaphorical representations of God without exception are myths, meaningful as such when understood to be mere hints and parallels, but they become superstitions when mistaken for the reality of God Himself.

Since every image conceals as much as it discloses, we come closest to God in the negation of images. But even in the Bible this Old Testament commandment was not fulfilled: the image of God's personality remained — His wrath and His love, His justice and His mercy. It is a commandment that cannot be fulfilled. Parmenides and Plato, with their speculative doctrines of being, the Indian Brahman philosophers, the Chinese Taoists attempted to apprehend without images the suprapersonal, pure, intangible reality of God — but in this they did not succeed. Human thought and human vision cannot dispense with the image. And though in philosophical thinking sensation and object almost vanished, perhaps ultimately some wisp of God's presence remains, with power to engender life.

Then, even after philosophy has rationally elucidated the deification of nature, the purely demonic, the aesthetic and superstitious, the specifically numinous, the deepest mystery is still not expelled.

Perhaps we can give some paraphrase of this presence of God at the end of philosophical endeavour.

It is the silence in the face of being. Speech ceases in the presence of that which is lost to us when it becomes object.

This ultimate can be attained only in the transcending of all thought. It cannot itself be transcended. Before it lies contentment with one's lot and the extinction of all desire.

Here is a haven and yet no fixed home. Here is a repose that can sustain us amid the inevitable unrest of our wanderings in the world.

Here thought must dissolve into radiance. Where there is no further question, there is also no answer. In the philosophical transcending of question and answer we arrive at the limit, at the stillness of being.

Another biblical injunction runs: *Thou shalt have no other gods before me.* At first this commandment implied a rejection of alien gods. Gaining in depth, it became a simple and unfathomable idea: there is only one God. The life of the man who believes in the one and only God rests on a foundation entirely different from that of a life with many gods. Concentration on the One gives to the decision of existence its real foundation. Infinite wealth implies diffusion; God's glory is not absolute unless it is grounded in the One. The quest for the One as the foundation of his life is an enduring problem for man, as actual as it was thousands of years ago.

A third biblical saying: *Thy will be done.* This fundamental attitude toward God means: Bow down before that which defies understanding, confident that it is situated above and not below the understandable. "Thy thoughts are not our thoughts, thy ways are not our ways."

Trust in this basic attitude makes possible an all-encompassing sense of thankfulness, a wordless, impersonal love.

Man stands before the godhead as the hidden God and can accept what is most terrible as His decision, fully aware that in whatever finite form he expresses this God it is spoken in human terms and hence false.

To sum up: Our attitude toward the godhead is defined by the commandments "No image and no likeness," "No other god," and by the attitude of acceptance expressed in the words "Thy will be done."

Reflection on God clarifies our faith. But to believe is not to see. God remains in the distance and remains question. To live by God does not mean to base oneself on calculable knowledge but to live as though we staked our existence on the assumption that God is.

To believe in God means to live by something which is not in the world, except in the polyvalent language of phenomena, which we call the hieroglyphs or symbols of transcendence.

The God of faith is the distant God, the hidden God, the indemonstrable God.

Hence I must recognize not only that I do not know God but even that I do not know whether I believe. Faith is no possession. It confers no secure knowledge, but it gives certainty in the practice of life.

Thus the believer lives in the enduring ambiguity of the objective, in enduring willingness to hear. He listens patiently and yet he is unswerving in his resolve. In the cloak of weakness he is strong, he is open, though in his real life he is resolute.

Reflection on God is typical of all significant philosophical thought: it does not bring secure knowledge, but to authentic self-hood it gives a free area for decision; the whole emphasis is on love in the world, on the reading of the symbols of transcendence, on the depth and breadth of that which is illumined by reason.

That is why all philosophical discourse is so incomplete. It calls for completion out of the being of him who hears it.

Philosophy does not give, it can only awaken — it can remind, and help to secure and preserve.

In it each of us understands what he actually knew before.

LEO TOLSTOY

Count Leo Tolstoy (1828–1910), author of such masterpieces as War and Peace *and* Anna Karenina, *struggled throughout his life with a number of profoundly felt philosophical questions. In particular, he, like Kierkegaard, sought to determine for himself the personal significance of Christianity. And, like Kierkegaard, he believed that his own society had abandoned Christianity for institutions and social conventions. In the last fifteen years of his life, Tolstoy preached a strict asceticism that he believed was consistent with the real meaning of Christianity. Regardless of whatever specific differences exist between his and Kierkegaard's vision of the Christian ideal, Christianity was for both a profound faith (as opposed to a rational doctrine) that affected every aspect of one's existence. In this excerpt from Tolstoy's* Confession, *he discusses his own spiritual crisis and the necessity of faith for salvation.*

Confession

IV

My life came to a stop. I could breathe, eat, drink, and sleep; indeed, I could not help but breathe, eat, drink, and sleep. But there was no life in me because I had no desires whose satisfaction I would have found reasonable. If I wanted something, I knew beforehand that it did not matter whether or not I got it.

If a fairy had come and offered to fulfill my every wish, I would not have known what to wish for. If in moments of intoxication I should have not desires but the habits of old desires, in moments of sobriety I knew that it was all a delusion, that I really desired nothing. I did not even want to discover truth anymore because I had guessed what it was. The truth was that life is meaningless.

It was as though I had lived a little, wandered a little, until I came to the precipice, and I clearly saw that there was nothing ahead except ruin. And there was no stopping, no turning back, no closing my eyes so I would not see that there was nothing ahead except the deception of life and of happiness and the reality of suffering and death, of complete annihilation.

I grew sick of life; some irresistible force was leading me to somehow get rid of it. It was not that I wanted to kill myself. The force that was leading me away from life was more powerful, more absolute, more all-encompassing than any desire. With all my strength I struggled to get away from life. The thought of suicide came to me as naturally then as the thought of improving life had come to me before. This thought was such a temptation that I had to use cunning against myself in order not to go through with it too hastily. I did not want to be in a hurry only because I wanted to use all my strength to untangle my thoughts. If I could not get them untangled, I told myself, I could always go ahead with it. And there I was, a fortunate man, carrying a rope from my room, where I was alone every night as I undressed, so that I would not hang myself from the beam between the closets. And I quit going hunting with a gun, so that I would not be too easily tempted to rid myself of life. I myself did not know what I wanted. I was afraid of life, I struggled to get rid of it, and yet I hoped for something from it.

And this was happening to me at a time when, from all indications, I should have been considered a completely happy man; this was when I was not yet fifty years old. I had a good, loving and beloved wife, fine children, and a large estate that was growing and expanding without any effort on my part. More than ever before I was respected by friends and acquaintances, praised by strangers, and I could claim a certain renown without really deluding myself. Moreover, I was not physically and mentally unhealthy; on the contrary, I enjoyed a physical and mental vigor such as I had rarely encountered among others my age. Physically, I could keep up with the peasants working in the fields; mentally, I could work eight and ten hours at a stretch without suffering any aftereffects from the strain. And in such a state of affairs I came to a point where I could not live; and even though I feared death, I had to employ ruses against myself to keep from committing suicide.

I described my spiritual condition to myself in this way: my life is some kind of stupid and evil practical joke that someone is playing on me. In spite of the fact that I did not acknowledge the existence of any "Someone" who might have created me, the notion that someone brought me into the world as a stupid and evil joke seemed to be the most natural way to describe my condition. . . .

"My family . . . ," I said to myself. But my family, my wife and children, are people too. They are subject to the same conditions as I: they must either live in the lie or face the terrible truth. Why should they live? Why should I love them? Why care for them, bring them up, and watch over them? So that they can sink into the despair that eats away at me, or to turn them over to stupidity? If I love them, then I cannot hide the truth from them. Every step they take in knowledge leads them to this truth. And the truth is death.

"Art, literature . . . ?" Under the influence of success and praise from others I had persuaded myself for a long time that this was something that may be done in spite of the approaching death that will annihilate everything — myself, my works, and the memory of them. But I soon saw that this, too, was a delusion. It became clear to me that art is an ornamentation of life, something that lures us into life. But life had lost its charm for me, so how was I to charm others? . . . It was no longer possible for me to be consoled by what I saw in the mirror, for I could see that my situation was stupid and despairing. It was good for me to rejoice when in the depths of my soul I believed that my life had meaning. Then this play of lights and shades, the play of the comical, the tragic, the moving, the beautiful, and the terrible elements in life had comforted me. But when I saw that life was meaningless and terrible the play in the mirror could no longer amuse me. . . .

But it did not stop here. Had I simply understood that life has no meaning, I might have been able to calmly accept it; I might have recognized that such was my lot. But I could not rest content at this. Had I been like a man who lives in a forest from which he knows there is no way out, I might have been able to go on living; but I was like a man lost in the forest who was terrified by the fact that he was lost, like a man who was rushing about, longing to find his way and knowing that every step was leading him into deeper confusion, and yet who could not help rushing about.

This was the horror. And in order to be delivered from this horror, I wanted to kill myself. I felt a horror of what awaited me; I knew that this horror was more terrible than my present situation, but I could not keep it away and I did not have the patience to wait for the end. No matter how convincing the argument was that a blood vessel in the heart would burst anyway or that something else would rupture and it would be all over, I could not patiently await the end. The horror of the darkness was too great, and I wanted to be free of it as quickly as possible by means of a rope or a bullet. It was this feeling, more powerful than any other, that was leading me toward suicide.

V

Several times I asked myself, "Can it be that I have overlooked something, that there is something which I have failed to understand? Is it not possible that this state of despair is common to everyone?" And I searched for an answer to my questions in every area of knowledge acquired by man. For a long time I carried on my painstaking search; I did not search casually, out of mere curiosity, but painfully, persistently, day and night, like a dying man seeking salvation. I found nothing.

I searched all areas of knowledge, and not only did I fail to find anything, but I was convinced that all those who had explored knowledge as I did had also come up with nothing. Not only had they found nothing, but they had clearly acknowledged the same thing that had brought me to despair: the only absolute knowledge attainable by man is that life is meaningless.

I searched everywhere. And thanks to a life spent in study and to my connections with the learned world, I had access to the most learned from all the various fields of knowledge. These scholars did not refuse to reveal to me the sum of their knowledge, not only through their books but in conversations with them; I knew everything that knowledge had to answer to the question of life.

For a long time I could not bring myself to believe that knowledge had no reply to the question of life other than the one it had come up with. For a long time I thought I might have misunderstood something, as I closely observed the gravity and seriousness in the tone of science, convinced in its position, while having nothing to do with the question of human life. For a long time I was timid around knowledge, and I thought that the absurdity of the answers given to my questions was not the fault of knowledge but was due to my own ignorance; but the thing was that this to me was no joke, no game, but a matter of life and death; and I finally came to the conclusion that my questions were the only legitimate questions serving as a basis for all knowledge and that it was not I but science that was guilty before my questions if it should pretend to answer these questions.

My question, the question that had brought me to the edge of suicide when I was fifty years old, was the simplest question lying in the soul of every human being, from a silly child to the wisest of the elders, the question without which life is impossible; such was the way I felt about the matter. The question is this: What will come of what I do today and tomorrow? What will come of my entire life?

Expressed differently, the question may be: Why should I live? Why should I wish for anything or do anything? Or to put it still differently: Is there any meaning in my life that will not be destroyed by my inevitably approaching death? . . .

The main thing was that my personal question, the question of what I am with all my desires, remained totally unanswered. I realized that these areas of knowledge may be very interesting and quite attractive, but their clarity and precision are inversely proportionate to their applicability to the questions of life. The less they have to do with the questions of life, the clearer and more precise they are; the more they attempt to provide answers to the questions of life, the more vague and unattractive they become. If we turn to those fields of knowledge that try to provide answers to the questions, to physiology, psychology, biology, sociology, then we encounter a striking poverty of thought and the greatest obscurity; we find in them a completely unjustified pretension to decide questions lying outside their scope, as well as incessant contradiction between one thinker and another and even thinkers contradicting themselves. If we turn to those fields of knowledge that are not concerned with answering the questions of life but only with answering their own special, scientific questions, then we may be carried away by the power of the human intellect, but we know beforehand that we shall find no answers to the question of life. These areas of knowledge completely ignore the question of life. They say, "We cannot tell you what you are and why you live; we do not have the answers to these questions, and we are not concerned with them. If you need to know about the laws of light, however, or about chemical compounds or the laws governing the development of organisms; if you need to know about the laws governing physical bodies, their forms and the relation between their size and number; if you need to know about the laws of your own mind, then for all this we have clear, precise, indubitable answers." . . .

Thus no matter how I twist and turn the speculative answers of philosophy, I can obtain nothing resembling an answer; not because, as in the case of the clear, experimental sciences, the answer does not relate to my question, but because even though the sum of the intellectual labor is here directed toward my question, there is no answer. And instead of an answer, all one can obtain is the very same question put in a complicated form.

VI

In my search for answers to the question of life I felt exactly as a man who is lost in a forest.

I came to a clearing, climbed a tree, and had a clear view of the endless space around me. But I could see that there was no house and that there could be no house; I went into the thick of the forest, into the darkness, but again I could see no house — only darkness.

Thus I wandered about in the forest of human knowledge. On one side of me were the clearings of mathematical and experimental sciences, revealing to me sharp horizons; but in no direction could I see a house. On the other side of me was the darkness of the speculative sciences, where every step I took plunged me deeper into darkness, and I was finally convinced that there could be no way out.

When I gave myself over to the bright light of knowledge, I was only diverting my eyes from the question. However clear and tempting the horizons that opened up to me might have been, however tempting it was to sink into the infinity of this knowledge, I soon realized that the clearer this knowledge was, the less I needed it, the less it answered my question.

"Well," I said to myself, "I know everything that science wants so much to know, but this path will not lead me to an answer to the question of the meaning of my life." In the realm of speculative science I saw that in spite of — or rather precisely because of — the fact that this knowledge was designed to answer my question, there could be no answer other than the one I had given myself: What is the meaning of my life? It has none. Or: What will come of my life? Nothing. Or: Why does everything that is exist, and why do I exist? Because it exists.

From one branch of human knowledge I received an endless number of precise answers to questions I had not asked, answers concerning the chemical composition of the stars, the movement of the sun toward the constellation Hercules, the origin of the species and of man, the forms of infinitely small atoms, and the vibration of infinitely small and imponderable particles of ether. But the answer given by this branch of knowledge to my question about the meaning of my life was only this: you are what you call your life; you are a temporary, random conglomeration of particles. The thing that you have been led to refer to as your life is simply the mutual interaction and alteration of these particles. This conglomeration will continue for a certain period of time; then the interaction of these particles will come to a halt, and the thing you call your life will come to an end and with it all your questions. You are a little lump of something randomly stuck together. The lump decomposes. The decomposition of this lump is known as your life. The lump falls apart, and thus the decomposition ends, as do all your questions. Thus the clear side of knowledge replies, and if it strictly follows its own principles, there is no more to be said.

It turns out, however, that such an answer does not constitute a reply to the question. I must know the meaning of my life, but to say that it is a particle of infinity not only fails to give it any meaning but destroys all possible meaning.

The experimental, exact side of knowledge may strike some vague agreement with the speculative side, saying that the meaning of life lies in development and in the contributions made to this development. But given the innaccuracy and obscurity of such a remark, it cannot be regarded as an answer. . . .

Thus my wanderings among the fields of knowledge not only failed to lead me out of my despair but rather increased it. One area of knowledge did not answer the question of life; the other branch of knowledge did indeed answer, all the more confirming my despair and showing me that the thing that had befallen me was not due to an error on my part or to a sick state of mind. On the contrary, this area of knowledge confirmed for me the fact that I had been thinking correctly and had been in agreement with the most powerful minds known to humanity.

I could not be deceived. All is vanity. Happy is he who has never been born; death is better than life; we must rid ourselves of life.

IX

I ran into a contradiction from which there were only two ways out: either the thing that I had referred to as reason was not as rational as I had thought, or the thing that I took to be irrational was not as irrational as I had thought. And I began to examine the course of the arguments that had come of my rational knowledge.

As I looked more closely at this course, I found it to be entirely correct. The conclusion that life is nothing was unavoidable; but I detected a mistake. The mistake was that my thinking did not correspond to the question I had raised. The question was: Why should I live? Or: Is there anything real and imperishable that will come of my illusory and perishable life? Or: What kind of meaning can my finite existence have in this infinite universe? In order to answer this question, I studied life.

It was obvious that the resolution of all the possible questions of life could not satisfy me because my question, no matter how simple it may seem at first glance, entails a demand to explain the finite by means of the infinite and the infinite by means of the finite.

I asked, "What is the meaning of my life beyond space, time, and causation?" And I answered, "What is the meaning of my life within space, time, and causation?" After a long time spent in the labor of thought, it followed that I could reply only that my life had no meaning at all.

Throughout my reasoning I was constantly comparing the finite to the finite and the infinite to the infinite; indeed, I could not do otherwise. Thus I concluded and had to conclude that force is force, matter is matter, will is will, infinity is infinity, nothing is nothing; and I could not get beyond that.

It was something similar to what happens in mathematics when we are trying to figure out how to solve an equation and all we can get is an identity. The method for solving the equation is correct, but all we get for an answer is $a = a$, or $x = x$, or $o = o$. The same thing was happening with my reasoning in regard to the question concerning the significance of my life. The answers that all the sciences give to this question are only identities. . . .

Having understood this, I realized that I could not search for an answer to my question in rational knowledge. The answer given by rational knowledge is merely an indication that an answer can be obtained only by formulating the question differently, that is, only when the relationship between the finite and the infinite is introduced into the question. I also realized that no matter how irrational and unattractive the answers given by faith, they have the advantage of bringing to every reply a relationship between the finite and the infinite, without which there can be no reply. However I may put the question of how I am to live, the answer is: according to the law of God. Is there anything real that will come of my life? Eternal torment or eternal happiness. What meaning is there which is not destroyed by death? Union with the infinite God, paradise.

Thus in addition to rational knowledge, which before had seemed to be the only knowledge, I was inevitably led to recognize a different type of knowledge, an irrational type, which all of humanity had: faith, which provides us with the possibility of living. As far as I was concerned, faith was as irrational as ever, but I could not fail to recognize that it alone provides humanity with an answer to the question of life, thus making it possible to live.

Rational knowledge led me to the conclusion that life is meaning-less; my life came to a halt, and I wanted to do away with myself. As I looked around at people, I saw that they were living, and I was convinced that they knew the meaning of life. Then I turned and looked at myself; as long as I knew the meaning of life, I lived. As it was with others, so it was with me: faith provided me with the meaning of life and the possibility of living. . . .

No matter what answers a given faith might provide for us, every answer of faith gives infinite meaning to the finite existence of man, meaning that is not destroyed by suffering, deprivation, and death. Therefore, the meaning of life and the possibility of living may be found in faith alone. I realized that the essential significance of faith lies not only in the "manifestation of things unseen" and so on, or in revelation (this is simply a description of one of the signs of faith); nor is it simply the relation between man and God (faith must first be determined and then God, not the other way around), or agreeing with what one has been told, even though this is what it is most often understood to be. Faith is the knowledge of the meaning of human life, whereby the individual does not destroy himself but lives. Faith is the force of life. If a man lives, then he must have faith in something. If he did not believe that he had some-thing he must live for, then he would not live. If he fails to see and understand the illusory nature of the finite, then he believes in the finite; if he understands the illusory nature of the finite, then he must believe in the infinite. Without faith it is impossible to live. . . .

XII

. . . This is what happened to me at the time: in the course of a whole year, when almost every minute I was asking myself whether I should end it all with a rope or a bullet, when I was occupied with the thoughts and observations I have described, my heart was tormented with an agonizing feeling. This feeling I can only describe as a search for God.

I say that this search for God was born not of reason but of an emotion because it was a search that arose not from my thought process — indeed, it was in direct opposition to my thinking — but from my heart. It was a feeling of dread, of loneliness, of forlornness in the midst of all that was alien to me; and it was a feeling of hope for someone's help.

In spite of the fact that I was convinced of the impossibility of proving the existence of God (Kant had shown me, and I had fully understood him, that there can be no such proof), I nonetheless searched for God in the hope that I might find him, and according to an old habit of prayer, I addressed the one for whom I searched and could not find. In my mind I would go over the conclusions of Kant and Schopenhauer regarding the impossibility of proving the existence of God, and I would try to refute them. Causation, I would say to myself, is not in the same category of thought as space and time. If I exist, then there is something that causes me to exist, the cause of all causes. And this cause of all that exists is called God; and I dwelled on this thought and tried with all my being to recognize the presence of this cause. As soon as I was conscious of the existence of such a power over me, I felt the possibility of life. But I asked myself, "What is this cause, this power? How am I to think about it? What is my relation to this thing I call God?" And only the answer that was familiar to me came into my head: "He is the creator, the provider of all things." I was not satisfied with this answer, and I felt that the thing I needed in order to live was still missing, I was overcome with horror, and I began to pray to the one whom I sought, that he might help me. And the more I prayed, the more clear it became to me that he did not hear me and that there was absolutely no one I could turn to. My heart full of despair over the fact that there is no God, I cried, "Lord, have mercy on me, save me! O Lord, my God, show me the way!" But no one had mercy on me, and I felt that my life had come to a stop.

But again and again and from various directions I kept coming back to the conviction that I could not have come into the world without any motive, cause, or meaning, that I could not be the fledgling fallen from a nest that I felt myself to be. If I lie on my back in the tall grass and cry out like a fallen fledgling, it is because my mother brought me into the world, kept me warm, fed me, and loved me. But where is my mother now? If I have been cast out, then who has cast me out? I cannot help but feel that someone who loved me gave birth to me. Who is this someone? Again, God.

"He sees and knows of my search, my despair, my struggle," I would say to myself. "He exists." And as soon as I acknowledged this for an instant, life immediately rose up within me, and I could sense the possi-

bility and even the joy of being. But again I would shift from the acknow-
ledgment of the existence of God to a consideration of my relation to him,
and again there arose before me the God who is our creator, the God of the
Trinity, who sent his son, our Redeemer. And again, isolated from me and
from the world, God would melt away before my eyes like a piece of ice;
again nothing remained, again the source of life withered away. I was
overcome with despair and felt that there was nothing for me to do but kill
myself. And, worst of all, I felt that I could not bring myself to go through
with it.

I slipped into these situations not two or three times but tens and
hundreds of times — now joy and vitality, now despair and a consciousness of the impossibility of life.

I remember one day in early spring when I was alone in the forest
listening to the sounds of the woods. I listened and thought about the one
thing that had constantly occupied me for the last three years. Again I was
searching for God. . . .

But at that point I took a closer look at myself and at what had been
happening within me; and I remembered the hundreds of times I had
gone through these deaths and revivals. I remembered that I had lived
only when I believed in God. Then, as now, I said to myself, "As long as I
know God, I live; when I forget, when I do not believe in him, I die."
What are these deaths and revivals? It is clear that I do not live whenever
I lose my faith in the existence of God, and I would have killed myself
long ago if I did not have some vague hope of finding God. I truly live only
whenever I am conscious of him and seek him. "What, then, do I seek?" a
voice cried out within me. "He is there, the one without whom there
could be no life." To know God and to live come to one and the same
thing. God is life.

"Live, seeking God, for there can be no life without God." And more
powerfully than ever a light shone within me and all around me, and this
light has not abandoned me since.

Thus I was saved from suicide. When and how this transformation
within me was accomplished, I could not say. Just as the life force within
me was gradually and imperceptibly destroyed, and I encountered the
impossibility of life, the halting of life, and the need to murder myself, so
too did this life force return to me gradually and imperceptibly. And the
strange thing is that the life force which returned to me was not new but
very old; it was the same force that had guided me during the early
periods of my life. In essence I returned to the first things, to the things of
childhood and youth. I returned to a faith in that will which gave birth to
me and which asked something of me; I returned to the conviction that
the single most important purpose in my life was to be better, to live
according to this will. I returned to the conviction that I could find the
expression of this will in something long hidden from me, something that

all of humanity had worked out for its own guidance; in short, I returned to a belief in God, in moral perfection, and in a tradition that instills life with meaning. The only difference was that I had once accepted all this on an unconscious level, while now I knew that I could not live without it.

What happened to me was something like the following. Unable to recall how I got there, I found myself in a boat that had been launched from some unknown shore; the way to the other shore was pointed out to me, the oars were placed in my inexperienced hands, and I was left alone. I worked the oars as best I knew how and rowed on. But the further I paddled toward the center, the faster became the current that took me off-course, and I encountered more and more people who, like myself, were being carried away by the current. There were a few who continued to row; some had thrown away their oars. There were large boats, enormous ships, filled with people; some struggled against the current, others gave themselves up to it. And, looking downstream at everyone being carried along by the current, the further I rowed, the more I forgot the way that had been pointed out to me. At the very center of the current, in the throng of boats and ships being carried downstream, I lost my way altogether and threw down my oars. All around me, in joy and triumph, people rushed downstream under sail and oar, assuring me and each other that there could be no other direction. And I believed them and moved along with them. And I was carried off a long way, so far that I heard the roar of the rapids in which I was bound to perish and saw boats being destroyed in them. Then I came to my senses. For a long time I could not understand what had happened to me. I saw before me the singular ruin toward which I was rushing headlong and which I feared, I could not see salvation anywhere, and I did not know what to do. But, looking back, I saw countless boats that were relentlessly struggling against the current, and I remembered the oars and the way to the shore and began to pull against the current and head back upstream toward it.

The shore was God, the stream was tradition, and the oars were the free will given to me to make it to the shore where I would be joined with God. Thus the force of life was renewed withing me, and I began to live once again.

FRIEDRICH DURRENMATT

This short story by Friedrich Durrenmatt (1921–   ), Swiss playwright, novelist, and story writer, might serve as a metaphor for the stages Kierkegaard describes in Stages on Life's Way.

The Tunnel

The young man who boarded his usual train that Sunday afternoon was twenty-four years old and fat. He was fat in order to protect himself, for anything he perceived out of the ordinary terrified him. Indeed, this clarity of vision was probably the only real ability he possessed, and even this was a burden to him. Although his fat gave a general protection to his body, he found it necessary to stuff every sort of hole in his body through which the terrifying influences might reach him. He smoked cigars (Ormond Brazil 10). He wore a pair of sunglasses over his ordinary glasses. He even stuffed his ears with wads of cotton wool. At twenty-four he was still dependent on his parents, a consequence of rather nebulous studies at the University. And the University was two hours away from home by train. Departure time five-fifty. Arrival at seven twenty-seven.

   And so this student, fat and twenty-four years old, boarded his usual Sunday train to attend a seminar the following day. The fact that he had already decided to skip class was irrelevant. As he left his home town the afternoon sun shone from a cloudless summer sky. It was pleasant weather for a trip he knew almost by heart. The train's route lay between the Alps and the Juras, past rich villages and towns, over a river and, after some twenty minutes further travel, into a little tunnel just beyond Burgdorf. The train was overcrowded and he had entered at one of the front cars. With considerable difficulty he worked his way toward the rear. Perspiring, and with two pairs of glasses, he offered an oafish appearance. All the travellers were sitting closely packed some even on suitcases. All the second-class compartments were relatively empty. The young man fought through the melee of families and recruits, students and lovers, falling against this one or that one as the train swayed, stumbling against stomachs and breasts until he came to a seat in the last car. At last he had found space enough to have a bench to himself, a pleasant surprise, since third-class coaches are seldom divided into compartments with benches. Opposite him, playing a solitary game of chess, he noted a man even fatter than himself, and on the same bench, near the corridor, sat a red-haired girl reading a novel. The young man gratefully chose the window seat on the empty bench. He had just lit an Ormond Brazil 10 when the train entered the little tunnel. Of course he had travelled this stretch many times before, almost every Saturday and Sunday throughout the past year, but he had never found the opportunity to examine the tunnel closely. He had, in fact, been only vaguely aware of it. Several times he had intended to give it his full attention, but each time he had been thinking of other matters, and each time the brief plunge into darkness had passed unnoticed, so fast was the train and so brief its plunge into the darkness of the little tunnel.

And even this time he had not been thinking of the tunnel and so had forgotten to take off his sunglasses. Outside the tunnel the sun had been shinning with all its force, flooding the hills and woods and the distant chain of the Juras with golden evening light. Even the little houses of the town through which they had just passed had seemed built of gold. This abrupt passage from light to darkness must then be the reason why the tunnel seemed so much longer than usual. He waited patiently in the dark compartment for the return to daylight. At any moment the first pale shimmer of daylight would gleam on his window-pane, widen as quickly as a flash of lightning, then close in powerfully with its full yellow brightness. Nevertheless, the darkness lasted. He took off his sunglasses. At about the same time the girl lit a cigarette. As her match flared orange he thought he detected a grim annoyance in her face. No doubt she resented the interruption in her perusal of her novel. He looked at his wristwatch. The luminous dial said six-ten.

He leaned back, settling himself in the corner between window and compartment wall, and directed his thoughts to the complications of his studies. No one really believed he was studying at all. He thought of the seminar he had to attend. Each of his activities seemed a pretext designed to achieve order behind the facade of routine pursuits. Perhaps what he sought was not order itself, but only a semblance of order. The art of an actor who used his fat, his cigars and his cotton wool as make-up for a genteel comedy, while all the while he knew himself to be a part of some monstrous farce. When he next looked at his watch the time was six-fifteen. The train was still in the tunnel. He felt confused. At last the light bulbs flickered and the compartment brightened. The red-haired girl returned to her novel and the fat gentleman resumed his solitary chess game. The whole compartment now appeared reflected in the window. But outside, on the other side of the window, the tunnel was still there.

He stepped into the corridor in which a tall man was walking up and down restlessly. He observed the light raincoat and the black scarf around the gentleman's neck. Surely there was no need for a scarf in this weather? A black scarf? He peered into the other compartments in the rear coach. The passengers were reading their newspapers or chatting. Normal. He returned to his corner and sat down. The tunnel must come to an end any minute now. At any second? His wrist watch read six-twenty. He felt an obscure annoyance with himself for not having paid more attention to the tunnel on previous trips. They had been in the tunnel for a quarter of an hour now. And surely, allowing for the speed of the train, it must be one of the longest tunnels in Switzerland. Or perhaps he had taken the wrong train. But he could recall no other tunnel of such length and importance within twenty minutes of his home. On impulse he asked the fat chess player if the train were indeed bound for Zurich. The man confirmed this. The student ventured again that he hadn't known that there was such a long tunnel on this part of the journey. The chess player was more than a little annoyed to have his difficult considerations interrupted a second time. He replied testily that in Switzerland there were a great many tunnels, in fact, an extraordinary number of tunnels, that he was actually travelling in Switzerland for the first time, but that an affluence of tunnels was the first thing one noticed about Switzerland, and indeed, his statistical almanac confirmed the fact that no country possessed such a positive abundance of tunnels as Switzerland! And he added that now he must excuse himself; he was very sorry, really, but a most difficult chess problem in regard to the Nimzowitsch Defense occupied his mind and he could afford no further diversions. The last remark was polite, but firm. It was evident that no further conversation could be expected from the chess player and, in any event, he could be of little use, since the route was new to him.

At that moment the conductor appeared, and the student had high hopes that his ticket would be refused. The official was pale and scrawny. He gave an impression of nervousness as he remarked to the girl near the door that she would have to change trains at Olten. Although Olten was also a regular stop on the Zurich run, the young man did not give up hope of being on the wrong train, so complete was his conviction that he had mistaken trains in boarding. He didn't doubt that he would have to pay extra fare, but he accepted the expense with equanimity. The return to daylight would be cheap at the price. He therefore handed his ticket to the conductor and said that his destination was Zurich. He accomplished the speech without once removing the Ormond Brazil 10 from his mouth.

"But the gentleman is on the right train," replied the conductor as he inspected the ticket.

"But we're going through a tunnel!" The young man had spoken with considerable anger. He was determined to put an end to the confusion. The official replied that they had just passed Herzogenbuchsee and would soon approach Langenthal where the train was due at six-twenty. The young man looked at his watch. Six-twenty. But they had been travelling through the tunnel for the past twenty minutes, he persisted. The conductor raised his brows.

"This is the Zurich train," he said, now looking for the first time toward the window. "Six-twenty," he said again, uneasily. "We'll be in Olten soon. Arrival time six thirty-seven. We must have gone into some bad weather suddenly. A storm. Yes. That's why it's dark."

The gentleman with the Nimzowitsch Defense problem entered the conversation now. He had been holding out his ticket (and holding up his game) for some time, but the conductor had not yet noticed him. "Nonsense," he interjected. "Nonsense! We're travelling through a tunnel. I can see the rock clearly. Looks like granite. Switzerland has more tunnels than all the rest of the world put together. Read it in a statistical almanac."

The conductor relieved him of his ticket, and repeated pleadingly that this was truly the Zurich train. Unmollified, the young man demanded to speak to the Chief Conductor. The ticket collector now felt his dignity to have been abused. He directed the student to the front of the train, but reiterated huffily that the train was going to Zurich, that the time was now six twenty-five, that in twelve minutes time (according to the summer schedule) the train would arrive in Olten, and that the young man should have no further doubts on that point. *He* travelled this train at least twelve times a month.

Nevertheless the young scholar set off to find the Chief Conductor. Movement through the crowded train now seemed even more difficult than before. The train must be travelling exceedingly fast. In any event, it was making a frightful racket. He stuffed the wads of cotton a little more firmly into his ears, for he had loosened them in order to speak to the ticket collector. The passengers were behaving calmly. This train was no different from any other Sunday afternoon train, and no one appeared worried. In the second-class compartments he came upon an Englishman standing by the corridor window. "Simplon," he was saying, as he tapped the pane with his pipe and beamed inanely.

Things were very much as usual in the dining car too. No seats were vacant, and neither waiters nor diners, occupied with Wiener Schnitzel and rice, made any comment on the tunnel. But there, near the exit of the dining car, he recognized the red bag of the Chief Conductor.

"What can I do for you, sir?" The Chief Conductor was a tall man, quiet behind a carefully groomed black mustache and neat rimless glasses.

"We have been in a tunnel for twenty-five minutes."

The Conductor did not look toward the windows, as the young man might have expected, but turned to a nearby waiter. "Give me a packet of Ormond 10," he said. "I smoke the same brand as the gentleman here." The waiter, however, indicated that the brand was not in stock, and the young man, glad of an opportunity for further conversation, proffered a Brazil.

"Thank you," replied the Conductor. "In Olten I shall hardly have time to buy any. You are doing me a great favor. Smoking is a most important business. Will you come this way, please?"

Mystified, the young man followed him into the freight car ahead of the diner.

"The next car is the locomotive," offered the official. "This is the front of the train."

A sickly yellow light burned amid the baggage. Most of the car lay in total darkness. The side doors were barred, as was the small window beside them, and through its irons the greater blackness of the tunnel seeped in. The trunks, many decorated with hotel stickers, the bicycles and the baby carriage that composed the cargo of the coach seemed haphazardly arranged. The Chief Conductor, an obviously precise man, hung his red bag on a nearby hook.

"What can I do for you?" he asked again, without, however, looking at the student. Instead, he began to enter neat columns in a book he had taken from his pocket.

"We have been in a tunnel since Burgdorf," answered the young man with determination. "There is no such enormous tunnel on this line. I know. I travel back and forth every week on this train."

The Chief Conductor continued to write. "Sir," he said, stepping close to his inquisitor, so close that their bodies almost touched, "sir, I have little to tell you. I have no idea how we got into this tunnel. I have no explanation for it. But I ask you to consider this. We are moving along on tracks: therefore this tunnel leads somewhere. We have no reason whatever to believe that anything is wrong with this tunnel, except, of course, that there seems to be no end to it." The Chief Conductor still held the unlit Ormond Brazil 10 between his lips. He had spoken extremely quietly, yet with such dignity and clarity, and with such assurance, that his words were audible despite the increased noise of the baggage car.

"Then I must ask you to stop the train," said the young man impatiently. "I really don't understand you. If there's something wrong with this tunnel — and it seems you can't explain even its existence — then your duty is to stop this train at once."

"Stop the train?" returned the older man slowly. It seemed he had already thought of that, but, as he informed his companion, it was a serious matter to stop a train. With this, he shut the book and laid it in the red bag which was swaying to and fro on its hook. Then he carefully lit the Ormond 10. The young man offered to pull the emergency brake overhead, and was on the point of releasing the lever, when suddenly he staggered forwards and was sent crashing against the wall. At the same moment, the baby carriage rolled toward him and several trunks slid by.

The Chief Conductor swayed strangely and began to move, hands out-stretched, through the freight car.

"We are going downhill!" he announced as he joined the young man now leaning against the wall. But the expected crash of hurtling train against granite tunnel did not occur. There was no shattering of tele-scoped coaches. Once again the train seemed to be running on a level. The door opened at the other end of the car. In the bright light of the diner, until the door swung to again, they could see the passengers merrily toasting one another's health.

"Come into the locomotive." At this point the Chief Conductor was peering thoughtfully, almost menacingly at the student. He opened the door nearby. As he did so a rush of tempestuous heat-laden air struck the pair with such force that they were driven back against the wall. At the same moment a frightful clatter resounded through the almost empty freight car.

"We'll have to climb over the engine," he cried into the younger man's ear. Despite his shouting, his voice was hardly audible. He then disappeared through the right-angle of the open doorway. The student followed cautiously in the direction of the swaying and brightly lit en-gine. He didn't know why he was climbing, but at this point determina-tion had overcome reason. He found himself on a pitching platform between the two cars, and clung desperately to the iron rails on both sides. Although the terrific draught moderated but slightly as he inched his way up to the locomotive, he dreaded the wind less than the immedi-ate nearness of the tunnel walls. They were hidden from him in the blackness, but were nevertheless frighteningly close. It was necessary to focus all his attention on the engine ahead, yet the pounding of the wheels and the hissing vibrating push of air against him gave him the feeling of careening, at the speed of a falling star, into a world of stone.

A board just wide enough to walk on crossed the gap between the cars and ran the length of the engine. Above and parallel to it, a curving metal rod served as railing. To reach the plank he would have to make a jump of nearly a yard. He braced himself, leapt, and pushed himself along the board. His progress was slow, since he had to press close to the outside of the engine to keep his foothold. It was not until he reached the long side of the engine and was fully exposed to the roaring hurricane of wind and to the menacing cliff walls now brilliantly illuminated by the engine lights that he began to realize his fear. But just then he was rescued by the Chief Conductor who pulled him through a small door into the engine. Exhausted, the young man lay against the wall. He was grateful for the sudden quiet. With the engine door shut, the steel walls of the giant locomotive deadened the noise almost completely.

"Well, we've lost the Ormond Brazil too," said the Conductor. "It wasn't a very sensible idea to light one before starting the climb, but they break so easily in one's pocket. It's their unusual length."

The young man was delighted to converse normally again. The close and terrifying rock walls had reminded him uncomfortably of his everyday world, of its ever similar days and years. The thought occurred to him that their boring similitude had perhaps been only a preparation for the present moment: that this was a moment of initiation, of truth, this departure from the surface of the earth and precipitous descent into the womb of the earth. He took another brown package from his right coat pocket and offered the Chief Conductor a new cigar. He took one himself, and carefully they lit their Brazils from the Conductor's lighter.

I am very fond of these Ormonds," said the older man, "but one must pull very hard on them. Otherwise they go out so easily."

For some reason these words made the student suspicious. Was the Conductor as uncomfortable as he about the tunnel? For the tunnel still ran on interminably, and his mind persisted in the thought that surely the tunnel must stop, even as a dream can end, all of a sudden.

"Six-forty," he said, consulting his watch. "We should be in Olten now." Even as he spoke, he thought of the hills and woods radiant only a short while ago in the late golden sun. The thought could have been present in both their minds. Nevertheless, the two men stood and smoked and leaned against their wall.

"Keller is my name," announced the Conductor as he puffed at his Brazil.

The student refused to change the topic of conversation.

"The climb to the engine was very dangerous, didn't you think? At least it was for me. I'm not used to that sort of thing. Anyway, I'd like to know why you've brought me here."

"I don't know," said Keller. "I wanted time to consider."

"Time to consider?"

"Yes," returned the Chief Conductor. "That's right." And he went on smoking. Just then the engine reeled over at a still steeper angle.

"We could go into the engineer's cabin," suggested Keller. He did not, however, leave his position against the wall. Annoyed by his companion's indecisiveness, the young man stepped briskly along the corridor to the driver's cabin, then abruptly stopped.

"Empty!" he said to the Conductor who had now moved up behind him. "The driver's seat is empty!" They went into the cabin. It was swaying too, for the engine was still tearing through the tunnel at enormous speed, bearing the train along with it, as though the weight of the coaches behind no longer counted.

"Allow me," said the Chief Conductor. He pressed some levers and pulled the emergency brake. There was no change. "We tried to stop the engine earlier. As soon as we noticed the alteration in the tracks. It didn't stop then either."

"It certainly isn't stopping now," said the other. He pointed to the speed indicator. "A hundred. Has the engine ever done a hundred before?"

"Good heavens! It has never gone so fast. Sixty-five at the most."

"Exactly. And the speed is increasing. Now the speedometer says a hundred and five. We must be falling." He went up to the window, but he couldn't keep his balance. He was pressed with his face against the glass, so fantastic was their speed. "The engine driver?" he shouted as he stared at the rock masses streaking towards him in the glare of the arc lights, disappearing above him and below him on either side of the engineer's cabin.

"He jumped off," Keller yelled back. He was now sitting on the floor, his back against the controls.

"When?" The student pursued the matter obstinately. Keller hesitated a while. He decided to relight his Ormond, an awkward task, for his legs were then at the same height as his head while the train continued its roll to one side.

"Five minutes after the switch. No use thinking to save him. Freight car man abandoned the train too."

"And you?" asked the student.

"I am in charge of this train. I, too, have always lived without hope."

"Without hope," repeated the young man. By then he was lying on the glass pane, face pressed against glass. Glass and engine and human flesh were pressed together above the abyss. "Back in the compartment," he thought, "we had entered the tunnel, but we didn't know that even then everything was already lost. We didn't think that anything had changed, and yet the shaft of the depths had already received us, and we had entered our abyss."

"I'll have to go to the rear," shouted the Chief Conductor. "The coaches will be in a panic. Everyone will be trying to get to the rear of the train."

"That's true." The student thought of the chessplayer and of the red-haired girl with her novel. He handed Keller his remaining packages of Ormond Brazil. "Take them. You'll lose your cigar again when you climb over."

"Aren't you coming?" The Conductor was once more on his feet and with difficulty he had begun to clamber up the funnel of the corridor. The student gazed at the useless instruments, at the useless ridiculous levers and switches shining silver-like in the glare of the cabin lights.

"A hundred and thirty," he called. "I don't think you'll be able to get to the coaches above us at this speed."

"It's my duty," shouted Keller over his shoulder.

"Certainly," returned the young man. He didn't bother turning his head to watch the other's senseless efforts.

"At least I have to try," yelled the Conductor. He was already far over the head of the fat young man. He braced elbows and thighs against slippery walls and seemed, indeed, to be making some progress. But just then the engine took a further turn downwards. It hurtled toward the interior of the earth, goal of all things, in its terrible plunge. Keller now was directly over his friend who lay face downwards on the silver gleaming window at the bottom of the driver's cabin. His strength gave. Suddenly he fell, crashed against the control panel and came to rest on the window beside his companion.

"What are we to do?" he cried, clinging to the young man's shoulders and shouting into his ear. The very fact that it was now necessary to shout alarmed him. The noise of the onrushing walls had destroyed even the quiet of the engine.

The younger man lay motionless on the pane of glass which separated him from the depths below. His fat body and weighty flesh were of no further use to him, no protection now.

"What are we to do?" persisted the Chief Conductor.

"Nothing," came the merciless reply. Merciless, yet not without a certain ghostly cheerfulness. Now, for the first time, his glasses were gone and his eyes were wide open. Greedily he sucked in the abyss through those wide-open eyes. Glass and metal splinters from the shattered control panel now studded his body. And still he refused to tear his thirsting eyes from the deadly spectacle below. As the first crack widened in the window beneath them, a current of air whistled into the cabin. It seized his two wads of cotton wool and swept them upwards like arrows into the corridor shaft overhead. He watched them briefly and spoke once more.

"Nothing. God let us fall. And now we'll come upon him."

chapter 3

God Is Dead and We Have Murdered Him: Nietzsche and the Attack on Morality

Every brute inversion knows the disinherited to whom the past no longer belongs, and not yet the future.

    Rilke

A philosopher: alas, a being who often runs away from himself, is often afraid of himself — but whose curiosity always makes him 'come to himself' again.

    Nietzsche, *Beyond Good and Evil,* no. 292

Although I know of no one who shares my views, as I have already said, I am conceited enough to think that I have not thought individually but collectively. I have the most curious feeling of solitude and multitude; of being a herald who has hastened on in advance without knowing whether the band of knights is following or not — in fact, whether they are still living.

    Nietzsche-Wagner Correspondence, p. 307

INTRODUCTION

Friedrich Nietzsche (1844–1899), like Kierkegaard, was not, strictly speaking, a philosopher. The son and grandson of Lutheran ministers, Nietzsche was trained as a philologist. Yet he profoundly changed the course of future philosophy; indeed, the spate of recent books on Nietzsche's philosophy (see the references at the end of this chapter) testifies to his enduring impact.

    Though Nietzsche, as far as we know, never read any of Kierkegaard's work, there are striking similarities in the two men's lives and views. For example, both Kierkegaard and Nietzsche were solitary individuals who experienced ill health much of their lives, Nietzsche from what was probably syphilis. Throughout his life, Nietzsche suffered from a fragile constitution, which included weak eyesight and a nervous stomach. In fact, he had to resign his post as Professor of Classical Philology at the University of Basel in Switzerland (which he received when he was only twenty-four) because of his deteriorating health. Nietzsche came to blame his medical problems on the excessive demands of the life of scholarship. Indeed, Nietzsche often wrote of the importance his illness played in his work:

> The daily battle against headache and the laughable diversity of my ailments demand such an amount of attention that I am running into the danger of becoming petty — but this is a counterweight to those very . . . high-flying tendencies that have such power over me that without some counterweight to them I would become a fool.
>
> Ecce Homo, *p. 26*

Both Kierkegaard and Nietzsche attacked organized religion, rejecting the weakness and mediocrity they thought essential to it. Like Kierkegaard, who viewed the "principle of association" as one which strengthens individuals numbers but weakens one ethically, so Nietzsche sought to combat the concept of "humanity" as well as the ideals of equality and unity among persons. "Insanity in individuals is something rare — but in groups, parties, nations, and epochs it is the rule." (*Beyond Good and Evil,* no. 156) Further, both Kierkegaard and Nietzsche viewed themselves as subversives. Just as the madman in Nietzsche's writing declares "I come too early," both Kierkegaard and Nietzsche felt out of place in their own times and cultures. Both had productive periods that lasted only ten years. Both wrote unremitting attacks on the cultural attitudes and values of their times. Nietzsche, for example, cites approvingly one review of one of his books: "Spiritual, just like material, explosive can serve a very useful purpose; it need not be misused for criminal ends. Only one does well, wherever such stuff is stored to declare plainly: 'This is dynamite!' " (Fuss and Shapiro, p. 92)[1]

In addition, both Kierkegaard and Nietzsche write in styles that are not typical of traditional philosophy. Their writings are frequently aphoristic, sometimes (at least superficially) contradictory, and often ambiguous. Nietzsche wrote that "the demand for an adequate mode of expression is senseless," (*Will to Power*, p. 625) and he consistently refused to limit himself to one writing style. This "stylistic pluralism" (Nehemas) has confused many readers of his. But Nietzsche tells us that his style intends quite deliberately to "create a distance" while opening

---

[1] The author of the quote is Joseph Viktor Widmann, a Swiss writer and editor of the *Berner Bund*. Interestingly, dynamite had been recently invented.

the ears of the audience to which he wishes to communicate. "One does not only wish to be understood when one writes; one wishes just as surely *not* to be understood." *(Gay Science,* p. 381) Like Kierkegaard, Nietzsche's style tends to be hyperbolic; this style of "shouting" guarantees that his readers — whatever reactions they might have to his work — will not be indifferent. Finally, Nietzsche almost never dwells on a particular subject. Nietzsche himself compares this technique to a cold bath where one must get in and out quickly.

Both Kierkegaard and Nietzsche view themselves more as diagnosticians of the maladies of their age than as theoreticians offering prescriptions. Nietzsche, however, rejects the most fundamental aspect of Kierkegaard's philosophical view: Christianity. Indeed, Nietzsche saw Christianity as the villain and urged that "Christianity is ripe for an autopsy." Nietzsche took pride in his willingness to lop off comforting beliefs, and his challenges to God and Christianity were profound. God, declares Nietzsche, is dead, leaving a void that only humans can seek to fill. But, though Nietzsche was an iconoclast, he was deeply troubled by the spiritual vacuum left by the death of God. Indeed, the following passage is one of the most wrenching in all of Nietzsche's writings:

The madman jumped into their midst and pierced them with his eyes. "Whither is God?" He cried; "I will tell you. *We have killed him* — you and I. All of us are his murderers. But how did we do this? How could we drink up the sea? Who gave us the sponge to wipe away the entire horizon? What were we doing when we unchained this earth from its sun? Whither is it moving now? Whither are we moving? Away from all suns? Are we not plunging continually? Backward, sideward, forward, in all directions? Is there still any up or down? Are we not straying as through an infinite nothing? Do we not feel the breath of empty space? Has it not become colder? Is not night continually closing in on us? Do we not need to light lanterns in the morning? Do we hear nothing as yet of the noise of the gravediggers who are burying God? Do we smell nothing as yet of the divine decomposition? Gods, too, decompose. God is dead. God remains dead. And we have killed him.

How shall we comfort ourselves, the murderers of all murderers? What was holiest and mightiest of all that the world has yet owned has bled to death under our knives: who will wipe this blood off us? What water is there for us to clean ourselves? What festivals of atonement, what sacred games shall we have to invent? Is not the greatness of this deed too great for us? Must we ourselves not become gods simply to appear worthy of it? There has never been a greater deed; and whoever is born after us — for the sake of this deed he will belong to a higher history than all history hitherto.

Gay Science, *p. 125*

And Nietzsche, like the madman, believes that few are truly ready to hear him:

> Here the madman fell silent and looked again at his listener; and they, too, were silent and stared at him in astonishment. At last he threw his lantern on the ground, and it broke into pieces and went out. "I have come too early," he said then; "my time is not yet. This tremendous event is still on its way, still wandering; it has not yet reached the ears of men. Lightning and thunder require time; the light of the stars requires time; deeds, though done, still require time to be seen and heard. This deed is still more distant from them than the most distant stars — *and yet they have done it themselves."*
>
> Gay Science, *p. 125*

For Nietzsche, "all religions are at bottom systems of cruelty," *(Genealogy of Morals,* p. 193) forcing us to sacrifice our own "instincts," reducing us to "ascetics" and "anti-natural fanatics." *(Beyond Good and Evil,* no. 55) Christianity has been tried; it is time, Nietzsche maintained, to discover something new.

> Why atheism nowadays? 'The father' in God is thoroughly refuted; equally so 'the judge,' 'the rewarder.' Also his 'free will': he does not hear — and even if he did, he would not know how to help. The worst is that he seems incapable of communicating himself clearly; is he uncertain? — This is what I have made out (by questioning and listening at a variety of conversations) to be the cause of the decline of European theism; it appears to me that though the religious instinct is in vigorous growth, — it rejects the theistic satisfaction with profound distrust.
>
> Beyond Good and Evil, *no. 53*

With Nietzsche's vision of atheism comes a kind of innocence, a rejection of the guilt and sin and asceticism that he believed inevitably accompany most modern religions, Christianity in particular. Such religions make us despise our bodies, ourselves; they make loving oneself a vice. Instead, Nietzsche sought to embrace this world and to reject the representatives of religion whom he calls "the preachers of death":

> There are the consumptives of the soul: they are hardly born before they begin to die and to long for doctrines of weariness and renunciation.
> They would like to be dead, and we should approve their wish! Let us guard against awakening these dead men and damaging these living coffins.
> They encounter an invalid or an old man or a corpse; and straightway they say 'Life is refuted!'
> But only they are refuted, they and their eye that sees only one aspect of existence.

> Muffled in deep depression, longing for the little accidents that bring about death: thus they wait and clench their teeth.
>
> Thus Spake Zarathustra, *p. 72*

Preaching of "eternal life" is, for Nietzsche, no different from teaching of death. Both are weary of life, weighed down by what he often refers to as the "spirit of gravity" (see pp. 209–10), which makes "earth and life heavy." This spirit of gravity, Nietzsche tells us, is the heaviest of burdens, for it represses the truth and places good and evil outside of each of us. We learn this heaviness almost from birth, when we are taught the notions of "good" and "evil" and are laden with the burden of values foreign to us. As a result, all morality becomes a common morality and life is a kind of barren desert. The spirit of gravity is the spirit of pessimism and nihilism. In its place, we must learn to love ourselves, to "stand and to walk and to run and to climb and to dance." And someday we will be weightless.

For Nietzsche, the death of God and the destruction of Christianity are world-historical events whose significance cannot be underestimated. He despises those "humanists" who reject God casually, "not wish(ing) to disturb anyone's peace of mind." ("David Strauss," p. 29) The end of Christianity is not an isolated setback whose recovery is simple and immediate. Rather, Christianity's demise opens up an abyss into which traditional concepts of morality, of goodness and evil, fall crashing.

> . . . The concept 'God' invented as the antithetical concept to life — everything harmful, noxious, slanderous, the whole mortal enmity against life, brought into one terrible unity! The concept 'the Beyond', 'real world' invented so as to deprive of value the *only* world which exists — so as to leave over no goal, no reason, no task for our earthly reality! The concept 'soul,' 'spirit,' finally even 'immortal soul,' invented so as to despise the body, so as to make it sick — 'holy' — so as to bring to all things in life which deserve serious attention, the questions of nutriment, residence, cleanliness, weather, a horrifying frivolity! Instead of health, 'salvation of the soul.' — which is to say a ridiculous choice between spasms of atonement and redemption hysteria! The concept 'sin' invented together with the instrument of torture which goes with it, the concept of 'free will,' as to confuse the instincts, so as to make mistrust of the instincts into second nature!
>
> Ecce Homo, *pp. 133–34*

Christianity has reversed concepts of morality and distorted all values. Nietzsche is not so concerned to prove Christianity "wrong" ("What have I to do with refutations!" [*Genealogy of Morals*, p. 4]) but rather to show the view for what it is.

In the concept of the 'selfless' of the 'self-denying' the actual badge of decadence, being lured by the harmful, no longer being able to discover where one's advantage lies, self-destruction, made the sign of value in general, made 'duty,' 'holiness,' the 'divine' in man! Finally — it is the most fearful — in the concept of the *good* man common cause made with everything weak, sick, ill-constituted, suffering from itself, all that *which ought to perish* — the law of *selection* crossed, an ideal made of opposition to the proud and well-constituted, to the affirmative man, to the man certain of the future and guaranteeing the future — the latter is henceforth called the evil man. . . . And this was all believed in *as morality*!

Genealogy of Morals, *p.4*

THE TRANSVALUATION OF VALUES

The falsification of everything real by morality stands there in all its glory; a pitiful psychology; the philosopher reduced to a country parson. — And for all that Plato *is to blame! He is still Europe's greatest misfortune.*

(Nietzsche, letter to Franz Overbeck, A *Self-Portrait from His Letters,* no. 114, p. 94)

Like Kierkegaard, Nietzsche saw the world in decline. The optimism of the Enlightenment is nowhere to be found in Nietzsche. In the preface to *The Will to Power*, for example, he writes:

What I relate is the history of the next two centuries. I describe what is coming, what can no longer come differently: *the advent of nihilism*. This history can be related even now; for necessity itself is at work here. This future speaks even now in a hundred signs, this destiny announces itself everywhere; for this music of the future all ears are cocked even now. For some time now, our whole European culture has been moving as toward a catastrophe, with a tortured tension that is growing from decade to decade: restlessly, violently, headlong, like a river that wants to reach the end, that no longer reflects, that is afraid to reflect. (p. 2)

The term *nihilism,* as we saw in chapter 1 (see pp. 40–41), was first coined in Russia in the second quarter of the nineteenth century. For Nietzsche, nihilism itself is the inevitable outcome of dependence on traditional absolutist morality. It is, therefore, the next logical step after Christianity and Enlightenment faith in progress. "*Radical nihilism* is the conviction of an absolute untenability of existence when it comes to the highest values one recognizes; plus the realization that we lack the least right to posit a beyond or an in-itself of things that might be 'divine' or morality incarnate." (*Will to Power,* p. 3) Indeed, for Nietzsche, "every purely moral value system . . . ends in nihilism." (p. 16) Nihilism is a transitional stage during which we realize that the values we've inherited are "shabby" and meaningless. Systems like Hegel's (see chapter 2, pp. 93–95) are finally seen for what they are: smoke screens meant to hide the fact that there are no absolute values, there is no goal or end to existence, and no real unity is possible. Nihilism is *not*, for Nietzsche, the problem; rather, it is a symptom of a complete breakdown, "a decline and recession of the power of the spirit." (*Will to Power*, p. 17) But it can also be, then, an indication of strength; "it is only late that one musters the courage for what one really knows." (p. 18)

Once we have smashed the false idols of objective right and wrong, we can begin to seek "new values." "He who has to be a creator in good and evil, truly, has first to be a destroyer and break values." (See p. 209.) Only the strongest are able to do this, for it means having to overcome two thousand years of Christianity. For Nietzsche this means being an "absolutely honest" or "straightforward" atheist untainted by any last vestiges of theology.

Nietzsche's training as a philologist provides him with the basis for this new understanding of morality. In considering this development (or genealogy) of morals, Nietzsche examines the dynamic in social relations from which morality emerges. What is most important about genealogy is that it reveals the origins of things we customarily take to be immutable facts. "The truth is hard," Nietzsche tells us, but as we begin to look at the origins of morality, a pattern emerges.

If we have the strength to overcome the lies we have been taught, we come to see that Christianity is but one perspective — neither absolute nor eternal. *The Genealogy of Morals* (see p. 196) begins with the statement, "We knowers are unknown to ourselves," and for Nietzsche there can be no truth without the recognition of the *subject* for whom it is the truth. For this reason Nietzsche rejects any form of dogmatism that claims to be "the" truth. As Zarathustra notes, "*the* way — that does not exist." (Part III, p. 11) It is part of the development of morality that its origin is forgotten; Nietzsche's "perspectivism" demands that that origin be explored. Nietzsche asks, "Under what conditions did man construct the value judgments *good* and *evil*? And what is their intrinsic worth?" (*Genealogy of Morals*, p. 151)

As the selection from *Beyond Good and Evil* (see pp. 190–95) notes, the noble person views himself or herself as the "creator of values." Each caste — master and slave — separates itself from the other, the master despising the slave, the slave full of what Nietzsche calls *ressentiment* for the master. The master's morality springs from a sense of power, whereas the slave's morality is "essentially the morality of utility." (*Beyond Good and Evil*, no. 260) Most likely, Nietzsche imagines, the morality of such a group will be based on denunciation and negativity. Unable to fight back in any real way, the slave creates an ideology that condemns power and material comfort as evil. Thus, "rancor" turns into something creative by "giving birth to values." (p. 198) The slave revolt in morality was an inversion of previous values; hence, what was considered good (e.g., wealth, power, even "world") becomes negative. In contrast, the "true morality" of the noble class grows out of triumphant self-affirmation, uniting action and morality, saying yes to all that is. The slave, however, "impotent and oppressed," is full of "bottled-up aggressions," (p. 199) and so must construct an illusion of happiness in reaction to the powerful. These "smalltime counterfeiters" are miserable, but they again twist values to reconstruct their misery as a sign of God's love:

> But they tell me that this very misery is the sign of their election by God, that one beats the dog one loves best, that this misery is perhaps also a preparation, a test, a kind of training, perhaps even more than that: something for which eventually they will be compensated with tremendous interest — in gold? No, in happiness. They call this *bliss*. (p. 202)

According to Nietzsche, the noble person takes pride in his or her self and in the accomplishments of that self. And the noble person's greatest delight comes in being different. The slave, in contrast, wants everyone to conform to one morality, since any sign of distinction would undermine the illusion that morality is a fact. Suffering, too, must be explained. We all ask "Whose fault is this?", and for Nietzsche, the worst part of suffering is that there is no answer to that question. But the "ascetic priest" comes along and gives a reason to suffering. He says, "Somebody must be at fault here, but that somebody is yourself" (p. 205); he thereby uses guilt to destroy life and to rob it of joy.

Is Nietzsche here guilty of what is now called the "genetic fallacy," that is, of confusing the origin of something with its nature or value? That the origin of some value, say, humility, is objectionable, does not entail that humility is itself objectionable. But this is not what Nietzsche is claiming. Rather, he wants to show that there are no "timeless and essential secrets" (Foucault, p. 142) behind values and practices. And, in exposing their origins, he believes he has shown that they are anti-life. This makes Nietzsche's own view perspectival, and he is aware of this. Does this undermine the value of Nietzsche's analysis? No, declares Nietzsche; indeed, he readily grants that "this also is only interpretation," adding, "so much the better." (*Beyond Good and Evil*, p. 22)

For Nietzsche, both slave and master offer perspectives on existence. As we have noted, for Nietzsche, there is no ultimate description of the world. Thus, no value is objectively true or false. As Zarathustra states, "unchanging good and evil does not exist." (p. 208)

. . . To speak of right and wrong *per se* makes no sense at all. No act of violence, rape, exploitation, destruction, is intrinsically 'unjust,' since life itself is violent, rapacious, exploitative, and destructive and cannot be conceived otherwise. Even more disturbingly, we have to admit that from the biological point of view legal conditions are necessarily exceptional conditions, since they limit the radical life-will bent on power and must finally subserve, as means, life's collective purpose, which is to create greater power constellations. To accept any legal system as sovereign and universal — to accept it, not merely as an instrument in the struggle of power complexes, but as a *weapon against struggle* . . . is an anti-vital principle which can only bring abut man's utter demoralization and indirectly, a reign of nothingness.

Genealogy of Morals, *p. 208*

This is why genealogy is so powerful, for it reveals the particular motivation behind a perspective like Christianity. This technique makes it impossible to treat any view as final and objective. Thus, for Nietzsche, there is no reason to call any particular act good or evil. Indeed, morality is counterfeit when it pretends to know "what 'good and evil' is." (*Will to Power*, p. 338) In a letter to a friend, Nietzsche conveys what he takes to be the significance of his work on values:

I've used these weeks to 'revalue values.' Do you understand this expression? When you come right down to it, the alchemist is the most praiseworthy of men: I mean the one who changes something negligible or contemptible into something of value, even gold. He alone enriches, the others merely exchange. My task is quite singular this time: I've asked myself what mankind has always hated, feared, and despised the most — and precisely out of this I've made my 'gold.'

Nietzsche: A Self-Portrait From His Letters, *p. 118*

Even though the "will to truth" is not the will to *one truth,* Nietzsche's analysis of the genealogy of morals does *not* entail either that there is no truth or that all interpretations of reality are equally good. If it did, then Nietzsche's critique of Christianity would make no sense. And Nietzsche frequently expresses a preference for one view over another. Nietzsche's overarching objective is to reject any form of dogmatism which claims to have the last word and demands that everyone therefore believe it. For this reason, though he is not antiscientific, he objects to claims that science can describe ultimate reality. Perhaps an analogy might help here: That no painting can ever hope to capture all of reality means neither that there is no truth at all in the painting nor that some paintings might not be better than others. Indeed, Nietzsche characterizes the view that there is no truth as an extreme form of nihilism which he ultimately rejects (see, for example, *Will to Power*, p. 15).

THE *UBERMENSCH*
AND THE WILL TO POWER

In *Ecce Homo,* his semiautobiographical work, Nietzsche criticizes morality as the most harmful of lies, as "incompatible with an ascending and affirmative life." (p. 128) "The harm the good do is the most harmful harm." (p. 130) Instead of fighting against life in the form of being "moral," one must create one's own values as they emerge from oneself. Nietzsche (like Kierkegaard) despises nothing more than conformity:

> Virtues are as dangerous as vices in so far as one lets them rule over one as authorities and laws from without and does not first produce them out of oneself, as one should do, as one's most personal self-defense and necessity, as conditions of precisely *our own* existence and growth, which we recognize and acknowledge independently of whether other men grow with us under similar or different conditions.
>
>   Will to Power, *no. 326*

But this independence of thought and action is rare. Living without absolutes is onerous. There is no final destination, only a journey. "Whoever has attained intellectual freedom even to a small extent cannot feel but as a wanderer upon the face of the earth — and not as a traveler *toward* some final destination; for that does not exist." (*Human, All Too Human,* p. 638) This journey requires great courage and is not for everyone.

As noted, for Nietzsche, two thousand years of Christianity have repressed the symptoms of nihilism. But the death of God brings the disease into the foreground. To say — like the nihilist — that all is meaningless is a reaction to two thousand years of "ultimate value" and is not necessarily true. Instead, we can — now as free spirits unweighted by gravity — propose new and better truths. Nihilism is then a stage, not the end. Creators of truths must be "hard," may need to kill even what they themselves hold most dear — as Zarathustra tells us, the "obvious." (*Thus Spake Zarathustra,* Part II, p.2) This brings us to a concept central to Nietzsche's later writings: the will to power.

It is not always clear what Nietzsche means by the concept of will to power. It is especially confusing since Neitzsche at times rejects even the existence of the will (see, for example, *Will to Power,* pp. 671, 689, 692). What Nietzsche rejects, though, is the "psychological" concept of will, particularly as that concept has been used to devalue human existence. Instead, Nietzsche insists that the will to power is in all of life, from the lowest forms to the highest, that which affirms and strengthens life. "Here we need a new, more definite formulation of the concept of 'life.' My formula for it is: Life is will to power." (*Will to Power,* p. 254)

The excerpt from *Thus Spake Zarathustra* (see pp. 206–20), for example, makes frequent references to this concept. "Only where life is, there is also will: not will to life, but—so I teach you—will to power!" (p. 208) For Nietzsche, all of life is governed by the will to power; it provides the dynamic energy behind the workings of the universe.

Nietzsche's concept of the will to power takes us directly to the *ubermensch* (or "overman") whose existence can begin to fill the void left by God's absence. "*I teach you the Superman*. Man is something that should be overcome. What have you done to overcome him?" (*Thus Spake Zarathustra*, p. 41) This notion of self-overcoming is one that reverberates throughout Nietzsche's writings.

The *ubermensch*, contrary to some interpretations, is neither an evolutionary goal nor a product of special breeding. Rather, the *ubermensch* represents what Nietzsche thinks we are capable of becoming. This overman is often at odds with the society which seeks to impede its development, so one must be sure that one's identity is not dependent on the group. Abandoning the herd is the only way back to oneself. Though the herd will call it a crime, this separation is an essential part of the process of self-overcoming. A true *ubermensch* knows that the value of life cannot be determined by objective criteria; thus, the assignment of any sort of value requires great strength and independence of spirit. A true *ubermensch* is "the ideal of the most high-spirited, alive, and world-affirming human being who has not only come to terms and learned to get along with whatever was and is, but who wants to have *what was and is* repeated into all eternity." (*Beyond Good and Evil*, p. 68)

Though Nietzsche admires people like Julius Caesar and Napoleon, his *ubermensch* is not necessarily a conqueror or a powerful person of state. Indeed, if a leader views himself or herself as merely expressing the "popular will," that individual is still under the sway of obedience and is not a true *ubermensch*. To be a true leader is first to be able to lead oneself. The *ubermensch* possesses a certain greatness of character, a nobility of spirit, and is one who *creates oneself*. Tyranny over others, then, is not an essential attribute of the *ubermensch;* yet, refraining from tyranny is not either, unless one has the power to be a tyrant and has made a deliberate decision to refrain from doing so. Julius Caesar, for example, was not to be admired for his military and political victories but rather because he mastered himself.

Lust for power can destroy the person who is not truly powerful. But in the *ubermensch* power is not a lust but a natural overflow of spirit. This doctrine of the *ubermensch* is consistent with Nietzsche's repudiation of morality. These "noble spirits" create themselves, without regard for social norms and values. They are great for that reason, yet they are fragile as well.

As on other issues, Nietzsche is not altogether clear in his discussions of the development of self. He urges us (*Gay Science*, p. 270; *Thus Spake Zarathustra*, Part IV, p. 1) to "become who you are," and the subtitle of *Ecce Homo* is "how one becomes what one is."

Since Nietzsche makes no distinction between being and becoming, the self cannot refer to any sort of goal that one has for action. Further, Nietzsche at times even characterizes the self as an illusion, arguing that conventional subject-predicate grammar confuses us into thinking that there is an agent. "The 'doer' is merely a fiction added to the deed — the deed is everything." (*Genealogy of Morals*, p. 13) In addition, Nietzsche's injunction to "become who you are" cannot be about potentiality and actuality, since that would imply that there *is* some actual self which is objectively determined and reachable. Nietzsche insists that there is no "final state"; but doesn't becoming what one is imply that one has finally arrived?

What, then, might Nietzsche mean? It appears that at least part of what he intends is a kind of personal integrity and acceptance of all that we are and all we have done. This kind of acceptance, Nietzsche believes, is compatible with continued change, since the self is not static; there is no room for "resting on one's laurels." (*Will to Power*, p. 108) This kind of constant self-creation and self-acceptance is extraordinarily difficult and is reserved only for the truly courageous. One must have the courage to say yes to one's life and all that it means. This does not, however, mean that any part of one's life (even the past) is fixed or inert. Rather, there is always room for reinterpretation, to move around the different elements of one's life while making new choices and decisions. But, always, "what returns, what finally comes home to me, is my own self." (*Thus Spake Zarathustra*, Part III, p. 1)

NIETZSCHE'S DOCTRINE OF ETERNAL RECURRENCE

> *Everything goes, everything returns; the wheel of existence rolls for ever. Everything dies, everything blossoms anew; the year of existence runs on for ever.*
>
> *Everything breaks, everything is joined anew; the same house of existence builds itself for ever. Everything departs, everything meets again; the ring of existence is true to itself for ever.*
>
> *Existence begins in every instant; the ball There rolls around every Here. The middle is everywhere. The path of eternity is crooked.*
>
> *Thus Spake Zarathustra*, p. 217

In "The Convalescent" of *Thus Spake Zarathustra* (see pp. 215–20), Zarathustra has lain comatose for seven full days, after having managed to face an "abysmal thought." This thought, the doctrine of eternal recurrence, is the view that "all things recur eternally and we ourselves with them, and that we have already existed an infinite number of times before and all things with us." (p. 219) This doctrine is probably the most difficult of all Nietzsche's teaching to understand and defend and has been a source of great puzzlement for his readers. Opponents of Nietzsche have used this doctrine as the basis for a repudiation of his philosophy; those more sympathetic to his views seem embarrassed by the notion of eternal recurrence and may even dismiss it as incidental to Nietzsche's general system.

But a careful reading of Nietzsche's work prevents us from dismissing this doctrine. Nietzsche viewed this idea as the pinnacle of his philosophic view and as consistent with his notion of the *ubermensch* and his repudiation of morality. Nietzsche tells us repeatedly how important this view is; indeed, it is, he writes, the basic conception of *Thus Spake Zarathustra*, (*Ecce Homo*, p. 99) with Zarathustra as its teacher. Nietzsche's notes suggest that he may have been planning a book called *The Eternal Recurrence*, but the sketches of it that appear at the end of *The Will to Power* (1053–1067) are unclear and may later have been repudiated by Nietzsche had he lived.

Nietzsche may have gotten the idea for the doctrine of eternal recurrence from the pre-Socratic philosopher Heraclitus or even from a contemporary of his, the German writer Heinrich Heine. Most interpreters of Nietzsche have understood eternal recurrence as a hypothesis that maintains that everything that has happened in the universe, is happening now, or will happen in the future has already happened and will happen again in exactly the same order into infinity.

> You teach that there is a great year of becoming, a colussus of a year:
>   this year must, like an hour-glass, turn itself over again and
>   again, so that it may run down and run out anew.
>
> So that all these years resemble one another, in the greatest things and
>   in the smallest, so that we ourselves resemble ourselves in
>   each great year, in the greatest things and in the smallest.
>   *Thus Spake Zarathustra*, p. 237

Regardless of how we interpret this notion, two important points are definite. First, this doctrine is consistent with Nietzsche's rejection of teleology. That is, if eternal recurrence is true, then it is clear that there is no end or goal toward which the universe aims. Nietzsche writes:

If the world had a goal, it must have been reached. If there were for it some unintended final state, this also must have been reached. If it were in any way capable of pausing and becoming fixed, of 'being,' if in the whole course of its becoming it possessed even for a moment this capability of 'being,' then all becoming would long since have come to an end, along with all thinking, all 'spirit.' The fact of 'spirit' as a form of becoming proves that the world has no goal, no final state, and is incapable of being.

Will to Power, *no. 1062*

Though Nietzsche tells us that the doctrine of eternal recurrence is "the most scientific of all possible hypotheses," (*Will to Power*, p. 55) he never tries to prove it in any real sense. It seems clear that there is no possibility of empirical support for such a hypothesis. Nietzsche does, however, think that this doctrine is consistent with developing modern science. For example, he insists that "the law of the conservation of energy demands *eternal recurrence.*" (*Will to Power*, no. 1063) For Nietzsche, there is a finite number of combinations possible in the ordering of events in the universe.

If the world may be thought of as a certain definite quantity of force and as a certain definite number of centers of force — and every other representation remains indefinite and therefore useless — it follows that, in the great dice game of existence, it must pass through a calculable number of combinations. In infinite time, every possible combination would at some time or another be realized; more: it would be realized an infinite number of times. And since between every combination and its next recurrence all other possible combinations would have to take place, and each of these combinations conditions the entire sequence of combinations in the same series, a circular movement of absolutely identical series is thus demonstrated: the world as a circular movement that has already repeated itself infinitely often and plays its game *in infinitum.*

Will to Power, *no. 1066*

Further, Nietzsche holds that eternal recurrence is the most powerful and yet also the most optimistic of any idea: "To me, on the contrary, everything seems far too valuable to be so fleeting: I seek an eternity for everything: ought one to pour the most precious salves and wines into the sea?—My consolation is that everything that has been is eternal: the sea will cast it up again." (*Will to Power*, no. 1065)

For Nietzsche, the truly great person is one who is willing to affirm every moment of his or her life, to affirm it since "escape is impossible." (*Will to Power*, no. 1058) Such a stance takes real courage, a courage that destroys even death, proclaiming "Was *that* life? Well then! Once more!" (*Thus Spake Zarathustra*, Part III, p. 178) Nietzsche's view of history is consistent with his work on eternal recurrence: "History can be borne only by strong personalities, weak ones are utterly extinguished by it." (*Uses and Disadvantages*, p. 86) This world is a world of the "eternally self-creating, the eternally self-destroying, this mystery world of the twofold voluptuous delight, my 'beyond good and evil,' without goal, unless the joy of the circle is itself a goal." (*Will to Power*, no. 1067)

As a theory of cosmology, Nietzsche's doctrine of eternal recurrence is problematic. Even if we disregard its lack of confirmability, there is no necessary connection between the amount of energy in the universe (even if it *is* finite) and the number of possible arrangements of that energy. Some commentators (e.g., Nehemas) have argued, however, that eternal recurrence is of least importance as a theory of the world and of most importance as a theory of the self.

In a section of *The Gay Science* entitled "The Greatest Weight," Nietzsche discusses the significance of eternal recurrence for individual existence:

> What if, some day or night a demon were to steal after you into your loneliness and say to you: 'This life as you now live it and have lived it, you will have to live once more and innumerable times more; and there will be nothing new in it, but every pain and every joy and every thought and sigh and everything unutterably small or great in your life will have to return to you, all in the same succession and sequence — even this spider and this moonlight between the trees, and even this moment and I myself. The eternal hourglass of existence is turned upside down again and again, and you with it, speck of dust!
>
> Gay Science, *no. 341*

This passage sheds some light on the "heaviness" of eternal recurrence and the courage required to affirm it. For Nietzsche, every thing is connected to every other thing. The world is "essentially a world of relationships" (*Will to Power*, p. 568) where meanings are imposed from some particular viewpoint. The true *ubermensch* says yes to life, changing each "thus it was " into a "thus I would have it." This is Nietzsche's important concept of *amor fati* (that one wants nothing to be different from what it is); there is nothing more affirming of one's life than to be willing to relive it innumerable times:

> Would you not throw yourself down and gnash your teeth and curse the demon who spoke thus? Or have you once experienced a tremendous moment when you would have answered him: 'You are a god and never have I heard anything more divine.' If this thought gained possession of you, it would change you as you are or perhaps crush you. The question in each and every thing, 'Do you desire this once more and innumerable times

more?' would lie upon your actions as the greatest weight. Or how well disposed would you have become to yourself and to life *to crave nothing more fervently* than this ultimate eternal confirmation and seal?

Gay Science, *no. 341*

But isn't this doctrine absurd? Why shouldn't we "fervently crave" some other state of affairs in our lives? Why shouldn't we wish to change pieces of our past? Isn't Nietzsche forcing us into an untenable position where we must reject or affirm wholeheartedly? Isn't some middle ground possible? For Nietzsche, the answer is no, because everything is interconnected; to change one fact about us is to change it all. According to Nietzsche,

> If we affirm one single moment, we thus affirm not only ourselves but all existence. For nothing is self-sufficient, neither in us ourselves nor in things; and if our soul has trembled with happiness and sounded like a harp string just once, all eternity was needed to produce this one event and in this single moment of affirmation all eternity was called good, redeemed, justified, and affirmed.
>
> Will to Power, *no. 1032*

Every one of our past actions — even if we might now regret it — makes us who we are today. As Zarathustra tells us, "Have you ever said Yes to a single joy?" Then "you have said Yes to all woe." (*Thus Spake Zarathustra,* Part IV, p. 19)

Is it possible that one's *yes* might be based on self-deception? That is, couldn't a morally repugnant or merely weak person also be willing to affirm his or her life? Nietzsche may have been aware of this possibility, but he did not address it. Living with eternal recurrence is limited only to the noblest spirits, and Nietzsche might argue that this ideal is one which would crush a weaker person. Or he might simply be willing to risk the consequences of his "immoralism."

To say yes is to take responsibility for the past. "Thus I willed it" means that every experience serves us. The noble figure does not take seriously even the worst of enemies. Rather than give in to the brooding of *ressentiment,* the true *ubermensch* finds the good in what someone has done to him or her and uses that as the basis for personal development. In such a way one gets the best of one's enemies.

CONCLUSION

Nietzsche's impact on contemporary thought has been enormous. His approach to philosophy via language is one that has endured in the tradition of linguistic philosophy. His criticism of the assumption that language make ontological claims on its users anticipates the analytic philosophers of the twentieth century. Nietzsche's ruthless analysis of what is is consistent with the tradition of positivism and empiricism. French historian Michel Foucault owes much to Nietzsche's use of genealogy and his rejection of ahistorical facts. Nietzsche's doctrine of the will was one of the first to anticipate modern psychoanalytic accounts of human behavior and motivation. Twentieth-century existentialists like Camus, Sartre, and de Beauvoir owe much to Nietzsche's views on religion and human purpose. Nietzsche's perspectivism prefigures the view of Sartre that human reality is constituted by signs. Martin Heidegger's analysis of Dasein as Being-in-the-World is indebted to Nietzsche's discussions of human subjectivity. Finally, the atheistic tendency in existentialism springs almost directly from the thought of Nietzsche. Perhaps he was, as he once ironically noted, "born posthumously."

The selections at the end of this chapter provide some examples of Nietzsche's concerns, his methodology, and the power and richness of his writing. In later chapters it will be more obvious to what extent existentialists are obliged to the genius of Nietzsche. Yet Nietzsche did not want followers. Indeed, Zarathustra tells us "only *when you have denied me will I return to you.*" And Nietzsche warns us all to take care that falling statues — the "holy," the revered — do not finally strike us dead. Every true creator, Nietzsche reminds us, must be "hard." Real courage requires that one seek oneself and not run from what is true or hide in the cliched and the safe. This notion of authenticity is one of the major themes of existentialist philosophy. For "he who looks into himself as into an enormous universe and carries the Milky Ways within himself, he also knows how irregular all Milky Ways are; they lead all the way into the chaos and labyrinth of existence." (*Gay Science*, p. 322)

QUESTIONS FOR CONSIDERATION

1. Can you affirm all of your life? Why or why not? What would it mean if you were able to do this?

2. Consider the three major doctrines of Nietzsche's philosophy: the will to power, the transvaluation of values, and eternal recurrence. Do these three views cohere? How are they mutually interdependent? Distinct?

3. Nietzsche frequently calls himself an "immoralist." Is he? Why or why not?

4. Hitler used many of Nietzsche's writings to defend and support his philosophy of fascism. Is fascism consistent with Nietzsche's view? Why or why not? Think about how the notion of the will to power might be relevant here.

5. Discuss some of the intersections between the philosophies of Nietzsche and Kierkegaard.
6. Is Nietzsche's condemnation of Christianity relevant to the Christianity of Kierkegaard or only traditional Christianity? Discuss and defend your position.
7. When you think of "becoming who you are," what comes to mind? What would doing this mean for you?

REFERENCES

Works by Nietzsche

Beyond Good and Evil. Translated by Helen Zimmern. New York: Modern Library, n.d.

"David Strauss: The Confessor and Writer." In *Untimely Meditations.* Translated by R. J. Hollingdale. Cambridge: Cambridge University Press, 1983.

Ecce Homo. Translated by R. J. Hollingdale. New York: Penguin Books, 1979.

The Gay Science. Translated by Walter Kaufmann. New York: Vintage Books, 1974.

The Genealogy of Morals. Translated by Francis Golffing. Garden City, N. Y.: Doubleday Anchor Books, 1956.

Human, All Too Human. Translated by R. J. Hollingdale. Cambridge: Cambridge University Press,1986.

Selected Letters of Friedrich Nietzsche. Edited by Christopher Middleton. Chicago: University of Chicago Press, 1969.

Thus Spake Zarathustra. Translated by R. J. Hollingdale. Baltimore: Penguin Books, 1961.

"Uses and Disadvantages of History." *In Untimely Meditations.* Translated by R. J. Hollingdale. Cambridge: Cambridge University Press, 1983.

The Will to Power. Translated by Walter Kaufmann and R. J. Hollingdale. New York: Vintage, 1967.

Other Works

BERGMANN, PETER. *Nietzsche: "The Last Antipolitical German."* Bloomington: Indiana University Press, 1987.

BERNSTEIN, JOHN A. *Nietzsche's Moral Philosophy.* Hackensack, N.J.: Fairleigh Dickinson, 1987.

DANNHAUSER, WERNER J. *Nietzsche's View of Socrates*. Ithaca, N.Y.: Cornell University Press, 1974.

DANTO, ARTHUR C. *Nietzsche as Philosopher*. New York: Macmillan, 1965.

DELEUZE, GILLES. *Nietzsche and Philosophy*. Translated by Hugh Tomlinson. New York: Columbia University Press, 1983.

DURR, VOLKER et al., eds. *Nietzsche: Literature and Values*. Madison: University of Wisconsin Press, 1987.

FOERSTER-NIETZSCHE, ELIZABETH, ed. *The Nietzsche-Wagner Correspondence*. Translated by Caroline V. Kerr. New York: Liveright, 1921.

FOUCAULT, MICHEL. "Nietzsche, Genealogy, History." In *Language, Counter-Memory, Practice,* edited by Donald F. Bouchard. Ithaca, N.Y.: Cornell University Press, 1977.

FUSS, PETER, and SHAPIRO, HENRY, eds. *Nietzsche: A Self-Portrait from His Letters*. Cambridge, Mass.: Harvard University Press, 1971.

HIGGINS, KATHLEEN. *Nietzsche's Zarathustra*. Philadelphia: Temple University Press, 1987.

LAMPERT, LAURENCE. *Nietzsche's Teaching*. New Haven, Conn.: Yale University Press, 1987.

NEHAMAS, ALEXANDER. *Nietzsche: Life as Literature*. Cambridge: Harvard University Press, 1985.

ROSENTHAL, BERNICE G., ed. *Nietzsche in Russia*. Princeton, N.J.: Princeton University Press, 1986.

SCHACHT, RICHARD. *Nietzsche*. London: Routledge, Kegan Paul, 1983.

SOLOMON, ROBERT, ed. *Nietzsche: A Collection of Critical Essays*. Garden City, N.Y.: Doubleday, 1973.

FRIEDRICH NIETZSCHE

Beyond Good and Evil, Nietzsche's critique of modernity, was written in 1886, shortly after the completion of Thus Spake Zarathustra. *It is an explanation of some of the ideas of* Zarathustra, *while at the same time a preparation for Nietzsche's final work,* The Will to Power. *Here Nietzsche developed his view of the meaning of "good" and "evil" and his critique of traditional doctrines of morality. In the following excerpt, Nietzsche explores the evolution of values.*

Beyond Good and Evil

CHAPTER V

THE NATURAL HISTORY OF MORALS

186

The moral sentiment in Europe at present is perhaps as subtle, belated, diverse, sensitive, and refined, as the "Science of Morals" belonging thereto is recent, initial, awkward, and coarse-fingered: — an interesting contrast, which sometimes becomes incarnate and obvious in the very person of a moralist. Indeed, the expression, "Science of Morals" is, in respect to what is designated thereby, far too presumptuous and counter to *good* taste, — which is always a foretaste of more modest expressions. One ought to avow with the utmost fairness *what* is still necessary here for a long time, *what* is alone proper for the present: namely, the collection of material, the comprehensive survey and classification of an immense domain of delicate sentiments of worth, and distinctions of worth, which live, grow, propagate, and perish — and perhaps attempts to give a clear idea of the recurring and more common forms of these living crystallisations — as preparation for a *theory of types* of morality. To be sure, people have not hitherto been so modest. All the philosophers, with a pedantic and ridiculous seriousness, demanded of themselves something very much higher, more pretentious, and ceremonious, when they concerned themselves with morality as a science: they wanted to *give a basis* to morality — and every philosopher hitherto has believed that he has given it a basis; morality itself, however, has been regarded as something "given." How far from their awkward pride was the seemingly insignifi-

From Friedrich Nietzsche, *Beyond Good and Evil,* translated by Helen Zimmern. Reprinted by permission of the publisher, Unwin Hyman Ltd.

cant problem — left in dust and decay — of a description of forms of morality, notwithstanding that the finest hands and senses could hardly be fine enough for it! It was precisely owing to moral philosophers knowing the moral facts imperfectly, in an arbitrary epitome, or an accidental abridgement — perhaps as the morality of their environment, their position, their church, their *Zeitgeist*, their climate and zone — it was precisely because they were badly instructed with regard to nations, eras, and past ages, and were by no means eager to know about these matters, that they did not even come in sight of the real problems of morals — problems which only disclose themselves by a comparison of *many* kinds of morality. In every "Science of Morals" hitherto, strange as it may sound, the problem of morality itself has been *omitted;* there has been no suspicion that there was anything problematic there! That which philosophers called "giving a basis to morality," and endeavoured to realise, has, when seen in a right light, proved merely a learned form of good *faith* in prevailing morality, a new means of its *expression*, consequently just a matter-of-fact within the sphere of a definite morality, yea, in its ultimate motive, a sort of denial that it is *lawful*, for this morality to be called in question — and in any case the reverse of the testing, analysing, doubting, and vivisecting of this very faith. . . .

199

Inasmuch as in all ages, as long as mankind has existed, there have also been human herds (family alliances, communities, tribes, peoples, states, churches), and always a great number who obey in proportion to the small number who command — in view, therefore, of the fact that obedience has been most practised and fostered among mankind hitherto, one may reasonably suppose that, generally speaking, the need thereof is now innate in every one, as a kind of *formal conscience* which gives the command: "Thou shalt unconditionally do something, unconditionally refrain from something"; in short, "Thou shalt." This need tries to satisfy itself and to fill its form with a content; according to its strength, impatience, and eagerness, it at once seizes as an omnivorous appetite with little selection, and accepts whatever is shouted into its ear by all sorts of commanders — parents, teachers, laws, class prejudices, or public opinion. The extraordinary limitation of human development, the hesitation, protractedness, frequent retrogression, and turning thereof, is attributable to the fact that the herd-instinct of obedience is transmitted best, and at the cost of the art of command. If one imagine this instinct increasing to its greatest extent, commanders and independent individuals will finally be lacking altogether; or they will suffer inwardly from a bad conscience, and will have to impose a deception on themselves in the first place in order to be able to command: just as if they also were only obeying. This condition of things actually exists in Europe at present — I call it the moral hypocrisy of the commanding class. They know no other way of protecting themselves from their bad conscience than by playing the role of executors of older and higher orders (of predecessors, of the constitution, of justice, of the law, or of God himself), or they even justify themselves by maxims from the current opinions of the herd, as "first servants of their people," or "instruments of the public weal." On the other hand, the gregarious European man nowadays assumes an air as if he were the only kind of man that is allowable; he glorifies his qualities, such as public spirit, kindness, deference, industry, temperance, modesty, indulgence, sympathy, by virtue of which he is gentle, endurable, and useful to the herd, as the peculiarly human virtues. In cases, however, where it is believed that the leader and bell-wether cannot be dispensed with, attempt after attempt is made nowadays to replace commanders by the summing together of clever gregarious men: all representative constitutions, for example, are of this origin. In spite of all, what a blessing, what a deliverance from a weight becoming unendurable, is the appearance of an absolute ruler for these gregarious Europeans — of this fact the effect of the appearance of Napoleon was the last great proof: the history of the influence of Napoleon is almost the history of the higher happiness to which the entire century has attained in its worthiest individuals and periods. . . .

259

To refrain mutually from injury, from violence, from exploitation, and put one's will on a par with that of others: this may result in a certain rough sense in good conduct among individuals when the necessary conditions are given (namely, the actual similarity of the individuals in amount of force and degree of worth, and their co-relation within one organisation). As soon, however, as one wished to take this principle more generally, and if possible even as *the fundamental principle of society*, it would immediately disclose what it really is — namely, a Will to the *denial* of life, a principle of dissolution and decay. Here one must think profoundly to the very basis and resist all sentimental weakness: life itself is *essentially* appropriation, injury, conquest of the strange and weak, suppression, severity, obtrusion of peculiar forms, incorporation, and at the least, putting it mildest, exploitation; — but why should one for ever use precisely these words on which for ages a disparaging purpose has been stamped? Even the organisation within which, as was previously supposed, the individuals treat each other as equal — it takes place in every healthy aristocracy — must itself, if it be a living and not a dying organisation, do all that towards other bodies, which the individuals within it refrain from doing to each other: it will have to be the incarnated

Will to Power, it will endeavour to grow, to gain ground, attract to itself and acquire ascendency — not owing to any morality or immorality, but because it *lives,* and because life *is* precisely Will to Power. On no point, however, is the ordinary consciousness of Europeans more unwilling to be corrected than on this matter; people now rave everywhere, even under the guise of science, about coming conditions of society in which "the exploiting character" is to be absent: — that sounds to my ears as if they promised to invent a mode of life which should refrain from all organic functions. "Exploitation" does not belong to a depraved, or imperfect and primitive society: it belongs to the *nature* of the living being as a primary organic function; it is a consequence of the intrinsic Will to Power, which is precisely the Will to Life. — Granting that as a theory this is a novelty — as a reality it is the *fundamental fact* of all history: let us be so far honest towards ourselves!

260

In a tour through the many finer and coarser moralities which have hitherto prevailed or still prevail on the earth, I found certain traits recurring regularly together, and connected with one another, until finally two primary types revealed themselves to me, and a radical distinction was brought to light. There is *master-morality* and *slave-morality;* — I would at once add, however, that in all higher and mixed civilisations, there are also attempts at the reconciliation of the two moralities; but one finds still oftener the confusion and mutual misunderstanding of them, indeed, sometimes their close juxtaposition — even in the same man, within one soul. The distinctions of moral values have either originated in a ruling caste, pleasantly conscious of being different from the ruled — or among the ruled class, the slaves and dependents of all sorts. In the first case, when it is the rulers who determine the conception "good," it is the exalted, proud disposition which is regarded as the distinguishing feature, and that which determines the order of rank. The noble type of man separates from himself the beings in whom the opposite of this exalted, proud disposition displays itself: he despises them. Let it at once be noted that in this first kind of morality the antithesis "good" and "bad" means practically the same as "noble" and "despicable"; — the antithesis "good" and *"evil"* is of a different origin. The cowardly, the timid, the insignificant, and those thinking merely of narrow utility are despised; moreover, also, the distrustful, with their constrained glances, the self-abasing, the dog-like kind of men who let themselves be abused, the mendicant flatterers, and above all the liars: — it is a fundamental belief of all aristocrats that the common people are untruthful. "We truthful ones" — the nobility in ancient Greece called themselves. It is obvious that everywhere the designations of moral value were at first applied to *men,* and were only derivatively and at a later period applied to *actions*; it is a gross mistake, therefore, when historians of morals start with questions like, "Why have sympathetic actions been praised?" The noble type of man regards *himself* as a determiner of values; he does not require to be approved of; he passes the judgment: "What is injurious to me is injurious in itself"; he knows that it is he himself only who confers honour on things; he is a *creator of values.* He honours whatever he recognizes in himself: such morality is self-glorification. In the foreground there is the feeling of plenitude, of power, which seeks to overflow, the happiness of high tension, the consciousness of a wealth which would fain give and bestow: — the noble man also helps the unfortunate, but not — or scarcely — out of pity, but rather from an impulse generated by the superabundance of power. The noble man honours in himself the powerful one, him also who has power over himself, who knows how to speak and how to keep silence, who takes pleasure in subjecting himself to severity and hardness, and has reverence for all that is severe and hard. "Wotan placed a hard heart in my breast," says an old Scandinavian Saga: it is thus rightly expressed from the soul of a proud Viking. Such a type of man is even proud of *not* being made for sympathy; the hero of the Saga therefore adds warningly: "He who has not a hard heart when young, will never have one." The noble and brave who think thus are the furthest removed from the morality which sees precisely in sympathy, or in acting for the good of others, or in *désintéressement,* the characteristic of the moral; faith in oneself, pride in oneself, a radical enmity and irony towards "selflessness," belong as definitely to noble morality, as do a careless scorn and precaution in presence of sympathy and the "warm heart." — It is the powerful who *know* how to honour, it is their art, their domain for invention. The profound reverence for age and for tradition — all law rests on this double reverence, — the belief and prejudice in favour of ancestors and unfavourable to newcomers, is typical in the morality of the powerful; and if, reversely, men of "modern ideas" believe almost instinctively in "progress" and the "future," and are more and more lacking in respect for old age, the ignoble origin of these "ideas" has complacently betrayed itself thereby. A morality of the ruling class, however, is more especially foreign and irritating to present-day taste in the sternness of its principle that one has duties only to one's equals; that one may act towards beings of a lower rank, towards all that is foreign, just as seems good to one, or "as the heart desires," and in any case "beyond good and evil": it is here that sympathy and similar sentiments can have a place. The ability and obligation to exercise prolonged gratitude and prolonged revenge — both only within the circle of equals, — artfulness in retaliation, *raffinement* of the idea in friendship, a certain necessity to have enemies (as outlets for the emotions of envy, quarrelsomeness, arrogance — in fact, in order to be a good *friend*): all these are typical characteristics of the noble morality, which, as has been pointed out, is not the morality of "modern ideas," and is therefore at present difficult to realise and also to unearth and disclose. — It is otherwise with the second type of morality, *slave-morality*. Supposing that the abused, the oppressed, the suffering, the unemancipated, the weary, and those uncertain of themselves, should moralise, what will be the common element in their moral estimates? Probably a pessimistic suspicion with regard to the entire situation of man will find expression, perhaps a condemnation of man, together with his situation. The slave has an unfavourable eye for the virtues of the powerful; he has a scepticism and distrust, a *refinement* of distrust of everything "good" that is there honoured — he would fain persuade himself that the very happiness there is not genuine. On the other hand, *those* qualities which serve to alleviate the existence of sufferers are brought into prominence and flooded with light; it is here that the sympathy, the kind, helping hand, the warm heart, patience, diligence, humility, and friendliness attain to honour; for here these are the most useful qualities, and almost the only means of supporting the burden of existence. Slave-morality is essentially the morality of utility. Here is the seat of the origin of the famous antithesis "good" and "evil": — power and dangerousness are assumed to reside in the evil, a certain dreadfulness, subtlety, and strength, which do not admit of being despised. According to slave-morality, therefore, the "evil" man arouses fear; according to master-morality, it is precisely the "good" man who arouses fear and seeks to arouse it, while the bad man is regarded as the despicable being. The contrast attains its maximum when, in accordance with the logical consequences of slave-morality, a shade of depreciation — it may be slight and well-intentioned — at last attaches itself to the "good" man of this morality; because, according to the servile mode of thought, the good man must in any case be the *safe* man: he is good-natured, easily deceived, perhaps a little stupid, *un bonhomme*. Everywhere that slave-morality gains the ascendency, language shows a tendency to approximate the significations of the words "good" and "stupid." — A last fundamental difference: the desire for *freedom*, the instinct for happiness and the refinements of the feeling of liberty belong as necessarily to slave-morals and morality, as artifice and enthusiasm in reverence and devotion are the regular symptoms of an aristocratic mode of thinking and estimating. — Hence we can understand without further detail why love *as a passion* — it is our European specialty — must absolutely be of noble origin. . . .

The Genealogy of Morals, *written one year after* Beyond Good and Evil, *is hardly less shocking today than when it was first written. This work is a scathing attack on religion, in particular those religions that glorify self-denial and asceticism.* The Genealogy of Morals *traces the evolution of what Nietzsche terms master and slave morality as the basis for the "manufacture of ideals." Nietzsche repudiates all ideas that signify "this hatred of humanity," this "loathing of the senses, of reason; this fear of beauty and happiness, this longing to escape from illusion." The following excerpt captures some of the passion and vehemence with which Nietzsche approaches these insights.*

The Genealogy of Morals

I

We knowers are unknown to ourselves, and for a good reason: how can we ever hope to find what we have never looked for? There is a sound adage which runs: "Where a man's treasure lies, there lies his heart." Our treasure lies in the beehives of our knowledge. We are perpetually on our way thither, being by nature winged insects and honey gatherers of the mind. The only thing that lies close to our heart is the desire to bring something home to the hive. As for the rest of life — so-called "experience" — who among us is serious enough for that? Or has time enough? When it comes to such matters, our heart is simply not in it — we don't even lend our ear. Rather, as a man divinely abstracted and self-absorbed into whose ears the bell has just drummed the twelve strokes of noon will suddenly awake with a start and ask himself what hour has actually struck, we sometimes rub our ears after the event and ask ourselves, astonished and at a loss, "What have we really experienced?" — or rather, "Who are we, really?" And we recount the twelve tremulous strokes of our experience, our life, our being, but unfortunately count wrong. The sad truth is that we remain necessarily strangers to ourselves, we don't understand our own substance, we *must* mistake ourselves; the axiom, "Each man is farthest from himself," will hold for us to all eternity. Of ourselves we are not "knowers". . . .

II

My ideas about the provenance of our moral prejudices (for that is to be the subject of the present work) found their first brief and tentative formulation in a collection of aphorisms called *Human, All Too Human: A*

Book for Free Spirits. I began that book one winter in Sorrento, at a moment when it was given me to pause, as a wanderer might pause, and to look back over the wild and dangerous territory my mind had crossed. It was the winter of 1876–77; the ideas themselves had come to me earlier, however. And it is those same ideas I wish to take up in the present treatise: let us hope that the long interval has done them good, making them stronger and more luminous. At all events, the fact that I still hold them fast today, that through all these years they have continued to intertwine and draw nourishment from each other, encourages me to believe that from the very beginning they were not isolated thoughts, nor random or sporadic ones, but sprang from a common root, from a primary desire for knowledge, legislating from deep down in increasingly precise terms, increasingly precise demands. A philosopher should proceed in no other way. We have no right to isolated thoughts, whether truthful or erroneous. Our thoughts should grow out of our values with the same necessity as the fruit out of the tree. Our yeas and nays, our ifs and buts should all be intimately related and bear testimony to one will, one health, one soil, one sun. Supposing you find these fruits unpalatable? What concern is that of the trees — or of us, the philosophers?

III

Because of a qualm peculiar to me and which I am loath to admit, since it refers to morals, or rather to anything that has ever been cried up as ethics — a qualm which, unbidden and irresistible, put me so at variance, from my earliest childhood, with environment, age, precepts, tradition that I feel almost entitled to call it my *a priori* — both my curiosity and my suspicions were focused betimes on the provenance of our notions of good and evil. Already at the age of thirteen I was exercised by the problem of evil. At an age when one's interests are "divided between childish games and God" I wrote my first essay on ethics. My solution of the problem was to give the honor to God, as is only just, and make him the father of evil. Was this what my *a priori* demanded of me — that new, immoral, or at any rate non-moral *a priori* — and that mysterious anti-Kantian "categorical imperative" to which I have hearkened more and more ever since, and not only hearkened? Fortunately I learned in good time to divorce the theological prejudice from the moral and no longer to seek the origin of evil *behind* the world. A certain amount of historical and philological training, together with a native fastidiousness in matters of psychology, before long transformed this problem into another, to wit, "Under what conditions did man construct the value judgments *good* and *evil*?" And what is their intrinsic worth? Have they thus far benefited or retarded mankind? Do they betoken misery, curtailment, degeneracy or, on the contrary, power, fullness of being, energy, courage in the face of life, and confidence in the future? A great variety of answers suggested themselves. I began to distinguish among periods, nations, individuals; I narrowed the problem down; the answers grew into new questions, investigations, suppositions, probabilities, until I had staked off at last my own domain, a whole hidden, growing and blooming world, secret gardens as it were, of whose existence no one must have an inkling. . . . How blessed are we knowers, provided we know to keep silent long enough!

VI

At first sight, this problem of pity and the ethics of pity (I am strongly opposed to our modern sentimentality in these matters) may seem very special, a marginal issue. But whoever sticks with it and learns how to ask questions will have the same experience that I had: a vast new panorama will open up before him; strange and vertiginous possibilities will invade him; every variety of suspicion, distrust, fear will come to the surface; his belief in ethics of any kind will begin to be shaken. Finally he will be forced to listen to a new claim. Let us articulate that new claim: we need a critique of all moral values; the intrinsic worth of these values must, first of all, be called in question. To this end we need to know the conditions from which those values have sprung and how they have developed and changed: morality as consequence, symptom, mask, *tartufferie*, sickness, misunderstanding; but, also, morality as cause, remedy, stimulant, inhibition, poison. Hitherto such knowledge has neither been forthcoming nor considered a desideratum. The intrinsic worth of these values was taken for granted as a fact of experience and put beyond question. Nobody, up to now, has doubted that the "good" man represents a higher value than the "evil," in terms of promoting and benefiting mankind generally, even taking the long view. But suppose the exact opposite were true. What if the "good" man represents not merely a retrogression but even a danger, a temptation, a narcotic drug enabling the present to live at the expense of the future? More comfortable, less hazardous, perhaps, but also baser, more petty — so that morality itself would be responsible for man, as a species, failing to reach the peak of magnificence of which he is capable? What if morality should turn out to be the danger of dangers? . . .

X

The slave revolt in morals begins by rancor turning creative and giving birth to values — the rancor of beings who, deprived of the direct outlet of action, compensate by an imaginary vengeance. All truly noble morality grows out of triumphant self-affirmation. Slave ethics, on the other hand, begins by saying *no* to an "outside," an "other," a non-self, and that *no* is its creative act. This reversal of direction of the evaluating look, this invariable looking outward instead of inward, is a fundamental feature of rancor. Slave ethics requires for its inception a sphere different from and hostile to its own. Physiologically speaking, it requires an outside stimulus in order to act at all; all its action is reaction. The opposite is true of aristocratic valuations: such values grow and act spontaneously, seeking out their contraries only in order to affirm themselves even more gratefully and delightedly. Here the negative concepts, *humble, base, bad*, are late, pallid counterparts of the positive, intense and passionate credo. "We noble, good, beautiful, happy ones." Aristocratic valuations may go amiss and do violence to reality, but this happens only with regard to spheres which they do not know well, or from the knowledge of which they austerely guard themselves: the aristocrat will, on occasion, misjudge a sphere which he holds in contempt, the sphere of the common man, the people. On the other hand we should remember that the emotion of contempt, of looking down, provided that it falsifies at all, is as nothing compared with the falsification which suppressed hatred, impotent vindictiveness, effects upon its opponent, though only in effigy. There is in all contempt too much casualness and nonchalance, too much blinking of facts and impatience, and too much inborn gaiety for it ever to make of its object a downright caricature and monster. Hear the almost benevolent nuances the Greek aristocracy, for example, puts into all its terms for the commoner; how emotions of compassion, consideration, indulgence, sugar-coat these words until, in the end, almost all terms referring to the common man survive as expressions for "unhappy," "pitiable" (cf. *deilos, deilaios, poneros, mochtheros*, the last two of which properly characterize the common man as a drudge and beast of burden); how, on the other hand, the words *bad, base, unhappy* have continued to strike a similar note for the Greek ear, with the timbre "unhappy" preponderating. The "wellborn" really felt that they were also the "happy." They did not have to construct their happiness factitiously by looking at their enemies, as all rancorous men are wont to do, and being fully active, energetic people they were incapable of divorcing happiness from action. They accounted activity a necessary part of happiness . . .

All this stands in utter contrast to what is called happiness among the impotent and oppressed, who are full of bottled-up aggressions. Their happiness is purely passive and takes the form of drugged tranquillity, stretching and yawning, peace, "sabbath," emotional slackness. Whereas the noble lives before his own conscience with confidence and frankness (*gennaios* "nobly bred" emphasizes the nuance "truthful" and perhaps also "ingenuous"), the rancorous person is neither truthful nor ingenuous nor honest and forthright with himself. His soul squints; his mind loves hide-outs, secret paths, and back doors; everything that is hidden seems to him his own world, his security, his comfort; he is expert in silence, in long memory, in waiting, in provisional self-depreciation, and in self-humiliation. A race of such men will, in the end, inevitably be cleverer than a race of aristocrats, and it will honor sharp-wittedness to a much greater degree, i.e., as an absolutely vital condition for its existence. Among the noble, mental acuteness always tends slightly to suggest luxury and overrefinement. The fact is that with them it is much less important than is the perfect functioning of the ruling, unconscious instincts or even a certain temerity to follow sudden impulses, court danger, or indulge spurts of violent rage, love, worship, gratitude, or vengeance. When a noble man feels resentment, it is absorbed in his instantaneous reaction and therefore does not poison him. Moreover, in countless cases where we might expect it, it never arises, while with weak and impotent people it occurs without fail. It is a sign of strong, rich temperaments that they cannot for long take seriously their enemies, their misfortunes, their *misdeeds;* for such characters have in them an excess of plastic curative power, and also a power of oblivion. (A good modern example of the latter is Mirabeau, who lacked all memory for insults and meannesses done him, and who was unable to forgive because he had forgotten). Such a man simply shakes off vermin which would get beneath another's skin — and only here, if anywhere on earth, is it possible to speak of "loving one's enemy." The noble person will respect his enemy, and respect is already a bridge to love. . . . Indeed he requires his enemy for himself, as his mark of distinction, nor could he tolerate any other enemy than one in whom he finds nothing to despise and much to esteem. Imagine, on the other hand, the "enemy" as conceived by the rancorous man! For this is his true creative achievement: he has conceived the "evil enemy," the Evil One, as a fundamental idea, and then as a pendant he has conceived a Good One — himself.

XI

The exact opposite is true of the noble-minded, who spontaneously creates the notion *good*, and later derives from it the conception of the *bad.* How ill-matched these two concepts look, placed side by side: the bad of noble origin, and the *evil* that has risen out of the cauldron of unquenched hatred! The first is a by-product, a complementary color, almost an afterthought; the second is the beginning, the original creative act of slave ethics. But neither is the conception of good the same in both cases, as we soon find out when we ask ourselves who it is that is really evil according to the code of rancor. The answer is: precisely the good one of the opposite code, that is the noble, the powerful — only colored, reinterpreted, reenvisaged by the poisonous eye of resentment. And we are the first to admit that anyone who knew these "good" ones only as enemies would find them evil enemies indeed. For these same men who, amongst themselves, are so strictly constrained by custom, worship, ritual, gratitude, and by mutual surveillance and jealousy, who are so resourceful in consideration, tenderness, loyalty, pride and friendship, when once they step outside their circle become little better than uncaged beasts of prey. Once abroad in the wilderness, they revel in the freedom from social constraint and compensate for their long confinement in the quietude of their own community. They revert to the innocence of wild animals: we can imagine them returning from an orgy of murder, arson, rape, and torture, jubilant and at peace with themselves as though they had committed a fraternity prank — convinced, moreover, that the poets for a long time to come will have something to sing about and to praise. Deep within all these noble races there lurks the beast of prey, bent on spoil and conquest. This hidden urge has to be satisfied from time to time, the beast let loose in the wilderness. This goes as well for the Roman, Arabian, German, Japanese nobility as for the Homeric heroes and the Scandinavian vikings. The noble races have everywhere left in their wake the catchword "barbarian." And even their highest culture shows an awareness of this trait and a certain pride in it (as we see, for example, in Pericles' famous funeral oration, when he tells the Athenians: "Our boldness has gained us access to every land and sea, and erected monuments to itself *for both good and evil*.") This "boldness" of noble races, so headstrong, absurd, incalculable, sudden, improbable (Pericles commends the Athenians especially for their *rathumia*), their utter indifference to safety and comfort, their terrible pleasure in destruction, their taste for cruelty — all these traits are embodied by their victims in the image of the "barbarian," the "evil enemy," the God or the Vandal. . . . If it were true, as passes current nowadays, that the real meaning of culture resides in its power to domesticate man's savage instincts, then we might be justified in viewing all those rancorous machinations by which the noble tribes, and their ideals, have been laid low as the true instruments of culture. But this would still not amount to saying that the *organizers* themselves represent culture. Rather, the exact opposite would be true, as is vividly shown by the current state of affairs. These carriers of the leveling and retributive instincts, these descendants of every European and extra-European slavedom, and especially of the pre-Aryan populations, represent human retrogression most flagrantly. Such "instruments of culture" are a disgrace to man and might make one suspicious of culture altogether. One might be justified in fearing the wild beast lurking within all noble races and in being on one's guard against it, but who would not a thousand times prefer fear when it is accompanied with admiration to security accompanied by the loathsome sight of perversion, dwarfishness, degeneracy? And is not the latter our predicament today? What accounts for our repugnance to man — for there is no question that he makes us suffer? Certainly not our fear of him, rather the fact that there is no longer anything to be feared from him; that the vermin "man" occupies the entire stage; that, tame, hopelessly mediocre, and savorless, he considers himself the apex of historical evolution; and not entirely without justice, since he is still somewhat removed from the mass of sickly and effete creatures whom Europe is beginning to stink of today.

XIV

Would anyone care to learn something about the way in which ideals are manufactured? Does anyone have the nerve? . . . Well then, go ahead! There's a chink through which you can peek into this murky shop. But wait just a moment, Mr. Foolhardy; your eyes must grow accustomed to the fickle light. . . . All right, tell me what's going on in there, audacious fellow; now I am the one who is listening.

"I can't see a thing, but I hear all the more. There's a low, cautious whispering in every nook and corner. I have a notion these people are lying. All the sounds are sugary and soft. No doubt you were right; they are transmuting weakness into merit."

"Go on."

"Impotence, which cannot retaliate, into kindness; pusillanimity into humility; submission before those one hates into obedience to One of whom they say that he has commanded this submission — they call him God. The inoffensiveness of the weak, his cowardice, his ineluctable standing and waiting at doors, are being given honorific titles such as patience; to be *unable* to avenge oneself is called to be *unwilling* to avenge oneself — even forgiveness ("for they know not what *they* do — we alone know what *they* do.") Also there's some talk of loving one's enemy — accompanied by much sweat."

"Go on."

"I'm sure they are quite miserable, all these whisperers and small-time counterfeiters, even though they huddle close together for warmth. But they tell me that this very misery is the sign of their election by God, that one beats the dogs one loves best, that this misery is perhaps also a preparation, a test, a kind of training, perhaps even more than that: something for which eventually they will be compensated with tremendous interest — in gold? No, in happiness. They call this *bliss*."

"Go on."

"Now they tell me that not only are they better than the mighty of this earth, whose spittle they must lick (not from fear — by no means — but because God commands us to honor our superiors), but they are even better off, or at least they will be better off someday. But I've had all I can stand. The smell is too much for me. This shop where they manufacture ideals seems to me to stink of lies."

"But just a moment. You haven't told me anything about the greatest feat of these black magicians, who precipitate the white milk of loving-kindness out of every kind of blackness. Haven't you noticed their most consummate sleight of hand, their boldest, finest, most brilliant trick? Just watch! These vermin, full of vindictive hatred, what are they brewing out of their own poisons? Have you ever heard vengeance and hatred mentioned? Would you ever guess, if you only listened to their words, that these are men bursting with hatred?"

"I see what you mean. I'll open my ears again — and stop my nose. Now I can make out what they seem to have been saying all along: 'We, the good ones, are also the just ones.' They call the thing they seek not retribution but the triumph of justice; the thing they hate is not their enemy, by no means — they hate injustice, ungodliness; the thing they hope for and believe in is not vengeance, the sweet exultation of vengeance ('sweeter than honey' as Homer said) but 'the triumph of God, who is just, over the godless'; what remains to them to love on this earth is not their brothers in hatred, but what they call their 'brothers in love' — all who are good and just."

"And what do they call that which comforts them in all their sufferings — their phantasmagoria of future bliss?"

"Do I hear correctly? They call it Judgment Day, the coming of *their* kingdom, the 'Kingdom of God.' Meanwhile they live in 'faith,' in 'love,' in 'hope.' "

"Stop! I've heard enough."

XV

If the reader has thoroughly grasped — and I demand that here especially he dig down deeply — that it cannot be the task of the healthy to wait on the sick, or to make them well, he will also have grasped another important thing: that for physicians and medical attendants we require men who are themselves sick. I believe that we have here the key to the meaning of the ascetic priest. We must look upon the ascetic priest as the predestined advocate and savior of a sick flock if we are to comprehend his tremendous historical mission. His dominion is over sufferers; he is instinctively propelled toward this empire, in which he can display his own peculiar gifts and even find a kind of happiness. He must be sick himself, he must be deeply akin to all the shipwrecked and diseased, if he is to understand them and be understood by them; yet he must also be strong, master over himself even more than over others, with a will to power that is intact, if he is to be their support, overlord, disciplinarian, tyrant, god. They are his flock, and he must defend them — against whom? Against the healthy, obviously, but also against their envy of the healthy; he must be the natural antagonist and *contemner* of all rude, violent, savage health and power. The priest is the earliest version of that delicate animal which contemns more readily than it hates. He would not be spared the task of warring with the beasts of prey, but his war will be a war of cunning ("intellect") rather than of brute force, as goes without saying. He might even be obliged to develop out of himself a new type of savage animal, or at least to adumbrate a new kind of ferocity in which the polar bear, the smooth, cold, patient tiger, and the fox would combine to form a new species, at once attractive and awe-inspiring. If the occasion should arise he might even step, with ursine dignity and calculated superiority, among the other wild animal species: herald and mouthpiece of even more mysterious powers, determined to sow in their midst pain, inner division, self-contradiction — confident of his rule over all sufferers. To be sure, he carries with him balms and ointments, but in order to cure he must first create patients. And even as he alleviates the pain of his patients he pours poison into their wounds. Such, then, is the supreme accomplishment of this magician and animal tamer, in whose orbit all that is sound becomes sick and all that is sick, tame. This strange shepherd actually succeeds very well in defending his sick flock. He defends them even against themselves, against all the wickedness and malice smoldering within the herd and whatever other troubles are bred among the sick. He fights a clever, hard, secret battle against anarchy and disintegration, always aware of the piling-up of rancor, that most dangerous of dynamites. His essential task is to set off the dynamite in such a way that the blast will injure neither himself nor the herd. In other words, it is up to the priest to redirect resentment toward a new object. For is it not true that every sufferer instinctively seeks a cause for his suffering; more specifically, an agent, a "guilty" agent who is susceptible to pain — in short some living being or other on whom he can vent his feelings directly or in effigy, under some pretext or other? The release of aggression is the best palliative for any kind of affliction. The wish to alleviate pain through strong emotional excitation is, to my mind, the true physiological motive behind all manifestations of resentment. I strongly disagree with those who would see here a mere defensive or prophylactic reaction to sudden injury or jeopardy, a mere reflex, such as a headless frog makes to throw off an acid. There is a fundamental difference between the two processes: in the one case the effort is simply to prevent further injury, in the other to *dull* by means of some violent emotion a secret, tormenting pain that is gradually becoming intolerable — to banish it momentarily from consciousness. For that purpose an emotion of maximum violence is required, and any pretext that comes to hand will serve. "*Somebody* must be responsible for my discomfort." This sort of reasoning is universal among sick people and holds all the more sway over them the more obscure the real physiological cause of their discomfort is to them. (That cause may lie in an affection of the sympathetic nerve, or an excessive secretion of bile, or a deficiency of alkaline sulphates and phosphates in the blood, or an abdominal obstruction which impedes the circulation of the blood, or a disorder of the ovaries, etc.) All sufferers alike excel in finding imaginary pretexts for their suffering. They revel in suspicion and gloat over imaginary injuries and slights; they ransack the bowels of their past and present for obscure and dubious incidents which give free rein to their torturous suspicions; they intoxicate themselves with the poison of their own minds. They tear open the most ancient wounds, fasten the guilt on friend, wife, child — whatever is closest to them. Every suffering sheep says to himself, "I suffer; it must be somebody's fault." But his shepherd, the ascetic priest, says to him, "You are quite right, my sheep, somebody must be at fault here, but that somebody is yourself. You alone are to blame — you alone are to blame for yourself." This is not only very bold but also abundantly false. But one thing, at least, has been accomplished: resentment has found a new target.

XVI

By now the reader should perceive what life's curative instinct, through the agency of the ascetic priest, has at least *tried* to accomplish, and what end is served by the temporary tyranny of such paradoxical and sophistical concepts as *guilt, sin* or *sinfulness, perdition, damnation.* The end is always to render the sick, up to a certain point, harmless, to make the incurable destroy themselves and to introvert the resentment of the less severely afflicted. In other words, the goal is to utilize the evil instincts of all sufferers for the purposes of self-discipline, self-surveillance, self-conquest. It goes without saying that a "medication" of this sort can never result in a physiologically effective cure, nor can it even be claimed that the vital instinct has really been tapped for the rehabilitation of the personality. All that this method achieved for a long time was the organization and concentration of the sick on one side (the word *church* is the popular term for this grouping), and a kind of provisional sequestration of the sounder and more fully "achieved" on the other; in short, the opening up of a chasm between sickness and health. And yet this was a great deal. (I proceed in this essay on an assumption which, addressing the kind of reader I do, I need not laboriously justify. I assume that sinfulness is not a basic human condition but merely the ethico-religious interpretation of physiological distemper. — The fact that a person thinks himself "guilty" or "sinful" is no proof that he *is* so, any more than the fact that a person feels healthy is a proof of his health. Take, for example, the famous witch trials. In those days even the most acute and humane judges had not the faintest doubt that the witches were guilty. The "witches" themselves had no doubt, and yet there was no guilt. — To state my assumption somewhat more broadly: "psychological pain" is not a fact but merely a causal interpretation of a set of facts which so far have eluded exact formulation — really no more than a fat word taking the place of a vague question mark. If anyone is unable to get rid of a psychological pain, the fault lies not in his "psyche" but, more likely, in his belly [to put it crudely, which does not mean that it should be understood crudely]. . . . The strong, healthy person digests his experiences [including every deed and misdeed] as he does his meals, even though he may have swallowed a tough morsel. If he can't get rid of an experience, then this kind of indigestion is every bit as physical as the other, and often, in fact, merely one of the consequences of the other. Let me add that one may hold such notions and yet be an enemy of all materialism.)

Nietzsche termed Zarathustra the greatest gift humankind had ever been given, and also the profoundest. It is in this work that he presents what he calls his most important idea, namely the doctrine of eternal recurrence. Thus Spake Zarathustra, *a book for everyone and no one, "invaded" Nietzsche in the summer of 1881 in Sils in the Swiss Alps. The first three books of this philosophical poem were composed in ten-day bursts in 1883, with months of reflection between. The last book was written at the beginning of 1885.* Thus Spake Zarathustra, *like* Beyond Good and Evil, *which was published just after it, is about the "philosophy of the future." Though neither text provides us with that new philosophy, they each suggest how such a philosophy might be possible. Nietzsche's Zarathustra, then, is both destroyer and creator. Like Nietzsche, he is an iconoclast deeply troubled by the spiritual vacuum left by the death of God. And like Nietzsche, he must "become hard" in order to create.*

Thus Spake Zarathustra

OF SELF-OVERCOMING

What urges you on and arouses your ardour, you wisest of men, do you call it 'will to truth'?

Will to the conceivability of all being: that is what *I* call your will!

You first want to *make* all being conceivable: for, with a healthy mistrust, you doubt whether it is in fact conceivable.

From Friedrich Nietzsche, *Thus Spake Zarathustra.* Translated by R. J. Hollingdale (Penguin Classics, 1961, 1969), copyright © R. J. Hollingdale, 1961, 1969. Reproduced by permission of Penguin Books Ltd.

But it must bend and accommodate itself to you! Thus will your will have it. It must become smooth and subject to the mind as the mind's mirror and reflection.

That is your entire will, you wisest men; it is a will to power; and that is so even when you talk of good and evil and of the assessment of values.

You want to create the world before which you can kneel: this is your ultimate hope and intoxication.

The ignorant, to be sure, the people — they are like a river down which a boat swims: and in the boat, solemn and disguised, sit the assessments of value.

You put your will and your values upon the river of becoming; what the people believe to be good and evil betrays to me an ancient will to power.

It was you, wisest men, who put such passengers in this boat and gave them splendour and proud names — you and your ruling will!

Now the river bears your boat along: it has to bear it. It is of small account if the breaking wave foams and angrily opposes its keel!

It is not the river that is your danger and the end of your good and evil, you wisest men, it is that will itself, the will to power, the unexhausted, procreating life-will.

But that you may understand my teaching about good and evil, I shall relate to you my teaching about life and about the nature of all living creatures.

I have followed the living creature, I have followed the greatest and the smallest paths, that I might understand its nature.

I caught its glance in a hundredfold mirror when its mouth was closed, that its eye might speak to me. And its eye did speak to me.

But wherever I found living creatures, there too I heard the language of obedience. All living creatures are obeying creatures.

And this is the second thing: he who cannot obey himself will be commanded. That is the nature of living creatures.

But this is the third thing I heard: that commanding is more difficult than obeying. And not only because the commander bears the burden of all who obey, and that this burden can easily crush him.

In all commanding there appeared to me to be an experiment and a risk: and the living creature always risks himself when he commands.

Yes, even when he commands himself: then also must he make amends for his commanding. He must become judge and avenger and victim of his own law.

How has this come about? thus I asked myself. What persuades the living creature to obey and to command and to practise obedience even in commanding?

Listen now to my teaching, you wisest men! Test in earnest whether I have crept into the heart of life itself and down to the roots of its heart!

Where I found a living creature, there I found will to power; and even in the will of the servant I found the will to be master.

The will of the weaker persuades it to serve the stronger; its will wants to be master over those weaker still: this delight alone it is unwilling to forgo.

And as the lesser surrenders to the greater, that it may have delight and power over the least of all, so the greatest, too, surrenders and for the sake of power stakes — life.

The devotion of the greatest is to encounter risk and danger and play dice for death.

And where sacrifice and service and loving glances are, there too is will to be master. There the weaker steals by secret paths into the castle and even into the heart of the more powerful — and steals the power.

And life itself told me this secret: 'Behold,' it said, 'I am that *which must overcome itself again and again.*

'To be sure, you call it will to procreate or impulse towards a goal, towards the higher, more distant, more manifold: but all this is one and one secret.

'I would rather perish than renounce this one thing; and truly, where there is perishing and the falling of leaves, behold, there life sacrifices itself — for the sake of power!

'That I have to be struggle and becoming and goal and conflict of goals: ah, he who divines my will surely divines, too, along what *crooked* paths it has to go!

'Whatever I create and however much I love it — soon I have to oppose it and my love: thus will my will have it.

'And you too, enlightened man, are only a path and footstep of my will: truly, my will to power walks with the feet of your will to truth!

'He who shot the doctrine of "will to existence" at truth certainly did not hit the truth: this will — does not exist!

'For what does not exist cannot will; but that which is in existence, how could it still want to come into existence?

'Only where life is, there is also will: not will to life, but — so I teach you — will to power!

'The living creature values many things higher than life itself; yet out of this evaluation itself speaks — the will to power!

Thus life once taught me: and with this teaching do I solve the riddle of your hearts, you wisest men.

Truly, I say to you: Unchanging good and evil does not exist! From out of themselves they must overcome themselves again and again.

You exert power with your values and doctrines of good and evil, you assessors of values; and this is your hidden love and the glittering, trembling, and overflowing of your souls.

But a mightier power and a new overcoming grow from out your values: egg and egg-shell break against them.

And he who has to be a creator in good and evil, truly, has first to be a destroyer and break values.

Thus the greatest evil belongs with the greatest good: this, however, is the creative good.

Let us *speak* of this, you wisest men, even if it is a bad thing. To be silent is worse; all suppressed truths become poisonous.

And let everything that can break upon our truths — break! There is many a house still to build!

Thus spoke Zarathustra.

OF THE SPIRIT OF GRAVITY

I

My glib tongue — is of the people; I speak too coarsely and warmly for silky rabbits. And my words sound even stranger to all inky fish and scribbling foxes.

My hand — is a fool's hand: woe to all tables and walls and whatever has room left for fool's scribbling, fool's doodling!

My foot — is a horse's foot: with it I trot and trample up hill, down dale, hither and thither over the fields, and am the Devil's own for joy when I am out at a gallop.

My stomach — is it perhaps an eagle's stomach? For it likes lamb's flesh best of all. But it is certainly a bird's stomach.

Nourished with innocent and few things, ready and impatient to fly, to fly away — that is my nature now: how should there not be something of the bird's nature in it!

And especially bird-like is that I am enemy to the Spirit of Gravity: and truly, mortal enemy, arch-enemy, born enemy! Oh where has my enmity not flown and strayed already!

I could sing a song about that — and I *will* sing one, although I am alone in an empty house and have to sing it to my own ears.

There are other singers, to be sure, whose voices are softened, whose hands are eloquent, whose eyes are expressive, whose hearts are awakened, only when the house is full: I am not one of them.

2

He who will one day teach men to fly will have moved all boundary-stones; all boundary-stones will themselves fly into the air to him, he will baptize the earth anew — as 'the weightless'.

The ostrich runs faster than any horse, but even he sticks his head heavily into heavy earth: that is what the man who cannot yet fly is like.

He calls earth and life heavy: and so *will* the Spirit of Gravity have it! But he who wants to become light and a bird must love himself — thus do *I* teach.

Not with the love of the sick and diseased, to be sure: for with them even self-love stinks!

One must learn to love oneself with a sound and healthy love, so that one may endure it with oneself and not go roaming about — thus do I teach.

Such roaming about calls itself 'love of one's neighbour': these words have been up to now the best for lying and dissembling, and especially for those who were oppressive to everybody.

And truly, to *learn* to love oneself is no commandment for today or for tomorrow. Rather is this art the finest, subtlest, ultimate, and most patient of all.

For all his possessions are well concealed from the possessor; and of all treasure pits, one's own is the last to be digged — the Spirit of Gravity is the cause of that.

Almost in the cradle are we presented with heavy words and values: this dowry calls itself 'Good' and 'Evil'. For its sake we are forgiven for being alive.

And we suffer little children to come to us, to prevent them in good time from loving themselves: the Spirit of Gravity is the cause of that.

And we — we bear loyally what we have been giving upon hard shoulders over rugged mountains! And when we sweat we are told: 'Yes, life is hard to bear!'

But only man is hard to bear! That is because he bears too many foreign things upon his shoulders. Like the camel, he kneels down and lets himself be well laden.

Especially the strong, weight-bearing man in whom dwell respect and awe: he has laden too many *foreign* heavy words and values upon himself — now life seems to him a desert!

And truly! Many things that are *one's own* are hard to bear, too! And much that is intrinsic in man is like the oyster, that is loathsome and slippery and hard to grasp —

so that a noble shell with noble embellishments must intercede for it. But one has to learn this art as well: to *have* a shell and a fair appearance and a prudent blindness!

Again, it is deceptive about many things in man that many a shell is inferior and wretched and too much of a shell. Much hidden goodness and power is never guessed at; the most exquisite dainties find no tasters!

Women, or the most exquisite of them, know this: a little fatter, a little thinner — oh, how much fate lies in so little!

Man is difficult to discover, most of all to himself; the spirit often tells lies about the soul. The Spirit of Gravity is the cause of that.

But he has discovered himself who says: This is *my* good and evil:

he has silenced thereby the mole and dwarf who says: 'Good for all, evil for all.'

Truly, I dislike also those who call everything good and this world the best of all. I call such people the all-contented.

All-contentedness that knows how to taste everything: that is not the best taste! I honour the obstinate, fastidious tongues and stomachs that have learned to say 'I' and 'Yes' and 'No'.

But to chew and digest everything — that is to have a really swinish nature! Always to say Ye-a — only the ass and those like him have learned that.

Deep yellow and burning red: that is to *my* taste — it mixes blood with all colours. But he who whitewashes his house betrays to me a whitewashed soul.

One loves mummies, the other phantoms; and both alike enemy to all flesh and blood — oh, how both offend my taste! For I love blood.

And I do not want to stay and dwell where everyone spews and spits: that is now *my* taste — I would rather live among thieves and perjurers. No one bears gold in his mouth.

More offensive to me, however, are all lickspittles; and the most offensive beast of a man I ever found I baptized Parasite: it would not love, yet wanted to live by love.

I call wretched all who have only one choice: to become an evil beast or an evil tamer of beasts: I would build no tabernacles among these men.

I also call wretched those who always have to *wait* — they offend my taste: all tax-collectors and shopkeepers and kings and other keepers of lands and shops.

Truly, I too have learned to wait, I have learned it from the very heart, but only to wait for *myself*. And above all I have learned to stand and to walk and to run and to jump and to climb and to dance.

This, however, is my teaching: He who wants to learn to fly one day must first learn to stand and to walk and to run and to climb and to dance — you cannot learn to fly by flying!

With rope-ladders I learned to climb to many a window, with agile legs I climbed up high masts: to sit upon high masts of knowledge seemed to me no small happiness —

to flicker like little flames upon high masts: a little light, to be sure, but yet a great comfort to castaway sailors and the shipwrecked!

I came to my truth by diverse paths and in diverse ways: it was not upon a single ladder that I climbed to the height where my eyes survey my distances.

And I have asked the way only unwillingly — that has always offended my taste! I have rather questioned and attempted the ways themselves.

All my progress has been an attempting and a questioning — and truly, one has to *learn* how to answer such questioning! That however — is to my taste:

not good taste, not bad taste, but *my* taste, which I no longer conceal and of which I am no longer ashamed.

'This — is now *my* way: where is yours?' Thus I answered those who asked me 'the way'. For *the* way — does not exist!

Thus spoke Zarathustra.

OF THE THREE EVIL THINGS

I

In a dream, in my last morning dream, I stood today upon a headland — beyond the world, I held a pair of scales and *weighed* the world.

Oh, that the dawn came to me too soon! It glowed me into wakefulness, the jealous dawn! It is always jealous of the glow of my morning dreams.

Measurable to him who has time, weighable to a good weigher, accessible to strong pinions, divinable to divine nutcrackers: thus did my dream find the world.

My dream, a bold sailor, half ship half hurricane, silent as a butterfly, impatient as a falcon: how did it have time and patience today for weighing of worlds?

Did my wisdom perhaps speak secretly to it, my laughing, wakeful day-wisdom that mocks all 'infinite worlds'? For my wisdom says: 'Where power is, there *number* becomes master: it has more power.'

How confidently did my dream gaze upon this finite world, eager neither for new things nor for old; neither in awe nor in supplication —

as if a round apple presented itself to my hand, a ripe, golden apple with a soft, cool, velvety skin — thus the world presented itself to me —

as if a tree nodded to me, a wide-branching, strong-willed tree, bent for reclining and as a footstool for the way-weary: thus the world stood upon my headland —

as if tender hands brought me a casket — a casket open for the delight of modest, adoring eyes: thus the world presented himself before me today —

not so enigmatic as to frighten away human love, not so explicit as to put to sleep human wisdom — a good, human thing was the world to me today, this world of which so many evil things are said!

How grateful I am to my morning dream, that today in the early morning I thus weighed the world! It came to me as a good, human thing, this dream and comforter of the heart!

And that I may do the same as it by day and learn and imitate its best aspects, I will now place the three most evil things upon the scales and weigh them well and humanly.

He who taught how to bless also taught how to curse: which are the three most-cursed things in the world? I will place these upon the scales.

Sensual pleasure, lust for power, selfishness: these three have hitherto been cursed the most and held in the worst and most unjust repute — these three will I weigh well and humanly.

Well then! Here is my headland and there is the sea: *it* rolls towards me, shaggy, fawning, the faithful old hundred-headed canine monster that I love.

Well then! Here I will hold the scales over the rolling sea:and I choose a witness, too, to look on — you, hermit tree, you heavy-odoured, broad-arched tree that I love!

Upon what bridge does the present go over to the hereafter? What compulsion compels the high to bend to the low? And what bids even the highest — to grow higher still?

Now the scales stand level and still: I have thrown in three weighty questions, the other scale bears three weighty answers.

2

Sensual pleasure: goad and stake to all hair-shirted despisers of the body and anathematized as 'the world' by all afterworldsmen: for it mocks and makes fools of all teachers of confusion and error.

Sensual pleasure: to the rabble the slow fire over which they are roasted; to all worm-eaten wood, to all stinking tatters, the ever-ready stewing-oven of lust.

Sensual pleasure: innocent and free to free hearts, the earth's garden-joy, an overflowing of thanks to the present from all the future.

Sensual pleasure: a sweet poison only to the withered, but to the lion-willed the great restorative and reverently-preserved wine of wines.

Sensual pleasure: the great symbolic happiness of a higher happiness and highest hope. For marriage is promised to many, and more than marriage —

to many that are stranger to one another than man and woman: and who has fully conceived *how strange* man and woman are to one another!

Sensual pleasure — but I will fence my thoughts round, and my words too: so that swine and hot fanatics shall not break into my garden!

Lust for power: the scourge of fire of the hardest-hearted; the cruel torment reserved by the cruellest for himself; the dark flame of living bonfires.

Lust for power: the wicked fly seated upon the vainest peoples; the mocker of all uncertain virtue; which rides upon every horse and every pride.

Lust for power: the earthquake that breaks and bursts open all that is decayed and hollow; the rolling, growling, punitive destroyer of white-washed sepulches; the flashing question-mark beside premature answers.

Lust for power: before its glance man crawls and bends and toils and becomes lower than the swine or the snake — until at last the cry of the great contempt bursts from him —

Lust for power: the fearsome teacher of the great contempt, who preaches in the face of cities and empires 'Away with you!' — until at last they themselves cry out 'Away with *me*!'

Lust for power: which, however, rises enticingly even to the pure and the solitary and up to self-sufficient heights, glowing like a love that paints purple delights enticingly on earthly heavens.

Lust for power: but who shall call it *lust*, when the height longs to stoop down after power! Truly, there is no sickness and lust in such a longing and descent!

That the lonely height may not always be solitary and sufficient to itself; that the mountain may descend to the valley and the wind of the heights to the lowlands —

Oh who shall find the rightful baptismal and virtuous name for such a longing! 'Bestowing virtue' — that is the name Zarathustra once gave the unnameable.

And then it also happened — and truly, it happened for the first time! — that his teaching glorified *selfishness*, the sound, healthy selfishness that issues from a mighty soul —

from a mighty soul, to which pertains the exalted body, the beautiful, victorious, refreshing body, around which everything becomes a mirror;

the supple, persuasive body, the dancer whose image and epitome is the self-rejoicing soul. The self-rejoicing of such bodies and souls calls itself: 'Virtue'.

Such self-rejoicing protects itself with its doctrines of good and bad as with sacred groves; with the names it gives its happiness it banishes from itself all that is contemptible.

It banishes from itself all that is cowardly; it says: Bad — that is to say, cowardly! He who is always worrying, sighing, complaining, and who gleans even the smallest advantage, seems contemptible to it.

It also despises all woeful wisdom: for truly, there is also a wisdom that blossoms in darkness, a night-shade wisdom, which is always sighing: 'All is vain!'

Timid mistrustfulness seems base to it, as do all who desire oaths instead of looks and hands; and all-too-mistrustful wisdom, for such is the nature of cowardly souls.

It regards as baser yet him who is quick to please, who, dog-like, lies upon his back, the humble man; and there is also a wisdom that is humble and dog-like and pious and quick to please.

Entirely hateful and loathsome to it is he who will never defend himself, who swallows down poisonous spittle and evil looks, the too-patient man who puts up with everything, is content with everything: for that is the nature of slaves.

Whether one be servile before gods and divine kicks, or before men and the silly opinions of men: it spits at slaves of *all* kinds, this glorious selfishness!

Bad: that is what it calls all that is broken-down and niggardly-servile, unclear, blinking eyes, oppressed hearts, and that false, yielding type of man who kisses with broad, cowardly lips.

And sham-wisdom: that is what it calls all wit that slaves and old men and weary men affect; and especially the whole bad, raving, over-clever priest-foolishness!

And to ill-use selfishness — precisely *that* has been virtue and called virtue. And 'selfless' — that is what, with good reason, all these world-weary cowards and Cross-spiders wished to be!

But now the day, the transformation, the sword of judgement, *the great noontide* comes to them all: then many things shall be revealed!

And he who declares the Ego healthy and holy and selfishness glorious — truly, he, a prophet, declares too what he knows: '*Behold, it comes, it is near, the great noontide!*'

Thus spoke Zarathustra.

THE CONVALESCENT

I

One morning, not long after his return to the cave, Zarathustra sprang up from his bed like a madman, cried with a terrible voice, and behaved as if someone else were lying on the bed and would not rise from it; and Zarathustra's voice rang out in such a way that his animals came to him in terror and from all the caves and hiding-places in the neighbour-hood of Zarathustra's cave all the creatures slipped away, flying, flutter-ing, creeping, jumping, according to the kind of foot or wing each had been given. Zarathustra, however, spoke these words:

Up, abysmal thought, up from my depths! I am your cockerel and dawn, sleepy worm: up! up! My voice shall soon crow you awake!

Loosen the fetters of your ears: listen! For I want to hear you! Up! Up! Here is thunder enough to make even the graves listen!

And wipe the sleep and all the dimness and blindness from your eyes! Hear me with your eyes, too: my voice is a medicine even for those born blind.

And once you are awake you shall stay awake for ever. It is not *my* way to awaken great-grandmothers from sleep in order to bid them — go back to sleep!

Are you moving, stretching, rattling? Up! Up! You shall not rattle, you shall — speak to me! Zarathustra the Godless calls you!

I, Zarathustra, the advocate of life, the advocate of suffering, the advocate of the circle — I call you, my most abysmal thought!

Ah! you are coming — I hear you! My abyss *speaks*, I have turned my ultimate depth into the light!

Ah! Come here! Give me your hand — ha! don't! Ha, ha! — Disgust, disgust, disgust — woe is me!

2

Hardly had Zarathustra spoken these words, however, when he fell down like a dead man and remained like a dead man for a long time. But when he again came to himself, he was pale and trembling and remained lying down and for a long time would neither eat nor drink. This condition lasted seven days; his animals, however, did not leave him by day or night, except that the eagle flew off to fetch food. And whatever he had collected and fetched he laid upon Zarathustra's bed: so that at last Zarathustra lay among yellow and red berries, grapes, rosy apples, sweet-smelling herbs and pine-cones. At his feet, however, two lambs were spread, which the eagle had, with difficulty, carried off from their shepherd.

At last, after seven days, Zarathustra raised himself in his bed, took a rosy apple in his hand, smelt it, and found its odour pleasant. Then his animals thought the time had come to speak with him.

'O Zarathustra,' they said, 'now you have lain like that seven days, with heavy eyes: will you not now get to your feet again?

'Step out of your cave: the world awaits you like a garden. The wind is laden with heavy fragrance that longs for you; and all the brooks would like to run after you.

'All things long for you, since you have been alone seven days — step out of your cave! All things want to be your physicians!

'Has perhaps a new knowledge come to you, a bitter, oppressive knowledge? You have lain like leavened dough, your soul has risen and overflowed its brim.'

'O my animals,' answered Zarathustra, 'go on talking and let me listen! Your talking is such refreshment: where there is talking, the world is like a garden to me. How sweet it is, that words and sounds of music exist: are words and music not rainbows and seeming bridges between things eternally separated?

'Every soul is a world of its own; for every soul every other soul is an afterworld.

'Appearance lies most beautifully among the most alike; for the smallest gap is the most difficult to bridge.

'For me — how could there be an outside-of-me? There is no outside! But we forget that, when we hear music; how sweet it is, that we forget!

'Are things not given names and musical sounds, so that man may refresh himself with things? Speech is a beautiful foolery: with it man dances over all things.

'How sweet is all speech and all the falsehoods of music! With music does our love dance upon many-coloured rainbows.'

'O Zarathustra,' said the animals then, 'all things themselves dance for such as think as we: they come and offer their hand and laugh and flee — and return.

'Everything goes, everything returns; the wheel of existence rolls for ever. Everything dies, everything blossoms anew; the year of existence runs on for ever.

'Everything breaks, everything is joined anew; the same house of existence builds itself for ever. Everything departs, everything meets again; the ring of existence is true to itself for ever.

'Existence begins in every instant; the ball There rolls around every Here. The middle is everywhere. The path of eternity is crooked.'

'O you buffoons and barrel-organs!' answered Zarathustra and smiled again; 'how well you know what had to be fulfilled in seven days:

'and how that monster crept into my throat and choked me! But I bit its head off and spat it away.

'And you — have already made a hurdy-gurdy song of it? I, however, lie here now, still weary from this biting and spitting away, still sick with my own redemption.

'*And you looked on at it all?* O my animals, are you, too, cruel? Did you desire to be spectators of my great pain, as men do? For man is the cruellest animal.

'More than anything on earth he enjoys tragedies, bullfights, and crucifixions; and when he invented Hell for himself, behold, it was his heaven on earth.

'When the great man cries out, straightway the little man comes running; his tongue is hanging from his mouth with lasciviousness. He, however, calls it his "pity".

'The little man, especially the poet — how zealously he accuses life in words! Listen to it, but do not overlook the delight that is in all accusation!

'Such accusers of life: life overcomes them with a glance of its eye. "Do you love me?" it says impudently; "just wait a little, I have no time for you yet."

'Man is the cruellest animal towards himself; and with all who call themselves "sinners" and "bearers of the Cross" and "penitents" do not overlook the sensual pleasure that is in this complaint and accusation!

'And I myself — do I want to be the accuser of man? Ah, my animals, this alone have I learned, that the wickedest in man is necessary for the best in him,

'that all that is most wicked in him is his best *strength* and the hardest stone for the highest creator; and that man must grow better *and* wickeder:

'To know: Man is wicked; *that* was to be tied to no torture-stake — but I cried as no one had cried before:

' "Alas, that his wickedest is so very small! Alas, that his best is so very small!"

'The great disgust at man — *it* choked me and had crept into my throat: and what the prophet prophesied: "It is all one, nothing is worth while, knowledge chokes."

'A long twilight limps in front of me, a mortally-weary, death-intoxicated sadness which speaks with a yawn.

' "The man of whom you are weary, the little man, recurs eternally" — thus my sadness yawned and dragged its feet and could not fall asleep.

'The human earth became to me a cave, its chest caved in, everything living became to me human decay and bones and mouldering past.

'My sighs sat upon all the graves of man and could no longer rise; my sighs and questions croaked and choked and gnawed and wailed by day and night:

' "Alas, man recurs eternally! The little man recurs eternally!"

'I had seen them both naked, the greatest man and the smallest man: all too similar to one another, even the greatest all too human!

'The greatest all too small! — that was my disgust at man! And eternal recurrence even for the smallest! that was my disgust at all existence!

'Ah, disgust! Disgust! Disgust!' Thus spoke Zarathustra and sighed and shuddered; for he remembered his sickness. But his animals would not let him speak further.

'Speak no further, convalescent!' — thus his animals answered him, 'but go out to where the world awaits you like a garden.

'Go out to the roses and bees and flocks of doves! But go out especially to the song-birds, so that you may learn *singing* from them!

'For convalescents should sing; let the healthy talk. And when the healthy man, too, desires song, he desires other songs than the convalescent.'

'O you buffoons and barrel-organs, do be quiet!' answered Zarathustra and smiled at his animals. 'How well you know what comfort I devised for myself in seven days!

'That I have to sing again — *that* comfort and *this* convalescence did I devise for myself: do you want to make another hurdy-gurdy song out of that, too?'

'Speak no further,' his animals answered once more; 'rather first prepare yourself a lyre, convalescent, a new lyre!

'For behold, O Zarathustra! New lyres are needed for your new songs.

'Sing and bubble over, O Zarathustra, heal your soul with new songs, so that you may bear your great destiny, that was never yet the destiny of any man!

'For your animals well know, O Zarathustra, who you are and must become: behold, *you are the teacher of the eternal recurrence,* that is now *your* destiny!

'That you have to be the first to teach this doctrine — how should this great destiny not also be your greatest danger and sickness!

'Behold, we know what you teach: that all things recur eternally and we ourselves with them, and that we have already existed an infinite number of times before and all things with us.

'You teach that there is a great year of becoming, a colossus of a year: this year must, like an hour-glass, turn itself over again and again, so that it may run down and run out anew:

'So that all these years resemble one another, in the greatest things and in the smallest, so that we ourselves resemble ourselves in each great year, in the greatest things and in the smallest.

'And if you should die now, O Zarathustra: behold, we know too what you would then say to yourself — but your animals ask you not to die yet!

'You would say — and without trembling, but rather gasping for happiness: for a great weight and oppression would have been lifted from you, most patient of men!

' "Now I die and decay," you would say, "and in an instant I shall be nothingness. Souls are as mortal as bodies.

' "But the complex of causes in which I am entangled will recur — it will create me again! I myself am part of these causes of the eternal recurrence.

' "I shall return, with this sun, with this earth, with this eagle, with this serpent — *not* to a new life or a better life or a similar life:

' "I shall return eternally to this identical and self-same life, in the greatest things and in the smallest, to teach once more the eternal recurrence of all things,

' "to speak once more the teaching of the great noontide of earth and man, to tell man of the Superman once more.

' "I spoke my teaching, I broke upon my teaching: thus my eternal fate will have it — as prophet do I perish!

' "Now the hour has come when he who is going down shall bless himself. Thus — *ends* Zarathustra's down-going." '

When the animals had spoken these words they fell silent and expected that Zarathustra would say something to them: but Zarathustra did not hear that they were silent. On the contrary, he lay still with closed eyes like a sleeper, although he was not asleep: for he was conversing with his soul. The serpent and the eagle, however, when they found him thus silent, respected the great stillness around him and discreetly withdrew.

FEODOR DOSTOYEVSKY

In his Genealogy of Morals, *Nietzsche tells us that "already at the age of thirteen I was exercised by the problem of evil." His solution to the problem was, he claims, to make God the "father of evil." In this selection from* The Brothers Karamazov, *Ivan the skeptic addresses this perennial problem of evil and its relation to the possibility of the existence of God. His examples provide a dramatic counterpoint to his devout brother Alyosha's declaration of faith.*

Rebellion

'I must make a confession to you,' Ivan began. 'I never could understand how one can love one's neighbours. In my view, it is one's neighbours that one can't possibly love, but only perhaps these who live far away. I read somewhere about "John the Merciful" (some saint) who, when a hungry and frozen stranger came to him and begged him to warm him, lay down with him in his bed and, putting his arms around him, began breathing into his mouth, which was festering and fetid from some awful disease. I'm convinced that he did so from heartache, from heartache that originated in a lie, for the sake of love arising from a sense of duty, for the sake of a penance he had imposed upon himself. To love a man, it's necessary that he should be hidden, for as soon as he shows his face, love is gone.'

'The elder Zossima has talked about it more than once,' observed Alyosha. 'He, too, declared that a man's face often prevented many people who were inexperienced in love from loving him. But then there's a great deal of love in mankind, almost Christ-like love, as I know myself, Ivan. . . .'

'Well, I'm afraid I don't know anything about it yet and I can't understand it, and an innumerable multitude of people are with me there. You see, the question is whether that is due to men's bad qualities or whether that is their nature. In my opinion, Christ's love for men is in a way a miracle that is impossible on earth. It is true he was a god. But we are no gods. Suppose, for instance, that I am capable of profound suffering, but no one else could ever know how much I suffer, because he is someone else and not I. Moreover, a man is rarely ready to admit that another man is suffering (as if it were some honour). Why doesn't he admit it, do you think? Because, I suppose, I have a bad smell or a stupid face, or because I once trod on his foot. Besides, there is suffering and suffering: there is humiliating suffering, which degrades me; a benefactor of mine, for instance, would not object to my being hungry, but he would not often tolerate some higher kind of suffering in me, for an idea, for instance. That he would only tolerate in exceptional cases, and even then he might look at me and suddenly realize that I haven't got the kind of face which, according to some fantastic notion of his, a man suffering for some idea ought to have. So he at once deprives me of all his benefactions, and not from an evil heart, either. Beggars, especially honourable beggars, should never show themselves in the streets, but ask for charity through the newspapers. Theoretically it is still possible to love one's neighbours, and sometimes even from a distance, but at close quarters almost never. If everything had been as on the stage, in the ballet, where, if beggars come in, they wear silken rags and tattered lace and beg for alms dancing gracefully, then it would still be possible to look at them with pleasure. But even then we might admire them but not love them. But enough of this. All I wanted is to make you see my point of view. I wanted to discuss the suffering of humanity in general, but perhaps we'd better confine ourselves to the sufferings of children. This will reduce the scope of my argument by a tenth, but I think we'd better confine our argument to the children. It's all the worse for me, of course. For, to begin with, one can love children even at close quarters and even with dirty and ugly faces (though I can't help feeling that children's faces are never ugly). Secondly, I won't talk about grown-ups because, besides being disgusting and undeserving of love, they have something to compensate them for it: they have eaten the apple and know good and evil and have become "like gods". They go on eating it still. But little children haven't eaten anything and so far are not guilty of anything. Do you love little children, Alyosha? I know you do and you will understand why I want to talk only about them now. If they, too, suffer terribly on earth, they do so, of course, for their fathers. They are punished for their fathers who have eaten the apple, but this is an argument from another world, an argument that is incomprehensible to the human heart here on earth. No innocent must suffer for another, and such innocents, too! You may be surprised at me, Alyosha, for I too love little children terribly. And note, please, that cruel men, passionate and carnal men, Karamazovs, are sometimes very fond of children. Children, while they are children, up to seven years, for instance, are very different from grown-up people: they seem to be quite different creatures with quite different natures. I knew a murderer in prison: in the course of his career he had murdered whole families in the houses he had broken into at night for the purpose of robbery, and while about it he had also murdered several children. But when he was in prison he showed a very peculiar affection for them. He used to stand by the window of his cell for hours watching the children playing in the prison yard. He trained one little boy to come up to his window and made great friends with him. You don't know why I'm telling you this, Alyosha? I'm afraid I have a headache and I'm feeling sad.'

'You speak with a strange air,' Alyosha observed uneasily, 'as though you were not quite yourself.'

'By the way, not so long ago a Bulgarian in Moscow told me,' Ivan went on, as though not bothering to listen to his brother, 'of the terrible atrocities committed all over Bulgaria by the Turks and Circassians who were afraid of a general uprising of the Slav population. They burn, kill, violate women and children, nail their prisoners' ears to fences and leave them like that till next morning when they hang them, and so on — it's impossible to imagine it all. And, indeed, people sometimes speak of man's "bestial" cruelty, but this is very unfair and insulting to the beasts: a beast can never be so cruel as a man, so ingeniously, so artistically cruel. A tiger merely gnaws and tears to pieces, that's all he knows. It would never occur to him to nail men's ears to a fence and leave them like that overnight, even if he were able to do it. These Turks, incidentally, seemed to derive a voluptuous pleasure from torturing children, cutting a child out of its mother's womb with a dagger and tossing babies up in the air and catching them on a bayonet before the eyes of their mothers. It was doing it before the eyes of their mothers that made it so enjoyable. But one incident I found particularly interesting. Imagine a baby in the arms of a trembling mother, surrounded by Turks who had just entered her house. They are having great fun: they fondle the baby, they laugh to make it laugh and they are successful: the baby laughs. At that moment the Turk points a pistol four inches from the baby's face. The boy laughs happily, stretches out his little hands to grab the pistol, when suddenly the artist pulls the trigger in the baby's face and blows his brains out. . . . Artistic, isn't it? Incidentally, I'm told the Turks are very fond of sweets.'

'Why are you telling me all this, Ivan?' asked Alyosha.

'I can't help thinking that if the devil doesn't exist and, therefore, man has created him, he has created him in his own image and likeness.'

'Just as he did God, you mean.'

'Oh, you're marvellous at "cracking the wind of the poor phrase", as Polonius says in *Hamlet*,' laughed Ivan. 'You've caught me there. All right. I'm glad. Your God is a fine one, if man created him in his own image and likeness. You asked me just now why I was telling you all this: you see, I'm a collector of certain interesting little facts and, you know, I'm jotting down and collecting from newspapers and books, from any-where, in fact, certain jolly little anecdotes, and I've already a good collection of them. The Turks, of course, have gone into my collection, but they are, after all, foreigners. I've also got lovely stories from home. Even better than the Turkish ones. We like corporal punishment, you know. The birch and the lash mostly. It's a national custom. With us nailed ears are unthinkable, for we are Europeans, after all. But the birch and the lash are something that is our own and cannot be taken away from us. Abroad they don't seem to have corporal punishment at all now. Whether they have reformed their habits or whether they've passed special legislation prohibiting flogging — I don't know, but they've made up for it by something else, something as purely national as ours. Indeed, it's so national that it seems to be quite impossible in our country, though I believe it is taking root here too, especially since the spread of the religious movement among our aristocracy. I have a very charming brochure, translated from the French, about the execution quite recently, only five years ago, of a murderer in Geneva. The murderer, Richard, a young fellow of three and twenty, I believe, repented and was converted to the Christian faith before his execution. This Richard fellow was an illegitimate child who at the age of six was given by his parents *as a present* to some shepherds in the Swiss mountains. The shepherds brought him up to work for them. He grew up among them like a little wild animal. The shepherds taught him nothing. On the contrary, when he was seven they sent him to take the cattle out to graze in the cold and wet, hungry and in rags. And it goes without saying that they never thought about it or felt remorse, being convinced that they had every right to treat him like that, for Richard had been given to them just as a chattel and they didn't even think it necessary to feed him. Richard himself testified how in those years, like the prodigal son in the Gospel, he was so hungry that he wished he could eat the mash given to the pigs, which were fattened for sale. But he wasn't given even that and he was beaten when he stole from the pigs. And that was how he spent all his childhood and his youth, till he grew up and, having grown strong, he himself went to steal. The savage began to earn his living as a day labourer in Geneva, and what he earned he spent on drink. He lived like a brute and finished up by killing and robbing an old man. He was caught, tried, and sentenced to death. There are no sentimentalists there, you see. In prison he was immediately surrounded by pastors and members of different Christian sects, philanthropic ladies, and so on. They taught him to read and write in prison, expounded the Gospel to him, exhorted him, tried their best to persuade him, wheedled, coaxed, and pressed him till he himself at last solemnly confessed his crime. He was converted and wrote to the court himself that he was a monster and that at last it had been vouchsafed to him by God to see the light and obtain grace. Everyone in Geneva was excited about him — the whole of philanthropic and religious Geneva. Everyone who was well-bred and belonged to the higher circles of Geneva society rushed to the prison to see him. They embraced and kissed Richard: "You are our brother! Grace has descended upon you!" Richard himself just wept with emotion: "Yes, grace has descended upon me!

Before in my childhood and youth I was glad of pigs' food, but now grace has descended upon me, too, and I'm dying in the Lord!" "Yes, yes, Richard, die in the Lord. You've shed blood and you must die in the Lord. Though it was not your fault that you knew not the Lord when you coveted the pigs' food and when you were beaten for stealing it (what you did was very wrong, for it is forbidden to steal), you've shed blood and you must die." And now the last day comes. Richard, weak and feeble, does nothing but cry and repeat every minute: "This is the happiest day of my life. I'm going to the Lord!" "Yes," cry the pastors, the judges, and the philanthropic ladies, "this is the happiest day of your life, for you are going to the Lord!" They all walked and drove in carriages behind the cart on which Richard was being taken to the scaffold. At last they arrived at the scaffold: "Die, brother," they cried to Richard, "die in the Lord, for His grace has descended upon you!" And so, covered with the kisses of his brothers, they dragged brother Richard on to the scaffold, placed him on the guillotine, and chopped off his head in a most brotherly fashion because grace had descended upon him too. Yes, that's characteristic. That brochure has been translated into Russian by some aristocratic Russian philanthropists of the Lutheran persuasion and sent gratis to the newspapers and other editorial offices for the enlightenment of the Russian people. The incident with Richard is so interesting because it's national. Though we may consider it absurd to cut off the head of a brother of ours because he has become our brother and because grace has descended upon him, we have, I repeat, our own national customs which are not much better. The most direct and spontaneous historic pastime we have is the infliction of pain by beating. Nekrassov has a poem about a peasant who flogs a horse about its eyes, "its gentle eyes". Who hasn't seen that? That is a truly Russian characteristic. He describes how a feeble nag, which has been pulling too heavy a load, sticks in the mud with its cart and cannot move. The peasant beats it, beats it savagely and, in the end, without realizing why he is doing it and intoxicated by the very act of beating, goes on showering heavy blows upon it. "Weak as you are, pull you must! I don't care if you die so long as you go on pulling!" The nag pulls hard but without avail, and he begins lashing the poor defenceless creature across its weeping, "gentle eyes". Beside itself with pain, it gives one tremendous pull, pulls out the cart, and off it goes, trembling all over and gasping for breath, moving sideways, with a curious sort of skipping motion, unnaturally and shamefully — it's horrible in Nekrassov. But it's only a horse and God has given us horses to be flogged. So the Tartars taught us and left us the whip as a present. But men, too, can be flogged. And there you have an educated and well-brought-up gentleman and his wife who birch their own little daughter, a child of seven — I have a full account of it. Daddy is glad that the twigs have knots, for, as he says, "it will sting more" and so he begins "stinging" his own daughter. I know for a fact that there are people who get so excited that they derive a sensual pleasure from every blow, literally a sensual pleasure, which grows progressively with every subsequent blow. They beat for a minute, five minutes, ten minutes. The more it goes on the more "stinging" do the blows become. The child screams, at last it can scream no more, it is gasping for breath. "Daddy, Daddy, dear Daddy!" The case, by some devilishly indecent chance, is finally brought to court. Counsel is engaged. The Russian people have long called an advocate — "a hired conscience". Counsel shouts in his client's defence: "It's such a simple thing, an ordinary domestic incident. A father has given a hiding to his daughter and, to our shame, it's been brought to court!" Convinced by him, the jurymen retire and bring in a verdict of not guilty. The public roars with delight that the torturer has been acquitted. Oh, what a pity I wasn't there! I'd have bawled out a proposal to found a scholarship in the name of the torturer! . . . Charming pictures. But I have still better ones about children. I've collected a great deal of facts about Russian children, Alyosha. A father and mother, "most respectable people of high social position, of good education and breeding", hated their little five-year-old daughter. You see, I repeat again most emphatically that this love of torturing children and only children is a peculiar characteristic of a great many people. All other individuals of the human species these torturers treat benevolently and mildly like educated and humane Europeans, but they are very fond of torturing children and, in a sense, this is their way of loving children. It's just the defencelessness of these little ones that tempts the torturers, the angelic trustfulness of the child, who has nowhere to go and no one to run to for protection — it is this that inflames the evil blood of the torturer. In every man, of course, a wild beast is hidden — the wild beast of irascibility, the wild beast of sensuous intoxication from the screams of the tortured victim. The wild beast let off the chain and allowed to roam free. The wild beast of diseases contracted in vice, gout, bad liver, and so on. This poor five-year-old girl was subjected to every possible torture by those educated parents. They beat her, birched her, kicked her, without themselves knowing why, till her body was covered with bruises; at last they reached the height of refinement: they shut her up all night, in the cold and frost, in the privy and because she didn't ask to get up at night (as though a child of five, sleeping its angelic, sound sleep, could be trained at her age to ask for such a thing), they smeared her face with excrement and made her eat it, and it was her mother, her mother who made her! And that mother could sleep at night, hearing the groans of the poor child locked up in that vile place! Do you realize what it means when a little creature like that, who's quite unable to understand what is happening to her, beats her little aching chest in that vile place, in the dark and cold, with her tiny fist and weeps searing, unresentful and gentle tears to "dear, kind God" to protect her? Can you understand all this absurd and horrible business, my friend and brother, you meek and humble novice? Can you understand why all this absurd and horrible business is so necessary and has been brought to pass? They tell me that without it man could not even have existed on earth, for he would not have known good and evil. But why must we know that confounded good and evil when it costs so much? Why, the whole world of knowledge isn't worth that child's tears to her "dear and kind God"! I'm not talking of the sufferings of grown-up people, for they have eaten the apple and to hell with them — let them all go to hell, but these little ones, these little ones! I'm sorry I'm torturing you, Alyosha. You're not yourself. I'll stop if you like.'

'Never mind, I want to suffer too,' murmured Alyosha.

'One more, only one more picture, and that, too, because it's so curious, so very characteristic, but mostly because I've only just read about it in some collection of Russian antiquities, in the *Archives* or *Antiquity*. I'll have to look it up, I'm afraid I've forgotten where I read it. It happened in the darkest days of serfdom, at the beginning of this century — and long live the liberator of the people! There was at the beginning of the century a General, a very rich landowner with the highest aristocratic connexions, but one of those (even then, it is true, rather an exception) who, after retiring from the army, are almost convinced that their service to the State has given them the power of life and death over their "subjects". There were such people in those days. Well, so the General went to live on his estate with its two thousand serfs, imagining himself to be God knows how big a fellow and treating his poorer neighbours as though they were his hangers-on and clowns. He had hundreds of hounds in his kennels and nearly a hundred whips — all mounted and wearing uniforms. One day, a serf-boy, a little boy of eight, threw a stone in play and hurt the paw of the General's favourite hound. "Why is my favourite dog lame?" He was told that the boy had thrown a stone at it and hurt its paw. "Oh, so it's you, is it?" said the General, looking him up and down. "Take him!" They took him. They took him away from his mother, and he spent the night in the lock-up. Early next morning the General, in full dress, went out hunting. He mounted his horse, surrounded by his hangers-on, his whips, and his huntsmen, all mounted. His house-serfs were all mustered to teach them a lesson, and in front of them all stood the child's mother. The boy was brought out of the lock-up. It was a bleak, cold, misty autumn day, a perfect day for hunting. The General ordered the boy to be undressed. The little boy was stripped naked. He shivered, panic-stricken and not daring to utter a sound. "Make him run!" ordered the General. "Run, run!" the whips shouted at him. The boy ran. "Sick him!" bawled the General, and set the whole pack of borzoi hounds on him. They hunted the child down before the eyes of his mother, and the hounds tore him to pieces! I believe the

General was afterwards deprived of the right to administer his estates. Well, what was one to do with him? Shoot him? Shoot him for the satisfaction of our moral feelings? Tell me, Alyosha!'

'Shoot him!' Alyosha said softly, raising his eyes to his brother with a pale, twisted sort of smile.

'Bravo!' yelled Ivan with something like rapture, 'If you say so, then — you're a fine hermit! So that's the sort of little demon dwelling in your heart, Alyosha Karamazov!'

'What I said was absurd, but — '

'Yes, but — that's the trouble, isn't it?' cried Ivan. 'Let me tell you, novice, that absurdities are only too necessary on earth. The world is founded on absurdities and perhaps without them nothing would come to pass in it. We know a thing or two!'

'What do you know?' . . .

Ivan was silent for a minute and his face suddenly became very sad.

'Listen to me: I took only children to make my case clearer. I don't say anything about the other human tears with which the earth is saturated from its crust to its centre — I have narrowed my subject on purpose. I am a bug and I acknowledge in all humility that I can't understand why everything has been arranged as it is. I suppose men themselves are to blame: they were given paradise, they wanted freedom and they stole the fire from heaven, knowing perfectly well that they would become unhappy, so why should we pity them? Oh, all that my pitiful earthly Euclidean mind can grasp is that suffering exists, that no one is to blame, that effect follows cause, simply and directly, that everything flows and finds its level — but then this is only Euclidean nonsense. I know that and I refuse to live by it! What do I care that no one is to blame, that effect follows cause simply and directly and that I know it — I must have retribution or I shall destroy myself. And retribution not somewhere in the infinity of space and time, but here on earth, and so that I could see it myself. I was a believer, and I want to see for myself. And if I'm dead by that time, let them resurrect me, for if it all happens without me, it will be too unfair. Surely the reason for my suffering was not that I as well as my evil deeds and sufferings may serve as manure for some future harmony for someone else. I want to see with my own eyes the lion lie down with the lamb and the murdered man rise up and embrace his murderer. I want to be there when everyone suddenly finds out what it has all been for. All religions on earth are based on this desire, and I am a believer. But then there are the children, and what am I to do with them? That is the question I cannot answer. I repeat for the hundredth time — there are lots of questions, but I've only taken the children, for in their case it is clear beyond the shadow of a doubt what I have to say. Listen: if all have to suffer so as to buy eternal harmony by their suffering, what have the children to do with it — tell me, please? It is entirely incomprehensible why they, too, should have to suffer and why they should have to buy harmony by their sufferings. Why should they, too, be used as dung for someone's future harmony? I understand solidarity in sin among men, I understand solidarity in retribution, too, but, surely, there can be no solidarity in sin with children, and if it is really true that they share their fathers' responsibility for all their fathers' crimes, then that truth is not, of course, of this world and it's incomprehensible to me. Some humorous fellow may say that it makes no difference since a child is bound to grow up and sin, but, then, he didn't grow up: he was torn to pieces by dogs at the age of eight. Oh, Alyosha, I'm not blaspheming! I understand, of course, what a cataclysm of the universe it will be when everything in heaven and on earth blends in one hymn of praise and everything that lives and has lived cries aloud: "Thou art just, O Lord, for thy ways are revealed!" Then, indeed, the mother will embrace the torturer who had her child torn to pieces by his dogs, and all three will cry aloud: "Thou art just, O Lord!", and then, of course, the crown of knowledge will have been attained and everything will be explained. But there's the rub: for it is that I cannot accept. And while I'm on earth, I hasten to take my own measures. For, you see, Alyosha, it may really happen that if I live to that moment, or rise again to see it, I shall perhaps myself cry aloud with the rest, as I look at the mother embracing her child's torturer: "Thou art just, O Lord!" But I do not want to cry aloud then. While there's still time, I make haste to arm myself against it, and that is why I renounce higher harmony altogether. It is not worth one little tear of that tortured little girl who beat herself on the breast and prayed to her "dear, kind Lord" in the stinking privy with her unexpiated tears! It is not worth it, because her tears remained unexpiated. They must be expiated, for otherwise there can be no harmony. But how, how are you to expiate them? Is it possible? Not, surely, by their being avenged? But what do I want them avenged for? What do I want a hell for torturers for? What good can hell do if they have already been tortured to death? And what sort of harmony is it, if there is a hell? I want to forgive. I want to embrace. I don't want any more suffering. And if the sufferings of children go to make up the sum of sufferings which is necessary for the purchase of truth, then I say beforehand that the entire truth is not worth such a price. And, finally, I do not want a mother to embrace the torturer who had her child torn to pieces by his dogs! She has no right to forgive him! If she likes, she can forgive him for herself, she can forgive the torturer for the immeasurable suffering he has inflicted upon her as a mother; but she has no right to forgive him for the sufferings of her tortured child. She has no right to forgive the torturer for that, even if her child were to forgive him! And if that is so, if they have no right to forgive him, what becomes of the harmony? Is there in the whole world a being who could or would have the right to forgive? I don't want harmony. I don't want it, out of the love I bear to mankind. I want to remain with my suffering unavenged. I'd rather remain with my suffering unavenged and my indignation unappeased, *even if I were wrong*. Besides, too high a price has been placed on harmony. We cannot afford to pay so much for admission. And therefore I hasten to return my ticket of admission. And indeed, if I am an honest man, I'm bound to hand it back as soon as possible. This I am doing. It is not God that I do not accept, Alyosha. I merely most respectfully return him the ticket.'

chapter 4

Existentialism
and the Problem of Being

Being is. Being is in-itself. Being is what it is.
   Sartre, *Being and Nothingness*

*Metaphysics is an enquiry over and above what-is, with a view to winning it back
again as such and in totality for our understanding.*
   Heidegger, "What Is Metaphysics?"

INTRODUCTION

Twentieth-century philosopher John Dewey has characterized philosophy as a "quest for certainty," and we saw in the introduction to this text
the powerful part Plato's philosophical system has played in that quest.
For Plato, the theory of Forms provides the basis for a reality that is
perfect and unchanging and for an epistemology (based on his view that
knowledge is recollection) that guarantees certainty. But such solutions
have their costs. For one, the material world, which changes and deteriorates — including the physical body — becomes suspect. That world is
the source of deception and illusion, and so cannot provide a foundation
for philosophical system building. As a result, we must shift our attention
away from the world of the changeable and become other-worldly. Finally, the Platonic system, in giving priority to the objective, tends to
devalue subjectivity, feeling, and ambiguity.

   The existentialist valorization of subjectivity, concrete experience,
and passion is only the beginning of the shift from Platonism. In addition,
the existentialist's attention to "negativities" like despair, anxiety, and
mortality take us even further. Finally, key to existentialism is its vision of
the dynamic between the individual and the world. While individuals in

the Platonic view can be separate from the world (and even the body), for the existentialist, *I* and *world* are inextricably connected; we are in space and in time in a vital dynamic which does not permit separation.

This is not to suggest that there is any one analysis to which all representatives of existentialism give assent. But existentialism is a positive philosophy that is grounded in a particular metaphysics. This chapter examines some of the similarities in the views of Heidegger, Sartre, and Merleau-Ponty on the nature of reality.

DESCARTES, HUSSERL, AND THE PHENOMENOLOGICAL TRADITION

Though the phenomenologist Edmund Husserl (1859–1938) is not an existentialist for a number of reasons, his writings had a major impact on the thought of many existentialist philosophers, in particular Heidegger, Sartre, and Merleau-Ponty. Sartre's major work, for example, *Being and Nothingness*, is particularly indebted to Husserl; indeed, it is subtitled *A Phenomenological Essay on Ontolgy*, where *ontology* is the "description of the phenomenon of being as it manifests itself." (*Being and Nothingness*, p. 7) To ground our discussion of Husserl, however, we must go back in the history of philosophy to the beginning of what is now known as the "modern period," to the works of René Descartes.

René Descartes (1596–1650) has been called the father of modern philosophy, and it is in Descartes that the modern conflict between faith and reason is powerfully exemplified. Descartes's scientific background predisposed him to reject beliefs lacking sufficient ground; indeed, he referred to such beliefs as "prejudice." His philosophical temperament, however, led Descartes to seek absolute knowledge; even the most highly probable claim failed to meet such a rigorous demand. Modern science, with its emphasis on experimentation and testing, could never give us certainty. Thus, we must look elsewhere for an absolute ground for philosophy. Finally, Descartes was a very devout Jesuit. He was not content to defend religion as a domain alien to reason; nor was he willing to accept that the scientific method required abandoning belief in God. How, then, does one reconcile these worlds?

Descartes used a method that is sometimes called radical skepticism. Unlike the skeptic who denies even the possibility of knowledge, Descartes adopted an attitude of doubt so as to determine what could provide a solid foundation for belief. Thus, he doubted everything that could possibly be questioned: for example, I know my senses often deceive me, so I refuse to trust their evidence; I have heard that amputees still feel phantom pain "in" a limb that is not present, so I even doubt the existence of my physical body; I may be dreaming and not in the place I believe myself to be; and there may be a malevolent god who tricks me into accepting all sorts of false beliefs. Once we have struck away at all of these beliefs, with what are we left?

For Descartes, no matter what else is open to question, one thing is certain: We are thinking beings (*cogito*). To doubt, to question, to ponder, to examine — these are all processes of thought that cannot be denied. Even if one *is* being deceived, there must be an "I" in order for there to be a being who *can* be deceived. As Descartes said, noticing that this truth "was so firm and so certain that the most extravagant suppositions of the skeptics were unable to shake it, I judged that I could accept it without scruple as the first principle of the philosophy I was seeking." (*Discourse*, p. 32)

Descartes believed this process of tearing down false beliefs to be constructive. That is, he sought to destroy so as to rebuild a structure whose foundation was solid. Just as we must begin to learn mathematics with simple statements like $1 + 1 = 2$, so we must move slowly and methodically to build a philosophical system. Once Descartes gives us the *cogito,* he then fills up the world with what he takes to be "clear and distinct" ideas: that God exists, that I have a body and that body and soul interact, and that there is a material world. We need not explore in great detail exactly how Descartes arrives at this destination, but several points are relevant. First, Descartes used deduction to move from one step to the next. For example, he believes that God exists based on the definition of God, that is, that God is a perfect being. And since God is a perfect being, then we know that God would not deceive us, and so the material world must exist. For Descartes, these steps in the argument are a priori; that is, they do not depend on our having had any particular experience. Second, Descartes, like Plato, is a dualist. But Descartes's dualism is not based on two worlds, one perfect and one imperfect. Rather, the Cartesian world divides up into matter and mind, entities having completely distinct qualities. Matter is, for example, extended, divisible, and mortal; in contrast, mind is without extension, indivisible, and immortal. Thus, the body is subject to all of the laws to which any material object must conform; whereas the soul has no extension, dimension, or any other properties attributed to matter.

How, then, does the mind interact with the body? Or, more concretely, how does the mind bring about bodily changes, like, for example, raising an arm? This is a puzzle for dualists, and Descartes posited that the pineal gland in the base of the neck accounts for the interaction between mind and body.

> Thus when we desire to imagine something we have never seen, this desire
> has the power of causing the gland to move in the manner requisite to drive
> the spirits towards the pores of the brain by the opening of which pores this

particular thing may be represented; thus when we wish to apply our attention for some time to the consideration of one particular object, this desire holds the gland for the time being inclined to the same side. Thus, finally, when we desire to walk or to move our body in some special way, this desire causes the gland to thrust the spirits towards the muscles which serve to bring about this result.

Passions, *pp. 350–51*

Yet the pineal gland is itself material. Thus, Descartes's solution is circular and fails to solve the problem of how spirit can interact with matter.

Descartes's return to the *cogito* as the basis for knowledge is a significant move in the history of philosophy. For Descartes, philosophy becomes the philosophy of the thinking subject. This turn toward inwardness, for Descartes, was the only way to ground knowledge. Yet it also may be a step toward closing the door from the *cogito* to the world "outside." How do we know that the world exists? Even if we cannot doubt that we are thinking, how do we know that our thoughts correspond to anything that is actually outside of us? For Descartes, we know it deductively, beginning with the thinking self, and moving logically to God and the reality of the natural world. And we know that any error must be a result of our own impatient will rushing ahead of intellect. But, since Descartes, many philosophers have questioned whether any purely logical process can give us existence. If we reject Descartes's deductive process, are we left with the private *cogito*, which knows its own feelings intimately, immediately and indubitably, but can never be sure of the existence of anything else?

Thus, Descartes's radical skepticism becomes for later philosophers more than just a methodology. Instead, it may be the end of systematizing. David Hume (1711–1776), for example, distinguished two kinds of statements: those that are definitional (abstract) and therefore certain (e.g., a triangle is a three-sided figure); and those that are based on experience and therefore never certain (e.g., a triangular sign means "yield"). He argued that a theory of metaphysics could not be based on the first sort of statement, since these are purely logical and do not provide us with anything positive about the external world; and it could not be based on the latter, since those statements are empirical and therefore probable at best. In a shocking move, Hume even questioned the notion of causation as a necessary relationship, arguing that our senses never reveal cause, but only the "constant conjunction" of certain events. Thus, he argued, our view that certain things cause other things is nothing but a matter of custom. One could apply such reasoning to virtually any metaphysical claim. If such is the case, then the search for a metaphysical system must be abandoned. According to Hume,

If we take in our hand any volume; of divinity or school metaphysics, for instance; let us ask, *Does it contain any abstract reasoning concerning quantity or number?* No. *Does it contain any experimental reasoning concerning matter of fact and existence?* No. Commit it then to the flames: For it can contain nothing but sophistry and illusion.

Enquiry, *p. 114*

Descartes also continues a tradition in philosophy which bifurcates the world of sense perception and the world of the intellect. The questions Descartes raised led to increasing suspicion of the senses. How do we know, for example, what is "in" us and what is "in" the object outside of us? Is the sweet taste of candy in the palate or in the candy itself? Some philosophers and even scientists (e.g., Galileo) tried to address this issue by distinguishing an object's primary qualities (like weight) and its secondary qualities (like color and taste). The former were thought to be in the object and hence essential to it; the latter were thought to be relative to the observer and hence subjective and "accidental." But from this move it is a short step to the philosophy of George Berkeley (1685–1753), who maintained that even perception of primary qualities could be relative to the "beholder." So, he argued, *esse* (to be) is *percipi,* (to be perceived). If what we mean by matter is a substance that exists outside of and independent of an observer, then, Berkeley claimed, matter does not exist. In this version of idealism (the view that *ideas* or *immaterial substances* are what are truly real), God is the ultimate perceiver, who gives stability and continuity to those ideas.

Finally, Immanuel Kant (1724–1824) sought to provide a basis for metaphysics. But he was vehement in his demand that we not expect more from reason than it can deliver. Indeed, Kant considered it one of the greatest accomplishments of his work that it exposed the "groundless pretensions" of reason. (*Critique of Pure Reason,* p. 100) His conclusion agrees with Hume that inductive statements cannot be the basis for the knowledge essential to metaphysics. Yet he was not willing to give up on metaphysical postulates like causation, order, and the existence of God. So he argued that the human mind structures reality in an active, dynamic way. In what Kant referred to as his "Copernican Revolution" in philosophy, he rejected the assumption of traditional philosophy that the mind is a passive recipient of data from the outside, and instead argued that knowledge is the result of the synthesizing activity of the knowing subject. It is the human mind, then, that bestows unity and coherence on the world. This structuring is not an activity of which we are conscious but is rather that which makes consciousness possible. Kant concludes that we perceive phenomena, but that there is an unknowable noumenal world ("things in themselves") that must be the basis for the phenomenal. Thus,

Kant, in attempting to save metaphysics, in a sense sealed its doom: Since we lack direct access to "reality in itself," we are limited to what we perceive. It is not surprising that philosophers since Kant (see especially chapter 3 for Nietzsche's repudiation of metaphysics) reject the possibility of metaphysics.

EDMUND HUSSERL AND THE PHENOMENOLOGICAL TRADITION

Like Descartes, Edmund Husserl, the founder of what has been called the phenomenological movement, sought certainty in his philosophy. Husserl too wished to rid himself of all "prejudice" and strive toward what he termed "genuine science." (*Cartesian Meditations*, p. 54) According to Husserl, Descartes's ambition to create a system of certainty was to be respected. Descartes, Husserl wrote, sought a "complete reforming of philosophy into a science grounded on an absolute foundation." (p. 1) For Husserl, "that aim shall indeed continually motivate the course of our meditations." (p. 8) Indeed, Husserl noted in one diary entry how important certainty was to him personally: "I have been through enough torments from lack of clarity and from doubt that wavers back and forth. . . . Only one need absorbs me: I must win clarity, else I cannot live; I cannot bear life unless I can believe that I shall achieve it." (Quoted in Speigelberg, p. 82)

Husserl uses the phrase *transcendental phenomenology* to describe his project, and he refers to it as being a "science of essential Being." In so doing, he emphasizes his commitment to pursuing certainty. In distinguishing transcendental phenomenology from empirical disciplines like psychology or anthropology, Husserl hoped to arrive at the "pure essences" of things. But no matter how earnestly Husserl wished for certainty, he rejected the nineteenth-century optimism that scientific method could provide it. And so, like Descartes, Husserl returns to the subject. This "subjective turn" is a defining feature of phenomenology.

Like Descartes, Husserl was looking for "presuppositionless" philosophy (*Ideas: General Introduction*, p. 20) and wanted to accept only that which is completely, to use Husserl's term, evident. Anything not absolutely certain should be set aside and "bracketed" as problematical, until later analysis justifies it. This is the Husserlian *epoche*, a term he borrowed from Greek skeptics who used it to designate the attitude they recommended that we adopt in the face of doubt and uncertainty. This attitude is one of suspension of judgment and noncommitment.

In the epoche, Husserl brackets "the existence of the world"; he terms this the "parenthesizing of the Objective world." (*Ideas: General*

Introduction, p. 15) This "natural standpoint" is that everyday point of view which is generally "taken for granted." (p. 15) To bracket that world is the first step to discovering the essences in that "natural unsophisticated standpoint of positive reality." (p. 15) The doubt Husserl demands of us is *not* disbelief, but rather a suspension of belief. Obviously, there are times when we do this when we truly are uncertain, but in the phenomenological stance, we suspend beliefs even when the experiences seem not at all ambiguous. For Husserl, when we suspend judgment on everyday matters of importance, we come to discover truths of great importance. In this way, "absolute subjectivity" becomes the basis for "absolute objectivity," since what survives the bracketing — the "residuum" (p. 33) — is *consciousness itself.*

Unlike Descartes (and like Kant), Husserl thought this science of certainty could not exist independent of the knowing subject. He uses the term *transcendental* like Kant. But, for Husserl, "transcendental subjectivity" or "transcendental ego" is not the "I" of everyday experience; rather, it is "the ego as subject of one's pure cogitationes." (*Cartesian Meditations*, pp. 2–3) So, Husserl wants to find the "indissoluble essential structures of transcendental subjectivity, which persist in and through all imaginable modifications." (*Ideas: General Introduction*, p. 12)

In performing this epoche, we discover ourselves as Transcendental ego, as pure conscious life given to us "antecedent to the natural being of the world." (*Cartesian Meditations*, p. 61) This epoche presupposes transcendent being, and it is Absolute.

In this process, one becomes aware that "my own phenomenologically self-contained essence can be posited in an *absolute* sense, as I am the Ego who invests the being of the world which I so constantly speak about with existential validity, as an existence (*Sein*) which wins for me from my own life's pure essence meaning and substantiated validity." (*Ideas: General Introductions*, pp. 5–6) "It [Absolute Being] only is non-relative, that is, relative only to itself; whereas the real world indeed exists, but in respect of essence is relative to transcendental subjectivity (*Ideas*, p. 19)

For Husserl, consciousness is always consciousness *of* something. He calls this property "intentionality." Intentionality is the fundamental property of this consciousness: "to be consciousness *of* something; as a *cogito*, to bear within itself its *cogitatum*." (*Cartesian Meditations*, p. 72) In reflecting on consciousness, we direct our attention to certain mental acts, for example, perceiving, valuing, remembering, and so forth. In observing pure consciousness, two domains of investigation come to the fore: the acts of ego revealed in reflection (and bracketed) and the objects of these acts of ego (these objects are in turn held in suspension by bracketing). If we do bracket all our judgments independent of the "flow of experience," then we restrict ourselves to considering only those phenomena which are part of that flow of experience (this is what it means to leave the natural standpoint and adopt the phenomenological standpoint). "I must lose the world by epoche in order to regain it by a universal self-examination." (*Cartesian Meditations*, p. 157)

In conducting this so-called "eidetic reduction," the essences of things are revealed to us, bringing us back from sense data to things-in-themselves. That is, once we exclude all that is "transcendentally posited," we end up with the pure phenomenon. (*Idea of Phenomenology*, p. 5) "Phenomenology aims at being a descriptive theory of the essence of pure transcendental experiences." (*Ideas: General Introduction*, p. 191) Though Husserl employs the Kantian term *phenomenon* to refer to the objects of our experience, he does not accept Kant's claim that there is another realm of Being inaccessible to us. This is how, for Husserl, we can avoid the Kantian problematic. For Husserl, the phenomenological method discloses a realm of being that is ultimate and indubitable (what Husserl calls "apodictic"); yet that realm is not *beyond* experience (like Kantian noumena) but is rather absolutely certain *within* experience. "*Thus to each psychic lived process there corresponds through the device of phenomenological reduction a pure phenomenon, which exhibits its intrinsic (immanent) essence . . . as an absolute datum.*" (*Idea of Phenomenology*, p. 45)

How can things be *for* consciousness without being constructed by consciousness? The answer lies in consciousness's intentionality, that consciousness is directed *out;* thus, consciousness does not construct its object but rather displays it. So Husserl agrees with Kant that human experience only provides us with phenomena. But he rejects Kant's view that the objects experienced are mental constructs. If we learn to use phenomenological method carefully and precisely, describing a "stream of experience" exactly as experienced, then we will move past relativism into apodicticity. For Husserl, this is almost like a religious conversion. Indeed, he quotes approvingly from St. Augustine (*in interiore homine habitat veritas;* truth dwells in the inner man) at the conclusion of his *Cartesian Meditations*.

So, for Husserl, Descartes must be rejected. Consciousness is not a thing but rather a flow of intentional acts. This system of thought, Husserl believed, could save metaphysics: "Upon the success of this science depends the possibility of a metaphysics, a science of being in the absolute and fundamental sense." (*Idea of Phenomenology*, p. 33) Later existentialist thinkers take up this notion of being; though their analyses are quite different from Husserl's, they owe much to his notions of intentionality and consciousness.

MARTIN HEIDEGGER: BEING REVEALED

Martin Heidegger (1889–1976), unlike Husserl, who was still attracted to the questions of traditional philosophy, wanted to rethink those questions and pose new ones. His project, he believed, was so unique that it might even require the transformation of language itself. Though Heidegger considered himself a phenomenologist, his approach was so different from Husserl's that the latter felt it necessary to distinguish their philosophies as being poles apart.

"Back to the things themselves" is the motto of phenomenology, and Heidegger, like Husserl, subscribes to this motto. But Heidegger rejects much of what is essential to Husserl's phenomenological method. For one, he maintains that the "natural standpoint" (which Husserl brackets) is the only place from which to begin an analysis of Being. Phenomenology, Heidegger claims, must look at the ordinary experience of the concretely existing human being; rather than try to analyze "essences," we must look instead at the "structures which are essential to" the human being's "state of being." (*Being and Time*, p. 421)

Thus, Heidegger rejects Husserl's transcendental idealism and his transcendental ego. For Heidegger, "things themselves" are not pure conscious events but rather are "the totality of what lies in the light of day or *can be brought to* the light." (*Being and Time*, p. 51) For Heidegger, phenomena are never "appearances": "in the phenomenological conception of 'phenomenon,' what one has in mind as that which shows itself is the Being of entities." (*Being and Time*, p. 60) Further, for Heidegger, phenomenology is simply a method; it does not designate the objects of its study but merely prescribes "how" such objects are to be understood.

Though Heidegger's thought went through changes during his lifetime, he never changed what was, by his own account, his one theme: the quest for Being. This quest, he says (p. 251) "covers the whole range of metaphysical problems." To understand Heidegger's metaphysics, one must understand what he means by this all-important concept. For Heidegger, Being (*Sein*) is not identical with individual beings. Rather, Being is that which "reveals itself as *physis*, 'nature,' which here does not yet mean a particular sphere of beings but rather beings as such as a whole, specifically in the sense of emerging presence." (*Basic Writing*, p. 129) Elsewhere, Heidegger speaks of philosophy as a dialogue between Being and being, with Being that permanent reality within which beings endure. So Being is a kind of ground or source for the concrete forms of existence.

For Heidegger, the question of Being does not refer to any particular events or beings, but rather to the metaphysical question of what it means for anything at all to be. "Why is there any Being at all — why not far rather Nothing?" (*Existence and Being*, p. 380) Or, as he says, what "helps what-is to become what it is?" (p. 255) These are clearly *not* scientific questions, yet, for Heidegger, our understanding of these questions grounds science as well as everyday life. Most of the time, we don't even think about Being; it had, Heidegger tells us, ceased to perplex us. We tend instead to focus on specific entities and forget about the Being of entities. "This Being can be covered up so extensively that it becomes forgotten and no question arises about it or about its meaning." (*Being and Time*, p. 59)

We can study Being using the phenomenological method, but Heidegger calls this project *ontology* to distinguish it from classical metaphysics. Indeed, Heidegger never wavered in his repudiation of the language of traditional metaphysics. "However, the question as to the essence of Being dies off, if it does not surrender the language of metaphysics, because metaphysical conception forbids thinking the question as to the essence of Being." (*Questions of Being*, p. 73) Or, as he wrote in *Being and Time*: "*Only as phenomenology is ontology possible.*" (p. 60)

It is difficult to make clear Heidegger's notion of Being, particularly since the English language does not distinguish the different senses of being to which Hiedegger refers. Other languages, in contrast, distinguish two kinds of Being. Greek, for example, has *to on* (the thing which is) and *to einai* (the Being of the thing which is); French has *l'être* (Being) and *l'étant* (being); and German has *das Seiende* (being) and *das Sein* (Being). English makes no such distinction, yet it is crucial to existentialist thinking.

Philosophers have often treated Being as the most universal (and hence the most empty) of categories. For Heidegger, Being is not an entity at all, but rather the "light" that illumines beings. Though the light is always there, we don't usually attend to it. Yet it makes possible our attending to specific beings. So Heidegger wants to use a concrete — i.e., phenomenological — approach to Being by beginning with *human* being as the starting point. For Heidegger, it is an irreducible and ultimate fact that humans exist in the world. The human being is there already; in fact, Heidegger uses the term *Dasein* to refer to this being-thereness of human being. Any analysis of Dasein's being, then, must be existential rather than transcendental.

For Heidegger, we can never prove the existence of the world. But if we don't begin with it, we end up with the disastrous philosophical consequences of Cartesianism or Kantianism or extreme skepticism. Heidegger rejects Husserl's notion of a presuppositionless philosophy, for the *world* of the everyday is always presupposed in all thinking. He rejects the criticism that this position is circular:

> (F)actically there is no circle at all in formulating our question as we have described. One can determine the nature of entities in their Being without

necessarily having the explicit concept of the meaning of Being at one's disposal. Otherwise there could have been no ontological knowledge heretofore. One would hardly deny that factically there has been such knowledge. Of course 'Being' has been presupposed in all ontology up till now, but not as a *concept* at one's disposal — not as the sort of thing we are seeking. This 'presupposing' of Being has rather the character of taking a look at it beforehand, so that in the light of it the entities presented to us get provisionally Articulated in their Being. This guiding activity of taking a look at Being arises from the average understanding of Being in which we always operate and which in the end belongs to the essential constitution of Dasein itself. Such 'presupposing' has nothing to do with laying down an axiom from which a sequence of propositions is deductively derived. It is quite impossible for there to be any 'circular argument' in formulating the question of the meaning of Being; for in answering this question, the issue is not one of grounding something by such a derivation; it is rather one of laying bare the grounds for it and exhibiting them.

Being and Time, *p. 27 (footnotes deleted)*

For Heidegger, the pure ego of Husserl is nothing but an empty abstraction. So we must begin with the only real *I:* the ego of Husserl's natural standpoint. This Dasein is not the human as primordial "knower" but rather the human as full of care or concern (*Sorge*). Care is *not*, for Heidegger, a property that Dasein sometimes has and sometimes does not have. Rather, care *is* Dasein.

One must bear in mind that Heidegger's project in describing Dasein's modes of Being is not primarily to describe Dasein. Rather, he believed that we could understand Being through an understanding of Dasein. "The analytic of Dasein . . . is to prepare the way for the problematic of fundamental ontology — *the question of the meaning of Being in general.*"(*Being and Time*, p. 227)

What does it mean to be human? For some, humans are toolmakers or language users or rational animals. For Heidegger, Dasein is primarily a being aware of Being, that is, a being whose very Being is an issue for it. *"Understanding of Being is itself a definite characteristic of Dasein's Being."* (*Being and Time*, p. 32) What does this mean? For Heidegger, it means that Dasein is distinctive in that it is an *ontological* being as well as one that is *ontic*. These terms are difficult at best to define, but, roughly speaking, by ontic (or *existentiell*) Heidegger means empirical or factual. The ontic world is the world of generalization; it is an object of study but one that is somewhat superficial and incomplete at best. In contrast, the ontological (or *existential*) is "a state of Being which is already underlying in every case" (*Being and Time*, p. 244) and which makes it possible for Dasein to have ontic concerns. To make this distinction more concrete, contrast the two senses of *knowledge* Kierkegaard discusses in relation to death (see chapter 1, p. 51). On the one hand, we know (in an ontic sense) a good deal of the "facts" of death; on the other hand, what underlies all this is the ontological awareness of our own dying. Dasein, then, is a being whose nature is ontological, open to Being, in contrast with pure objects in the world:

> Dasein is an entity which does not just occur among other entities. Rather it is ontically distinguished by the fact that, in its very Being, that Being is an *issue* for it. But in that case, this is a constitutive state of Dasein's Being, and this implies that Dasein, in its Being, has a relationship towards that Being — a relationship which itself is one of Being. And this means further that there is some way in which Dasein understands itself in its Being, and that to some degree it does so explicitly. It is peculiar to this entity that with and through its Being, this Being is disclosed to it. *Understanding of Being is itself a definite characteristic of Dasein's Being.* Dasein is ontically distinctive in that it *is* ontological.
>
> Being and Time, p. 12 (*footnotes deleted*)

Dasein is ontologically distinctive in a number of ways. For one, Dasein does not have a nature; it is a being who is possibility, who can choose itself in any given moment. Further, Dasein has attitudes toward the world, a relationship. Dasein is "in-the-world" in a way that is very different from the way water is in a glass or a chair is in the room. Dasein is not side-by-side with the world, but is unitary "Being-in-the-world." Heidegger uses hyphens deliberately to convey the inextricable connectedness of this dynamic. Finally, Dasein is ontological in the sense that it can raise questions about its own Being. Since it is Dasein alone of all beings who seeks Being, understanding Dasein is a necessary first step in the quest. In this process, Heidegger finds three fundamental aspects of Dasein, which he analyzes: facticity, existentiality, and forfeiture.

First, Heidegger analyzes the feature of Dasein he refers to as "facticity." Facticity refers to Dasein's "thrownness" in the world. For Heidegger, Dasein is already in the world, a world into which it has been thrown. This world is not the world of astrophysics — the immense, infinite cosmos — but rather the world as it is *our* world. We don't have complete control over this world, yet it is ours to appropriate. In the world of facticity we experience things as "readiness-to-hand," that is, we relate to everything (even natural objects, like trees) as having some instrumental purpose. Protagoras (see chapter 1) was not far off: We *are* the measure of all things. And it is only when there is some disruption in this world of the ready-to-hand — our car won't start, our typewriter jams, we lose a contact lens — that we even notice these instruments and find that we are surrounded by them. This mode, then, always refers back to Dasein and its needs and purposes; it makes clear how Dasein is a being of concern. Since we determine what is ready-to-hand by our specific concerns and projects, then we define their value in those terms. Thus, it is only *"when an assignment has been disturbed* — when something is unusable for some purpose" or that something we need is missing — that the "assignment becomes explicit." (*Being and Time*, p. 74) In this way, the environment discloses itself to us.

The term *existentiality* does not refer to the way in which rocks and trees exist, but to Dasein's awareness both of its connection to world and of its future possibilities. "The Being of Dasein means ahead-of-itself-Being-already-in-the-world," (*Being and Time*, p. 236) and it is this mode of Dasein's existence that makes Care understandable. Dasein is always "beyond itself" without a set nature (despite facticity), full of possibility. As Heidegger notes (p. 259), Dasein's basis is transcendent, that is, it is already "beyond what-is-in-totality."

Dasein is always reaching outside itself; its very being is aiming at what it is not yet. Thus, Dasein is immersed in temporality. Time is not, however, to be understood as superficial clock time. Heidegger claims that the expressions "there is Being" and "there is Time" reveal something fundamentally existential about Dasein's being. In German, the idiom *es gibt* means "there is," but literally translated, it means "it gives." For Heidegger, this is not just an irrelevant linguistic quirk. Rather, being and time are forms of "presencing," which "give themselves" to Dasein.

> How are we to determine this giving of presencing that prevails in the present, in the past, in the future? Does this giving lie in this, that it reaches us, or does it reach us because it is in itself a reaching? The latter. Approaching, being not yet present, at the same time gives and brings about what is no longer present. The reciprocal relation of both at the same time gives and brings about the present.
>
> *Being and Time*, p. 39

So, in Dasein, the past, present, and future all blend.

Finally, "forfeiture" is a fundamental attribute of Dasein. In Dasein's immersion in the world, it tends to forget Being for beings. Dasein's everyday mode tends to be a public one, where *das Man* (the "they") or the anonymous crowd provides an escape from an awareness of Being. Chapter 1 (see pp. 58–72) discusses Heidegger's analysis of Being-toward-Death and the role *das Man* plays in that structure of Being. But he uses this notion in other contexts as well, showing how Dasein's falling back on *das Man* keeps Dasein from being authentic (see chapter 7, pp. 448–51, for a discussion of the existential notion of authenticity). How do I return from *verfallen* (a state of *in*authenticity or "fallenness") to knowledge of Being? For Heidegger, it is through the experience of dread.

Our dread has no identifiable, specific object to which it corresponds. This experience may result from but is not limited to an awareness of our Being-toward-Death. But other, more everyday experiences can provoke dread. In fact, Heidegger reminds us that the experience of dread may be as deep as the experience that causes it is shallow (see, for example, p. 261). This dread reminds us of possibility. When we face possibility, we see that we are free and also that we will die someday. This experience sets us free from the illusions of the 'they,' individuating each of us and making authenticity possible.

Heidegger's later work picks up with this notion of dread to focus on the experience of Nothingness. Indeed, "Nothing" plays a very important role in many of Heidegger's works after *Being and Time*. For Heidegger, to face Nothingness (in the form of dread) is to overcome that forgetfulness which pulls us away from Being. Thus, there must be a powerful dynamic between Being and Nothingness. The excerpt at the end of this chapter from Heidegger's essay "What is Metaphysics?" shows his preoccupation with nothing. "(W)hy worry about this Nothing? 'Nothing' is absolutely rejected by science and abandoned as null and void (*das Nichtige*)." (p. 253) Most of us, like the scientist, want to know "nothing of Nothing." And, Heidegger notes, there is good reason for this: The moment we try to think about Nothing, we end up in contradiction. Since thought is always thought *of* something, then thought could not be of nothing. But, for Heidegger, "Nothing is more original than the Not and negation," (p. 254) for "the very possibility of negation as an act of reason, and consequently reason itself, are somehow dependent on Nothing." (pp. 254–55) Yet, how can the Nothing "be" anything? Again, as in *Being and Time*, Heidegger looks at the experiences of the everyday — boredom and being in love, for example — to try to learn more about Nothing. "Does there ever occur in human existence," he asks, "a mood of this kind, through which we are brought face to face with Nothing itself?" (p. 256) He finds this in the experience of dread: "Dread reveals Nothing." (p. 257) And it is for Heidegger Nothing that makes the revelation of Being possible. For Heidegger, nothing is not the opposite of what-is; it is "integral to the Being of what-is." (p. 262) Thus, an analysis of Nothing leads us to Metaphysics, since we have seen that "Going beyond what-is is of the essence of Dasein." And this " 'going beyond' is metaphysics itself." (p. 263)

Science can never substitute for metaphysics, because scientific investigation can never find Being. Only with courage can one find Being, for the revelation of Being brings with it awe and dread. Only Dasein is capable of such courage: Dasein "alone of all beings, when addressed by the voice of Being, experiences the marvel of all marvels: that what-is *is*." (postscript to "What Is Metaphysics?", not excerpted) Indeed, for Heidegger, Dasein is the "seat-holder for Nothingness." (*Question of Being*, p. 97)

Heidegger and his students have maintained that the entire body of his work is a seamless web relating to the quest for Being. Yet some critics of Heidegger have argued that his later philosophy succumbed to irrationalism and mysticism. The excerpt (pp. 251–64) may give some hint of Heidegger's tendency toward unusual uses of language and his anti-intellectualism (the introduction to this text, p. 16, quotes a passage from the postscript to this essay in which Heidegger condemns "exact thinking.") Further, Heidegger states explicitly that language cannot do justice to Being, and later in his life he argued that poetry (not philosophy) is the path to Being. In a final section of "What Is Metaphysics?", Heidegger tells us that the best we can do is a "speechless thanking . . . which alone does homage to the grace wherewith Being had endowed the nature of Dasein, in order that he may take over in his relationship to Being the guardianship of Being." (*Basic Writings*, p. 389) For many, such statements have uncomfortably religious overtones. Heidegger never finished the project he set out to accomplish in *Being and Time;* but, regardless of one's response to his philosophical views, his thinking has had an enormous impact on twentieth-century existentialism.

SARTRE, MERLEAU-PONTY, AND THE PHENOMENOLOGICAL TRADITION

Merleau-Ponty's opening remarks in the excerpt following this chapter provide an eloquent account of the relationship between phenomenology and existentialist thought. Though phenomenology is about essences, it also is about putting those essences back into existence and not assuming an other-worldly reality. It is, then, about facticity, about using human experience as the starting point. It is transcendental, in that it brackets the natural standpoint; yet it also begins with the world "already there," and "all its efforts are concentrated upon re-achieving a direct and primitive contact with the world, and endowing that contact with a philosophical status." (p. 265) Finally, while phenomenology hopes to be a "rigorous science," it also seeks to provide an account of time, space, and the world as lived. With these paradoxes, each phenomenologist's style of philosophizing is unique; this certainly includes Sartre and Merleau-Ponty, who use the term *phenomenology* despite striking contrasts in their views.

Like Heidegger, both Sartre and Merleau-Ponty maintain that we cannot prove the existence of the world. Rather, it is presupposed in all of our projects and in all of our thinking. Descartes's methodical doubt is really an artifice, for "the world is there before any possible analysis of mine." Thus, "it would be artificial to make it the outcome of a series of syntheses which link, in the first place sensations, then aspects of the object corresponding to different perspectives, when both are nothing but products of analysis, with no sort of prior reality." (p. 268)

Sartre too rejects attempts to prove the existence of the world. For Sartre, the world is already there, and attempts to prove it must presuppose it. Sartre makes important use of Husserl's concept of intentionality in this context, though he objects to the use to which Husserl put it. Since consciousness is always intentional, it is always directed out. "To say that consciousness is consciousness of something is to say that it must produce itself as a revealed-revelation of a being which is not it and which gives itself as already existing when consciousness reveals it." (p. 281) Sartre rejects the Cartesian notion of consciousness as a "thing" which reveals being outside of it. Rather, Sartre tells us, subjectivity cannot constitute the objective and consciousness, as real subjectivity, is "nothing." "If we wish at any price to make the being of the phenomenon depend on consciousness, the object must be distinguished from consciousness not by its *presence* but by its *absence*." (p. 279) Consciousness, for Sartre, being always intentional, is "born *supported by* a being which is not itself." (p. 280)

Thus, for Sartre, the phenomenological method does reveal the being that is outside of it. There is no other realm of noumena "behind one's shoulder" and thus no distinction between essences and appearances. Dasein is not simply the being whose being is in question, but "a being such that in its being, its being is in question in so far as this being implies a being other than itself." (p. 281)

For both Sartre and Merleau-Ponty, the human mind (whether as intellect or sense perception) does not construct a world. If such were the case, then we would constantly be piecing together bits of perception with bits of thought to try to weave together a whole which is the world. But in fact no such process takes place. Rather, "perception is not even an act, a deliberate taking up of a position; it is the background from which all acts stand out, and is presupposed by them." (Merleau-Ponty, p. 269) "There is no inner man, man is in the world, and only in the world does he know himself." This is why, for example, Sartre calls his project in *Being and Nothingness* "a phenomenological essay on ontology" to distinguish it from metaphysical inquiries, which seek to go beyond Being by asking about the why's of things in the world. Ontology, in contrast, studies "the structures of being of the existent taken as a totality," being descriptive rather than explanatory.

In saying that there is no distinction between essence and appearance, Sartre and Merleau-Ponty are not saying that we can fully know the beings outside of us. There is no complete inventory we can ever hope to compile that would flesh out fully all of the aspects of an object. Sartre refers to this world of objects as being-in-itself (*en soi*), which is distinct from consciousness, or being-for-itself (*pour soi*). Being-in-itself, for Sartre, is just what it is. Unlike human being, which is not what it is and is what it is not, Being-in-itself is without possibility.

For Sartre, then, the in-itself is passive and inert, it is "dumb-packed-togetherness." The for-itself, in contrast, is empty, absolute freedom, insubstantial. In fact, the for-itself is more like a hole in being than any sort of being at all. The for-itself is forever engaged in a struggle to fill itself up, to become the in-itself. Yet this is paradoxical, for it can never be an object. The for-itself cannot be without the in-itself, and it can only be a revelation of Being because it is *not*-Being. Indeed, Sartre claims that we are the beings "by whom nothingness comes into the world."

The excerpt from *Being and Nothingness* at the end of this chapter (pp. 279–91) gives Sartre's analysis of Being-in-itself: "It (being-in-itself) is what it is." And this means that "by itself it can not even be what it is not; . . . it can encompass no negation. It is full positivity. It knows no otherness; it never posits itself as *other-than-another-being*. It can support no connection with the other. It is itself indefinitely and it exhausts itself in being."

In contrast, *pour soi* is always in the world and in space and in time in very different ways. The human being is a "being of distances," (p. 287) a being who is not what it is and is what it is not. "Nothingness lies coiled in the heart of being — like a worm," (p. 291) Sartre says. And, for Sartre, the human being — *pour soi* — is a being of negation. We are not our past, for it has already occurred; yet we are not our future, for that has yet to occur. And, when we try to capture the present moment, we find that it has already disappeared. We are not an object, yet we yearn to be "filled up" and complete. This quest is, however, futile. Ironically, the moment when *pour soi* is complete is when it dies, and then the body becomes *en soi*.

Sartre, like Nietzsche, rejects the existence of God. He argues that the notion that God exists is a contradictory one. In God, *en soi* and *pour soi* are one, yet this, for Sartre, is impossible. And, Sartre claims, if God exists, then human freedom (see chapter 5) is not possible, for God must have some part in human projects and activities. And if God plays no role in our affairs, then the concept is a superfluous one.

Without God, the world is one of contingency where there is no reason for anything to be in contrast to anything else. The introduction to this text, pages 1–21, discusses the notion of contingency and in particular makes references to Sartre's classic *Nausea*. In that novel, Roquentin comes face to face with the fact of contingency, that there is no necessary reason for any particular thing to be. If such is the case, then there is no reason for our own existence. The world of ontic beings is one that is too much for us (*de trop*); we can never explain it or take it all in. But this does not mean that there is some hidden reality "behind" the appearance. Rather, "the being of an existence is exactly what it *appears*." (Sartre, *Being and Nothingness*, p. 4) Things do not depend on our whims or our perception of them. For example, the reality of the pen that I am holding is that it is *not I*. But it is my consciousness of being which is not-I which produces consciousness. Thus, world and consciousness are reciprocal notions.

CONCLUSION

The word *exist* has its origin in Latin, and it literally means "to stand out." Though today we think of *existence* as fairly passive — consider the phrase "mere existence" — the word has been endowed with a dynamic meaning in existential ontology. For existentialists, we are immersed in Being. We — as Dasein — are the only being for whom Being is an issue. We are ontological beings who exist always in-situation; we are thrown into the world, a world rich and independent of our will. It is a world that is *de trop,* too much, contingent, gratuitous. It cannot ever be taken in completely by consciousness.

Heidegger once wrote that the restoration of metaphysics was the only way to avoid plunging into nihilism. (*Question of Being,* p. 93) Whether or not one accepts such a claim, it does appear that the questions metaphysicians ask are some of the most fundamental and serious of any. We need to ask whether, in this post-Cartesian era, metaphysics is still possible.

The excerpts that follow are not a definitive picture of existential ontology. Such a picture is not possible here, for the three authors excerpted — Merleau-Ponty, Heidegger, and Sartre — not only disagree with each other as much as they agree, but also have each written hundreds of pages on this topic. But these selections suggest some of the ways in which their views provide the basis for many of the themes recurrent in existentialism.

QUESTIONS FOR CONSIDERATION

1. What is metaphysics? How is ontology different from metaphysics?
2. What is phenomenology? From what you have read of the philosophers here (not including Husserl), what is it about their philosophies and/or styles of philosophizing that might count as phenomenological?
3. Consider each of the perspectives on metaphysics this chapter outlines in conjunction with some of the characteristics of existentialism discussed in the introduction to this text. What similarities do you find?

4. Does Heidegger's concept of Being make sense to you? What about his concept of Nothing? Why or why not?

5. How would an existentialist metaphysic respond to the skeptic who doubts the existence of the external world? Is this answer satisfactory to you?

6. What sorts of metaphysical implications follow if God does not exist?

7. Is Sartre a dualist? Think about his analysis of the structures of *pour soi* and *en soi* and defend your answer.

8. How are the ontic and the ontological different? How does Heidegger use these terms? Other philosophers?

9. Using the excerpt from Heidegger's "What is Metaphysics?" (pp. 251–64) and the excerpt from Sartre's *Being and Nothingness*, (pp. 279–91) what differences exist between Heidegger's concept of Nothing and Sartre's?

REFERENCES

BERKELEY, GEORGE. *Three Dialogues Between Hylas and Philonous.* Edited by Robert Merrihew Adams. Indianapolis: Hackett Publishing, 1979.

DESAN, WILFRID. *The Tragic Finale: An Essay on the Philosophy of Jean Paul Sartre.* New York: Harper Torchbooks, 1954.

DESCARTES, RENE. *Discourse on Method.* Translated by Donald A. Cress. Indianapolis: Hackett Publishing, 1980.

———. *Meditations on First Philosophy.* Translated by Donald A. Cress. Indianapolis: Hackett Publishing, 1979.

———. *The Passions of the Soul.* Translated by Elizabeth S. Haldane and G. R. T. Ross. Cambridge, Mass.: Cambridge University Press, 1911.

GRENE, MARJORIE. *Sartre.* Lanham, Md.: University Press of America, 1983.

HEIDEGGER, MARTIN. *Basic Writings.* Edited by David Farrell Krell. New York: Harper & Row, 1957.

———. *Being and Time.* Translated by John Macquarrie and Edward Robinson. New York: Harper & Row, 1962.

———. *Discourse on Thinking.* Translated by John M. Anderson and E. Hans Freund. New York: Harper & Row, 1966.

———. *Existence and Being.* Translated by R. F. C. Hull and Alan Crick. Chicago: Henry Regnery, 1949.

———. *Kant and the Problem of Metaphysics.* Translated by James S. Churchill. Bloomington: Indiana University Press, 1962.

————. *The Question of Being.* Translated by Jean T. Wilde and William Kluback. New Haven, Conn.: College and University Press, 1958.

————. "What Is Metaphysics?" Translated by R. F. C. Hull and Alan Crick. In *Basic Writings,* edited by David Farrell Krell. New York: Harper and Row, 1962.

HUME, DAVID. *An Enquiry Concerning Human Understanding.* Edited by Eric Steinberg. Indianapolis: Hackett Publishing, 1977.

HUSSERL, EDMUND. *Cartesian Meditations: An Introduction to Phenomenology.* Translated by Dorion Cairns. The Hague: Martinus Nijhoff, 1960.

————. *Ideas: General Introduction to Pure Phenomenology.* Translated by W. R. Boyce Gibson. London: George Allen & Unwin, 1958.

————. *The Idea of Phenomenology.* Translated by William P. Alston and George Nakhnikian. The Hague: Martinus Nijhoff, 1964.

KANT, IMMANUEL. *Critique of Pure Reason.* Translated by Norman Kemp Smith. New York: St. Martin's Press, 1965.

MARCEL, GABRIEL. *The Existential Background of Human Dignity.* Cambridge, Mass.: Harvard University Press, 1963.

————. *The Philosophy of Existentialism.* Translated by Manya Harari. Secaucus, N.J.: Citadel Press, 1973.

MCCORMICK, PETER, and ELLISTON, F. A., eds. *Husserl: Short Works.* Notre Dame, Indiana: University of Notre Dame Press, 1981.

MERLEAU-PONTY, MAURICE. *The Phenomenology of Perception.* Translated by Colin Smith. London: Routledge and Kegan Paul, 1962.

SARTRE, JEAN-PAUL. *Being and Nothingness.* Translated by Hazel Barnes. New York: Washington Square Books, 1966.

SCHACHT, RICHARD. *Hegel and After: Studies in Continental Philosophy between Kant and Sartre.* Pittsburgh: University of Pittsburgh Press, 1975.

SPEIGELBERG, HERBERT. *The Phenomenological Movement.* The Hague: Martinus Nijhoff, 1965.

WILSHIRE, BRUCE. *Metaphysics.* New York: Pegasus, 1969.

MARTIN HEIDEGGER

Though Martin Heidegger (see also chapter 2, p. 58, for a longer biography of Heidegger) was never a formal student of Husserl, he worked closely with him at the University of Freiburg, and Husserl led him in step-by-step training in the phenomenological method. Believing Heidegger to be the heir he had sought, Husserl secured for Heidegger succession to his professorship. But Heidegger's approach was radically different from Husserl's, and Heidegger soon dissociated himself from the phenomenological movement and from Husserl personally. For Heidegger, the object to be studied is Being, not beings. Thus, Heidegger's concern is not to create a rigorous science of indubitable knowledge, but rather to create an ontology using the phenomenological method. The following excerpt gives an example of Heidegger's approach to the study of Being.

What Is Metaphysics?

"What is metaphysics?" The question leads one to expect a discussion about metaphysics. Such is not our intention. Instead, we shall discuss a definite metaphysical question, thus, as it will appear, landing ourselves straight into metaphysics. Only in this way can we make it really possible for metaphysics to speak for itself.

Our project begins with the presentation of a metaphysical question, then goes on to its development and ends with its answer.

THE PRESENTATION OF A METAPHYSICAL QUESTION

Seen from the point of view of sound common sense, Philosophy, according to Hegel, is the "world stood on its head". Hence the peculiar nature of our task calls for some preliminary definition. This arises out of the dual nature of metaphysical questioning.

Firstly, every metaphysical question always covers the whole range of metaphysical problems. In every case it is itself the whole. Secondly, every metaphysical question can only be put in such a way that the questioner as such is by his very questioning involved in the question.

From this we derive the following pointer: metaphysical questioning has to be put as a whole and has always to be based on the essential

"What Is Metaphysics?" reprinted from Martin Heidegger, *Existence and Being*, translated by R. F. C. Hull and Alan Crick, by permission of Henry Regnery, 1949. Footnotes deleted and postscript omitted.

situation of existence, which puts the question. We question here and now, on our own account. Our existence — a community of scientists, teachers and students — is ruled by science. What essential things are happening to us in the foundations of our existence, now that science has become our passion?

The fields of the sciences lie far apart. Their methodologies are fundamentally different. This disrupted multiplicity of disciplines is to-day only held together by the technical organisation of the Universities and their faculties, and maintained as a unit of meaning by the practical aims of those faculties. As against this, however, the root of the sciences in their essential ground has atrophied.

And yet — insofar as we follow their most specific intentions — in all the sciences we are related to what-is. Precisely from the point of view of the sciences no field takes precedence over another, neither Nature over History nor vice versa. No one methodology is superior to another. Mathematical knowledge is no stricter than philological or historical knowledge. It has merely the characteristic of "exactness", which is not to be identified with strictness. To demand exactitude of history would be to offend against the idea of the kind of strictness that pertains to the human-istic sciences. The world-relationship which runs through all the sci-ences as such constrains them to seek what-is *in itself*, with a view to rendering it, according to its quiddity (*Wasgehalt*) and its modality (*Seinsart*), an object of investigation and basic definition. What the sci-ences accomplish, ideally speaking, is an approximation to the essential nature of all things.

This distinct world-relationship to what-is in itself is sustained and guided by a freely chosen attitude on the part of our human existence. It is true that the pre-scientific and extra-scientific activities of man also relate to what-is. But the distinction of science lies in the fact that, in an alto-gether specific manner, it and it alone explicitly allows the object itself the first and last word. In this objectivity of questioning, definition and proof there is a certain limited submission to what-is, so that this may reveal itself. This submissive attitude taken up by scientific theory be-comes the basis of a possibility: the possibility of science acquiring a leadership of its own, albeit limited, in the whole field of human exis-tence. The world-relationship of science and the attitude of man respon-sible for it can, of course, only be fully understood when we see and understand what is going on in the world-relationship so maintained. Man — one entity (*Seiendes*) among others — "pursues" science. In this "pursuit" what is happening is nothing less than the irruption of a partic-ular entity called "Man" into the whole of what-is, in such a way that in and through this irruption what-is manifests itself *as* and *how* it is. The manner in which the revelatory irruption occurs is the chief thing that helps what-is to become what it is.

This triple process of world-relationship, attitude, and irruption — a radical unity — introduces something of the inspiring simplicity and intensity of *Da-sein* into scientific existence. If we now explicitly take possession of scientific *Da-sein* as clarified by us, we much necessarily say:

That to which the world-relationship refers is what-is — and nothing else.

That by which every attitude is moulded is what-is — and nothing more.

That with which scientific exposition effects its "irruption" is what-is — and beyond that, nothing.

But is it not remarkable that precisely at that point where scientific man makes sure of his surest possession he should speak of something else? What is to be investigated is what-is — and nothing else; only what-is — and nothing more; simply and solely what-is — and beyond that, nothing.

But what about this "nothing"? Is it only an accident that we speak like that quite naturally? Is it only a manner of speaking — and nothing more?

But why worry about this Nothing? "Nothing" is absolutely rejected by science and abandoned as null and void (*das Nichtige*). But if we abandon Nothing in this way are we not, by that act, really admitting it? Can we, though, speak of an admission when we admit Nothing? But perhaps this sort of cross-talk is already degenerating into an empty wrangling about words.

Science, on the other hand, has to assert its soberness and seriousness afresh and declare that it is concerned solely with what-is. Nothing — how can it be for science anything other than a horror and a phantasm? If science is right then one thing stands firm: science wishes to know nothing of Nothing. Such is after all the strictly scientific approach to Nothing. We know it by wishing to know nothing of Nothing.

Science wishes to know nothing of Nothing. Even so the fact remains that at the very point where science tries to put its own essence in words it invokes the aid of Nothing. It has recourse to the very thing it rejects. What sort of schizophrenia is this?

A consideration of our momentary existence as one ruled by science has landed us in the thick of an argument. In the course of this argument a question has already presented itself. The question only requires putting specifically: What about Nothing?

THE DEVELOPMENT OF THE QUESTION

The development of our enquiry into Nothing is bound to lead us to a position where either the answer will prove possible or the impossibility of an answer will become evident. "Nothing" is admitted. Science, by adopting an attitude of superior indifference, abandons it as that which "is not".

All the same we shall endeavour to enquire into Nothing. What is Nothing? Even the initial approach to this question shows us something out of the ordinary. So questioning, we postulate Nothing as something that somehow or other "is" — as an entity (*Seiendes*). But it is nothing of the sort. The question as to the what and wherefore of Nothing turns the thing questioned into its opposite. The question deprives itself of its own object.

Accordingly, every answer to this question is impossible from the start. For it necessarily moves in the form that Nothing "is" this, that or the other. Question and answer are equally nonsensical in themselves where Nothing is concerned.

Hence even the rejection by science is superfluous. The commonly cited basic rule of all thinking — the proposition that contradiction must be avoided — and common "logic" rule out the question. For thinking, which is essentially always thinking about something, would, in thinking of Nothing, be forced to act against its own nature.

Because we continually meet with failure as soon as we try to turn Nothing into a subject, our enquiry into Nothing is already at an end — always assuming, of course, that in this enquiry "logic" is the highest court of appeal, that reason is the means and thinking the way to an original comprehension of Nothing and its possible revelation.

But, it may be asked, can the law of "logic" be assailed? Is not reason indeed the master in this enquiry into Nothing? It is in fact only with reason's help that we can define Nothing in the first place and postulate it as a problem — though a problem that consumes only itself. For Nothing is the negation (*Verneinung*) of the totality of what-is: that which is absolutely not. But at this point we bring Nothing into the higher category of the Negative (*Nichthaftes*) and therefore of what is negated. But according to the overriding and unassailable teachings of "logic" negation is a specific act of reason. How, then, in our enquiry into Nothing and into the very possibility of holding such an enquiry can we dismiss reason? Yet is it so sure just what we are postulating? Does the Not (*das Nicht*), the state of being negated (*die Verneintheit*) and hence negation itself (*Verneinung*), in fact represent that higher category under which Nothing takes its place as a special kind of thing negated? Does Nothing "exist" only because the Not, i.e. negation exists? Or is it the other way about? Does negation and the Not exist only because Nothing exists? This has not been decided — indeed, it has not even been explicitly asked. We assert: "Nothing" is more original than the Not and negation.

If this thesis is correct then the very possibility of negation as an act of reason, and consequently reason itself, are somehow dependent on

Nothing. How, then, can reason attempt to decide this issue? May not the apparent nonsensicality of the question and answer where Nothing is concerned only rest, perhaps, on the blind obstinacy of the roving intellect?

If, however, we refuse to be led astray by the formal impossibility of an enquiry into Nothing and still continue to enquire in the face of it, we must at least satisfy what remains the fundamental pre-requisite for the full pursuit of any enquiry. If Nothing as such is still to be enquired into, it follows that it must be "given" in advance. We must be able to encounter it.

Where shall we seek Nothing? Where shall we find Nothing? In order to find something must we not know beforehand that it is there? Indeed we must! First and foremost we can only look if we have presupposed the presence of a thing to be looked for. But here the thing we are looking for is Nothing. Is there after all a seeking without presupposition, a seeking complemented by a pure finding?

However that may be, we do know "Nothing" if only as a term we bandy about every day. This ordinary hackneyed Nothing, so completely taken for granted and rolling off our tongue so casually — we can even give an off-hand "definition" of it:

Nothing is the complete negation of the totality of what-is.

Does not this characteristic of Nothing point, after all, in the direction from which alone it may meet us?

The totality of what-is must be given beforehand so as to succumb as such to the negation from which Nothing is then bound to emerge.

But, even apart from the questionableness of this relationship between negation and Nothing, how are we, as finite beings, to render the whole of what-is in its totality accessible *in itself* — let alone to ourselves? We can, at a pinch, think of the whole of what-is as an "idea" and then negate what we have thus imagined in our thoughts and "think" it negated. In this way we arrive at the formal concept of an imaginary Nothing, but never Nothing itself. But Nothing is nothing, and between the imaginary and the "authentic" (*eigentlich*) Nothing no difference can obtain, if Nothing represents complete lack of differentiation. But the "authentic" Nothing — is this not once again that latent and nonsensical idea of a Nothing that "is"? Once again and for the last time rational objections have tried to hold up our search, whose legitimacy can only be attested by a searching experience of Nothing.

As certainly as we shall never comprehend absolutely the totality of what-is, it is equally certain that we find ourselves placed in the midst of what-is and that this is somehow revealed in totality. Ultimately there is an essential difference between comprehending the totality of what-is and finding ourselves in the midst of what-is-in-totality. The former is absolutely impossible. The latter is going on in existence all the time.

Naturally enough it looks as if, in our everyday activities, we were always holding on to this or that actuality (*Seiendes*), as if we were lost in this or that region of what-is. However fragmentary the daily round may appear it still maintains what-is, in however shadowy a fashion, within the unity of a "whole". Even when, or rather, precisely when we are not absorbed in things or in our own selves, this "wholeness" comes over us — for example, in real boredom. Real boredom is still far off when this book or that play, this activity or that stretch of idleness merely bores us. Real boredom comes when "one is bored". This profound boredom, drifting hither and thither in the abysses of existence like a mute fog, draws all things, all men and oneself along with them, together in a queer kind of indifference. This boredom reveals what-is in totality.

There is another possibility of such revelation, and this is in the joy we feel in the presence of the being — not merely the person — of some-one we love.

Because of these moods in which, as we say, we "are" this or that (i.e. bored, happy, etc.) we find ourselves (*befinden uns*) in the midst of what-is-in-totality, wholly pervaded by it. The affective state in which we find ourselves not only discloses, according to the mood we are in, what-is in totality, but this disclosure is at the same time far from being a mere chance occurrence and is the ground-phenomenon of our *Da-sein*.

Our "feelings," as we call them, are not just the fleeting concomitant of our mental or volitional behaviour, nor are they simply the cause and occasion of such behaviour, nor yet a state that is merely "there" and in which we come to some kind of understanding with ourselves.

Yet, at the very moment when our moods thus bring us face to face with what-is-in-totality they hide the Nothing we are seeking. We are now less than ever of the opinion that mere negation of what-is-in-totality as revealed by these moods of ours can in fact lead us to Nothing. This could only happen in the first place in a mood so peculiarly revelatory in its import as to reveal Nothing itself.

Does there ever occur in human existence a mood of this kind, through which we are brought face to face with Nothing itself?

This may and actually does occur, albeit rather seldom and for moments only in the key-mood of dread (*Angst*). By "dread" we do not mean "anxiety" (*Aengstlichkeit*), which is common enough and is akin to nervousness (*Furchtsamkeit*) — a mood that comes over us only too eas-ily. Dread differs absolutely from fear (*Furcht*). We are always *afraid* of this or that definite thing, which threatens us in this or that definite way. "Fear of" is generally "fear about" something. Since fear has this charac-teristic limitation — "of" and "about" — the man who is afraid, the ner-vous man, is always bound by the thing he is afraid of or by the state in which he finds himself. In his efforts to save himself from this "some-thing" he becomes uncertain in relation to other things; in fact, he "loses his bearings" generally.

In dread no such confusion can occur. It would be truer to say that dread is pervaded by a peculiar kind of peace. And although dread is always "dread of", it is not dread of this or that. "Dread of" is always a dreadful feeling "about" — but not about this or that. The indefiniteness of *what* we dread is not just lack of definition: it represents the essential impossibility of defining the "what". The indefiniteness is brought out in an illustration familiar to everybody.

In dread, as we say, "one feels something uncanny". What is this "something" (*es*) and this "one"? We are unable to say what gives "one" that uncanny feeling. "One" just feels it generally (*im Ganzen*). All things, and we with them, sink into a sort of indifference. But not in the sense that everything simply disappears; rather, in the very act of drawing away from us everything turns towards us. This withdrawal of what-is-in-totality, which then crowds round us in dread, this is what oppresses us. There is nothing to hold on to. The only thing that remains and overwhelms us whilst what-is slips away, is this "nothing".

Dread reveals Nothing.

In dread we are "in suspense" (*wir schweben*). Or, to put it more precisely, dread holds us in suspense because it makes what-is-in-totality slip away from us. Hence we too, as existents in the midst of what-is, slip away from ourselves along with it. For this reason it is not "you" or "I" that has the uncanny feeling, but "one". In the trepidation of this suspense where there is nothing to hold on to, pure *Da-sein* is all that remains.

Dread strikes us dumb. Because what-is-in-totality slips away and thus forces Nothing to the fore, all affirmation (lit. "Is"-saying: *"Ist"-Sagen*) fails in the face of it. The fact that when we are caught in the uncanniness of dread we often try to break the empty silence by words spoken at random, only proves the presence of Nothing. We ourselves confirm that dread reveals Nothing — when we have got over our dread. In the lucid vision which supervenes while yet the experience is fresh in our memory we must needs say that what we were afraid of was "actually" (*eigentlich:* also "authentic") Nothing. And indeed Nothing itself, Nothing as such, was there.

With this key-mood of dread, therefore, we have reached that event in our *Da-sein* which reveals Nothing, and which must therefore be the starting-point of our enquiry.

What about Nothing?

THE ANSWER TO THE QUESTION

The answer which alone is important for our purpose has already been found if we take care to ensure that we really do keep to the problem of Nothing. This necessitates changing man into his *Da-sein* — a change always occasioned in us by dread — so that we may apprehend Nothing as and how it reveals itself in dread. At the same time we have finally to dismiss those characteristics of Nothing which have not emerged as a result of our enquiry.

"Nothing" is revealed in dread, but not as something that "is". Neither can it be taken as an object. Dread is not an apprehension of Nothing. All the same, Nothing is revealed in and through dread, yet not, again, in the sense that Nothing appears as if detached and apart from what-is-in-totality when we have that "uncanny" feeling. We would say rather: in dread Nothing functions as if *at one with* what-is-in-totality. What do we mean by "at one with "?

In dread what-is-in-totality becomes untenable (*hinfällig*). How? What-is is not annihilated (*vernichtet*) by dread, so as to leave Nothing over. How could it, seeing that dread finds itself completely powerless in face of what-is-in-totality! What rather happens is that Nothing shows itself as essentially belonging to what-is while this is slipping away in totality.

In dread there is no annihilation of the whole of what-is in itself: but equally we cannot negate what-is-in-totality in order to reach Nothing. Apart from the fact that the explicitness of a negative statement is foreign to the nature of dread as such, we would always come too late with any such negation intended to demonstrate Nothing. For Nothing is anterior to it. As we said, Nothing is "at one with" what-is as this slips away in totality.

In dread there is a retreat from something, though it is not so much a flight as a spell-bound (*gebannt*) peace. This "retreat from" has its source in Nothing. The latter does not attract: its nature is to repel. This "repelling from itself" is essentially an "expelling into": a conscious gradual relegation to the vanishing what-is-in-totality (*das entgleitenlassende Verweisen auf das versinkende Seiende im Ganzen*). And this total relegation to the vanishing what-is-in-totality — such being the form in which Nothing crowds round us in dread — is the essence of Nothing: nihilation. Nihilation is neither an annihilation (*Vernichtung*) of what-is, nor does it spring from negation (*Verneinung*). Nihilation cannot be reckoned in terms of annihilation or negation at all. Nothing "nihilates" (*nichtet*) of itself.

Nihilation is not a fortuitous event; but, understood as the relegation to the vanishing what-is-in-totality, it reveals the latter in all its till now undisclosed strangeness as the pure "Other" — contrasted with Nothing.

Only in the clear night of dread's Nothingness is what-is as such revealed in all its original overtness (*Offenheit*): that it "is" and is not Nothing. This verbal appendix "and not Nothing" is, however, not an *a posteriori* explanation but an *a priori* which alone makes possible any revelation of what-is. The essence of Nothing as original nihilation lies in this: that it alone brings *Da-sein* face to face with what-is as such.

Only on the basis of the original manifestness of Nothing can our human *Da-sein* advance towards and enter into what-is. But insofar as *Da-sein* naturally relates to what-is, as that which it is not and which itself is, Da-sein *qua Da-sein* always proceeds from Nothing as manifest.

Da-sein means *being projected into* Nothing (*Hineingehaltenheit in das Nichts*).

Projecting into Nothing, *Da-sein* is already beyond what-is-in-totality. This "being beyond" (*Hinaussein*) what-is we call Transcendence. Were *Da-sein* not, in its essential basis, transcendent, that is to say, were it not projected from the start into Nothing, it could never relate to what-is, hence could have no self-relationship.

Without the original manifest character of Nothing there is no self-hood and no freedom.

Here we have the answer to our question about Nothing. Nothing is neither an object nor anything that "is" at all. Nothing occurs neither by itself nor "apart from" what-is, as a sort of adjunct. Nothing is that which makes the revelation of what-is as such possible for our human existence. Nothing not merely provides the conceptual opposite of what-is but is also an original part of essence (*Wesen*). It is in the Being (*Sein*) of what-is that the nihilation of Nothing (*das Nichten des Nichts*) occurs.

But now we must voice a suspicion which has been withheld far too long already. If it is only through "projecting into Nothing" that our *Da-sein* relates to what-is, in other words, has any existence, and if Nothing is only made manifest originally in dread, should we not have to be in a continual suspense of dread in order to exist at all? Have we not, however, ourselves admitted that this original dread is a rare thing? But above all, we all exist and are related to actualities which we ourselves are not and which we ourselves are — without this dread. Is not this dread, therefore, an arbitrary invention and the Nothing attributed to it an exaggeration?

Yet what do we mean when we say that this original dread only occurs in rare moments? Nothing but this: that as far as we are concerned and, indeed, generally speaking, Nothing is always distorted out of its original state. By what? By the fact that in one way or another we completely lose ourselves in what-is. The more we turn to what-is in our dealings the less we allow it to slip away, and the more we turn aside from Nothing. But all the more certainly do we thrust ourselves into the open superficies of existence.

And yet this perpetual if ambiguous aversion from Nothing accords, within certain limits, with the essential meaning of Nothing. It — Nothing in the sense of nihilation — relegates us to what-is. Nothing "nihilates" unceasingly, without our really knowing what is happening — at least, not with our everyday knowledge.

What could provide more telling evidence of the perpetual, far-reaching and yet ever-dissimulated overtness of Nothing in our existence, than negation? This is supposed to belong to the very nature of human thought. But negation cannot by any stretch of imagination produce the Not out of itself as a means of distinguishing and contrasting given things, thrusting this Not between them, as it were. How indeed could negation produce the Not out of itself, seeing that it can only negate when something is there to be negated? But how can a thing that is or ought to be negated be seen as something negative (*nichthaft*) unless all thinking as such is on the look-out for the Not? But the Not can only manifest itself when its source — the nihilation of Nothing and hence Nothing itself — is drawn out of concealment. The Not does not come into being through negation, but negation is based on the Not, which derives from the nihilation of Nothing. Nor is negation only a mode of nihilating behaviour, i.e. behaviour based *a priori* on the nihilation of Nothing.

Herewith we have proved the above thesis in all essentials: Nothing is the source of negation, not the other way about. If this breaks the sovereignty of reason in the field of enquiry into Nothing and Being, then the fate of the rule of "logic" in philosophy is also decided. The very idea of "logic" disintegrates in the vortex of a more original questioning.

However often and however variously negation — whether explicit or not — permeates all thinking, it cannot *of itself* be a completely valid witness to the manifestation of Nothing as an essential part of *Da-sein*. For negation cannot be cited either as the sole or even the chief mode of nihilation, with which, because of the nihilation of Nothing, *Da-sein* is saturated. More abysmal than the mere propriety of rational negation is the harshness of opposition and the violence of loathing. More responsible the pain of refusal and the mercilessness of an interdict. More oppressive the bitterness of renunciation.

These possible modes of nihilating behaviour, through which our *Da-sein* endures, even if it does not master, the fact of our being thrown upon the world are not modes of negation merely. That does not prevent them from expressing themselves in and through negation. Indeed, it is only then that the empty expanse of negation is really revealed. The permeation of *Da-sein* by nihilating modes of behaviour points to the perpetual, ever-dissimulated manifestness of Nothing, which only dread reveals in all its originality. Here, of course, we have the reason why original dread is generally repressed in *Da-sein*. Dread is there, but sleeping. All *Da-sein* quivers with its breathing: the pulsation is slightest in beings that are timorous, and is imperceptible in the "Yea, yea!" and "Nay, nay!" of busy people; it is readiest in the reserved, and surest of all in the courageous. But this last pulsation only occurs for the sake of that for which it expends itself, so as to safeguard the supreme greatness of *Da-sein*.

The dread felt by the courageous cannot be contrasted with the joy or even the comfortable enjoyment of a peaceable life. It stands — on the hither side of all such contrasts — in secret union with the serenity and gentleness of creative longing.

Original dread can be awakened in *Da-sein* at any time. It need not be awakened by any unusual occurrence. Its action corresponds in depth to the shallowness of its possible cause. It is always on the brink, yet only seldom does it take the leap and drag us with it into the state of suspense.

Because our *Da-sein* projects into Nothing on this basis of hidden dread, man becomes the "stand-in" (*Platzhalter*) for Nothing. So finite are we that we cannot, of our own resolution and will, bring ourselves originally face to face with Nothing. So bottomlessly does finalisation (*Verendlichung*) dig into existence that our freedom's peculiar and profoundest finality fails.

This projection into Nothing on the basis of hidden dread is the overcoming of what-is-in-totality: Transcendence.

Our enquiry into Nothing will, we said, lead us straight to metaphysics. The name "metaphysics" derives from the Greek τὰ μετὰ τὰ φυσικά. This quaint title was later interpreted as characterising the sort of enquiry which goes μετά — trans, beyond — what-is as such.

Metaphysics is an enquiry over and above what-is, with a view to winning it back again as such and in totality for our understanding.

In our quest for Nothing there is similar "going beyond" what-is, conceived as what-is-in-totality. It therefore turns out to be a "metaphysical" question. We said in the beginning that such questioning had a double characteristic: every metaphysical question at once embraces the whole of metaphysics, and in every question the being (*Da-sein*) that questions is himself caught up in the question.

To what extent does the question about Nothing span and pervade the whole of metaphysics?

Since ancient times metaphysics has expressed itself on the subject of Nothing in the highly ambiguous proposition: *ex nihilo nihil fit* — nothing comes from nothing. Even though the proposition as argued never made Nothing itself the real problem, it nevertheless brought out very explicitly, from the prevailing notions about Nothing, the overriding fundamental concept of what-is.

Classical metaphysics conceives Nothing as signifying Not-being (*Nichtseiendes*), that is to say, unformed matter which is powerless to form itself into "being" and cannot therefore present an appearance (εἶδος). What has "being" is the self-creating product (*Gebilde*) which presents itself as such in an image (*Bild*), i.e. something seen (*Anblick*). The origin, law and limits of this ontological concept are discussed as little as Nothing itself.

Christian dogma, on the other hand, denies the truth of the proposition *ex nihilo nihil fit* and gives a twist to the meaning of Nothing, so that it now comes to mean the absolute absence of all "being" outside God: *ex nihilo fit — ens creatum:* the created being is made out of nothing. "Nothing" is now the conceptual opposite of what truly and authentically (*eigentlich*) "is"; it becomes the *summum ens,* God as *ens increatum.* Here, too, the interpretation of Nothing points to the fundamental concept of what-is. Metaphysical discussion of what-is, however, moves on the same plane as the enquiry into Nothing. In both cases the questions concerning Being (*Sein*) and Nothing as such remain unasked. Hence we need not be worried by the difficulty that if God creates "out of nothing" he above all must be able to relate himself to Nothing. But if God is God he cannot know Nothing, assuming that the "Absolute" excludes from itself all nullity (*Nichtigkeit*).

This crude historical reminder shows Nothing as the conceptual opposite of what truly and authentically "is", i.e. as the negation of it. But once Nothing is somehow made a problem this contrast not only undergoes clearer definition but also arouses the true and authentic metaphysical question regarding the Being of what-is. Nothing ceases to be the vague opposite of what-is: it now reveals itself as integral to the Being of what-is.

"Pure Being and pure Nothing are thus one and the same". This proposition of Hegel's (*Science of Logic,* vol. I, **Werke** III, p. 74) is correct. Being and Nothing hang together, but not because the two things — from the point of view of the Hegelian concept of thought — are one in their indefiniteness and immediateness, but because Being itself is finite in essence and is only revealed in the Transcendence of *Da-sein* as projected into Nothing.

If indeed the question of Being as such is the all-embracing question of metaphysics, then the question of Nothing proves to be such as to span the whole metaphysical field. But at the same time the question of Nothing pervades the whole of metaphysics only because it forces us to face the problem of the origin of negation, that is to say, forces a decision about the legitimacy of the rule of "logic" in metaphysics.

The old proposition *ex nihilo nihil fit* will then acquire a different meaning, and one appropriate to the problem of Being itself, so as to run: *ex nihilo omne ens qua ens fit:* every being, so far as it is a being, is made out of nothing. Only in the Nothingness of *Da-sein* can what-is-in-totality — and this in accordance with its peculiar possibilities, i.e. in a finite manner — come to itself. To what extent, then, has the enquiry into Nothing, if indeed it be a metaphysical one, included our own questing *Da-sein?*

Our *Da-sein* as experienced here and now is, we said, ruled by science. If our *Da-sein,* so ruled, is put into this question concerning Nothing, then it follows that it must have been put in question by this question.

The simplicity and intensity of scientific *Da-sein* consist in this: that it relates in a special manner to what-is and to this alone. Science would like to abandon Nothing with a superior gesture. But now, in this question of Nothing, it becomes evident that scientific *Da-sein* is only possible when projected into Nothing at the outset. Science can only come to terms with itself when it does not abandon Nothing. The alleged soberness and superiority of science becomes ridiculous if it fails to take Nothing seriously. Only because Nothing is obvious can science turn what-is into an object of investigation. Only when science proceeds from metaphysics can it conquer its essential task ever afresh, which consists not in the accumulation and classification of knowledge but in the perpetual discovery of the whole realm of truth, whether of Nature or of History.

Only because Nothing is revealed in the very basis of our *Da-sein* is it possible for the utter strangeness of what-is to dawn on us. Only when the strangeness of what-is forces itself upon us does it awaken and invite our wonder. Only because of wonder, that is to say, the revelation of Nothing, does the "Why?" spring to our lips. Only because this "Why?" is possible as such can we seek for reasons and proofs in a definite way. Only because we can ask and prove are we fated to become enquirers in this life.

The enquiry into Nothing puts us, the enquirers, ourselves in question. It is a metaphysical one.

Man's *Da-sein* can only relate to what-is by projecting into Nothing. Going beyond what-is is of the essence of *Da-sein*. But this "going beyond" is metaphysics itself. That is why metaphysics belongs to the nature of man. It is neither a department of scholastic philosophy nor a field of chance ideas. Metaphysics is the ground-phenomenon of *Da-sein*. It is *Da-sein* itself. Because the truth of metaphysics is so unfathomable there is always the lurking danger of profoundest error. Hence no scientific discipline can hope to equal the seriousness of metaphysics. Philosophy can never be measured with the yard-stick of the idea of science.

Once the question we have developed as to the nature of Nothing is really asked by and among our own selves, then we are not bringing in metaphysics from the outside. Nor are we simply "transporting" ourselves into it. It is completely out of our power to transport ourselves into metaphysics because, in so far as we exist, we are already there. Φύσει γὰρ, ὦ φίλει, ἔνεστί τις φιλοσοφία τῇ τοῦ ἀνδρὸς διανοίᾳ (Plato: Phaedrus 279a).* While man exists there will be philosophising of some sort. Philosophy, as we call it, is the setting in motion of metaphysics; and in metaphysics philosophy comes to itself and sets about its explicit tasks. Philosophy is only set in motion by leaping with all its being, as only it

---

* "For by nature, my friend, man's mind dwells in philosophy."

can, into the ground-possibilities of being as a whole. For this leap the following things are of crucial importance: firstly, leaving room for what-is-in-totality; secondly, letting oneself go into Nothing, that is to say, freeing oneself from the idols we all have and to which we are wont to go cringing; lastly, letting this "suspense" range where it will, so that it may continually swing back again to the ground-question of metaphysics, which is wrested from Nothing itself:

Why is there any Being at all — why not far rather Nothing?

MAURICE MERLEAU-PONTY

Maurice Merleau-Ponty (1908–1961) is often mistakenly considered a mere intellectual appendage to Sartre. In fact, though, his views are quite different. Specifically, his work is an important attempt to argue against the Cartesian model of human being. In his most important work, The Phenomenology of Perception, *he argues against Sartre that it is not consciousness, but the human body, that is intentional, that our bodies are not mere objects in the world but rather they are our Being in the world, the perspective from which we judge and value and perceive. This excerpt is from the preface of that work.*

Preface

What is phenomenology? It may seem strange that this question has still to be asked half a century after the first works of Husserl. The fact remains that it has by no means been answered. Phenomenology is the study of essences; and according to it, all problems amount to finding definitions of essences: the essence of perception, or the essence of consciousness, for example. But phenomenology is also a philosophy which puts essences back into existence, and does not expect to arrive at an understanding of man and the world from any starting point other than that of their 'facticity'. It is a transcendental philosophy which places in abeyance the assertions arising out of the natural attitude, the better to understand them; but it is also a philosophy for which the world is always 'already there' before reflection begins — as an inalienable presence; and all its efforts are concentrated upon re-achieving a direct and primitive contact with the world, and endowing that contact with a philosophical status. It is the search for a philosophy which shall be a 'rigorous science', but it also offers an account of space, time and the world as we 'live' them. It tries to give a direct description of our experience as it is, without taking account of its psychological origin and the causal explanations which the scientist, the historian or the sociologist may be able to provide. Yet Husserl in his last works mentions a 'genetic phenomenology',[1] and even a 'constructive phenomenology'.[2] One may try to do away with these contradictions by making a distinction between Husserl's and

---

[1] *Méditations cartésiennes*, pp. 120 ff.

[2] See the unpublished *6th Méditation cartésienne*, edited by Eugen Fink, to which G. Berger has kindly referred us.

From Maurice M. Merleau-Ponty, *The Phenomenology of Perception*, translated by Colin Smith, 1962. Reprinted by permission of Routledge & Kegan Paul.

Heidegger's phenomenologies; yet the whole of *Sein und Zeit* springs from an indication given by Husserl and amounts to no more than an explicit account of the 'natürlicher Weltbegriff' or the 'Lebenswelt' which Husserl, towards the end of his life, identified as the central theme of phenomenology, with the result that the contradiction reappears in Husserl's own philosophy. The reader pressed for time will be inclined to give up the idea of covering a doctrine which says everything, and will wonder whether a philosophy which cannot define its scope deserves all the discussion which has gone on around it, and whether he is not faced rather by a myth or a fashion.

Even if this were the case, there would still be a need to understand the prestige of the myth and the origin of the fashion, and the opinion of the responsible philosopher must be that *phenomenology can be practised and identified as a manner or style of thinking, that it existed as a movement before arriving at complete awareness of itself as a philosophy.* It has been long on the way, and its adherents have discovered it in every quarter, certainly in Hegel and Kierkegaard, but equally in Marx, Nietzsche and Freud. A purely linguistic examination of the texts in question would yield no proof; we find in texts only what we put into them, and if ever any kind of history has suggested the interpretations which should be put on it, it is the history of philosophy. We shall find in ourselves, and nowhere else, the unity and true meaning of phenomenology. It is less a question of counting up quotations than of determining and expressing in concrete form this *phenomenology for ourselves* which has given a number of present-day readers the impression, on reading Husserl or Heidegger, not so much of encountering a new philosophy as of recognizing what they had been waiting for. Phenomenology is accessible only through a phenomenological method. Let us, therefore, try systematically to bring together the celebrated phenomenological themes as they have grown spontaneously together in life. Perhaps we shall then understand why phenomenology has for so long remained at an initial stage, as a problem to be solved and a hope to be realized.

It is a matter of describing, not of explaining or analysing. Husserl's first directive to phenomenology, in its early stages, to be a 'descriptive psychology', or to return to the 'things themselves', is from the start a rejection of science. I am not the outcome or the meeting-point of numerous causal agencies which determine my bodily or psychological make-up. I cannot conceive myself as nothing but a bit of the world, a mere object of biological, psychological or sociological investigation. I cannot shut myself up within the realm of science. All my knowledge of the world, even my scientific knowledge, is gained from my own particular point of view, or from some experience of the world without which the symbols of science would be meaningless. The whole universe of science is built upon the world as directly experienced, and if we want to subject science itself to rigorous scrutiny and arrive at a precise assessment of its meaning and scope, we must begin by reawakening the basic experience of the world of which science is the second-order expression. Science has not and never will have, by its nature, the same significance *qua* form of being as the world which we perceive, for the simple reason that it is a rationale or explanation of that world. I am, not a 'living creature' nor even a 'man', nor again even 'a consciousness' endowed with all the characteristics which zoology, social anatomy or inductive psychology recognize in these various products of the natural or historical process — I am the absolute source, my existence does not stem from my antecedents, from my physical and social environment; instead it moves out towards them and sustains them, for I alone bring into being myself (and therefore into being in the only sense that the word can have for me) the tradition which I elect to carry on, or the horizon whose distance from me would be abolished — since that distance is not one of its properties — if I were not there to scan it with my gaze. Scientific points of view, according to which my existence is a moment of the world's, are always both naïve and at the same time dishonest, because they take for granted, without explicitly mentioning it, the other point of view, namely that of consciousness, through which from the outset a world forms itself round me and begins to exist for me. To return to things themselves is to return to that world which precedes knowledge, of which knowledge always *speaks,* and in relation to which every scientific schematization is an abstract and derivative sign-language, as is geography in relation to the countryside in which we have learnt beforehand what a forest, a prairie or a river is.

This move is absolutely distinct from the idealist return to consciousness, and the demand for a pure description excludes equally the procedure of analytical reflection on the one hand, and that of scientific explanation on the other. Descartes and particularly Kant *detached* the subject, or consciousness, by showing that I could not possibly apprehend anything as existing unless I first of all experienced myself as existing in the act of apprehending it. They presented consciousness, the absolute certainty of my existence for myself, as the condition of there being anything at all; and the act of relating as the basis of relatedness. It is true that the act of relating is nothing if divorced from the spectacle of the world in which relations are found; the unity of consciousness in Kant is achieved simultaneously with that of the world. And in Descartes methodical doubt does not deprive us of anything, since the whole world, at least in so far as we experience it, is reinstated in the *Cogito,* enjoying equal certainty, and simply labelled 'thought of . . .'. But the relations between subject and world are not strictly bilateral: if they were, the certainty of the world would, in Descartes, be immediately given with that of the *Cogito,* and Kant would not have talked about his 'Copernican revolution'. Analytical reflection starts from our experience of the world and goes back to the subject as to a condition of possibility distinct from that experience, revealing the all-embracing synthesis as that without which there would be no world. To this extent it ceases to remain part of our experience and offers, in place of an account, a reconstruction. It is understandable, in view of this, that Husserl, having accused Kant of adopting a 'faculty psychologism',[3] should have urged, in place of a noetic analysis which bases the world on the synthesizing activity of the subject, his own *'noematic reflection'* which remains within the object and, instead of begetting it, brings to light its fundamental unity.

The world is there before any possible analysis of mine, and it would be artificial to make it the outcome of a series of syntheses which link, in the first place sensations, then aspects of the object corresponding to different perspectives, when both are nothing but products of analysis, with no sort of prior reality. Analytical reflection believes that it can trace back the course followed by a prior constituting act and arrive, in the 'inner man' — to use Saint Augustine's expression — at a constituting power which has always been identical with that inner self. Thus reflection is carried away by itself and installs itself in an impregnable subjectivity, as yet untouched by being and time. But this is very ingenuous, or at least it is an imcomplete form of reflection which loses sight of its own beginning. When I begin to reflect my reflection bears upon an unreflective experience; moreover my reflection cannot be unaware of itself as an event, and so it appears to itself in the light of a truly creative act, of a changed structure of consciousness, and yet it has to recognize, as having priority over its own operations, the world which is given to the subject because the subject is given to himself. The real has to be described, not constructed or formed. Which means that I cannot put perception into the same category as the syntheses represented by judgements, acts or predications. My field of perception is constantly filled with a play of colours, noises and fleeting tactile sensations which I cannot relate precisely to the context of my clearly perceived world, yet which I nevertheless immediately 'place' in the world, without ever confusing them with my daydreams. Equally constantly I weave dreams round things. I imagine people and things whose presence is not incompatible with the context, yet who are not in fact involved in it: they are ahead of reality, in the realm of the imaginary. If the reality of my perception were based solely on the intrinsic coherence of 'representations', it ought to be for ever hesitant and, being wrapped up in my conjectures on probabilities, I ought to be ceaselessly taking apart misleading syntheses, and reinstating in reality stray phenomena which I had excluded in the first place. But this does not happen. The real is a closely woven fabric. It does not await our

---

[3] *Logische Untersuchungen, Prolegomena zur reinen Logik,* p. 93.

judgement before incorporating the most surprising phenomena, or before rejecting the most plausible figments of our imagination. Perception is not a science of the world, it is not even an act, a deliberate taking up of a position; it is the background from which all acts stand out, and is presupposed by them. The world is not an object such that I have in my possession the law of its making; it is the natural setting of, and field for, all my thoughts and all my explicit perceptions. Truth does not 'inhabit' only 'the inner man', or more accurately, there is no inner man, man is in the world, and only in the world does he know himself. When I return to myself from an excursion into the realm of dogmatic common sense or of science, I find, not a source of intrinsic truth, but a subject destined to the world.

All of which reveals the true meaning of the famous phenomenological reduction. There is probably no question over which Husserl spent more time — or to which he more often returned, since the 'problematic of reduction' occupies an important place in his unpublished work. For a long time, and even in recent texts, the reduction is presented as the return to a transcendental consciousness before which the world is spread out and completely transparent, quickened through and through by a series of apperceptions which it is the philosopher's tasks to reconstitute on the basis of their outcome. Thus my sensation of redness is *perceived as* the manifestation of a certain redness experienced, this in turn as the manifestation of a red surface, which is the manifestation of a piece of red cardboard, and this finally is the manifestation or outline of a red thing, namely this book. We are to understand, then, that it is the apprehension of a certain *hylè*, as indicating a phenomenon of a higher degree, the *Sinngebung*, or active meaning-giving operation which may be said to define consciousness, so that the world is nothing but 'world-as-meaning', and the phenomenological reduction is idealistic, in the sense that there is here a transcendental idealism which treats the world as an indivisible unity of value shared by Peter and Paul, in which their perspectives blend. 'Peter's consciousness' and 'Paul's consciousness' are in communication, the perception of the world 'by Peter' is not Peter's doing any more than its perception 'by Paul' is Paul's doing; in each case it is the doing of pre-personal forms of consciousness, whose communication raises no problem, since it is demanded by the very definition of consciousness, meaning or truth. In so far as I am a consciousness, that is, in so far as something has meaning for me, I am neither here nor there, neither Peter nor Paul; I am in no way distinguishable from an 'other' consciousness, since we are immediately in touch with the world and since the world is, by definition, unique, being the system in which all truths cohere. A logically consistent transcendental idealism rids the world of its opacity and its transcendence. The world is precisely that thing of which we form a representation, not as men or as empirical subjects, but in so far as we are all one light and participate in the One without destroying its unity. Analytical reflection knows nothing of the problem of other minds, or of that of the world, because it insists that with the first glimmer of consciousness there appears in me theoretically the power of reaching some universal truth, and that the other person, being equally without thisness, location or body, the Alter and the Ego are one and the same in the true world which is the unifier of minds. There is no difficulty in understanding how *I* can conceive the Other, because the I and consequently the Other are not conceived as part of the woven stuff of phenomena; they have validity rather than existence. There is nothing hidden behind these faces and gestures, no domain to which I have no access, merely a little shadow which owes its very existence to the light. For Husserl, on the contrary, it is well known that there is a problem of other people, and the *alter ego* is a paradox. If the other is truly for himself alone, beyond his being for me, and if we are for each other and not both for God, we must necessarily have some appearance for each other. He must and I must have an outer appearance, and there must be, besides the perspective of the For Oneself — my view of myself and the other's of himself — a perspective of For Others — my view of others and theirs of me. Of course, these two perspectives, in each one of us, cannot be simply juxtaposed, *for in that case it is not I that the other would see, nor he that I should see.* I must be the exterior that I present others, and the body of the other must be the other himself. This paradox and the dialectic of the Ego and the Alter are possible only provided that the Ego and the Alter Ego are defined by their situation and are not freed from all inherence; that is, provided that philosophy does not culminate in a return to the self, and that I discover by reflection not only my presence to myself, but also the possibility of an 'outside spectator'; that is, again, provided that at the very moment when I experience my existence — at the ultimate extremity of reflection — I fall short of the ultimate density which would place me outside time, and that I discover within myself a kind of internal weakness standing in the way of my being totally individualized: a weakness which exposes me to the gaze of others as a man among men or at least as a consciousness among consciousnesses. Hitherto the *Cogito* depreciated the perception of others, teaching me as it did that the I is accessible only to itself, since it defined *me* as the thought which I have of myself, and which clearly I am alone in having, at least in this ultimate sense. For the 'other' to be more than an empty word, it is necessary that my existence should never be reduced to my bare awareness of existing, but that it should take in also the awareness that *one* may have of it, and thus include my incarnation in some nature and the possibility, at least, of a historical situation. The *Cogito* must reveal me in a situation, and it is on this condition alone that transcendental subjectivity can, as Husserl puts it[4] *be* an intersubjectivity. As a meditating Ego, I can clearly distinguish from myself the world and things, since I certainly do not exist in the way in which things exist. I must even set aside from myself my body understood as a thing among things, as a collection of physico-chemical processes. But even if the *cogitatio*, which I thus discover, is without location in objective time and space, it is not without place in the phenomenological world. The world, which I distinguished from myself as the totality of things or of processes linked by causal relationships, I rediscover 'in me' as the permanent horizon of all my *cogitationes* and as a dimension in relation to which I am constantly situating myself. The true *Cogito* does not define the subject's existence in terms of the thought he has of existing, and furthermore does not convert the indubitability of the world into the indubitability of thought about the world, nor finally does it replace the world itself by the world as meaning. On the contrary it recognizes my thought itself as an inalienable fact, and does away with any kind of idealism in revealing me as 'being-in-the-world'.

It is because we are through and through compounded of relationships with the world that for us the only way to become aware of the fact is to suspend the resultant activity, to refuse it our complicity (to look at it *ohne mitzumachen*, as Husserl often says), or yet again, to put it 'out of play'. Not because we reject the certainties of common sense and a natural attitude to things — they are, on the contrary, the constant theme of philosophy — but because, being the presupposed basis of any thought, they are taken for granted, and go unnoticed, and because in order to arouse them and bring them to view, we have to suspend for a moment our recognition of them. The best formulation of the reduction is probably that given by Eugen Fink, Husserl's assistant, when he spoke of 'wonder' in the face of the world.[5] Reflection does not withdraw from the world towards the unity of consciousness as the world's basis; it steps back to watch the forms of transcendence fly up like sparks from a fire; it slackens the intentional threads which attach us to the world and thus brings them to our notice; it alone is consciousness of the world because it reveals that world as strange and paradoxical. Husserl's transcendental is not Kant's and Husserl accuses Kant's philosophy of being 'worldly', because it *makes use* of our relation to the world, which is the motive force of the transcendental deduction, and makes the world immanent in the subject, instead of *being filled with wonder* at it and conceiving the subject as a process of transcendence towards the world. All the misunderstandings with his interpreters, with the existentialist 'dissidents' and

---

[4] *Die Krisis der europäischen Wissenschaften und die transzendentale Phänomenologie*, III (unpublished).
[5] *Die phänomenologische Philosophie Edmund Husserls in der gegenwärtigen Kritik*, pp. 331 and ff.

finally with himself, have arisen from the fact that in order to see the world and grasp it as paradoxical, we must break with our familiar acceptance of it and, also, from the fact that from this break we can learn nothing but the unmotivated upsurge of the world. The most important lesson which the reduction teaches us is the impossibility of a complete reduction. This is why Husserl is constantly re-examining the possibility of the reduction. If we were absolute mind, the reduction would present no problem. But since, on the contrary, we are in the world, since indeed our reflections are carried out in the temporal flux on to which we are trying to seize (since they *sich einströmen*, as Husserl says), there is no thought which embraces all our thought. The philosopher, as the unpublished works declare, is a perpetual beginner, which means that he takes for granted nothing that men, learned or otherwise, believe they know. It means also that philosophy itself must not take itself for granted, in so far as it may have managed to say something true; that it is an ever-renewed experiment in making its own beginning; that it consists wholly in the description of this beginning, and finally, that radical reflection amounts to a consciousness of its own dependence on an unreflective life which is its initial situation, unchanging, given once and for all. Far from being, as has been thought, a procedure of idealistic philosophy, phenomenological reduction belongs to existential philosophy: Heidegger's 'being-in-the-world' appears only against the background of the phenomenological reduction.

A misunderstanding of a similar kind confuses the notion of the 'essences' in Husserl. Every reduction, says Husserl, as well as being transcendental is necessarily eidetic. That means that we cannot subject our perception of the world to philosophical scrutiny without ceasing to be identified with that act of positing the world, with that interest in it which delimits us, without drawing back from our commitment which is itself thus made to appear as a spectacle, without passing from the *fact* of our existence to its *nature*, from the Dasein to the Wesen. But it is clear that the essence is here not the end, but a means, that our effective involvement in the world is precisely what has to be understood and made amenable to conceptualization, for it is what polarizes all our conceptual particularizations. The need to proceed by way of essences does not mean that philosophy takes them as its object, but, on the contrary, that our existence is too tightly held in the world to be able to know itself as such at the moment of its involvement, and that it requires the field of ideality in order to become acquainted with and to prevail over its facticity. The Vienna Circle, as is well known, lays it down categorically that we can enter into relations only with meanings. For example, 'consciousness' is not for the Vienna Circle identifiable with what we are. It is a complex meaning which has developed late in time, which should be handled with care, and only after the many meanings which have contributed, throughout the word's semantic development, to the formation of its present one have been made explicit. Logical positivism of this kind is the antithesis of Husserl's thought. Whatever the subtle changes of meaning which have ultimately brought us, as a linguistic acquisition, the word and concept of consciousness, we enjoy direct access to what it designates. For we have the experience of ourselves, of that consciousness which we are, and it is on the basis of this experience that all linguistic connotations are assessed, and precisely through it that language comes to have any meaning at all for us. 'It is that as yet dumb experience . . . which we are concerned to lead to the pure expression of its own meaning.'[6] Husserl's essences are destined to bring back all the living relationships of experience, as the fisherman's net draws up from the depths of the ocean quivering fish and seaweed. Jean Wahl is therefore wrong in saying that 'Husserl separates essences from existence'.[7] The separated essences are those of language. It is the office of language to cause essences to exist in a state of separation which is in fact merely apparent, since through language they still rest upon the ante-predicative life of consciousness. In the silence of primary consciousness can be seen appearing not only what words mean, but also what things mean: the core of primary meaning round which the acts of naming and expression take shape.

Seeking the essence of consciousness will therefore not consist in developing the *Wortbedeutung* of consciousness and escaping from existence into the universe of things said; it will consist in rediscovering my actual presence to myself, the fact of my consciousness which is in the last resort what the word and the concept of consciousness mean. Looking for the world's essence is not looking for what it is as an idea once it has been reduced to a theme of discourse; it is looking for what it is as a fact for us, before any thematization. Sensationalism 'reduces' the world by noticing that after all we never experience anything but states of ourselves. Transcendental idealism too 'reduces' the world since, in so far as it guarantees the world, it does so by regarding it as thought or consciousness of the world, and as the mere correlative of our knowledge, with the result that it becomes immanent in consciousness and the aseity of things is thereby done away with. The eidetic reduction is, on the other hand, the determination to bring the world to light as it is before any falling back on ourselves has occurred, it is the ambition to make reflection emulate the unreflective life of consciousness. I aim at and perceive a world. If I said, as do the sensationalists, that we have here only 'states of consciousness', and if I tried to distinguish my perceptions from my dreams with the aid

---

[6] *Méditations cartésiennes*, p. 33.
[7] *Réalisme, dialectique et mystère*, l'Arbalète, Autumn, 1942, unpaginated.

of 'criteria', I should overlook the phenomenon of the world. For if I am able to talk about 'dreams' and 'reality', to bother my head about the distinction between imaginary and real, and cast doubt upon the 'real', it is because this distinction is already made by me before any analysis; it is because I have an experience of the real as of the imaginary, and the problem then becomes one not of asking how critical thought can provide for itself secondary equivalents of this distinction, but of making explicit our primordial knowledge of the 'real', of describing our perception of the world as that upon which our idea of truth is forever based. We must not, therefore, wonder whether we really perceive a world, we must instead say: the world is what we perceive. In more general terms we must not wonder whether our self-evident truths are real truths, or whether, through some perversity inherent in our minds, that which is self-evident for us might not be illusory in relation to some truth in itself. For in so far as we talk about illusion, it is because we have identified illusions, and done so solely in the light of some perception which at the same time gave assurance of its own truth. It follows that doubt, or the fear of being mistaken, testifies as soon as it arises to our power of unmasking error, and that it could never finally tear us away from truth. We are in the realm of truth and it is 'the experience of truth' which is self-evident.[8] To seek the essence of perception is to declare that perception is, not presumed true, but defined as access to truth. So, if I now wanted, according to idealistic principles, to base this *de facto* self-evident truth, this irresistible belief, on some absolute self-evident truth, that is, on the absolute clarity which my thoughts have for me; if I tried to find in myself a creative thought which bodied forth the framework of the world or illumined it through and through, I should once more prove unfaithful to my experience of the world, and should be looking for what makes that experience possible instead of looking for what it is. The self-evidence of perception is not adequate thought or apodeictic self-evidence.[9] The world is not what I think, but what I live through. I am open to the world, I have no doubt that I am in communication with it, but I do not possess it; it is inexhaustible. 'There is a world', or rather: 'There is the world'; I can never completely account for this ever-reiterated assertion in my life. This facticity of the world is what constitutes the *Weltlichkeit der Welt*, what causes the world to be the world; just as the facticity of the *cogito* is not an imperfection in itself, but rather what assures me of my existence. The eidetic method is the method of a phenomenological positivism which bases the possible on the real.

[8] *Das Erlebnis der Wahrheit (Logische Untersuchungen, Prolegomena zur reinen Logik)* p. 190.
[9] There is no apodeictic self-evidence, the *Formale und transzendentale Logik* (p. 142) says in effect.

We can now consider the notion of intentionality, too often cited as the main discovery of phenomenology, whereas it is understandable only through the reduction. "All consciousness is consciousness of something'; there is nothing new in that. Kant showed, in the *Refutation of Idealism*, that inner perception is impossible without outer perception, that the world, as a collection of connected phenomena, is anticipated in the consciousness of my unity, and is the means whereby I come into being as a consciousness. What distinguishes intentionality from the Kantian relation to a possible object is that the unity of the world, before being posited by knowledge in a specific act of identification, is 'lived' as ready-made or already there. Kant himself shows in the *Critique of Judgement* that there exists a unity of the imagination and the understanding and a unity of subjects *before the object,* and that, in experiencing the beautiful, for example, I am aware of a harmony between sensation and concept, between myself and others, which is itself without any concept. Here the subject is no longer the universal thinker of a system of objects rigorously interrelated, the positing power who subjects the manifold to the law of the understanding, in so far as he is to be able to put together a world — he discovers and enjoys his own nature as spontaneously in harmony with the law of the understanding. But if the subject has a nature, then the hidden art of the imagination must condition the categorical activity. It is no longer merely the aesthetic judgement, but knowledge too which rests upon this art, an art which forms the basis of the unity of consciousness and of consciousnesses.

Husserl takes up again the *Critique of Judgement* when he talks about a teleology of consciousness. It is not a matter of duplicating human consciousness with some absolute thought which, from outside, is imagined as assigning to it its aims. It is a question of recognizing consciousness itself as a project of the world, meant for the world which it neither embraces nor possesses, but towards which it is perpetually directed — and the world as this pre-objective individual whose imperious unity decrees what knowledge shall take as its goal. This is why Husserl distinguishes between intentionality of act, which is that of our judgements and of those occasions when we voluntarily take up a position — the only intentionality discussed in the *Critique of Pure Reason* — and operative intentionality *(fungierende Intentionalität),* or that which produces the natural and antepredicative unity of the world and of our life, being apparent in our desires, our evaluations and in the landscape we see, more clearly than in objective knowledge, and furnishing the text which our knowledge tries to translate into precise language. Our relationship to the world, as it is untiringly enunciated within us, is not a thing which can be any further clarified by analysis; philosophy can only place it once more before our eyes and present it for our ratification.

Through this broadened notion of intentionality, phenomenological 'comprehension' is distinguished from traditional 'intellection', which is confined to 'true and immutable natures', and so phenomenology can become a phenomenology of origins. Whether we are concerned with a thing perceived, a historical event or a doctrine, to 'understand' is to take in the total intention — not only what these things are for representation (the 'properties' of the thing perceived, the mass of 'historical facts', the 'ideas' introduced by the doctrine) — but the unique mode of existing expressed in the properties of the pebble, the glass or the piece of wax, in all the events of a revolution, in all the thoughts of a philosopher. It is a matter, in the case of each civilization, of finding the Idea in the Hegelian sense, that is, not a law of the physico-mathematical type, discoverable by objective thought, but that formula which sums up some unique manner of behaviour towards others, towards Nature, time and death: a certain way of patterning the world which the historian should be capable of seizing upon and making his own. These are the *dimensions* of history. In this context there is not a human word, not a gesture, even one which is the outcome of habit or absent-mindedness, which has not some meaning. For example, I may have been under the impression that I lapsed into silence through weariness, or some minister may have thought he had uttered merely an appropriate platitude, yet my silence or his words immediately take on a significance, because my fatigue or his falling back upon a ready-made formula are not accidental, for they express a certain lack of interest, and hence some degree of adoption of a definite position in relation to the situation.

When an event is considered at close quarters, at the moment when it is lived through, everything seems subject to chance: one man's ambition, some lucky encounter, some local circumstance or other appears to have been decisive. But chance happenings offset each other, and facts in their multiplicity coalesce and show up a certain way of taking a stand in relation to the human situation, reveal in fact an *event* which has its definite outline and about which we can talk. Should the starting-point for the understanding of history be ideology, or politics, or religion, or economics? Should we try to understand a doctrine from its overt content, or from the psychological make-up and the biography of its author? We must seek an understanding from all these angles simultaneously, everything has meaning, and we shall find this same structure of being underlying all relationships. All these views are true provided that they are not isolated, that we delve deeply into history and reach the unique core of existential meaning which emerges in each perspective. It is true, as Marx says, that history does not walk on its head, but it is also true that it does not think with its feet. Or one should say rather that it is neither its 'head' not its 'feet' that we have to worry about, but its body. All economic and psychological explanations of a doctrine are true, since the thinker never thinks from any starting-point but the one constituted by what he is. Reflection even on a doctrine will be complete only if it succeeds in linking up with the doctrine's history and the extraneous explanations of it, and in putting back the causes and meaning of the doctrine in an existential structure. There is, as Husserl says, a 'genesis of meaning' (*Sinngenesis*), which alone, in the last resort, teaches us what the doctrine 'means.' Like understanding, criticism must be pursued at all levels, and naturally, it will be insufficient, for the refutation of a doctrine, to relate it to some accidental event in the author's life: its significance goes beyond, and there is no pure accident in existence or in coexistence, since both absorb random events and transmute them into the rational.

Finally, as it is indivisible in the present, history is equally so in its sequences. Considered in the light of its fundamental dimensions, all periods of history appear as manifestations of a single existence, or as episodes in a single drama — without our knowing whether it has an ending. Because we are in the world, we are *condemned to meaning*, and we cannot do or say anything without its acquiring a name in history.

Probably the chief gain from phenomenology is to have united extreme subjectivism and extreme objectivism in its notion of the world or of rationality. Rationality is precisely measured by the experiences in which it is disclosed. To say that there exists rationality is to say that perspectives blend, perceptions confirm each other, a meaning emerges. But it should not be set in a realm apart, transposed into absolute Spirit, or into a world in the realist sense. The phenomenological world is not pure being, but the sense which is revealed where the paths of my various experiences intersect, and also where my own and other people's intersect and engage each other like gears. It is thus inseparable from subjectivity and intersubjectivity, which find their unity when I either take up my past experiences in those of the present, or other people's in my own. For the first time the philosopher's thinking is sufficiently conscious not to anticipate itself and endow its own results with reified form in the world. The philosopher tries to conceive the world, others and himself and their interrelations. But the meditating Ego, the 'impartial spectator' (*uninteressierter Zuschauer*)[10] do not rediscover an already given rationality, they 'establish themselves',[11] and establish it, by an act of initiative which has no guarantee in being, its justification resting entirely on the effective power which it confers on us of taking our own history upon ourselves.

The phenomenological world is not the bringing to explicit expression of a pre-existing being, but the laying down of being. Philosophy is not the reflection of a pre-existing truth, but, like art, the act of bringing

[10] *6th Méditation cartésienne* (unpublished).
[11] Ibid.

truth into being. One may well ask how this creation is *possible*, and if it does not recapture in things a pre-existing Reason. The answer is that the only pre-existent Logos is the world itself, and that the philosophy which brings it into visible existence does not begin by being *possible*; it is actual or real like the world of which it is a part, and no explanatory hypothesis is clearer than the act whereby we take up this unfinished world in an effort to complete and conceive it. Rationality is not a *problem*. There is behind it no unknown quantity which has to be determined by deduction, or, beginning with it, demonstrated inductively. We witness every minute the miracle of related experiences, and yet nobody knows better than we do how this miracle is worked, for we are ourselves this network of relationships. The world and reason are not problematical. We may say, if we wish, that they are mysterious, but their mystery defines them: there can be no question of dispelling it by some 'solution', it is on the hither side of all solutions. True philosophy consists in relearning to look at the world, and in this sense a historical account can give meaning to the world quite as 'deeply' as a philosophical treatise. We take our fate in our hands, we become responsible for our history through reflection, but equally by a decision on which we stake our life, and in both cases what is involved is a violent act which is validated by being performed.

Phenomenology, as a disclosure of the world, rests on itself, or rather provides its own foundation. All knowledge is sustained by a 'ground' of postulates and finally by our communication with the world as primary embodiment of rationality. Philosophy, as radical reflection, dispenses in principle with this resource. As, however, it too is in history, it too exploits the world and constituted reason. It must therefore put to itself the question which it puts to all branches of knowledge, and so duplicate itself infinitely, being, as Husserl says, a dialogue or infinite meditation, and, in so far as it remains faithful to its intention, never knowing where it is going. The unfinished nature of phenomenology and the inchoative atmosphere which has surrounded it are not to be taken as a sign of failure, they were inevitable because phenomenology's task was to reveal the mystery of the world and of reason. If phenomenology was a movement before becoming a doctrine or a philosophical system, this was attributable neither to accident, nor to fraudulent intent. It is as painstaking as the works of Balzac, Proust, Valéry or Cézanne — by reason of the same kind of attentiveness and wonder, the same demand for awareness, the same will to seize the meaning of the world or of history as that meaning comes into being. In this way it merges into the general effort of modern thought.

JEAN-PAUL SARTRE

Sartre tells us that we are "not justified in considering any of its [his system's] parts in isolation from the whole," so no excerpt can do justice to the complex subtleties of his overall view. But following are two brief selections from his most well-known work, Being and Nothingness, *which has become the principal text of the modern existentialist movement. These selections provide an introduction to Sartre's analysis of Being.*

Being For-Itself and In-Itself

THE ONTOLOGICAL PROOF

Being has not been given its due. We believed we had dispensed with granting transphenomenality to the being of the phenomenon because we had discovered the transphenomenality of the being of consciousness. We are going to see, on the contrary, that this very transphenomenality requires that of the being of the phenomenon. There is an "ontological proof" to be derived not from the reflective *cogito* but from the *pre-reflective* being of the *percipiens*. This we shall now try to demonstrate.

All consciousness is consciousness *of* something. This definition of consciousness can be taken in two very distinct senses: either we understand by this that consciousness is constitutive of the being of its object, or it means that consciousness in its inmost nature is a relation to a transcendent being. But the first interpretation of the formula destroys itself: to be conscious *of* something is to be confronted with a concrete and full presence which *is not* consciousness. Of course one can be conscious of an absence. But this absence appears necessarily as a pre-condition of presence. As we have seen, consciousness is a real subjectivity and the impression is a subjective plenitude. But this subjectivity can not go out of itself to posit a transcendent object in such a way as to endow it with a plenitude of impressions.[1] If then we wish at any price to make the being of the phenomenon depend on consciousness, the object must be distinguished from consciousness not by its *presence* but by its *absence*, not by its plenitude, but by its nothingness. If being belongs to consciousness, the object is not consciousness, not to the extent that it is another being, but that it is non-being. This is the appeal to the infinite of which we

---

[1] Tr. *I.e.*, in such a way that the impressions are objectified into qualities of the thing.

From Jean-Paul Sartre, *Being and Nothingness*, translated by Hazel Barnes, pp. 21 30, 49 56.

spoke in the first section of this work. For Husserl, for example, the animation of the hyletic nucleus by the only intentions which can find their fulfillment (*Erfüllung*) in this *hyle* is not enough to bring us outside of subjectivity. The truly objectifying intentions are empty intentions, those which aim beyond the present subjective appearance at the infinite totality of the series of appearances.

We must further understand that the intentions aim at appearances which are never to be given at one time. It is an impossibility on principle for the terms of an infinite series to exist all at the same time before consciousness, along with the real absence of all these terms except for the one which is the foundation of objectivity. If present these impressions — even in infinite number — would dissolve in the subjective; it is their absence which gives them objective being. Thus the being of the object is pure non-being. It is defined as a *lack*. It is that which escapes, that which by definition will never be given, that which offers itself only in fleeting and successive profiles.

But how can non-being be the foundation of being? How can the absent, *expected* subjective become thereby the objective? A great joy which I hope for, a grief which I dread, acquire from that fact a certain transcendence. This I admit. But that transcendence in immanence does not bring us out of the subjective. It is true that things give themselves in profile; that is, simply by appearances. And it is true that each appearance refers to other appearances. But each of them is already in itself alone a *transcendent being*, not a subjective material of impressions — a *plenitude of being*, not a lack — a *presence*, not an absence. It is futile by a sleight of hand to attempt to found the *reality* of the object on the subjective plenitude of impressions and its *objectivity* on non-being; the objective will never come out of the subjective nor the transcendent from immanence, nor being from non-being. But, we are told, Husserl defines consciousness precisely as a transcendence. In truth he does. This is what he posits. This is his essential discovery. But from the moment that he makes of the *noema* and *unreal*, a correlate *of* the *noesis*, a noema whose *esse* is *percipi*, he is totally unfaithful to his principle.

Consciousness is consciousness *of* something. This means that transcendence is the constitutive structure of consciousness; that is, that consciousness is born *supported by* a being which is not itself. This is what we call the ontological proof. No doubt someone will reply that the existence of the demand of consciousness does not prove that this demand ought to be satisfied. But this objection can not hold up against an analysis of what Husserl calls intentionality, though, to be sure, he misunderstood its essential character. To say that consciousness is consciousness of something means that for consciousness there is no being outside of that precise obligation to be a revealing intuition of something — *i.e.*, of a transcendent being. Not only does pure subjectivity, if initially given, fail to transcend itself to posit the objective; a "pure" subjectivity disappears. What can properly be called subjectivity is consciousness (of) consciousness. But this consciousness (of being) consciousness must be qualified in some way, and it can be qualified only as revealing intuition or it is nothing. Now a revealing intuition implies something revealed. Absolute subjectivity can be established only in the face of something revealed; immanence can be defined only within the apprehension of a transcendent. It might appear that there is an echo here of Kant's refutation of problematical idealism. But we ought rather to think of Descartes. We are here on the ground of being, not of knowledge. It is not a question of showing that the phenomena of inner sense imply the existence of objective spatial phenomena, but that consciousness implies in its being a non-conscious and transphenomenal being. In particular there is no point in replying that in fact subjectivity implies objectivity and that it constitutes itself in constituting the objective; we have seen that subjectivity is powerless to constitute the objective. To say that consciousness is consciousness of something is to say that it must produce itself as a revealed-revelation of a being which is not it and which gives itself as already existing when consciousness reveals it.

Thus we have left pure appearance and have arrived at full being. Consciousness is a being whose existence posits its essence and inversely it is consciousness of a being, whose essence implies its existence; that is, in which appearance lays claim to *being*. Being is everywhere. Certainly we could apply to consciousness the definition which Heidegger reserves for *Dasein* and say that it is a being such that in its being, its being is in question. But it would be necessary to complete the definition and formulate it more like this: *consciousness is a being such that in its being, its being is in question in so far as this being implies a being other than itself.*

We must understand that this being is no other than the transphenomenal being of phenomena and not a noumenal being which is hidden behind them. It is the being of this table, of this package of tobacco, of the lamp, more generally the being of the world which is implied by consciousness. It requires simply that the being of that which *appears* does not exist *only* in so far as it appears. The transphenomenal being of what exists *for consciousness* is itself in itself (*lui-même en soi*).

BEING-IN-ITSELF

We can now form a few definite conclusions about the *phenomenon of being*, which we have considered in order to make the preceding observations. Consciousness is the revealed-revelation of existents, and existents appear before consciousness on the foundation of their being.

Nevertheless the primary characteristic of the being of an existent is never to reveal itself completely to consciousness. An existent can not be stripped of its being; being is the ever present foundation of the existent; it is everywhere in it and nowhere. There is no being which is not the being of a certain mode of being, none which can not be apprehended through the mode of being which manifests being and veils it at the same time. Consciousness can always pass beyond the existent, not toward its being, but toward the *meaning of this being.* That is why we call it ontic-ontological, since a fundamental characteristic of its transcendence is to transcend the ontic toward the ontological. The meaning of the being of the existent in so far as it reveals itself to consciousness is the phenomenon of being. This meaning has itself a being, based on which it manifests itself.

It is from this point of view that we can understand the famous Scholastic argument according to which there is a vicious circle in every proposition which concerns being, since any judgment about being already implies being. But in actuality there is no vicious circle, for it is not necessary again to pass beyond the being of this meaning toward its meaning; the meaning of being is valid for the being of every phenomenon, including its own being. The phenomenon of being is not being, as we have already noted. But it indicates being and requires it — although, in truth, the ontological proof which we mentioned above is not valid *especially* or *uniquely* for it; there is *one* ontological proof valid for the whole domain of consciousness. But this proof is sufficient to justify all the information which we can derive from the phenomenon of being. The phenomenon of being, like every primary phenomenon, is immediately disclosed to consciousness. We have at each instant what Heidegger calls a pre-ontological comprehension of it; that is, one which is not accompanied by a fixing in concepts and elucidation. For us at present, then, there is no question of considering this phenomenon for the sake of trying to fix the meaning of being. We must observe always:

(1) That this elucidation of the meaning of being is valid only for the being of the phenomenon. Since the being of consciousness is radically different, its meaning will necessitate a particular elucidation, in terms of the revealed-revelation of another type of being, being-for-itself (*l'être-pour-soi*), which we shall define later and which is opposed to the being-in-itself (*l'être-en-soi*) of the phenomenon.

(2) That the elucidation of the meaning of being-in-itself which we are going to attempt here can be only provisional. The aspects which will be revealed *imply* other significations which ultimately we must apprehend and determine. In particular the preceding reflections have permitted us to distinguish two absolutely separated regions of being: the being of the *pre-reflective cogito* and the being of the phenomenon. But although the concept of being has this peculiarity of being divided into two

regions without communication, we must nevertheless explain how these two regions can be placed under the same heading. That will necessitate the investigation of these two types of being, and it is evident that we can not truly grasp the meaning of either one until we can establish their true connection with the notion of being in general and the relations which unite them. We have indeed established by the examination of non-positional self-consciousness that the being of the phenomenon can on no account act upon consciousness. In this way we have ruled out a *realistic* conception of the relations of the phenomenon with consciousness.

We have shown also by the examination of the spontaneity of the non-reflective cogito that consciousness can not get out of its subjectivity if the latter has been initially given, and that consciousness can not act upon transcendent being nor without contradiction admit of the passive elements necessary in order to constitute a transcendent being arising from them. Thus we have ruled out the *idealist* solution of the problem. It appears that we have barred all doors and that we are now condemned to regard transcendent being and consciousness as two closed totalities without possible communication. It will be necessary to show that the problem allows a solution other than realism or idealism.

A certain number of characteristics can be fixed on immediately because for the most part they follow naturally from what we have just said.

A clear view of the phenomenon of being has often been obscured by a very common prejudice which we shall call "creationism." Since people supposed that God had given being to the world, being always appeared tainted with a certain passivity. But a creation *ex nihilo* can not explain the coming to pass of being; for if being is conceived in a subjectivity, even a divine subjectivity, it remains a mode of intra-subjective being. Such subjectivity can not have even the *representation* of an objectivity, and consequently it can not even be affected with the will to create the objective. Furthermore being, if it is suddenly placed outside the subjective by the fulguration of which Leibniz speaks, can only affirm itself as distinct from and opposed to its creator; otherwise it dissolves in him. The theory of perpetual creation, by removing from being what the Germans call *Selbständigkeit*, makes it disappear in the divine subjectivity. If being exists as over against God, it is its own support; it does not preserve the least trace of divine creation. In a word, even if it had been created, being-in-itself would be *inexplicable* in terms of creation; for it assumes its being beyond the creation.

This is equivalent to saying that being is uncreated. But we need not conclude that being creates itself, which would suppose that it is prior to itself. Being can not be *causa sui* in the manner of consciousness. Being is *itself.* This means that it is neither passivity nor activity. Both of these notions are *human* and designate human conduct or the instruments of human conduct. There is activity when a conscious being uses means with an end in view. And we call those objects passive on which our activity is exercised, inasmuch as they do not spontaneously aim at the end which we make them serve. In a word, man is active and the means which he employs are called passive. These concepts, put absolutely, lose all meaning. In particular, being is not active; in order for there to be an end and means, there must be being. For an even stronger reason it can not be passive, for in order to be passive, it must be. The self-consistency of being is beyond the active as it is beyond the passive.

Being is equally beyond negation as beyond affirmation. Affirmation is always affirmation of something; that is, the act of affirming is distinguished from the thing affirmed. But if we suppose an affirmation in which the affirmed comes to fulfill the affirming and is confused with it, this affirmation can not be affirmed — owing to too much of plenitude and the immediate inherence of the noema in the noesis. It is there that we find being — if we are to define it more clearly — in connection with consciousness. It is the noema in the noesis; that is, the inherence in itself without the least distance. From this point of view, we should not call it "immanence," for immanence in spite of all *connection* with self is still that very slight withdrawal which can be realized — away from the self. But being is not a connection with itself. It is *itself*. It is an immanence which can not realize itself, an affirmation which can not affirm itself, an activity which can not act, because it is glued to itself. Everything happens as if, in order to free the affirmation *of* self from the heart of being, there is necessary a decompression of being. Let us not, however, think that being is merely *one* undifferentiated self-affirmation; the undifferentiation of the in-itself is beyond an infinity of self-affirmations, inasmuch as there is an infinity of modes of self-affirming. We may summarize these first conclusions by saying that being is in itself.

But if being is in itself, this means that it does not refer to itself as self-consciousness does. It is this self. It is itself so completely that the perpetual reflection which constitutes the self is dissolved in an identity. That is why being is at bottom beyond the *self*, and our first formula can be only an approximation due to the requirements of language. In fact being is opaque to itself precisely because it is filled with itself. This can be better expressed by saying that *being is what it is*. This statement is in appearance strictly analytical. Actually it is far from being reduced to that principle of identity which is the unconditioned principle of all analytical judgments. First the formula designates a particular region of being, that of *being in-itself*. We shall see that the being of *for-itself* is defined, on the contrary, as being what it is not and not being what it is. The question here then is of a regional principle and is as such synthetical. Furthermore it is necessary to oppose this formula — being in-itself *is* what it is — to that which designates the being of consciousness. The latter in fact, as we shall see, *has to be* what it is.

This instructs us as to the special meaning which must be given to the "is" in the phrase, being *is* what it is. From the moment that beings exist who have to be what they are, the fact of being what they are is no longer a purely axiomatic characteristic; it is a contingent principle of being in-itself. In this sense, the principle of identity, the principle of analytical judgments, is also a regional synthetical principle of being. It designates the opacity of being-in-itself. This opacity has nothing to do with our *position* in relation to the in-itself; it is not that we are obliged *to apprehend it and to observe it* because we are "without." Being-in-itself has no *within* which is opposed to a *without* and which is analogous to a judgment, a law, a consciousness of itself. The in-itself has nothing secret; it is *solid (massif)*. In a sense we can designate it as a synthesis. But it is the most indissoluble of all: the synthesis of itself with itself.

The result is evidently that being is isolated in its being and that it does not enter into any connection with what is not itself. Transition, becoming, anything which permits us to say that being is not yet what it will be and that it is already what it is not — all that is forbidden on principle. For being is the being of becoming and due to this fact it is beyond becoming. It is what it is. This means that by itself it can not even be what it is not; we have seen indeed that it can encompass no negation. It is full positivity. It knows no otherness; it never posits itself as *other-than-another-being*. It can support no connection with the other. It is itself indefinitely and it exhausts itself in being. From this point of view we shall see later that it is not subject to temporality. It is, and when it gives way, one can not even say that it no longer is. Or, at least, a consciousness can be conscious of it as no longer being, precisely because consciousness is temporal. But being itself does not exist as a lack there where it was; the full positivity of being is re-formed on its giving way. It was and at present other beings are: that is all.

Finally — this will be our third characteristic — being-in-itself *is*. This means that being can neither be derived from the possible nor reduced to the necessary. Necessity concerns the connection between ideal propositions but not that of existents. An existing phenomenon can never be derived from another existent qua existent. This is what we shall call the *contingency* of being-in-itself. But neither can being-in-itself be derived from a *possibility*. The possible is a structure of the *for-itself*; that is, it belongs to the other region of being. Being-in-itself is never either possible or impossible. It *is*. This is what consciousness expresses in anthropomorphic terms by saying that being is superfluous (*de trop*) — that is, that consciousness absolutely can not derive being from anything, either from another being, or from a possibility, or from a necessary law. Uncreated, without reason for being, without any connection with another being, being-in-itself is *de trop* for eternity.

Being is. Being is in-itself. Being is what it is. These are the three characteristics which the preliminary examination of the phenomenon of being allows us to assign to the being of phenomena. For the moment it is impossible to push our investigation further. This is not yet the examination of the *in-itself* — which is never anything but what it is — which will allow us to establish and to explain its relations with the for-itself. Thus we have left "appearances" and have been led progressively to posit two types of being, the in-itself and the for-itself, concerning which we have as yet only superficial and incomplete information. A multitude of questions remain unanswered: What is the ultimate meaning of these two types of being? For what reasons do they both belong to *being* in general? What is the meaning of that being which includes within itself these two radically separated regions of being? If idealism and realism both fail to explain the relations which *in fact* unite these regions which *in theory* are without communication, what other solution can we find for this problem? And how can the being of the phenomenon be transphenomenal?

It is to attempt to reply to these questions that I have written the present work.

THE PHENOMENOLOGICAL CONCEPT OF NOTHINGNESS

There is another possible way of conceiving being and nothingness as complements. One could view them as two equally necessary components of the real without making being "pass into" nothingness — as Hegel does — and without insisting on the posteriority of nothingness as we attempted to do. We might on the contrary emphasize the reciprocal forces of repulsion which being and non-being exercise on each other, the real in some way being the tension resulting from these antagonistic forces. It is toward this new conception that Heidegger is oriented.[2]

We need not look far to see the progress which Heidegger's theory of nothingness has made over that of Hegel. First, being and non-being are no longer empty abstractions. Heidegger in his most important work has shown the legitimacy of raising the question concerning being; the latter has no longer the character of a Scholastic universal which it still retained with Hegel. There is a meaning of being which must be clarified; there is a "pre-ontological comprehension" of being which is involved in every kind of conduct belonging to human reality" — *i.e.*, in each of its projects. Similarly difficulties which customarily arise as soon

---

[2] Heidegger, *Qu'est-ce que la metaphysique.* (Translated by Corbin. Paris: Gallimard. 1938.) ["What Is Metaphysics?" Translated by R. F. C. Hull and Alan Crick. From *Existence and Being*, ed. by Werner Brock. Chicago: Henry Regnery, 1949.]

as a philosopher touches on the problem of Nothingness are shown to be without foundation; they are important in so far as they limit the function of the understanding, and they show simply that this problem is not *within the province* of the understanding. There exist on the other hand numerous attitudes of "human reality" which imply a "comprehension" of nothingness: hate, prohibitions, regret, *etc.* For *Dasein* there is even a permanent possibility of finding oneself "face to face" with nothingness and discovering it as a phenomenon: this possibility is anguish.

Heidegger, while establishing the possibilities of a concrete apprehension of Nothingness, never falls into the error which Hegel made; he does not preserve a being for Non-Being, not even an abstract being. Nothing is not; it nihilates itself.[3] It is supported and conditioned by transcendence. We know that for Heidegger the being of human reality is defined as "being-in-the-world." The world is a synthetic complex of instrumental realities inasmuch as they point one to another in ever widening circles, and inasmuch as man makes himself known in terms of this complex which he is. This means both that "human reality" springs forth *invested* with being and "finds itself" (*sich befinden*) in being — and also that human reality causes being, which surrounds it, to be disposed around human reality in the form of the world.

But human reality can make being appear as organized totality in the world only by surpassing being. All determination for Heidegger is surpassing since it supposes a withdrawal taken from a particular point of view. This passing beyond the world, which is a condition of the very rising up of the world as such, is effected by the *Dasein* which directs the surpassing *toward itself*. The characteristic of selfness (*Selbstheit*), in fact, is that man is always separated from what he is by all the breadth of the being which he is not. He makes himself known to himself from the other side of the world and he looks from the horizon toward himself to recover his inner being. Man is "a being of distances." In the movement of turning inward which traverses all of being, being arises and organizes itself as the world without there being either priority of the movement over the world, or the world over the movement. But this appearance of the self beyond the world — that is, beyond the totality of the real — is an emergence of "human reality" in nothingness. It is in nothingness alone that being can be surpassed. At the same time it is from the point of view of beyond the world that being is organized into the world, which means on the one hand that human reality rises up as an emergence of being in non-being and on the other hand that the world is "suspended"

---

[3] Tr. Heidegger uses the by now famous expression "*Das Nichts nichtet*" or "Nothing nothings." I think "nihilate" is a closer equivalent to Sartre's *néantise* than "annihilate" because the fundamental meaning of the term is "to make nothing" rather than "to destroy or do away with." *Nichtet, néantise* and *nihilate* are all, of course, equally without foundation in the dictionaries of the respective languages.

in nothingness. Anguish is the discovery of this double, perpetual nihil-ation. It is in terms of this surpassing of the world that *Dasein* manages to realize the contingency of the world; that is, to raise the question, "How does it happen that there is something rather than nothing?" Thus the contingency of the world appears to human reality in so far as human reality has established itself in nothingness in order to apprehend the contingency.

Here then is nothingness surrounding being on every side and at the same time expelled from being. Here nothingness is given as that by which the world receives its outlines as the world. Can this solution satisfy us?

Certainly it can not be denied that the apprehension of the world qua world is a nihilation. From the moment the world appears qua world it gives itself as *being only that*. The necessary counterpart of this appre-hension then is indeed the emergence of "human reality" in nothing-ness. But where does "human reality" get its power of emerging thus in non-being? Without a doubt Heidegger is right in insisting on the fact that negation derives its foundation from nothingness. But if nothingness provides a ground for negation, it is because nothingness envelops the *not* within itself as its essential structure. In other words, it is not as undifferentiated emptiness or as a disguised otherness that nothingness provides the ground for negation. Nothingness stands at the origin of the negative judgment because it is itself negation. It founds the negation as an *act* because it is the negation as *being*. Nothingness can be nothing-ness only by nihilating itself expressly as nothingness of the world; that is, in its nihilation it must direct itself expressly toward this world in order to constitute itself as refusal of the world. Nothingness carries being in its heart. But how does the emergence account for this nihilating refusal? Transcendence, which is "the pro-ject of self beyond," is far from being able to establish nothingness; on the contrary, it is nothingness which is at the very heart of transcendence and which conditions it.

Now the characteristic of Heidegger's philosophy is to describe *Dasein* by using positive terms which hide the implicit negations. *Dasein* is "outside of itself, in the world"; it is "a being of distances"; it is care; it is "its own possibilities," *etc*. All this amounts to saying that *Dasein* "is not" in itself, that it "is not" in immediate proximity to itself, and that it "surpasses" the world inasmuch as it posits itself as *not being in itself* and as *not being the world*. In this sense Hegel is right rather than Heidegger when he states that Mind is the negative. Actually we can put to each of them the same question, phrased slightly differently. We should say to Hegel: "It is not sufficient to posit mind as mediation and the negative; it is necessary to demonstrate negativity as the structure of being of mind. What must mind be in order to be able to constitute itself as negative?" And we can ask the same question of Heidegger in these words: "If negation is the original structure of transcendence, what must be the original structure of 'human reality' in order for it to be able to transcend the world?" In both cases we are shown a negating activity and there is no concern to ground this activity upon a negative being. Heidegger in addition makes of Nothingness a sort of intentional correlate of transcendence, without seeing that he has already inserted it into transcendence itself as its original structure.

Furthermore what is the use of affirming that Nothingness provides the ground for negation, if it is merely to enable us to form subsequently a theory of non-being which by definition separates Nothingness from all concrete negation? If I emerge in nothingness *beyond* the world, how can this extra-mundane nothingness furnish a foundation for those little pools of non-being which we encounter each instant in the depth of being. I say, "Pierre is not there," "I have no more money," *etc.* Is it really necessary to surpass the world toward nothingness and to return subsequently to being in order to provide a ground for these everyday judgments? And how can the operation be affected? To accomplish it we are not required to make the world slip into nothingness; standing within the limits of being, we simply deny an attribute to a subject. Will someone say that each attribute refused, each being denied is taken up by one and the same extra-mundane nothingness, that non-being is like the fullness of what is not, that the world is suspended in non-being as the real is suspended in the heart of possibilities? In this case each negation would necessarily have for origin a particular surpassing: the surpassing of one being toward another. But what is this surpassing, if not simply the Hegelian mediation — and have we not already and in vain sought in Hegel the nihilating ground of the mediation? Furthermore even if the explanation is valid for the simple, radical negations which deny to a determined object any kind of presence in the depth of being (*e.g.,* "Centaurs *do not exist*" — "*There is no* reason for him to be late" — "The ancient Greeks *did not practice* polygamy"), negations which, if need be, can contribute to constituting Nothingness as a sort of geometrical place for unfulfilled projects, all inexact representations, all vanished beings or those of which the idea is only a fiction — even so this interpretation of non-being would no longer be valid for a certain kind of reality which is in truth the most frequent: namely, those negations which include non-being in their being. How can we hold that these are at once partly within the universe and partly outside in extra-mundane nothingness?

Take for example the notion of distance, which conditions the determination of a location, the localization of a point. It is easy to see that it possesses a negative moment. Two points are distant when they are *separated* by a certain length. The length, a positive attribute of a segment of a straight line, intervenes here by virtue of the negation of an absolute, undifferentiated proximity. Someone might perhaps seek to reduce distance to *being only* the length of the segment of which the two points considered, A and B, would be the limits. But does he not see that he has changed the direction of attention in this case and that he has, under cover of the same word, given another object to intuition? The organized complex which is constituted by the segment *with* its two limiting terms can furnish actually two different objects to knowledge. We can in fact give the *segment* as immediate object of intuition, in which case this segment represents a full, concrete tension, of which the length is a positive attribute and the two points A and B appear only as a moment of the whole; that is, as they are implicated by the segment itself as its limits. Then the negation, expelled from the segment and its length, takes refuge in the two *limits:* to say that point B is a limit of the segment is to say that the segment *does not* extend beyond this point. Negation is here a secondary structure of the object. If, on the other hand, we direct our attention to the two points A and B, they arise as immediate objects of intuition on the ground of space. The segment disappears as a full, concrete object; it is apprehended in terms of two points as the emptiness, the negativity which separates them. Negation is not subject to the points, which cease to be *limits* in order to impregnate the very length of the segment with distance. Thus the total form constituted by the segment and its two limits with its inner structure of negation is capable of letting itself be apprehended in two ways. Rather there are two forms, and the condition of the appearance of the one is the disintegration of the other, exactly as in perception we constitute a particular object as a *figure* by rejecting another so as to make of it a *ground*, and conversely. In both instances we find the same quantity of negation which at one time passes into the notion of limits and at another into the notion of distance, but which in each case can not be suppressed. Will someone object that the idea of distance is psychological and that it designates only the extension which must be *cleared* in order to go from point A to point B? We shall reply that the same negation is included in this *to clear* since this notion expresses precisely the passive resistance of the remoteness. We will willingly admit with Heidegger that "human reality" is "remote-from-itself"; that is, that is rises in the world as that which creates distances and at the same time causes them to be removed (*ent-fernend*). But this remoteness-from-self, even if it is the necessary condition in order that *there may be* remoteness in general, envelops remoteness in itself as the negative structure which must be surmounted. It will be useless to attempt to reduce distance to the simple result of a *measurement*. What has become evident in the course of the preceding discussion is that the two points and the segment which is enclosed between them have the indissoluble unity of what the Germans call a *Gestalt*. Negation is the cement which realizes this unity. It defines precisely the immediate relation which connects these two points and which presents them to intuition as the indissoluble unity of the distance. This negation can be covered over only by claiming to reduce distance to the measurement of a length, for negation is the *raison d'être* of that measurement.

What we have just shown by the examination of *distance*, we could just as well have brought out by describing realities like absence, change, otherness, repulsion, regret, distraction, *etc*. There is an infinite number of realities which are not only objects of judgment, but which are experienced, opposed, feared, *etc.*, by the human being and which in their inner structure are inhabited by negation, as by a necessary condition of their existence. We shall call them *négatités*.[4] Kant caught a glimpse of their significance when he spoke of regulative concepts (*e.g.* the immortality of the soul), types of syntheses of negative and positive in which negation is the condition of positivity. The function of negation varies according to the nature of the object considered. Between wholly positive realities (which however retain negation as the condition of the sharpness of their outlines, as that which fixes them as what they are) and those in which the positivity is only an appearance concealing a hole of nothingness, all gradations are possible. In any case it is impossible to throw these negations back into an extra-mundane nothingness since they are dispersed in being, are supported by being, and are conditions of reality. Nothingness beyond the world accounts for absolute negation; but we have just discovered a swarm of ultra-mundane beings which possess as much reality and efficacy as other beings, but which enclose within themselves non-being. They require an explanation which remains within the limits of the real. Nothingness, if it is supported by being, vanishes *qua nothingness,* and we fall back upon being. Nothingness can be nihilated only on the foundation of being; if nothingness can be given, it is neither before nor after being, nor in a general way outside of being. Nothingness lies coiled in the heart of being — like a worm.

---

[4] Tr. A word coined by Sartre with no equivalent term in English.

chapter 5

Freedom and Responsibility

. . . [N]othing is more unbearable, once one has it, than freedom. I suppose this was why I asked her to marry me; to give myself something to be moored to. Perhaps this was why, in Spain, she decided that she wanted to marry me. But people can't, unhappily, invent their mooring posts, their lovers and their friends, any more than they can invent their parents. Life gives these and also takes them away and the great difficulty is to say Yes to life.

        James Baldwin, *Giovanni's Room*, p. 10

To live is to feel ourselves fatally obliged to exercise our liberty, to decide what we are going to be in this world. Not for a single moment is our activity of decision allowed to rest. Even when in desperation we abandon ourselves to whatever may happen, we have decided not to decide.

        Ortega y Gasset, *The Revolt of the Masses*, p. 48

. . . Freedom does not begin when parents are rejected or buried; freedom dies when parents are born.
    He is free who is unaware of his origin.
    He is free who is born of an egg dropped in the woods.
    He is free who is spat out from the sky and touches the earth without a pang of gratitude.

        Milan Kundera, *Life Is Elsewhere*, p. 121

INTRODUCTION

The term *freedom* has a multitude of meanings in both popular and philosophical literature. We read of freedom of speech and freedom of religion; we debate about what countries are free, or we examine the merits of the free market. We hear of academic freedom, freedom from want, and even freedom to die.

Central to the tradition of Western liberal political theory has been the concept of freedom as freedom from coercion. For example, I cannot be free if you hold me at gunpoint and demand "your money or your life." In this sense, one is said to be free if one is not being compelled to act in ways one would not otherwise choose to act. This absence of freedom might come in the form of natural constraints (I could not have a picnic because of the hurricane) or obstacles created by other persons (I could not elope because you blocked all the exits).

Some theorists have sought to broaden this concept of freedom to include more than the mere absence of coercion. They have argued that freedom means not simply the absence of natural or artifically imposed obstacles (negative freedom), but also the positive power to act on the basis of one's desires. In this more expansive sense of freedom, I may be said to be unfree if my poverty or my lack of education keeps me from realizing my goals. In this sense, the absence of coercion is a necessary but not sufficient condition for freedom.

Some recent analyses of freedom have noted a problem in traditional views of freedom: If freedom (in the aforementioned definitions) implies the ability to act on a choice from among alternatives, we are left with the possibility of a society of happy slaves — individuals who are indoctrinated through direct or indirect means of control — who always get what they desire but whose desires are themselves carefully manipulated by those in power. In such a case, there is no coercion in the ordinary sense, but such a society is not free. Thus, freedom also seems to imply the ability to understand the nature of the alternatives available to us, to be able to evaluate alternatives rationally, and to make deliberate choices from among those alternatives. This deeper sense of freedom is not only about whether we can act on our choices, but rather whether we in fact *choose* those choices freely.

This new formulation leaves open the question as to what extent individuals in a given society are truly free: Does the pervasiveness of advertising in our own society, for example, keep us from being free to make real choices about the kinds of lives we want to lead? Does sex-role socialization limit our freedom to create our own individual personalities? How do we know which aspects of our character are of our own creation and which are products of processes beyond our control? Since Homo sapiens requires teaching to develop those traits we characterize as human, are we all — to some extent — manipulated by the representatives of culture in the process of earning our membership in the human race?

It is easy to discern through observation whether we are free in these narrow senses. If we observe a mugger holding a gun on someone or note that someone suffers from epilepsy or discover that someone is being held in prison, we can with little controversy assume that that person's freedom is limited. But if more obvious constraints are removed, are we justified in assuming that that person is free? Even if we assume that some actions are the result of an agent's free choice, by what criteria do we distinguish those actions from actions that result from socialization or some other form of psychic compulsion? Should we believe someone's self-report which informs us that one has "freely chosen" a particular occupation or style of dress or food preference? Couldn't one — like the happy slave — be mistaken about the extent of one's freedom? It is not uncommon to discover long after an event has occurred what its real motivation was. Perhaps we are all under a mild hypnotic trance of which we are unaware but whose power is irresistible.

These concerns are pivotal to determining responsibility in the moral realm. Ordinarily, we assign responsibility for an action when the person freely chooses his or her action. For example, I will not blame you if your car goes out of control during an epileptic seizure. I might, however, blame you for the decision to drive if you knew that you were prone to such seizures. Responsibility — in the form of either blame or praise — is generally thought to imply *choice*. The statement "I was not responsible" could mean one of two things: It might mean, "I did not do it," or it might mean, "I did it but I could not help doing it." Thus, Hamlet *did* kill Laertes, but we would not consider him a murderer since he did not know that his sword was tipped with poison. Had he known, he presumably would have acted otherwise. The defense attorney for accused killer Richard Speck did not try to show that Speck did not commit the crime, but rather that he could not help doing what he did because of the presence of an extra Y chromosome in his genetic make-up. Laurence Harvey, in the classic thriller *The Manchurian Candidate*, kills because he has been brainwashed by enemy agents.

The first sense of responsibility (which we refer to as "causal responsiblity") is descriptive. For example, if I ask for a causal answer to Agatha Christie's question "Who killed Roger Ackroyd?", I am attempting to ascertain whose actions led to the death of Ackroyd. On the other hand, if I am asking about the *murderer* of Roger Ackroyd, I am raising a normative question, which implies blame or, possibly, if Ackroyd had been a nefarious villain, praise. To say that one ought to have done as one did or that one ought to have done otherwise is absurd unless one could have made different choices. Praise and blame, therefore, imply choice. We do not, for example, hold responsible very young children and nonhuman animals. Indeed, we distinguish the "programmed" behavior of certain beings (animals, human babies, even machines) from *conduct*, which is the result of free and deliberate choice.

Earlier we characterized the philosophy of existentialism with the statement "Existence precedes essence." The introduction to this text and chapter 4 in particular explored this formula as a metaphysical statement about the nature of Being. This statement is, at bottom, about freedom. If it is true that existence precedes essence, then human beings have no fixed nature. Rather, it is our very choices that bring into being who we are. And, since the world is contingent, there is nothing that necessarily grounds our choices. We are free and must decide; even *not* deciding is a form of decision. And our freedom is inextricably inter-twined with our responsibity for those choices we make. Let us, then, look more carefully at the notion of *choice*.

FREE WILL AND DETERMINISM

Before the modern era, philosophers and scientists tended to operate on a *teleological* model of the world; that is, their focus was on the idea of *purpose*. Assuming that the universe was a perfect creation of a supreme intelligence, such thinkers sought to construct theoretical systems to explain the reasons for the world's functioning as it does. Many of these metaphysicians developed deductive models borrowed from mathemat-ics with "indubitable" axioms and hypotheses which followed from them. One could, then, "deduce" why some event rather than another occurred and why the universe is set up in the way that it is.

Modern science began when people stopped asking about purposes and started asking instead about causes. Gradually, a mechanistic para-digm came to replace the teleological. Scientists, for example, came to discover that the motions of the heavenly bodies followed certain laws that could be expressed mathematically. Observation, experimentation, and the search for such laws took the place of metaphysical speculation and intuition. The world was treated as analogous to a vast machine whose parts work together. And when one begins to operate in terms of causes and effects, the possibility of science as a predictive discipline emerges.

At first these shifts in thinking did little to undermine belief either in God as the basis for the world or the reality of human freedom. Newton, for example, repeatedly refers in his works to a divine creator whose intelligence is responsible for the world's order. Indeed, what better basis for natural laws than a supreme being who, much like a human sovereign, enacts laws and makes sure that they are carried out? Others argued that mechanistic principles applied only to the world of the mate-rial; hence, humans are exempt from this inexorable causality by virtue of our possession of a soul. Descartes, for example, maintained that God had given us a will which, though responsible for sin and error, was the basis for our freedom. Both intellectual error and moral sin were, according to Descartes, the results of a failure to restrain the will. But it is always possible to control the will, and this possibility is the basis for free will.

This freedom is, Descartes believed, a great gift from God, for it is "limited by no boundaries." Indeed, "nothing else in me is so perfect or so great," and it is in this respect "that I bear an image and likeness of God." (*Meditations*, p. 37)

Despite these attempts to reconcile human freedom with the laws of nature, it was not much of a leap to apply those laws to human beings as well. Philosopher Thomas Hobbes (1588–1679), for example, was a materialist who denied the existence of any immaterial soul or spirit in human beings. Instead, he sought to interpret the workings of human nature in accordance with the laws of physics, maintaining that all human behavior is the behavior of matter and hence to be understood in accordance with the same laws which we ascribe to matter. All human action, he believed, was the result of the operation of the motives of desire and aversion; these motives Hobbes took to be varieties of physical force.

> In deliberation, the last appetite, or aversion, immediately adhering to the action, or to the omission thereof, is that we call the *will;* the act, not the faculty, of *willing.* And beasts that have *deliberation,* must necessarily also have *will.* . . . *Will,* therefore, *is the last appetite in deliberating.*
>
> *Leviathan, p. 127*

An act of will for Hobbes, therefore, is simply the "last appetite." So, for Hobbes, to say that one is free is only to say that one is able to do that which one wills.

Baron D'Holbach (1723–1789), a materialist and an atheist, took Hobbes's views of human nature even further to reject human freedom:

> Man is a being purely physical; in whatever manner he is considered, he is connected to universal nature, and submitted to the necessary and immutable laws that she imposes on all the beings she contains, according to their peculiar essences or to particular species. Man's life is a line that nature commands him to describe upon the surface of the earth, without his own consent; his organization does in no way depend upon himself; his ideas come to him involuntarily; his habits are in the power of those who cause him to contract them; he is unceasingly modified by causes, whether visible or concealed, over which he has no control, which necessarily regulate his mode of existence; give the hue to his way of thinking, and determine his manner of acting. He is good or bad, happy or miserable, wise or foolish, reasonable or irrational, without his will being for any thing in these various states. Nevertheless, in despite of the shackles by which he is bound, it is pretended he is a free agent, or that independent of the causes by which he is moved, he determines his own will, and regulates his own condition.
>
> *System of Nature, p. 110*

This view of D'Holbach is today known as *determinism,* the view that all human behavior is caused. Where does one find "uncaused events"? The concept, determinists argue, makes no sense. Just as disciplines like physics, chemistry, and biology depend on the assumption of universal causality as the basis for scientific progress, so too do anthropology, psychology, and sociology require that we view the human world as one governed by causality.

In human behavior the analogue for cause in the physical world is motivation. Motivation may be external (you push me) or internal (I feel angry and push you back), but it is the cause for whatever choices we make. We do that for which we have the strongest motive, and that depends on personal preferences, which depend on a number of factors related to heredity and environment. Determinists argue that notions like Descartes's "free will" undetermined by anything else seem to make human choice completely random, capricious, and inexplicable. On the contrary, we now know a good deal about the impact of biological variables on human behavior; and we can thank Freud for our acceptance of the notion that some motives are unconscious even to the agent himself or herself.

Contemporary determinist psychologist B. F. Skinner maintains, much like Hobbes, that eventually a science of the nervous system based on direct observation rather than inference will describe the neural states and events which immediately precede instances of behavior. These events in turn will be found to be preceded by other neurological events, and these in turn by others. This series will lead us back to events outside the nervous system, and, eventually, outside the organism. Determinists argue that such a framework represents progress, for, instead of blaming the agent for "wrongdoing" (which is really only socially disapproved conduct), we look for those causally antecedent conditions which resulted in the behavior and seek to modify those:

> We do not hold people responsible for their reflexes — e.g. coughing in church. We hold them responsible for their operant behavior — e.g. for whispering in church or remaining in church while coughing. But there are variables which are responsible for whispering as well as coughing, and these may be just as inexorable. When we recognize this, we are likely to drop the notion of responsibility altogether and with it the doctrine of free will as an inner causal agent.

> *Science and Human Behavior, p. 115*

Thus, as our preceding discussion makes clear, if a choice is one we could not have avoided making, then it is one for which we are not morally responsible. And since the choices we make could not have been avoided, for the determinist, we are not morally responsible for any of our actions.[1]

For Skinner, the only real question is whether we plan society to insure that conditioning is positive or let the conditioning occur haphazardly:

> If we are not to rely solely upon accident for the innovations which give rise to cultural evolution, we must accept the fact that some kind of control of human behavior is inevitable. We cannot use good sense in human affairs unless someone engages in the design and construction of environmental conditions which affect the behavior of [people]. Environmental changes have always been the condition for the improvement of cultural patterns, and we can hardly use the more effective methods of science without making changes on a grander scale. We are all controlled by the world in which we live, and part of that world has been and will be constructed by men. The question is this: Are we to be controlled by accident, by tyrants, or by ourselves in effective cultural design?
>
> *"Freedom and the Control of Men," p. 51*

The critic of determinism draws to a great extent on the human feeling of freedom, the sense that there are many occasions when we make real choices and that we could have done other than what we did do. Libertarianism about free will (not to be confused with the political theory of the same name, which concerns political rights and freedoms) maintains that: (1) there are some actions that are determined by ourselves without being determined in turn by something else; (2) if an action is self-determined, then the agent could have done otherwise; (3) if the agent could have done otherwise, then the action is free; and (4) we are only responsible for those actions that are determined by ourselves.

Thus, for the libertarian, at least some of our actions are free, and we are responsible for them. Thus, the libertarian rejects determinism. Some go as far as philosopher William James does to argue for indeterminacy even in the natural world (in the form of randomness or chance):

> Indeterminate future volitions *do* mean chance. Let us not fear to shout if from the house-tops if need be; for we now know that the idea of chance is, at bottom, exactly the same thing as the idea of gift — the one simply being a

---

[1] This analysis deliberately conflates two versions of determinism, labeled by William James in his essay "The Dilemma of Determinism" as "hard" and "soft." Though soft determinists accept the premise that there is no uncaused (free) human action, they reject the hard claim that there is no responsibility for conduct. Instead, the key question for the soft determinist is whether action springs from character; that is, did I do what I wanted to do? If so, the soft determinist finds me responsible, even though the wants themselves are not freely chosen. This distinction makes little difference for our purposes here.

disparaging, and the other a eulogistic, name for anything on which we have no effective *claim*.

"The Dilemma of Determinism," pp. 158–59

Others accept determinism in the natural order but reject it as regards human conduct. The following statement from philosopher C. A. Campbell is typical of this version of libertarianism:

> In my view there never were in the established results of physical science cogent reasons for believing that the apparently universal determinism of inorganic processes holds good also of the processes of the human body.
>
> *In Defense of Free Will, p. 216*

EXISTENTIALISM AND THE DILEMMA OF FREE WILL

Determinists have very powerful arsenals of arguments with which to defend their position. Increasingly, empirical disciplines like psychology and sociology make clear the antecedent conditions leading to behavior. Modern psychiatry has demonstrated quite convincingly the unconscious motives frequently operating in human behavior. Ever more sophisticated technology has enabled us to study the brain to discover the neurophysiological basis for much of our feelings and conduct. Even something seemingly as trivial as one's place in the birth order of one's family is now known to be relevant to the development of certain personality traits. Further, determinists maintain that the absence of a known cause for some behavior is only a confession of our own ignorance and not a rebuttal of determinism itself.

What arguments can libertarians marshal? It seems futile to search for an uncaused event, since a determinist can easily posit a known or a hypothetical cause. Must one resort to some totally unscientific perspective to accomodate human freedom? Further, how can humans be responsible if our actions are uncaused, and therefore random and capricious? What is human character if not a basis for predicting what actions one is likely to perform? How do existentialists — for whom freedom is the basis for Dasein's existence — answer these questions?

We have seen that one of the major characteristics of existentialist thinking is its focus on the concreteness of human experience. For existentialism, the starting point of philosophy is not abstract thought or even the abstract thinking subject but rather the totality of the human being thrown into the world of daily affairs. Feeling, thought, and action cannot be separated into neat compartments; rather, the human being is a unity which always already exists and must be analyzed "in situation." "I act" and "I think" and "I feel" are not opposed to one another; in a sense, we might say action is inclusive, involving the whole person in dynamic interaction with the world. According to Sartre, action is "a choice of myself in the world and by the same token . . . a discovery of the world." (*Being and Nothingness*, p. 594)

But we are not simply our actions in a functional sense. Our actions are not simply the observable deeds one might record on camera; we are more than the roles we play or the tasks we perform. Rather, we make ourselves through our actions. Thus, every action we perform is full of meaning.

For Sartre, the for-itself is essentially nothingness, and its primary mode of being in the world is "neantisation" or nihilation (see chapter 4). This negating capacity occurs in everyday acts of knowledge; indeed it is the "cement" for our being in the world. Only what "is not" is able to understand what "is." Through this nihilation, the human being is able to organize and divide up the world. In this sense, humans are *signifying beings,* and all objects are signs.

> Because we are men and because we live in the world of men, of work, and of conflicts, all the objects which surround us are signs. By themselves they indicate their use and scarcely mask the real project of those who have made them such *for us* and who address us through them. But their particular ordering, under this or that circumstance, retraces for us an individual action, a project, an event. . . . Everything at every instant is always signifying, and significations reveal to us men and relations among men across the structures of society.
>
> *Search for a Method, pp. 155–56*

Thus, nothing has meaning independent of those human beings who endow the world with meaning. There is no a priori meaning attached to any object in the world. Rather, we endow all of those objects with meaning as they become parts of human projects. A stop sign, for example, has no meaning separate from the driving conventions of which it is a part. The size, the shape, the color, even the letters mean nothing in themselves. The sign does not make us stop any more than arriving at our destination does. Rather, we choose to give the sign significance and make the decision to come to a halt.

Though few other existentialists adopt this concept of the *pour soi* exactly as Sartre does, nonetheless if existence comes before essence, human reality must constantly create and recreate itself. Indeed, for existentialist thinkers, human reality *is* freedom. In order to make this equation more than a mere rhetorical flourish, we must explain what the basis for this freedom is.

The problem with most free-will theorists is that they have sought to objectify freedom, to analyze it as an object that can be perceived and either confirmed or disconfirmed from the outside. But the moment one adopts this perspective, the determinist has won. For existentialists, freedom is not something but rather nothing. It is not found "in" certain actions but is rather the basis for action.

How do we know this? For Kant, we know that we are free because it is a necessary postulate for morality. For many existentialists, we know that we are free because of our experience of anxiety. Anxiety (or anguish or dread) occurs in the confrontation with possibility. Our anguish reminds us that we are without any excuse but also without any justification. Our anguish reminds us that we must decide our future. Orestes, in Sartre's play *The Flies*, is a murderer "without remorse"; yet he must live with the flies, the concrete symbol of his own anguish. Unlike his sister Electra, who tries to flee from her own freedom, Orestes knows that he must choose and must live with his choices. When Zeus reminds him who his creator is, Orestes responds, "The moment you created me I ceased to be yours." Orestes' freedom is, however, a terrible burden that he must shoulder; indeed, Sartre calls this "dreadful freedom."

The freedom of existentialism, then, is not the optimistic freedom of the "humanists"; it is the freedom that is the burden we bear for our choices. As Sartre writes, (p. 311), the basis of freedom "coincides with the nothingness which is at the heart of man." Freedom is possibility, but we also recognize that every decision we make closes off some possibilities and opens up others. A choice of vocation, for example, means that there are a multitude of other vocations we renounce. Every decision implies what Kierkegaard referred to as a "leap," for we must go beyond our concrete circumstances. We must, as Sartre and Marcel put it, "engage" — almost as though every decision we make is a kind of promissory note. That most of us fail to experience this anxiety does not show this analysis to be in error. Most of us, through our addiction to habit and custom, flee from this experience of anxiety (see chapter 7 for a detailed discussion of "bad faith"). The deadening nature of conformity does not, for existentialists, free us from responsibility, for we can always say *no*.

Herein lies the beginning of a resolution of the determinist/libertarian debate on the issue of freedom. For existentialists, the determinist is correct that the world is governed by causality. The libertarian is misguided in looking for an "uncaused cause," for there is no such thing. But that does not mean that we must conclude that there is no human freedom. As we have noted, making a choice involves a kind of "leap." This leap signals to us that there is no absolute ground for our choice. Every action does have an end. In this sense, the determinist is not wrong. But this means that all our actions are *intentional*, or they would not be actions. According to Sartre,

> [T]o speak of an act without a cause is to speak of an act which would lack the intentional structure of every act; and the proponents of free will by searching for it on the level of the act which is in the process of being performed can only end up by rendering the act absurd.
>
> *Being and Nothingness, pp. 563–64*

It is true that it is impossible to find an act without a motive, but the motive — though an integral part of the act — does not *cause* the act.

The mistake the determinist makes is in viewing causes and motives as *things*. But they are not facts whose meaning is determined outside of us. Rather, they are signs whose significance depends on our projects. The libertarian, though, is mistaken in looking for isolated cases of free acts. There are not "holes" of freedom to which one might point. "It is therefore the positing of my ultimate ends which characterizes my being and which is identical with the sudden thrust of the freedom which is mine." (p. 314) This thrust, according to Sartre, is an *existence:* "it has nothing to do with an essence or with a property of a being which would be engendered conjointly with an idea." (p. 314)

The real question, then, is what serves as the cause of our action, and, for existentialists, it is our own consciousness which confers value and makes of the in-itself a cause. This value is always directed toward the future and "is therefore in itself a négatité." (*Being and Nothingness,* p. 564) Indeed, that we have an intention signals a lack of some sort. Our act is the expression of freedom, where act, motive, and end "are all constituted in a single upsurge." (p. 565) In the excerpt at the end of this chapter Sartre uses the terms *continuum* and *plenum* to refer to the dynamic that exists for Dasein of cause, act, and end. (p. 311) In the process of acting, we decide our end and our motive.

> Thus the motive makes itself understood as what it is by means of the ensemble of beings which are 'not,' by ideal existences, and by the future. Just as the future turns back upon the present and the past in order to elucidate them, so it is the ensemble of my projects which turns back in order to confer upon the *motive* its structure as a motive. It is only because I escape the in-itself by nihiliating myself toward my possibilities that this in-itself can take on value as cause or motive.
>
> *Being and Nothingness, p. 564*

Causes and motives for existentialists have meaning only as part of a project yet to occur. Dasein is transcendence; for example, I must be able to be not-me in order to be able to give value to the in-itself. Thus, nothing can "determine" my action. This is not to say that there are no objective facts about the world. But those "facts" can only be revealed to a for-itself who then "chooses itself in this or that particular way." (p. 316)

In Sartre's example, the knife is "objectively" an instrument with a blade and a handle. But we can use that knife to cut, or as a makeshift hammer, or as a decorative ornament on a wall.

> Two important consequences result. (1) No factual state whatever it may be (the political and economic structure of society, the psychological 'state,' etc.) is capable by itself of motivating any act whatsoever. For an act is a projection of the for-itself toward what is not, and what is can in no way determine by itself what is not. (2) No factual state can determine conscious-ness to apprehend it as a négatité or as a lack.
>
> *Being and Nothingness, p. 562*

The cause, then, does not determine the action and only appears to us through the project. According to Merleau-Ponty, "what misleads us on this, is that we often look for freedom in the voluntary deliberation which examines one motive after another and seems to opt for the weightiest or most convincing." But, in reality, "the deliberation follows the deci-sion, and it is my secret decision which brings the motives to light." (p. 325)

Freedom for existentialism, then, is difficult to define precisely because it *has no* essence. But this does not mean that it is indescribable. According to Sartre,

> . . . (m)y freedom is perpetually in question in my being; it is not a quality added on or a *property* of my nature. It is very exactly the stuff of my being; and as in my being, my being is in question, I must necessarily possess a certain comprehension of freedom.
>
> *Being and Nothingness, p. 566*

Just as we are aware that the for-itself is what it is not and is not what it is, so we are aware that we are free. Causes are transcendent, they cannot be trapped.

> In vain shall I seek to catch hold of them; I escape them by my very existence. I am condemned to exist forever beyond my essence, beyond the causes and motives of my act. I am condemned to be free. This means that no limits to my freedom can be found except freedom itself or, if you prefer, that we are not free to cease being free. To the extent that the for-itself wishes to hide its own nothingness from itself and to incorporate the in-itself as its true mode of being, it is trying also to hide its freedom from itself.
>
> *Being and Nothingness, p. 567*

We may mistakenly confer the status of necessary cause to a motive because once we have acted, our motive becomes *past* and so appears to be "thingified." But we confer value on those motives, based on our projects, which can change in an instant, nihilating the value we once gave them. This does not mean that our actions are capricious or our choices irrational. Our actions are indeed comprehensible, but this does not mean that they are causally determined.

> Every project is comprehensible as a project of itself toward a possible. It is comprehensible first in so far as it offers a rational content which is immediately apprehensible — I place my knapsack on the ground *in order to* rest for a moment. This means that we immediately apprehend the possible which it projects and the end at which it aims. In the second place it is comprehensible in that the possible under consideration refers to other possibles, these to still others, and so on to the ultimate possibility which I am.
>
> *Being and Nothingness, p. 592*

Motives are not burdens that are imposed on our actions. Even feelings are freely chosen; Sartre tells us we should not, strictly speaking, say "I am sad," but rather, "I make myself sad." "Character" does not really exist, for character is final and definite and Dasein is always in-the-making. Even our temperament, our predispositions, are of our choosing. As Merleau-Ponty notes: "My temperament exists only for the second order knowledge that I gain about myself when I see myself as others see me, and in so far as I recognize it, confer value upon it, and in that sense, choose it." (p. 325)

This is not to deny that there are relevant material circumstances. Heidegger uses the concept *geworfenheit* — thrownness — to suggest that we are already in the thick of things; Sartre writes of "facticity" to describe what is "given" to us: e.g., class background, family, nation of birth, and so forth. But these "situations" do not determine action. Indeed, they may be aids or obstacles, and there is no a priori way to judge which is which.

> What is an obstacle for me may not be so for another. There is no obstacle in an absolute sense, but the obstacle reveals its coefficient of adversity across freely invented and freely acquired techniques. The obstacle reveals this efficient also in terms of the value of the end posited by freedom. The rock will not be an obstacle if I wish at any cost to arrive at the top of the mountain. On the other hand, it will discourage me if I have freely fixed limits to my desire of making the projected climb.
>
> *Being and Nothingness, p. 628*

Or, as Merleau-Ponty explains: "One and the same project being given, one rock will appear as an obstacle, and another, being more negotiable, as a means." (p. 329) Thus, it is "freedom which brings into being the obstacles to freedom." (p. 329) "Without facticity freedom would not exist — as a power of nihilation and of choice — and without freedom facticity would not be discovered and would have no meaning." (Sartre, *Being and Nothingness*, pp. 636–37)

Even our past does not determine our future, for we must decide our relationship to our own history. We "surpass" the given by the simple fact of living it. We do have a past but we are beyond our past. In fact, it is only Dasein who can give the past significance. Ontic beings cannot. As Sartre wrote,

> . . . To surpass all that is also to preserve it. . . . By projecting ourselves toward our possible so as to escape the contradictions of our existence, we unveil them, and they are revealed in our very action although this action is richer than they are and gives us access to a social world in which new contradictions will involve us in new conduct.
>
> *Search, p. 101*

Like Sartre, Merleau-Ponty (see excerpt beginning p. 324) argues that one cannot be "a little" free. "It is inconceivable that I should be free in certain of my actions and determined in others." (p. 325) And "once I am free, I am not to be counted among things, and I must then be uninterruptedly free." (p. 325) Although, like all ontic beings, we are unable to change the brute fact of our past, Dasein alone can decide its relation to its past and give it significance. It is ridiculous to complain about what we could have been, to bemoan the "if onlys." Indeed, in a sense, we are even responsible for our own birth. Though it is of course true that we did not ask to be born, it is also true that we choose to be born in our ongoing relation to future projects. To say, "I did not ask to be born," is to try to flee responsibilities. Yet we are also responsible for that desire to flee responsibility. Just as we create our own relationship with our past, so we create our own relationship to our birth in our choices and attitudes. (See excerpt from *Being and Nothingness*, pp. 321–23.)

Thus, we begin and end with responsibility. We live with the anguish of knowing that we cannot choose not to choose. Indeed, we carry the weight of the world on our shoulders. Everything that happens to us is *ours*. As Sartre states, "the peculiar character of human-reality is that it is without excuse." (p. 322) Our anguish reveals that all projects can be changed or modified. Not only are we without excuse; we are also without justification. The choices we make "serve as the foundation for the ensemble of significations which constitute reality," (p. 319) but these choices are completely contingent. Since Dasein is the one by whom it happens that there *is* a world, we then have complete responsibility for that world. "It is therefore senseless to think of complaining since nothing foreign has decided what we feel, what we live, or what we are." (p. 321)

Not all existentialists paint as gloomy a picture of freedom as Sartre. The excerpt at the end of this chapter from Gabriel Marcel conjoins a discussion of freedom with that of hope. Coming from a theistic perspective, Marcel argues that every human being is irreplaceable, and he rejects Sartre's emphasis on despair. Sartre, he writes, treats freedom "as a radical deficiency" rather than "as an achievement." (p. 340) But for Marcel, we are not automatically free except in the emptiest of senses. Freedom, he claims, must be won; "freedom is a conquest — always partial, always precarious, always challenged." (p. 341) Freedom can only be assessed in specific situations.

The existential analysis of freedom has had important implications for psychiatry as well as philosophy. Our excerpt from psychiatrist Viktor Frankl's *The Unheard Cry for Meaning* employs existential categories in a therapeutic context. Like Sartre, Frankl claims that the conditions of facticity do not completely condition us. "(I)t is up to him whether or not he succumbs and surrenders to the conditions." (p. 346) Himself a survivor of concentration camps, Frankl bears witness "to the unexpected extent to which man is capable of defying and braving even the worst conditions conceivable." (p. 346) This is much like Sartre's claim that there is no situation that is inhuman. Frankl says,

> Ultimately, man is not subject to the conditions that confront him; rather, these conditions are subject to his decision. Wittingly or unwittingly, he decides whether he will face up or give in, whether or not he will let himself be determined by the conditions. Of course, it could be objected that such decisions are themselves determined. But it is obvious that this results in a *regressus in infinitum*. . . . 'All choices are caused but they are caused by the chooser.' (See pp. 346–47.)

Like all existentialists, theists as well as nontheists, Frankl reaffirms (even for his psychiatric patients) the openness of Dasein.

> When the self-transcendence of existence is denied, existence itself is distorted. It is reified. Being is reduced to a mere thing. Being human is de-personalized. And, what is most important, the subject is made into an object. (See p. 349.)

CONCLUSION

Much of the focus of this chapter has been on Sartre's analysis of freedom. This is not to suggest either that all existentialists agree with his explication or that Sartre's view is nonproblematic. Rather, there are two reasons why Sartre's framework receives so much attention here: (1) Sartre's discussion of freedom is probably — of all representative existentialist thinkers — the most developed and in-depth aproach to the topic; and (2) Sartre's discussion of freedom is probably the most extreme form of freedom defended in the history of philosophy.

Yet Sartre's characterization of freedom is not completely idiosyncratic. Indeed, his emphasis on choice and possibility, his insistence on personal responsibility, and his treatment of anguish have a history in the writings of Pascal, Kierkegaard, Dostoyevsky, Marcel, and, to some extent, Heidegger. In this conclusion we consider what is problematic in Sartre's view; in doing so, we may articulate some key criticisms that apply not only to Sartre's framework but also more generally to existential treatments of freedom.

Freedom is central to existentialism and fundamental to Sartre's system. *Pour soi* is essentially nihilation, seeking (but always failing) to become complete. Sartre repeatedly insists that human beings have no essence, since the for-itself is pure and undefinable freedom. But if to be human is to be "condemned to be free," is this not a notion of human nature? Elsewhere Sartre writes of a "universal human condition," but how is this different from an essence or nature? If the for-itself is essentially "lack" or "desire," seeking futilely to become God, isn't there a limit on our freedom and an essence to our nature? Though Sartre may be more extreme on this point than other existentialists, these questions force a reexamination of what it means to claim that existence precedes essence.

Second, Sartre insists that obstacles do not exist a priori; rather, our choices make some things obstacles, others assets, and others irrelevant. A rainstorm may be a blessing to a farmer during a drought, a disappointment for an outing, and insignificant if we've planned to stay home and read. But is Sartre right in claiming that we are absolutely free, no matter what our concrete situation? Is our freedom really limitless? And don't present choices influence the range of possible future options? Are we really absolutely free to change a project at any given moment? Even other existentialists like Karl Jaspers and Maurice Merleau-Ponty have criticized this approach as simplistic.

Finally, one must wonder what political and ethical implications follow from such an extreme view of freedom. If we are all absolutely free and completely responsible, why should we make any effort to improve the social conditions of any given person or society? Sartre tells us (see p. 321) that the soldier who is drafted is totally responsible for the war. As responsible as if he had enlisted? As responsible as his commanding officer? As the rulers of the nations engaged in the war? If freedom is truly absolute, then we cannot distinguish levels of power and levels of responsibility. Indeed, Sartre's view seems to trivialize all differences among individuals and to make facticity irrelevant.

There is evidence that Sartre changed his view on freedom later in his philosophical career: "I still believe that individual freedom is total, ontologically speaking, but on the other hand I am more and more convinced that this freedom is conditioned and limited by circumstances." (1956, quoted in *The Tragic Finale*, p. xvi) Yet he also, even later, insisted:

> The idea I have never ceased to develop is that in the end you are always responsible for what is made of you. Even if you can do nothing else besides assume this responsibility. I believe that a man can always make something out of what is made of him. This is freedom. . . .
>
> *New Left Review interview, London, 1970*

Our goal here, though, is not to settle on what was Sartre's final position on human freedom. What we must recognize is that — for existentialism — human being *is* freedom. But that freedom is also a burden. It reminds us that we can never be complete, no matter what we may do. "As long as we are alive," writes Merleau-Ponty, "our situation is open." (p. 331)

QUESTIONS FOR CONSIDERATION

1. Sartre states (see excerpt, p. 321) that the soldier in a war is responsible for the war. Do you agree? What implications follow from such a view of responsibility?

2. Consider Sartre's view of the relation between our past and our freedom. Does the past determine the future? Since there are many aspects of our past that we did *not* choose, is Sartre wrong in his claim that we are all free to choose ourselves? Take, for example, the adult who was physically abused as a child; is he or she free? What might Sartre say?

3. What does it mean for something to be possible? How is the notion of possibility related to human freedom?

4. What is the relation between freedom and the inevitability of death?

5. The first part of this chapter distinguishes freedom from coercion from psychic or ontological freedom. What sort of political system would be consistent with an existentialist view of freedom? That is, what — if any — coercive measures would an "ideal" existentialist society adopt?

6. Is God's existence consistent with human freedom? Why or why not?

7. Sartre claims that every event is an opportunity. What does this mean? Is he right?

REFERENCES

BALDWIN, JAMES. *Giovanni's Room*. New York: Laurel, 1985.

CAMPBELL, C. A. *In Defense of Free Will, an Inaugural Lecture*. Glasgow: Jackson, Son and Co., 1938.

DESAN, WILFRID. *The Tragic Finale: An Essay on the Philosophy of Jean-Paul Sartre*. New York: Harper & Row, 1954.

DESCARTES, RÉNE. *Meditations on First Philosophy*. Translated by Donald A. Cress. Indianapolis: Hackett Publishing, 1979.

HOBBES, THOMAS. *Leviathan*. Edited by C. B. Macpherson. Baltimore: Penguin Books, 1971.

HOLBACH, BARON D'. *System of Nature*. London: Kearsley, 1797.

HOSPERS, JOHN. "Meaning and Free Will." *Philosophy and Phenomenological Research* 10 (1950): 313–30.

JAMES, WILLIAM. "The Dilemma of Determinism." In *Essays on Faith and Morals*, edited by R. B. Perry, pp. 145–83. New York: New American Library, 1962.

KUNDERA, MILAN. *Life Is Elsewhere*. Baltimore: Penguin Books, 1986.

MARCEL, GABRIEL. *Homo Viator: An Introduction to a Metaphysic of Hope*. Translated by Emma Craufurd. New York: Harper & Row, 1962.

———. "Mortality, Hope, and Freedom." In *The Existential Background of Human Dignity*, pp. 136–53. Cambridge: Harvard University Press, 1963.

———. *The Mystery of Being*. translated by G. S. Fraser. Chicago: Henry Regnery Co., 1950.

———. "The Ontological Mystery." In *The Existential Background of Human Dignity*, pp. 75–93. Cambridge, Mass.: Harvard University Press, 1963.

ORTEGA Y GASSET, JOSE. *The Revolt of the Masses*. Translated anonymously. New York: W. W. Norton & Co., 1960.

SARTRE, JEAN-PAUL. *Being and Nothingness*. Translated by Hazel E. Barnes. New York: Washington Square Press, 1964.

———. *Search for a Method*. Translated by Hazel E. Barnes. *New York: Vintage Books, 1968.*

SKINNER, B. F. "Freedom and the Control of Men." *The American Scholar*, 25, (1955–1956), pp. 47–65.

———. *Science and Human Behavior*. New York: The Free Press, 1953.

———. *Walden Two. New York: Macmillan, 1960.*

JEAN-PAUL SARTRE

Sartre's libertarianism (or what some now call "agency theory") is one of the most radical theories of freedom. In this excerpt from Being and Nothingness, *Sartre explores the notion of will and its relation to human possibility and choice. He argues that the for-itself is always inescapably free, and that that freedom is a burden at the heart of human existence. The excerpt concludes with a brief discussion of the concept of responsibility, which once again makes clear how radical a view Sartre's is.*

Being and Nothingness

The ultimate meaning of determinism is to establish within us an unbroken continuity of existence in itself. The motive conceived as a psychic fact — *i.e.*, as a full and given reality — is, in the deterministic view, articulated without any break with the decision and the act, both of which are equally conceived as psychic givens. The in-itself has got hold of all these "data"; the motive provokes the act as the physical causes its effect; everything is real, everything is full. Thus the refusal of freedom can be conceived only as an attempt to apprehend oneself as being-in-itself; it amounts to the same thing. Human reality may be defined as a being such that in its being its freedom is at stake because human reality perpetually tries to refuse to recognize its freedom. Psychologically in each one of us this amounts to trying to take the causes and motives as *things*. We try to confer permanence upon them. We attempt to hide from ourselves that their nature and their weight depend each moment on the meaning which I give to them; we take them for constants. This amounts to considering the meaning which I gave to them just now or yesterday — which is irremediable because it is *past* — and extrapolating from it a character fixed still in the present. I attempt to persuade myself that the cause *is* as it was. Thus it would pass whole and untouched from my past consciousness to my present consciousness. It would inhabit my consciousness. This amounts to trying to give an essence to the for-itself. In the same way people will posit ends as transcendences, which is not an error. But instead of seeing that the transcendences there posited are maintained in their being by my own transcendence, people will assume that I encounter them upon my surging up in the world; they come from God, from nature, from "my" nature, from society. These ends ready made and pre-human will therefore define the meaning of my act even

From *Being and Nothingness*, translated by Hazel Barnes, pp. 567–79, 597–602, 707–11.
©Philosophical Library, 1956.

before I conceive it, just as causes as pure psychic givens will produce it
without my even being aware of them.

Cause, act, and end constitute a *continuum*, a *plenum*. These abortive attempts to stifle freedom under the weight of being (they collapse
with the sudden upsurge of anguish before freedom) show sufficiently
that freedom in its foundation coincides with the nothingness which is at
the heart of man. Human-reality is free because it *is not enough*. It is free
because it is perpetually wrenched away from itself and because it has
been separated by a nothingness from what it is and from what it will be.
It is free, finally, because its present being is itself a nothingness in the
form of the "reflection-reflecting." Man is free because he is not himself
but presence to himself. The being which is what it is can not be free.
Freedom is precisely the nothingness which *is made-to-be* at the heart of
man and which forces human-reality *to make itself* instead of *to be*. As we
have seen, for human reality,to be is to *choose oneself;* nothing comes to it
either from the outside or from within which it can *receive or accept*.
Without any help whatsoever, it is entirely abandoned to the intolerable
necessity of making itself be — down to the slightest detail. Thus
freedom is not *a* being; it is *the being* of man — *i.e.*, his nothingness of
being. If we start by conceiving of man as a plenum, it is absurd to try to
find in him afterwards moments or psychic regions in which he would be
free. As well look for emptiness in a container which one has filled
beforehand up to the brim! Man can not be sometimes slave and sometimes free; he is wholly and forever free or he is not free at all.

These observations can lead us, if we know how to use them, to new
discoveries. They will enable us first to bring to light the relations between freedom and what we call the "will." There is a fairly common
tendency to seek to identify free acts with voluntary acts and to restrict
the deterministic explanation to the world of the passions. In short the
point of view of Descartes. The Cartesian will is free, but there are
"passions of the soul." Again Descartes will attempt a physiological
interpretation of these passions. Later there will be an attempt to instate a
purely psychological determinism. Intellectualistic analyses such as
Proust, for example, attempts with respect to jealousy or snobbery can
serve as illustrations for this concept of the passional "mechanism." In
this case it would be necessary to conceive of man as simultaneously free
and determined, and the essential problem would be that of the relations
between this unconditioned freedom and the determined processes of
the psychic life: how will it master the passions, how will it utilize them
for its own benefit? A wisdom which comes from ancient times — the
wisdom of the Stoics — will teach us to come to terms with these passions
so as to master them; in short it will counsel us how to conduct ourselves
with regard to affectivity as man does with respect to nature in general
when he obeys it in order better to control it. Human reality therefore

appears as a free power besieged by an ensemble of determined processes. One will distinguish wholly free acts, determined processes over which the free will has power, and processes which on principle escape the human-will.

It is clear that we shall not be able to accept such a conception. But let us try better to understand the reasons for our refusal. There is one objection which is obvious and which we shall not waste time in developing; this is that such a trenchant duality is inconceivable at the heart of the psychic unity. How in fact could we conceive of a being which could be *one* and which nevertheless on the one hand would be constituted as a series of facts determined by one another — hence existents in exteriority — and which on the other hand would be constituted as a spontaneity determining itself to be and revealing only itself? A *priori* this spontaneity would be capable of no action on a determinism already *constituted*. On what could it act? On the object itself (the present psychic fact)? But how could it modify an in-itself which by definition is and can be only what it is? On the actual law of the process? This is self-contradictory. On the antecedents of the process? But it amounts to the same thing whether we act on the present psychic fact in order to modify it in itself or act upon it in order to modify its consequences. And in each case we encounter the same impossibility which we pointed out earlier. Moreover, what instrument would this spontaneity have at its disposal? If the hand can clasp, it is because it can be clasped. Spontaneity, since by definition it is *beyond reach*, can not in turn *reach*; it can produce only itself. And if it could dispose of a special instrument, it would then be necessary to conceive of this as of an intermediary nature between free will and determined passions — which is not admissible. For different reasons the passions could get no hold upon the will. Indeed it is impossible for a determined process to act upon a spontaneity, exactly as it is impossible for objects to act upon consciousness. Thus any synthesis of two types of existents is impossible; they are not homogeneous; they will remain each one in its incommunicable solitude. The only bond which a nihilating spontaneity could maintain with mechanical processes would be the fact that it *produces itself by an internal negation directed toward these existents*. But then the spontaneity will exist precisely only in so far as it denies concerning itself that it is these passions. Henceforth the ensemble of the determined πάθος will of necessity be apprehended by spontaneity as a pure transcendent; that is, as what is necessarily *outside*, as what *is not* it.[1] This internal negation would therefore have for its effect only the dissolution of the πάθος in the world, and the πάθος would exist as some sort of object in the midst of the

---

[1] Tr. I.e., is not spontaneity.

world for a free spontaneity which would be simultaneously will and consciousness. This discussion shows that two solutions and only two are possible: either man is wholly determined (which is inadmissible, especially because a determined consciousness — *i.e.*, a consciousness externally motivated — becomes itself pure exteriority and ceases to be consciousness) or else man is wholly free.

But these observations are still not our primary concern. They have only a negative bearing. The study of the will should, on the contrary, enable us to advance further in our understanding of freedom. And this is why the fact which strikes us first is that if the will is to be autonomous, then it is impossible for us to consider it as a *given* psychic fact; that is, in-itself. It can not belong to the category defined by the psychologist as "states of consciousness." Here as everywhere else we assert that the state of consciousness is a pure idol of a positive psychology. If the will is to be freedom, then it is of necessity negativity and the power of nihilation. But then we no longer can see why autonomy shoud be preserved for the will. In fact it is hard to conceive of those holes of nihilation which would be the volitions and which would surge up in the otherwise dense and full web of the passions and of the πάθος in general. If the will is nihilation, then the ensemble of the psychic must likewise be nihilation. Moreover — and we shall soon return to this point — where do we get the idea that the "fact" of passion or that pure, simple desire is not nihilating? Is not passion first a project and an enterprise? Does it not exactly posit a state of affairs as intolerable? And is it not thereby forced to effect a withdrawal in relation to this state of affairs and to nihilate it by isolating it and by considering it in the light of an end — *i.e.*, of a non-being? And does not passion have its own ends which are recognized precisely at the same moment at which it posits them as non-existent? And if nihilation is precisely the being of freedom, how can we refuse autonomy to the passions in order to grant it to the will?

But this is not all: the will, far from being the unique or at least the privileged manifestation of freedom, actually — like every event of the for-itself — must presuppose the foundation of an original freedom in order to be able to constitute itself as will. The will in fact is posited as a reflective decision in relation to certain ends. But it does not create these ends. It is rather a mode of being in relation to them: it decrees that the pursuit of these ends will be reflective and deliberative. Passion can posit the same ends. For example, if I am threatened, I can run away at top speed because of my fear of dying. This passional fact nevertheless posits implicitly as a supreme end the value of life. Another person in the same situation will, on the contrary, understand that he must remain at his post even if resistance at first appears more dangerous than flight; he "will stand firm." But his goal, although better understood and explicitly posited, remains the same as in the case of the emotional reaction. It is simply that the methods of attaining it are more clearly conceived; certain of them are rejected as dubious or inefficacious, others are more solidly organized. The difference here depends on the choice of means and on the degree of reflection and of making explicit, not on the end. Yet the one who flees is said to be "passionate," and we reserve the term "voluntary" for the man who resists. Therefore the question is of a difference of subjective attitude in relation to a transcendent end. But if we wish to avoid the error which we denounced earlier and not consider these transcendent ends as pre-human and as an *a priori* limit to our transcendence, then we are indeed compelled to recognize that they are the temporalizing projection of our freedom. Human reality can not receive its ends, as we have seen, either from outside or from a so-called inner "nature." It chooses them and by this very choice confers upon them a transcendent existence as the external limit of its projects. From this point of view — and if it is understood that the existence of the *Dasein* precedes and commands its essence — human reality in and through its very upsurge decides to define its own being by its ends. It is therefore the positing of my ultimate ends which characterizes my being and which is identical with the sudden thrust of the freedom which is mine. And this thrust is an *existence;* it has nothing to do with an essence or with a property of a being which would be engendered conjointly with an idea.

Thus since freedom is identical with my existence, it is the foundation of ends which I shall attempt to attain either by the will or by passionate efforts. Therefore it can not be limited to voluntary acts. Volitions, on the contrary, like passions are certain subjective attitudes by which we attempt to attain the ends posited by original freedom. By original freedom, of course, we should not understand a freedom which would be *prior* to the voluntary or passionate act but rather a foundation which is strictly contemporary with the will or the passion and which these *manifest*, each in its own way. Neither should we oppose freedom to the will or to passion as the "profound self" of Bergson is opposed to the superficial self; the for-itself is wholly selfness and can not have a "profound self," unless by this we mean certain transcendent structures of the psyche. Freedom is nothing but the *existence* of our will or of our passions in so far as this existence is the nihilation of facticity; that is, the existence of a being which is its being in the mode of having to be it. We shall return to this point. In any case let us remember that the will is determined within the compass of motives and ends already posited by the for-itself in a transcendent projection of itself toward its possibles. If this were not so, how could we understand deliberation, which is an evaluation of means in relation to already existing ends?

If these ends are already posited, then what remains to be decided at each moment is the way in which I shall conduct myself with respect to them; in other words, the attitude which I shall assume. Shall I act by volition or by passion? Who can decide except me? In fact, if we admit that circumstances decide for me (for example, I can act by volition when faced with a minor danger but if the peril increases, I shall fall into passion), we thereby suppress all freedom. It would indeed be absurd to declare that the will is autonomous when it appears but that external circumstances strictly determine the moment of its appearance. But, on the other hand, how can it be maintained that a will which does not yet exist can suddenly decide to shatter the chain of the passions and suddenly stand forth on the fragments of these chains? Such a conception would lead us to consider the will as a *power* which sometimes would manifest itself to consciousness and at other times would remain hidden, but which would in any case possess the permanence and the existence "in-itself" of a property. This is precisely what is inadmissible. It is, however, certain that common opinion conceives of the moral life as a struggle between a will-thing and passion-substances. There is here a sort of psychological Manichaeism which is absolutely insupportable.

Actually it is not enough to will; it is necessary to will to will. Take, for example, a given situation: I can react to it emotionally. We have shown elsewhere that emotion is not a physiological tempest;[2] it is a reply adapted to the situation; it is a type of conduct, the meaning and form of which are the object of an intention of consciousness which aims at attaining a particular end by particular means. In fear, fainting and cataplexie[3] aim at suppressing the danger by suppressing the consciousness of the danger. There is an *intention* of losing consciousness in order to do away with the formidable world in which consciousness is engaged and which comes into being through consciousness. Therefore we have to do with magical behavior provoking the symbolic satisfactions of our desires and revealing by the same stroke a magical stratum of the world. In contrast to this conduct voluntary and rational conduct will consider the situation scientifically, will reject the magical, and will apply itself to realizing determined series and instrumental complexes which will enable us to resolve the problems. It will organize a system of means by taking its stand on instrumental determinism. Suddenly it will reveal a technical world; that is, a world in which each instrumental-complex refers to another larger complex and so on. But what will make me decide to choose the magical aspect or the technical aspect of the world? It can not be the world itself, for this in order to be manifested waits to be discovered. Therefore it is necessary that the for-itself in its project must choose being the one by whom the world is revealed as magical or rational; that is, the for-itself must as a free project of itself give to itself

---

[2] *Esquisse d'une théorie des émotions.* Hermann, 1939.

[3] Tr. A word invented by Preyer to refer to a sudden inhibiting numbness produced by any shock.

magical or rational existence. It is responsible for either one, for the for-itself can *be* only if it has chosen itself. Therefore the for-itself appears as the free foundation of its emotions as of its volitions. My fear *is* free and manifests my freedom; I have put all my freedom into my fear, and I have chosen myself as fearful in this or that circumstance. Under other circumstances I shall exist as deliberate and courageous, and I shall have put all my freedom into my courage. In relation to freedom there is no privileged psychic phenomenon. All my "modes of being" manifest freedom equally since they are all ways of being my own nothingness.

This will be even more apparent in the description of what we called the "causes and motives" of action. We have outlined that description in the preceding pages; at present it will be well to return to it and take it up again in more precise terms. Did we not say indeed that passion is the *motive* of the act — or again that the passional act is that which has passion for its motive? And does not the will appear as the decision which follows deliberation concerning causes and motives? What then is a cause? What is a motive?

Generally by cause we mean the reason for the act; that is, the ensemble of rational considerations which justify it. If the government decides on a conversion of Government bonds, it will give the causes for its act: the lessening of the national debt, the rehabilitation of the Treasury. Similarly it is by *causes* that historians are accustomed to explain the acts of ministers or monarchs; they will seek the *causes* for a declaration of war: the occasion is propitious, the attacked country is disorganized because of internal troubles; it is time to put an end to an economic conflict which is in danger of lasting interminably. If Clovis is converted to Catholicism, then inasmuch as so many barbarian kings are Arians, it is because Clovis sees an opportunity of getting into the good graces of the episcopate which is all powerful in Gaul. And so on. One will note here that the cause is characterized as an objective appreciation of the situation. The cause of Clovis' conversion is the political and religious state of Gaul; it is the relative strengths of the episcopate, the great landowners, and the common people. What motivates the conversion of the bonds is the state of the national debt. Nevertheless this objective appreciation can be made only in the light of a presupposed end and within the limits of a project of the for-itself toward this end. In order for the power of the episcopate to be revealed to Clovis as the cause of his conversion (that is, in order for him to be able to envisage the objective consequences which this conversion could have) it is necessary first for him to posit as an end the conquest of Gaul. If we suppose that Clovis has other ends, he can find in the situation of the Church causes for his becoming Arian or remaining pagan. It is even possible that in the consideration of the Church he can even find no cause for acting in any way at all; he will then discover nothing in relation to this subject; he will leave the situation of the episcopate in the state of "unrevealed," in a total obscurity. We shall therefore use the term *cause* for the objective apprehension of a determined situation as this situation is revealed in the light of a certain end as being able to serve as the means for attaining this end.

The motive, on the contrary, is generally considered as a subjective fact. It is the ensemble of the desires, emotions, and passions which urge me to accomplish a certain act. The historian looks for motives and takes them into account only as a last resort when the causes are not sufficient to explain the act under consideration. . . .In contrast to the historian the psychologist will by preference look for motives; usually he supposes, in fact, that they are "contained in" the state of consciousness which has provoked the action. The ideal rational act would therefore be the one for which the motives would be practically nil and which would be uniquely inspired by an objective appreciation of the situation. The irrational or passionate act will be characterized by the reverse proportion.

It remains for us to explain the relation between causes and motives in the everyday case in which they exist side by side. For example, I can join the Socialist party because I judge that this party serves the interests of justice and of humanity or because I believe that it will become the principal historical force in the years which will follow my joining: these are causes. And at the same time I can have motives: a feeling of pity or charity for certain classes of the oppressed, a feeling of shame at being on the "good side of the barricade," as Gide says, or again an inferiority complex, a desire to shock my relatives, *etc.* What can be meant by the statement that I have joined the Socialist party for these causes *and* these motives? Evidently we are dealing with two radically distinct layers of meaning. How are we to compare them? How are we to determine the part played by each of them in the decision under consideration? This difficulty, which certainly is the greatest of those raised by the current distinction between causes and motives, has never been resolved; few people indeed have so much as caught a glimpse of it. Actually under a different name it amounts to positing the existence of a conflict between the will and the passions. But if the classic theory is discovered to be incapable of assigning to cause and motive their proper influence in the simple instance when they join together to produce a single decision, it will be wholly impossible[4] for it to explain or even to conceive of a conflict between causes and motives, a conflict in which each group would urge its individual decision. Therefore we must start over again from the beginning.

To be sure, the cause is objective; it is the state of contemporary things as it is revealed to a consciousness. It is *objective* that the Roman plebs and aristocracy were corrupted by the time of Constantine or that

[4] Tr. Sartre says "wholly possible" (*tout à fait possible*) which I feel sure is a misprint.

the Catholic Church is ready to favor a monarch who at the time of Clovis will help it triumph over Arianism. Nevertheless this state of affairs can be revealed only to a for-itself since in general the for-itself is the being by which "there is" a world. Better yet, it can be revealed only to a for-itself which chooses itself in this or that particular way — that is, to a for-itself which has made its own individuality. The for-itself must of necessity have projected itself in this or that way in order to discover the instrumental implications of instrumental-things. . . .[T]his potentiality can be revealed only if the situation is surpassed toward a state of things which does not yet exist — in short, toward a nothingness. In a word the world gives counsel only if one questions it, and one can question it only for a well-determined end.

Therefore the cause, far from determining the action, appears only in and through the project of an action. It is in and through the project of imposing his rule on all of Gaul that the state of the Western Church appears objectively to Clovis as a cause for his conversion. In other words the consciousness which carves out the cause in the ensemble of the world has already its own structure; it has given its own ends to itself, it has projected itself toward its possibles, and it has its own manner of hanging on to its possibilities: this peculiar manner of holding to its possibles is here affectivity. This internal organization which consciousness has given to itself in the form of non-positional self-consciousness is strictly correlative with the carving out of causes in the world. . . .

Earlier we posed a question: I have yielded to fatigue, we said, and doubtless I *could have* done otherwise but *at what price?* At present we are in a position to answer this. Our analysis, in fact, has just shown us that this act was not *gratuitous*. To be sure, it was not explained by a motive or a cause conceived as the content of a prior state of consciousness, but it had to be interpreted in terms of an original project of which it formed an integral part. Hence it becomes evident that we can not suppose that the act could have been modified without at the same time supposing a fundamental modification of my original choice of myself. This way of yielding to fatigue and of letting myself fall down at the side of the road expresses a certain initial stiffening against my body and the inanimate in-itself. It is placed within the compass of a certain view of the world in which difficulties can appear "not worth the trouble of being tolerated"; or, to be exact, since the motive is a pure non-thetic consciousness and consequently an initial project of itself toward an absolute end (a certain aspect of the in-itself-for-itself), it is an apprehension of the world (warmth, distance from the city, uselessness of effort, *etc.*) as the cause of my ceasing to walk. Thus this *possible* — to stop – *theoretically* takes on its meaning only in and through the hierarchy of the possibles which I am in terms of the ultimate and initial possible. This does not imply that I *must necessarily* stop but merely that I can refuse to stop only by a radical conversion of my being-in-the-world; that is, by an abrupt metamorphosis of my initial project — *i.e.*, by another choice of myself and of my ends. Moreover this modification is always possible.

The anguish which, when this possibility is revealed; manifests our freedom to our consciousness is witness of this perpetual modifiability of our initial project. In anguish we do not simply apprehend the fact that the possibles which we project are perpetually eaten away by our freedom-to-come; in addition we apprehend our choice — *i.e.*, ourselves — *as unjustifiable*. This means that we apprehend our choice as not deriving from any prior reality but rather as being about to serve as foundation for the ensemble of significations which constitute reality. Unjustifiability is not only the subjective recognition of the absolute contingency of our being but also that of the interiorization and recovery of this contingency on our own account. For the choice — as we shall see — issues from the contingency of the in-itself which it nihilates and transports it to the level of the gratuitous determination of the for-itself by itself. Thus we are perpetually engaged in our choice and perpetually conscious of the fact that we ourselves can abruptly invert this choice and "reverse steam"; for we project the future by our very being, but our existential freedom perpetually eats it away as we make known to ourselves what we are by means of the future but without getting a grip on this future which remains always possible without ever passing to the rank of the *real*. Thus we are perpetually *threatened* by the nihilation of our actual choice and perpetually threatened with choosing ourselves — and consequently with becoming — other than we are. By the sole fact that our choice is absolute, it is *fragile;* that is, by positing our freedom by means of it, we posit by the same stroke the perpetual possibility that the choice may become a "here and now" which has been made-past in the interests of a "beyond" which I shall be.

Nevertheless let us thoroughly understand that our actual choice is such that it furnishes us with no *motive* for making it past by means of a further choice. In fact, it is this original choice which originally creates all causes and all motives which can guide us to partial actions; it is this which arranges the world with its meaning, its instrumental-complexes, and its coefficient of adversity. The absolute change which threatens us from our birth until our death remains perpetually unpredictable and incomprehensible. Even if we envisage other fundamental attitudes as *possible*, we shall never consider them except from outside, as the behavior of Others. And if we attempt to refer our conduct to them, they shall not for all that lose their character as external and as transcended-transcendences. To "understand" them in fact would be already to have chosen them. . . .

Thus every fundamental choice defines the direction of the pursued-pursuit at the same time that it temporalizes itself. This does not mean that it *gives an initial thrust* or that there is something settled — which I can exploit to my profit so long as I hold myself within the limits of this choice. On the contrary, the nihilation is pursued continuously, and consequently the free and continuous recovery of the choice is obligatory. This recovery, however, is not made from *instant to instant* while I freely reassume my choice. This is because there is no instant. The recovery is so narrowly joined to the ensemble of the process that it has no instantaneous meaning and can not have any. But precisely because it is free and perpetually recovered by freedom, my choice is limited by freedom itself; that is, it is haunted by the specter of the instant. In so far as I *shall reassume* my choice, the making-past of the process will be effected in perfect ontological continuity with the present. The process which is made-past remains organized with the present nihilation in the form of a *practical knowing;* that is, meaning which is lived and interiorized without ever being an *object* for the consciousness which projects itself toward its own ends. But precisely because I am free I always have the possibility of positing my immediate past as an object. This means that even though my prior consciousness was a pure non-positional consciousness (of) the past while it constituted itself as an internal negation of the co-present real and made its meaning known to itself by its ends posited as "reassumed," now at the time of the new choice, consciousness posits its own past as an object, that is, it *evaluates* its past and takes its bearings in relation to it. This act of objectivizing the immediate past is the same as the new choice of other ends; it contributes to causing the instant to spring forth as the nihilating rupture of the temporalization. . . .

III. FREEDOM AND RESPONSIBILITY

Although the considerations which are about to follow are of interest primarily to the ethicist, it may nevertheless be worthwhile after these descriptions and arguments to return to the freedom of the for-itself and to try to understand what the fact of this freedom represents for human destiny.

The essential consequence of our earlier remarks is that man being condemned to be free carries the weight of the whole world on his shoulders; he is responsible for the world and for himself as a way of being. We are taking the word "responsibility" in its ordinary sense as "consciousness (of) being the incontestable author of an event or of an object." In this sense the responsibility of the for-itself is overwhelming since he[5] is the one by whom it happens that *there is* a world; since he is

[5] footnote deleted

also the one who makes himself be, then whatever may be the situation in which he finds himself, the for-itself must wholly assume this situation with its peculiar coefficient of adversity, even though it be insupportable. He must assume the situation with the proud consciousness of being the author of it, for the very worst disadvantages or the worst threats which can endanger my person have meaning only in and through my project; and it is on the ground of the engagement which I am that they appear. It is therefore senseless to think of complaining since nothing foreign has decided what we feel, what we live, or what we are.

Furthermore this absolute responsibility is not resignation; it is simply the logical requirement of the consequences of our freedom. What happens to me happens through me, and I can neither affect myself with it nor revolt against it nor resign myself to it. Moreover everything which happens to me is *mine*. By this we must understand first of all that I am always equal to what happens to me *qua* man, for what happens to a man through other men and through himself can be only human. The most terrible situations of war, the worst tortures do not create a non-human state of things; there is no non-human situation. It is only through fear, flight, and recourse to magical types of conduct that I shall decide on the non-human, but this decision is human, and I shall carry the entire responsibility for it. But in addition the situation is *mine* because it is the image of my free choice of myself, and everything which it presents to me is *mine* in that this represents me and symbolizes me. Is it not I who decide the coefficient of adversity in things and even their unpredictability by deciding myself?

Thus there are no *accidents* in a life; a community event which suddenly bursts forth and involves me in it does not come from the outside. If I am mobilized in a war, this war is *my* war; it is in my image and I deserve it. I deserve it first because I could always get out of it by suicide or by desertion; these ultimate possibles are those which must always be present for us when there is a question of envisaging a situation. For lack of getting out of it, I have *chosen* it. This can be due to inertia, to cowardice in the face of public opinion, or because I prefer certain other values to the value of the refusal to join in the war (the good opinion of my relatives, the honor of my family, *etc.*). Any way you look at it, it is a matter of a choice. This choice will be repeated later on again and again without a break until the end of the war. Therefore we must agree with the statement by J. Romains, "In war there are no innocent victims."[6] If therefore I have preferred war to death or to dishonor, everything takes place as if I bore the entire responsibility for this war. Of course others have declared it, and one might be tempted perhaps to consider me as a simple accomplice. But this notion of complicity has

---

[6] J. Romains, *Les hommes de bonne volonté*. Vol. III: "Prélude à Verdun."

only a juridical sense, and it does not hold here. For it depended on me that for me and by me this war should not exist, and I have decided that it does exist. There was no compulsion here, for the compulsion could have got no hold on a freedom. I did not have any excuse; for as we have said repeatedly in this book, the peculiar character of human-reality is that it is without excuse. Therefore it remains for me only to lay claim to this war.

But in addition the war is *mine* because by the sole fact that it arises in a situation which I cause to be and that I can discover it there only by engaging myself for or against it, I can no longer distinguish at present the choice which I make of myself from the choice which I make of the war. To live this war is to choose myself through it and to choose it through my choice of myself. There can be no question of considering it as "four years of vacation" or as a "reprieve," as a "recess," the essential part of my responsibilities being elsewhere in my married, family, or professional life. In this war which I have chosen I choose myself from day to day, and I make it mine by making myself. If it is going to be four empty years, then it is I who bear the responsibility for this.

Finally, as we pointed out earlier, each person is an absolute choice of self from the standpoint of a world of knowledges and of techniques which this choice both assumes and illumines; each person is an absolute upsurge at an absolute date and is perfectly unthinkable at another date. It is therefore a waste of time to ask what I should have been if this war had not broken out, for I have chosen myself as one of the possible meanings of the epoch which imperceptibly led to war. I am not distinct from this same epoch; I could not be transported to another epoch without contradiction. Thus *I am* this war which restricts and limits and makes comprehensible the period which preceded it. In this sense we may define more precisely the responsibility of the for-itself if to the earlier quoted statement, "There are no innocent victims," we add the words, "We have the war we deserve." Thus, totally free, undistinguishable from the period for which I have chosen to be the meaning, as profoundly responsible for the war as if I had myself declared it, unable to live without integrating it in *my* situation, engaging myself in it wholly and stamping it with my seal, I must be without remorse or regrets as I am without excuse; for from the instant of my upsurge into being, I carry the weight of the world by myself alone without anything or any person being able to lighten it.

Yet this responsibility is of a very particular type. Someone will say, "I did not ask to be born." This is a naïve way of throwing greater emphasis on our facticity. I am responsible for everything, in fact, except for my very responsibility, for I am not the foundation of my being. Therefore everything takes place as if I were compelled to be responsible. I am *abandoned* in the world, not in the sense that I might remain abandoned and passive in a hostile universe like a board floating on the water, but rather in the sense that I find myself suddenly alone and without help, engaged in a world for which I bear the whole responsibility without being able, whatever I do, to tear myself away from this responsibility for an instant. For I am responsible for my very desire of fleeing responsibilities. To make myself passive in the world, to refuse to act upon things and upon Others is still to choose myself, and suicide is one mode among others of being-in-the-world. Yet I find an absolute responsibility for the fact that my facticity (here the fact of my birth) is directly inapprehensible and even inconceivable, for this fact of my birth never appears as a brute fact but always across a projective reconstruction of my for-itself. I am ashamed of being born or I am astonished at it or I rejoice over it, or in attempting to get rid of my life I affirm that I live and I assume this life as bad. Thus in a certain sense I *choose* being born. This choice itself is integrally affected with facticity since I am not able not to choose, but this facticity in turn will appear only in so far as I surpass it toward my ends. Thus facticity is everywhere but inapprehensible; I never encounter anything except my responsibility. That is why I can not ask, "*Why* was I born?" or curse the day of my birth or declare that I did not ask to be born, for these various attitudes toward my birth — *i.e.*, toward the *fact* that I realize a presence in the world — are absolutely nothing else but ways of assuming this birth in full responsibility and of making it *mine*. Here again I encounter only myself and my projects so that finally my abandonment — *i.e.*, my facticity — consists simply in the fact that I am condemned to be wholly responsible for myself. I am the being which *is* in such a way that in its being its being is in question. And this "is" of my being *is* as present and inapprehensible.

Under these conditions since every event in the world can be revealed to me only as an *opportunity* (an opportunity made use of, lacked, neglected, *etc.*), or better yet since everything which happens to us can be considered as a *chance* (*i.e.*, can appear to us only as a way of realizing this being which is in question in our being) and since others as transcendences-transcended are themselves only *opportunities* and *chances*, the responsibility of the for-itself extends to the entire world as a peopled-world. It is precisely thus that the for-itself apprehends itself in anguish; that is, as a being which is neither the foundation of its own being nor of the Other's being nor of the in-itselfs which form the world, but a being which is compelled to decide the meaning of being — within it and everywhere outside of it. The one who realizes in anguish his condition as *being* thrown into a responsibility which extends to his very abandonment has no longer either remorse or regret or excuse; he is no longer anything but a freedom which perfectly reveals itself and whose being resides in this very revelation. But as we pointed out at the beginning of this work, most of the time we flee anguish in bad faith.

MAURICE MERLEAU-PONTY

Maurice Merleau-Ponty (see also chapter 4) was a phenomenologist whose primary work was in philosophical psychology. Like Sartre, he viewed freedom as implicit in the capacity of consciousness to transcend its situation and choose from a variety of options. Unlike Sartre, he did not view such freedom as total. By our choices, we do create ourselves, he agreed. But, as the following excerpt indicates, for Merleau-Ponty there is a "sedimentation of our life" through those choices. This "sedimentation" makes some choices more "probable" than others. The following selection clarifies Merleau-Ponty's positive view on this subject and his disagreements with Sartre.

Freedom

Again, it is clear that no causal relationship is conceivable between the subject and his body, his world or his society. Only at the cost of losing the basis of all my certainties can I question what is conveyed to me by my presence to myself. Now the moment I turn to myself in order to describe myself, I have a glimpse of an anonymous flux, a comprehensive project in which there are so far no 'states of consciousness', nor, *a fortiori*, qualifications of any sort. For myself I am neither 'jealous', nor 'inquisitive', nor 'hunchbacked', nor 'a civil servant'. It is often a matter of surprise that the cripple or the invalid can put up with himself. The reason is that such people are not for themselves deformed or at death's door. Until the final coma, the dying man is inhabited by a consciousness, he is all that he sees, and enjoys this much of an outlet. Consciousness can never objectify itself into invalid-consciousness or cripple-consciousness, and even if the old man complains of his age or the cripple of his deformity, they can do so only by comparing themselves with others, or seeing themselves through the eyes of others, that is, by taking a statistical and objective view of themselves, so that such complaints are never absolutely genuine: when he is back in the heart of his own consciousness, each of us feels beyond his limitations and thereupon resigns himself to them. They are the price which we automatically pay for being in the world, a formality which we take for granted. Hence we may speak disparagingly of our looks and still not want to change our face for another. No idiosyncrasy can, seemingly, be attached to the insuperable generality of consciousness, nor can any limit be set to this immeasurable power of escape. In order to be determined (in the two senses of that

From Maurice Merleau-Ponty, *The Phenomenology of Perception*, translated by Colin Smith, 1962. Reprinted with permission of Routledge & Kegan Paul.

word) by an external factor, it is necessary that I should be a thing. Neither my freedom nor my universality can admit of any eclipse. It is inconceivable that I should be free in certain of my actions and determined in others: how should we understand a dormant freedom that gave full scope to determinism? And if it is assumed that it is snuffed out when it is not in action, how could it be rekindled? If *per impossibile* I had once succeeded in *making myself into* a thing, how should I subsequently reconvert myself to consciousness? Once I am free, I am not to be counted among things, and I must then be uninterruptedly free. Once my actions cease to be mine, I shall never recover them, and if I lose my hold on the world, it will never be restored to me. It is equally inconceivable that my liberty should be attenuated; one cannot be to some extent free, and if, as is often said, motives incline me in a certain direction, one of two things happens: either they are strong enough to force me to act, in which case there is no freedom, or else they are not strong enough, and then freedom is complete, and as great in the worst torments as in the peace of one's home. We ought, therefore, to reject not only the idea of causality, but also that of motivation.[1] The alleged motive does not burden my decision; on the contrary my decision lends the motive its force. Everything that I 'am' in virtue of nature or history — hunchbacked, handsome or Jewish — I never am completely for myself, as we have just explained: and I may well be these things for other people, nevertheless I remain free to posit another person as a consciousness whose views strike through to my very being, or on the other hand merely as an object. It is also true that this option is itself a form of constraint: if I am ugly, I have the choice between being an object of disapproval or disapproving of others. I am left free to be a masochist or a sadist, but not free to ignore others. But this dilemma, which is given as part of the human lot, is not one for me as pure consciousness: it is still I who makes another to be for me and makes each of us be as human beings. Moreover, even if existence as a human being were imposed upon me, the manner alone being left to my choice, and considering this choice itself and ignoring the small number of forms it might take, it would still be a free choice. If it is said that my temperament inclines me particularly to either sadism or masochism, it is still merely a manner of speaking, for my temperament exists only for the second order knowledge that I gain about myself when I see myself as others see me, and in so far as I recognize it, confer value upon it, and in that sense, choose it. What misleads us on this, is that we often look for freedom in the voluntary deliberation which examines one motive after another and seems to opt for the weightiest or most convincing. In reality the deliberation follows the decision, and it is my secret decision which brings the motives to light, for it would be difficult to conceive what the force of a

---

[1] See J. P. Sartre, *L'Être et le Néant*, pp. 508 and ff.

motive might be in the absence of a decision which it confirms or to which it runs counter. When I have abandoned a project, the motives which I thought held me to it suddenly lose their force and collapse. In order to resuscitate them, an effort is required on my part to reopen time and set me back to the moment preceding the making of the decision. Even while I am deliberating, already I find it an effort to suspend time's flow, and to keep open a situation which I feel is closed by a decision which is already there and which I am holding off. That is why it so often happens that after giving up a plan I experience a feeling of relief: 'After all, I wasn't all that involved'; the debate was purely a matter of form, and the deliberation a mere parody, for I had decided against from the start.

We often see the weakness of the will brought forward as an argument against freedom. And indeed, although I can will myself to adopt a course of conduct and act the part of a warrior or a seducer, it is not within my power to be a warrior or seducer with ease and in a way that 'comes naturally'; really to *be* one, that is. But neither should we seek freedom in the act of will, which is, in its very meaning, something short of an act. We have recourse to an act of will only in order to go against our true decision, and, as it were, for the purpose of proving our powerlessness. If we had really and truly made the conduct of the warrior or the seducer our own, then we should *be* one or the other. Even what are called obstacles to freedom are in reality deployed by it. An unclimbable rock face, a large or small, vertical or slanting rock, are things which have no meaning for anyone who is not intending to surmount them, for a subject whose projects do not carve out such determinate forms from the uniform mass of the *in itself* and cause an orientated world to arise — a significance in things. There is, then, ultimately nothing that can set limits to freedom, except those limits that freedom itself has set in the form of its various initiatives, so that the subject has simply the external world that he gives himself. Since it is the latter who, on coming into being, brings to light significance and value in things, and since no thing can impinge upon it except through acquiring, thanks to it, significance and value, there is no action of things on the subject, but merely a signification (in the active sense), a centrifugal *Sinngebung*. The choice would seem to lie between scientism's conception of causality, which is incompatible with the consciousness which we have of ourselves, and the assertion of an absolute freedom divorced from the outside. . . . Either they all lie within our power, or none does.

The result, however, of this first reflection on freedom would appear to be to rule it out altogether. If indeed it is the case that our freedom is the same in all our actions, and even in our passions, if it is not to be measured in terms of our conduct, and if the slave displays freedom as much by living in fear as by breaking his chains, then it cannot be held that there is such a thing as *free action*, freedom being anterior to all actions. In any case it will not be possible to declare: 'Here freedom makes its appearance', since free action, in order to be discernible, has to stand out against a background of life from which it is entirely, or almost entirely, absent. We may say in this case that it is everywhere, but equally nowhere. In the name of freedom we reject the idea of acquisition, since freedom has become a primordial acquisition and, as it were, our state of nature. Since we do not have to provide it, it is the gift granted to us of having no gift, it is the nature of consciousness which consists in having no nature, and in no case can it find external expression or a place in our life. The idea of action, therefore, disappears: nothing can pass from us to the world, since we are nothing that can be specified, and since the non-being which constitutes us could not possibly find its way into the world's plenum. There are merely intentions immediately followed by their effects, and we are very near to the Kantian idea of an intention which is tantamount to the act, which Scheler countered with the argument that the cripple who would like to be able to save a drowning man and the good swimmer who actually saves him do not have the same experience of autonomy. The very idea of choice vanishes, for to choose is to choose *something* in which freedom sees, at least for a moment, a symbol of itself. There is free choice only if freedom comes into play in its decision, and posits the situation chosen as a situation of freedom. A freedom which has no need to be exercised because it is already acquired could not commit itself in this way: it knows that the following instant will find it, come what may, just as free and just as indeterminant. The very notion of freedom demands that our decision should plunge into the future, that something should have been *done* by it, that the subsequent instant should benefit from its predecessor and, though not necessitated, should be at least required by it. If freedom is doing, it is necessary that what it does should not be immediately undone by a new freedom. Each instant, therefore, must not be a closed world; one instant must be able to commit its successors and, a decision once taken and action once begun, I must have something acquired at my disposal, I must benefit from my impetus, I must be inclined to carry on, and there must be a bent or propensity of the mind. It was Descartes who held that conservation demands a power as great as does creation; a view which implies a realistic notion of the instant. It is true that the instant is not a philosopher's fiction. It is the point at which one project is brought to fruition and another begun[2] — the point at which my gaze is transferred from one end to another, it is the *Augen-Blick*. But this break in time cannot occur unless each of the two spans is of a piece. Consciousness, it is said, is, though not atomized into instants, at least haunted by the spectre of the instant which it is obliged continually to exorcise by a free act. We shall

[2] J. P. Sartre, *L'Être et le Néant*, p. 544.

soon see that we have indeed always the power to interrupt, but it implies in any case a power to *begin,* for there would be no severance unless freedom had taken up its abode somewhere and were preparing to move it. Unless there are cycles of behaviour, open situations requiring a certain completion and capable of constituting a background to either a confirmatory or transformatory decision, we never experience freedom. The choice of intelligible character is excluded, not only because there is no time anterior to time, but because choice presupposes a prior commitment and because the idea of an initial choice involves a contradiction. If freedom is to have *room* in which to move, if it is to be describable as freedom, there must be something to hold it away from its objectives, it must have a *field,* which means that there must be for it special possibilities, or realities which tend to cling to being. As J. P. Sartre himself observes, dreaming is incompatible with freedom because, in the realm of imagination, we have no sooner taken a certain significance as our goal than we already believe that we have intuitively brought it into being, in short, because there is no obstacle and nothing *to do.*[3] It is established that freedom is not to be confused with those abstract decisions of will at grips with motives or passions, for the classical conception of deliberation is relevant only to a freedom 'in bad faith' which secretly harbours antagonistic motives without being prepared to act on them, and so itself manufactures the alleged proofs of its impotence. We can see, beneath these noisy debates and these fruitless efforts to 'construct' ourselves, the tacit decisions whereby we have marked out round ourselves the field of possibility, and it is true that nothing is done as long as we cling to these fixed points, and everything is easy as soon as we have weighed anchor. This is why our freedom is not to be sought in spurious discussion on the conflict between a style of life which we have no wish to reappraise and circumstances suggestive of another: the real choice is that of whole character and our manner of being in the world. But either this total choice is never uttered, since it is the silent upsurge of our being in the world, in which case it is not clear in what sense it could be said to be ours, since this freedom glides over itself and is the equivalent of a fate — or else our choice of ourselves is truly a choice, a conversion involving our whole existence. In this case, however, there is presupposed a previous acquisition which the choice sets out to modify and it founds a new tradition: this lead us to ask whether the perpetual severance in terms of which we initially defined freedom is not simply the negative aspect of our universal commitment to a world, and whether our indifference to each determinate thing does not express merely our involvement in all; whether the ready-made freedom from which we started is not reducible to a power of initiative, which cannot be trans-

---

[3] Ibid., p. 562.

formed into *doing* without taking up some proposition of the world, and whether, in short, concrete and actual freedom is not indeed to be found in this exchange. It is true that nothing has *significance* and value for anyone but *me* and through anyone but me, but this proposition remains indeterminate and is still indistinguishable from the Kantian idea of a consciousness which 'finds in things only what it has put into them', and from the idealist refutation of realism, as long as we fail to make clear how we understand significance and the self. . . .

When I say that this rock is unclimbable, it is certain that this attribute, like that of being big or little, straight and oblique, and indeed like all attributes in general, can be conferred upon it only by the project of climbing it, and by a human presence. It is, therefore, freedom which brings into being the obstacles to freedom, so that the latter can be set over against it as its bounds. However, it is clear that, one and the same project being given, one rock will appear as an obstacle, and another, being more negotiable, as a means. My freedom, then, does not so contrive it that this way there is an obstacle, and that way a way through, it arranges for there to be obstacles and ways through in general; it does not draw the particular outline of this world, but merely lays down its general structures. It may be objected that there is no difference; if my freedom conditions the structure of the 'there is', that of the 'here' and the 'there', it is present wherever these structures arise. We cannot distinguish the quality of 'obstacle' from the obstacle itself, and relate one to freedom and the other to the world in itself which, without freedom, would be merely an amorphous and unnameable mass. It is not, therefore, outside myself that I am able to find a limit to my freedom. But do I not find it in myself? We must indeed distinguish between my express intentions, for example the plan I now make to climb those mountains, and general intentions which evaluate the potentialities of my environment. Whether or not I have decided to climb them, these mountains appear high to me, because they exceed my body's power to take them in its stride, and, even if I have just read *Micromégas*, I cannot so contrive it that they are small for me. Underlying myself as a thinking subject, who am able to take my place at will on Sirius or on the earth's surface, there is, therefore, as it were a natural self which does not budge from its terrestrial situation and which constantly adumbrates absolute valuations. What is more, my projects as a thinking being are clearly modelled on the latter; if I elect to see things from the point of view of Sirius, it is still to my terrestrial experience that I must have recourse in order to do so; I may say, for example, that the Alps are *molehills*. In so far as I have hands, feet, a body, I sustain around me intentions which are not dependent upon my decisions and which affect my surroundings in a way which I do not choose. These intentions are general in a double sense: firstly in the sense that they constitute a system in which all possible objects are simultaneously included; if the mountain appears high and upright, the tree appears small and sloping; and furthermore in the sense that they are not simply mine, they originate from other than myself, and I am not surprised to find them in all psycho-physical subjects organized as I am. . . . It is, there-fore, true that there are no obstacles in themselves, but the self which qualifies them as such is not some acosmic subject; it runs ahead of itself in relation to things in order to confer upon them the form of things. There is an autochthonous significance of the world which is constituted in the dealings which our incarnate existence has with it, and which provides the ground of every deliberate *Sinngebung.*

This is true not only of an impersonal and, all in all, abstract function such as 'external perception'. There is something comparable present in all evaluations. It has been perceptively remarked that pain and fatigue can never be regarded as causes which 'act' upon my liberty, and that, in so far as I may experience either at any given moment, they do not have their origin outside me, but always have a significance and express my attitude towards the world. Pain makes me give away and say what I ought to have kept to myself, fatigue makes me break my journey. We all know the moment at which we decide no longer to endure pain or fatigue, and when, simultaneously, they become intolerable in fact. Tiredness does not halt my companion, because he likes the clamminess of his body, the heat of the road and the sun, in short, because he likes to feel himself in the midst of things, to feel their rays converging upon him, to be the cynosure of all this light, and an objective of touch for the earth's crust. My own fatigue brings me to a halt because I dislike it, because I have chosen differently my manner of being in the world, because, for instance, I endeavour, not to be in nature, but rather to win the recogni-tion of others. I am free in relation to fatigue to precisely the extent that I am free in relation to my being in the world, free to make my way by transforming it.[4] But here once more we must recognize a sort of sedi-mentation of our life: an attitude towards the world, when it has received frequent confirmation, acquires a favoured status for us. Yet since freedom does not tolerate any motive in its path, my habitual being in the world is at each moment equally precarious, and the complexes which I have allowed to develop over the years always remain equally soothing, and the free act can with no difficulty blow them sky-high. However, having built our life upon an inferiority complex which has been opera-tive for twenty years, it is not *probable* that we shall change. It is clear what a summary rationalism might say in reply to such a hybrid notion: there are no degrees of possibility; either the free act is no longer possi-ble, or it is still possible, in which case freedom is complete. In short, 'probable' is meaningless. It is a notion belonging to statistical thought,

---

[4] J. P. Sartre, *L'Être et le Néant*, pp. 531 and ff.

which is not thought at all, since it does not concern any particular thing actually existing, any moment of time, any concrete event. 'It is improbable that Paul will give up writing bad books' means nothing, since Paul may well decide to write no more such books. The probable is everywhere and nowhere, a reified fiction, with only a psychological existence; it is not an ingredient of the world. And yet we have already met it a little while ago in the perceived *world*. The mountain is great or small to the extent that, as a perceived thing, it is to be found in the field of my possible actions, and in relation to a level which is not only that of my individual life, but that of 'any man'. Generality and probability are not fictions, but phenomena; we must therefore find a phenomenological basis for statistical thought. It belongs necessarily to a being which is fixed, situated and surrounded by things in the world. 'It is improbable' that I should at this moment destroy an inferiority complex in which I have been content to live for twenty years. That means that I have committed myself to inferiority, that I have made it my abode, that this past, though not a fate, has at least a specific weight and is not a set of events over there, at a distance from me, but the atmosphere of my present. The rationalist's dilemma: either the free act is possible, or it is not — either the event originates in me or is imposed on me from the outside, does not apply to our relations with the world and with our past. Our freedom does not destroy our situation, but gears itself to it: as long as we are alive, our situation is open, which implies both that it calls up specially favoured modes of resolution, and also that it is powerless to bring one into being by itself. . . .

What, then, becomes of the freedom we spoke about at the outset, if this point of view is taken? I can no longer pretend to be a cipher, and to choose myself continually from the starting point of nothing at all. If it is through subjectivity that nothingness appears in the world, it can equally be said that it is through the world that nothingness comes into being. I am a general refusal to be anything, accompanied surreptitiously by a continual acceptance of such and such a qualified form of being. *For even this general refusal is still one manner of being, and has its place in the world*. It is true that I can at any moment interrupt my projects. But what *is* this power? It is the power to begin something else, for we never remain suspended in nothingness. We are always in a plenum, in being, just as a face, even in repose, even in death, is always doomed to express something (there are people whose faces, in death, bear expressions of surprise, or peace, or discretion), and just as silence is still a modality of the world of sound. I may defy all accepted form, and spurn everything, for there is no case in which I am utterly committed: but in this case I do not withdraw into my freedom, I commit myself elsewhere. Instead of thinking about my bereavement, I look at my nails, or have lunch, or engage in politics. Far from its being the case that my freedom is always unattended, it is never without an accomplice, and its power of perpetually tearing itself away finds its fulcrum in my universal commitment in the world. My actual freedom is not on the hither side of my being, but before me, in things. We must not say that I continually choose myself, on the excuse that I *might* continually refuse what I am. Not to refuse is not the same thing as to choose. We could identify drift and action only by depriving the implicit of all phenomenal value, and at every instant arraying the world before us in perfect transparency, that is, by destroying the world's 'worldliness'. Consciousness holds itself responsible for everything, and takes everything upon itself, but it has nothing of its own and makes its life in the world. We are led to conceive freedom as a choice continually remade as long as we do not bring in the notion of a generalized or natural time. We have seen that there is no natural time, if we understand thereby a time of things without subjectivity. There is, however, at least a generalized time, and this is what the common notion of time envisages. It is the perpetual reiteration of the sequence of past, present, and future. It is, as it were, a constant disappointment and failure. This is what is expressed by saying that it is continuous: the present which it brings to us is never a present for good, since it is already over when it appears, and the future has, in it, only the appearance of a goal towards which we make our way, since it quickly comes into the present, whereupon we turn towards a fresh future. This time is the time of our bodily functions, which like it, are cyclic, and it is also that of nature with which we co-exist. It offers us only the adumbration and the abstract form of a commitment, since it continually erodes itself and undoes that which it has just done. As long as we place in opposition, with no mediator, the For Itself and the In Itself, and fail to perceive, between ourselves and the world, this natural foreshadowing of a subjectivity, this prepersonal time which rests upon itself, acts are needed to sustain the upsurge of time, and everything becomes equally a matter of choice, the respiratory reflex no less than the moral decision, conservation no less than creation. As far as we are concerned, consciousness attributes this power of universal constitution to itself only if it ignores the event which upholds it and is the occasion of its birth. A consciousness for which the world 'can be taken for granted', which finds it 'already constituted' and present even in consciousness itself, does not *absolutely* choose either its being or its manner of being.

What then is freedom? To be born is both to be born of the world and to be born into the world. The world is already constituted, but also never completely constituted; in the first case we are acted upon, in the second we are open to an infinite number of possibilities. But this analysis is still abstract, for we exist in both ways *at once*. There is, therefore, never determinism and never absolute choice, I am never a thing and never bare consciousness. In fact, even our own pieces of initiative, even the situations which we have chosen, bear us on, once they have been entered upon by virtue of a state rather than an act. The generality of the 'rôle' and of the situation comes to the aid of decision, and in this exchange between the situation and the person who takes it up, it is impossible to determine precisely the 'share contributed by the situation' and the 'share contributed by freedom'. Let us suppose that a man is tortured to make him talk. If he refuses to give the names and addresses which it is desired to extract from him, this does not arise from a solitary and unsupported decision: the man still feels himself to be with his comrades, and, being still involved in the common struggle, he is as it were incapable of talking. Or else, for months or years, he has, in his mind, faced this test and staked his whole life upon it. Or finally, he wants to prove, by coming through it, what he has always thought and said about freedom. These motives do not cancel out freedom, but at least ensure that it does not go unbuttressed in being. What withstands pain is not, in short, a bare consciousness, but the prisoner with his comrades or with those he loves and under whose gaze he lives; or else the awareness of his proudly willed solitude, which again is a certain mode of the *Mit-Sein*. And probably the individual in his prison daily reawakens these phantoms, which give back to him the strength he gave to them. But conversely, in so far as he has committed himself to this action, formed a bond with his comrades or adopted this morality, it is because the historical situation, the comrades, the world around him seemed to him to expect that conduct from him. The analysis could be pursued endlessly in this way. We choose our world and the world chooses us. What is certain, in any case, is that we can at no time set aside within ourselves a redoubt to which being does not find its way through, without seeing this freedom, immediately and by the very fact of being a living experience, take on the appearance of being and become a motive and a buttress. Taken concretely, freedom is always a meeting of the inner and the outer — even the prehuman and prehistoric freedom with which we began — and it shrinks without ever disappearing altogether in direct proportion to the lessening of the *tolerance* allowed by the bodily and institutional data of our lives. There is, as Husserl says, on the one hand a 'field of freedom' and on the other a 'conditioned freedom'; not that freedom is absolute within the limits of this field and non-existent outside it (like the perceptual field, this one has no traceable boundaries), but because I enjoy immediate and remote possibilities. Our commitments sustain our power and there is no freedom without some power. Our freedom, it is said, is either total or non-existent. This dilemma belongs to objective thought and its stable-companion, analytical reflection. If indeed we place ourselves within being, it must necessarily be the case that our actions must have their origin outside us, and if we revert to constituting consciousness, they must originate within. But we have learnt precisely to recognize the order of phenomena. We are involved in the world and with others in an inextricable tangle. The idea of situation rules out absolute freedom at the source of our commitments, and equally, indeed, at their terminus. No commitment, not even commitment in the Hegelian State, can make me leave behind all differences and free me for anything. This universality itself, from the mere fact of its being experienced, would stand out as a particularity against the world's background, for existence both generalizes and particularizes everything at which it aims, and cannot ever be finally complete.

The synthesis of *in itself* and *for itself* which brings Hegelian freedom into being has, however, its truth. In a sense, it is the very definition of existence, since it is effected at every moment before our eyes in the phenomenon of presence, only to be quickly re-enacted, since it does not conjure away our finitude. By taking up a present, I draw together and transform my past, altering its significance, freeing and detaching myself from it. But I do so only by committing myself somewhere else. Psychoanalytical treatment does not bring about its cure by producing direct awareness of the past, but in the first place by binding the subject to his doctor through new existential relationships. It is not a matter of giving scientific assent to the psychoanalytical interpretation, and discovering a notional significance for the past; it is a matter of reliving this or that as significant, and this the patient succeeds in doing only by seeing his past in the perspective of his co-existence with the doctor. The complex is not dissolved by a non-instrumental freedom, but rather displaced by a new pulsation of time with its own supports and motives. The same applies in all cases of coming to awareness: they are real only if they are sustained by a new commitment. Now this commitment too is entered into in the sphere of the implicit, and is therefore valid only for a certain temporal cycle. The choice which we make of our life is always based on a certain givenness. My freedom can draw life away from its spontaneous course, but only by a series of unobtrusive deflections which necessitate first of all following its course — not by any absolute creation. All explanations of my conduct in terms of my past, my temperament and my environment are therefore true, provided that they be regarded not as separable contributions, but as moments of my total being, the significance of which I am entitled to make explicit in various ways, without its ever being possible to say whether I confer their meaning upon them or receive it from them. I am a psychological and historical structure, and have received, with existence, a manner of existing, a style. All my actions and thoughts stand in a relationship to this structure, and even a philosopher's thought is merely a way of making explicit his hold on the world, and what he is. The fact remains that I am free, not in spite of, or on the hither side of, these motivations, but by means of them. For this significant life, this certain significance of nature and history which I am, does not limit my access to the world, but on the contrary is my means of entering into communication with it. It is by being unrestrictedly and unreservedly what I am at present that I have a chance of moving forward; it is by living my time that I am able to understand other times, by plunging into the present and the world, by taking on deliberately what I am fortuitously, by willing what I will and doing what I do, that I can go further. I can miss being free only if I try to bypass my natural and social situation by refusing to take it up, in the first place, instead of assuming it in order to join up with the natural and human world. Nothing determines me from outside, not because nothing acts upon me, but, on the contrary, because I am from the start outside myself and open to the world. We are *true* through and through, and have with us, by the mere fact of belonging to the world, and not merely being in the world in the way that things are, all that we need to transcend ourselves. We need to have no fear that our choices or actions restrict our liberty, since choice and action alone cuts us loose from our anchorage. Just as reflection borrows its wish for absolute sufficiency from the perception which causes a thing to appear, and as in this way idealism tacitly uses that 'primary opinion' which it would like to destroy as opinion, so freedom flounders in the contradictions of commitment, and fails to realize that, without the roots which it thrusts into the world, it would not be freedom at all. Shall I make this promise? Shall I risk my life for so little? Shall I give up my liberty in order to save liberty? There is no theoretical reply to these questions. But there are these *things* which stand, irrefutable, there is before you this person whom you love, there are these men whose existence around you is that of slaves, and *your* freedom cannot be willed without leaving behind its singular relevance, and without willing freedom *for all*. Whether it is a question of things or of historical situations, philosophy has no other function than to teach us to see them clearly once more, and it is true to say that it comes into being by destroying itself as separate philosophy. But what is here required is silence, for only the hero lives out his relation to men and the world. 'Your son is caught in the fire; you are the one who will save him. . . . If there is an obstacle, you would be ready to give your shoulder provided only that you can charge down that obstacle. Your abode is your act itself. Your act is you. . . . You give yourself in exchange. . . . Your significance shows itself, effulgent. It is your duty, your hatred, your love, your steadfastness, your ingenuity. . . . Man is but a network of relationships, and these alone matter to him.'[5]

[5] A. de Saint-Exupéry, *Pilote de Guerre*, pp. 171, 174, 176.

GABRIEL MARCEL

Gabriel Marcel (1889–1973) is a leading twentieth-century existentialist thinker. A convert to Catholicism, he wrote consistently of the connections between faith and human purpose and the need for today's individual to reject mass "techniques" and specialization. Like Sartre, Marcel criticizes the notion that freedom is a thing or even an attribute of Dasein. But, where for Sartre we are "condemned to be free," Marcel insists on the connection between freedom and hope. And, like Merleau-Ponty, he emphasizes the limitations of one's concrete conditions. Whether this difference results from a contrasting interpretation of our nature or is inextricably tied to Marcel's theism is an open question. In his analysis of "fraternity" as linked to freedom, he foreshadows the discussion in chapter 6 of "The Other."

Mortality, Hope, and Freedom

There is a temptation which seems for many men of our time to be almost irresistible to argue from the fact of man's mortality that he is negligible as an individual, and to transfer to the collective and to society that regard of which he has been judged positively unworthy. But to reason in this way is to follow a road which leads to tyranny and to servitude. Now the paradox which we considered briefly in the preceding chapter is that we can, on the contrary, find in man's finitude itself the principle of his essential dignity. How is this possible? We have to take as a point of departure the fact that man is the only being known to us who knows himself to be mortal. Moreover, in the perspective we have adopted this fact reveals that man transcends the society to which a certain type of "reason" pretends to sacrifice him: for this very society, if it has a destiny, is not conscious of it, is incapable of having a conception of it, and *a fortiori* of mastering it. In the final reckoning, then, the priority rests with the individual.

In any case, we must not fail to note that the fact of this knowledge of one's own mortality involves the same indeterminateness with regard to value that I drew attention to earlier: from this ambiguous situation we can emerge only on condition that we pass beyond the limits of the ego. In the text of *Les Coeurs avides* which I have cited, Arnaud was meditating not on his own mortality, but on that of his father. And this meditation was suffused with a compassion which was also a form of piety. It is precisely the nature of this piety which is to be accounted for, without, however, assuming that it can be reduced to something simpler and "self-evident" in the Cartesian sense.

I believe that our first obligation is resolutely to avoid the reductionist interpretation which would see in this piety a weakened and faded survival of superstitious fears. Of course, such attempts at derivation will always be possible, but they would all be open to the central objection that almost inevitably applies to any claim that "such and such is *nothing but* this or that" in other words, to the denial of the distinctive quality of a given experience in the name of genetic considerations. The truth would seem to be rather that piety toward the dead, or toward those whose death we anticipate, fulfills a demand for compensation, which pertains perhaps to a secret modality of justice. Everything happens as if the pious man — and I take this adjective in the most nonconfessional sense — felt called upon to oppose to this process of deterioration, operating on the level of corruptible flesh, an inverse movement directed upward, or one might say towards exaltation, had that word not lost its noble and etymological connotation. But here we must probe still deeper. What takes place — and that usually beyond the reach of explicit formulation — is the confidence that in death one's being will raise itself to an integrity which life lived would perhaps not have allowed it, because of life's perpetually dispersed, tortured, and torn character. The famous line of Mallarmé, "Tel qu'en lui-même enfin l'éternité le change,"[1] happily renders this accession to eternity.

It is true that what is sometimes disclosed at the end of a life is its fundamental nullity, its inanity, or, what is even worse than nothingness, a perverted will embodied in a chain of actions, a will to destroy everything of man's which makes for communication and peace. But it seems to me that it would always be difficult to hold to such a judgment; inevitably, something comes to attenuate its force and to refocus it into a question. For this same being who seemed to have willed evil was either deprived of love, in which case it is as if at the close of his existence he himself became accuser, or else he was loved, and this love to which he could not respond cannot help but take on the character of an intercession. But it is true that this word "intercession" can have meaning only if it is unspoken, and if the intersubjective consciousness refuses to admit or, *a fortiori*, to proclaim the finality of death. This is not the place to enter directly into the complex and involved argument which I have elsewhere devoted to the problem of survival, and which I have already touched upon in connection with *L'Iconoclaste*. Here I would draw attention to just one or two points:

To begin with, it seems to me that whatever our religious or agnostic position we have to reject any negativist dogmatism, which is usually

[1] "As eternity at last gives him back to himself." (Tr.)

founded on a superannuated scientism. Furthermore, we must acknowledge that, contrary to the claim of societies under the domination of an official atheism, which allow themselves to be ruled by the logic of that same atheism, the exclusion of human life from any extension into the realm of the invisible is by no means reflected in a greater respect for human life or a more solicitous treatment of it; nor has it benefited from the fact that theoretically it is regarded as a good whose loss is irretrievable. I am rather inclined to think that in the societies in question a devaluation of life has come about in the sense that one might speak of a currency devaluation. Wars and revolutions with their fearful consumption of human lives have had such an effect. I recall the comment of a well-known general, made in the presence of a relative of mine who was a General Staff Officer, on the day after a bloody offensive action during the first World War: "Men are replaceable." Scandalous, and even sacrilegious words, for in fact a human individual is precisely *that which is not replaceable*. But it must be emphasized that our time, more than any other, has succeeded in introducing a merchandising distinction between "wholesale" and "retail" into a domain from which it should have been forever excluded. But that is one consequence among many others of a materialism that in our time pervades not only our opinions but our way of life, and which, with an inconsistency that does no honor to human nature, is even coexistent in some people — I would not say with authentic religious beliefs, but with the ghosts of such beliefs. . . .

But, generally speaking, philosophers, up to the present time, have paid almost no attention to certain structural characteristics of the human being which allow for the insertion of freedom into the fabric of our existence. Once more, unless one is the champion of a scientific materialism which seems to be plainly dated, I do not see how it can be seriously maintained that survival after death is purely and simply unthinkable. A margin of incertitude remains, and it is open to reflection as an aspect of the mystery involved in our destiny. And surely it would be equally wrong to regard this margin as fixed and constant, and therefore independent of the ways in which we tend to orient our existence in this world. It is plain that the more each one of us takes himself for a center, considering others only in relation to himself, the more the idea of the beyond will be emptied of all meaning, for this world beyond will then appear as a senseless prolongation. That is its character in a perspective like Sartre's where "the other" is thought of primarily as a threat to my integrity, or, in other words, my self-sufficiency.* On the contrary, the more the other, or others, will have become an integral part of my experience, the more I will be led to recognize their irreducible value as well as

* See chapter 6, pp. 371–81, for a discussion of Sartre's view of interpersonal relationships.

the difficulty *for us* of achieving a lasting harmony here below; and the more necessary it will be to conceive a mode of existence which is different from the one we have known, and which will lead us toward the real and *pleromatic* unity where we will be all in all.

I am by no means underestimating the force of the objection which is unfailingly provoked by such an assertion. It will be ascribed to the kind of wishful thinking which rigorous reflection is obliged to reject.

But it is at this juncture that the reflections on hope which I was led to develop in the midst of the second World War become relevant. I took as my point of departure the idea that desire and hope must be carefully distinguished, and that Spinoza in particular erred in identifying them. I had already observed in *Positions et approches concrètes* that the opposition is not, as Spinoza said, between fear and hope, but rather between fear and desire, and I added that the negative correlative of hope is to adopt the perspective of the worst, as the defeatist does, for example. But ten years after this book was written I tried in a more searching way to cast light on some of the fundamental characteristics of hope, basing my reflection on the situation which was ours as Frenchmen, namely, defeat and oppression by the enemy, or, more plainly still, the situation of prisoners awaiting liberation. What was revealed to me then, in a *syneidesis* like those to which I referred earlier, is that hope is always tied to an experience of captivity: "But I appear to myself as captive if I am conscious not only of being thrown into a situation, but engaged by it — under external constraint — in a mode of existence which carries with it restrictions of all kinds on my own action . . .Such a situation makes it impossible for me to rise to an experienced plenitude either of feeling or of thought." But what I realize correlatively is that the subject of "I hope" is not reducible to the ego which is the subject of desire, or, in other words, that the subject of "I hope" excludes all claims. Such claims are in a certain way present in optimism, as found in someone who, confronted with a tragic situation, declares in the name of a wisdom to which he apparently lays claim, "I tell you that things will work out" — while his defeatist interlocutor will say with the same assurance, "Well, I say that nothing will work out and the worst will happen." It is as if hope were situated in another dimension of which it could be said that it is that of humility and patience, a patience which is perhaps a profound and secret characteristic of life. If then we say, as we must, that hope is the act by which the temptation to despair is actively overcome, we must add that this victory is not necessarily accompanied by a feeling of effort; it is even linked to relaxation rather than to tension. But it should be stressed that this relaxation is not, and must not be, a slackening. . . .I mentioned patience above, but it is obvious that this is the very opposite of passivity. We must in fact beware of falling prey to the same confusion to which I have drawn attention in connection with receptivity. As regards hope, nothing could be more mistaken than to see it as a kind of inactive hovering over an event which is expected to come to pass all by itself. It is indeed true that hope or patience can sink to the level where a sense of ease becomes mere slackening. I might quote here a few lines from "Phénoménologie de l'espérance," in *Homo Viator*. I was answering the objection that might be made to the assertion that patience is generally operative in a person — a child, or someone who is sick, for example — while hope operates with respect to a situation which does not seem capable of being personalized:

> On reflection, the gap nonetheless tends to narrow, possibly because I have or have not hope in the being for whom I bear responsibility, and one may justifiably ask oneself whether "I have hope in thee" is not really the most authentic form of the verb "I hope." But this does not exhaust the matter; the nature of the test is revealed in its effect on me, in the way it impinges on my being, insofar as it leaves me open to a permanent alteration. So it is that illness, for example, may make me into that deformed being typified as the professional sick person, who thinks of himself as such and contracts into the *habitus* of a sick person — the same processes holding true in the case of captivity or exile. Insofar as I hope, I release myself from an inner determinism comparable to a cramp, by which I risk — in a testing experience — settling into one of those degraded, fragmented, and finally somnambulistic expressions of the human person, which engenders despair above all because it involves fascination.[2]

This last remark seems to me of the greatest importance, because it underscores the obsessional character of despair. . . .

The philosophic context into which the reflection on freedom is brought into this chapter is likely to surprise the reader. He will ask why we need stress a connection between freedom and hope which does not seem apparent. Here, the controlling fact for me was that, as we have seen — particularly in a certain existential line of thought — an absolutely opposite relation was being articulated. When a philosopher like Sartre dares to write that man is condemned to be free, so that freedom is no longer treated as an achievement but rather as a radical deficiency, there is a great temptation to place freedom at the heart of despair, having only to invent some Marxist device in order to escape the dilemma thereby created. In an existential perspective of that kind one would be disposed to define the free man as the rootless man, knowing and wanting himself as such. This becomes apparent in the literature which we see around us by a peculiar sort of fraternization between the intellectual and the "beatnik," and it is only by exhaustive — though by no means deceptive — dialectical acrobatics that the anarchism so defined by this frater-

---

[2] *Homo Viator*, trans. E. Craufurd (London: Gollanez, 1951), p. 41.

nity can be transmuted into a Marxism which, while certainly heterodox, will try in spite of everything to be accepted or tolerated by the orthodox Marxists. . . .

To begin with, we must take note of the significant fact that not one of us can really say, "I am free." There is no meaning in the statement that man *is* free, and there is of course still less in claiming, with Rousseau, that he is *born* free; there is no more fatal error than that which consists in regarding freedom as an attribute. I am tempted to say that it is exactly the opposite. It is far more appropriate to say that every one of us has to make himself into a free man; that within the bounds of the possible he has to take advantage of the structural conditions of which I have spoken, which make freedom possible. In other words, freedom is a conquest — always partial, always precarious, always challenged. And we should remind ourselves again that it is in the midst of a situation of captivity that freedom can be born, at first in the shape of the aspiration to be free. But the word "aspiration" is misleading; it can correspond to a simple "I should like" which is separated by an abyss from "I want" (*je veux*). And in fact we have seen that hope is itself irreducible to aspiration, since it implies a patience, a vigilance, and a firmness of purpose which are incompatible with a simple "I should like."

To say that the freest man is the one who has the most hope is perhaps above all to indicate that he is the man who has been able to give his existence the richest significance, or stake the most on it. But this is enough to exclude absolutely the pure dilettante, that is, the one who, living only for himself, seeks solely to collect such experiences as will awaken in him, each time with different shades and nuances, a feeling of exaltation which fulfills him for that moment. But from such a flame, can anything remain in the end but ashes?

In the line of thought that I have tried to formulate in the course of this book, it is evident that the stakes I have alluded to here can only be conceived of on the level of intersubjectivity, or, if you wish, fraternity, and perhaps everything that has been said up to now will be clarified if we now postulate that the freest man is also the most fraternal.

But this formula acquires its full meaning only if we bring to light the implications of the word "fraternal." The fraternal man is linked to his neighbor, but in such a way that this tie not only does not fetter him, but frees him from himself. Now what I have tried to show is that this freedom is of primary importance, for each one of us tends to become a prisoner of himself, not only in respect to his material interests, his passions, or simply his prejudices, but still more essentially in the predisposition which inclines him to be centered on himself, and to view everything only from his own perspective. The fraternal man, on the contrary, is somehow enriched by everything which enriches his brother, in that communion which exists between his brother and himself.

But it is not hard to see the role that hope plays here. For to love one's brothers is above all to have hope in them, that is, to go beyond that in their conduct which almost always begins by bruising or disappointing us. And on the other hand experience undeniably shows that the hope which we put in them can help to transform them, while, inversely, if by our thought we enclose them in what strikes us as their nature, we contribute to stopping their spiritual growth. This is manifestly true for the educator. But there is a sense in which it may be said that fraternity implies a mutual education.

Moreover, it seems to me necessary to stress that fraternity excludes the spirit of abstraction and the ideologies in which that spirit tends always to be embodied. Here I come back to what I said before on the difference between equality and fraternity. It might be said that the spirit of abstraction always leads to a kind of segregation, the class segregation practiced in communist countries being in this respect no better than racial segregation. But what is fraternity if not the refusal of all forms of segregation? This refusal, of course, is actually the negative side of the emphasis placed on the universal. But the danger is ever-present, as I have shown, that the universal may wither or deteriorate into a purely abstract relation, and it is precisely to this deterioration that the spirit of fraternity is opposed. Again: fraternity implies a dynamism which is in fact that of love, and not — as with equality — that of the rectifying spirit. But this is of course no more than a schematic way of presenting an opposition which in concrete reality is not always clearly discernible. . . .

In this perspective, nothing seems more absurd than to treat freedom as an attribute, when it can never be more than a partial and precarious victory. To become aware of this, we have only to imagine the confusion into which each of us would be plunged if we were asked, "Are you free?" To such a question no answer is possible, because in fact the question is meaningless. It can only take on meaning if it becomes specific. Suppose, instead, that I am asked, "Do you consider that such and such a step was freely taken — for instance, with reference to your career?" Even in this case a reflection centered on the existential, that is, no longer obsessed with causality — an obsession from which contemporary thought, especially that of Bergson, has helped to free us — will bring to light the difficulties involved in trying to answer such a question honestly. Let us imagine, for example, the case of a man who, without any wish to do so, is obliged to study medicine merely because his father, himself, aged or ill, has passionately desired his son to succeed him in the practice of that profession. If you should ask this young man, "Do you consider that you have freely chosen this profession?" he would no doubt be greatly embarrassed. He would certainly acknowledge having undergone pressure from his father, but it is possible that he would refuse absolutely to consider that pressure as a constraint, or *coactio*. Perhaps he would ascribe to affection or to a sense of duty what others would interpret rather as blackmail, and so he would refuse to admit that his choice was not a free one. But it must be understood as well — and this point seems to me most important, bearing as it does on what I have said previously in connection with *Un Homme de Dieu* — that perhaps in the actual content of life his own way of interpreting his choice in retrospect would be considerably modified. If his professional life is a failure, if he perceives that he should in fact have oriented his existence quite differently, it is probable that he will be inclined to lay stress, resentfully, on the pressure suffered, which would appear a posteriori as a constraint. The reverse would be the case if, having taken a liking to his work, he has on the contrary found success in it and is satisfied that his life has been worthwhile.

Along these lines, one might be tempted to say that the essential question can be formulated only in a personal form, and in the first person, and only from that moment where our life stretches behind us like a well-traveled landscape, reconstructing the progress — so often halting and problematic — that has been ours. At that moment, it seems to me, we can ask ourselves, "Am I conscious of having been a free man?" Certainly it is then that the question takes on meaning, although it is manifestly impossible to answer it by a simple yes or no.

VIKTOR E. FRANKL

Famed psychiatrist Viktor E. Frankl (1905–   ) survived three years in Nazi concentration camps and is the founder of a school of psychotherapy now known as Logotherapy. All of Frankl's writings emphasize the "human dimension" of the search for meaning. The feeling of meaninglessness is, he states, the "mass neurosis" of our age and must be taken more seriously by the psychoanalytic community. His writings borrow much from the tradition of existentialism (though he is critical of certain aspects of that philosophy). In the following excerpt, he discusses his view of freedom and its connection to the therapeutic relationship.

Determinism and Humanism: Critique of Pan-Determinism

The two perennial philosophical issues, the problem of body and mind, and the problem of free choice (or, as it might be expressed, determinism versus indeterminism), cannot be solved. But at least it is possible to identify the reason why they are unsolvable.

The body-mind problem can be reduced to the question: How is it possible to conceive of that unity in diversity which could be the definition of man? And who would deny that there is diversity in man? As Konrad Lorenz says: "The wall separating the two great incommensurables, the physiological and psychological, is unsurmountable. Even the extension of scientific research into the field of psychophysics did not bring us closer to the solution of the body-mind problem."[1] As to the hope that future research might bring a solution, Werner Heisenberg is equally pessimistic, contending that "we do not expect a direct way of understanding between bodily movements and psychological processes, for even in the exact sciences reality breaks down into separate levels."

In fact, we are living in an age of what I would call the pluralism of science, and the individual sciences depict reality in such different ways that the pictures contradict each other. However, it is my contention that the *contradictions do not contradict* the unity of reality. This holds true also of the human reality. In order to demonstrate this, let us recall that each science, as it were, cuts out a cross section of reality. Let us now follow the implications of this analogy from geometry:

[1] *Uber tierisches und menschliches Verhalten*, Munich, 1965, pp. 362 and 372.

If we cut two orthogonal cross sections from a cylinder, the horizontal cross section represents the cylinder as a circle whereas the vertical cross section represents it as a square. But as we know, nobody has managed as yet to transform a circle into a square. Similarly, none has succeeded as yet in bridging the gap between the somatic and psychological aspects of the human reality. And, we may add, nobody is likely to succeed, because the *coincidentia oppositorum,* as Nicholas of Cusa has called it, is not possible within any cross section but only beyond all of them in the next higher dimension. It is no different with man. On the biological level, in the plane of biology, we are confronted with the somatic aspects of man, and on the psychological level, in the plane of psychology, with his psychological aspects. Thus, within the planes of both scientific approaches we are facing diversity but missing the unity in man, because this unity is available only in the human dimension. Only in the human dimension lies the *"unitas multiplex,"* as man has been defined by Thomas Aquinas. This unity is not really a unity *in* diversity but rather a unity *in spite of* diversity.

What is true of the oneness of man, also holds for his openness:

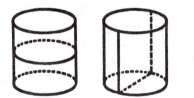

Going back to the cylinder, let us now imagine that it is not a solid but an open vessel, say, a cup. In that case, what will the cross sections be like? While the horizontal one still is a closed circle, in the vertical plane the cup is now seen as an open figure. But as soon as we realize that both figures are mere cross sections, the closedness of one figure is perfectly compatible with the openness of the other. Something analogous holds for man. He too is sometimes portrayed as if he were merely a closed system within which cause-effect relations, such as conditioned or unconditioned reflexes, are operant. On the other hand, being human is profoundly characterized as being open to the world, as Max Scheler, Arnold Gehlen and Adolf Portmann have shown. Or, as Martin Heidegger said, being human is "being in the world." What I have called the self-transcendence of existence denotes the fundamental fact that being human means relating to something, or someone, other than oneself, be it a meaning to fulfill, or human beings to encounter. And existence falters and collapses unless this self-transcendent quality is lived out.

That the self-transcendent quality of existence, the openness of being human, is touched by one cross section and missed by another is understandable. Closedness and openness have become compatible. And I think that the same holds true of freedom and determinism. There is determinism in the psychological dimension, and freedom in the noö-logical dimension, which is the human dimension, the dimension of human phenomena. As to the body-mind problem, we wound up with the phrase "unity in spite of diversity." As to the problem of free choice, we are winding up with the phrase "freedom in spite of determinism." It parallels the phrase once coined by Nicolai Hartmann, "autonomy in spite of dependency."

As a human phenomenon, however, freedom is all too human. Human freedom is finite freedom. Man is not free from conditions. But he is free to take a stand in regard to them. The conditions do not completely condition him. Within limits it is up to him whether or not he succumbs and surrenders to the conditions. He may as well rise above them and by so doing open up and enter the human dimension. As I once put it: As a professor in two fields, neurology and psychiatry, I am fully aware of the extent to which man is subject to biological, psychological and sociological conditions. But in addition to being a professor in two fields I am a survivor of four camps — concentration camps, that is — and as such I also bear witness to the unexpected extent to which man is capable of defying and braving even the worst conditions conceivable. Sigmund Freud once said, "Let us attempt to expose a number of the most diverse people uniformly to hunger. With the increase of the imperative urge of hunger all individual differences will blur, and in their stead will appear the uniform expression of the one unstilled urge." In the concentration camps, however, the reverse was true. People became more diverse. The beast was unmasked — and so was the saint. The hunger was the same but people were different. In truth, calories do not count.

Ultimately, man is not subject to the conditions that confront him; rather, these conditions are subject to his decision. Wittingly or unwittingly, he decides whether he will face up or give in, whether or not he will let himself be determined by the conditions. Of course, it could be objected that such decisions are themselves determined. But it is obvious that this results in a *regressus in infinitum*. A statement by Magda B. Arnold epitomizes this state of affairs and lends itself as an apt conclusion of the discussion: "All choices are caused but they are caused by the chooser."[2]

Interdisciplinary research covers more than one cross section. It prevents one-sidedness. Regarding the problem of free choice, it prevents us from denying, on the one hand, the deterministic and mechanistic aspects of the human reality, or on the other hand, the human freedom to transcend them. This freedom is not denied by determinism but rather by what I am used to calling pan-determinism. In other words, the alternatives really are pan-determinism versus determinism, rather than determinism versus indeterminism. And as to Freud, he only espoused pan-determinism in theory. In practice, he was anything but blind to the human freedom to change, to improve, for instance, when he once defined the goal of psychoanalysis as giving "the patient's ego the freedom to choose one way or the other."[3]

Human freedom implies man's capacity to detach himself from himself. I like to illustrate this capacity with the following story: During World War I a Jewish army doctor was sitting together with his gentile friend, an aristocratic colonel, in a foxhole when heavy shooting began. Teasingly, the colonel said, "You are afraid, aren't you? Just another proof that the Aryan race is superior to the Semitic one." "Sure, I am afraid," was the doctor's answer. "But who is superior? If you, my dear colonel, were as afraid as I am, you would have run away long ago." What counts is not our fears and anxieties as such, but the attitude we adopt toward them. This attitude is freely chosen.

The freedom of choosing an attitude toward our psychological make-up even extends to the pathological aspects of this make-up. Time and again, we psychiatrists meet patients whose response to their delusions is anything but pathological. I have met paranoiacs who, out of their delusional ideas of persecution, have killed their alleged enemies; but I have also met paranoiacs who have forgiven their supposed adversaries. The latter have not acted out of mental illness but rather reacted to this illness out of their humanness. To speak of suicide rather than homicide, there are cases of depression who commit suicide, and there are cases who manage to overcome the suicidal impulse for the sake of a cause or a person. They are too committed to commit suicide, as it were.

I for one am convinced that a psychosis such as a paranoia or an endogenous depression is somatogenic. More specifically, its etiology is biochemical — even though more often than not its exact nature could not yet be determined. Yet we are not justified in making fatalistic inferences. They would not be valid even in cases in which biochemistry is

[2] *The Human Person*, New York, 1954, p. 40.
[3] *The Ego and the Id.* London, 1927, p. 72.

based on heredity. In context with the latter, for instance, I never weary of quoting Johannes Lange, who once reported a case of identical twin brothers. One brother wound up as a cunning criminal. The other wound up as a cunning criminologist. Being cunning might well be a matter of heredity. But becoming a criminal or a criminologist, as the case may be, is a matter of attitude. Heredity is no more than the material from which man builds himself. It is no more than the stones that are, or are not, refused and rejected by the builder. But the builder himself is not built of stones. . . .

Fatalism on the part of the psychiatrist is likely to reinforce fatalism on the part of the patient, which is characteristic of neurosis, anyway. And what is true of psychiatry also holds for sociatry. Pan-determinism serves the criminal as an alibi: it is the mechanisms within him that are blamed. Such an argument, however, proves to be self-defeating. If the defendant alleges that he really was not free and responsible when he committed his crime, the judge may claim the same when passing sentence.

Actually, criminals, at least once the judgment has been passed, do not wish to be regarded as mere victims of psychodynamic mechanisms or conditioning processes. As Scheler once pointed out, man has a *right* to be considered guilty and to be punished. To explain his guilt away by looking at him as the victim of circumstances also means taking away his human dignity. I would say that it is a prerogative of man to become guilty. To be sure, it also is his responsibility to overcome guilt. . . .

Let us turn determinism against pan-determinism. That is, let us attempt a strictly causal explanation of the latter: Let us ask ourselves what are the causes of pan-determinism. I would say that it is lack of discrimination that causes pan-determinism. On the one hand, causes are confounded with reasons. On the other hand, causes are confounded with conditions. What, then, is the difference between causes and reasons? If you cut onions you weep — your tears have a cause. But you have no reason to weep. But if a loved one dies, you have reason to weep. If you do rock climbing and arrive at a height of 10,000 feet you may have to cope with a feeling of oppression and anxiety. This may stem from either a cause or a reason. Lack of oxygen may be the cause. But if you know that you are badly equipped or poorly trained, anxiety has a reason.

Being human has been defined as "being in the world." The world includes reasons and meanings. But reasons and meanings are excluded if you conceive of man as a closed system. What is left is causes and effects. The effects are represented by conditioned reflexes or responses to stimuli. The causes are represented by conditioning processes or drives and instincts. Drives and instincts push but reasons and meanings pull. If you conceive of man in terms of a closed system you notice only forces that push but no motives that pull. Consider the front doors of any American hotel. From inside the lobby you notice only the sign "push."

The sign "pull" is visible only from without. Man has doors as does the hotel. He is no closed monad, and psychology degenerates into some sort of monadology unless it recognizes his openness to the world. This openness of existence is reflected by its self-transcendence. The self-transcendent quality of the human reality in turn is reflected in the "intentional" quality of human phenomena, as Franz Brentano and Edmund Husserl term it. Human phenomena refer and point to "intentional objects."[4] Reasons and meanings represent such objects. They are the logos for which the psyche is reaching out. If psychology is to be worthy of its name it has to recognize both halves of this name, the logos as well as the psyche.

When the self-transcendence of existence is denied, existence itself is distorted. It is reified. Being is reduced to a mere thing. Being human is de-personalized. And, what is most important, the subject is made into an object. This is due to the fact that it is the characteristic of a subject that it relates to objects. And it is a characteristic of man that he relates to intentional objects in terms of values and meanings which serve as reasons and motives. If self-transcendence is denied and the door to meanings and values is closed, reasons and motives are replaced by conditioning processes, and it is up to the "hidden persuaders" to do the conditioning, to manipulate man. It is reification that opens the door to manipulation. And vice versa. If one is to manipulate human beings he first has to reify them, and, to this end, indoctrinate them along the lines of pan-determinism. "Only by dispossessing autonomous man," says B. F. Skinner, "can we turn the real causes of human behavior — from the inaccessible to the manipulable."[5] I quite simply think, first of all, that conditioning processes are not the real causes of human behavior; secondly, that the real cause is something accessible, provided that the humanness of human behavior is not denied on *a priori* grounds; and, thirdly, that the humanness of human behavior cannot be revealed unless we recognize that the real "cause" of a given individual's behavior is not a cause but, rather, a reason.

Causes are confused not only with reasons but also with conditions. In a way, however, causes are conditions. They are sufficient conditions in contrast to conditions in the strict sense of necessary conditions. Incidentally, there are not only necessary conditions but also what I would call possible conditions. By this I mean releases and triggers. So-called psychosomatic diseases, for example, are not caused by psychological factors — that is to say, they are not psychogenic as are neuroses. Rather,

---

[4] Herbert Spiegelberg, *The Phenomenological Movement*, Vol. 2, 1960, p. 721.
[5] *Beyond Freedom and Dignity*, New York: Alfred A. Knopf, 1971. (Remainder of footnote deleted.)

psychosomatic diseases are somatic diseases that have been triggered off by psychological factors.

A sufficient condition is sufficient to create and engender a phenomenon: i.e., the phenomenon is determined by such a cause not only in its essence but also in its existence. By contrast, a necessary condition is a precondition. It is a prerequisite. There are cases of mental retardation, for example, that are due to a hypofunction of the thyroid gland. If such a patient is given thyroid extract his I.Q. improves and increases. Does that mean that spirit is nothing but thyroid substance, as said in a book I once had to review? I would rather say that thyroid substance is "nothing but" a necessary condition which the author confounded with a sufficient condition. For a change, let us turn to a hypofunction of the adrenocortical glands. I myself have published two papers based on laboratory research to the effect that there are cases of depersonalization resulting from the hypofunction of the adrenocortical glands. If such a patient is given desoxycorticosterone acetate he again feels like a person. The sense of selfhood is restored. Does that mean that the self is nothing but desoxycorticosterone acetate?

Here we reach the point at which pan-determinism turns into reductionism. Indeed, it is the lack of discrimination between causes and conditions that allows reductionism to deduce a human phenomenon from, and reduce it to, a subhuman phenomenon. However, in being derived from a subhuman phenomenon, the human phenomenon is turned into a mere epiphenomenon.

Reductionism is the nihilism of today. It is true that Jean-Paul Sartre's brand of existentialism hinges on the pivots "Being and Nothingness," but the lesson to be learned from existentialism is a hyphenated nothingness, namely, the no-thingness of the human being. A human being is not one thing among other things. Things determine each other. Man, however, determines himself. Rather, he decides whether or not he lets himself be determined, be it by the drives and instincts that push him, or the reasons and meanings that pull him.

The nihilism of yesterday taught nothingness. Reductionism now is preaching nothing-but-ness. Man is said to be nothing but a computer or a "naked ape." It is perfectly legitimate to use the computer as a model, say, for the functioning of our central nervous system. The *analogia entis* extends and is valid down to the computer. However, there are also dimensional differences which are disregarded and neglected by reductionism. Consider, for example, the typically reductionist theory of conscience according to which this uniquely human phenomenon is nothing but the result of conditioning processes. The behavior of a dog that has wet the carpet and slinks under the couch with its tail between its legs does not manifest conscience but something I would rather call anticipatory anxiety — specifically, the fearful expectation of punishment. This might well be the result of conditioning processes. It has nothing to do with conscience, however, because true conscience has nothing to do with the expectation of punishment. As long as a man is still motivated either by the fear of punishment or by the hope of reward — or, for that matter, by the wish to appease the superego — conscience has not had its say as yet. . . .

Thus far we have discussed causes over against reasons and necessary conditions over against sufficient conditions. However, there is a third discrimination we have to consider. What is usually understood by "sufficient conditions" is efficient causes as opposed to final causes. Now my contention is that final causes, or for that matter meanings and purposes, are perceptible and only to a scientific approach that is appropriate to them. The pan-determinist who contends that there are no meanings and purposes is like a man "who would study organic existence," to quote Johann Wolfgang von Goethe. He

> First drives out the soul with stern persistence;
> Then the parts in his hand he may hold and class,
> But the spiritual link is lost, alas!
> *Encheireisin naturae,* this Chemistry names,
> Nor knows how herself she banters and blames!
>   Faust, *Part I*

There is a "missing link" indeed. Meaning is missing in the world as described by many a science. This, however, does not imply that the world is void of meaning, but only that many a science is blind to it. Meaning is scotomized by many a science. It is not demonstrated by every scientific approach; it is not touched by every "cross section," to stick to our simile. Consider a curve that lies in a vertical plane.

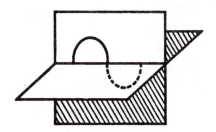

What is left of this line in a horizontal plane is no more than three points, isolated points, disconnected points, points without a meaningful connection between them. The meaningful connections lie above and below the horizontal plane. Might it not be the same with those events which science sees as random, for example, chance mutations? And is it not conceivable that there is a hidden meaning, a higher or a deeper meaning that eludes the cross section because it lies above or below it as do the higher and the lower parts of the curve? The fact remains that not everything can be explained in meaningful terms. But what now can be explained is at least the reason why this is *necessarily* the case.

If this is true of meaning, how much more does it hold for ultimate meaning. *The more comprehensive the meaning, the less comprehensible it is.* Infinite meaning is necessarily beyond the comprehension of a finite being. Here is the point at which science gives up and wisdom takes over. Blaise Pascal once said, *"Le coeur a ses raisons, que la raison ne connait point"* (the heart has reasons that reason does not know). There is, indeed, what is called the wisdom of the heart. Or one may call it the ontological self-understanding. A phenomenological analysis of the way in which the man in the street, out of the wisdom of the heart, understands himself, may teach us that there is more to being human than being the battleground of the clashing claims of ego, id and superego, as Fulton J. Sheen once mockingly put it, and there is more to being human than being a pawn and plaything of conditioning processes or drives and instincts. From the man in the street we may learn that being human means being confronted continuously with situations which are each at once chance and challenge, giving us a chance to fulfill ourselves by meeting the challenge to fulfill its meaning. Each situation is a call, first to listen, and then to respond.

And now the point is reached at which the circle is closed. We departed from determinism as a limitation of freedom and have arrived at humanism as an expansion of freedom. Freedom is part of the story and half of the truth. Being free is but the negative aspect of the whole phenomenon whose positive aspect is being responsible. Freedom may degenerate into mere arbitrariness unless it is lived in terms of responsibleness. That is why I would recommend that the Statue of Liberty on the East Coast be supplemented by a Statue of Responsibility on the West Coast.

FEODOR DOSTOYEVSKY

In this excerpt from The Brothers Karamazov, *Ivan tells a story that revolves around Christ's return to earth in the sixteenth century. In this "poem," The Grand Inquisitor, after arresting Christ for heresy, confronts him on the subject of human freedom. Ivan asks his brother Alyosha who is humanity's real savior — the one who offers us freedom or the one who offers us bread.*

The Grand Inquisitor

The action of my poem takes place in Spain, in Seville, during the most terrible time of the Inquisition, when fires were lighted every day throughout the land to the glory of God and

> In the splendid autos-da-fé
> Wicked heretics were burnt.

Oh, of course, this was not the second coming when, as he promised, he would appear at the end of time in all his heavenly glory, and which would be as sudden "as the lightning cometh out of the east, and shineth even unto the west". No, all he wanted was to visit his children only for a moment and just where the stakes of the heretics were crackling in the flames. In his infinite mercy he once more walked among men in the semblance of man as he had walked among men for thirty-three years fifteen centuries ago. He came down into the hot "streets and lanes" of the southern city just at the moment when, a day before, nearly a hundred heretics had been burnt all at once by the cardinal, the Grand Inquisitor, *ad majorem gloriam Dei* in "a magnificent auto da fé", in the presence of the king, the court, the knights, the cardinals, and the fairest ladies of the Court and the whole population of Seville. He appeared quietly, incon- spicuously, but everyone — and that is why it is so strange — recognized him. That might have been one of the finest passages in my poem — I mean, why they recognized him. The people are drawn to him by an irresistible force, they surround him, they throng about him, they follow him. He walks among them in silence with a gentle smile of infinite compassion. The sun of love burns in his heart, rays of Light, of Enlight- enment, and of Power stream from his eyes and, pouring over the people, stir their hearts with responsive love. He stretches forth his hands to them, blesses them, and a healing virtue comes from contact with him, even with his garments. An old man, blind from childhood, cries out to him from the midst of the crowd, "O Lord, heal me so that I may see thee", and it is as though scales fell from his eyes, and the blind man sees him. The people weep and kiss the ground upon which he walks. Children scatter flowers before him, sing and cry out to him: "Hosannah!" "It is he, it is he himself," they all repeat. "It must be he, it can be no one but he." He stops on the steps of the Cathedral of Seville at the moment when a child's little, open white coffin is brought in with weeping into the church: in it lies a girl of seven, the only daughter of a prominent citizen. The dead child is covered with flowers. "He will raise up your child", people shout from the crowd to the weeping mother. The canon, who has come out to meet the coffin, looks on perplexed and knits his brows. But presently a cry of the dead child's mother is heard. She throws herself at his feet. "If it is thou," she cries, holding out her hands to him, "then raise my child from the dead!" The funeral cortège halts. The coffin is lowered on to the steps at his feet. He gazes with compassion and his lips once again utter softly the words, "Talitha cumi" — "and the damsel arose". The little girl rises in the coffin, sits up, and looks around her with surprise in her smiling, wide-open eyes. In her hands she holds the nosegay of white roses with which she lay in her coffin. There are cries, sobs, and confusion among the people, and it is at that very moment that the Cardinal himself, the Grand Inquisitor, passes by the cathedral in the square. He is an old man of nearly ninety, tall and erect, with a shrivelled face and sunken eyes, from which, though, a light like a fiery spark still gleams. Oh, he is not wearing his splendid cardinal robes in which he appeared before the people the day before, when the enemies of the Roman faith were being burnt — no, at that moment he is wearing only his old, coarse, monk's cassock. He is followed at a distance by his sombre assistants and his slaves and his "sacred" guard. He stops in front of the crowd and watches from a distance. He sees everything. He sees the coffin set down at *his* feet, he sees the young girl raised from the dead, and his face darkens. He knits his grey, beetling brows and his eyes flash with an ominous fire. He stretches forth his finger and commands the guards to seize *him*. And so great is his power and so accustomed are the people to obey him, so humble and submissive are they to his will, that the crowd immediately makes way for the guards and, amid the death-like hush that descends upon the square, they lay hands upon *him* and lead him away. The crowd, like one man, at once bows down to the ground before the old Inquisitor, who blesses them in silence and passes on. The guards take their Prisoner to the dark, narrow, vaulted prison in the old building of the Sacred Court and lock him in there. The day passes and night falls, the dark, hot and "breathless" Seville night. The air is "heavy with the scent of laurel and lemon". Amid the profound darkness, the iron door of the prison is suddenly opened and the old Grand Inquisitor himself slowly enters the prison with a light in his hand. He is alone and the door at once closes behind him. He stops in the doorway and gazes for a long time, for more than a minute, into his face. At last he approaches him slowly, puts the lamp on the table and says to him:

' "Is it you? You?" '

'But, receiving no answer, he adds quickly: "Do not answer, be silent. And, indeed, what can you say? I know too well what you would say. Besides, you have no right to add anything to what you have said already in the days of old. Why, then, did you come to meddle with us? For you have come to meddle with us, and you know it. But do you know what is going to happen tomorrow? I know not who you are and I don't want to know: whether it is you or only someone who looks like him, I do not know, but tomorrow I shall condemn you and burn you at the stake as the vilest of heretics, and the same people who today kissed your feet, will at the first sign from me rush to rake up the coals at your stake tomorrow. Do you know that? Yes, perhaps you do know it," he added after a moment of deep reflection without taking his eyes off his prisoner for an instant.'

'I'm afraid I don't quite understand it, Ivan,' said Alyosha, who had been listening in silence all the time, with a smile. 'Is it just a wild fantasy, or has the old man made some mistake, some impossible *qui pro quo?*'

'You can assume it to be the latter,' laughed Ivan, 'if our modern realism has spoilt you so much that you can't bear anything fantastic. If you prefer a *qui pro quo,* then let it be so. It is true,' he laughed again, 'the old man was ninety and he might have long ago gone mad about his fixed idea. He might, too, have been struck by the Prisoner's appearance. It might, finally, have been simply delirium. A vision the ninety-year-old man had before his death, particularly as he had been greatly affected by the burning of a hundred heretics at the auto-da-fé the day before. What difference does it make to us whether it was a *qui pro quo* or a wild fantasy? The only thing that matters is that the old man should speak out, that at last he does speak out and says aloud what he has been thinking in silence for ninety years.'

'And is the Prisoner also silent? Does he look at him without uttering a word?'

'Yes,' Ivan laughed again, 'that's how it should be in all such cases. The old man himself tells him that *he* has no right to add anything to what had already been said before. If you like, this is the most fundamental feature of Roman Catholicism, in my opinion at any rate: "Everything," he tells him, "has been handed over by you to the Pope and, therefore, everything is now in the Pope's hands, and there's no need for you to come at all now — at any rate, do not interfere for the time being." They not only speak, but also write in that sense. The Jesuits do at any rate. I've read it myself in the works of their theologians. "Have you the right to reveal to us even one of the mysteries of the world you have come from?" my old man asks him and replies for him himself. "No, you have not. So that you may not add anything to what has been said before and so as not to deprive men of the freedom which you upheld so strongly when you were on earth. All that you might reveal anew would encroach on men's freedom of faith, for it would come as a miracle, and their freedom of faith was dearer to you than anything even in those days, fifteen hundred years ago. Was it not you who said so often in those days, 'I shall make you free'? But now you have seen those 'free' men," the old man adds suddenly with a pensive smile. "Yes, this business has cost us a great deal," he goes on, looking sternly at him, "but we've completed it at last in your name. For fifteen centuries we've been troubled by this freedom, but now it's over and done with for good. You don't believe that it is all over? You look meekly at me and do not deign even to be indignant with me? I want you to know that now — yes, today — these men are more than ever convinced that they are absolutely free, and yet they themselves have brought their freedom to us and humbly laid it at our feet. But it was we who did it. And was that what you wanted? Was that the kind of freedom you wanted?" '

'I'm afraid I don't understand again,' Alyosha interrupted. 'Is he being ironical, is he laughing?'

'Not in the least. You see, he glories in the fact that he and his followers have at last vanquished freedom and have done so in order to make men happy. "For," he tells him, "it is only now (he is, of course, speaking of the Inquisition), that it has become possible for the first time to think of the happiness of men. Man is born a rebel, and can rebels be happy? You were warned," he says to him. "There has been no lack of warnings and signs, but you did not heed the warnings. You rejected the only way by which men might be made happy, but, fortunately, in departing, you handed on the work to us. You have promised and you have confirmed it by your own word. You have given us the right to bind and unbind, and of course you can't possibly think of depriving us of that right now. Why, then, have you come to interfere with us?" '

'And what's the meaning of "there has been no lack of warnings and signs"?' asked Alyosha.

'That, you see, is the chief thing about which the old man has to speak out.

' "The terrible and wise spirit, the spirit of self-destruction and non-existence," the old man went on, "the great spirit talked with you in the wilderness and we are told in the books that he apparently 'tempted' you. Is that so? And could anything truer have been said than what he revealed to you in his three questions and what you rejected, and what in the books are called 'temptations'? And yet if ever there has been on earth a real, prodigious miracle, it was on that day, on the day of the three temptations. Indeed, it was in the emergence of those three questions that the miracle lay. If it were possible to imagine, for the sake of argument, that those three questions of the terrible spirit had been lost without leaving a trace in the books and that we had to rediscover, restore, and invent them afresh and that to do so we had to gather together all the wise men of the earth — rulers, high priests, scholars, philosophers, poets — and set them the task of devising and inventing three questions which would not only correspond to the magnitude of the occasion, but, in addition, express in three words, in three short human sentences, the whole future history of the world and of mankind, do you think that the entire wisdom of the earth, gathered together, could have invented anything equal in depth and force to the three questions which were actually put to you at the time by the wise and mighty spirit in the wilderness? From those questions alone, from the miracle of their appearance, one can see that what one is dealing with here is not the human, transient mind, but the absolute and everlasting one. For in those three questions the whole future history of mankind is, as it were, anticipated and combined in one whole and three images are presented in which all the insoluble historical contradictions of human nature all over the world will meet. At the time it could not be so clearly seen, for the future was still unknown, but now, after fifteen centuries have gone by, we can see that everything in those three questions was so perfectly divined and foretold and has been so completely proved to be true that nothing can be added or taken from them.

' "Decide yourself who was right — you or he who questioned you then? Call to your mind the first question; its meaning, though not in these words, was this: 'You want to go into the world and you are going empty-handed, with some promise of freedom, which men in their simplicity and their innate lawlessness cannot even comprehend, which they fear and dread — for nothing has ever been more unendurable to man and to human society than freedom! And do you see the stones in this parched and barren desert? Turn them into loaves, and mankind will run after you like a flock of sheep, grateful and obedient, though for ever trembling with fear that you might withdraw your hand and they would no longer have your loaves.' But you did not want to deprive man of freedom and rejected the offer, for, you thought, what sort of freedom is it if obedience is bought with loaves of bread? You replied that man does not live by bread alone, but do you know that for the sake of that earthly bread the spirit of the earth will rise up against you and will join battle with you and conquer you, and all will follow him, crying 'Who is like this beast? He has given us fire from heaven!' Do you know that ages will pass and mankind will proclaim in its wisdom and science that there is no crime and, therefore, no sin, but that there are only hungry people. 'Feed them first and then demand virtue of them!' — that is what they will inscribe on their banner which they will raise against you and which will destroy your temple. A new building will rise where your temple stood, the dreadful Tower of Babel will rise up again, and though, like the first one, it will not be completed, yet you might have prevented the new tower and have shortened the sufferings of men by a thousand years — for it is to us that they will come at last, after breaking their hearts for a thousand years with their tower! Then they will look for us again under the ground, hidden in the catacombs (for we shall again be persecuted and tortured), and they will find us and cry out to us, 'Feed us, for those who have promised us fire from heaven have not given it to us!' And then we shall finish building their tower, for he who feeds them will complete it, and we alone shall feed them in your name, and we shall lie to them that it is in your name. Oh, without us they will never, never feed themselves. No science will give them bread so long as they remain free. But in the end they will lay their freedom at our feet and say to us, 'We don't mind being your slaves so long as you feed us!' They will, at last, realize themselves that there cannot be enough freedom and bread for everybody, for they will never, never be able to let everyone have his fair share! They will also be convinced that they can never be free because they are weak, vicious, worthless, and rebellious. You promised them bread from heaven, but, I repeat again, can it compare with earthly bread in the eyes of the weak, always vicious and always ignoble race of man? And if for the sake of the bread from heaven thousands and tens of thousands will follow you, what is to become of the millions and scores of thousands of millions of creatures who will not have the strength to give up the earthly bread for the bread of heaven? Or are only the scores of thousands of the great and strong dear to you, and are the remaining millions, numerous as the sand of the sea, who are weak but love you, to serve only as the material for the great and the strong? No, to us the weak, too, are dear. They are vicious and rebellious, but in the end they will become obedient too. They will marvel at us and they will regard us as gods because, having become their masters, we consented to endure freedom and rule over them — so dreadful will freedom become to them in the end! But we shall tell them that we do your bidding and rule in your name. We shall deceive them again, for we shall not let you come near us again. That deception will be our suffering, for we shall be forced to lie. That was the meaning of the first question in the wilderness, and that was what you rejected in the name of freedom, which you put above everything else. And yet in that question lay hidden the great secret of this world. By accepting 'the loaves', you would have satisfied man's universal and everlasting craving, both as an individual and as mankind as a whole, which can be summed up in the words 'whom shall I worship?' Man, so long as he remains free, has no more constant and agonizing anxiety than to find as quickly as possible someone to worship. But man seeks to worship only what is incontestable, so incontestable, indeed, that all men at once agree to worship it all together. For the chief concern of those miserable creatures is not only to find something that I or someone else can worship, but to find something that all believe in and worship, and the absolutely essential thing is that they should do so *all together*. It is this need for *universal* worship that is the chief torment of every man individually and of mankind as a whole from the beginning of time. For the sake of that universal worship they have put each other to the sword. They have set up gods and called upon each other, 'Give up your gods and come and worship ours, or else death to you and to your gods!' And so it will be to the end of the world, even when the gods have vanished from the earth: they will prostrate themselves before idols just the same. You knew, you couldn't help knowing this fundamental mystery of human nature, but you rejected the only absolute banner, which was offered to you, to make all men worship you alone incontestably — the banner of earthly bread, which you rejected in the name of freedom and the bread from heaven. And look what you have done further — and all again in the name of freedom! I tell you man has no more agonizing anxiety than to find someone to whom he can hand over with all speed the gift of freedom with which the unhappy creature is born. But only he can gain possession of men's freedom who is able to set their conscience at ease. With the bread you were given an incontestable banner: give him bread and man will worship you, for there is nothing more incontestable than bread; but if at the same time someone besides yourself should gain possession of his conscience — oh, then he will even throw away your bread and follow him who has ensnared his conscience. You were right about that. For the mystery of human life is not only in living, but in knowing why one lives. Without a clear idea of what to live for man will not consent to live and will rather destroy himself than remain on the earth, though he were surrounded by loaves of bread. That is so, but what became of it? Instead of gaining possession of men's freedom, you gave them greater freedom than ever! Or did you forget that a tranquil mind and even death is dearer to man than the free choice in the knowledge of good and evil? There is nothing more alluring to man than this freedom of conscience, but there is nothing more tormenting, either. And instead of firm foundations for appeasing man's conscience once and for all, you chose everything that was exceptional, enigmatic, and vague, you chose everything that was beyond the strength of men, acting, consequently, as though you did not love them at all — you who came to give your life for them! Instead of taking possession of men's freedom you multiplied it and burdened the spiritual kingdom of man with its sufferings for ever. You wanted man's free love so that he should follow you freely, fascinated and captivated by you. Instead of the strict ancient law, man had in future to decide for himself with a free heart what is good and what is evil, having only your image before him for guidance. But did it never occur to you that he would at last reject and call in question even your image and your truth, if he were weighed down by so fearful a burden as freedom of choice? They will at last cry aloud that the truth is not in you, for it was impossible to leave them in greater confusion and suffering than you have done by leaving them with so many cares and insoluble problems. It was you yourself, therefore, who laid the foundation for the destruction of your kingdom and you ought not to blame anyone else for it. And yet, is that all that was offered to you? There are three forces, the only three forces that are able to conquer and hold captive for ever the conscience of these weak rebels for their own happiness — these forces are: miracle, mystery, and authority. You rejected all three and yourself set the example for doing so. When the wise and terrible spirit set you on a pinnacle of the temple and said to you: 'If thou be the Son of God, cast thyself down: for it is written, He shall give his angels charge concerning thee: and in their hands they shall bear thee up, lest at any time thou dash thy foot against a stone, and thou shalt prove then how great is thy faith in thy Father.' But, having heard him, you rejected his proposal and did not give way and did not cast yourself down. Oh, of course, you acted proudly and magnificently, like God. But men, the weak, rebellious race of men, are they gods? Oh, you understood perfectly then that in taking one step, in making a move to cast yourself down, you would at once have tempted God and have lost all your faith in him, and you would have been dashed to pieces against the earth which you came to save, and the wise spirit that tempted you would have rejoiced. But, I repeat, are there many like you? And could you really assume for a moment that men, too, could be equal to such a temptation? Is the nature of man such that he can reject a miracle and at the most fearful moments of life, the moments of his most fearful, fundamental, and agonizing spiritual problems, stick to the free decision of the heart? Oh, you knew that your great deed would be preserved in books, that it would go down to the end of time and the extreme ends of the earth, and you hoped that, following you, man would remain with God and ask for no miracle. But you did not know that as soon as man rejected miracle he would at once reject God as well, for what man seeks is not so much God as miracles. And since man is unable to carry on without a miracle, he will create new miracles for himself, miracles of his own, and will worship the miracle of the witch-doctor and the sorcery of the wise woman, rebel, heretic and infidel though he is a hundred times over. You did not come down from the cross when they shouted to you, mocking and deriding you: 'If thou be the Son of God, come down from the cross.' You did not come down because, again, you did not want to enslave man by a miracle and because you hungered for a faith based on free will and not on miracles. You hungered for freely given love and not for the servile raptures of the slave before the might that has terrified him once and for all. But here, too, your judgment of men was too high, for they are slaves, though rebels by nature. Look round and judge: fifteen centuries have passed, go and have a look at them: whom have you raised up to yourself? I swear, man has been created a weaker and baser creature than you thought him to be! Can he, can he do what you did? In respecting him so greatly, you acted as though you ceased to feel any compassion for him, for you asked too much of him — you who have loved him more than yourself! Had you respected him less, you would have asked less of him, and that would have been more like love, for his burden would have been lighter. He is weak and base. What does it matter if he does rebel against our authority everywhere now and is proud of his rebellion? It is the pride of a child and of a schoolboy. They are little children rioting in class and driving out their teacher. But an end will come to the transports of the children, too. They will pay dearly for it. They will tear down the temples and drench the earth with blood. But they will realize at last, the foolish children, that although they are rebels, they are impotent rebels who are unable to keep up with their rebellion. Dissolving into foolish tears, they will admit at last that he who created them rebels must undoubtedly have meant to laugh at them. They will say so in despair, and their utterance will be a blasphemy which will make them still more unhappy, for man's nature cannot endure blasphemy and in the end will always avenge it on itself. And so, unrest, confusion, and unhappiness — this is the present lot of men after all you suffered for their freedom! Your great prophet tells in a vision and in an allegory that he saw all those who took part in the first resurrection and that there were twelve thousand of them from each tribe. But if there were so many then, they, too, were not like men, but gods. They had borne your cross, they had endured scores of years of the hungry and barren wilderness, feeding on locusts and roots — and you can indeed point with pride to those children of freedom, freely given love, and free and magnificent sacrifice in your name. But remember that there were only a few thousand of them, and they, too, gods. But what of the rest? And why are the rest, the weak ones, to blame if they were not able to endure all that the mighty ones endured? Why is the weak soul to blame for being unable to receive gifts to terrible? Surely, you did not come only to the chosen and for the chosen? But if so, there is a mystery here and we cannot understand it. And if it is a mystery, then we, too, were entitled to preach a mystery and to teach them that it is neither the free verdict of their hearts nor love that matters, but the mystery which they must obey blindly, even against their conscience. So we have done. We have corrected your great work and have based it on *miracle, mystery, and au-*

thority. And men rejoiced that they were once more led like sheep and that the terrible gift which had brought them so much suffering had at last been lifted from their hearts. Were we right in doing and teaching this? Tell me. Did we not love mankind when we admitted so humbly its impotence and lovingly lightened its burden and allowed men's weak nature even to sin, so long as it was with our permission? Why, then, have you come to meddle with us now? And why are you looking at me silently and so penetratingly with your gentle eyes? Get angry. I do not want your love because I do not love you myself. And what have I to hide from you? Or don't I know to whom I am speaking? All I have to tell you is already known to you. I can read it in your eyes. And would I conceal our secret from you? Perhaps it is just what you want to hear from my lips. Well, then, listen. We are not with you but with *him:* that is our secret! It's a long time — eight centuries — since we left you and went over to *him.* Exactly eight centuries ago we took from him what you rejected with scorn, the last gift he offered you, after having shown you all the kingdoms of the earth: we took from him Rome and the sword of Caesar and proclaimed ourselves the rulers of the earth, the sole rulers, though to this day we have not succeeded in bringing our work to total completion. But whose fault is it? Oh, this work is only beginning, but it has begun. We shall have to wait a long time for its completion and the earth will have yet much to suffer, but we shall reach our goal and be Caesars and it is then that we shall think about the universal happiness of man. And yet even in those days you could have taken up the sword of Caesar. Why did you reject that last gift? By accepting that third counsel of the mighty spirit, you would have accomplished all that man seeks on earth, that is to say, whom to worship, to whom to entrust his conscience and how at last to unite all in a common, harmonious, and incontestable ant-hill, for the need of universal unity is the third and last torment of men. . . . By accepting the world and Caesar's purple, you would have founded the world state and given universal peace. For who is to wield dominion over men if not those who have taken possession of their consciences and in whose hands is their bread? And so we have taken the sword of Caesar and, having taken it, we of course rejected you and followed *him.* Oh, many more centuries are yet to pass of the excesses of their free mind, of their science and cannibalism, for, having begun to build their Tower of Babel without us, they will end up with cannibalism. But then the beast will come crawling up to us and will lick our feet and will bespatter them with tears of blood from its eyes. And we shall sit upon the beast and raise the cup, and on it will be written: 'Mystery!' And then, and only then, will the reign of peace and happiness come to men. You pride yourself upon your chosen ones, but you have only the chosen ones, while we will bring peace to all. But that is not all: how many of those chosen ones, of those mighty ones who could have become the chosen ones, have at last grown tired of waiting for you and have carried and will go on carrying the powers of their spirit and the ardours of their hearts to another field and will end by raising their *free* banner against you? But you raised that banner yourself. With us, however, all will be happy and will no longer rise in rebellion nor exterminate one another, as they do everywhere under your freedom. Oh, we will convince them that only then will they become free when they have resigned their freedom to us and have submitted to us. And what do you think? Shall we be right or shall we be lying? They will themselves be convinced that we are right, for they will remember the horrors of slavery and confusion to which your freedom brought them. Freedom, a free mind and science will lead them into such a jungle and bring them face to face with such marvels and insoluble mysteries that some of them, the recalcitrant and the fierce, will destroy themselves, others, recalcitrant but weak, will destroy one another, and the rest, weak and unhappy, will come crawling to our feet and cry aloud: 'Yes, you were right, you alone possessed his mystery, and we come back to you — save us from ourselves!' In receiving loaves from us, they will, of course, see clearly that we are taking the loaves made by their own hands in order to distribute them among themselves, without any miracle. They will see that we have not made stones into loaves, but they will, in truth, be more pleased with receiving them from our hands than with the bread itself! For they will remember only too well that before, without us, the bread they made turned to stones in their hands, but that when they came back to us, the very stones turned to bread in their hands. They will appreciate only too well what it means to submit themselves to us for ever! And until men understand this, they will be unhappy. And who, pray, was more than anyone responsible for that lack of understanding? Who divided the flock and scattered it on unknown paths? But the flock will be gathered together again and will submit once more, and this time it will be for good. Then we shall give them quiet, humble happiness, the happiness of weak creatures, such as they were created. Oh, we shall at last persuade them not to be proud, for you raised them up and by virtue of that taught them to be proud; we shall prove to them that they are weak, that they are mere pitiable children, but that the happiness of a child is the sweetest of all. They will grow timid and begin looking up to us and cling to us in fear as chicks to the hen. They will marvel at us and be terrified of us and be proud that we are so mighty and so wise as to be able to tame such a turbulent flock of thousands of millions. They will be helpless and in constant fear of our wrath, their minds will grow timid, their eyes will always be shedding tears like women and children, but at the slightest sign from us they will be just as ready to pass to mirth and laughter, to bright-eyed gladness and happy childish song. Yes, we shall force them to work, but in their leisure hours we shall make their life like a children's game, with children's songs, in chorus, and with innocent dances. Oh, we shall permit them to sin, too, for they are weak and helpless, and they will love us like children for allowing them to sin. We shall tell them that every sin can be expiated, if committed with our permission; that we allow them to sin because we love them all and as for the punishment for their sins — oh well, we shall take it upon ourselves. And we shall take it upon ourselves, and they will adore us as benefactors who have taken their sins upon ourselves before God. And they will have no secrets from us. We shall allow or forbid them to live with their wives and mistresses, to have or not have children — everything according to the measure of their obedience — and they will submit themselves to us gladly and cheerfully. The most tormenting secrets of their conscience — everything, everything they will bring to us, and we shall give them our decision for it all, and they will be glad to believe in our decision, because it will relieve them of their great anxiety and of their present terrible torments of coming to a free decision themselves. And they will all be happy, all the millions of creatures, except the hundred thousand who rule over them. For we alone, we who guard the mystery, we alone shall be unhappy. There will be thousands of millions of happy infants and one hundred thousand sufferers who have taken upon themselves the curse of knowledge of good and evil. Peacefully they will die, peacefully will they pass away in your name, and beyond the grave they will find nothing but death. But we shall keep the secret and for their own happiness will entice them with the reward of heaven and eternity. For even if there were anything at all in the next world, it would not of course be for such as they. They declare and prophesy that you will come and be victorious again, that you will come with your chosen ones, with your proud and mighty ones, but we shall declare that they have only saved themselves, while we have saved all. It is said that the whore, who sits upon the beast and holds in her hands the *mystery,* will be put to shame, that the weak will rise up again, that they will rend her purple and strip naked her 'vile' body. But then I will rise and point out to you the thousands of millions of happy babes who have known no sin. And we who, for their happiness, have taken their sins upon ourselves, we shall stand before you and say, 'Judge us if you can and if you dare.' Know that I am not afraid of you. Know that I, too, was in the wilderness, that I, too, fed upon locusts and roots, that I, too, blessed freedom, with which you have blessed men, and that I, too, was preparing to stand among your chosen ones, among the strong and mighty, thirsting 'to make myself of the number'. But I woke up and refused to serve madness. I went back and joined the hosts of those who have *corrected your work.* I went away from the proud and returned to the meek for the happiness of the meek. What I say to you will come to pass and our kingdom will be established. I repeat, tomorrow you will behold the obedient flock which at a mere sign from me will rush to heap up the hot coals against the stake at which I shall burn you because you have come to meddle with us. For if anyone has ever deserved our fire, it is you. Tomorrow I shall burn you. *Dixi!*" '

Ivan stopped. He had got worked up as he talked and he spoke with enthusiasm; but when he had finished, he suddenly smiled.

Alyosha, who had listened to him in silence, tried many times towards the end to interrupt him, restraining his great agitation with an effort. But now he suddenly burst into speech, as though carried away beyond control.

'But,' he cried, reddening, 'this is absurd! Your poem is in praise of Jesus and not in his disparagement as — as you wanted it to be. And who will believe you about freedom? Is that the way to understand it? Is that the way it is understood by the Greek Orthodox Church? It's Rome, and not the whole of Rome, either — it's not true. They are the worst among the Catholics — the Inquisitors, the Jesuits! . . . And, besides, there could never have been such a fantastic person as your Inquisitor. What are those sins of men they take upon themselves? Who are these keepers of the mystery who have taken some sort of curse upon themselves for the happiness of men? When have they been seen? We know the Jesuits, people speak ill of them — do you really think they are the people in your poem? They are certainly not the same at all. . . . They are simply the Romish army for the future establishment of a universal government on earth, with the Emperor — the Pontiff of Rome — at its head. That is their ideal, but without any mystery or lofty sadness about it. . . . It's the most ordinary lust for power, for filthy earthly gains, enslavement — something like a future regime of serfdom with them as the landowners — that is all they are after. Perhaps they don't even believe in God. Your suffering Inquisitor is nothing but a fantasy. . . .'

'Wait, wait,' Ivan laughed, 'don't be so excited! You say it's a fantasy — very well, I don't deny it. Of course it's a fantasy. But, look here, you don't really think that the Catholic movement in the last few centuries is really nothing but a lust for power for the sake of some filthy gains. . . . It isn't by any chance Father Paissy's teachings, is it?'

'No, no, on the contrary, Father Paissy once said something of the same kind as you, but,' Alyosha suddenly recollected himself, 'of course, it's not the same thing at all. Not the same thing at all!'

'A very valuable piece of information all the same in spite of your "not the same thing at all". What I'd like to ask you is why your Jesuits and Inquisitors have united only for some vile material gains? Why shouldn't there be among them a sufferer tormented by great sorrow and loving humanity? You see, let us suppose that among all those who are only out for filthy material gains there's one, just one, who is like my old Inquisitor, who had himself fed on roots in the wilderness, a man possessed, who was eager to mortify his flesh so as to become free and perfect; and yet one who had loved humanity all his life and whose eyes were suddenly opened and who saw that it was no great moral felicity to attain complete control over his will and at the same time achieve the conviction that millions of other God's creatures had been created as a mockery, that they would never be able to cope with their freedom, that no giants would ever arise from the pitiful rebels to complete the tower, that the great idealist had not in mind such boobies when he dreamt of his harmony. Realizing that, he returned and joined — the clever fellows. That could have happened, couldn't it?

'Whom did he join? What clever fellows?' cried Alyosha, almost passionately. 'They are not so clever and they have no such mysteries and secrets. Except perhaps only godlessness, that's all their secret. Your inquisitor doesn't believe in God — that's all his secret!'

'Well, suppose it is so! At last you've guessed it! And, in fact it really is so. That really is his whole secret. But is that not suffering, particularly for a man like him who had sacrificed his whole life for a great cause in the wilderness and has not cured himself of his love of humanity? In his last remaining years he comes to the clear conviction that it is only the advice of the great and terrible spirit that could bring some sort of supportable order into the life of the feeble rebels, "the unfinished experimental creatures created as a mockery". And so, convinced of that, he sees that one has to follow the instructions of the wise spirit, that terrible spirit of death and destruction. He therefore accepts lies and deceptions and leads men consciously to death and destruction. Keeps deceiving them all the way, so that they should not notice where they are being led, for he is anxious that those miserable, blind creatures should at least on the way think themselves happy. And, mind you, the deception is in the name of him in whose ideal the old man believed so passionately all his life! Is not that a calamity? And even if there were only one such man at the head of the whole army of men "craving for power for the sake of filthy gains" — would not even one such man be sufficient to make a tragedy? Moreover, one man like that, standing at the head of the movement, is enough for the emergence of a real leading idea of the entire Roman Church with all its armies and Jesuits — the highest idea of this Church. I tell you frankly it's my firm belief that there was never any scarcity of such single individuals among those who stood at the head of the movement. . . .

'I'm sure it exists and, indeed, it must be so. I can't help feeling that something of the same kind of mystery exists also among the freemasons at the basis of their organization. That is why the Catholics hate the freemasons so much, for they regard them as their competitors who are breaking up the unity of their idea, while there should be only one flock and one shepherd. However, I feel that in defending my theory I must appear to you as an author who resents your criticism. Let's drop it.'

'You're probably a freemason yourself!' Alyosha cried, unable to restrain himself. 'You don't believe in God,' he added, but this time in great sorrow. He imagined, besides, that his brother was looking mockingly at him. 'How does your poem end?' he asked suddenly, his eyes fixed on the ground. 'Or was that the end?'

'I intended to end it as follows: when the Inquisitor finished speaking, he waited for some time for the Prisoner's reply. His silence distressed him. He saw that the Prisoner had been listening intently to him all the time, looking gently into his face and evidently not wishing to say anything in reply. The old man would have liked him to say something, however bitter and terrible. But he suddenly approached the old man and kissed him gently on his bloodless, aged lips. That was all his answer. The old man gave a start. There was an imperceptible movement at the corners of his mouth; he went to the door, opened it and said to him: "Go, and come no more — don't come at all — never, never!" And he let him out into "the dark streets and lanes of the city". The Prisoner went away.'

'And the old man?'

'The kiss glows in his heart, but the old man sticks to his idea.'

'And you together with him?' Alyosha cried sorrowfully. 'You too?'

Ivan laughed.

chapter 6

The Other and the Body

The existence of other people is a difficulty and an outrage for objective thought.
Merleau-Ponty, *The Phenomenology of Perception*, p. 349

INTRODUCTION

In her memoirs, Simone de Beauvoir tells how she and Sartre used to worry almost to the point of obsession over the problems associated with the existence of other people. Together they would observe the strangers who frequented the same cafes and invent life histories for those strangers. Of course, these life histories were very likely inaccurate, yet they served the purpose of endowing their creators with a certain control. Such fictionalized accounts, because they are nonreciprocal, take away the Other's mystery and, in effect, erase the Other as subject.

These sorts of concerns are relatively recent to philosophy. For Plato and Aristotle, for example, the existence of the Other does not loom as a major consideration. It is assumed that we can know other people and can judge the behavior of those people by the same standards by which we judge ourselves. This is not to suggest that these early philosophers viewed the Other as identical to the self. Indeed, they insisted on the importance of certain distinctions, including sex, class, and character. But they never doubted — such differences notwithstanding — that one can *know* the Other.

The modern period beginning with Descartes ushered in an era of new questions about other beings and their relation to self. One important consequence, as we saw in chapter 4, pp. 232–36, is the separation between mental and physical entities. Descartes's dualism claimed that

368

"mind" was housed in the body "more intimately than a pilot in a ship," but he left it a mystery as to how this interaction occurs. In fact, he was finally driven to hypothesize that it was the pineal gland which was the meeting place for body/mind interaction. According to Descartes, body and mind are completely distinct: The former is material, divisible, and destructible, while the latter is immaterial, indivisible, and indestructible. Thus, the body is subject to all of the laws to which any material object must conform; whereas the soul has no extension, dimension, or any other properties attributed to matter. According to Descartes,

> Although . . . I have a body that is very closely joined to me, nevertheless, because on the one hand I have a clear and distinct idea of myself — insofar as I am a thing that thinks and not an extended thing — and because on the other hand I have a distinct idea of a body — insofar as it is merely an extended thing, and not a thing that thinks — it is therefore certain that I am truly distinct from my body, and that I can exist without it.
>
> *Meditations*, p. 49

And, for Descartes, our knowledge of our minds is better than our knowledge of our bodies; indeed, "nothing can be more easy and more evidently perceived by me than my mind." (*Meditations*, p. 23) Given that the self is mental, yet housed in a material substance, we might assume that the same is true for others. But, since we alone have privileged access to that self and no other, how can we be sure what is the nature of the Other?

For Descartes, the privileged access we possess to our own thoughts and feelings is immediate and infallible. But we do not have such access to the mind of the Other, nor does the Other have access to our mind. We can observe the Other's behavior, but what we see or touch or hear is *physical.* And since mind and body are completely separate and since the senses can deceive, we have no way of knowing with certainty what the Other is experiencing. For example, you may of course be deceiving me deliberately; but, even if you are sincere, I do not have direct access to your soul; your expressions of joy or pain or anger may result from thoughts and feelings very different from my own. Indeed, you might even be a highly sophisticated automaton trained to observe and to act out human feeling. Am I, then, trapped in an isolated world of my individual *cogito*, unable to reach the Other directly?

The modern concern with the Other makes sense when one looks at the social and cultural contexts from which it springs. The developing awareness of differences in other cultures, for example, gave rise not only to disciplines like anthropology, but also increasingly to questions about how to interpret those differences and even whether an outsider (expert or layperson) is capable of truly understanding the meaning of those cultural norms.

Further, the growing attention (in particular, in the writings of socialists and Marxists) to issues of competition among social classes emphasized the differences in those classes and the struggles between classes, some to maintain power and others to seize it. Chapter 1 (pp. 43–47) outlines a discussion of the "problem of alienation," which is very much a product of post-Cartesianism. Developing science, with its growing emphasis on mechanistic explanations and its skepticism regarding traditional (especially religious) value systems, led to a heightened sense of separation, not only of humans from nature but also of humans from one other. This sense of "homelessness" heightens the feeling of separation from others. Where do we fit in nature? What is special about our own existence? Who are we? What sort of bond — if any — do we share with others?

Ironically, even liberalism in political theory, despite its preoccupation with group norms and democratic process, masks a problem of the Other. This ideology is based on the view that individual citizens, despite their conflicting interests and values, grudgingly create social arrangements in order to enhance the possibility of personal survival. Thus, liberal democratic theory rests on the assumption that human beings, though they necessarily interact with one another in their daily transactions, are socially and metaphysically autonomous "atoms."

Finally, as we saw in our chapters on Kierkegaard (pp. 91–161) and Nietzsche (pp. 171–230), many of the thinkers of the nineteenth century came to view the interests of the group as antithetical to the interests of the individual. The group, the "they," the "herd" — whatever term we use — may keep us from realizing our own potential. The notion of inauthenticity recurs in existentialist thought, and it is often linked to our Being with (and for) others.

Thus, it is in the philosophy and popular thinking of the modern era that the "otherness of others" has become a problem. And much of contemporary existentialist thought has been devoted to considering this issue. In fiction as well as nonfiction, one sees as a recurrent theme the tension between the individual and others. In Heidegger's analysis of death, *das Man* prevents our ontological awareness of our Being-toward-Death. In Sartre's play *No Exit*, hell is not a place of physical torture but rather a room with three people judging one another. In Kierkegaard's analysis of the stages on life's way (see pp. 104–7), the last stage — the religious — is where the individual is totally individualized and face-to-face with God. Nietzsche's Zarathustra is a wanderer without ties to family or community.

There is no one coherent existential view of the Other. This chapter, then, explores three attempts to frame an analysis of our relations with others, our intersubjectivity. This selection of representative thinkers is not an endorsement of any particular view or set of views. Rather, each reveals some important aspect of existentialist thinking. The first, Sartre's view, is one of the most well-known discussions of Being-with-Others. This analysis springs from Sartre's atheism and his phenomenology of consciousness. It was popularized in many of Sartre's fictional works and given more systematic philosophic attention in treatises like *Being and Nothingness*. Second, we examine the view of philosopher Martin Buber, whose analysis of the interpersonal emerges in his most famous work, *I and Thou*. Buber's discussion is grounded in his theism and his mysticism, and is a powerful counterpoint to Sartre's model. Finally, we explore the work of Simone de Beauvoir. Her masterpiece *The Second Sex* goes decidedly beyond Sartre's framework. More specifically, she reveals how one might blend feminist theory and existentialism to ground an analysis of the body and of interpersonal relationships. Selections from each of these works follow this chapter.

JEAN-PAUL SARTRE: "HELL IS OTHER PEOPLE"

It is ironic that, in a philosophy as individualistic as existentialism, the Other plays such an important role. We have seen that existentialist thinkers emphasize that one must face one's death alone; that one is responsible for one's life; and that certain kinds of systems and groups tend to erase the value of the individual's concrete existence. But the other side of existentialism is its focus on Being-in-the-world; and Being-in-the-world is not only (or even primarily) about being with objects, but rather being with others in our community. The very existence of language is proof of our communal existence. It may be too strong to say that language *is* thought, but — at the very least — it is language that makes thought accessible, and language is a public phenomenon.

For centuries, the Other was treated philosophically as another object of perception like any other material object. Thus, for example, I see John in the same way that I see a tree or a book. But as we consider this experience more carefully, we realize that the Other's existence is not like the existence of any object. Our experience of other human beings is qualitatively different from our experience of objects, for objects — as mere ontic beings or Sartre's "dumb-packed-togetherness" — cannot go beyond what they are. Objects are fixed, without possibility; and any changes in nature that objects do undergo must come from forces outside of them. But the existence of other human beings is clearly different. The Other is already there, is in the world, in a way that identifies the Other as another being like ourselves. The surest proof of this is our embarrassment when another stares at us. We can look until we're bored of looking, for example, at the chair across from us; but if there were another person in that chair, the experience of looking is very different. Thus, the Other is not an object, like that chair; the other is some new kind of "not-me."

Existentialists do not attempt to prove the existence of other minds any more than they seek to prove the existence of an external world. Any such proof is necessarily circular, as it must presuppose that which it is attempting to demonstrate. Where Descartes's dualism required that he bring in God to reassure us of the existence of the material world and the presence of other minds, materialist views like, for example, B. F. Skinner's "behaviorism" (see chapter 5, pp. 297–98), maintain that we can infer the existence of other selves with feelings like our own from behavioral cues similar to our own. Neither approach satisfies us existentially. Descartes's *cogito* is a completely sterile notion — it is thinking emptied of content and separate from the world; this *cogito* has no character — how could it possibly be the *I* of our everyday subjective experiences? Further, even if we are convinced that other selves exist, this *cogito* is not individuated, so whence does difference among selves arise? In contrast, materialists (in their various forms; e.g., Skinner's behaviorism) cannot explain the difference in how we experience other persons and other objects. The physical similarity between our material being and that of another does not seem sufficient to explain this powerful difference in our subjective awareness.

In chapter 4 we explored briefly the impact of Husserl's phenomenological approach on existentialism. Husserl viewed the transcendental ego as absolute subjectivity and sought to bracket the "natural standpoint" of everyday experience. What remains after this bracketing is that pure transcendental ego which is our very own. And Husserl's notion of intentionality provides the bridge between ego and world. But this epoché is a release from all otherness and all Others in a "uniquely philosophical solitude." (*Crisis*, pp. 187–188) Though Husserl tried to provide an analysis of other-egos, his absolute ego is still primary and original; it is that which constitutes the world, and so, that which constitutes the other as well. Later existentialists, however, have maintained that Husserl found subjectivity at the expense of the subject and have sought to return to the subject in its lived-world in order to analyze the phenomenon of intersubjectivity.

For existentialists, the world is already there as an "inalienable presence" (Merleau-Ponty, *Phenomenology*, p. viii) before reflection begins, so any proof is either absurd or superfluous. Similarly, we are already being-with-Others. We do not need a rational proof of this, for it is a matter of intuition, not cognition. Indeed, for Sartre, the Other is a presence (like ourselves) and we experience this presence in our awareness of *shame* in the face of the Other. In Sartre's play *No Exit*, for example, three characters are in hell ("where night never comes and people are always seen"), where there is neither fire and brimstone nor satanic torture, but only the constant presence of the Other. At one point, one member of the group, Garcin, suggests that they all sit down quietly, simply "look at the floor" and "try to forget the others are there." (p.23) But this is, as Inez points out, clearly impossible:

> To forget about the others? How utterly absurd! I *feel* you there, in every pore. Your silence clamors in my ears. You can nail up your mouth, cut your tongue out — but you can't prevent your *being there*. (p. 23)

For Sartre, we encounter the Other everywhere we turn. Our world is, as he puts it, "haunted" by the Other's presence. Even if we are alone, we experience the Other's presence when we read a book written by an Other, live in an apartment owned by an Other, or use a product made by an Other. The world, then, is not simply made up of objects whose meanings we provide; rather, the world is full of a plurality of meanings that are independent of our choices.

Thus, for Sartre, our awareness of the presence of the Other does not depend on linguistic communication of any sort: "Can you stop your thoughts? I can hear them ticking away like a clock, tick-tock, tick-tock, and I'm certain you hear mine." (*No Exit*, p. 23) And, unlike Garcin, who seeks to look away, Inez plans to "look you in the eyes and fight it out face to face." But no strategy "works" in any permanent way.

There are no mirrors in the hell Sartre creates in *No Exit;* mirrors are objects, and however much we gaze at them, they do not gaze back. What would it mean to depend on the Other to be a mirror? In the following passage from *No Exit*, Estelle, after realizing that there are no mirrors available, tries to use Inez as her mirror to guide her in applying her make-up:

> Estelle: I've six big mirrors in my bedroom. There they are. I can see them. But they don't see me. They're reflecting the carpet, the settee, the window — but how empty it is, a glass in which I'm absent! When I talked to people I always made sure there was one near by in which I could see myself. I watched myself talking. And somehow it kept me alert, seeing myself as the others saw me. . . . Oh dear! My lipstick! I'm sure I've put it on all crooked. No, I can't do without a looking-glass for ever and ever, I simply can't.
> Inez: Suppose I try to be your glass? Come and pay me a vist, dear. Here's a place for you on my sofa.
> Estelle: But — [points to Garcin]
> Inez: Oh, he doesn't count.
> Estelle: But we're going to — to hurt each other. You said it yourself.
> Inez: Do I look as if I wanted to hurt you?

Estelle: One never can tell.

Inez: Much more likely *you'll* hurt *me.* Still, what does it matter? If I've got to suffer, it may as well be at your hands, your pretty hands. Sit down. Come closer. Closer. Look into my eyes. What do you see?

Estelle: Oh, I'm there! But so tiny I can't see myself properly.

Inez: But I can. Every inch of you. Now ask me questions. I'll be as candid as any looking-glass. [Estelle seems rather embarrassed and turns to Garcin, as if appealing to him for help.]

Estelle: Please, Mr. Garcin. Sure our chatter isn't boring you? [Garcin makes no reply.]

Inez: Don't worry about him. As I said, he doesn't count. We're by our-selves. . . . Ask away.

Estelle: Are my lips all right?

Inez: Show! No, they're a bit smudgy.

Estelle: I thought as much. Luckily [throws a quick glance at Garcin] no one's seen me. I'll try again.

Inez: That's better. No. Follow the line of your lips. Wait! I'll guide your hand. There. That's quite good.

Estelle: As good as when I came in?

Inez: Far better. Crueler. Your mouth looks quite diabolical that way.

Estelle: Good gracious! And you say you like it! How maddening, not being able to see for myself! You're quite sure, Miss Serrano, that it's all right now?

Inez: Won't you call me Inez?

Estelle: Are you sure it looks all right?

Inez: You're lovely, Estelle.

Estelle: But how can I rely upon your taste? Is it the same as *my* taste? Oh, how sickening it all is, enough to drive one crazy!

Inez: I have your taste, my dear, because I like you so much. Look at me. No, straight. Now smile. I'm not so ugly, either. Am I not nicer than your glass?

Estelle: Oh, I don't know. You scare me rather. My reflection in the glass never did that; of course, I knew it so well. Like something I had tamed. . . . I'm going to smile, and my smile will sink down into your pupils, and heaven knows what it will become.

Inez: And why shouldn't you "tame" me? [The women gaze at each other, Estelle with a sort of fearful fascination.] Listen! I want you to call me Inez. We must be great friends.

Estelle: I don't make friends with women very easily.

Inez: Not with postal clerks, you mean? Hullo, what's that — that nasty red spot at the bottom of your cheek? A pimple?

Estelle: A pimple? Oh, how simply foul! Where?

Inez: There. . . . You know the way they catch larks — with a mirror? I'm your lark-mirror, my dear, and you can't escape me. . . . There isn't any pimple, not a trace of one. So what about it? Suppose the mirror started telling lies? Or suppose I covered my eyes — as he is doing — and refused to look at you, all that loveliness of yours would be wasted on the desert air.

No, don't be afraid, I can't help looking at you, I shan't turn my eyes away.
And I'll be nice to you, ever so nice. Only you must be nice to me, too.[1]

Estelle is aware that the reality of Inez is profoundly different from that of
a mirror. Her mirror reflection, she tells us, never scared her; but Inez's
look frightens her. A reflection in glass is familiar and can be "tamed."
But how does Estelle "tame" Inez? How does she know how she is being
seen by her? Mirrors can't lie or make demands or refuse to reflect; the
Other, because she is a subject like Estelle, can refuse to do her bidding.
Estelle describes this feeling of losing control as "sickening," and it is
this experience Sartre has in mind as paradigmatic of intersubjectivity.

For Sartre, this sort of conflict is the original sense of being-for-
another. (See p. 404.) For example, I cannot control the Other as I control
my pen or my book — the Other, like me, is a being who also confers his
or her own meaning on the world. Even if we are engaged in some shared
project, this common project is not the same for each of us. According to
Merleau-Ponty,

> (I)t does not appear in the selfsame light to both of us, we are not both
> equally enthusiastic about it, or at any rate not in quite the same way, simply
> because Paul is Paul and I am myself. Although his consciousness and mine,
> working through our respective situations, may contrive to produce a com-
> mon situation in which they can communicate, it is nevertheless from the
> subjectivity of each of us that each one projects this 'one and only' world.
> (*Phenomenology of Perception*, p. 356)

Any encounter with another subject forces us to experience a different dimension of our own being. Rather than controlling the world
through *our* assignation of values, we are now at the mercy of another
meaning maker. As Sartre wrote,

> As soon as a freedom other than mine arises confronting me, I begin to exist
> in a new dimension of being; and this time it is not a question of my
> conferring a meaning on brute existents or of accepting responsibility on my
> own account for the meaning which Others have conferred on certain ob-
> jects. It is I myself who see a meaning conferred upon me, and I do not have
> the recourse of accepting the responsibility of this meaning which I have
> since it can not be given to me except in the form of an empty indication.
>
> *Being and Nothingness*, p. 671

[1] Excerpt from Jean-Paul Sartre, *No Exit*, translated by Stuart Gilbert (Alfred A.
Knopf, 1946), pp. 20–22. Reprinted with permission of Alfred A. Knopf, Inc.

Others treat us in certain ways suggesting their judgments of us; we learn of this in our relations with them:

> Thus something of myself — according to this new dimension — exists in the manner of the *given;* at least *for me,* since this being which I am *is suffered,* it *is* without *being existed.* I learn of it and suffer it in and through the relations which I enter into with others, in and through their conduct with regard to me.
>
> *Being and Nothingness, p. 671*

Thus, in the face of the Other, we are no longer master of our situation. The Other is capable of organizing the world differently from us. As Merleau-Ponty wrote, "No sooner has my gaze fallen upon a living body in process of acting than the objects surrounding it immediately take on a fresh layer of significance: they are no longer simply what I myself could make of them, they are what this other pattern of behavior is about to make of them." (*Phenomenology,* p. 353) Every subject, then, has his or her own view of the world, and this view may include us without our being able to control how we are seen. When another subject looks at us, we are suddenly "located," like a thing, in time and in space; the Other sees us as we cannot see ourselves and as no nonsubject (say, for example, a dog) sees us. This is how we know that the Other is truly a subject like us and not simply another object in the world or even a very sophisticated robot.

The language Sartre uses to describe this experience of *Mitsein* (being with others) is highly charged and dramatic. For example, the selection at the end of this chapter describes the experience of being looked at while staring through a keyhole. (p. 398) As I look at the people in the room, I make objects of them. Unnoticed, I observe their actions and establish a "worldly" relation between them and me; this world is *my* world. But there is also the ever-present possibility of my becoming an object for someone else. Suppose someone does come by and catches me "in the act"? My immediate feeling is of shame, of being caught; I suddenly have become an object for that Other. When the Other looks at me — whether it is the *I* peeping through the keyhole or the *I* reading on a park bench or the *I* whistling as I walk down the street — that look constitutes a disruption of my world. Sartre uses the vivid phrase "internal hemorrhage" (p. 400) to describe this feeling.

The shame that I experience when the other looks at me is *not* the shame of being caught in the act of doing something "wrong," for it can occur at any moment and is not limited to acts I may be less than proud of. This is, quite simply, the experience of being *seen* (p. 402) in a situation that reflects both my freedom and my limitation (what Sartre calls "facticity"). The Other's look "seems to go in front of" his or her eyes, (p. 398) making it clear that the Other is a being ahead-of-itself and that I am vulnerable. In fact, when we are looked at by an Other, we cease to perceive the Other's eyes. By the mere appearance of the Other, I am put in the position of passing judgment on myself as on an object, for it is as an object that I appear to the Other. Suddenly, what was once *my* world is taken in by the other's look and made into a part of that world; I become one more object among all other "instrumentalities" in that arrangement. The "flow of blood" is trapped and localized as the Other's look fixes me as an object. (p. 401) Everything takes place as if it were outside of me, and this experience is certain proof of the Other's freedom.

For Sartre, this new organization of my world, which is a result of the Other's look at me, results in a kind of self-alienation. Suddenly, my potentiality "decomposes" (p. 398) under the Other's look and I appear to have a "nature." It is not that I perceive myself as losing my freedom "in order to become a thing, but my nature is — over there, outside my lived freedom — as a given attribute of this being which I am for the Other." (p. 402) This experience is akin, according to Sartre, to Adam's and Eve's original fall from grace. "My original fall is the existence of the Other." (p. 402) And even if the Other's presence is a "false alarm," I still experience my being-for-others in my rapid heart-beat, red face, and constant guardedness. Even if I "tremble at the slightest noise, if each creak announces to me a look, this is because I am already in the state of being looked-at." (*Being and Nothingness*, p. 370)

The shame we experience before the Other — an "immediate shudder that runs through me from head to foot"(*Being and Nothingness*, p. 302) — is the shame, Sartre claims, of recognition. We can laugh at a caricature of ourselves, but the Other's look is no caricature. "I recognize that I *am* as the Other sees me." (*Being and Nothingness*, p. 302). For example, as I sit here, my dog stares at me as I stare at this piece of paper on which I write. But I can stare endlessly at the paper and be stared at endlessly by my dog without feeling the immediate and visceral strain of shame that the Other's gaze provokes in me. For Sartre, the shame I feel is not just the awareness that I possess a body; if that were all, then any material object (e.g., I bump my knee on the coffee table) could reveal that to me. Rather, my realization of myself as an object is inseparable from my awareness that the Other is a subject and that I can never see myself with the Other's consciousness. In Sartre's version of the Greek story of Orestes, *The Flies,* King Aegistheus reveals how his subjects' freedom enslaves him:

> Since I came to the throne, all I said, all my acts, have been aimed at building up an image of myself. I wish each of my subjects to keep that image in the foreground of his mind, and to feel, even when alone, that my eyes are on him, severely judging his own most private thoughts. But I have

been trapped in my own net. I have come to see myself only as they see me. I peer into the dark pit of their souls, and there, deep down, I see the image that I have built up. I shudder, but I cannot take my eyes off it. Almighty Zeus, who am I? Am I anything more than the dread that others have of me? (p. 103)

The for-itself, as we have seen, in striving to become in-itself, is striving to become God. The search is futile, but this continual evasion of and flight toward the in-itself is the burden of freedom. There cannot be many gods, so we seek to annihilate the Other, or the Other will annihilate us. The process that Sartre describes is one of alienation in which we become objectified. "In fact my wrenching away from myself and the upsurge of the Other's freedom are one; I can feel them and live them only as an ensemble; I cannot even try to conceive of one without the other." (*Being and Nothingness*, p. 367) We need no rational proof that we exist, for the Other's look makes clear without doubt that we are individuated consciousness. "Each look makes us prove concretely — and in the indubitable certainty of the *cogito* — that we exist for all living men; that is, that there are (some) consciousnesses from whom I exist." (p. 374)

Thus, there is an ever-present conflict in our being-for-others. We must try to recover ourselves from the Other by making an object of the Other; "for I cannot be *an object for an object*." (*Being and Nothingness*, p. 384) But this success is never permanent: "(O)ne look on the part of the Other is sufficient to make all these schemes collapse and to make me experience once more the transfiguration of the Other." Either we must become an object for the other, or the Other must become an object for us. (p. 394) Only the dead are totally and finally objects, for they have lost all possibility.

This discussion is interwoven with Sartre's analysis of the body. Unlike most traditional philosophers, Sartre views the body as central to our being in the world. Indeed, it is the reference to which all things point. The for-itself is not like a soul united to or housed in a body; rather, it *is* its body. The body is at one and the same time a point of view and a point of departure. It is our center of reference, but it is also "the surpassed," for it reveals the world to us and, in doing so, reveals our contingent being. This is the basis for our feeling of ontological nausea, which is the basis for all other ontic nauseas.

But the body also exists for the Other, as for example, both I and the Other are building our worlds with ourselves as centers. To understand how I exist as body-for-other is also to understand how the other exists for-me. The body of the Other may be in-itself, but it is not in-itself in the way in which a human corpse is. "The Other's body is *meaningful*." (*Being and Nothingness*, p. 452) Like me (and unlike a corpse), the

Other's body conveys a world of meanings and defines and creates itself through its instrumental relations with objects. I apprehend the Other's body in terms of a total situation, for I cannot understand the Other except in a context. When I see your tears, for example, I do not perceive your tears or your eyes or your hand wiping the tears. Rather, I perceive a person who is unhappy. My relation with the Other is always "reciprocal and moving" (p. 404) unlike my relations with objects, which are static and unilateral. So the body of the Other is always "body more than body."

The Other, like me, is for-itself, that is, it is not what it is and it is what it is not. And, as for-itself, I both pursue and flee from the in-itself. Indeed, for Sartre, the for-itself *is* flight because it is the foundation of all negativity and hence all relation. To affirm my own subject-self, I seek to possess the Other, to assimilate the Other's freedom into my own. But this unity with the Other is not possible. For Sartre, there is an almost unbearable tension in this dynamic. I cannot make the Other disappear or take on an object-status, for that would negate *my* being-for-others. At the same time, though, the Other is making of *me* an object in his or her world. I want to grab hold of the Other's freedom, not for the mere desire for power, but, as Sartre says, to possess the other's freedom *as* freedom. (p. 407)

These dynamics have important repercussions for concrete relations with others. The Other's existence reveals to me the being I am without my being able to control or even conceive of that being. Through the Other's look, the meaning of my being moves outside me, giving the Other an advantage over me. This ontological conflict, Sartre tells us, leads to two strategies. One he identifies as *love* (pp. 404–12) where I try to assimilate the lover's freedom as part of the "project of recovering myself." (p. 404) The lover wants to possess the beloved, to become one with the lover. But this is obviously impossible. And, though the lover wants to possess the Other, it is not as an object or a robot that I want you to love me; indeed, only the fact that you are another for-itself who is freedom allows me to love you at all. Yet I cannot know you as you are to yourself. Even if I could magically read your mind, it would still be from the perspective of my own lived experience and not yours. So I engage in an endless and futile struggle to be both me *and* Other. And the tension in love is the awareness that, at any moment, I could be seen as object by my lover, or the two of us might be seen by a third party. Such looks would devastate the feeling of love that I have.

Some of us, in recognition of the futility of love, try a second strategy, which Sartre identifies as indifference, desire, hate, and sadism. In this approach, we flee the in-itself by making the Other into an object. But this too is a failure. We may succeed in ignoring the Other, but our indifference leaves us painfully alone in our freedom. Likewise, sadism is always a failure, as one glance of the victim (like Aegistheus' subjects) reveals to us freedom; the victim's submission is deceptive and unstable. As Sartre says, "what the sadist seeks to appropriate is in actuality the transcended freedom of the victim." (p. 417) But this freedom is out of the reach of the sadist, for "it is precisely in and through the Other's absolute freedom that there exists" a world in which there is sadism. (p. 417) Even hate makes clear that the Other contaminates us, and it fails to prevent the Other from existing as consciousness and freedom. Indeed, when such hate becomes obsessive, it may bestow even *more* power on the Other.

Each of these strategies is "on principle" doomed to failure, (p. 416) yet there is no escape from them. As one strategy fails, so is the other born. According to Sartre,

> This means that we can never hold a consistent attitude toward the Other unless he is simultaneously revealed to us as subject and as object, as transcendence-transcending and as transcendence-transcended — which is on principle impossible. Thus ceaselessly tossed from being-a-look to being-looked-at, falling from one to the other in alternate revolutions, we are always, no matter what attitude is adopted, in a state of instability in relation to the Other.
>
> *Being and Nothingness*, p. 529

The excerpt from *Being and Nothingness* that follows this chapter provides some of Sartre's analysis of these two modes of concrete being with others. Though Sartre implies that there are other possible ways of being with others, he also suggests that he views these two modes as basic and all others as mere variations on them. "The Other is on principle inapprehensible; he flees me when I seek him and possesses me when I flee him" (p. 529) says Sartre, and he gives us no reason to believe that any other dynamic is possible.

Sartre is very aware of the criticism that he has ignored the possibility of real community. Yet, for Sartre, the essence of intersubjectivity is inevitably conflict. Despite our common experiences of "we" and "us," those experiences are still, for Sartre, profoundly rooted in a battle of transcendence. The "we" who sit together on the subway or rush to the exit of a burning building or study in the library — all these are nothing but artificial collections of individuals.

Since Sartre suggests in *Being and Nothingness* that his concern is to flesh out an analysis of relationships in bad faith, some have maintained that his view of intersubjectivity is not as bleak as it seems. And there is reason to believe that he may have changed his view of the possibilities for genuine love. In a series of interviews in the weekly *Le Nouvel Observateur*, Sartre hinted that he might have erred in his analysis of the interpersonal. "I left each individual too independent in my theory of others," he concluded. "Today, I consider that everything which occurs in one consciousness in a given moment is necessarily tied to, often engendered by . . . the existence of others. . . . What is real is the relationship between thee and me." In the next breath, though, he claimed that he did not regard himself as an old man; rather, he said, it is "the others who are my old age." Regardless, though, of how we interpret the variety of messages he left, Sartre never provided a positive analysis of being-with-others. Thus, we turn to philosopher Martin Buber for an analysis of authentic being-with-others.

EXISTENTIAL DIALOGISM: MARTIN BUBER AND THE SEARCH FOR RELATION

Martin Buber, rather than exploring relationships in bad faith, seeks instead to develop a more complete exposition of what it means to speak of authentic being-with-others. Buber does not disagree with those existentialists who are critical of modern-day being-with-others. Indeed, he acknowledges that real dialogue has become rare today, tending to be disguised monologue or the relaying of purely technical information. Whether we are on the job, at a cocktail party, or in the presence of our friends, our conversations tend toward the inauthentic, our communications conventional and one-sided. This is not to say that people have become egoistic; indeed, Buber notes that even the social do-gooder may not enter into a genuine dialogue with those whom he or she is helping. Real dialogue requires that we truly *see* the other person. According to Buber,

> The basic movement of the life of dialogue is the turning towards the other. That, indeed, seems to happen every hour and quite trivially. If you look at someone and address him you turn to him, of course with the body, but also in the requisite measure with the soul, in that you direct attention to him. But what of all this is an essential action, done with the essential being? In this way, that out of the incomprehensibility of what lies to hand this one person steps forth and becomes a presence.
>
> *Between Man and Man*, p. 7

This sort of dialogue is, for Buber, the basis for real community, in contrast to what he calls "collectivity." "Collectivity is based on an organized atrophy of personal existence, community on its increase and confirmation in life lived towards one another." (*Between Man*, p. 10) Further, in a collectivity, individuals are bundled (rather than bound) together: "Individuals packed together, armed and equipped in common, with only as much life from man to man as will inflame the marching step." (p. 10)

No one is free from the responsibility of dialogue. For Buber, this activity is not reserved for the intellectual. It is even possible to achieve the life of dialogue in the workplace:

> He [a manager] practices it when he is inwardly aware, with a latent and disciplined fantasy, of the multitude of these persons, whom naturally he cannot separately know and remember as such; so that now, when one of them for some reason or other steps really as an individual into the circle of his vision and the realm of his decision, he is aware of him without strain not as a number with a human mask but as a person. He practises it when he comprehends and handles these persons as persons — for the greatest part necessarily indirectly, by means of a system of mediation which varies according to the extent, nature and structure of the undertaking, but also directly, in the parts which concern him by way of organization.
>
> *Between Man,* p. 23

This dialogue is the basis for what Buber terms the I-Thou relationship. For Buber, this relationship is primordial, and makes the individual I and the individual Thou possible. Many of our relationships, including those with other people, are I-It relationships. In the I-It relationship, we live in a world of instruments. Relationships between things are external; that is, it does not matter to the chair if we move it or even destroy it. In contrast, relations between people are internal. When we treat an Other as an object, we are not really open to the presence of the Other; we, in Kant's words, treat others as means to our ends rather than as ends in themselves. Racism, sexism, exploitation, and psychological manipulation are examples of I-It relationships.

There are other, more subtle, forms of the I-It: parents who fail to listen to their children; scholars who succumb to memorization and one-upmanship rather than develop a real passion for learning. And we can easily think of variations of these inauthentic relationships. There might be, for example, a we-we relationship, which fails to nurture any sort of individuality or difference, for such diversity might be threatening to the we. Or there could be the us-them in which anyone who has not succeeded in gaining membership in the group is automatically the enemy. In all these models, there is an genuine failure to be open to the Other.

Buber's analysis is not necessarily a normative one. Indeed, it is not always wrong to treat others as means to our ends. For example, I ask you for directions, you teach me to play guitar, you operate to remove my appendix. In these cases, no one is deceived or manipulated or made worse by the I-It relationship; indeed, such relationships may be mutually advantageous. But Buber believes there is more potential in being human.

For Buber, the I-Thou relationship involves one's whole being.

More specifically, he refers to it as a "confirmation" in which I really become myself through the Other and you really become you through me. Thus, for Buber, there is no I without Thou. The dialogue between an I and a Thou is never one-sided or domineering; rather, there is giving *and* receiving in this "personal meeting." Every I-Thou relationship is unique and exclusive — "it fills the firmament — not as if there were nothing else, but everything else lives in *its* light." (Buber, *I and Thou*, p. 126) Unlike Sartre, who sees the Other as a threat to freedom, Buber finds real freedom in the I-Thou: "Here I and You confront each other freely in a reciprocity that is not involved in or tainted by any causality; here man finds guaranteed the freedom of his being and of being." (p. 100)

According to Buber, when we say *I*, we are never really in isolation: We are either with objects or with persons. In a true personal meeting, there is no split between the active and the passive, between the giver and the receiver. In such a relationship, one is dependent yet free:

> Yes, in the pure relationship you felt altogether dependent, as you could never possibly feel in any other — and yet also altogether free as never and nowhere else; created — and creative. You no longer felt the one, limited by the other; you felt both without bounds, both at once.
>
> *I and Thou*, p. 130

Buber insists that this relationship is not derived from any other experience; rather, it is ultimate and absolute. There is no doubt that we cannot live without "its"; yet, at the same time, if we have *only* the it we are not really human. And love, for Buber, is the responsibility of an I for a Thou. It is *between* two persons, not just in each of them.

For Buber, we find God in the I-Thou relationship. Indeed, God is the eternal Thou, a Being who can never be an object, an It. Buber's masterpiece *I and Thou* deals with our direct relationship with God. In this sense, Buber springs directly out of Jewish religious tradition in that one can at any time return to and be accepted by God. His view is not, however, meant to be mystical or to take us away from the everyday world; rather, his view infuses the sacred into the everyday:

> The clear and firm structure of the I-You relationship, familiar to anyone with a candid heart and the courage to stake it, is not mystical. To understand it we must sometimes step out of our habits of thought, but not out of the primal norms that determine man's thoughts about what is actual. Both in the realm of nature and in the realm of spirit — the spirit that lives on in sayings and works and the spirit that strives to become sayings and works — what acts on us may be understood as the action of what has being.
>
> *I and Thou*, p. 177

Not only is our relationship with God direct, it is also, like all other I-Thou relationships, reciprocal. Buber's view here is paradoxical:

> That you need God more than anything, you know at all times in your heart. But don't you know also that God needs you — in the fullness of his eternity, you? How would man exist if God did not need him, and how would you exist? You need God in order to be, and God needs you — for that which is the meaning of your life. Teachings and poems try to say more, and say too much: how murky and presumptuous is the chatter of "the emerging God" — but the emergence of the living God we know unswervingly in our hearts.
>
> *I and Thou,* p. 130

Like Buber, theist Gabriel Marcel believes that the I lives in ontological harmony with every other Thou. For Marcel, "the more I think of my own being, the more I realize that this being does not depend on its own jurisdiction," and "the more I am, the more I affirm myself as being, the less I posit myself as autonomous." (*Being and Having,* p. 192) The Other can be our savior rather than our enemy. But this requires that we give up our own egocentrism. According to Marcel,

> This surely means that I must puncture the illusion, infinite persistent it is true, that I am possessed of unquestionable privileges which make me the centre of my universe, while other people are either mere obstructions to be removed or circumvented, or else those echoing amplifiers, whose purpose is to foster my self-complacency. I propose to call this illusion moral egocentricity, thus marking clearly how deeply it has become rooted in our very nature. In fact, just as any notions we may have of cosmography do not rid us from the immediate impression that the sun and stars go round the earth, so it is not possible for us to escape completely here below from the preconceived idea which makes each one tend to establish himself as the centre around which all the rest have no other function but to gravitate.
>
> *Homo Viator,* p. 19

Marcel uses the notion of "presence" to refer to one's openness to the Being of others. It is linked to "the urge to make ourselves recognised by some other person, some witness, helper, rival, or adversary." (*Homo Viator,* p. 15) Like Buber, he views God as the foundation for this connection with others. "That means — and there is nothing which is more important to keep in view — that the knowledge of an individual being cannot be separated from the act of love or charity by which this being is accepted in all which makes of him a unique creature or, if you like, the image of God." (*Homo Viator,* p. 23–24)

For both Marcel and Buber, we must reach out beyond our "narrow selves" to that which is beyond us but also depends on us for its existence.

This relationship is reciprocal, and through it one affirms oneself and the being of the Other. Where Sartre focuses on the shame we experience in the Other's gaze, Marcel and Buber emphasize the kind of confirmation we can receive in authentic relations with Others. The little child who exclaims, "Look what I found!" seeks this sort of affirmation; likewise, as adults, we can gain self-knowledge and fulfillment from others. We can share secrets and projects, lend assistance to one another, and discover mutual needs and even a common history. For example, when I hear that you attended the same college as I or grew up in the same town or even that we have the same birthday, we develop an immediate connection. And there is much more than we even realize that connects us, that makes us allies rather than enemies.

We saw in chapter 2 that Kierkegaard views the Other as a hindrance to our potential to reach the final stage on life's way, the religious stage. The examples of Abraham's willingness to sacrifice Isaac, and his own traumatic rejection of marriage, represent, for Kierkegaard, the "knight of faith," the individual whose actions cannot even be understood. Christianity, for Kierkegaard, is not a religion for the masses; indeed, the notion of a "Christian nation" is, he tells us, a contradiction. But for Marcel and Buber, the Other is not a hindrance to our religious development; rather, our connectedness to Others is the basis for our connectedness to God. It is, as Sartre says, a circle, but it is not a vicious one.

FEMINISM AND EXISTENTIALISM: WOMAN AS OTHER

> "Between us there is reciprocity. . . . At the moment when you recognize a consciousness in me, you know that I recognize one in you too."
> Simone de Beauvoir, *L'invitee*, p. 312

The introduction to Simone de Beauvoir's *Second Sex* tells the reader that de Beauvoir approaches her topic from the perspective of an existentialist ethics. De Beauvoir maintains that this perspective is well suited to her subject, which is *Woman*. Everyone seems to agree, she acknowledges, on the basic facts: for example, that women comprise 50 percent of the human species, and that women come equipped with certain biological features, like a uterus. But, she notes, there are times when people claim a woman is "not womanly enough" or when social commentators complain that femininity itself is in danger. These kinds of statements might suggest that there is something fragile about being a woman, and that in fact there is more to being a woman than possessing ovaries. But what is that "more"?

Increasingly, de Beauvoir comments, we are inclined to say that there are no real differences between men and women, and that women — like men — are just human. But for de Beauvoir this view is overly simplistic. One can, she says, simply take a walk down the street and one will realize that there are very real differences between men and women. Whether those differences will someday disappear is irrelevant, for the fact is that they now exist.

According to de Beauvoir, a man never presents himself first as a member of a particular sex; a woman always does. For "man" is not just male, he is also generic "man," as in "all men are mortal" or "mankind." Women, according to de Beauvoir, are always defined in contrast. This applies even to discussions of the body:

> Woman has ovaries, a uterus; these peculiarities imprison her in her subjectivity, circumscribe her within the limits of her own nature. It is often said that she thinks with her glands. Man superbly ignores the fact that his anatomy also includes glands, such as the testicles, and that they secrete hormones. He thinks of his body as a direct and normal connection with the world, which he believes he apprehends objectively, whereas he regards the body of a woman as a hindrance, a prison, weighed down by everything peculiar to it.
>
> *Second Sex,* p. xviii

Thus, man defines woman in terms relative to him. "He is the subject, he is the Absolute — she is the Other." (p. xix) Here, de Beauvoir's existentialist framework begins to provide the basis for her analysis.

As we have seen, Sartre's phenomenology of interpersonal relationships exposes a dynamic of consciousness struggling against consciousness to gain ascendency. De Beauvoir in *The Second Sex* presupposes much of this framework. She maintains, for example, that culture itself tends to be based on separation rather than collectivity, and that hostility and opposition between subjects are fundamental data of social reality.

But no Other voluntarily agrees to be an object. Rather, the Subject must be submissive enough to accept this control. In this context, Woman must be submissive enough to allow herself to be defined relative to the subject, Man. How has this occurred, since women and men exist in virtually equal numbers and have throughout time?

De Beauvoir argues that this situation is a result of the social, emotional, and biological interconnections of men and women. Unlike other oppressed groups, women do not see themselves as united in a similar plight. They do not all hate their enemies; indeed, they are probably their wives or their sisters or their mothers. Women do not share a common history or a common language or a common culture. Consequently, the oppression of women is pervasive and extremely difficult to eradicate. This is all the more true, since some women reap the advantages of their association with powerful males.

De Beauvoir in *The Second Sex* comes to the conclusion that women are inferior to men. But, she argues, it is an example of bad faith (see chapter 7 for a discussion of the ethical implications of bad faith) to maintain that this is a permanent condition. To do so would be to give women and men a fixed and static nature, and this obviously violates the existentialist analysis of Dasein as freedom and possibility. Furthermore, de Beauvoir argues, it is woman's socialization which has made her inferior to men. She has been restricted physically by her clothes, intellectually by inadequate education, and morally by her lack of independence. Even when women resign themselves to this inferiority, there is no "innate" basis for it. According to de Beauvoir,

> It has been often asserted that if she resigns herself to such submission, it means that she is inferior to boys materially and morally and is incapable of rivalry with them: abandoning a hopeless contest, she leaves to a member of the superior caste the task of assuring her happiness. But the fact is that her resignation comes not from any predetermined inferiority: on the contrary, it is that which gives rise to all her insufficiencies; that resignation has its source in the adolescent girl's past, in the society around her, and particularly in the future assigned to her.
>
> *The Second Sex,* p. 368

Women, too, can be in bad faith in accepting their object-status. At times this decision is advantageous, as it relieves the woman of any responsibility for her situation. Furthermore, women have learned all sorts of means by which to deceive men into thinking that they are the inferior sex.

> (L)ike all the oppressed, woman deliberately dissembles her objective actuality; the slave, the servant, the indigent, all who depend upon the caprices of a master, have learned to turn toward him a changeless smile or an enigmatic impassivity; their real sentiments, their actual behavior, are carefully hidden. And moreover woman is taught from adolescence to lie to men, to scheme, to be wily. In speaking to them she wears an artificial expression on her face; she is cautious, hypocritical, play-acting.
>
> *The Second Sex,* p. 292

But, regardless, de Beauvoir argues that it is men who have the most to gain from the objectification of women. They can, for example, feel superior, and so "the most mediocre of males feels himself a demigod as compared with women." (*The Second Sex,* p. xxviii) Most men will not make bald assertions about women's inferiority, but will rather expose their privileged subject-status in more subtle ways, for example, through overprotectiveness or trivializing comments.

For de Beauvoir, the oppression of women is an "absolute evil." (*The Second Sex,* p. xxxiii) Every individual, she argues, every *pour soi,* can only justify its existence by its freedom, by constantly reaching out into the future in its own individual transcendence. To refuse this for oneself or to limit it in another is to attempt to make of Dasein an *en-soi;* but this is, for de Beauvoir, a degradation. To do so is to fall back into "stagnation," into the "brutish life of subjection to given condition." (p. xxxiii) De Beauvoir rejects the notion that one in such circumstances can be called happy, for happiness never "consists in being at rest"; and the *en-soi* is always at rest, (p. xxxiii) it is exactly what it is and nothing more. As she states in the *Ethics of Ambiguity* (see chapter 7), there is no absolute justification for our actions, but we must always reach out toward freedom.

Thus, there is no "destiny" for Woman (see p. 426). It is true that there is a battle between the sexes, but this too results from situation and not "nature." "All oppression creates a state of war," says de Beauvoir, (p. 427) and it is in self-defense that Woman tries to deceive, dominate, or beguile Man. There is no point in blaming one or the other sex, for the situation has been with us too long. De Beauvoir (see p. 433) discusses what liberation might mean for women, and she argues that it is essential that women make decisions for themselves. It has been too long that others have done that for her: "Woman is determined not by her hormones or by mysterious instincts, but by the manner in which her body and her relation to the world are modified through the action of others than herself." (p. 434)

Some feminists maintain that de Beauvoir has undermined her argument through her acceptance of male values, like assertiveness and activity. They argue that de Beauvoir has overlooked the values of "women's culture," like qualities of nurturing, sensitivity, and so forth. It is especially ironic that the last sentence of *The Second Sex* (see p. 439) affirms the "brotherhood" of all humanity. But de Beauvoir might respond that character traits that arise out of oppression, out of otherness, must not be affirmed. Since, as an existentialist, her view is based on freedom, she rejects any attributes that emerge in response to limiting situations. Though her view of freedom does not seem to be as absolute as that of Sartre, she nonetheless makes freedom what distinguishes human being from any other sort of freedom. For women, then, to be human is to reaffirm ourselves in that freedom.

CONCLUSION

Though existentialists may disagree on the specifics of the analysis, all are preoccupied with the problem of intersubjectivity. Indeed, they emphasize the paradoxical nature of being human: While we require the teaching of others to enable us to become human, we also resist the notion that we are those others' creations. Like Estelle in *No Exit*, we crave the "look" of the other at the same time that we realize, in frustration, that we cannot control how the other looks at us.

This chapter has explored three very different analyses of human intersubjectivity. Though each one acknowledges the importance of that intersubjectivity, each differs in its perspective on that importance. For Sartre, being-with-others is essentially problematic; as for-itself, as possibility, we are forever forced to battle with another for-itself over which of us will be reduced to object status. In contrast, for Buber (and others, like Marcel) intersubjectivity (though not without its tensions) is a means *back* to ourselves. To be a person, according to this view, is essentially to exist with others. Finally, de Beauvoir uses the concepts of existentialism to look at one particular dynamic, namely the dynamic of patriarchy, to show how Woman becomes "created" Other. The excerpts that follow clarify the contributions each framework makes.

QUESTIONS FOR CONSIDERATION

1. Sartre's view of interpersonal relationships has a good deal to do with his notion of freedom. Do freedoms have to be in conflict, as Sartre claims?
2. Can you think of relationships that do not follow the model that Sartre describes? What do you think Sartre would say about your example(s)?
3. Does Buber's view depend on belief in God? Why or why not?
4. Where does the notion of possession fit into Sartre's framework? What does it mean to want to "possess the freedom of the Other"?
5. How is de Beauvoir an existentialist? How is she a feminist? How do these two views mesh? How might they be incompatible?
6. In what ways has Woman been considered Other in contemporary society?
7. Is it possible to treat others as Thou? Defend your position.
8. Look again at the excerpt from Marcel at the end of chapter 5 (see

pp. 336–43). How is Marcel's view of freedom related to his analysis of interpersonal relationships?

REFERENCES

AYER, ALFRED J. "One's Knowledge of Other Minds." *Theoria* 19 (1953), pp. 1–20.

BUBER, MARTIN. *Between Man and Man.* Translated by Ronald Gregor Smith. New York: Macmillan, 1965.

———. *I and Thou.* Translated by Walter Kaufmann. New York: Charles Scribner's Sons, 1970.

DE BEAUVOIR, SIMONE. *L'Invitee.* Paris: Gallimard, 1943.

———. *The Second Sex.* Translated by H. M. Parshley. New York: Vintage Books, 1952.

DESCARTES, RÉNE. *Meditations on First Philosophy.* Translated by Donald A. Cress. Indianapolis: Hackett Publishing Co., 1979.

———. *The Passions of the Soul.* Translated by Elizabeth S. Haldane and G. R. T. Ross. Cambridge: Cambridge University Press, 1911.

HEIDEGGER, MARTIN. *Being and Time.* Translated by John Macquarrie and Edward Robinson. New York: Harper & Row, 1962.

HUSSERL, EDMUND. *The Crisis of European Sciences and Transcendental Phenomenology.* Translated by D. Carr. Evanston, Ill.: Northwestern University Press, 1970.

MARCEL, GABRIEL. *Being and Having: An Existentialist Diary.* New York: Harper and Row, 1965.

———. *Homo Viator: An Introduction to a Metaphysic of Hope.* Translated by Emma Craufurd. New York: Harper & Row, 1962.

———. *The Mystery of Being.* Translated by G. S. Fraser. Chicago: Henry Regnery Co., 1950.

MERLEAU-PONTY, MAURICE. *The Phenomenology of Perception.* Translated by Colin Smith. London: Routledge and Kegan Paul, 1962. See especially pages 67–201 and 346–65.

SARTRE, JEAN-PAUL. "Playboy Interview: Jean-Paul Sartre — Candid Conversation." *Playboy* 12 (1965):69–77.

———. *Being and Nothingness.* Translated by Hazel Barnes. New York: Washington Square Press, 1956.

———. *The Devil and the Good Lord.* Translated by Kitty Black. New York: Vintage Books, 1960.

———. *The Flies.* In *No Exit and Three Other Plays,* translated by Stuart Gilbert. New York: Vintage Books, 1946.

————. *No Exit.* In *No Exit and Three Other Plays,* translated by Stuart Gilbert. New York: Vintage Books, 1946.

THEUNISSEN, MICHAEL. *The Other: Studies in the Social Ontology of Husserl, Heidegger, Sartre, and Buber.* Translated by Christopher Macann. Cambridge: Massachusetts Institute of Technology Press, 1986.

WOODWARD, KENNETH L. (with Scott Sullivan), "Jean-Paul Sartre — 1905–1980." *Newsweek,* April 28, 1980, p. 77.

JEAN-PAUL SARTRE

Sartre is perhaps most famous (or infamous) for analysis of interpersonal relationships. In his fiction as well as in his major philosophical treatises like Being and Nothingness *(from which the following excerpt comes), he expresses a profound pessimism over the possibility of authentic relationships. Whether he leaves any room for a positive model of the intersubjective is open to debate. But there is no doubt that his focus is on the essential conflict that exists between self and the Other.*

Being and Nothingness

IV. THE LOOK

This woman whom I see coming toward me, this man who is passing by in the street, this beggar whom I hear calling before my window, all are for me *objects* — of that there is no doubt. Thus it is true that at least one of the modalities of the Other's presence to me is *object-ness*. But we have seen that if this relation of object-ness is the fundamental relation between the Other and myself, then the Other's existence remains purely conjectural. Now it is not only conjectural but *probable* that this voice which I hear is that of a man and not a song on a phonograph; it is infinitely *probable* that the passerby whom I see is a man and not a perfected robot. This means that without going beyond the limits of probability and indeed because of this very probability, my apprehension of the Other as an object essentially refers me to a fundamental apprehension of the Other in which he will not be revealed to me as an object but as a "presence in person." In short, if the Other is to be a probable object and not a dream of an object, then his object-ness must of necessity refer not to an original solitude beyond my reach, but to a fundamental connection in which the Other is manifested in some way other than through the knowledge which I have of him. The classical theories are right in considering that every perceived human organism *refers* to something and that this to which it refers is the foundation and guarantee of its probability. Their mistake lies in believing that this reference indicates a separate existence, a consciousness which would be behind its perceptible manifestations as the noumenon is behind the Kantian *Empfindung*. Whether or not this consciousness exists in a separate state, the face which I see does not refer to it; it is not this consciousness which is the

From Jean-Paul Sartre, *Being and Nothingness,* translated by Hazel Barnes, pp. 340–53, 377–81, 474–82, 490–93, 494–95, 521–26. Footnotes deleted. Reprinted by permission of the Philosophical Library.

truth of the probable object which I perceive. In actual fact the reference to a twin upsurge in which the Other is presence for me to a "being-in-a-pair-with-the-Other," and this is given outside of knowledge proper even if the latter be conceived as an obscure and unexpressible form on the order of intuition. In other words, the problem of Others has generally been treated as if the primary relation by which the Other is discovered is object-ness; that is, as if the Other were first revealed — directly or indirectly — to our perception. But since this perception by its very nature *refers* to something other than to itself and since it can refer neither to an infinite series of appearances of the same type — as an idealism the perception of the table or of the chair does — nor to an isolated entity located on principle outside my reach, its essence must be to refer to a primary relation between my consciousness and the Other's. This relation, in which the Other must be given to me directly as a subject although in connection with me, is the fundamental relation, the very type of my being-for-others.

Nevertheless the reference here cannot be to any mystic or ineffable experience. It is in the reality of everyday life that the Other appears to us, and this probability refers to everyday reality. The problem is precisely this: there is in everyday reality an original relation to the Other which can be constantly pointed to and which consequently can be revealed to me outside all reference to a religious or mystic unknowable. In order to understand it I must question more exactly this ordinary appearance of the Other in the field of my perception; since this appearance refers to that fundamental relation, the appearance must be capable of revealing to us, at least as a reality aimed at, the relation to which it refers.

I am in a public park. Not far away there is a lawn and along the edge of that lawn there are benches. A man passes by those benches. I see this man; I apprehend him as an object and at the same time as a man. What does this signify? What do I mean when I assert that this object *is a man?*

If I were to think of him as being only a puppet, I should apply to him the categories which I ordinarily use to group temporal-spatial "things." That is, I should apprehend him as being "beside" the benches, two yards and twenty inches from the lawn, as exercising a certain pressure on the ground, *etc.* His relation with other objects would be of the purely additive type; this means that I could have him disappear without the relations of the other objects around him being perceptibly *changed.* In short, no new relation would appear *through him* between those things in my universe: grouped and synthesized *from my point of view* into instrumental complexes, they would *from his* disintegrate into multiplicities of indifferent relations. Perceiving him as a *man*, on the other hand, is not to apprehend an additive relation between the chair and him; it is to register an organization *without distance* of the things in my universe around that privileged object. To be sure, the lawn remains two yards and twenty inches away from him, but it is also *as a lawn* bound to him in a relation which at once both transcends distance and contains it. Instead of the two terms of the distance being indifferent, interchangeable, and in a reciprocal relation, the distance *is unfolded starting from* the man whom I see and *extending up to* the lawn as the synthetic upsurge of a univocal relation. We are dealing with a relation which is without *parts,* given at one stroke, inside of which there unfolds a spatiality which is not *my* spatiality; for instead of a grouping *toward me* of the objects, there is now an orientation *which flees from me.*

Of course this relation without distance and without parts is in no way that original relation of the Other to me which I am seeking. In the first place, it concerns only the man and the things in the world. In addition it is still an object of knowledge; I shall express it, for example, by saying that this man sees the lawn, or that in spite of the prohibiting sign he is preparing to walk on the grass, *etc.* Finally it still retains a pure character of probability: First, it is *probable* that this object is a man. Second, even granted that he is a man, it remains only probable that he sees the lawn at the moment that I perceive him; it is possible that he is dreaming of some project without exactly being aware of what is around him, or that he is blind, *etc., etc.* Nevertheless this new relation of the object-man to the object-lawn has a particular character; it is simultaneously given to me as a whole, since it is there in the world as an object which I can know (it is, in fact, an objective relation which I express by saying: Pierre has glanced at this watch, Jean has looked out the window, *etc.*), and at the same time it entirely escapes me. To the extent that the man-as-object is the fundamental term of this relation, to the extent that the relation *reaches toward him,* it escapes me. I can not put myself at the center of it. The distance which unfolds between the lawn and the man across the synthetic upsurge of this primary relation is a negation of the distance which I establish — as a pure type of external negation — between these two objects. The distance appears as a pure *disintegration* of the relations which I apprehend between the objects of my universe. It is not I who realize this disintegration; it appears to me as a relation which I aim at emptily across the distances which I originally established between things. It stands as a background of things, a background which on principle escapes me and which is conferred on them from without. Thus the appearance among the objects of *my* universe of an element of disintegration in that universe is what I mean by the appearance of a man in my universe.

The Other is first the permanent flight of things toward a goal which I apprehend as an object at a certain distance from me but which escapes me inasmuch as it unfolds about itself its own distances. Moreover this disintegration grows by degrees; if there exists between the lawn and the Other a relation which is without distance and which creates distance, then there exists necessarily a relation between the Other and the statue which stands on a pedestal *in the middle of* the lawn, and a relation between the Other and the big chestnut trees which border the walk; there is a total space which is grouped around the Other, and this space is made *with my space;* there is a regrouping in which I take part but which escapes me, a regrouping of all the objects which people my universe. This regrouping does not stop there. The grass is something qualified; it is *this* green grass which exists for the Other; in this sense the very quality of the object, its deep, raw green is in direct relation to this man. This green turns toward the Other a face which escapes me. I apprehend the relation of the green to the Other as an objective relation, but I can not apprehend the green *as* it appears to the Other. Thus suddenly an object has appeared which has stolen the world from me. Everything is in place; everything still exists for me; but everything is traversed by an invisible flight and fixed in the direction of a new object. The appearance of the Other in the world corresponds therefore to a fixed sliding of the whole universe, to a decentralization of the world which undermines the centralization which I am simultaneously effecting.

But *The Other* is still an object *for me.* He belongs to *my distances;* the man is there, twenty paces from me, he is turning his back on me. As such he is again two yards, twenty inches from the lawn, six yards from the statue; hence the disintegration of my universe is contained within the limits of this same universe; we are not dealing here with a flight of the world toward nothingness or outside itself. Rather it appears that the world has a kind of drain hole in the middle of its being and that it is perpetually flowing off through this hole. The universe, the flow, and the drain hole are all once again recovered, reapprehended, and fixed as an object. All this is there *for me* as a partial structure of the world, even though the total disintegration of the universe is involved. Moreover these disintegrations may often be contained within more narrow limits. There, for example, is a man who is reading while he walks. The disintegration of the universe which he represents is purely virtual: he has ears which do not hear, eyes which see nothing except his book. Between his book and him I apprehend an undeniable relation without distance of the same type as that which earlier connected the walker with the grass. But this time the form has closed in on itself. There is a full object for me to grasp. In the midst of the world I can say "man-reading" as I could say "cold stone," "fine rain." I apprehend a closed "Gestalt" in which the *reading* forms the essential quality; for the rest, it remains blind and mute, lets itself be known and perceived as a pure and simple temporal-spatial thing, and seems to be related to the rest of the world by a purely indifferent externality. The quality "man-reading" as the relation of the man to the book is simply a little particular crack in my universe. At the heart of this solid, visible form he makes himself a particular emptying.

The form is massive only in appearance; its peculiar meaning is to be — in the midst of my universe, at ten paces from me, at the heart of that massivity — a closely consolidated and localized flight.

None of this enables us to leave the level on which the Other is an *object*. At most we are dealing with a particular type of objectivity akin to that which Husserl designated by the term *absence* without, however, his noting that the Other is defined not as the absence of a consciousness in relation to the body which I see but by the absence of the world which I perceive, an absence discovered at the very heart of my perception of this world. On this level the Other is an object in the world, an object which can be defined by the world. But this relation of flight and of absence on the part of the world in relation to me is only probable. If it is this which defines the objectivity of the Other, then to what original presence of the Other does it refer? At present we can give this answer: if the Other-as-object is defined in connection with the world as the object which sees what I see, then my fundamental connection with the Other-as-subject must be able to be referred back to my permanent possibility of *being seen* by the Other. It is in and through the revelation of my being-as-object for the Other that I must be able to apprehend the presence of his being-as-subject. For just as the Other is a probable object for me-as-subject, so I can discover myself in the process of becoming a probable object for only a certain subject. This revelation can not derive from the fact that *my universe is an object for the Other-as-object, as if* the Other's look after having wandered over the lawn and the surrounding objects came following a definite path to place itself on me. I have observed that I can not be an object for an object. A radical conversion of the Other is necessary if he is to escape objectivity. Therefore I can not consider the look which the Other directs on me as one of the possible manifestations of his objective being; the Other can not look at *me* as he looks at the grass. Furthermore my objectivity can not itself derive *for me* from the objectivity of the world since I am precisely the one by whom *there is* a world; that is, the one who on principle can not be an object for himself.

Thus this relation which I call "being-seen-by-another," far from being merely one of the relations signified by the word *man*, represents an irreducible fact which can not be deduced either from the essence of the Other-as-object, or from my being-as-subject. On the contrary, if the concept of the Other-as-object is to have any meaning, this can be only as the result of the conversion and the degradation of that original relation. In a word, my apprehension of the Other in the world as *probably being* a man refers to my permanent possibility of *being-seen-by-him;* that is, to the permanent possibility that a subject who sees me may be substituted for the object seen by me. "Being-seen-by-the-Other" is the *truth* of "seeing-the-Other." Thus the notion of the Other can not under any circumstances aim at a solitary, extra-mundane consciousness which I can not even think. The man is defined by his relation to the world and by his relation to myself. He is that object in the world which determines an internal flow of the universe, an internal hemorrhage. He is the subject who is revealed to me in that flight of myself toward objectivation. But the original relation of myself to the Other is not only an absent truth aimed at across the concrete presence of an object in my universe; it is also a concrete, daily relation which at each instant I experience. At each instant the Other *is looking at me*. It is easy therefore for us to attempt with concrete examples to describe this fundamental connection which must form the basis of any theory concerning the Other. If the Other is on principle the *one who looks at me*, then we must be able to explain the meaning of the Other's look.

Every look directed toward me is manifested in connection with the appearance of a sensible form in our perceptive field, but contrary to what might be expected, it is not connected with any determined form. Of course what *most often* manifests a look is the convergence of two ocular globes in my direction. But the look will be given just as well on occasion when there is a rustling of branches, or the sound of a footstep followed by silence, or the slight opening of a shutter, or a light movement of a curtain. During an attack men who are crawling through the brush apprehend as a *look to be avoided,* not two eyes, but a white farmhouse which is outlined against the sky at the top of a little hill. It is obvious that the object thus constituted still manifests the look as being probable. It is only probable that behind the bush which has just moved there is someone hiding who is watching me. But this probability need not detain us for the moment; we shall return to this point later. What is important first is to define the look in itself. Now the bush, the farmhouse are not the look; they only represent the *eye*, for the eye is not at first apprehended as a sensible organ of vision but as the support for the look. They never refer therefore to the actual eye of the watcher hidden behind the curtain, behind a window in the farmhouse. In themselves they are already eyes. On the other hand neither is the look one quality among others of the object which functions as an eye, nor is it the total form of that object, nor a "worldly" relation which is established between that object and me. On the contrary, far from perceiving the look *on* the objects which manifest it, my apprehension of a look turned toward me appears on the ground of the destruction of the eyes which "look at me." If I apprehend the look, I cease to perceive the eyes; they are there, they remain in the field of my perception as pure *presentations*, but I do not make any use of them; they are neutralized, put out of play; they are no longer the object of a thesis but remain in that state of "disconnection" in which the world is put by a consciousness practicing the phenomenological reduction prescribed by Husserl. It is never when eyes are looking at you that you can find them beautiful or ugly, that you can remark on their color. The Other's look hides his eyes; he seems to go *in front of them.* This illusion stems from the fact that eyes as objects of my perception remain at a precise distance which unfolds from me to them (in a word, I am present to the eyes without distance, but they are distant from the place where I "find my-self") whereas the look is upon me without distance while at the same time it holds me at a distance — that is, its immediate presence to me unfolds a distance which removes me from it. I can not therefore direct my attention on the look without at the same stroke causing my perception to decompose and pass into the background. There is produced here something analogous to what I attempted to show elsewhere in connection with the subject of the imagination. We can not, I said then, perceive and imagine simultaneously; it must be either one or the other. I should willingly say here: we can not perceive the world and at the same time apprehend a look fastened upon us; it must be either one or the other. This is because to perceive is to *look at,* and to apprehend a look is not to apprehend a look-as-object in the world (unless the look is not directed upon us); it is to be conscious of *being looked at.* The look which the *eyes* manifest, no matter what kind of eyes they are, is a pure reference to myself. What I apprehend immediately when I hear the branches crackling behind me is not that *there is someone there;* it is that I am vulnerable, that I have a body which can be hurt, that I occupy a place and that I can not in any case escape from the space in which I am without defense — in short, that I *am seen.* Thus the look is first an intermediary which refers from me to myself. What is the nature of this intermediary? What does *being seen* mean for me?

Let us imagine that moved by jealousy, curiosity, or vice I have just glued my ear to the door and looked through a keyhole. I am alone and on the level of a non-thetic self-consciousness. This means first of all that there is no self to inhabit my consciousness, nothing therefore to which I can refer my acts in order to qualify them. They are in no way *known;* I am *my acts* and hence they carry in themselves their whole justification. I am a pure consciousness *of* things, and things, caught up in the circuit of my selfness, offer to me their potentialities as the proof of my non-thetic consciousness (of) my own possibilities. This means that behind that door a spectacle is presented as "to be seen," a conversation as "to be heard." The door, the keyhole are at once both instruments and obstacles; they are presented as "to be handled with care"; the keyhole is given as "to be looked through close by and a little to one side," *etc.* Hence from this moment "I do what I have to do." No transcending view comes to confer upon my acts the character of a *given* on which a judgment can be brought to bear. My consciousness sticks to my acts, it *is* my acts; and my acts are commanded only by the ends to be attained and by the instruments to be employed. My attitude, for example, has no "outside"; it is a pure process of relating the instrument (the keyhole) to the end to be attained (the spectacle to be seen), a pure mode of losing myself in the world, of causing myself to be drunk in by things as ink is by a blotter in order that an instrumental-complex oriented toward an end may be synthetically detached on the ground of the world. The order is the reverse of causal order. It is the end to be attained which organizes all the moments which precede it. The end justifies the means; the means do not exist for themselves and outside the end.

Moreover the ensemble exists only in relation to a free project of my possibilities. Jealousy, as the possibility which I *am*, organizes this instrumental complex by transcending it toward itself. But I *am* this jealousy; I do not *know* it. If I contemplated it instead of making it, then only the worldly complex in instrumentality could teach it to me. This ensemble in the world with its double and inverted determination (there is a spectacle to be seen behind the door only because I am jealous, but my jealousy is nothing except the simple objective fact that *there is* a sight *to be seen* behind the door) — this we shall call *situation*. This situation reflects to me at once both my facticity and my freedom; on the occasion of a certain objective structure of the world which surrounds me, it refers my freedom to me in the form of tasks to be freely done. There is no constraint here since my freedom eats into my possibles and since correlatively the potentialities of the world indicate and offer only themselves. Moreover I can not truly define myself as *being* in a situation: first because I am not a positional consciousness of myself; second because I am my own nothingness. In this sense — and since I am what I am not and since I am not what I am — I can not even define myself as truly *being* in the process of listening at doors. I escape this provisional definition of myself by means of all my transcendence. There as we have seen is the origin of bad faith. Thus not only am I unable to *know* myself, but my very being escapes — although I *am* that very escape from my being — and I am absolutely nothing. There is nothing *there* but a pure nothingness encircling a certain objective ensemble and throwing it into relief outlined upon the world, but this ensemble is a real system, a disposition of means in view of an end.

But all of a sudden I hear footsteps in the hall. Someone is looking at me! What does this mean? It means that I am suddenly affected in my being and that essential modifications appear in my structure — modifications which I can apprehend and fix conceptually by means of the reflective *cogito*.

First of all, I now exist as *myself* for my unreflective consciousness. It is this irruption of the self which has been most often described: I see *myself* because *somebody* sees me — as it is usually expressed. This way of putting it is not wholly exact. But let us look more carefully. So long as we considered the for-itself in its isolation, we were able to maintain that the unreflective consciousness can not be inhabited by a self; the self was given in the form of an object and only for the reflective consciousness. But here the self comes to haunt the unreflective consciousness. Now the unreflective consciousness is a consciousness *of* the world. Therefore for the unreflective consciousness the self exists on the level of objects in the world; this role which devolved only on the reflective conscious- ness — the making-present of the self — belongs now to the unreflective consciousness. Only the reflective consciousness has the self directly for an object. The unreflective consciousness does not apprehend the *person* directly or as *its* object; the person is presented to consciousness *in so far as the person is an object for the Other.* This means that all of a sudden I am conscious of myself as escaping myself, not in that I am the foundation of my own nothingness but in that I have my foundation outside myself. I am for myself only as I am a pure reference to the Other.

Nevertheless we must not conclude here that the object is the Other and that the *Ego* present to my consciousness is a secondary structure or a meaning of the Other-as-object; the Other is not an object here and can not be an object, as we have shown, unless by the same stroke *my* self ceases to be an object-for-the-Other and vanishes. Thus I do not aim at the Other as an object nor at my *Ego* as an object for myself; I do not even direct an empty intention toward that *Ego* as toward an object presently out of my reach. In fact it is separated from me by a nothingness which I can not fill since I apprehend it *as not being for me* and since on principle it exists for the *Other.* Therefore I do not aim at it as if it could someday be given me but on the contrary in so far as it on principle flees from me and will never belong to me. Nevertheless I *am that Ego*; I do not reject it as a strange image, but it is present to me as a self which I *am* without *knowing* it; for I discover it in shame and, in other instances, in pride. It is shame or pride which reveals to me the Other's look and myself at the end of that look. It is the shame or pride which makes me *live,* not *know* the situation of being looked at.

Now, shame, as we noted at the beginning of this chapter, is shame of *self;* it is the *recognition* of the fact that I *am* indeed that object which the Other is looking at and judging. I can be ashamed only as my freedom escapes me in order to become a *given* object. Thus originally the bond between my unreflective consciousness and my *Ego,* which is being looked at, is a bond not of knowing but of being. Beyond any knowledge which I can have, I am this self which another knows. And this self which I am — this I am in a world which the Other has made alien to me, for the Other's look embraces my being and correlatively the walls, the door, the keyhole. All these instrumental-things, in the midst of which I am, now turn toward the Other a face which on principle escapes me. Thus I am my *Ego* for the Other in the midst of a world which flows toward the Other. Earlier we were able to call this internal hemorrhage the flow of *my* world toward the Other-as-object. This was because the flow of blood was trapped and localized by the very fact that I fixed as an object in my world that Other toward which this world was bleeding. Thus not a drop of blood was lost; all was recovered, surrounded, localized although in a being which I could not penetrate. Here on the contrary the flight is without limit; it is lost externally; the world flows out of the world and I flow outside myself. The Other's look makes me be beyond my being in this world and puts me in the midst of the world which is at once *this world* and beyond this world. What sort of relations can I enter into with this being which I am and which shame reveals to me?

In the first place there is a relation of being. I *am* this being. I do not for an instant think of denying it; my shame is a confession. I shall be able later to use bad faith so as to hide it from myself, but bad faith is also a confession since it is an effort to flee the being which I am. But I am this being, neither in the mode of "having to be" nor in that of "was"; I do not found it in its being; I can not produce it directly. But neither is it the indirect, strict effect of my acts as when my shadow on the ground or my reflection in the mirror is moved in correlation with the gestures which I make. This being which I am preserves a certain indetermination, a certain unpredictability. And these new characteristics do not come only from the fact that I can not *know* the Other; they stem also and especially from the fact that the Other is free. Or to be exact and to reverse the terms, the Other's freedom is revealed to me across the uneasy indetermination of the being which I am for him. Thus this being is not my possible; it is not always in question at the heart of my freedom. On the contrary, it is the limit of my freedom, its "backstage" in the sense that we speak of "behind the scenes." It is given to me as a burden which I carry without ever being able to turn back to know it, without even being able to realize its weight. If it is comparable to my shadow, it is like a shadow which is projected on a moving and unpredictable material such that no table of reference can be provided for calculating the distortions resulting from these movements. Yet we still have to do with *my* being and not with an image of my being. We are dealing with my being as it is written in and by the Other's freedom. Everything takes place as if I had a dimension of being from which I was separated by a radical nothingness; and this nothingness is the Other's freedom. The Other has to make my being-for-him *be* in so far as he has to be his being. Thus each of my free conducts engages me in a new environment where the very stuff of my being is the unpredictable freedom of another. Yet by my very shame I claim as mine that freedom of another. I affirm a profound unity of consciousness, not that harmony of monads which has sometimes been taken as a guarantee of objectivity but a unity of being; for I accept and wish that others should confer upon me a being which I recognize.

Shame reveals to me that I *am* this being, not in the mode of "was" or of "having to be" but *in-itself*. When I am alone, I can not realize my "being-seated"; at most it can be said that I simultaneously both am it and am not it. But in order for me to be what I am, it suffices merely that the Other look at me. It is not for myself, to be sure; I myself shall never succeed at realizing this being-seated which I grasp in the Other's look. I shall remain forever a consciousness. But it is for the Other. Once more the nihilating escape of the for-itself is fixed, once more the in-itself closes in upon the for-itself. But once more this metamorphosis is effected *at a distance*. For the Other *I am seated* as this inkwell *is on* the table; for the Other, *I am leaning over* the keyhole as this tree *is bent* by the wind. Thus for the Other I have stripped myself of transcendence. This is because my transcendence becomes for whoever makes himself a witness of it (*i.e.*, determines himself *as not being* my transcendence) a purely established transcendence, a given-transcendence; that is, it acquires a nature by the sole fact that the *Other* confers on it an outside. This is accomplished, not by any distortion or by a refraction which the Other would impose on my transcendence through his categories, but by his very being. If there is an Other, whatever or whoever he may be, whatever may be his relations with me, and without his acting upon me in any way except by the pure upsurge of his being — then I have an outside, I have a *nature*. My original fall is the existence of the Other. Shame — like pride — is the apprehension of myself as a nature although that very nature escapes me and is unknowable as such. Strictly speaking, it is not that I perceive myself losing my freedom in order to become a *thing*, but my nature is — over there, outside my lived freedom — as a given attribute of this being which I am for the Other.

I grasp the Other's look at the very center of my *act* as the solidification and alienation of my own possibilities. In fear or in anxious or prudent anticipation, I perceive that these possibilities which I *am* and which are the condition of my transcendence are given also to another, given as about to be transcended in turn by his own possibilities. The Other as a look is only that — my transcendence transcended. Of course I still *am* my possibilities in the mode of non-thetic consciousness (of) these possibilities. But at the same time the look alienates them from me. Hitherto I grasped these possibilities thetically on the world and in the world in the form of the potentialities of instruments: the dark corner in the hallway referred to me the possibility of hiding — as a simple potential quality of its shadow, as the invitation of its darkness. This quality or instrumentality of the object belonged to it alone and was given as an objective, ideal property marking its real belonging to that complex which we have called *situation*. But with the Other's look a new organization of complexes comes to superimpose itself on the first. To apprehend myself as seen is, in fact, to apprehend myself as seen *in the world* and from the standpoint of the world. The look does not carve me out in the universe; it comes to search for me at the heart of my situation and grasps me only in irresolvable relations with instruments. If I am seen as seated, I must be seen as "seated-on-a-chair," if I am grasped as bent over, it is as "bent-over-the-keyhole," *etc*. But suddenly the alienation of myself, which is the act of being-looked-at, involves the alienation of the world which I organize. I am seen as seated on this chair with the result that I do not see it at all, that it is impossible for me to see it, that it escapes me so as to organize itself into a new and differently oriented complex — with other relations and other distances in the midst of other objects which similarly have for me a secret face.

Thus I, who in so far as I am my possibles, am what I am not and am not what I am — behold now I *am* somebody! And the one who I am — and who on principle escapes me — I am he *in the midst of the world* in so far as he escapes me. Due to this fact my relation to an object or the potentiality of an object decomposes under the Other's look and appears to me in the world as my possibility of utilizing the object, but only as this possibility on principle escapes me; that is, in so far as it is surpassed by the Other toward his own possibilities.

. . . Thus my being-for-others — *i.e.*, my Me-as-object — is not an image cut off from me and growing in a strange consciousness. It is a perfectly real being, *my* being as the condition of my selfness confronting the Other and of the Other's selfness confronting me. It is my *being-outside* — not a being passively submitted to which would itself have come to me from outside, but an outside assumed and recognized as *my* outside. In fact it is possible for me to deny that the Other is me only in so far as the Other is himself a *subject*. If I immediately refused the Other as pure object — that is, as existing in the midst of the world — it would not be the Other which I refused but rather an object which on principle had nothing in common with subjectivity. I should remain defenseless before a total assimilation of myself to the Other for failing to take precautions within the true province of the Other — subjectivity — which is also *my* province. But this limit can neither come from me nor be thought by me, for I can not limit myself; otherwise I should be a finite totality. On the other hand, in Spinoza's terms, thought can be limited only by thought. Consciousness can be limited only by my consciousness. Now we can grasp the nature of my Self as-object: it is the limit between two consciousnesses as it is produced by the limiting consciousness and assumed by the limited consciousness. And we must understand it in the two senses of the word "limit." On the side of the limiting, indeed, the limit is apprehended as the container which contains me and surrounds me, the shell of emptiness which pleads for me as a totality while putting me out of play; on the side of the limited, it is wholly a phenomenon of selfness and is as the mathematical limit is to the series which progresses toward it without ever reaching it. Every being which I have to be is at its limit like an asymptotic curve to a straight line. Thus I am a detotalized and indefinite totality, contained within a finite totality which surrounds me at a distance and which I am outside myself without ever being able either to realize it or even to touch it. . . .

I. FIRST ATTITUDE TOWARD OTHERS: LOVE, LANGUAGE, MASOCHISM

Everything which may be said of me in my relations with the Other applies to him as well. While I attempt to free myself from the hold of the Other, the Other is trying to free himself from mine; while I seek to enslave the Other, the Other seeks to enslave me. We are by no means dealing with unilateral relations with an object-in-itself, but with reciprocal and moving relations. The following descriptions of concrete behavior must therefore be envisaged within the perspective of *conflict*. Conflict is the original meaning of being-for-others.

If we start with the first revelation of the Other as a *look*, we must recognize that we experience our inapprehensible being-for-others in the form of a *possession*. I am possessed by the Other; the Other's look fashions my body in its nakedness, causes it to be born, sculptures it, produces it as it *is*, sees it as I shall never see it. The Other holds a secret — the secret of what I am. He makes me be and thereby he possesses me, and this possession is nothing other than the consciousness of possessing me. I in the recognition of my object-state have proof that he has this consciousness. By virtue of consciousness the Other is for me simultaneously the one who has stolen my being from me and the one who causes "there to be" a being which is my being. Thus I have a comprehension of this ontological structure: I am responsible for my being-for-others, but I am not the foundation of it. It appears to me therefore in the form of a contingent given for which I am nevertheless responsible; the Other founds my being in so far as this being is in the form of the "there is." But he is not responsible for my being although he founds it in complete freedom — in and by means of his free transcendence. Thus to the extent that I am revealed to myself as responsible for my being, I *lay claim to* this being which I am; that is, I wish to recover it, or, more exactly, I am the project of the recovery of my being. I want to stretch out my hand and grab hold of this being which is presented to me as *my being* but at a distance — like the dinner of Tantalus; I want to found it by my very freedom. For if in one sense my being-as-object is an unbearable contingency and the pure "possession" of myself by another, still in another sense this being stands as the indication of what I should be obliged to recover and found in order to be the foundation of myself. But this is conceivable only if I assimilate the Other's freedom. Thus my project of recovering myself is fundamentally a project of absorbing the Other.

Nevertheless this project must leave the Other's nature intact. Two consequences result: (1) I do not thereby cease to assert the Other — that is, to deny concerning myself that I am the Other. Since the Other is the foundation of my being, he could not be dissolved in me without my being-for-others disappearing. Therefore if I project the realization of unity for the Other, this means that I project my assimilation of the Other's Otherness as my own possibility. In fact the problem for me is to make myself be by acquiring the possibility of taking the Other's point of view on myself. It is not a matter of acquiring a pure, abstract faculty of knowledge. It is not the pure *category* of the Other which I project appropriating to myself. This category is not conceived nor even conceivable. But on the occasion of concrete experience with the Other, an experience suffered and realized, it is this concrete Other as an absolute reality whom in his otherness I wish to incorporate into myself. (2) The Other whom I wish to assimilate is by no means the Other-as-object. Or, if you prefer, my project of incorporating the Other in no way corresponds to a recapturing of my for-itself as myself and to a surpassing of the Other's transcendence toward my own possibilities. For me it is not a question of obliterating my object-state by making an object of the Other, which would amount to *releasing* myself from my being-for-others. Quite the contrary, I want to assimilate the Other as the Other-looking-at-me, and this project of assimilation includes an augmented recognition of my being-looked-at. In short, in order to maintain before me the Other's freedom which is looking at me, I identify myself totally with my being-looked-at. And since my being-as-object is the only possible relation between me and the Other, it is this being-as-object which alone can serve me as an instrument to effect my assimilation of the *other freedom.*

Thus as a reaction to the failure of the third ekstasis, the for-itself wishes to be identified with the Other's freedom as founding its own being-in-itself. To be other to oneself — the ideal always aimed at concretely in the form of being *this Other* to oneself — is the primary value of my relations with the Other. This means that my being-for-others is haunted by the indication of an absolute-being which would be itself as other and other as itself and which, by freely giving to itself its being-itself as other and its being-other as itself, would be the very being of the ontological proof — that is, God. This ideal can not be realized without my surmounting the original contingency of my relations to the Other; that is, by overcoming the fact that there is no relation of internal negativity between the negation by which the Other is made other than I and the negation by which I am made other than the Other. We have seen that this contingency is insurmountable; it is the *fact of* my relations with the Other, just as my body is the *fact* of my being-in-the-world. Unity with the Other is therefore *in fact* unrealizable. It is also unrealizable *in theory,* for the assimilation of the for-itself and the Other in a single transcendence would necessarily involve the disappearance of the characteristic of otherness in the Other. Thus the condition on which I project the identification of myself with the Other is that I persist in denying that I am the Other. Finally this project of unification is the source of *conflict* since while I experience myself as an object for the Other and while I project assimilating him in and by means of this experience, the Other apprehends me as an object in the midst of the world and does not project identifying me with himself. It would therefore be necessary — since being-for-others includes a double internal negation — to act upon the internal negation by which the Other transcends my transcendence and makes me exist for the Other; that is, *to act upon the Other's freedom.*

This unrealizable ideal which haunts my project of myself in the presence of the Other is not to be identified with love in so far as love is an enterprise; *i.e.,* an organic ensemble of projects toward my own possibilities. But it is the ideal of love, its motivation and its end, its unique value. Love as the primitive relation to the Other is the ensemble of the projects by which I aim at realizing this value.

These projects put me in direct connection with the Other's freedom. It is in this sense that love is a conflict. We have observed that the Other's freedom is the foundation of my being. But precisely because I exist by means of the Other's freedom, I have no security; I am in danger in this freedom. It moulds my being and *makes me be,* it confers values upon me and removes them from me; and my being receives from it a perpetual passive escape from self. Irresponsible and beyond reach, this protean freedom in which I have engaged myself can in turn engage me in a thousand different ways of being. My project of recovering my being can be realized only if I get hold of this freedom and reduce it to being a freedom subject to my freedom. At the same time it is the only way in which I can act on the free negation of interiority by which the Other constitutes me as an Other; that is the only way in which I can prepare the way for a future identification of the Other with me. This will be clearer perhaps if we study the problem from a purely psychological aspect. Why does the lover want to be *loved?* If Love were in fact a pure desire for physical possession, it could in many cases be easily satisfied. Proust's hero, for example, who installs his mistress in his home, who can see her and possess her at any hour of the day, who has been able to make her completely dependent on him economically, ought to be free from worry. Yet we know that he is, on the contrary, continually gnawed by anxiety. Through her consciousness Albertine escapes Marcel even when he is at her side, and that is why he knows relief only when he gazes on her while she sleeps. It is certain then that the lover wishes to capture a "consciousness." But why does he wish it? And how?

The notion of "ownership," by which love is so often explained, is not actually primary. Why should I want to appropriate the Other if it were not precisely that the Other makes me be? But this implies precisely a certain mode of appropriation; it is the Other's freedom as such that we want to get hold of. Not because of a desire for power. The tyrant scorns love, he is content with fear. If he seeks to win the love of his subjects, it is for political reasons; and if he finds a more economical way to enslave them, he adopts it immediately. On the other hand, the man who wants to be loved does not desire the enslavement of the beloved. He is not bent on becoming the object of passion which flows forth mechanically. He does not want to possess an automaton, and if we want to humiliate him, we need only try to persuade him that the beloved's passion is the result of a psychological determinism. The lover will then feel that both his love and his being are cheapened. If Tristan and Isolde fall madly in love because of a love potion, they are less interesting. The total enslavement of the beloved kills the love of the lover. The end is surpassed; if the beloved is transformed into an automaton, the lover finds himself alone. Thus the lover does not desire to possess the beloved as one possesses a thing; he demands a special type of appropriation. He wants to possess a freedom as freedom.

On the other hand, the lover can not be satisfied with that superior form of freedom which is a free and voluntary engagement. Who would be content with a love given as pure loyalty to a sworn oath? Who would be satisfied with the words, "I love you because I have freely engaged myself to love you and because I do not wish to go back on my word." Thus the lover demands a pledge, yet is irritated by a pledge. He wants to be loved by a freedom but demands that this freedom as freedom should no longer be free. He wishes that the Other's freedom should determine itself to become love — and this not only at the beginning of the affair but at each instant — and at the same time he wants this freedom to be captured *by itself*, to turn back upon itself, as in madness, as in a dream, so as to will its own captivity. This captivity must be a resignation that is both free and yet chained in our hands. In love it is not a determinism of the passions which we desire in the Other nor a freedom beyond reach; it is a freedom which *plays the role of* a determinism of the passions and which is caught in its own role. For himself the lover does not demand that he be the *cause* of this radical modification of freedom but that he be the unique and privileged occasion of it. In fact he could not want to be the cause of it without immediately submerging the beloved in the midst of the world as a tool which can be transcended. That is not the essence of love. On the contrary, in Love the Lover wants to be "the whole World" for the beloved. This means that he puts himself on the side of the world; he is the one who assumes and symbolizes the world; he is a *this* which includes all other *thises*. He is and consents to be an *object*. But on the other hand, he wants to be the object in which the Other's freedom consents to lose itself, the object in which the Other consents to find his being and his *raison d'être* as his second facticity — the object-limit of transcendence, that toward which the Other's transcendence transcends all other objects but which it can in no way transcend. And everywhere he desires the circle of the Other's freedom; that is, at each instant as the Other's freedom accepts this limit to his transcendence, this acceptance is *already* present as the motivation of the acceptance considered. It is in the capacity of an end already chosen that the lover wishes to be chosen as an end. This allows us to grasp what basically the lover demands of the beloved; he does not want to *act* on the Other's freedom but to exist *a priori* as the objective limit of this freedom; that is, to be given at one stroke along with it and in its very upsurge as the limit which the freedom must accept in order to be free. By this very fact, what he demands is a limiting, a gluing down of the Other's freedom by itself; this limit of structure is in fact a *given,* and the very appearance of the given as the limit of freedom means that the freedom *makes itself exist* within the given by being its own prohibition against surpassing it. This prohibition is envisaged by the lover *simultaneously* as something lived — that is, something suffered (in a word, as a facticity) and as something freely consented to. It must be freely consented to since it must be effected only with the upsurge of a freedom which chooses itself as freedom. But it must be only what is lived since it must be an impossibility always present, a facticity which surges back to the heart of the Other's freedom. This is expressed psychologically by the demand that the free decision to love me, which the beloved formerly has taken, must slip in as a magically determining motivation *within* his present free engagement.

Now we can grasp the meaning of this demand: the facticity which is to be a factual limit for the Other in my demand to be loved and which is to result in being *his own* facticity — this is *my* facticity. It is in so far as I am the object which the Other makes come into being that I must be the inherent limit to his very transcendence. Thus the Other by his upsurge into being makes me be as unsurpassable and absolute, not as a nihilating For-itself but as a being-for-others-in-the-midst-of-the-world. Thus to want to be loved is to invest the Other with one's own facticity; it is to wish to compel him to re-create you perpetually as the condition of a freedom which submits itself and which is engaged; it is to wish both that freedom found fact and that fact have preeminence over freedom. If this end could be attained, it would result in the first place in my being *secure* within the Other's consciousness. First because the motive of my uneasiness and my shame is the fact that I apprehend and experience myself in my being-for-others as that which can always be surpassed toward something else, that which is the pure object of a value judgment, a pure means, a pure tool. My uneasiness stems from the fact that I assume necessarily and freely that being which another makes me be in an absolute freedom. "God knows what I am for him! God knows what he thinks of me!" This means "God knows what he makes me be." I am haunted by this being which I fear to encounter someday at the turn of a path, this being which is so strange to me and which is yet *my being* and which I know that I shall never encounter in spite of all my efforts to do so. But if the Other loves me then I become the *unsurpassable,* which means that I must be the absolute end. In this sense I am saved from *instrumentality.* My existence in the midst of the world becomes the exact correlate of my transcendence-for-myself since my independence is absolutely safeguarded. The object which the Other must make me be is an object-transcendence, an absolute center of reference around which all the instrumental-things of the world are ordered as pure *means.* At the same time, as the absolute limit of freedom — *i.e.,* of the absolute source of all values — I am protected against any eventual devalorization. I am the absolute value. To the extent that I assume my being-for-others, I assume myself as value. Thus to want to be loved is to want to be placed beyond the whole system of values posited by the Other and to be the condition of all valorization and the objective foundation of all values. This demand is the usual theme of lovers' conversations, whether as in *La Porte Etroite,* the woman who wants to be loved identifies herself with an ascetic morality of self-surpassing and wishes to embody the ideal limit of this surpassing — or as more usually happens, the woman in love demands that the beloved in his acts should sacrifice traditional morality for her and is anxious to know whether the beloved would betray his friends for her, "would steal for her," "would kill for her," *etc.*

From this point of view, my being must escape the *look* of the beloved, or rather it must be the object of a look with another structure. I must no longer be seen on the ground of the world as a "this" among other "thises," but the world must be revealed in terms of me. In fact to the extent that the upsurge of freedom makes a world exist, I must be, as the limiting-condition of this upsurge, the very condition of the upsurge of a world. I must be the one whose function is to makes trees and water exist, to make cities and fields and other men exist, in order to give them later to the Other who arranges them into a world, just as the mother in matrilineal communities receives titles and the family name not to keep them herself but to transfer them immediately to her children. In one sense if I am to be loved, I am the object by whose agency the world will exist for the Other; in another sense I am the world. Instead of being a "this" detaching itself on the ground of the world, I am the ground-as-object on which the world detaches itself. Thus I am reassured; the Other's look no longer paralyzes me with finitude. It no longer fixes my being in *what I am.* I can no longer be *looked at* as ugly, as small, as cowardly, since these characteristics necessarily represent a factual limitation of my being and an apprehension of my finitude as finitude. To be sure, my possibles remain transcended possibilities, dead-possibilities; but I possess all possibles. I am all the dead-possibilities in the world; hence I cease to be the being who is understood from the standpoint of other beings or of its acts. In the loving intuition which I demand, I am to be given as an absolute totality in terms of which all its peculiar acts and all beings are to be understood. One could say, slightly modifying a famous pronouncement of the Stoics, that "the beloved can fail in three ways." The ideal of the sage and the ideal of the man who wants to be loved actually coincide in this that both want to be an object-as-totality accessible to a global intuition which will apprehend the beloved's or the sage's actions in the world as partial structures which are interpreted in terms of the totality. Just as wisdom is proposed as a state to be attained by an absolute metamorphosis, so the Other's freedom must be absolutely metamorphosed in order to allow me to attain the state of being loved. . . .

The problem of my being-for-others remains therefore without solution. The lovers remain each one for himself in a total subjectivity; nothing comes to relieve them of their duty to make themselves exist each one for himself; nothing comes to relieve their contingency nor to save them from facticity. At least each one has succeeded in escaping danger from the Other's freedom — but altogether differently than he expected. He escapes not because the Other makes him be as the object-limit of his transcendence but because the Other experiences him as subjectivity and wishes to experience him only as such. Again the gain is perpetually compromised. At the start, each of the consciousnesses can at any moment free itself from its chains and suddenly contemplate the other as an *object*. Then the spell is broken; the Other becomes one mean among means. He is indeed an object for others as the lover desires but an object-as-tool, a perpetually transcended object. The illusion, the game of mirrors which makes the concrete reality of love, suddenly ceases. Later in the experience of love each consciousness seeks to shelter its being-for-others in the Other's freedom. This supposes that the Other is beyond the world as pure subjectivity, as the absolute by which the world comes into being. But it suffices that the lovers should be *looked at* together by a third person in order for each one to experience not only his own objectivation but that of the other as well. Immediately the Other is no longer for me the absolute transcendence which founds me in my being; he is a transcendence-transcended, not by me but by another. My original relation to him — *i.e.*, my relation of being the beloved for my lover, is fixed as a dead-possibility. It is no longer the experienced relation between a limiting object of all transcendence and the freedom which founds it; it is a love-as-object which is wholly alienated toward the third. Such is the true reason why lovers seek solitude. It is because the appearance of a third person, whoever he may be, is the destruction of their love. But factual solitude (*e.g.*, we are alone in my room) is by no means a theoretical solitude. Even if nobody sees us, we exist for *all* consciousness and we are conscious of existing for all. The result is that love as a fundamental mode of being-for-others holds in its being-for-others the seed of its own destruction.

We have just defined the triple destructibility of love: in the first place it is, in essence, a deception and a reference to infinity since to love is to wish to be loved, hence to wish that the Other wish that I love him. A pre-ontological comprehension of this deception is given in the very impulse of love — hence the lover's perpetual dissatisfaction. It does not come, as is so often said, from the unworthiness of being loved but from an implicit comprehension of the fact that the amorous intuition is, as a fundamental-intuition, an ideal out of reach. The more I am loved, the more I lose my *being*, the more I am thrown back on my own responsibilities, on my own power to be. In the second place the Other's awakening is always possible; at any moment he can make me appear as an object — hence the lover's perpetual insecurity. In the third place love is an absolute which is perpetually *made relative* by others. One would have to be alone in the world with the beloved in order for love to preserve its character as an absolute axis of reference — hence the lover's perpetual shame (or pride — which here amounts to the same thing).

Thus it is useless for me to have tried to lose myself in objectivity; my passion will have availed me nothing. The Other has referred me to my own unjustifiable subjectivity — either by himself or through others. This result can provoke a total despair and a new attempt to realize the identification of the Other and myself. Its ideal will then be the opposite of that which we have just described; instead of projecting the absorbing of the Other while preserving in him his otherness, I shall project causing myself to be absorbed by the Other and losing myself in his subjectivity in order to get rid of my own. This enterprise will be expressed concretely by the *masochistic* attitude. Since the Other is the foundation of my being-for-others, if I relied on the Other to make me exist, I should no longer be anything more than a being-in-itself founded in its being by a freedom. Here it is my own subjectivity which is considered as an obstacle to the primordial act by which the Other would found me in my being. It is my own subjectivity which above all must be denied by *my own freedom.* I attempt therefore to engage myself wholly in my being-as-object. I refuse to be anything more than an object. I rest upon the Other, and as I experience this being-as-object in shame, I will and I love my shame as the profound sign of my objectivity. As the Other apprehends me as object by means of *actual desire,* I wish to be desired, I make myself in shame an object of desire.

This attitude would resemble that of love if instead of seeking to exist for the Other as the object-limit of his transcendence, I did not rather insist on making myself be treated as one object among others, as an instrument to be used. Now it is *my* transcendence which is to be denied, not his. This time I do not have to project capturing his freedom; on the contrary I hope that this freedom may *be* and *will* itself to be radically free. Thus the more I shall enjoy the abdication of my transcendence. Finally I project being nothing more than an *object;* that is, radically an *in-itself.* But inasmuch as a freedom which will have absorbed mine will be the foundation of this in-itself, my being will become again the foundation of itself. Masochism, like sadism, is the assumption of guilt. I am guilty due to the very fact that I am an object, I am guilty toward myself since I consent to my absolute alienation. I am guilty toward the Other, for I furnish him with the occasion of being guilty — that is, of radically missing my freedom as such. Masochism is an attempt not to fascinate the Other by means of my objectivity but to cause myself to be fascinated by my objectivity-for-others; that is, to cause myself to be constituted as an object by the Other in such a way that I non-thetically apprehend my subjectivity as a *nothing* in the presence of the in-itself which I represent to the Other's eyes. Masochism is characterized as a species of vertigo, vertigo not before a precipice of rock and earth but before the abyss of the Other's subjectivity.

But masochism is and must be itself a failure. In order to cause myself to be fascinated by my self-as-object, I should necessarily have to be able to realize the intuitive apprehension of this object such as it is *for the Other,* a thing which is on principle impossible. Thus I am far from being able to be fascinated by this alienated Me, which remains on principle inapprehensible. It is useless for the masochist to get down on his knees, to show himself in ridiculous positions, to cause himself to be used as a simple lifeless instrument. It is *for the Other* that he will be obscene or simply passive, for the Other that he will *undergo* these postures; for himself he is forever condemned to *give them to himself.* It is in and through his transcendence that he disposes of himself as a being to be transcended. The more he tries to taste his objectivity, the more he will be submerged by the consciousness of his subjectivity — hence his anguish. Even the masochist who pays a woman to whip him is treating her as an instrument and by this very fact posits himself in transcendence in relation to her. . . .

II. SECOND ATTITUDE TOWARD OTHERS: INDIFFERENCE, DESIRE, HATE, SADISM

The failure of the first attitude toward the Other can be the occasion for my assuming the second. But of course neither of the two is really first; each of them is a fundamental reaction to being-for-others as an original situation. It can happen therefore that due to the very impossibility of my identifying myself with the Other's consciousness through the intermediacy of my object-ness for him, I am led to turn deliberately toward the

Other and *look* at him. In this case to look at the Other's look is to posit oneself in one's own freedom and to attempt on the ground of this freedom to confront the Other's freedom. The meaning of the conflict thus sought would be to bring out into the open the struggle of two freedoms confronted as freedoms. But this intention must be immediately disappointed, for by the sole fact that I assert myself in my freedom confronting the Other, I make the Other a transcendence-transcended — that is, an object. It is the story of that failure which we are about to investigate. We can grasp its general pattern. I direct my look upon the Other who is looking at me. But a look can not be looked at. As soon as I look in the direction of the look it disappears, and I no longer see anything but eyes. At this instant the Other becomes a being which I possess and which recognizes my freedom. It seems that my goal has been achieved since I possess the being who has the key to my object-state and since I can cause him to make proof of my freedom in a thousand different ways. But in reality the whole structure has collapsed, for the being which remains within my hands is an Other-as-object. As such he has lost the key to my being-as-object, and he possesses a pure and simple image of me which is nothing but one of its objective affects and which no longer touches me. If he experiences the effects of my freedom, if I can act upon his being in a thousand different ways and transcend his possibilities with all my possibilities, this is only in so far as he is an object in the world and as such is outside the state of recognizing my freedom. My disappointment is complete since I seek to appropriate the Other's freedom and perceive suddenly that I can act upon the Other only in so far as this freedom has collapsed beneath my look. This disappointment will be the result of my further attempts to seek again for the Other's freedom across the object which he is for me and to find privileged attitudes or conduct which would appropriate this freedom across a total appropriation of the Other's body. These attempts, as one may suspect, are on principle doomed to failure.

But it can happen also that "to look at the look" is my original reaction to my being-for-others. This means that in my upsurge into the world, I can choose myself as looking at the Other's look and can build my subjectivity upon the collapse of the subjectivity of the Other. It is this attitude which we shall call *indifference toward others*. Then we are dealing with a kind of *blindness* with respect to others. But the term "blindness" must not lead us astray. I do not suffer this blindness as a state. I *am* my own blindness with regard to others, and this blindness includes an implicit comprehension of being-for-others; that is, of the Other's transcendence as a look. This comprehension is simply what I myself determine to hide from myself. I practice then a sort of factual solipsism; others are those forms which pass by in the street, those magic objects which are capable of acting at a distance and upon which I can act by means of determined conduct. I scarcely notice them; I act as if I were alone in the world. I brush against "people" as I brush against a wall; I avoid them as I avoid obstacles. Their freedom-as-object is for me only their "coefficient of adversity." I do not even imagine that they can *look at* me. Of course they have some knowledge of me, but this knowledge does not touch me. It is a question of pure modifications of their being which do not pass from them to me and which are tainted with what we call a "suffered-subjectivity" or "subjectivity-as-object"; that is, they express what they are, not what I am, and they are the effect of my action upon them. Those "people" are functions: the ticket-collector is only the function of collecting tickets; the café waiter is nothing but the function of serving the patrons. . . .

Now we can see the meaning of the sadist's demand: grace reveals freedom as a property of the Other-as-object and refers obscurely — just as do the contradictions in the sensible world in the case of Platonic recollection — to a transcendent Beyond of which we preserve only a confused memory and which we can reach only be a radical modification of our being; that is, by resolutely assuming our being-for-others. Grace both unveils and veils the Other's flesh, or if you prefer, it unveils the flesh in order immediately to veil it; in grace flesh is the inaccessible Other. The sadist aims at destroying grace in order *actually* to constitute another synthesis of the Other. He wants to make the Other's flesh appear; and in its very appearance the flesh will destroy grace, and facticity will reabsorb the Other's freedom-as-object. This reabsorption is not annihilation; for the sadist it is the Other-as-free who is manifested as flesh. The identity of the Other-as-object is not destroyed through these avatars, but the relations between flesh and freedom are reversed. In grace freedom contained and veiled facticity; in the new synthesis to be effected it is facticity which contains and hides freedom. The sadist aims therefore at making the flesh appear abruptly and by compulsion; that is, by the aid not of his own flesh but of his body as instrument. He aims at making the Other assume attitudes and positions such that his body appears under the aspect of the *obscene;* thus the sadist himself remains on the level of instrumental appropriation since he causes flesh to be born by exerting force upon the Other, and the Other becomes an instrument in his hands. The sadist handles the Other's body, leans on the Other's shoulders so as to bend him toward the earth and to make his haunches stick up, *etc.* On the other hand, the goal of this instrumental utilization is immanent in the very utilization; the sadist treats the Other as an instrument in order to make the Other's flesh appear. The sadist is the being who apprehends the Other as the instrument whose function is his own incarnation. The ideal of the sadist will therefore be to achieve the moment when the Other will be already flesh without ceasing to be an instrument, flesh to cause the birth of flesh, the moment at which the thighs, for example, already offer themselves in an obscene expanding passivity, and yet are instruments which are managed, which are pushed aside, which are bent so as to make the buttocks stick out in order in turn to incarnate them. But let us not be deceived here. What the sadist thus so tenaciously seeks, what he wants to knead with his hands and bend under his wrists is the Other's freedom. The freedom is there in that flesh; it is freedom which is this flesh since there is a facticity of the Other. It is therefore this freedom which the sadist tries to appropriate.

Thus the sadist's effort is to ensnare the Other in his flesh by means of violence and pain, by appropriating the Other's body in such a way that he treats it as flesh so as to cause flesh to be born. But this appropriation surpasses the body which it appropriates, for its purpose is to possess the body only in so far as the Other's freedom has been ensnared within it. This is why the sadist will want manifest proofs of this enslavement of the Other's freedom through the flesh. He will aim at making the Other ask for pardon, he will use torture and threats to force the Other to humiliate himself, to deny what he holds most dear. It is often said that this is done through the will to dominate or thirst for power. But this explanation is either vague or absurd. It is the will to dominate which should be explained first. This can not be prior to sadism as its foundation, for in the same way and on the same plane as sadism, it is born from anxiety in the face of the Other. In fact, if the sadist is pleased upon obtaining a denial by means of torture, this is for a reason analogous to that which allows us to interpret the meaning of *Love*. We have seen in fact that Love does not demand the abolition of the Other's freedom but rather his enslavement as freedom; that is, freedom's self-enslavement. Similarly the sadist does not seek to suppress the freedom of the one whom he tortures but to force this freedom freely to identify itself with the tortured flesh. This is why the moment of pleasure for the torturer is that in which the victim betrays or humiliates himself.

In fact no matter what pressure is exerted on the victim, the abjuration remains *free;* it is a spontaneous production, a response to a situation; it manifests human-reality. No matter what resistance the victim has offered, no matter how long he has waited before begging for mercy, he would have been able despite all to wait ten minutes, one minute, one second longer. He has *determined* the moment at which the pain became unbearable. The proof of this is the fact that he will later live out his abjuration in remorse and shame. Thus he is entirely responsible for it. On the other hand the sadist for his part considers himself entirely the cause of it. If the victim resists and refuses to beg for mercy, the game is only that much more pleasing. One more turn of the screw, one extra twist and the resistance will finally give in. The sadist posits himself as "having all the time in the world." He is calm, he does not hurry. He uses his instruments like a technician; he tries them one after another as the locksmith tries various keys in a keyhole. He enjoys this ambiguous and contradictory situation. On the one hand indeed he is the one who patiently at the heart of universal determinism employs means in view of an end which will be *automatically* attained — just as the lock will automatically open when the locksmith finds the "right" key; on the other hand, this determined end can be realized only with the Other's free and complete cooperation. Therefore until the last the end remains both predictable and unpredictable. For the sadist the object realized is ambiguous, contradictory, without equilibrium since it is both the strict consequence of a technical utilization of determinism and the manifestation of an unconditioned freedom. The spectacle which is offered to the sadist is that of a freedom which struggles against the expanding of the flesh and which finally freely chooses to be submerged in the flesh. At the moment of the abjuration the result sought is attained: the body is wholly flesh, panting and obscene; it holds the position which the torturers have given to it, not that which it would have assumed by itself; the cords which bind it hold it as an inert thing, and thereby it has ceased to be the object which moves spontaneously. In the abjuration a freedom chooses to be wholly identified with this body; this distorted and heaving body is the very image of a broken and enslaved freedom.

These few remarks do not aim at exhausting the problem of sadism. We wanted only to show that it is as a seed in desire itself, as the failure of desire; in fact as soon as I seek to *take* the Other's body, which through my incarnation I have induced to incarnate itself, I break the reciprocity of incarnation, I surpass my body toward its own possibilities, and I orient myself in the direction of sadism. Thus sadism and masochism are the two reefs on which desire may founder — whether I surpass my troubled disturbance toward an appropriation of the Other's flesh or, intoxicated with my own trouble, pay attention only to my flesh and ask nothing of the Other except that he should be the look which aids me in realizing my flesh. It is because of this inconstancy on the part of desire and its perpetual oscillation between these two perils that "normal" sexuality is commonly designated as "sadistic-masochistic."

Nevertheless sadism too — like blind indifference and like desire — bears within itself the cause of its own failure. In the first place there is a profound incompatibility between the apprehension of the body as flesh and its instrumental utilization. If I make an instrument out of flesh, it refers me to other instruments and to potentialities, in short to a future; it is partially justified in its *being-there* by the situation which I create around myself, just as the presence of nails and of a picture to be nailed on the wall justifies the existence of the hammer. Suddenly the body's character as flesh — that is, its unutilizable facticity — gives way to that of an instrumental-thing. The complex "flesh-as-instrument" which the sadist has attempted to create disintegrates. This profound disintegration can be hidden so long as the flesh is the instrument to reveal flesh, for in this way I constitute an instrument with an immanent end. But when the incarnation is achieved, when I have indeed before me a panting body, then I no longer know how to *utilize* this flesh. No goal can be assigned to it, precisely because I have effected the appearance of its absolute contingency. It is *there,* and it is there *for nothing.* As such I can not get hold of it as flesh; I can not integrate it in a complex system of instrumentality without its materiality as flesh, its "fleshliness" immediately escaping me. I can only remain disconcerted before it in a state of contemplative astonishment or else incarnate myself in turn and allow myself again to be troubled, so as to place myself once more at least on the level where flesh is revealed to flesh in its entire "fleshliness." Thus sadism at the very moment when its goal is going to be attained gives way to desire. Sadism is the failure of desire, and desire is the failure of sadism. One can get out of the circle only by means of satiation and so-called "physical possession." In this a new synthesis of sadism and of desire is given. The tumescence of sex manifests incarnation, the fact of "entering into" or of being "penetrated" symbolically realizes the sadistic and masochistic attempt to appropriate. But if pleasure enables us to get out of the circle, this is because it kills both the desire and the sadistic passion without satisfying them.

At the same time and on a totally different level sadism harbors a new motive for failure. What the sadist seeks to appropriate is in actuality the transcendent freedom of the victim. But this freedom remains on principle out of reach. And the more the sadist persists in treating the other as an instrument, the more this freedom escapes him. He can act upon the freedom only by making it an objective property of the Other-as-object; that is, on freedom in the midst of the world with its dead-possibilities. But since the sadist's goal is to recover his being-for-others, he misses it on principle, for the only Other with whom he has to do is the Other in the world who has only "images in his head" of the sadist assaulting him.

The sadist discovers his error when his victim *looks at* him; that is, when the sadist experiences the absolute alienation of his being in the Other's freedom; he realizes then not only that he has not recovered his *being-outside* but also that the activity by which he seeks to recover it is itself transcended and fixed in "sadism" as an *habitus* and a property with its cortege of dead-possibilities and that this transformation takes place through and for the Other whom he wishes to enslave. He discovers then that he can not act on the Other's freedom even by forcing the Other to humiliate himself and to beg for mercy, for it is precisely in and through the Other's absolute freedom that there exists a world in which there are sadism and instruments of torture and a hundred pretexts for being humiliated and for foreswearing oneself.

MARTIN BUBER

Martin Buber (1878–1965) taught philosophy from 1938 to 1951 at Hebrew University in Jerusalem. He is best known for his revival of the Jewish mystical movement called Hasidism. From this interest in Hasidic thought evolved his I-Thou (here translated "You") philosophy of human relationships. The following excerpt gives some sense of the power of his writing.

I and Thou

Man becomes an I through a You. What confronts us comes and vanishes, relational events take shape and scatter, and through these changes crystallizes, more and more each time, the consciousness of the constant partner, the I-consciousness. To be sure, for a long time it appears only woven into the relation to a You, discernible as that which reaches for but is not a You; but it comes closer and closer to the bursting point until one day the bonds are broken and the I confronts its detached self for a moment like a You — and then it takes possession of itself and henceforth enters into relations in full consciousness.

Only now can the other basic word be put together. For although the You of the relation always paled again, it never became the It of an I — an object of detached perception and experience, which is what it will become henceforth — but as it were an It for itself, something previously unnoticed that was waiting for the new relational event. Of course, the maturing body* as the carrier of its sensations and the executor of its drives stood out from its environment, but only in the next-to-each-other where one finds one's way, not yet in the absolute separation of I and object. Now, however, the detached I is transformed — reduced from substantial fullness to the functional one-dimensionality of a subject that experiences and uses objects — and thus approaches all the "It for itself," overpowers it and joins with it to form the other basic word. The man who has acquired an I and says I-It assumes a position before things but does not confront them in the current of reciprocity. He bends down to examine particulars under the objectifying magnifying glass of close scrutiny, or he uses the objectifying telescope of distant vision to arrange them as mere scenery. In his contemplation he isolates them without any feeling for the exclusive or joins them without any world feeling. The former

*All footnotes deleted.

could be attained only through relation, and the latter only by starting from that. Only now he experiences things as aggregates of qualities. Qualities, to be sure, had remained in his memory after every encounter, as belonging to the remembered You; but only now things seem to him to be constructed of their qualities. Only by drawing on his memory of the relation — dreamlike, visual, or conceptual, depending on the kind of man he is — he supplements the core that revealed itself powerfully in the You, embracing all qualities: the substance. Only now does he place things in a spatio-temporal-causal context; only now does each receive its place, its course, its measurability, its conditionality. The You also appears in space, but only in an exclusive confrontation in which everything else can only be background from which it emerges, not its boundary and measure. The You appears in time, but in that of a process that is fulfilled in itself — a process lived through not as a piece that is a part of a constant and organized sequence but in a "duration" whose purely intensive dimension can be determined only by starting from the You. It appears simultaneously as acting on and as acted upon, but not as if it had been fitted into a causal chain; rather as, in its reciprocity with the I, the beginning and end of the event. This is part of the basic truth of the human world: only It can be put in order. Only as things cease to be our You and become our It do they become subject to coordination. The You knows no system of coordinates.

But having got this far, we must also make another pronouncement without which this piece of the basic truth would remain an unfit fragment: an ordered world is not the world order. There are moments of the secret ground in which world order is beheld as present. Then the tone is heard all of a sudden whose uninterpretable score the ordered world is. These moments are immortal; none are more evanescent. They leave no content that could be preserved, but their force enters into the creation and into man's knowledge, and the radiation of its force penetrates the ordered world and thaws it again and again. Thus the history of the individual, thus the history of the race.

* * *

The world is twofold for man in accordance with his twofold attitude.

He perceives the being that surrounds him, plain things and beings as things; he perceives what happens around him, plain processes and actions as processes, things that consist of qualities and processes that consist of moments, things recorded in terms of spatial coordinates and processes recorded in terms of temporal coordinates, things and processes that are bounded by other things and processes and capable of being measured against and compared with those others — an ordered world, a detached world. This world is somewhat reliable; it has density and duration; its articulation can be surveyed; one can get it out again and again; one recounts it with one's eyes closed and then checks with one's eyes open. There it stands — right next to your skin if you think of it that way, or nestled in your soul if you prefer that: it is your object and remains that, according to your pleasure — and remains primally alien both outside and inside you. You perceive it and take it for your "truth", it permits itself to be taken by you, but it does not give itself to you. It is only *about* it that you can come to an understanding with others; although it takes a somewhat different form for everybody, it is prepared to be a common object for you; but you cannot encounter others in it. Without it you cannot remain alive; its reliability preserves you; but if you were to die into it, then you would be buried in nothingness.

Or man encounters being and becoming as what confronts him — always only *one* being and every thing only as a being. What is there reveals itself to him in the occurrence, and what occurs there happens to him as being. Nothing else is present but this one, but this one cosmically. Measure and comparison have fled. It is up to you how much of the immeasurable becomes reality for you. The encounters do not order themselves to become a world, but each is for you a sign of the world order. They have no association with each other, but every one guarantees your association with the world. The world that appears to you in this way is unreliable, for it appears always new to you, and you cannot take it by its word. It lacks density, for everything in it permeates everything else. It lacks duration, for it comes even when not called and vanishes even when you cling to it. It cannot be surveyed: if you try to make it surveyable, you lose it. It comes — comes to fetch you — and if it does not reach you or encounter you it vanishes, but it comes again, transformed. It does not stand outside you, it touches your ground; and if you say "soul of my soul" you have not said too much. But beware of trying to transpose it into your soul — that way you destroy it. It is your present; you have a present only insofar as you have it; and you can make it into an object for you and experience and use it — you must do that again and again — and then you have no present any more. Between you and it there is a reciprocity of giving: you say You to it and give yourself to it; it says You to you and gives itself to you. You cannot come to an understanding *about* it with others; you are lonely with it; but it teaches you to encounter others and to stand your ground in such encounters; and through the grace of its advents and the melancholy of its departures it leads you to that You in which the lines of relation, though parallel, intersect. It does not help you to survive; it only helps you to have intimations of eternity.

The It-world hangs together in space and time.

The You-world does not hang together in space and time.

The individual You *must* become an It when the event of relation has run its course.

The individual It *can* become a You by entering into the event of relation.

These are the two basic privileges of the It-world. They induce man to consider the It-world as the world in which one has to live and also can live comfortably — and that even offers us all sorts of stimulations and excitements, activities and knowledge. In this firm and wholesome chronicle the You-moments appear as queer lyric-dramatic episodes. Their spell may be seductive, but they pull us dangerously to extremes, loosening the well-tried structure, leaving behind more doubt than satisfaction, shaking up our security — altogether uncanny, altogether indispensable. Since one must after all return into "the world," why not stay in it in the first place? Why not call to order that which confronts us and send it home into objectivity? And when one cannot get around saying You, perhaps to one's father, wife, companion — why not say You and mean It? After all, producing the sound "You" with one's vocal cords does not by any means entail speaking the uncanny basic word. Even whispering an amorous You with one's soul is hardly dangerous as long as in all seriousness one means nothing but experiencing and using.

One cannot live in the pure present: it would consume us if care were not taken that it is overcome quickly and thoroughly. But in pure past one can live; in fact, only there can a life be arranged. One only has to fill every moment with experiencing and using, and it ceases to burn.

And in all the seriousness of truth, listen: without It a human being cannot live. But whoever lives only with that is not human. . . .

* * *

— One can understand how the It-world, left to itself, untouched and unthawed by the emergence of any You, should become alienated and turn into an incubus; but how does it happen that, as you say, the I of man is deactualized? Whether it lives in relation or outside it, the I remains assured of itself in its self-consciousness, which is a strong thread of gold on which the changing states are strung. Whether I say, "I see you" or "I see the tree," seeing may not be equally actual in both cases, but the I is equally actual in both.

— Let us examine, let us examine ourselves to see whether this is so. The linguistic form proves nothing. After all, many a spoken You really means an It to which one merely says You from habit, thoughtlessly. And many a spoken It really means a You whose presence one may remember with one's whole being, although one is far away. Similarly, there are innumerable occasions when I is only an indispensable pronoun, only a necessary abbreviation for "This one there who is speaking." But self-consciousness? If one sentence truly intends the You of a relation and the other one the It of an experience, and if the I in both sentences is thus intended in truth, do both sentences issue from the same self-consciousness?

The I of the basic word I-You is different from that of the basic word I-It.

The I of the basic word I-It appears as an ego and becomes conscious of itself as a subject (of experience and use).

The I of the basic word I-You appears as a person and becomes conscious of itself as subjectivity (without any dependent genetive).

Egos appear by setting themselves apart from other egos.

Persons appear by entering into relation to other persons.

One is the spiritual form of natural differentiation, the other that of natural association.

The purpose of setting oneself apart is to experience and use, and the purpose of that is "living" — which means dying one human life long.

The purpose of relation is the relation itself — touching the You. For as soon as we touch a You, we are touched by a breath of eternal life.

Whoever stands in relation, participates in an actuality; that is, in a being that is neither merely a part of him nor merely outside him. All actuality is an activity in which I participate without being able to appropriate it. Where there is no participation, there is no actuality. Where there is self-appropriation, there is no actuality. The more directly the You is touched, the more perfect is the participation.

The I is actual through its participation in actuality. The more perfect the participation is, the more actual the I becomes.

But the I that steps out of the event of the relation into detachment and the self-consciousness accompanying that, does not lose its actuality. Participation remains in it as a living potentiality. To use words that originally refer to the highest relation but may also be applied to all others: the seed remains in him. This is the realm of subjectivity in which the I apprehends simultaneously its association and its detachment. Genuine subjectivity can be understood only dynamically, as the vibration of the I in its lonely truth. This is also the place where the desire for ever higher and more unconditional relation and for perfect participation in being arises and keeps rising. In subjectivity the spiritual substance of the person matures.

The person becomes conscious of himself as participating in being, as being-with, and thus as a being. The ego becomes conscious of himself as being this way and not that. The person says, "I am"; the ego says, "That is how I am." "Know thyself" means to the person: know yourself as being. To the ego it means: know your being-that-way. By setting himself apart from others, the ego moves away from being.

This does not mean that the person "gives up" his being-that-way, his being different; only, this is not the decisive perspective but merely the necessary and meaningful form of being. The ego, on the other hand, wallows in his being-that-way — or rather for the most part in the fiction of his being-that-way — a fiction that he has devised for himself. For at bottom self-knowledge usually means to him the fabrication of an effective apparition of the self that has the power to deceive him even more thoroughly; and through the contemplation and veneration of this apparition one seeks the semblance of knowledge of one's own being-that-way, while actual knowledge of it would lead one to self-destruction — or rebirth.

The person beholds his self; the ego occupies himself with his My: my manner, my race, my works, my genius.

The ego does not participate in any actuality nor does he gain any. He sets himself apart from everything else and tries to possess as much as possible by means of experience and use. That is *his* dynamics: setting himself apart and taking possession — and the object is always It, that which is not actual. He knows himself as a subject, but this subject can appropriate as much as it wants to, it will never gain any substance: it remains like a point, functional, that which experiences, that which uses, nothing more. All of its extensive and multifarious being-that-way, all of its eager "individuality" cannot help it to gain any substance.

There are not two kinds of human beings, but there are two poles of humanity.

No human being is pure person, and none is pure ego; none is entirely actual, none entirely lacking in actuality. Each lives in a twofold I. But some men are so person-oriented that one may call them persons, while others are so ego-oriented that one may call them egos. Between these and those true history takes place.

The more a human being, the more humanity is dominated by the ego, the more does the I fall prey to inactuality. In such ages the person in the human being and in humanity comes to lead a subterranean, hidden, as it were invalid existence — until it is summoned.

*   *   *

How much of a person a man is depends on how strong the I of the basic word I-You is in the human duality of his I.

The way he says I — what he means when he says I — decides where a man belongs and where he goes. The word "I" is the true shibboleth of humanity.

Listen to it!

How dissonant the I of the ego sounds! When it issues from tragic lips, tense with some self-contradiction that they try to hold back, it can move us to great pity. When it issues from chaotic lips that savagely, heedlessly, unconsciously represent contradiction, it can make us shudder. When the lips are vain and smooth, it sounds embarrassing or disgusting.

Those who pronounce the severed I, wallowing in the capital letter, uncover the shame of the world spirit that has been debased to mere spirituality.

But how beautiful and legitimate the vivid and emphatic I of Socrates sounds! It is the I of infinite conversation, and the air of conversation is present on all its ways, even before his judges, even in the final hour in prison. This I lived in that relation to man which is embodied in conversation. It believed in the actuality of men and went out toward them. Thus it stood together with them in actuality and is never severed from it. Even solitude cannot spell forsakenness, and when the human world falls silent for him, he hears his *daimonion* say You.

How beautiful and legitimate the full I of Goethe sounds! It is the I of pure intercourse with nature. Nature yields to it and speaks ceaselessly with it; she reveals her mysteries to it and yet does not betray her mystery. It believes in her and says to the rose: "So it is You" — and at once shares the same actuality with the rose. Hence, when it returns to itself, the spirit of actuality stays with it; the vision of the sun clings to the blessed eye that recalls its own likeness to the sun, and the friendship of the elements accompanies man into the calm of dying and rebirth.

Thus the "adequate, true, and pure" I-saying of the representatives of association, the Socratic and the Goethean persons, resounds through the ages.

And to anticipate and choose an image from the realm of unconditional relation: how powerful, even overpowering, is Jesus' I-saying, and how legitimate to the point of being a matter of course! For it is the I of the unconditional relation in which man calls his You "Father" in such a way that he himself becomes nothing but a son. Whenever he says I, he can only mean the I of the holy basic word that has become unconditional for him. If detachment ever touches him, it is surpassed by association, and it is from this that he speaks to others. In vain you seek to reduce this I to something that derives its power from itself, nor can you limit this You to anything that dwells in us. Both would once again deactualize the actual, the present relation. I and You remain; everyone can speak the You and then becomes I; everyone can say Father and then becomes son; actuality abides. . . .

Extended, the lines of relationships intersect in the eternal You.

Every single You is a glimpse of that. Through every single You the basic word addresses the eternal You. The mediatorship of the You of all beings accounts for the fullness of our relationships to them — and for the lack of fulfillment. The innate You is actualized each time without ever being perfected. It attains perfection solely in the immediate relationship to the You that in accordance with its nature cannot become an It.

Men have addressed their eternal You by many names. When they sang of what they had thus named, they still meant You: the first myths were hymns of praise. Then the names entered into the It-language; men felt impelled more and more to think of and to talk about their eternal You as an It. But all names of God remain hallowed — because they have been used not only to speak *of* God but also to speak *to* him.

Some would deny any legitimate use of the word God because it has been misused so much. Certainly it is the most burdened of all human words. Precisely for that reason it is the most imperishable and unavoidable. And how much weight has all erroneous talk about God's nature and works (although there never has been nor can be any such talk that is not erroneous) compared with the one truth that all men who have addressed God really meant him? For whoever pronounces the word God and really means You, addresses, no matter what his delusion, the true You of his life that cannot be restricted by any other and to whom he stands in a relationship that includes all others.

But whoever abhors the name and fancies that he is godless — when he addresses with his whole devoted being the You of his life that cannot be restricted by any other, he addresses God.

SIMONE DE BEAUVOIR

Simone de Beauvoir (1908–1986) was born in Paris and educated at the Sorbonne. She suffers, along with Merleau-Ponty, the disadvantage of being viewed in the shadow of Sartre, either as his disciple or companion. But de Beauvoir is one of the foremost novelists of the twentieth century, and though she did not see herself primarily as a philosopher, she is one of the major existentialist thinkers of the period. In her book The Ethics of Ambiguity *(see chapter 7), she provides us with an analysis of an existential ethic that is original and carefully developed.*

The Second Sex *was first published in France in 1949, and it has become a monument in feminist analysis. In it de Beauvoir uses the major concepts of existentialism (such as bad faith and the in-itself and for-itself) to illuminate the position of women in patriarchal society. In the following excerpt, she concludes her analysis with an overview and some recommendations for the future.*

The Second Sex

No, woman is not our brother; through indolence and depravity we have made of her a being apart, unknown, having no weapon other than her sex, which not only means constant strife but is moreover an unfair weapon of the eternal little slave's mistrust — adoring or hating, but never our frank companion, a being set apart as if in *esprit de corps* and freemasonry.

Many men would still subscribe to these words of Laforgue; many think that there will always be "strife and dispute," as Montaigne put it, and that fraternity will never be possible. The fact is that today neither men nor women are satisfied with each other. But the question is to know whether there is an original curse that condemns them to rend each other or whether the conflicts in which they are opposed merely mark a transitional moment in human history.

We have seen that in spite of legends no physiological destiny imposes an eternal hostility upon Male and Female as such; even the famous praying mantis devours her male only for want of other food and for the good of the species: it is to this, the species, that all individuals are subordinated, from the top to the bottom of the scale of animal life. Moreover, humanity is something more than a mere species: it is a historical development; it is to be defined by the manner in which it deals with its natural, fixed characteristics, its *facticité*. Indeed, even with the most extreme bad faith in the world, it is impossible to demonstrate the existence of a rivalry between the human male and female of a truly physiological nature. Further, their hostility may be allocated rather to that intermediate terrain between biology and psychology: psychoanalysis. Woman, we are told, envies man his penis and wishes to castrate him; but the childish desire for the penis is important in the life of the adult woman only if she feels her femininity as a mutilation; and then it is as a symbol of all the privileges of manhood that she wishes to appropriate the male organ. We may readily agree that her dream of castration has this symbolic significance: she wishes, it is thought, to deprive the male of his transcendence.

But her desire, as we have seen, is much more ambiguous: she wishes, in a contradictory fashion, *to have* this transcendence, which is to suppose that she at once respects it and denies it, that she intends at once to throw herself into it and keep it within herself. This is to say that the drama does not unfold on a sexual level; further, sexuality has never seemed to us to define a destiny, to furnish in itself the key to human behavior, but to express the totality of a situation that it only helps to define. The battle of the sexes is not immediately implied in the anatomy of man and woman. The truth is that when one evokes it, one takes for granted that in the timeless realm of Ideas a battle is being waged between those vague essences the Eternal Feminine and the Eternal Masculine; and one neglects the fact that this titanic combat assumes on earth two totally different forms, corresponding with two different moments of history.

The woman who is shut up in an immanence endeavors to hold man in that prison also; thus the prison will be confused with the world, and woman will no longer suffer from being confined there: mother, wife, sweetheart are the jailers. Society, being codified by man, decrees that woman is inferior: she can do away with this inferiority only by destroying the male's superiority. She sets about mutilating, dominating man, she contradicts him, she denies his truth and his values. But in doing this she is only defending herself; it was neither a changeless essence nor a mistaken choice that doomed her to immanence, to inferiority. They were imposed upon her. All oppression creates a state of war. And this is no exception. The existent who is regarded as inessential cannot fail to demand the re-establishment of her sovereignty.

Today the combat takes a different shape; instead of wishing to put man in prison, woman endeavors to escape from one; she no longer seeks to drag him into the realms of immanence but to emerge, herself, into the light of transcendence. Now the attitude of the males creates a new conflict: it is with a bad grace that the man lets her go. He is very well pleased to remain the sovereign subject, the absolute superior, the essential being; he refuses to accept his companion as an equal in any concrete way. She replies to his lack of confidence in her by assuming an aggressive attitude. It is no longer a question of a war between individuals each shut up in his or her sphere: a caste claiming its rights goes over the top and it is resisted by the privileged caste. Here two transcendences are face to face; instead of displaying mutual recognition, each free being wishes to dominate the other.

This difference of attitude is manifest on the sexual plane as on the spiritual plane. The "feminine" woman in making herself prey tries to reduce man, also, to her carnal passivity; she occupies herself in catching him in her trap, in enchaining him by means of the desire she arouses in him in submissively making herself a thing. The emancipated woman, on the contrary, wants to be active, a taker, and refuses the passivity man means to impose on her. Thus Elise and her emulators deny the values of the activities of virile type; they put the flesh above the spirit, contingence above liberty, their routine wisdom above creative audacity. But the "modern" woman accepts masculine values: she prides herself on thinking, taking action, working, creating, on the same terms as men; instead of seeking to disparage them, she declares herself their equal.

In so far as she expresses herself in definite action, this claim is legitimate, and male insolence must then bear the blame. But in men's defense it must be said that women are wont to confuse the issue. A Mabel Dodge Luhan intended to subjugate D. H. Lawrence by her feminine charms so as to dominate him spiritually thereafter; many women, in order to show by their successes their equivalence to men, try to secure male support by sexual means; they play on both sides, demanding old-fashioned respect and modern esteem, banking on their old magic and their new rights. It is understandable that a man becomes irritated and puts himself on the defensive; but he is also double-dealing when he requires woman to play the game fairly while he denies them the indispensable trump cards through distrust and hostility. Indeed, the struggle cannot be clearly drawn between them, since woman is opaque in her very being; she stands before man not as a subject but as an object paradoxically endued with subjectivity; she takes herself simultaneously as *self* and as *other,* a contradiction that entails baffling consequences. When she makes weapons at once of her weakness and of her strength, it is not a matter of designing calculation: she seeks salvation spontaneously in the way that has been imposed on her, that of passivity, at the same time when she is actively demanding her sovereignty; and no doubt this procedure is unfair tactics, but it is dictated to her by the ambiguous situation assigned her. Man, however, becomes indignant when he treats her as a free and independent being and then realizes that she is still a trap for him; if he gratifies and satisfies her in her posture as prey, he finds her claims to autonomy irritating; whatever he does, he feels tricked and she feels wronged.

The quarrel will go on as long as men and women fail to recognize each other as peers; that is to say, as long as femininity is perpetuated as such. Which sex is the more eager to maintain it? Woman, who is being emancipated from it, wishes none the less to retain its privileges; and man, in that case, wants her to assume its limitations. "It is easier to accuse one sex than to excuse the other," says Montaigne. It is vain to apportion praise and blame. The truth is that if the vicious circle is so hard to break, it is because the two sexes are each the victim at once of the other and of itself. Between two adversaries confronting each other in their pure liberty, an agreement could be easily reached: the more so as the war profits neither. But the complexity of the whole affair derives from the fact that each camp is giving aid and comfort to the enemy; woman is pursuing a dream of submission, man a dream of identification. Want of authenticity does not pay: each blames the other for the unhappiness he or she has incurred in yielding to the temptations of the easy way; what man and woman loathe in each other is the shattering frustration of each one's own bad faith and baseness.

We have seen why men enslaved women in the first place; the devaluation of femininity has been a necessary step in human evolution, but it might have led to a collaboration between the two sexes; oppression is to be explained by the tendency of the existent to flee from himself by means of identification with the other, whom he oppresses to that end. In each individual man that tendency exists today; and the vast majority yield to it. The husband wants to find himself in his wife, the lover in his mistress, in the form of a stone image; he is seeking in her the myth of his virility, of his sovereignty, of his immediate reality. "My husband never goes to the movies," says his wife, and the dubious masculine opinion is graved in the marble of eternity. But he is himself the slave of his double: what an effort to build up an image in which he is always in danger! In spite of everything his success in this depends upon the capricious freedom of women: he must constantly try to keep this propitious to him. Man is concerned with the effort to appear male, important, superior; he pretends so as to get pretense in return; he, too, is aggressive, uneasy; he feels hostility for women because he is afraid of them, he is afraid of them because he is afraid of the personage, the image, with which he identifies himself. What time and strength he squanders in liquidating, sublimating, tranferring complexes, in talking about women, in seducing them, in fearing them! He would be liberated himself in their liberation. But this is precisely what he dreads. And so he obstinately persists in the mystifications intended to keep woman in her chains.

That she is being tricked, many men have realized, "What a misfortune to be a woman! And yet the misfortune, when one is a woman, is at bottom not to comprehend that it is one," says Kirkegaard.* For a long time there have been efforts to disguise this misfortune. For example, guardianship has been done away with: women have been given "protectors," and if they are invested with the rights of the old-time guardians, it is in woman's own interest. To forbid her working, to keep her at home, is to defend her against herself and to assure her happiness. We have seen what poetic veils are thrown over her monotonous burdens of housekeeping and maternity: in exchange for her liberty she has received the false treasures of her "femininity." Balzac illustrates this maneuver very well in counseling man to treat her as a slave while persuading her that she is a queen. Less cynical, many men try to convince themselves that she is really privileged. There are American sociologists who seriously teach today the theory of "low-class gain." In France, also, it has often been proclaimed — although in a less scientific manner — that the workers are very fortunate in not being obliged to "keep up appearances" and still more so the bums who can dress in rags and sleep on the sidewalks, pleasures forbidden to the Count de Beaumont and the Wendels. Like the carefree wretches gaily scratching at their vermin, like the merry Negroes laughing under the lash and those joyous Tunisian Arabs burying their starved children with a smile, woman enjoys that incomparable privilege: irresponsibility. Free from troublesome burdens and cares, she obviously has "the better part." But it is disturbing that with an obstinate perversity — connected no doubt with original sin — down through the centuries and in all countries, the people who have the better part are always crying to their benefactors: "It is too much! I will be satisfied with yours!" But the munificent capitalists, the generous colonists, the superb males, stick to their guns: "Keep the better part, hold on to it!"

It must be admitted that the males find in woman more complicity than the oppressor usually finds in the oppressed. And in bad faith they take authorization from this to declare that she had *desired* the destiny they have imposed on her. We have seen that all the main features of her training combine to bar her from the roads of revolt and adventure. Society in general — beginning with her respected parents — lies to her by praising the lofty values of love, devotion, the gift of herself, and then concealing from her the fact that neither lover nor husband nor yet her children will be inclined to accept the burdensome charge of all that. She cheerfully believes these lies because they invite her to follow the easy slope: in this other commit their worst crime against her; throughout her life from childhood on, they damage and corrupt her by designating as her

* Footnote deleted

true vocation this submission, which is the temptation of every existent in the anxiety of liberty. If a child is taught idleness by being amused all day long and never being led to study, or shown its usefulness, it will hardly be said, when he grows up, that he chose to be incapable and ignorant; yet this is how woman is brought up, without ever being impressed with the necessity of taking charge of her own existence. So she readily lets herself come to count on the protection, love, assistance, and supervision of others, she lets herself be fascinated with the hope of self-realization without *doing* anything. She does wrong in yielding to the temptation; but man is in no position to blame her, since he has led her into the temptation. When conflict arises between them, each will hold the other responsible for the situation; she will reproach him with having made her what she is: "No one taught me to reason or to earn my own living"; he will reproach her with having accepted the consequences: "You don't know anything, you are an incompetent," and so on. Each sex thinks it can justify itself by taking the offensive; but the wrongs done by one do not make the other innocent.

The innumerable conflicts that set men and women against one another come from the fact that neither is prepared to assume all the consequences of this situation which the one has offered and the other accepted. The doubtful concept of "equality in inequality," which the one uses to mask his despotism and the other to mask her cowardice, does not stand the test of experience: in their exchanges, woman appeals to the theoretical equality she has been guaranteed, and man the concrete inequality that exists. The result is that in every association an endless debate goes on concerning the ambiguous meaning of the words *give* and *take:* she complains of giving her all, he protests that she takes his all. Woman has to learn that exchanges — it is a fundamental law of political economy — are based on the value the merchandise offered has for the buyer, and not for the seller: she has been deceived in being persuaded that her worth is priceless. The truth is that for man she is an amusement, a pleasure, company, an inessential boon; he is for her the meaning, the justification of her existence. The exchange, therefore, is not of two items of equal value.

This inequality will be especially brought out in the fact that the time they spend together — which fallaciously seems to be the same time — does not have the same value for both partners. During the evening the lover spends with his mistress he could be doing something of advantage to his career, seeing friends, cultivating business relationships, seeking recreation; for a man normally integrated in society, time is a positive value: money, reputation, pleasure. For the idle, bored woman, on the contrary, it is a burden she wishes to get rid of; when she succeeds in killing time, it is a benefit to her: the man's presence is pure profit. In a liaison what most clearly interests the man, in many cases, is the sexual benefit he gets from it: if need be, he can be content to spend no more time with his mistress than is required for the sexual act; but — with exceptions — what she, on her part, wants is to kill all the excess time she has on her hands; and — like the storekeeper who will not sell potatoes unless the customer will take turnips also — she will not yield her body unless her lover will take hours of conversation and "going out" into the bargain. A balance is reached if, on the whole, the cost does not seem too high to the man, and this depends, of course, on the strength of his desire and the importance he gives to what is to be sacrificed. But if the woman demands — offers — too much time, she becomes wholly intrusive, like the river overflowing its banks, and the man will prefer to have nothing rather than too much. Then she reduces her demands; but very often the balance is reached at the cost of a double tension: she feels that the man has "had" her at a bargain, and he thinks her price is too high. This analysis, of course, is put in somewhat humorous terms; but — except for those affairs of jealous and exclusive passion in which the man wants total possession of the woman — this conflict constantly appears in cases of affection, desire, and even love. He always has "other things to do" with his time; whereas she has time to burn; and he considers much of the time she gives him not as a gift but as a burden.

As a rule he consents to assume the burden because he knows very well that he is on the privileged side, he has a bad conscience; and if he is of reasonable good will he tries to compensate for the inequality by being generous. He prides himself on his compassion, however, and at the first clash he treats the woman as ungrateful and thinks, with some irritation: "I'm too good to her." She feels she is behaving like a beggar when she is convinced of the high value of her gifts, and that humiliates her.

Here we find the explanation of the cruelty that woman often shows she is capable of practicing; she has a good conscience because she is on the unprivileged side; she feels she is under no obligation to deal gently with the favored caste, and her only thought is to defend herself. She will even be very happy if she has occasion to show her resentment to a lover who has not been able to satisfy all her demands: since he does not give her enough, she takes savage delight in taking back everything from him. At this point the wounded lover suddenly discovers the value *in toto* of a liaison each moment of which he held more or less in contempt: he is ready to promise her everything, even though he will feel exploited again when he has to make good. He accuses his mistress of blackmailing him: she calls him stingy; both feel wronged.

Once again it is useless to apportion blame and excuses: justice can never be done in the midst of injustice. A colonial administrator has no possibility of acting rightly toward the natives, nor a general toward his soldiers; the only solution is to be neither colonist nor military chief; but a man could not prevent himself from being a man. So there he is, culpable in spite of himself and laboring under the effects of a fault he did not himself commit; and here she is, victim and shrew in spite of herself. Sometimes he rebels and becomes cruel, but then he makes himself an accomplice of the injustice, and the fault becomes really his. Sometimes he lets himself be annihilated, devoured, by his demanding victim; but in that case he feels duped. Often he stops at a compromise that at once belittles him and leaves him ill at ease. A well-disposed man will be more tortured by the situation than the woman herself: in a sense it is always better to be on the side of the vanquished; but if she is well-disposed also, incapable of self-sufficiency, reluctant to crush the man with the weight of her destiny, she struggles in hopeless confusion.

In daily life we meet with an abundance of these cases which are incapable of satisfactory solution because they are determined by unsatisfactory conditions. A man who is compelled to go on materially and morally supporting a woman whom he no longer loves feels he is victimized; but if he abandons without resources the woman who has pledged her whole life to him, she will be quite as unjustly victimized. The evil originates not in the perversity of individuals — and bad faith first appears when each blames the other — it originates rather in a situation against which all individual action is powerless. Women are "clinging," they are a dead weight, and they suffer for it; the point is that their situation is like that of a parasite sucking out the living strength of another organism. Let them be provided with living strength of their own, let them have the means to attack the world and wrest from it their own subsistence, and their dependence will be abolished — that of man also. There is no doubt that both men and women will profit greatly from the new situation.

A world where men and women would be equal is easy to visualize, for that precisely is what the Soviet Revolution *promised:* women raised and trained exactly like men were to work under the same conditions and for the same wages. Erotic liberty was to be recognized by custom, but the sexual act was not to be considered a "service" to be paid for; woman was to be *obliged* to provide herself with other ways of earning a living; marriage was to be based on a free agreement that the spouses could break at will; maternity was to be voluntary, which meant that contraception and abortion were to be authorized and that, on the other hand, all mothers and their children were to have exactly the same rights, in or out of marriage; pregnancy leaves were to be paid for by the State, which would assume charge of the children, signifying not that they would be *taken away* from their parents, but that they would not be *abandoned* to them.

But is it enough to change laws, institutions, customs, public opinion, and the whole social context, for men and women to become truly equal? "Women will always be women," say the skeptics. Other seers prophesy that in casting off their femininity they will not succeed in changing themselves into men and they will become monsters. This would be to admit that the woman of today is a creation of nature; it must be repeated once more that in human society nothing is natural and that woman, like much else, is a product elaborated by civilization. The intervention of others in her destiny is fundamental: if this action took a different direction, it would produce a quite different result. Woman is determined not by her hormones or by mysterious instincts, but by the manner in which her body and her relation to the world are modified through the action of others than herself. The abyss that separates the adolescent boy and girl has been deliberately opened out between them since earliest childhood; later on, woman could not be other than what she *was made*, and that past was bound to shadow her for life. If we appreciate its influence, we see clearly that her destiny is not predetermined for all eternity.

We must not believe, certainly, that a change is woman's economic condition alone is enough to transform her, though this factor has been and remains the basic factor in her evolution; but until it has brought about the moral, social, cultural, and other consequences that it promises and requires, the new woman cannot appear. At this moment they have been realized nowhere, in Russia no more than in France or the United States; and this explains why the woman of today is torn between the past and the future. She appears most often as a "true woman" disguised as a man, and she feels herself as ill at ease in her flesh as in her masculine garb. She must shed her old skin and cut her own new clothes. This she could do only through a social evolution. No single educator could fashion a *female human being* today who would be the exact homologue of the *male human being;* if she is raised like a boy, the young girl feels she is an oddity and thereby she is given a new kind of sex specification. Stendhal understood this when he said: "The forest must be planted all at once." But if we imagine, on the contrary, a society in which the equality of the sexes would be concretely realized, this equality would find new expression in each individual.

If the little girl were brought up from the first with the same demands and rewards, the same severity and the same freedom, as her brothers, taking part in the same studies, the same games, promised the same future, surrounded with women and men who seemed to her undoubted equals, the meanings of the castration complex and of the oedipus complex would be profoundly modified. Assuming on the same basis as the father the material and moral responsibility of the couple, the mother would enjoy the same lasting prestige; the child would perceive around her an androgynous world and not a masculine world. Were she emotionally more attracted to her father — which is not even sure — her love for him would be tinged with a will to emulation and not a feeling of powerlessness; she would not be oriented toward passivity. Authorized to test her powers in work and sports, competing actively with the boys, she would not find the absence of the penis — compensated by the promise of a child — enough to give rise to an inferiority complex; correlatively, the boy would not have a superiority complex if it were not instilled into him and if he looked up to women with as much respect as to men. The little girl would not seek sterile compensation in narcissism and dreaming, she would not take her fate for granted; she would be interested in what she was *doing,* she would throw herself without reserve into undertakings.

I have already pointed out how much easier the transformation of puberty would be if she looked beyond it, like the boys, toward a free adult future: menstruation horrifies her only because it is an abrupt descent into femininity. She would also take her young eroticism in much more tranquil fashion if she did not feel a frightened disgust for her destiny as a whole; coherent sexual information would do much to help her over this crisis. And thanks to coeducational schooling, the august mystery of Man would have no occasion to enter her mind: it would be eliminated by everyday familiarity and open rivalry.

Objections raised against this system always imply respect for sexual taboos; but the effort to inhibit all sex curiosity and pleasure in the child is quite useless; one succeeds only in creating repressions, obsessions, neuroses. The excessive sentimentality, homosexual fervors, and platonic crushes of adolescent girls, with all their train of silliness and frivolity, are much more injurious than a little childish sex play and a few definite sex experiences. It would be beneficial above all for the young girl not to be influenced against taking charge herself of her own existence, for then she would not seek a demigod in the male — merely a comrade, a friend, a partner. Eroticism and love would take on the nature of free transcendence and not that of resignation; she could experience them as a relation between equals. There is no intention, of course, to remove by a stroke of the pen all the difficulties that the child has to overcome in changing into an adult; the most intelligent, the most tolerant education could not relieve the child of experiencing things for herself; what could be asked is that obstacles should not be piled gratuitously in her path. Progress is already shown by the fact that "vicious" little girls are no longer cauterized with a red-hot iron. Psychoanalysis has given parents some instruction, but the conditions under which, at the present time, the sexual training and initiation of woman are accomplished are so deplorable that none of the objections advanced against the idea of a radical change could be considered valid. It is not a question of abolishing in woman the contingencies and miseries of the human condition, but of giving her the means for transcending them.

Woman is the victim of no mysterious fatality; the peculiarities that identify her as specifically a woman get their importance from the significance placed upon them. They can be surmounted, in the future, when they are regarded in new perspectives. Thus, as we have seen, through her erotic experience woman feels — and often detests — the domination of the male; but this is no reason to conclude that her ovaries condemn her to live forever on her knees. Virile aggressiveness seems like a lordly privilege only within a system that in its entirety conspires to affirm masculine sovereignty; and woman *feels* herself profoundly passive in the sexual act only because she already *thinks* of herself as such. Many modern women who lay claim to their dignity as human beings still envisage their erotic life from the standpoint of a tradition of slavery: since it seems to them humiliating to lie beneath the man, to be penetrated by him, they grow tense in frigidity. But if the reality were different, the meaning expressed symbolically in amorous gestures and postures would be different, too: a woman who pays and dominates her lover can, for example, take pride in her superb idleness and consider that she is enslaving the male who is actively exerting himself. And here and now there are many sexually well-balanced couples whose notions of victory and defeat are giving place to the idea of an exchange.

As a matter of fact, man, like woman, is flesh, therefore passive, the plaything of his hormones and of the species, the restless prey of his desires. And she, like him, in the midst of the carnal fever, is a consenting, a voluntary gift, an activity; they live out in their several fashions the strange ambiguity of existence made body. In those combats where they think they confront one another, it is really against the self that each one struggles, projecting into the partner that part of the self which is repudiated; instead of living out the ambiguities of their situation, each tries to make the other bear the abjection and tries to reserve the honor for the self. If, however, both should assume the ambiguity with a clear-sighted modesty, correlative of an authentic pride, they would see each other as equals and would live out their erotic drama in amity. The fact that we are human beings is infinitely more important than all the peculiarities that distinguish human beings from one another; it is never the given that confers superiorities: "virtue," as the ancients called it, is defined at the level of "that which depends on us." In both sexes is played out the same drama of the flesh and the spirit, of finitude and transcendence; both are gnawed away by time and laid in wait for by death, they have the same essential need for one another; and they can gain from their liberty the same glory. If they were to taste it, they would no longer be tempted to dispute fallacious privileges, and fraternity between them could then come into existence.

I shall be told that all this is utopian fancy, because woman cannot be "made over" unless society has first made her really the equal of man. Conservatives have never failed in such circumstances to refer to that vicious circle; history, however, does not revolve. If a caste is kept in a state of inferiority, no doubt it remains inferior; but liberty can break the circle. Let the Negroes vote and they become worthy of having the vote: let woman be given responsibilities and she is able to assume them. The fact is that oppressors cannot be expected to make a move of gratuitous generosity; but at one time the revolt of the oppressed, at another time even the very evolution of the privileged caste itself, creates new situations; thus men have been led, in their own interest, to give partial emancipation to woman: it remains only for women to continue their ascent, and the successes they are obtaining are an encouragement for them to do so. It seems almost certain that sooner or later they will arrive at complete economic and social equality, which will bring about an inner metamorphosis.

However this may be, there will be some to object that if such a world is possible it is not desirable. When woman is "the same" as her male, life will lose its salt and spice. This argument, also, has lost its novelty: those interested in perpetuating present conditions are always in tears about the marvelous past that is about to disappear, without having so much as a smile for the young future. It is quite true that doing away with the slave trade meant death to the great plantations, magnificent with azaleas and camellias, it meant ruin to the whole refined Southern civilization. The attics of time have received its rare old laces along with the clear pure voices of the Sistine *castrati*,* and there is a certain "feminine charm" that is also on the way to the same dusty repository. I agree that he would be a barbarian indeed who failed to appreciate exquisite flowers, rare lace, the crystal-clear voice of the eunuch, and feminine charm.

When the "charming woman" shows herself in all her splendor, she is a much more exalting object than the "idiotic paintings, over-doors, scenery, showman's garish signs, popular chromos," that excited Rimbaud; adorned with the most modern artifices, beautified according to the newest techniques, she comes down from the remoteness of the ages, from Thebes, from Crete, from Chichén-Itzá; and she is also the totem set up deep in the African jungle; she is a helicopter and she is a bird; and there is this, the greatest wonder of all: under her tinted hair the forest murmur becomes a thought, and words issue from her breasts. Men stretch forth avid hands toward the marvel, but when they grasp it is gone; the wife, the mistress, speak like everybody else through their mouths: their words are worth just what they are worth; their breasts also. Does such a fugitive miracle — and one so rare — justify us in perpetuating a situation that is baneful for both sexes? One can appreciate the

* Males who were castrated (eunuchs)

beauty of flowers, the charm of women, and appreciate them at their true value; if these treasures cost blood or misery, they must be sacrificed.

But in truth this sacrifice seems to men a peculiarly heavy one; few of them really wish in their hearts for woman to succeed in making it; those among them who hold woman in contempt see in the sacrifice nothing for them to gain, those who cherish her see too much that they would lose. And it is true that the evolution now in progress threatens more than feminine charm alone: in beginning to exist for herself, woman will relinquish the function as double and mediator to which she owes her privileged place in the masculine universe; to man, caught between the silence of nature and the demanding presence of other free beings, a creature who is at once his like and a passive thing seems a great treasure. The guise in which he conceives his companion may be mythical, but the experiences for which she is the source or the pretext are none the less real: there are hardly any more precious, more intimate, more ardent. There is no denying that feminine dependence, inferiority, woe, give women their special character; assuredly woman's autonomy, if it spares men many troubles, will also deny them many conveniences; assuredly there are certain forms of the sexual adventure which will be lost in the world of tomorrow. But this does not mean that love, happiness, poetry, dream, will be banished from it.

Let us not forget that our lack of imagination always depopulates the future; for us it is only an abstraction; each one of us secretly deplores the absence there of the one who was himself. But the humanity of tomorrow will be living flesh and in its conscious liberty; that time will be its present and it will in turn prefer it. New relations of flesh and sentiment of which we have no conception will arise between the sexes; already, indeed, there have appeared between men and women friendships, rivalries, complicities, comradeships — chaste or sensual — which past centuries could not have conceived. To mention one point, nothing could seem to me more debatable than the opinion that dooms the new world to uniformity and hence to boredom. I fail to see that this present world is free from boredom or that liberty ever creates uniformity.

To begin with, there will always be certain differences between man and woman; her eroticism, and therefore her sexual world, have a special form of their own and therefore cannot fail to engender a sensuality, a sensitivity, of a special nature. This means that her relations to her own body, to that of the male, to the child, will never be identical with those the male bears to his own body, to that of the female, and to the child; those who make much of "equality in difference" could not with good grace refuse to grant me the possible existence of differences in equality. Then again, it is institutions that create uniformity. Young and pretty, the slaves of the harem are always the same in the sultan's embrace; Christianity gave eroticism its savor of sin and legend when it endowed the human female with a soul; if society restores her sovereign individuality to woman, it will not thereby destroy the power of love's embrace to move the heart.

It is nonsense to assert that revelry, vice, esctasy, passion, would become impossible if man and woman were equal in concrete matters; the contradictions that put the flesh in opposition to the spirit, the instant to time, the swoon of immanence to the challenge of transcendence, the absolute of pleasure to the nothingness of forgetting, will never be resolved; in sexuality will always be materialized the tension, the anguish, the joy, the frustration, and the triumph of existence. To emancipate woman is to refuse to confine her to the relations she bears to man, not to deny them to her; let her have her independent existence and she will continue none the less to exist for him *also:* mutually recognizing each other as subject, each will yet remain for the other an *other.* The reciprocity of their relations will not do away with the miracles — desire, possession, love, dream, adventure — worked by the division of human beings into two separate categories; and the words that move us — giving, conquering, uniting — will not lose their meaning. On the contrary, when we abolish the slavery of half of humanity, together with the whole system of hypocrisy that it implies, then the "division" of humanity will reveal its genuine significance and the human couple will find its true form. "The direct, natural, necessary relation of human creatures is the *relation of man to woman,*" Marx has said.* "The nature of this relation determines to what point man himself is to be considered as a *generic being,* as mankind; the relation of man to woman is the most natural relation of human being to human being. By it is shown, therefore, to what point the *natural* behavior of man has become *human* or to what point the *human* being has become his *natural* being, to what point his *human nature* has become his *nature.*"

The case could not be better stated. It is for man to establish the reign of liberty in the midst of the world of the given. To gain the supreme victory, it is necessary, for one thing, that by and through their natural differentiation men and women unequivocally affirm their brotherhood.

* *Philosophical Works,* Vol. VI (Marx's italics)

chapter 7

Existentialism
and the Moral Life

Every existing thing is born without reason, prolongs itself out of weakness, and dies by chance.

Sartre, *Nausea*

Even when I make a cup of coffee I change the world.

Sartre, *Playboy* interview

INTRODUCTION

Human beings share subject-status in a world of objects. To use Heidegger's terminology, each of us is a Dasein who is in the world in a way that is radically different from the being of purely ontic beings. We are self-conscious, "entrusted with our own Being." Dasein is in the world in the sense that it is with the world through its Care (or, again in Heidegger's original term, *Sorge*). This Care is our unique ability to project ourselves into the future, the ability to live always ahead of ourselves. But there is a tragic ambiguity in this reality, for each of us must also live with the consciousness of mortality.

As we have seen, traditional philosophical theories have attempted to mask these painful realities. De Beauvoir (p. 459) notes the strategies such philosophers have employed. Dualists deny death and maintain that each of us is an immortal soul, which survives the physical death of the body. Straightforward materialists, in contrast, reduce mind to matter, dismissing the existential significance of the anguish that accompanies awareness of finitude. Neither the dualist nor the materialist gives priority to our anxiety in Being-toward-Death and our dread in relation to that nothingness which is the end of all possibility. Existentialists, as we have seen, make this anguish fundamental to and constitutive of Dasein's reality. And, whatever individual existentialist thinkers have concluded about despair, all agree that it must be the starting point for thinking about what it means to be an ontological being.

These considerations play a key role in our examination of the possibility of an existential ethic. Broadly speaking, ethics is the study of values, of what one ought to do. It is therefore prescriptive rather than descriptive. That is, any ethical statement recommends that we do or forbear from doing some action. When, for example, I maintain that killing is wrong, I recommend to members of my moral community that they not kill. Even if I stipulate exceptions to this principle — for example, that it is wrong to kill except in self-defense — I am nonetheless prescribing that the only sort of permissible killing is that which occurs when one is acting in self-defense. Though we may disagree as to what constitutes an act of self-defense (e.g., does this include capital punishment? killing in wartime? abortion?), we nonetheless have a guideline for human conduct. Even the most sincere assent to an ethical principle does not, however, guarantee that one will behave in the prescribed manner. We are not angels from whom correct actions emanate automatically from correct beliefs. We may lack a will strong enough to follow through on our moral convictions, particularly when doing so requires some measure of sacrifice. Regardless of our actual conduct, however, values provide ideals by which we judge action — our own and others' — as right or wrong.

Traditional ethical theories have sought to define the "good life" and to provide an objective basis for ethical action. Aristotle (384–322 B.C.), for example, maintained that a good action was one which followed the "golden mean." By this he meant that one ought not to act in ways that were extreme, that is, either in excess or defect. So, for example, one ought to be generous but not stingy or extravagant. Ethical theorists Jeremy Bentham (1748–1832) and John Stuart Mill (1806–1873) defended a view known as utilitarianism. The basic principle of utilitarianism — termed by Bentham the "greatest happiness" principle — urges that we choose those actions which maximize utility.

Whatever we desire, Mill argued, is desired because it leads to happiness. If happiness is the end of all human action, then "it necessarily follows that it must be the criterion of morality, since a part is included in the whole." (*Utilitarianism*, p. 49) By "happiness" utilitarians are not referring to those states of complete rapture or ecstasy we sometimes encounter; indeed, a moral system founded on such rare and ephemeral moments would be quite a strange one. Instead, utilitarians urge us to seek those experiences that are likely to provide pleasure and to avoid those likely to lead to pain. But the greatest happiness principle is not one of crude egoism. Rather, Mill insists that each of us must determine what course of action will maximize utility and include in that calculation all those whose interests are likely to be affected by the decision. Thus, utilitarian theory is based on the importance of consequences in judging the morality of an action: that is, if X leads to good consequences, then X is a good action.

The German philosopher Immanuel Kant (1724–1804) rejected such theories for their focus on feelings like pleasure and pain, arguing that the capacity to pursue pleasure is not unique to our species. Rather, he maintained, the basis for human conduct must be that which distinguishes us from other animals: our ability to act on the basis of duty. His "categorical imperative" that one should "act so as to will one's act to be universal law" requires that we view ethics as a rational endeavor. To will an act to be universal is to acknowledge one's nature as moral lawmaker and to imagine a world in which everyone does what one is about to do. If, for example, I wonder whether I may make a promise knowing that I intend not to keep it, I must be willing to allow giving false promises to be universal law. But such a maxim would destroy itself almost as soon as I try to will it; or, as Kant puts it: "For by such a law there would really be no promises at all, since in vain would my willing future actions be professed to other people who would not believe what I professed, or if they over-hastily did believe, then they would pay me back in like coin." (*Grounding*, p. 15) For Kant, reason dictates morality. We must do what is right not simply because it is "prudent" to do so. Since prudence is contingent and unpredictable, it cannot be the basis for morality. Rather, we must do what is right because it is our duty.

This brief introduction hardly does justice to the richness and scope of traditional Kantian and utilitarian theory. Nor does it consider alternative ethical theories or any of the recent modifications of Kantianism and utilitarianism with their attendant strengths and weaknesses. It does, however, lay a foundation on which to consider some of the features of ethical theory in general. As we have seen, some of these theories view certain end results (e.g., self-interest, happiness, pleasure) as primary in judging an action. Others maintain that there are central features of actions (e.g., motivation, intention, etc.) that make them right or wrong regardless of the consequences that follow from them. What all of these ethical theories share is the assumption that ethics is objective, that is, that there are certain kinds of actions that are objectively right or wrong. And each theory holds that the faculty of reason is capable of understanding the objective nature of ethics and the conditions one must meet to achieve a good end. For some theories, this determination is based on an externally imposed order, such as, for example, the will of God. For other theories, it is human nature that provides the ground for ethics. But no theory is ambiguous: Each has fairly clear criteria for determining whether actions are right or wrong, and each is capable of those determinations in advance of the action. Though these theories may enable us to take into account the particular circumstances of a given situation (a utilitarian, for example, would want to know what particular action will lead to maximum happiness, and that will vary depending on circumstances), virtually all traditional theories in ethics posit that there are right and wrong actions. This means, then, given the law of contradiction, that if *X* is right, then *not-X* must be wrong.

Thus, no matter what particular ethical view we hold, we can use the values of that system to judge our actions and the actions of others, and we can use that system as an objective guideline for determining future conduct. Though even members of the same school of ethics may disagree about what is the correct course in a given situation, all must agree that there is *some* right action and all others are wrong. Disagreement, then, would occur over the application of the criteria rather than the criteria themselves.

Existentialists, however, make subjectivity the beginning and the end of human experience. Yet this emphasis on subjectivity makes ethics problematic. We have seen, for example, how Kierkegaard's religious stage (see chapter 2) "suspends the ethical" as one makes a leap of faith in obedience to God. This leap is ultimately unconditioned and leaves the knight of faith completely alone. In contrast, the ethical life is essentially one of community, of rules and norms, of family life, of the universal. One cannot, in Kant's language, will Abraham's act to be universal law. How could one will a world in which fathers kill their sons? Yet, for Kierkegaard, this is precisely what makes Abraham a hero. There are no rules or guidelines for how to be a "knight of faith." If there were, those very rules would undermine themselves. Similarly, Nietzsche calls himself an "immoralist," and his attack on morality is an attack on those traditional values which, he believed, elevate the herd and glorify weakness. His injunction to "self-overcome" is one that provides neither concrete strategies to follow nor substantive criteria to determine whether one has reached that goal.

Twentieth-century existentialists have also been ambivalent about (if not hostile to) ethics. Heidegger, for example, explicitly maintains that ethics is not a concern central to his philosophy, though there is no doubt that much of what he says has key implications for ethical analysis (see, for example, the discussion of authenticity, p. 52). At the end of *Being and Nothingness,* Sartre promises us a longer work on ethics, but his philosophical interests moved him in other directions and he never delivered on that promise. He did write a long essay, *Existentialism Is a Humanism,* in response to his critics: the communists, who saw existentialism as bourgeois, individualistic, and ahistorical; and the Catholics, who claimed that the view led to despair, degraded humanity, and "forgot the smile of a child." But this essay is flawed, and Sartre later repudiated it. Camus wrote extensively on issues (e.g., suicide in *The Myth of Sisyphus*) central to ethical theory; but he left no systematic work on the issue. It is Simone de Beauvoir, whose book *The Ethics of Ambiguity* is excerpted at the end of this chapter, who most conscientiously attempted to outline a framework for an existential ethic and to respond to critics of that view. The introduction to this chapter owes much to her analysis.

Many of the characteristics of existentialism outlined in the introduction to this text seem, at least superficially, to undermine the possibility of ethics. If ethics is about community, how can a philosophy which elevates the individual above the group have an ethic? If ethics requires consistency and predictability, does existentialism's insistence on the changeability of concrete experience and its rejection of rules preclude an ethical system? Can we be ethical and be absolutely free? How can we speak of "right" and "wrong" action in a world that is fundamentally subjective? How can we prescribe for ourselves, or for others? Finally, it appears that every ethical system presupposes that our actions *mean* something, that is, that they *matter*, not only in terms of the general community but also in terms of who we are. If the world is absurd and, finally, meaningless, doesn't existentialism deny "the reality and seriousness of human undertakings"? (Sartre, *Existentialism*, p. 12) Indeed, why be ethical at all?

This chapter considers these questions, using primarily the works of twentieth-century atheistic existentialists. We have chosen this branch of existentialism for a number of reasons: first, because chapter 3 is an examination of existential theism whose implications for ethics can be fleshed out by the reader; second, because the thinkers whose writing is our focus (primarily de Beauvoir) have struggled seriously and at great length with the questions raised in the preceding paragraph; and, finally, because these questions are probably most difficult for one who professes to be both existentialist *and* atheist.

ETHICS AND FREEDOM

In the twentieth century, existentialists like Camus, de Beauvoir, and Sartre begin with what we have termed "dreadful freedom." Nietzsche proclaimed that "God is dead," but God's absence leaves us with a terrible void (see pp. 174–75). We cannot allow ourselves to be seduced by those naive atheists "who would like to abolish God with the least possible expense." (Sartre, *Existentialism*, p. 25) It is of no use to substitute "human nature" or "progress" or "*a priori* values" for the God we have lost and pretend that no change has occurred. Rather, we must recognize that, without God, we have lost the very ground for our Being. We must see that we are thrown into the world without necessary reason, that we are free and totally responsible. All absolutes — absolute truth, absolute necessity, and absolute moral values — die when God dies.

Traditional ethical systems have run from the ambiguity that results from freedom and subjectivity and replaced it with rigid systems of right and wrong conduct. But such systems, existentialists maintain, overestimate the power of the human intellect and undervalue the richness and complexity of human experience. To say that existence precedes essence is to say that we begin as nothing. There is no human nature, nothing but what we make of ourselves. "First of all, man exists, turns up, appears on the scene, and, only afterwards, defines himself." (Sartre, *Existentialism*, p. 18) Ethics, then, must be a creative venture, as we organize our own worlds of meaning around our actions.

Sartre characterizes human reality as *pour soi*, as nothingness. Heidegger maintains that Dasein's essential Being is possibility. Whatever we call it, however, human reality is what it is not and not what it is. We are our pasts, which have already occurred; we are our futures, which have not yet occurred. We struggle to become *en soi*, to be complete, to be filled up. Yet this struggle is futile, and, ironically, is ended only when we die and *pour soi* finally becomes *en soi*. We struggle vainly to become God.

We are, then, essentially nothingness, a lack, a possibility. But this only means that there are no external reasons for what we do, that nothing is necessary. We must justify ourselves, for there is no God and no human nature that can provide that ground for us. We must give ourselves our reasons for what we are, recognizing that we can choose anything. There are no unconditioned values, for that would make a thing of values and rob us of our freedom. In a vain attempt to become God, we become human. According to de Beauvoir (see p. 557), "It is not granted him to exist without tending toward this being which he will never be [i.e., God]. But it is possible for him to want this tension even with the failure which it involves." To strive to become God is, then, to court failure. But in the process of failing to be both *en soi* and *pour soi*, we become *possibility*. Accepting this failure, de Beauvoir's "tension," is a positive affirmation of existence. As we saw in chapter 5, this possibility is dizzying. Looking into the openness that is our future is like staring down into a bottomless chasm. Without *a priori* values, we experience a sense of anguish and a sense of forlornness: We have no basis on which to decide, yet we must decide. "We are alone, with no excuses." (Sartre, *Existentialism*, p. 27)

We are, then, the source of our values. And those values spring from what Sartre calls *projects* (see p. 558): "Value is this lack-in-being of which freedom *makes itself* a lack; and it is because the latter makes itself a lack that value appears. It is desire which creates the desirable, and the project which sets up the end." Through our desire, we create a project, and in that process our values appear. These values emerge from us, not God or human nature. Since existence precedes essence, we are fully responsible for ourselves. We cannot wish ourselves other than we are, for we are our acts, our projects. As a result, the persons we are, are the person we have chosen to be. This fact fills us with anguish, forlornness, and despair. If God does not exist, we face our responsibilities alone. There is nothing that legitimizes us. "We have no excuse behind us, nor justification before us." (Sartre, *Existentialism*, p. 27) We are responsible even for our passion. And, given that the future is nothingness, possibility, there is always the chance that our plans will not lead to the results for which we had aimed. Of course there are — for every one of us — an infinite number of "I could haves." This is simply obvious, for all of us are freedom. But what counts about us is the sum total of all our deeds. For existentialism, "I choose," "I act," and "I am" are virtually interchangeable phrases.

It is impossible to answer precisely why one chooses anything, but for existentialism we create with our own vision of the future in mind. Each decision we make is a renewal of the old one or a choice of new goals. And with no excuse behind us (e.g., fate or God) nor justification before us (e.g., approval from others, absolute values, etc.) we simply *choose*. The for-itself, because it is essentially nothingness, is desire; *pour soi* constantly needs a project by which one creates one's own choices and motives.

Thus, it is only an existential ethic that endows human conduct with any real significance. Without forgiveness or justification from God, without compensation in heaven or punishment in hell, we alone give our existence its importance. Our acts are definitive, they create who we are. Indeed, we carry the responsibility for the world on our shoulders. We are, in Camus's words, "without appeal." But this is not, existentialists maintain, a posture of pessimism. To say that one is "without appeal" is not to condemn that life or to complain about it. Rather, as de Beauvoir makes clear (see p. 447), it is to assert that there is nothing outside of existence and that values emerge from that existence.

EXISTENTIALISM AND VALUES

Isn't all this subjective? Indeed. But what else could it be? For existentialists, the basis for all projects is subjective. Unlike Kantian theory with its impersonal "rational individual" who acts as lawmaker, existentialism addresses itself to the actions of concrete individuals in concrete situations in "dreadful freedom." Sartre's story about his troubled student may be helpful here.

[The boy's] father was on bad terms with his mother, and moreover, was inclined to be a collaborationist; his older brother had been killed in the

German offensive of 1940, and the young man, with somewhat immature but generous feelings, wanted to avenge him. His mother lived alone with him, very much upset by the half-treason of her husband and the death of her older son; the boy was her only consolation.

The boy was faced with the choice of leaving for England and joining the Free French Forces — that is, leaving his mother behind — or remaining with his mother and helping her to carry on. He was fully aware that the woman lived only for him and that his going-off — and perhaps his death — would plunge her into despair. He was also aware that every act that he did for his mother's sake was a sure thing, in the sense that it was helping her to carry on, whereas every effort he made toward going off and fighting was an uncertain move which might run aground and prove completely useless; for example, on the way to England he might, while passing through Spain, be detained indefinitely in a Spanish camp; he might reach England or Algiers and be stuck in an office at a desk job. As a result, he was faced with two very different kinds of action: one, concrete, immediate, but concerning only one individual; the other concerned an incomparably vaster group, a national collectivity, but for that very reason was dubious, and might be interrupted en route. And, at the same time, he was wavering between two kinds of ethics. On the one hand, an ethics of sympathy, of personal devotion; on the other, a broader ethics, but one whose efficacy was more dubious. He had to choose between the two.

> *Existentialism*, pp. 28–30

This student obviously faces a profound dilemma. What could help him choose? Should he stay with his mother or help the cause of the resistance? How would our traditional theories help here? What would Aristotle advise us? That is to say, how do we determine what is the golden mean? Christian doctrine might tell us to love our neighbor or to be charitable, but who is one's neighbor here? Or, what would it mean to maximize utility in this case? The student might be killed moments after joining the resistance, in which case no one is helped and his mother is worse off as a result. Or he might stay with his mother and feel guilt and regret, failing to maximize pleasure. How can he predict the future here? As a Kantian, one must ask what should be willed to be universal law. Can't we will both that all children help their aging parents *and* that all citizens participate to the best of their abilities in just causes? To which of these moral "universals" should we give assent? According to Sartre,

The Kantian ethics says, 'Never treat any person as a means, but as an end.' Very well, if I stay with my mother, I'll treat her as an end and not as a means; but by virtue of this fact, I'm running the risk of treating the people around me who are fighting, as means; and, conversely, if I go to join those who are fighting, I'll be treating them as an end, and, by doing that, I run the risk of treating my mother as a means.

> *Existentialism*, pp. 30–31

Even a seemingly simpler theory such as egoism — do whatever is in one's own self-interest — seems unenlightening here, precisely because it is not clear what is in our self-interest. We can even disregard value systems entirely and act on the basis of how we feel. But, as Sartre points out, the only way to determine the strength of a feeling is by performing whatever particular action confirms that feeling. We can seek out advice, as did Sartre's young student, but we must choose our advisor ("choosing your adviser is involving yourself," according to Sartre), and we must interpret the advice and decide whether to act on it. No matter what, we must make a choice. And yet no choice is objectively right or wrong.

Perhaps all ethical choices are like this one. Perhaps objective theories with their textbook approaches to life and their vague notions of value fail us in real flesh-and-blood situations. Perhaps no a priori code of ethics is truly instructive in the tough cases, which are common enough in human experience. For existentialists, it is important to recognize that in choosing we determine our values; it is not an ethical principle that instructs us as to how we should behave, but rather it is our actions that create value.

Sartre believes that this process begins with what he calls the "original project," when one first becomes aware of oneself as a separate entity and projects a desired relationship between oneself and the world. This drama extends throughout one's life, as each individual decision is necessarily either a renewed choice of that original goal or an assertion of new goals. Thus, we choose ourselves constantly. In a sense, it is not enough to say that we have freedom; rather, we *are* freedom. Sartre even insists that we cannot fall back on the cliché that we "did not ask to be born," for the very fact that we are here means that we are choosing to be born (see chapter 5, pp. 322–23). We are thrown into the world and are of the world. We have no choice but to involve ourselves in that world through our projects. This may seem harsh, but "it prompts people to understand that reality alone is what counts, that dreams, expectations, and hopes warrant no more than to define a man as a disappointed dream, as miscarried hopes, as vain expectations." (Sartre, *Existentialism*, p. 39)

EXISTENTIALISM AND LIVING AUTHENTICALLY

Though we cannot choose not to be free, we can try to escape from this freedom in a number of ways. We can blame our behavior on circumstances or society or we can argue that we "had no alternative"; or we can assert that our values "demanded" a certain course of action. At times we blame our pasts for our present behavior. Like Pontius Pilate, we can try to wash our hands of the anguish of our decisions. The inauthentic person is afraid to face the ambiguous character of human reality. Rather than confront the experience of anguish such a realization provokes, this individual creates a system in which ambiguity and anguish are inadmissible. Philosopher and theologian Paul Tillich refers to this sort of response to freedom as pathological.

> Existential anxiety of doubt drives the person toward the creation of certitude in systems of meaning, which are supported by tradition and authority. In spite of the element of doubt which is implied in man's finite spirituality, and in spite of the threat of meaninglessness implied in man's estrangement, anxiety is reduced by these ways of producing and preserving certitude. Neurotic anxiety builds a narrow castle of certitude which can be defended and is defended with the utmost tenacity. Man's power of asking is prevented from becoming actual in this sphere, and if there is a danger of its becoming actualized by questions asked from the outside he reacts with a fanatical rejection. However the castle of undoubted certitude is not built on the rock of reality. The inability of the neurotic to have a full encounter with reality makes his doubts as well as his certitudes unrealistic. He puts both in the wrong place. . . . [H]e is without the courage to take the anxiety of emptiness or doubt and meaninglessness upon himself.
>
> *Courage to Be,* pp. 76–77

Like Tillich, other extentialists emphasize the notion of courage in the face of anxiety. Many do not, however, face this challenge forthrightly. Some (Sartre calls them the cowards — *les laches*) are the serious-minded who hide their freedom by way of deterministic excuses and social norms. Others (Sartre's term is stinkers — *les salauds*) try to pretend that their existence is necessary and not contingent. But "bad faith" (Heidegger's "inauthenticity") does not free us from real responsibility. According to de Beauvoir, no one is passive: "no one can know the peace of the tomb while he is alive." (*Ethics of Ambiguity,* p. 43) And even though we have a past, we must still choose the form that past will take for us. Bad faith is a lie to oneself, an attempt to be what one is not. But it is not a deliberate lie by one in possession of appropriate information. It is a refusal to take responsibility for one's being. The authentic individual faces something the inauthentic is afraid to face, namely the "subjective tension of freedom." (*Ethics of Ambiguity,* p. 48)

The excerpt from Sartre at the end of this chapter makes clear that, in bad faith, we seek to flee from the fact that consciousness is what it is not and is not what it is. Because of the nature of consciousness, the risk of bad faith is always present; it is *pour soi*'s futile attempt to be *en soi*, to be complete and absolute. Bad faith is indeed a form of faith, not a cynical lie or a real belief. Bad faith tries to hide from itself the realization that, at bottom, all values are arbitrary.

Thus, for representatives of existentialism, that view is a philosophy of action, not quietism, and dignity, not degradation. A philosophy of subjectivity and freedom requires that we act and make our deeds paramount in the process of self-creation. According to de Beauvoir,

> What the existentialist says is that the coward makes himself cowardly, that the hero makes himself heroic. There's always a possibility for the coward not to be cowardly any more and for the hero to stop being heroic. What counts is total involvement; some one particular action or set of circumstances is not total involvement.
>
> *Ethics of Ambiguity*, pp. 41–42

In Sartre's play *No Exit*, for example, three characters are condemned to hell. Garcin is a man who was a political coward and betrayed his comrades; Inez is a lesbian who is killed in her lover's suicide; Estelle is an adulterer who has killed her young baby. But Sartre does not suggest that any of their actions was objectively wrong. Rather it is their inauthentic relationship to their conduct that has condemned them to hell. Garcin, for example, bemoans the fact that he "died too soon" and "wasn't allowed time to do my deeds." But Inez's response rejects his inauthentic excuses: "One always dies too soon — or too late. And yet one's whole life is complete at that moment, with a line drawn neatly under it, ready for the summing up. You are — your life, and nothing else." (p. 45) Throughout *No Exit* each character engages in a struggle with the others for the validation of his or her life. Yet it is clear that others cannot provide that for us. Freedom is dreadful precisely because we stand alone; we are forlorn. According to Sartre,

> We all hide deep within ourselves a scandalous rupture . . . we know all the anguish of being wrong and not being able to consider ourselves in the wrong, of being right and not feeling ourselves right; we all oscillate between the temptation to prefer ourselves to all because our consciousness is for us the center of the world and that of preferring everything to our consciousness.
>
> *Saint Genet*, p. 547

Contrast this with the character Orestes in Sartre's play, *The Flies*. Orestes makes a decision to kill his mother and stepfather. Though his sister Electra has goaded him to perform the act, he never blames her for his decision. Indeed, she is the classic actor in bad faith, for once the deed is done she cowers before the seriousness of it all and wishes it undone. Orestes, in contrast, willingly kills; but at the same time he cannot deny the gravity of his act, and at the end of the play he leaves his innocence behind him and takes away the flies that will plague him until his death. The worst sort of murderer, Sartre writes, is the one who feels remorse. "I carry the weight of the world by myself alone without anything or any person being able to lighten it." (*Being and Nothingness*; see p. 322)

Heidegger also addresses the issue of inauthenticity, though ethics is not a central concern in his writing. He writes of the "they" (*das Man*) that provides the escape route for inauthentic existence. We can get lost in "theyness" and fail to realize the choices we are making.

> With Dasein's lostness in the 'they', that factical potentiality-for-Being which is closest to it (the tasks, rules, and standards, the urgency and extent, of concernful and solicitous Being-in-the-world) has already been decided upon. The 'they' has always kept Dasein from taking hold of these possibilities of Being. The 'they' even hides the manner in which it has tacitly relieved Dasein of the burden of explicit *choosing* these possibilities. It remains indefinite who has 'really' done the choosing. So Dasein makes no choices, gets carried along by the nobody, and thus ensnares itself in inauthenticity.
>
> *Being and Time*, p. 268

We are the only animals capable of bad faith, for we are the only animals capable of being "at a distance" from ourselves. Human beings live in a creative dynamic with the world, and in that dynamic, that resistance, we discover the world. The person in bad faith tries to hide from the experience of anguish and isolation that is inevitable when we realize that we always miss our goal. *Pour soi* can never be *en soi;* we are essentially and always incomplete. Zeus in *The Flies* tells Orestes that "as long as they have their eyes fixed on me, they forget to look into themselves," (p. 103) and the person in bad faith cannot tolerate that inward glance. The person in bad faith cannot tolerate the experience of "nausea," which is about contingency and ambiguity.

EXISTENTIALIST ETHICS: EXAMINING THE CRITICAL RESPONSES

If our projects define value, if desire creates what is desirable, then can there be any limits to what is ethical? It would appear that any project can create meaning out of possibility. If so, then any project would create value. But this appears to be circular and provides us with no basis by which we can assess a given project or by which we may choose from among projects. Are all projects equally justified? Is any project ever impermissible? Would not any of our actions — by virtue of their being a human action — be ethical? If so, wouldn't this mean the repudiation of all ethics? Given our complete freedom, we may choose any project at all. But are all projects of equal value? Was Dostoyevsky right when he warned in *The Brothers Karamazov* that "if God does not exist, then all is permitted"?

What, then, keeps us from choosing projects that oppress others? If we are truly "without appeal," must we also be without recourse to condemnation? As the readings at the end of this chapter demonstrate, there are clearly no recipes for being ethical. If life is like a work of art, then the best we can do is "propose methods." (p. 590) Indeed, existentialists maintain that our attitudes and our actions, though there are no a priori values that determine them, involve all humanity. And we cannot avoid this involvement, for it is how we define ourselves. Freedom, they claim, must seek itself as its own end, not in any abstract sense but rather in every given concrete situation. But what does this mean? Is the freedom of the existentialists just an empty formula, or is there any content to it?

Contemporary existentialists insist that we need the freedom of others as a recognition of our own subjectivity. "We have to respect freedom only when it is intended for freedom, not when it strays, flees itself, and resigns itself," wrote de Beauvoir. (*Ethics of Ambiguity*, pp. 90–91) Thus, there may be criteria for determining whether an action is right or wrong. According to de Beauvoir, "To want existence, to want to disclose the world, and to want men to be free are one and the same will." (p. 87) Likewise, Sartre wrote, "I can take freedom as my goal only if I take that of others as a goal as well." (*Existentialism*, p. 54) Thus, we need not respect the "freedom" of the slaveowner to own slaves or the "freedom" of a Caligula to murder all those in his disfavor. "A freedom which is interested only in denying freedom must be denied." (de Beauvoir, *Ethics of Ambiguity*, p. 91) Once we realize that all values come from within, we must always choose freedom as the basis for all such values. But does this reduce existential ethics to another version of objectivism? Are there, that is, objective criteria by which we can then determine an action's rightness or wrongness? Sartre, for example, chose to use his freedom to work for the cause of the French resistance against fascism. Can we assume that he would accept the choice of another to work for fascism? What about the Nazi who claims to be willing to affirm the world that his or her actions create? We all can now agree that Nazi war criminal Adolph Eichmann's declaration that he was "only following orders" is an obvious example of an actor in bad faith. But we can doubtless imagine another sort of Eichmann who goes to his grave affirming his belief in his life's mission. Can an existential ethic — an ethic that rejects all a priori values — condemn his conduct? What if Eichmann were to accept his freedom and his anguish, to reject all excuses? According to existentialism, an ethical person must act authentically, out of integrity. One is obliged to affirm one's actions as they are relevant to one as a person. Is being a Nazi consistent with such a notion of integrity? Can we imagine a

Nazi voicing the following words that Orestes proclaims at the conclusion of *The Flies*? "You see me, men of Argos, you understand that my crime is wholly mine; I claim it as my own, for all to know; it is my glory, my life's work, and you can neither punish me nor pity me. That is why I fill you with fear." (p. 126) And when Electra asks Orestes where they will go, he responds "Towards ourselves." (p. 124) But Electra cannot join him:

> I won't hear any more from you. All you have to offer me is misery and squalor. Help! Zeus, king of gods and men, my king, take me in your arms, carry me from this place, and shelter me. I will obey your law, I will be your creature and your slave, I will embrace your knees. Save me from the flies, from my brother, from myself! Do not leave me lonely and and I will give up my whole life to atonement. I repent, Zeus. I bitterly repent. (p. 124)

For contemporary existentialists, we answer to ourselves. Our lives are without absolute meaning, yet we endow them with the only sort of meaning that is possible, namely, contingent, subjective meaning. According to de Beauvoir,

> In order for this world to have any importance, in order for our understanding to have a meaning and to be worthy of sacrifices, we must affirm the concrete and particular thickness of this world and the individual reality of our projects and ourselves.
> *Ethics of Ambiguity*, p. 106

In response to critics who maintain that existentialism's logical outcome is pessimism and nihilism, de Beauvoir holds that the opposite is true:

> (I)f the individual is set up as a unique and irreducible value, the word sacrifice regains all its meaning; what a man loses in renouncing his plans, his future, and his life no longer appears as a negligible thing. Even if he decides that in order to justify his life he must consent to limiting its course, even if he accepts dying, there is a wrench at the heart of this acceptance, for freedom demands both that it recover itself as an absolute and that it prolongs its movement indefinitely.
> *Ethics of Ambiguity*, p. 107

That we live only once, that we are our deeds, that we have no excuses — all of these, for existentialism, give profound value and importance to our projects. No one can say absolutely that our actions are right or wrong, but no one can say that they don't matter.

Camus's play *The Just Assassins* gives his view of the moral limits to human action. In the preface to the work, Camus tells us that his goal was to show that "action itself had limits." (p. x) The play tells the story of a group of Russian revolutionaries who plot to kill the Grand Duke, in particular the story of Kaliayev, who is assigned to throw the bomb at the Duke's carriage. Camus states that his admiration for Kaliayev and his lover, Dora, is "complete." Like Sartre and de Beauvoir, Camus believes that there must be parameters to what may count as justified, even if done for a just cause. "There is no good and just action but what recognizes those limits and, if it must go beyond them, at least accepts death." (p. x) Kaliayev, for example, states before he is about to be executed: "If I did not die — it's then I'd be a murderer," (p. 288) and he takes full responsibility for his action. His last words are: "If I have proved equal to the task assigned, of protesting with all the manhood in me against violence, may death consummate my task with the purity of the ideal that inspired it." (p. 294) Is everything permitted? Dora claims that "even in destruction there's a right way and a wrong way." (p. 258)

No project is inherently valuable or valueless. Camus, for example, imagines Sisyphus, condemned by the gods to roll a rock up a hill for all of eternity, to be happy. This futile and endless task is not so different from the tasks of ants or bees programmed to perform the same behaviors over time. But it is different in the sense that the story of Sisyphus is a tragedy because Sisyphus is conscious. Sisyphus is the absurd person in an absurd world. But Camus imagines that Sisyphus is happy. He is happy not because his project has inherent worth (indeed, it was not even chosen by him), but because of his relationship to his project.

> I leave Sisyphus at the foot of the mountain! One always finds one's burden again. But Sisyphus teaches the higher fidelity that negates the gods and raises rocks. He too concludes that all is well. This universe henceforth without a master seems to him neither sterile nor futile. Each atom of that stone, each mineral flake of that night-filled mountain, in itself forms a world. The struggle itself toward the heights is enough to fill a person's heart. One must imagine Sisyphus happy.
>
> *The Myth of Sisyphus*, p. 91

Camus has written that "if the world were clear, art would not exist." (p. 73) Perhaps one might change Camus's statement for our context: if the world were clear, ethics would not exist.

CONCLUSION

At the conclusion of his most well-known work, *Being and Nothingness,* Sartre raises a number of questions relating to freedom, responsibility, and being in the world. But, he tells us, "these questions, which refer us to a pure and not an accessory reflection, can find their reply only on the ethical plane." (p. 798) Though Sartre at that point promised "we shall devote to them a future work," that future work never appeared.

We began our examination of existentialism in this text with a discussion of the characteristic themes of that philosophy. We emphasized existentialism's richness and diversity, its rejection of all sorts of "crystal palaces," and its focus on human experience as it is subjectively lived. Though it is clear that there are many systematic thinkers in this tradition, they all have tended to agree that the meaning of human experience cannot be captured in tidy formulae and all-encompassing systems.

Thus, it is appropriate that we end our investigation with a look at the possibilities for an existentialist ethic. We find that we are faced with similar questions to those we have asked in previous chapters. With subjectivity at its core and possibility always on the horizon, existentialists have sought to explain how we create values. Such values have no absolute meaning but rather emerge from our own subjective projects and concerns.

Does this view contradict the very meaning of an ethic? Must we, like Neitzsche, all proclaim ourselves "immoralists"? Do values become nothing more than subjective preferences? Have we lost our ability to criticize? No doubt an existential ethic must be profoundly different from traditional ethical views. The following readings discuss in more depth just how different existentialism is.

QUESTIONS FOR CONSIDERATION

1. Richard Rorty has described existentialism as an "intrinsically reactive movement of thought." (*Philosophy and the Mirror of Nature*, Princeton University Press, 1979, p. 366) Having explored the different facets of existential philosophy, does this criticism seem fair to you? Why or why not?

2. Sartre asks us to imagine that a storm has destroyed a farmer's crops. The destruction, he tells us, does not come from the in-itself, for that is simply a rearrangement of matter. Rather, the destruction comes from our own assignment of meaning to the act. What sorts of implications follow for ethics in this view? Is Sartre right?

3. Charles Taylor, in a criticism of Sartrian ethics, maintains that Sartre leaves the agent with "no language in which the superiority of one alternative over the other can be articulated." As a result, he claims, "choice fades into non-choice." ("Responsibility for Self," in *The Identity of Persons*, edited by A. Rorty, pp. 291–92. Berkeley: University of California Press, 1976) Consider this criticism with respect to the discussion and readings from this chapter. If you disagree with

Taylor's objection, how might you posit a "superiority of alternatives"?

4. Is the concept of authenticity the same as the concept of integrity? Is it an ethical notion at all? Why or why not?

5. What do you think Sartre's troubled student should have done? On what do you base your decision? Are all (most?) ethical dilemmas like this one?

6. How is Sartre's discussion of bad faith linked to his discussion of freedom (see chapter 5)?

7. Would an existentialist have to defend a "self-affirming" Eichmann? Why or why not?

REFERENCES

ARISTOTLE. *Nichomachean Ethics.* Translated by Richard McKeon. New York: Modern Library, 1947.

CAMUS, ALBERT. *The Just Assassins.* Translated by Stuart Gilbert. New York: Vintage Books, 1954.

————. *The Myth of Sisyphus.* Translated by Justin O'Brien. New York: Alfred A. Knopf, 1955.

DE BEAUVOIR, SIMONE. *The Blood of Others.* Translated by Roger Senhouse and Yvonne Moyse. New York: Pantheon, 1948.

————. *The Ethics of Ambiguity.* Translated by Bernard Frechtman. Secaucus, N.J.: The Citadel Press, 1948.

FRANKENA, WILLIAM K. *Ethics.* Englewood Cliffs, N.J.: Prentice-Hall, 1963.

HARMAN, GILBERT. *The Nature of Morality; an Introduction to Ethics.* New York: Oxford University Press, 1977.

HEIDEGGER, MARTIN. *Being and Time.* Translated by John Macquarrie and Edward Robinson. New York: Harper and Row, 1962.

KANT, IMMANUEL. *Grounding for the Metaphysics of Morals.* Translated by James W. Ellington. Indianapolis: Hackett Publishing, 1981.

————. *Lectures on Ethics.* Translated by Louis Infield. Indianapolis: Hackett Publishing Co., 1963.

MACINTYRE, ALASDAIR. *A Short History of Ethics.* New York: Macmillan, 1966.

MAYO, BERNARD. *The Philosophy of Right and Wrong.* London: Routledge & Kegan Paul, 1986.

MILL, JOHN STUART. *Utilitarianism.* Edited by Oskar Piest. Indianapolis: Bobbs-Merrill Educational Publishing, 1957.

OLSON, ROBERT G. *Ethics: A Short Introduction.* New York: Random House, 1978.

Playboy Interview: "Jean-Paul Sartre — Candid Conversation." *Playboy* 12 (May, 1965), pp. 69–77.

SARTRE, JEAN-PAUL. *Being and Nothingness.* Translated by Hazel Barnes. New York: Washington Square Books, 1956.

———. *Existentialism* (or *Existentialism Is a Humanism*). Translated by Bernard Frechtman. New York: Philosophical Library, 1947.

———. *The Flies.* In *No Exit and Three Other Plays,* translated by Stuart Gilbert. New York: Vintage Books, 1946.

———. *Nausea.* Translated by Lloyd Alexander. New York: New Directions, 1964.

———. *No Exit.* In *No Exit and Three Other Plays,* translated by Stuart Gilbert. New York: Vintage Books, 1946.

———. *Saint Genet, Comedian et Martyr.* Paris: Gallimard, 1952.

TILLICH, PAUL. *The Courage to Be.* New Haven, Conn.: Yale University Press, 1952.

SIMONE DE BEAUVOIR

Simone de Beauvoir (1908–1986) (see p. 426 for a more detailed biography) is the author of novels such as The Blood of Others *and* She Came to Stay, *a number of autobiographical works, such as* A Very Easy Death *and* Memoirs of a Dutiful Daughter, *and philosophical works, such as* The Second Sex *and* The Ethics of Ambiguity *(1948). Though de Beauvoir's thinking is often treated as a mere extension of Sartre's,* The Ethics of Ambiguity *is in fact an original explication of the possibility of an existential ethic, a project that Sartre promised but never delivered. In this excerpt from the first chapter of that work, de Beauvoir makes freedom central to an ethic of existentialism and maintains that there is an inextricable connection between freedom and morality.*

The Ethics of Ambiguity

"Life in itself is neither good nor evil, it is the place of good and evil, according to what you make it."
— Montaigne

"The continuous work of our life," says Montaigne, "is to build death." He quotes the Latin poets: *Prima, quae vitam dedit, hora corpsit.* And again: *Nascentes morimur.* Man knows and thinks this tragic ambivalence which the animal and the plant merely undergo. A new paradox is thereby introduced into his destiny. "Rational animal," "thinking reed," he escapes from his natural condition without, however, freeing himself from it. He is still a part of this world of which he is a consciousness. He asserts himself as a pure internality against which no external power can take hold, and he also experiences himself as a thing crushed by the dark weight of other things. At every moment he can grasp the non-temporal truth of his existence. But between the past which no longer is and the future which is not yet, this moment when he exists is nothing. This privilege, which he alone possesses, of being a sovereign and unique subject amidst a universe of objects, is what he shares with all his fellow-men. In turn an object for others, he is nothing more than an individual in the collectivity on which he depends.

As long as there have been men and they have lived, they have all felt this tragic ambiguity of their condition, but as long as there have been philosophers and they have thought, most of them have tried to mask it. They have striven to reduce mind to matter, or to reabsorb matter into mind, or to merge them within a single substance. Those who have accepted the dualism have established a hierarchy between body and soul which permits of considering as negligible the part of the self which cannot be saved. They have denied death, either by integrating it with life or by promising to man immortality. Or, again they have denied life, considering it as a veil of illusion beneath which is hidden the truth of Nirvana.

And the ethics which they have proposed to their disciples has always pursued the same goal. It has been a matter of eliminating the ambiguity by making oneself pure inwardness or pure externality, by escaping from the sensible world or by being engulfed in it, by yielding to eternity or enclosing oneself in the pure moment. Hegel, with more ingenuity, tried to reject none of the aspects of man's condition and to reconcile them all. According to his system, the moment is preserved in the development of time; Nature asserts itself in the face of Spirit which denies it while assuming it; the individual is again found in the collectivity within which he is lost; and each man's death is fulfilled by being canceled out into the Life of Mankind. One can thus repose in a marvelous optimism where even the bloody wars simply express the fertile restlessness of the Spirit.

At the present time there still exist many doctrines which choose to leave in the shadow certain troubling aspects of a too complex situation. But their attempt to lie to us is in vain. Cowardice doesn't pay. Those reasonable metaphysics, those consoling ethics with which they would like to entice us only accentuate the disorder from which we suffer. Men of today seem to feel more acutely than ever the paradox of their condition. They know themselves to be the supreme end to which all action should be subordinated, but the exigencies of action force them to treat one another as instruments or obstacles, as means. The more widespread their mastery of the world, the more they find themselves crushed by uncontrollable forces. Though they are masters of the atomic bomb, yet it is created only to destroy them. Each one has the incomparable taste in his mouth of his own life, and yet each feels himself more insignificant than an insect within the immense collectivity whose limits are one with the earth's. Perhaps in no other age have they manifested their grandeur more brilliantly, and in no other age has this grandeur been so horribly flouted. In spite of so many stubborn lies, at every moment, at every opportunity, the truth comes to light, the truth of life and death, of my solitude and my bond with the world, of my freedom and my servitude, of the insignificance and the sovereign importance of each man and all men. There was Stalingrad and there was Buchenwald, and neither of the two wipes out the other. Since we do not succeed in fleeing it, let us therefore try to look the truth in the face. Let us try to assume our fundamental ambiguity. It is in the knowledge of the genuine conditions of our life that we must draw our strength to live and our reason for acting.

From the very beginning, existentialism defined itself as a philosophy of ambiguity. It was by affirming the irreducible character of ambiguity that Kierkegaard opposed himself to Hegel, and it is by ambiguity that, in our own generation, Sartre, in *Being and Nothingness*, fundamentally defined man, that being whose being is not to be, that subjectivity which realizes itself only as a presence in the world, that engaged freedom, that surging of the for-oneself which is immediately given for others. But it is also claimed that existentialism is a philosophy of the absurd and of despair. It encloses man in a sterile anguish, in an empty subjectivity. It is incapable of furnishing him with any principle for making choices. Let him do as he pleases. In any case, the game is lost. Does not Sartre declare, in effect, that man is a "useless passion," that he tries in vain to realize the synthesis of the for-oneself and the in-oneself, to make himself God? It is true. But it is also true that the most optimistic ethics have all begun by emphasizing the element of failure involved in the condition of man; without failure, no ethics; for a being who, from the very start, would be an exact co-incidence with himself, in a perfect plenitude, the notion of having-to-be would have no meaning. One does not offer an ethics to a God. It is impossible to propose any to man if one defines him as nature, as something given. The so-called psychological or empirical ethics manage to establish themselves only by introducing surreptitiously some flaw within the man-thing which they have first defined. Hegel tells us in the last part of *The Phenomenology of Mind* that moral consciousness can exist only to the extent that there is disagreement between nature and morality. It would disappear if the ethical law became the natural law. To such an extent that by a paradoxical "displacement," if moral action is the absolute goal, the absolute goal is also that moral action may not be present. This means that there can be a having-to-be only for a being who, according to the existentialist definition, questions himself in his being, a being who is at a distance from himself and who has to be his being.

Well and good. But it is still necessary for the failure to be surmounted, and existentialist ontology does not allow this hope. Man's passion is useless; he has no means for becoming the being that he is not. That too is true. And it is also true that in *Being and Nothingness* Sartre has insisted above all on the abortive aspect of the human adventure. It is only in the last pages that he opens up the perspective for an ethics. However, if we reflect upon his descriptions of existence, we perceive that they are far from condemning man without recourse.

The failure described in *Being and Nothingness* is definitive, but it is also ambiguous. Man, Sartre tells us, is "a being who *makes himself* a lack of being *in order that there might be* being." That means, first of all, that his passion is not inflicted upon him from without. He chooses it. It is his very being and, as such, does not imply the idea of unhappiness. If this choice is considered as useless, it is because there exists no absolute value before the passion of man, outside of it, in relation to which one might distinguish the useless from the useful. The word "useful" has not yet received a meaning on the level of description where *Being and Nothingness* is situated. It can be defined only in the human world established by man's projects and the ends he sets up. In the original helplessness from which man surges up, nothing is useful, nothing is useless. It must therefore be understood that the passion to which man has acquiesced finds no external justification. No outside appeal, no objective necessity permits of its being called useful. It *has* no reason to will itself. But this does not mean that it can not justify itself, that it can not *give itself* reasons for being that it does not *have*. And indeed Sartre tells us that man makes himself this lack of being *in order that* there might be being. The term *in order that* clearly indicates an intentionality. It is not in vain that man nullifies being. Thanks to him, being is disclosed and he desires this disclosure. There is an original type of attachment to being which is not the relationship "wanting to be" but rather "wanting to disclose being." Now, here there is not failure, but rather success. This end, which man proposes to himself by making himself lack of being, is, in effect, realized by him. By uprooting himself from the world, man makes himself present to the world and makes the world present to him. I should like to be the landscape which I am contemplating, I should like this sky, this quiet water to think themselves within me, that it might be I whom they express in flesh and bone, and I remain at a distance. But it is also by this distance that the sky and the water exist before me. My contemplation is an excruciation only because it is also a joy. I can not appropriate the snow field where I slide. It remains foreign, forbidden, but I take delight in this very effort toward an impossible possession. I experience it as a triumph, not as a defeat. This means that man, in his vain attempt to *be* God, makes himself exist *as* man, and if he is satisfied with this existence, he coincides exactly with himself. It is not granted him to exist without tending toward this being which he will never be. But it is possible for him to want this tension even with the failure which it involves. His being is lack of being, but this lack has a way of being which is precisely existence. In Hegelian terms it might be said that we have here a negation of the negation by which the positive is re-established. Man makes himself a lack, but he can deny the lack as lack and affirm himself as a positive existence. He then assumes the failure. And the condemned action, insofar as it is an effort to be, finds it validity insofar as it is a manifestation of existence. However, rather than being a Hegelian act of surpassing, it is a matter of a conversion. For in Hegel the surpassed terms are preserved only as abstract moments, whereas we consider that existence still remains a negativity in the positive affirmation of itself. And it does not appear, in its turn, as the term of a further synthesis. The failure is not surpassed, but assumed. Existence asserts itself as an absolute which must seek its justification within itself and not suppress itself, even though it may be lost by preserving itself. To attain his truth, man must not attempt to dispel the ambiguity of his being but, on the contrary, accept the task of realizing it. He rejoins himself only to the extent that he agrees to remain at a distance from himself. This conversion is sharply distinguished from the Stoic conversion in that it does not claim to oppose to the sensible universe a formal freedom which is without content. To exist genuinely is not to deny this spontaneous movement of my transcendence, but only to refuse to lose myself in it. Existentialist conversion should rather be compared to Husserlian reduction: let man put his will to be "in parentheses" and he will thereby be brought to the consciousness of his true condition. And just as phenomenological reduction prevents the errors of dogmatism by suspending all affirmation concerning the mode of reality of the external world, whose flesh and bone presence the reduction does not, however, contest, so existentialist conversion does not suppress my instincts, desires, plans, and passions. It merely prevents any possibility of failure by refusing to set up as absolutes the ends toward which my transcendence thrusts itself, and by considering them in their connection with the freedom which projects them.

The first implication of such an attitude is that the genuine man will not agree to recognize any foreign absolute. When a man projects into an ideal heaven that impossible synthesis of the for-itself and the in-itself that is called God, it is because he wishes the regard of this existing Being to change his existence into being; but if he agrees not to be in order to exist genuinely, he will abandon the dream of an inhuman objectivity. He will understand that it is not a matter of being right in the eyes of a God, but of being right in his own eyes. Renouncing the thought of seeking the guarantee for his existence outside of himself, he will also refuse to believe in unconditioned values which would set themselves up athwart his freedom like things. Value is this lacking-being of which freedom *makes itself* a lack; and it is because the latter makes itself a lack that value appears. It is desire which creates the desirable, and the project which sets up the end. It is human existence which makes values spring up in the world on the basis of which it will be able to judge the enterprise in which it will be engaged. But first it locates itself beyond any pessimism, as beyond any optimism, for the fact of its original springing forth is a pure contingency. Before existence there is no more reason to exist than not to exist. The lack of existence can not be evaluated since it is the fact on the basis of which all evaluation is defined. It can not be compared to anything for there is nothing outside of it to serve as a term of comparison. This rejection of any extrinsic justification also confirms the rejection of an original pessimism which we posited at the beginning. Since it is unjustifiable from without, to declare from without that it is unjustifiable is not to condemn it. And the truth is that outside of existence there is nobody. Man exists. For him it is not a question of wondering whether his presence in the world is useful, whether life is worth the trouble of being lived. These questions make no sense. It is a matter of knowing whether he wants to live and under what conditions.

But if man is free to define for himself the conditions of a life which is valid in his own eyes, can he not choose whatever he likes and act however he likes? Dostoievsky asserted, "If God does not exist, everything is permitted." Today's believers use this formula for their own advantage. To re-establish man at the heart of his destiny is, they claim, to repudiate all ethics. However, far from God's absence authorizing all license, the contrary is the case, because man is abandoned on the earth, because his acts are definitive, absolute engagements. He bears the responsibility for a world which is not the work of a strange power, but of himself, where his defeats are inscribed, and his victories as well. A God can pardon, efface, and compensate. But if God does not exist, man's faults are inexpiable. If it is claimed that, whatever the case may be, this earthly stake has no importance, this is precisely because one invokes that inhuman objectivity which we declined at the start. One can not start by saying that our earthly destiny *has* or *has not* importance, for it depends upon us to give it importance. It is up to man to make it important to be a man, and he alone can feel his success or failure. And if it is again said that nothing forces him to try to justify his being in this way, then one is playing upon the notion of freedom in a dishonest way. The believer is also free to sin. The divine law is imposed upon him only from the moment he decides to save his soul. In the Christian religion, though one speaks very little about them today, there are also the damned. Thus, on the early plane, a life which does not seek to ground itself will be a pure contingency. But it is permitted to wish to give itself a meaning and a truth, and it then meets rigorous demands within its own heart.

However, even among the proponents of secular ethics, there are many who charge existentialism with offering no objective content to the moral act. It is said that this philosophy is subjective, even solipsistic. If he is once enclosed within himself, how can man get out? But there too we have a great deal of dishonesty. It is rather well known that the fact of being a subject is a universal fact and that the Cartesian *cogito* expresses both the most individual experience and the most objective truth. By affirming that the source of all values resides in the freedom of man, existentialism merely carries on the tradition of Kant, Fichte, and Hegel, who, in the words of Hegel himself, "have taken for their point of departure the principle according to which the essence of right and duty and the essence of the thinking and willing subject are absolutely identical." The idea that defines all humanism is that the world is not a given world, foreign to man, one to which he has to force himself to yield from without. It is the world willed by man, insofar as his will expresses his genuine reality.

Some will answer, "All well and good. But Kant escapes solipsism because for him genuine reality is the human person insofar as it transcends its empirical embodiment and chooses to be universal." And doubtless Hegel asserted that the "right of individuals to their particularity is equally contained in ethical substantiality, since particularity is the extreme, phenomenal modality in which moral reality exists (*Philosophy of Right*, § 154)." But for him particularity appears only as a moment of the totality in which it must surpass itself. Whereas for existentialism, it is not impersonal universal man who is the source of values, but the plurality of concrete, particular men projecting themselves toward their ends on the basis of situations whose particularity is as radical and as irreducible as subjectivity itself. How could men, originally separated, get together?

And, indeed, we are coming to the real situation of the problem. But to state it is not to demonstrate that it can not be resolved. On the contrary, we must here again invoke the notion of Hegelian "displacement." There is an ethics only if there is a problem to solve. And it can be said, by inverting the preceding line of argument, that the ethics which have given solutions by effacing the fact of the separation of men are not valid precisely because there *is* this separation. An ethics of ambiguity will be one which will refuse to deny *a priori* that separate existants can, at the same time, be bound to each other, that their individual freedoms can forge laws valid for all.

Before undertaking the quest for a solution, it is interesting to note that the notion of situation and the recognition of separation which it implies are not peculiar to existentialism. We also meet it in Marxism which, from one point of view, can be considered as an apotheosis of subjectivity. Like all radical humanism, Marxism rejects the idea of an inhuman objectivity and locates itself in the tradition of Kant and Hegel. Unlike the old kind of utopian socialism which confronted earthly order with the archetypes of Justice, Order, and Good, Marx does not consider that certain human situations are, in themselves and absolutely, preferable to others. It is the needs of people, the revolt of a class, which define aims and goals. It is from within a rejected situation, in the light of this rejection, that a new state appears as desirable; only the will of men decides; and it is on the basis of a certain individual act of rooting itself in the historical and economic world that this will thrusts itself toward the future and then chooses a perspective where such words as goal, progress, efficacy, success, failure, action, adversaries, instruments, and obstacles, have a meaning. Then certain acts can be regarded as good and others as bad.

In order for the universe of revolutionary values to arise, a subjective movement must create them in revolt and hope. And this movement appears so essential to Marxists that if an intellectual or a bourgeois also claims to want revolution, they distrust him. They think that it is only from the outside, by abstract recognition, that the bourgeois intellectual can adhere to these values which he himself has not set up. Regardless of what he does, his situation makes it impossible for the ends pursued by proletarians to be absolutely his ends too, since it is not the very impulse of his life which has begotten them.

However, in Marxism, if it is true that the goal and the meaning of action are defined by human wills, these wills do not appear as free. They are the reflection of objective conditions by which the situation of the class or the people under consideration is defined. In the present moment of the development of capitalism, the proletariat can not help wanting its elimination as a class. Subjectivity is re-absorbed into the objectivity of the given world. Revolt, need, hope, rejection, and desire are only the resultants of external forces. The psychology of behavior endeavors to explain this alchemy.

It is known that that is the essential point on which existentialist ontology is opposed to dialectical materialism. We think that the meaning of the situation does not impose itself on the consciousness of a passive subject, that it surges up only by the disclosure which a free subject effects in his project. It appears evident to us that in order to adhere to Marxism, to enroll in a party, and in one rather than another, to be actively attached to it, even a Marxist needs a decision whose source is only in himself. And this autonomy is not the privilege (or the defect) of the intellectual or the bourgeois. The proletariat, taken as a whole, as a class, can become conscious of its situation in more than one way. It can want the revolution to be brought about by one party or another. It can let itself be lured on, as happened to the German proletariat, or can sleep in the dull comfort which capitalism grants it, as does the American proletariat. It may be said that in all these cases it is betraying; still, it must be free to betray. Or, if one pretends to distinguish the real proletariat from a treacherous proletariat, or a misguided or unconscious or mystified one, then it is no longer a flesh and blood proletariat that one is dealing with, but the idea of a proletariat, one of those ideas which Marx ridiculed.

Besides, in practice, Marxism does not *always* deny freedom. The very notion of action would lose all meaning if history were a mechanical unrolling in which man appears only as a passive conductor of outside forces. By acting, as also by preaching action, the Marxist revolutionary asserts himself as a veritable agent; he assumes himself to be free. And it is even curious to note that most Marxists of today — unlike Marx him-self — feel no repugnance at the edifying dullness of moralizing speeches. They do not limit themselves to finding fault with their adver-saries in the name of historical realism. When they tax them with coward-ice, lying, selfishness, and venality, they very well mean to condemn them in the name of a moralism superior to history. Likewise, in the eulogies which they bestow upon each other they exalt the eternal vir-tues, courage, abnegation, lucidity, integrity. It may be said that all these words are used for propagandistic purposes, that it is only a matter of expedient language. But this is to admit that this language is heard, that it awakens an echo in the hearts of those to whom it is addressed. Now, neither scorn nor esteem would have any meaning if one regarded the acts of a man as a purely mechanical resultant. In order for men to become indignant or to admire, they must be conscious of their own freedom and the freedom of others. Thus, everything occurs within each man and in the collective tactics as if men were free. But then what revelation can a coherent humanism hope to oppose to the testimony which man brings to bear upon himself? So Marxists often find themselves having to confirm this belief in freedom, even if they have to reconcile it with determina-tion as well as they can.

However, while this concession is wrested from them by the very practice of action, it is in the name of action that they attempt to condemn a philosophy of freedom. They declare authoritatively that the existence of freedom would make any concerted enterprise impossible. According to them, if the individual were not constrained by the external world to want this rather than that, there would be nothing to defend him against his whims. Here, in different language, we again meet the charge formu-lated by the respectful believer of supernatural imperatives. In the eyes of the Marxist, as of the Christian, it seems that to act freely is to give up justifying one's acts. This is a curious reversal of the Kantian "you must; therefore, you can." Kant postulates freedom in the name of morality. The Marxist, on the contrary, declares, "You must; therefore, you can not." To him a man's action seems valid only if the man has not helped set it going by an internal movement. To admit the ontological possibility of a choice is already to betray the Cause. Does this mean that the revolutionary attitude in any way gives up being a moral attitude? It would be logical, since we observed with Hegel that it is only insofar as the choice is not realized at first that it can be set up as a moral choice. But here again Marxist thought hesitates. It sneers at idealistic ethics which do not bite into the world; but its scoffing signifies that there can be no ethics outside of action, not that action lowers itself to the level of a simple natural process. It is quite evident that the revolutionary enterprise has a human meaning. Lenin's remark, which says, in substance, "I call any action useful to the party moral action; I call it immoral if it is harmful to the party," cuts two ways. On the one hand, he refuses to accept outdated values, but he also sees in political operation a total manifestation of man as having-to-be at the same time as being. Lenin refuses to set up ethics abstractly because he means to realize it effectively. And yet a moral idea is present in the words, writings, and acts of Marxists. It is contradictory, then, to reject with horror the moment of choice which is precisely the moment when spirit passes into nature, the moment of the concrete fulfillment of man and morality.

As for us, whatever the case may be, we believe in freedom. Is it true that this belief must lead us to despair? Must we grant this curious paradox: that from the moment a man recognizes himself as free, he is prohibited from wishing for anything?

On the contrary, it appears to us that by turning toward this freedom we are going to discover a principle of action whose range will be universal. The characteristic feature of all ethics is to consider human life as a game that can be won or lost and to teach man the means of winning. Now, we have seen that the original scheme of man is ambiguous: he wants to be, and to the extent that he coincides with this wish, he fails. All the plans in which this will to be is actualized are condemned; and the ends circumscribed by these plans remain mirages. Human transcendence is vainly engulfed in those miscarried attempts. But man also wills himself to be a disclosure of being, and if he coincides with this wish, he wins, for the fact is that the world becomes present by his presence in it. But the disclosure implies a perpetual tension to keep being at a certain distance, to tear oneself from the world, and to assert oneself as a freedom. To wish for the disclosure of the world and to assert oneself as freedom are one and the same movement. Freedom is the source from which all significations and all values spring. It is the original condition of all justification of existence. The man who seeks to justify his life must want freedom itself absolutely and above everything else. At the same time that it requires the realization of concrete ends, of particular projects, it requires itself universally. It is not a ready-made value which offers itself from the outside to my abstract adherence, but it appears (not on the plane of facility, but on the moral plane) as a cause of itself. It is necessarily summoned up by the values which it sets up and through which it sets itself up. It can not establish a denial of itself, for in denying itself, it would deny the possibility of any foundation. To will oneself moral and to will oneself free are one and the same decision.

It seems that the Hegelian notion of "displacement" which we relied on a little while ago is now turning against us. There is ethics only if ethical action is not present. Now, Sartre declares that every man is free, that there is no way of his not being free. When he wants to escape his destiny, he is still fleeing it. Does not this presence of a so to speak natural freedom contradict the notion of ethical freedom? What meaning can there be in the words *to will oneself* free, since at the beginning we *are* free? It is contradictory to set freedom up as something conquered if at first it is something given.

This objection would mean something only if freedom were a thing or a quality naturally attached to a thing. Then, in effect, one would either have it or not have it. But the fact is that it merges with the very movement of this ambiguous reality which is called existence and which *is* only by making itself be; to such an extent that it is precisely only by having to be conquered that it gives itself. To will oneself free is to effect the transition from nature to morality by establishing a genuine freedom on the original upsurge of our existence.

Every man is originally free, in the sense that he spontaneously casts himself into the world. But if we consider this spontaneity in its facticity, it appears to us only as a pure contingency, an upsuring as stupid as the clinamen of the Epicurean atom which turned up at any moment whatsoever from any direction whatsoever. And it was quite necessary for the atom to arrive somewhere. But its movement was not justified by this result which had not been chosen. It remained absurd. Thus, human spontaneity always projects itself toward something. The psychoanalyst discovers a meaning even in abortive acts and attacks of hysteria. But in order for this meaning to justify the transcendence which discloses it, it must itself be founded, which it will never be if I do not choose to found it myself. Now, I can evade this choice. We have said that it would be contradictory deliberately to will oneself not free. But one can choose not to will himself free. In laziness, heedlessness, capriciousness, cowardice, impatience, one contests the meaning of the project at the very moment that one defines it. The spontaneity of the subject is then merely a vain living palpitation, its movement toward the object is a flight, and itself is an absence. To convert the absence into presence, to convert my flight into will, I must assume my project positively. It is not a matter of retiring into the completely inner and, moreover, abstract movement of a given spontaneity, but of adhering to the concrete and particular movement by which this spontaneity defines itself by thrusting itself toward an end. It is through this end that it sets up that my spontaneity confirms itself by reflecting upon itself. Then, by a single movement, my will, establishing the content of the act, is legitimized by it. I realize my escape toward the other as a freedom when, assuming the presence of the object, I thereby assume myself before it as a presence. But this justification requires a constant tension. My project is never founded; it founds itself. To avoid the anguish of this permanent choice, one may attempt to flee into the object itself, to engulf one's own presence in it. In the servitude of the serious, the original spontaneity strives to deny itself. It strives in vain, and meanwhile it then fails to fulfill itself as moral freedom.

We have just described only the subjective and formal aspect of this freedom. But we also ought to ask ourselves whether one can will oneself free in any matter, whatsoever it may be. It must first be observed that this will is developed in the course of time. It is in time that the goal is pursued and that freedom confirms itself. And this assumes that it is realized as a unity in the unfolding of time. One escapes the absurdity of the clinamen only by escaping the absurdity of the pure moment. An existence would be unable to found itself if moment by moment it crumbled into nothingness. That is why no moral question presents itself to the child as long as he is still incapable of recognizing himself in the past or seeing himself in the future. It is only when the moments of his life begin to be organized into behaviour that he can decide and choose. The value of the chosen end is confirmed and, reciprocally, the genuineness of the choice is manifested concretely through patience, courage, and fidelity. If I leave behind an act which I have accomplished, it becomes a thing by falling into the past. It is no longer anything but a stupid and opaque fact. In order to prevent this metamorphosis, I must ceaselessly return to it and justify it in the unity of the project in which I am engaged. Setting up the movement of my transcendence requires that I never let it uselessly fall back upon itself, that I prolong it indefinitely. Thus I can not genuinely desire an end today without desiring it through my whole existence, insofar as it is the future of this present moment and insofar as it is the surpassed past of days to come. To will is to engage myself to persevere in my will. This does not mean that I ought not aim at any limited end. I may desire absolutely and forever a revelation of a moment. This means that the value of this provisional end will be confirmed indefinitely. But this living confirmation can not be merely contemplative and verbal. It is carried out in an act. The goal toward which I surpass myself must appear to me as a point of departure toward a new act of surpassing. Thus, a creative freedom develops happily without ever congealing into unjustified facticity. The creator leans upon anterior creations in order to create the possibility of new creations. His present project embraces the past and places confidence in the freedom to come, a confidence which is never disappointed. It discloses being at the end of a further disclosure. At each moment freedom is confirmed through all creation.

However, man does not create the world. He succeeds in disclosing it only through the resistance which the world opposes to him. The will is defined only by raising obstacles, and by the contingency of facticity certain obstacles let themselves be conquered, and others do not. This is what Descartes expressed when he said that the freedom of man is infinite, but his power is limited. How can the presence of these limits be reconciled with the idea of a freedom confirming itself as a unity and an indefinite movement?

In the face of an obstacle which it is impossible to overcome, stubbornness is stupid. If I persist in beating my fist against a stone wall, my freedom exhausts itself in this useless gesture without succeeding in giving itself a content. It debases itself in a vain contingency. Yet, there is hardly a sadder virtue than resignation. It transforms into phantoms and contingent reveries projects which had at the beginning been set up as will and freedom. A young man has hoped for a happy or useful or glorious life. If the man he has become looks upon these miscarried attempts at his adolescence with disillusioned indifference, there they are, forever frozen in the dead past. When an effort fails, one declares bitterly that he has lost time and wasted his powers. The failure condemns that whole part of ourselves which we had engaged in the effort. It was to escape this dilemma that the Stoics preached indifference. We could indeed assert our freedom against all constraint if we agreed to renounce the particularity of our projects. If a door refuses to open, let us accept not opening it and there we are free. But by doing that, one manages only to save an abstract notion of freedom. It is emptied of all content and all truth. The power of man ceases to be limited because it is annulled. It is the particularity of the project which determines the limitation of the power, but it is also what gives the project its content and permits it to be set up. There are people who are filled with such horror at the idea of a defeat that they keep themselves from ever doing anything. But no one would dream of considering this gloomy passivity as the triumph of freedom.

The truth is that in order for my freedom not to risk coming to grief against the obstacle which its very engagement has raised, in order that it might still pursue its movement in the face of the failure, it must, by giving itself a particular content, aim by means of it at an end which is nothing else but precisely the free movement of existence. Popular opinion is quite right in admiring a man who, having been ruined or having suffered an accident, knows how to gain the upper hand, that is, renew his engagement in the world, thereby strongly asserting the independence of freedom in relation to thing. Thus, when the sick Van Gogh calmly accepted the prospect of a future in which he would be unable to paint any more, there was no sterile resignation. For him painting was a personal way of life and of communication with others which in another form could be continued even in an asylum. The past will be integrated and freedom will be confirmed in a renunciation of this kind. It will be lived in both heartbreak and joy. In heartbreak, because the project is then robbed of its particularity — it sacrifices its flesh and blood. But in joy, since at the moment one releases his hold, he again finds his hands free and ready to stretch out toward a new future. But this act of passing beyond is conceivable only if what the content has in view is not to bar up the future, but, on the contrary, to plan new possibilities. This brings us back by another route to what we had already indicated. My freedom must not seek to trap being but to disclose it. The disclosure is the transition from being to existence. The goal which my freedom aims at is conquering existence across the always inadequate density of being.

However, such salvation is only possible if, despite obstacles and failures, a man preserves the disposal of his future, if the situation opens up more possibilities to him. In case his transcendence is cut off from his goal or there is no longer any hold on objects which might give it a valid content, his spontaneity is dissipated without founding anything. Then he may not justify his existence positively and he feels its contingency with wretched disgust. There is no more obnoxious way to punish a man than to force him to perform acts which make no sense to him, as when one empties and fills the same ditch indefinitely, when one makes soldiers who are being punished march up and down, or when one forces a schoolboy to copy lines. Revolts broke out in Italy in September 1946 because the unemployed were set to breaking pebbles which served no purpose whatever. As is well known, this was also the weakness which ruined the national workshops in 1848. This mystification of useless effort is more intolerable than fatigue. Life imprisonment is the most horrible of punishments because it preserves existence in its pure facticity but forbids it all legitimation. A freedom can not will itself without willing itself as an indefinite movement. It must absolutely reject the constraints which arrest its drive toward itself. This rejection takes on a positive aspect when the constraint is natural. One rejects the illness by curing it. But it again assumes the negative aspect of revolt when the oppressor is a human freedom. One can not deny being: the in-itself is, and negation has no hold over this being, this pure positivity; one does not escape this fullness: a destroyed house *is* a ruin; a broken chain *is* scrap iron: one attains only signification and, through it, the for-itself which is projected there; the for-itself carries nothingness in its heart and can be annihilated, whether in the very upsurge of its existence or through the world in which it exists. The prison is repudiated as such when the prisoner escapes. But revolt, insofar as it is pure negative movement, remains abstract. It is fulfilled as freedom only by returning to the positive, that is, by giving itself a content through action, escape, political struggle, revolution. Human transcendence then seeks, with the destruction of the given situation, the whole future which will flow from its victory. It resumes its indefinite rapport with itself. There are limited situations where this return to the positive is impossible, where the future is radically blocked off. Revolt can then be achieved only in the definitive rejection of the imposed situation, in suicide.

It can be seen that, on the one hand, freedom can always save itself, for it is realized as a disclosure of existence through its very failures, and it can again confirm itself by a death freely chosen. But, on the other hand, the situations which it discloses through its project toward itself do not appear as equivalents. It regards as privileged situations those which permit it to realize itself as indefinite movement; that is, it wishes to pass beyond everything which limits its power; and yet, this power is always limited. Thus, just as life is identified with the will-to-live, freedom always appears as a movement of liberation. It is only by prolonging itself through the freedom of others that it manages to surpass death itself and to realize itself as an indefinite unity. Later on we shall see what problems such a relationship raises. For the time being it is enough for us to have established the fact that the words "to will oneself free" have a positive and concrete meaning. If man wishes to save his existence, as only he himself can do, his original spontaneity must be raised to the height of moral freedom by taking itself as an end through the disclosure of a particular content.

But a new question is immediately raised. If man has one and only one way to save his existence, how can he choose not to choose it in all cases? How is a bad willing possible? We meet with this problem in all ethics, since it is precisely the possibility of a perverted willing which gives a meaning to the idea of virtue. We know the answer of Socrates, of Plato, of Spinoza: "No one is willfully bad." And if Good is a transcendent thing which is more or less foreign to man, one imagines that the mistake can be explained by error. But if one grants that the moral world is the world genuinely willed by man, all possibility of error is eliminated. Moreover, in Kantian ethics, which is at the origin of all ethics of autonomy, it is very difficult to account for an evil will. As the choice of his character which the subject makes is achieved in the intelligible world by a purely rational will, one can not understand how the latter expressly rejects the law which it gives to itself. But this is because Kantianism defined man as a pure positivity, and it therefore recognized no other possibility in him than coincidence with himself. We, too, define morality by this adhesion to the self; and this is why we say that man can not positively decide between the negation and the assumption of his freedom, for as soon as he decides, he assumes it. He can not positively will not to be free for such a willing would be self-destructive. Only, unlike Kant, we do not see man as being essentially a positive will. On the contrary, he is first defined as a negativity. He is first at a distance from himself. He can coincide with himself only by agreeing never to rejoin himself. There is within him a perpetual playing with the negative, and he thereby escapes himself, he escapes his freedom. And it is precisely because an evil will is here possible that the words "to will oneself free" have a meaning. Therefore, not only do we assert that the existentialist doctrine permits the elaboration of an ethics, but it even appears to us as the only philosophy in which an ethics has its place. For, in a metaphysics of transcendence, in the classical sense of the term, evil is reduced to error; and in humanistic philosophies it is impossible to account for it, man being defined as complete in a complete world. Existentialism alone gives — like religions — a real role to evil, and it is this, perhaps, which make its judgments so gloomy. Men do not like to feel themselves in danger. Yet, it is because there are real dangers, real failures and real earthly damnation that words like victory, wisdom, or joy have meaning. Nothing is decided in advance, and it is because man has something to lose and because he can lose that he can also win.

Therefore, in the very condition of man there enters the possibility of not fulfilling this condition. In order to fulfill it he must assume himself as a being who "makes himself a lack of being so that there might be being." But the trick of dishonesty permits stopping at any moment whatsoever. One may hesitate to make oneself a lack of being, one may withdraw before existence, or one may falsely assert oneself as being, or assert oneself as nothingness. One may realize his freedom only as an abstract independence, or, on the contrary, reject with despair the distance which separates us from being. All errors are possible since man is a negativity, and they are motivated by the anguish he feels in the face of his freedom. Concretely, men slide incoherently from one attitude to another. We shall limit ourselves to describing in their abstract form those which we have just indicated.

JEAN-PAUL SARTRE

At the end of the previous selection from The Ethics of Ambiguity, *Simone de Beauvoir notes that existentialism (along with religion) accords a real place to evil, since it acknowledges the possibility of failure as well as triumph. Since we are incomplete (and never will be complete except in death), there is always the possibility of not fulfilling our projects. To avoid the anguish of this dreadful possibility, we may opt for dishonesty. The following excerpt from Sartre's* Being and Nothingness *analyzes some of the forms that dishonesty — bad faith — can take.*

Bad Faith

I. BAD FAITH AND FALSEHOOD

THE human being is not only the being by whom *négatités* are disclosed in the world; he is also the one who can take negative attitudes with respect to himself. In our Introduction we defined consciousness as "a being such that in its being, its being is in question in so far as this being implies a being other than itself." But now that we have examined the meaning of "the question," we can at present also write the formula thus: "Consciousness is a being, the nature of which is to be conscious of the nothingness of its being." In a prohibition or a veto, for example, the human being denies a future transcendence. But this negation is not explicative. My consciousness is not restricted to *envisioning* a *négatité*. It constitutes itself in its own flesh as the nihilation of a possibility which another human reality projects as *its* possibility. For that reason it must arise in the world as a *No;* it is as a No that the slave first apprehends the master, or that the prisoner who is trying to escape sees the guard who is watching him. There are even men (*e.g.,* caretakers, overseers, gaolers), whose social reality is uniquely that of the No, who will live and die, having forever been only a No upon the earth. Others, so as to make the No a part of their very subjectivity, establish their human personality as a perpetual negation. This is the meaning and function of what Scheler calls "the man of resentment" — in reality, the No. But there exist more subtle behaviors, the description of which will lead us further into the inwardness of consciousness. Irony is one of these. In irony a man annihilates what he posits within one and the same act; he leads us to believe in

From "Bad Faith," in *Being and Nothingness,* translated by Hazel Barnes, pp. 86–116. © Philosophical Library, 1956. Deletions as noted.

order not to be believed; he affirms to deny and denies to affirm; he creates a positive object but it has no being other than its nothingness. Thus attitudes of negation toward the self permit us to raise a new question: What are we to say is the being of man who has the possibility of denying himself? But it is out of the question to discuss the attitude of "self-negation" in its universality. The kinds of behavior which can be ranked under this heading are too diverse; we risk retaining only the abstract form of them. It is best to choose and to examine one determined attitude which is essential to human reality and which is such that consciousness instead of directing its negation outward turns it toward itself. This attitude, it seems to me, is *bad faith (mauvaise foi).*

Frequently this is identified with falsehood. We say indifferently of a person that he shows signs of bad faith or that he lies to himself. We shall willingly grant that bad faith is a lie to oneself, on condition that we distinguish the lie to oneself from lying in general. Lying is a negative attitude, we will agree to that. But this negation does not bear on consciousness itself; it aims only at the transcendent. The essence of the lie implies in fact that the liar actually is in complete possession of the truth which he is hiding. A man does not lie about what he is ignorant of; he does not lie when he spreads an error of which he himself is the dupe; he does not lie when he is mistaken. The ideal description of the liar would be a cynical consciousness, affirming truth within himself, denying it in his words, and denying that negation as such. Now this doubly negative attitude rests on the transcendent; the fact expressed is transcendent since it does not exist, and the original negation rests on a *truth;* that is, on a particular type of transcendence. As for the inner negation which I effect correlatively with the affirmation for myself of the truth, this rests on *words;* that is, on an event in the world. Furthermore the inner disposition of the liar is positive; it could be the object of an affirmative judgment. The liar intends to deceive and he does not seek to hide this intention from himself nor to disguise the translucency of consciousness; on the contrary, he has recourse to it when there is a question of deciding secondary behavior. It explicitly exercises a regulatory control over all attitudes. As for his flaunted intention of telling the truth ("I'd never want to deceive you! This is true! I swear it!") — all this, of course, is the object of an inner negation, but also it is not recognized by the liar as *his* intention. It is played, imitated, it is the intention of the character which he plays in the eyes of his questioner, but this character, precisely because he *does not exist,* is a transcendent. Thus the lie does not put into the play the inner structure of present consciousness; all the negations which constitute it bear on objects which by this fact are removed from consciousness. The lie then does not require special ontological foundation, and the explanations which the existence of negation in general requires are valid without change in the case of deceit. Of course we have described the ideal lie; doubtless it happens often enough that the liar is more or less the victim of his lie, that he half persuades himself of it. But these common, popular forms of the lie are also degenerate aspects of it; they represent intermediaries between falsehood and bad faith. The lie is a behavior of transcendence.

The lie is also a normal phenomenon of what Heidegger calls the "*mit-sein.*"[1] It presupposes my existence, the existence of the *Other*, my existence *for* the Other, and the existence of the Other *for* me. Thus there is no difficulty in holding that the liar must make the project of the lie in entire clarity and that he must possess a complete comprehension of the lie and of the truth which he is altering. It is sufficient that an over-all opacity hide his intentions from the *Other;* it is sufficient that the Other can take the lie for truth. By the lie consciousness affirms that it exists by nature as *hidden from the Other;* it utilizes for its own profit the ontological duality of myself and myself in the eyes of the Other.

The situation can not be the same for bad faith if this, as we have said, is indeed a lie to oneself. To be sure, the one who practices bad faith is hiding a displeasing truth or presenting as truth a pleasing untruth. Bad faith then has in appearance the structure of falsehood. Only what changes everything is the fact that in bad faith it is from myself that I am hiding the truth. Thus the duality of the deceiver and the deceived does not exist here. Bad faith on the contrary implies in essence the unity of a *single* consciousness. This does not mean that it can not be conditioned by the *mit-sein* like all other phenomena of human reality, but the *mit-sein* can call forth bad faith only by presenting itself as *a situation* which bad faith permits surpassing; bad faith does not come from outside to human reality. One does not undergo his bad faith; one is not infected with it; it is not a *state.* But consciousness affects itself with bad faith. There must be an original intention and a project of bad faith; this project implies a comprehension of bad faith as such and a pre-reflective apprehension (of) consciousness as affecting itself with bad faith. It follows first that the one to whom the lie is told and the one who lies are one and the same person, which means that I must know in my capacity as deceiver the truth which is hidden from me in my capacity as the one deceived. Better yet I must know the truth very exactly *in order* to conceal it more carefully — and this not at two different moments, which at a pinch would allow us to re-establish a semblance of duality — but in the unitary structure of a single project. How then can the lie subsist if the duality which conditions it is suppressed?

To this difficulty is added another which is derived from the total translucency of consciousness. That which affects itself with bad faith must be conscious (of) its bad faith since the being of consciousness is

---

[1] Tr. a "being-with" others in the world.

consciousness of being. It appears then that I must be in good faith, at least to the extent that I am conscious of my bad faith. But then this whole psychic system is annihilated. We must agree in fact that if I deliberately and cynically attempt to lie to myself, I fail completely in this undertaking; the lie falls back and collapses beneath my look; it is ruined *from behind* by the very consciousness of lying to myself which pitilessly constitutes itself well within my project as its very condition. We have here an *evanescent* phenomenon which exists only in and through its own differentiation. To be sure, these phenomena are frequent and we shall see that there is in fact an "evanescence" of bad faith, which, it is evident, vacillates continually between good faith and cynicism: Even though the existence of bad faith is very precarious, and though it belongs to the kind of psychic structures which we might call *metastable*,[2] it presents nonetheless an autonomous and durable form. It can even be the normal aspect of life for a very great number of people. A person can *live* in bad faith, which does not mean that he does not have abrupt awakenings to cynicism or to good faith, but which implies a constant and particular style of life. Our embarrassment then appears extreme since we can neither reject nor comprehend bad faith.

To escape from these difficulties people gladly have recourse to the unconscious. In the psychoanalytical interpretation, for example, they use the hypothesis of a censor, conceived as a line of demarcation with customs, passport division, currency control, *etc.*, to re-establish the duality of the deceiver and the deceived. Here instinct or, if you prefer, original drives and complexes of drives constituted by our individual history, make up *reality*. It is neither *true* nor *false* since it does not *exist for itself*. It simply *is*, exactly like this table, which is neither true nor false *in itself* but simply *real*. As for the conscious symbols of the instinct, this interpretation takes them not for appearances but for real psychic facts. Fear, forgetting, dreams exist really in the capacity of concrete facts of consciousness in the same way as the words and the attitudes of the liar are concrete, really existing patterns of behavior. The subject has the same relation to these phenomena as the deceived to the behavior of the deceiver. He establishes them in their reality and must interpret them. There is a *truth* in the activities of the deceiver; if the deceived could reattach them to the situation where the deceiver establishes himself and to his project of the lie, they would become integral parts of truth, by virtue of being lying conduct. Similarly there is a truth in the symbolic acts; it is what the psychoanalyst discovers when he reattaches them to the historical situation of the patient, to the unconscious complexes which they express, to the blocking of the censor. Thus the subject deceives himself about the *meaning* of his conduct, he apprehends it in

---

[2] Tr. Sartre's own word, meaning subject to sudden changes or transition.

its concrete existence but not in its *truth*, simply because he cannot derive it from an original situation and from a psychic constitution which remain alien to him.

By the distinction between the "id" and the "ego," Freud has cut the psychic whole into two. I *am* the ego but I *am* not the *id*. I hold no privileged position in relation to my unconscious psyche. I *am* my own psychic phenomena in so far as I establish them in their conscious reality. For example I am the impulse to steal this or that book from this bookstall. I am an integral part of the impulse; I bring it to light and I determine myself hand-in-hand with it to commit the theft. But I *am* not those psychic facts, in so far as I receive them passively and am obliged to resort to hypotheses about their origin and their true meaning, just as the scholar makes conjectures about the nature and essence of an external phenomenon. This theft, for example, which I interpret as an immediate impulse determined by the rarity, the interest, or the price of the volume which I am going to steal — it is in truth a process derived from self-punishment, which is attached more or less directly to an Oedipus complex. The impulse toward the theft contains a truth which can be reached only by more or less probable hypotheses. The criterion of this truth will be the number of conscious psychic facts which it explains; from a more pragmatic point of view it will be also the success of the psychiatric cure which it allows. Finally the discovery of this truth will necessitate the cooperation of the psychoanalyst, who appears as the *mediator* between my unconscious drives and my conscious life. The Other appears as being able to effect the synthesis between the unconscious thesis and the conscious antithesis. I can know myself only through the mediation of the other, which means that I stand in relation to *my* "id," in the position of the *Other*. If I have a little knowledge of psychoanalysis, I can, under circumstances particularly favorable, try to psychoanalyze myself. But this attempt can succeed only if I distrust every kind of intuition, only if I apply to my case *from the outside*, abstract schemes and rules already learned. As for the results, whether they are obtained by my efforts alone or with the cooperation of a technician, they will never have the certainty which intuition confers; they will possess simply the always increasing probability of scientific hypotheses. The hypothesis of the Oedipus complex, like the atomic theory, is nothing but an "experimental idea"; as Pierce said, it is not to be distinguished from the totality of experiences which it allows to be realized and the results which it enables us to foresee. Thus psychoanalysis substitutes for the notion of bad faith, the idea of a lie without a liar; it allows me to understand how it is possible for me to be lied to without lying to myself since it places me in the same relation to myself that the Other is in respect to me; it replaces the duality of the deceiver and the deceived, the essential condition of the lie, by that of the "id" and the "ego." It introduces into my subjectivity the deepest intersubjective structure of the *mit-sein*. Can this explanation satisfy us?

Considered more closely the psychoanalytic theory is not as simple as it first appears. It is not accurate to hold that the "id" is presented as a thing in relation to the hypothesis of the psychoanalyst, for a thing is indifferent to the conjectures which we make concerning it, while the "id" on the contrary is sensitive to them when we approach the truth. Freud in fact reports resistance when at the end of the first period the doctor is approaching the truth. This resistance is objective behavior apprehended from without: the patient shows defiance, refuses to speak, gives fantastic accounts of his dreams, sometimes even removes himself completely from the psychoanalytic treatment. It is a fair question to ask what part of himself can thus resist. It can not be the "Ego," envisaged as a psychic totality of the facts of consciousness; this could not suspect that the psychiatrist is approaching the end since the ego's relation to the *meaning* of its own reactions is exactly like that of the psychiatrist himself. At the very most it is possible for the ego to appreciate objectively the degree of probability in the hypotheses set forth, as a witness of the psychoanalysis might be able to do, according to the number of subjective facts which they explain. Furthermore, this probability would appear to the ego to border on certainty, which he could not take offense at since most of the time it is he who by a *conscious* decision is in pursuit of the psychoanalytic therapy. Are we to say that the patient is disturbed by the daily revelations which the psychoanalyst makes to him and that he seeks to remove himself, at the same time pretending in his own eyes to wish to continue the treatment? In this case it is no longer possible to resort to the unconscious to explain bad faith; it is there in full consciousness, with all its contradictions. But this is not the way that the psychoanalyst means to explain this resistance; for him it is secret and deep, it comes from afar; it has its roots in the very thing which the psychoanalyst is trying to make clear.

Furthermore it is equally impossible to explain the resistance as emanating from the complex which the psychoanalyst wishes to bring to light. The complex as such is rather the collaborator of the psychoanalyst since it aims at expressing itself in clear consciousness, since it plays tricks on the censor and seeks to elude it. The only level on which we can locate the refusal of the subject is that of the censor. It alone can comprehend the questions or the revelations of the psychoanalyst as approaching more or less near to the real drives which it strives to repress — it alone because it alone *knows* what it is repressing.

If we reject the language and the materialistic mythology of psychoanalysis, we perceive that the censor in order to apply its activity with discernment must know what it is repressing. In fact if we abandon all the metaphors representing the repression as the impact of blind forces, we are compelled to admit that the censor must choose and in order to choose must be aware of so doing. How could it happen otherwise that the censor allows lawful sexual impulses to pass through, that it permits needs (hunger, thirst, sleep) to be expressed in clear consciousness? And how are we to explain that it can relax its surveillance, that it can even be deceived by the disguises of the instinct? But it is not sufficient that it discern the condemned drives; it must also apprehend them *as to be repressed,* which implies in it at the very least an awareness of its activity. In a word, how could the censor discern the impulses needing to be repressed without being conscious of discerning them? How can we conceive of a knowledge which is ignorant of itself? To know is to know that one knows, said Alain. Let us say rather: All knowing is consciousness of knowing. Thus the resistance of the patient implies on the level of the censor an awareness of the thing repressed as such, a comprehension of the end toward which the questions of the psychoanalyst are leading, and an act of synthetic connection by which it compares the *truth* of the repressed complex to the psychoanalytic hypothesis which aims at it. These various operations in their turn imply that the censor is conscious (of) itself. But what type of self-consciousness can the censor have? It must be the consciousness (of) being conscious of the drive to be repressed, but precisely *in order not be conscious of it.* What does this mean if not that the censor is in bad faith?

II. PATTERNS OF BAD FAITH

If we wish to get out of this difficulty, we should examine more closely the patterns of bad faith and attempt a description of them. This description will permit us perhaps to fix more exactly the conditions for the possibility of bad faith; that is, to reply to the question we raised at the outset: "What must be the being of man if he is to be capable of bad faith?"

Take the example of a woman who has consented to go out with a particular man for the first time. She knows very well the intentions which the man who is speaking to her cherishes regarding her. She knows also that it will be necessary sooner or later for her to make a decision. But she does not want to realize the urgency; she concerns herself only with what is respectful and discreet in the attitude of her companion. She does not apprehend this conduct as an attempt to achieve what we call "the first approach"; that is, she does not want to see possibilities of temporal development which his conduct presents. She restricts this behavior to what is in the present; she does not wish to read in the phrases which he addresses to her anything other than their explicit meaning. If he says to her, "I find you so attractive!" she disarms this phrase of its sexual background; she attaches to the conversation and to the behavior of the speaker, the immediate meanings, which she imagines as objective qualities. The man who is speaking to her appears to her sincere and respectful as the table is round or square, as the wall coloring is blue or gray. The qualities thus attached to the person she is listening to are in this way fixed in a permanence like that of things, which is no other than the projection of the strict present of the qualities into the temporal flux. This is because she does not quite know what she wants. She is profoundly aware of the desire which she inspires, but the desire cruel and naked would humiliate and horrify her. Yet she would find no charm in a respect which would be only respect. In order to satisfy her, there must be a feeling which is addressed wholly to her *personality* — *i.e.*, to her full freedom — and which would be a recognition of her freedom. But at the same time this feeling must be wholly desire; that is, it must address itself to her body as object. This time then she refuses to apprehend the desire for what it is; she does not even give it a name; she recognizes it only to the extent that it transcends itself toward admiration, esteem, respect and that it is wholly absorbed in the more refined forms which it produces, to the extent of no longer figuring anymore as a sort of warmth and density. But then suppose he takes her hand. This act of her companion risks changing the situation by calling for an immediate decision. To leave the hand there is to consent in herself to flirt, to engage herself. To withdraw it is to break the troubled and unstable harmony which gives the hour its charm. The aim is to postpone the moment of decision as long as possible. We know what happens next; the young woman leaves her hand there, but she *does not notice* that she is leaving it. She does not notice because it happens by chance that she is at this moment all intellect. She draws her companion up to the most lofty regions of sentimental speculation; she speaks of Life, of her life, she shows herself in her essential aspect — a personality, a consciousness. And during this time the divorce of the body from the soul is accomplished; the hand rests inert between the warm hands of her companion — neither consenting nor re-sisting — a thing.

We shall say that this woman is in bad faith. But we see immediately that she uses various procedures in order to maintain herself in this bad faith. She has disarmed the actions of her companion by reducing them to being only what they are; that is, to existing in the mode of the in-itself. But she permits herself to enjoy his desire, to the extent that she will apprehend it as not being what it is, will recognize its transcendence. Finally while sensing profoundly the presence of her own body — to the point of being aroused, perhaps — she realizes herself as *not being* her own body, and she contemplates it as though from above as a passive object to which events can *happen* but which can neither provoke them nor avoid them because all its possibilities are outside of it. What unity do we find in these various aspects of bad faith? It is a certain art of forming contradictory concepts which unite in themselves both an idea and the negation of that idea. The basic concept which is thus engendered uti-lizes the double property of the human being, who is at once a *facticity* and a *transcendence*. These two aspects of human reality are and ought to be capable of a valid coordination. But bad faith does not wish either to coordinate them or to surmount them in a synthesis. Bad faith seeks to affirm their identity while preserving their differences. It must affirm facticity as *being* transcendence and transcendence as *being* facticity, in such a way that at the instant when a person apprehends the one, he can find himself abruptly faced with the other. . . .

We can see the use which bad faith can make of these judgments which all aim at establishing that I am not what I am. If I were only what I *am*, I could, for example, seriously consider an adverse criticism which someone makes of me, question myself scrupulously, and perhaps be compelled to recognize the truth in it. But thanks to transcendence, I am not subject to all that I am. I do not even have to discuss the justice of the reproach. As Suzanne says to Figaro, "To prove that I am right would be to recognize that I can be wrong." I am on a plane where no reproach can touch me since what I really am is my transcendence. I flee from myself, I escape myself, I leave my tattered garment in the hands of the fault-finder. But the ambiguity necessary for bad faith comes from the fact that I affirm here that I *am* my transcendence in the mode of being of a thing. It is only thus, in fact, that I can feel that I escape all reproaches. It is in the sense that our young woman purifies the desire of anything humiliating by being willing to consider it only as pure transcendence, which she avoids even naming. But inversely "I Am Too Great for Myself," while showing our transcendence changed into facticity, is the source of an affinity of excuses for our failures or our weaknesses. Similarly the young coquette maintains transcendence to the extent that the respect, the esteem manifested by the actions of her admirer are already on the plane of the transcendent. But she arrests this transcendence, she glues it down with all the facticity of the present; respect is nothing other than respect, it is an arrested surpassing which no longer surpasses itself toward anything.

But although this *metastable* concept of "transcendence-facticity" is one of the most basic instruments of bad faith, it is not the only one of its kind. We can equally well use another kind of duplicity derived from human reality which we will express roughly by saying that its being-for itself implies complementarily a being-for-others. Upon any one of my conducts it is always possible to converge two looks, mine and that of the Other. The conduct will not present exactly the same structure in each case. But as we shall see later, as each look perceives it, there is between these two aspects of my being, no difference between appearance and being — as if I were to my self the truth of myself and as if the Other possesses only a deformed image of me. The equal dignity of being, possessed by my being-for-others and by my being-for-myself, permits a perpetually disintegrating synthesis and a perpetual game of escape from the for-itself to the for-others and from the for-others to the for-itself. We have seen also the use which our young lady made of our being-in-the-midst-of-the-world — *i.e.*, of our inert presence as a passive object among other objects — in order to relieve herself, suddenly from the functions of her being-in-the world — that is, from the being which causes there to be a world by projecting itself beyond the world toward its own possibilities. Let us note finally the confusing syntheses which play on the nihilating ambiguity of these temporal ekstases, affirming at once that I am what I have been (the man who deliberately *arrests himself* at one period in his life and refuses to take into consideration the later changes) and that I am not what I have been (the man who in the face of reproaches or rancor dissociates himself from his past by insisting on his freedom and on his perpetual re-creation). In all these concepts, which have only a transitive role in the reasoning and which are eliminated from the conclusion (like the imaginaries in the computations of physicists), we find again the same structure. We have to deal with human reality as a being which is what it is not and which is not what it is. . . .

If man is what he is, bad faith is forever impossible and candor ceases to be his ideal and becomes instead his being. But is man what he is? And more generally, how can he *be* what he is when he exists as consciousness of being? If candor or sincerity is a universal value, it is evident that the maxim "one must be what one is" does not serve solely as a regulating principle for judgments and concepts by which I express what I am. It posits not merely an ideal of knowing but an ideal of *being;* it proposes for us an absolute equivalence of being with itself as a prototype of being. In this sense it is necessary that we *make ourselves* what we are. But what *are we* then if we have the constant obligation to make ourselves what we are, if our mode of being is having the obligation to be what we are?

Let us consider this waiter in the café. His movement is quick and forward, a little too precise, a little too rapid. He comes toward the patrons with a step a little too quick. He bends forward a little too eagerly; his voice, his eyes express an interest a little too solicitous for the order of the customer. Finally there he returns, trying to imitate in his walk the inflexible stiffness of some kind of automaton while carrying his tray with the recklessness of a tight-rope-walker by putting it in a perpetually unstable, perpetually broken equilibrium which he perpetually re-establishes by a light movement of the arm and hand. All his behavior seems to us a game. He applies himself to chaining his movements as if they were mechanisms, the one regulating the other; his gestures and even his voice seem to be mechanisms; he gives himself the quickness and pitiless rapidity of things. He is playing, he is amusing himself. But what is he playing? We need not watch long before we can explain it: he is playing at *being* a waiter in a café. There is nothing there to surprise us.

The game is a kind of marking out and investigation. The child plays with his body in order to explore it, to take inventory of it; the waiter in the café plays with his condition in order to *realize* it. This obligation is not different from that which is imposed on all tradesmen. Their condition is wholly one of ceremony. The public demands of them that they realize it as a ceremony; there is the dance of the grocer, of the tailor, of the auctioneer, by which they endeavor to persuade their clientele that they are nothing but a grocer, an auctioneer, a tailor. A grocer who dreams is offensive to the buyer, because such a grocer is not wholly a grocer. Society demands that he limit himself to his function as a grocer, just as the soldier at attention makes himself into a soldier-thing with a direct regard which does not see at all, which is no longer meant to see, since it is the rule and not the interest of the moment which determines the point he must fix his eyes on (the sight "fixed at ten paces"). There are indeed many precautions to imprison a man in what he is, as if we lived in perpetual fear that he might escape from it, that he might break away and suddenly elude his condition.

In a parallel situation, from within, the waiter in the café can not be immediately a café waiter in the sense that this inkwell *is* an inkwell, or the glass is a glass. It is by no means that he can not form reflective judgments or concepts concerning his condition. He knows well what it "means": the obligation of getting up at five o'clock, of sweeping the floor of the shop before the restaurant opens, of starting the coffee pot going, *etc.* He knows the rights which it allows: the right to the tips, the right to belong to a union, *etc.* But all these concepts, all these judgments refer to the transcendent. It is a matter of abstract possibilities, of rights and duties conferred on a "person possessing rights." And it is precisely this person *who I have to be* (if I am the waiter in question) and who I am not. It is not that I do not wish to be this person or that I want this person to be different. But rather there is no common measure between his being and mine. It is a "representation" for others and for myself, which means that I can be he only in *representation*. But if I represent myself as him, I am not he; I am separated from him as the object from the subject, separated *by nothing*, but this nothing isolates me from him. I can not be he, I can only play *at being* him; that is, imagine to myself that I am he. And thereby I affect him with nothingness. In vain do I fulfill the functions of a café waiter. I can be he only in the neutralized mode, as the actor is Hamlet, by mechanically making the *typical gestures* of my state and by aiming at myself as an imaginary café waiter through those gestures taken as an "analogue." What I attempt to realize is a being-in-itself of the café waiter, as if it were not just in my power to confer their value and their urgency upon my duties and the rights of my position, as if it were not my free choice to get up each morning at five o'clock or to remain in bed, even though it meant getting fired. As if from the very fact that I sustain this role in existence I did not transcend it on every side, as if I did not constitute myself as one *beyond* my condition. Yet there is no doubt that I *am* in a sense a café waiter — otherwise could I not just as well call myself a diplomat or a reporter? But if I am one, this can not be in the mode of being in-itself. I am a waiter in the mode of *being what I am not*.

Furthermore we are dealing with more than mere social positions; I am never any one of my attitudes, any one of my actions. The good speaker is the one who *plays* at speaking, because he can not *be speaking*. The attentive pupil who wishes to *be* attentive, his eyes riveted on the teacher, his ears wide open, so exhausts himself in playing the attentive role that he ends up by no longer hearing anything. Perpetually absent to my body, to my acts, I am despite myself that "divine absence" of which Valéry speaks. I can not say either that I *am* here or that I *am* not here, in the sense that we say "that box of matches *is* on the table"; this would be to confuse my "being-in-the-world" with a "being-in-the-midst-of-the-world." Nor that I *am* standing, nor that I *am* seated; this would be to confuse my body with the idiosyncratic totality of which it is only one of the structures. On all sides I escape being and yet — I am.

But take a mode of being which concerns only myself: I am sad. One might think that surely I am the sadness in the mode of being what I am. What is the sadness, however, if not the intentional unity which comes to reassemble and animate the totality of my conduct? It is the meaning of this dull look with which I view the world, of my bowed shoulders, of my lowered head, of the listlessness in my whole body. But at the very moment when I adopt each of these attitudes, do I not know that I shall not be able to hold on to it? Let a stranger suddenly appear and I will lift up my head, I will assume a lively cheerfulness. What will remain of my sadness except that I obligingly promise it an appointment for later after the departure of the visitor! Moreover is not this sadness itself a *conduct?* Is it not consciousness which affects itself with sadness as a magical recourse against a situation too urgent? And in this case even, should we not say that being sad means first to make oneself sad? That may be, someone will say, but after all doesn't giving oneself the being of sadness mean to *receive* this being? It makes no difference from where I receive it. The fact is that a consciousness which affects itself with sadness is sad precisely for this reason. But it is difficult to comprehend the nature of consciousness; the being-sad is not a ready-made being which I give to myself as I can give this book to my friend. I do not possess the property of *affecting myself with being.* If I make myself sad, I must continue to make myself sad from beginning to end. I can not treat my sadness as an impulse finally achieved and put it on file without re-creating it, nor can I carry it in the manner of an inert body which continues its movement after the initial shock. There is no inertia in consciousness. If I make myself sad, it is because I *am* not sad — the being of the sadness escapes me by and in the very act by which I affect myself with it. The being-in-itself of sadness perpetually haunts my consciousness (of) being sad, but it is as a value which I can not realize; it stands as a regulative meaning of my sadness, not as its constitutive modality.

Someone may say that my consciousness at least *is*, whatever may be the object or the state of which it makes itself consciousness. But how do we distinguish my consciousness (of) being sad from sadness? Is it not all one? It is true in a way that my consciousness *is*, if one means by this that for another it is a part of the totality of being on which judgments can be brought to bear. But it should be noted, as Husserl clearly understood, that my consciousness appears originally to the Other as an absence. It is the object always present as the *meaning* of all my attitudes and all my conduct — and always absent, for it gives itself to the intuition of another as a perpetual question — still better, as a perpetual freedom. When Pierre looks at me, I know of course that he is looking at me. His eyes, things in the world, are fixed on my body, a thing in the world — that is the objective fact of which I can say: it *is*. But it is also a fact *in the world*. The meaning of this look is not a fact in the world, and this is what makes me uncomfortable. Although I make smiles, promises, threats, nothing can get hold of the approbation, the free judgment which I seek; I know that it is always beyond. I sense it in my very attitude, which is no longer like that of the worker toward the things he uses as instruments. My reactions, to the extent that I project myself toward the Other, are no longer for myself but are rather mere *presentations;* they await being constituted as graceful or uncouth, sincere or insincere, *etc.*, by an apprehension which will be provoked by my efforts only if of itself it lends them force (that is, only in so far as it causes itself to be provoked from the outside), *which is its own mediator with the transcendent.* Thus the objective fact of the being-in-itself of the Other's consciousness is posited in order to disappear in negativity and in freedom: the Other's consciousness is as not-being; its being-in-itself "here and now" is not-to-be.

The Other's consciousness is what it is not.

Furthermore the being of my own consciousness does not appear to me as the consciousness of the Other. It *is* because it makes itself, since its being is consciousness of being. But this means that making sustains being; consciousness has to be its own being, it is never sustained by being; it sustains being in the heart of subjectivity, which means once again that it is inhabited by being but that it is not being: *consciousness is not what it is.*

Under these conditions what can be the significance of the ideal of sincerity except as a task impossible to achieve, of which the very meaning is in contradiction with the structure of my consciousness. To be sincere, we said, is to be what one is. That supposes that I am not originally what I am. But here naturally Kant's "You ought, therefore you can" is implicitly understood. I can *become* sincere; this is what my duty and my effort to achieve sincerity imply. But we definitely establish that the original structure of "not being what one is" renders impossible in advance all movement toward being in itself or "being what one is." And this impossibility is not hidden from consciousness; on the contrary, it is the very stuff of consciousness; it is the embarrassing constraint which we constantly experience; it is our very incapacity to recognize ourselves, to constitute ourselves as being what we are. It is this necessity which means that, as soon as we posit ourselves as a certain being, by a legitimate judgment, based on inner experience or correctly deduced from *a priori* or empirical premises, then by that very positing we surpass this being — and that not toward another being but toward emptiness, toward *nothing.*

How then can we blame another for not being sincere or rejoice in our own sincerity since this sincerity appears to us at the same time to be impossible? How can we in conversation, in confession, in introspection, even attempt sincerity since the effort will by its very nature be doomed to failure and since at the very time when we announce it we have a prejudicative comprehension of its futility? In introspection I try to determine exactly what I am, to make up my mind to be my true self without delay — even though it means consequently to set about searching for ways to change myself. But what does this mean if not that I am constituting myself as a thing? Shall I determine the ensemble of purposes and motivations which have pushed me to do this or that action? But this is already to postulate a causal determinism which constitutes the flow of my states of consciousness as a succession of physical states. Shall I uncover in myself "drives," even though it be to affirm them in shame? But is this not deliberately to forget that these drives are realized with my consent, that they are not forces of nature but that I lend them their efficacy by a perpetually renewed decision concerning their value? Shall I pass judgment on my character, on my nature? Is this not to veil from myself at that moment what I know only too well, that I thus judge a past to which by definition my present is not subject? The proof of this is that the same man who in sincerity posits that he is what in actuality he was, is indignant at the reproach of another and tries to disarm it by asserting that he can no longer be what he was. We are readily astonished and upset when the penalties of the court affect a man who in his new freedom *is no longer* the guilty person he was. But at the same time we require of this man that he recognize himself as *being* this guilty one. What then is sincerity except precisely a phenomenon of bad faith? Have we not shown indeed that in bad faith human reality is constituted as a being which is what it is not and which is not what it is?

Let us take an example: A homosexual frequently has an intolerable feeling of guilt, and his whole existence is determined in relation to this feeling. One will readily foresee that he is in bad faith. In fact it frequently happens that this man, while recognizing his homosexual inclination, while avowing each and every particular misdeed which he has committed, refuses with all his strength to consider himself "*a paederast.*" His case is always "different," peculiar; there enters into it something of a game, of chance, of bad luck; the mistakes are all in the past; they are explained by a certain conception of the beautiful which women can not satisfy; we should see in them the results of a restless search, rather than the manifestations of a deeply rooted tendency, *etc., etc.* Here is assuredly a man in bad faith who borders on the comic since, acknowledging all the facts which are imputed to him, he refuses to draw from them the conclusion which they impose. His friend, who is his most severe critic, becomes irritated with this duplicity. The critic asks only one thing — and perhaps then he will show himself indulgent: that the guilty one recognize himself as guilty, that the homosexual declare frankly — whether humbly or boastfully matters little — "I am a paederast." We ask here: Who is in bad faith? The homosexual or the champion of sincerity?

The homosexual recognizes his faults, but he struggles with all his strength against the crushing view that his mistakes constitute for him a *destiny.* He does not wish to let himself be considered as a thing. He has an obscure but strong feeling that a homosexual is not a homosexual as this table is a table or as this red-haired man is red-haired. It seems to him that he has escaped from each mistake as soon as he has posited it and recognized it; he even feels that the psychic duration by itself cleanses him from each misdeed, constitutes for him an undetermined future, causes him to be born anew. Is he wrong? Does he not recognize in himself the peculiar, irreducible character of human reality? His attitude includes then an undeniable comprehension of truth. But at the same time he needs this perpetual rebirth, this constant escape in order to live; he must constantly put himself beyond reach in order to avoid the terrible judgment of collectivity. Thus he plays on the word *being*. He would be right actually if he understood the phrase "I am not a paederast" in the sense of "I am not what I am." That is, if he declared to himself, "To the extent that a pattern of conduct is defined as the conduct of a paederast and to the extent that I have adopted this conduct, I am a paederast. But to the extent that human reality can not be finally defined by patterns of conduct, I am not one." But instead he slides surreptitiously toward a different connotation of the word "being." He understands "not being" in the sense of "not-being-in itself." He lays claim to "not being a paederast" in the sense in which this table *is not* an inkwell. He is in bad faith.

But the champion of sincerity is not ignorant of the transcendence of human reality, and he knows how at need to appeal to it for his own advantage. He makes use of it even and brings it up in the present argument. Does he not wish first in the name of sincerity, then of freedom, that the homosexual reflect on himself and acknowledge himself as a homosexual? Does he not let the other understand that such a confession will win indulgence for him? What does this mean if not that the man who will acknowledge himself as a homosexual will no longer be *the same* as the homosexual whom he acknowledges being and that he will escape into the region of freedom and of good will? The critic asks the man then to be what he is in order no longer to be what he is. It is the profound meaning of the saying, "A sin confessed is half pardoned." The critic demands of the guilty one that he constitute himself as a thing, precisely in order no longer to treat him as a thing. And this contradiction is constitutive of the demand of sincerity. Who can not see how offensive to the Other and how reassuring for me is a statement such as, "He's just a paederast," which removes a disturbing freedom from a trait and which aims at henceforth constituting all the acts of the Other as consequences following strictly from his essence. That is actually what the critic is demanding of his victim — that he constitute himself as a thing, that he should entrust his freedom to his friend as a fief, in order that the friend should return it to him subsequently — like a suzerain to his vassal. The champion of sincerity is in bad faith to the degree that in order to reassure himself, he pretends to judge, to the extent that he demands that freedom as freedom constitute itself as a thing. We have here only one episode in that battle to the death of consciousness which Hegel calls "the relation of the master and the slave." A person appeals to another and demands that in the name of his nature as consciousness he should radically destroy himself as consciousness, but while making this appeal he leads the other to hope for a rebirth beyond this destruction.

Very well, someone will say, but our man is abusing sincerity, playing one side against the other. We should not ask for sincerity in the relation of the *mit-sein* but rather where it is pure — in the relations of a person with himself. But who can not see that objective sincerity is constituted in the same way? Who can not see that the sincere man constitutes himself as a thing in order to escape the condition of a thing by the same act of sincerity? The man who confesses that he is evil has exchanged his disturbing "freedom-for-evil" for an inanimate character of evil; he *is* evil, he clings to himself, he is what he is. But by the same stroke, he escapes from that *thing*, since it is he who contemplates it, since it depends on him to maintain it under his glance or to let it collapse in an infinity of particular acts. He derives a *merit* from his sincerity, and the deserving man is not the evil man as he is evil but as he is beyond his evilness. At the same time the evil is disarmed since it is nothing, save on the plane of determinism, and since in confessing it I posit my freedom in respect to it; my future is virgin; everything is allowed to me.

Thus the essential structure of sincerity does not differ from that of bad faith since the sincere man constitutes himself as what he is *in order not to be it*. This explains the truth recognized by all that one can fall into bad faith through being sincere. As Valéry pointed out, this is the case with Stendhal. Total, constant sincerity as a constant effort to adhere to oneself is by nature a constant effort to dissociate oneself from oneself. A person frees himself from himself by the very act by which he makes himself an object for himself. To draw up a perpetual inventory of what one is means constantly to redeny oneself and to take refuge in a sphere where one is no longer anything but a pure, free regard. The goal of bad faith, as we said, is to put oneself out of reach; it is an escape. Now we see that we must use the same terms to define sincerity. What does this mean?

In the final analysis the goal of sincerity and the goal of bad faith are not so different. To be sure, there is a sincerity which bears on the past and which does not concern us here; I am sincere if I confess *having had* this pleasure or that intention. We shall see that if this sincerity is possible, it is because in his fall into the past, the being of man is constituted as a being-in-itself. But here our concern is only with the sincerity which aims at itself in present immanence. What is its goal? To bring me to confess to myself what I am in order that I may finally coincide with my being; in a word, to cause myself to be, in the mode of the in-itself, what I am in the mode of "not being what I am." Its assumption is that fundamentally I am already, in the mode of the in-itself, what I have to be. Thus we find at the base of sincerity a continual game of mirror and reflection, a perpetual passage from the being which is what it is to the being which is not what it is and inversely from the being which is not what it is to the being which is what it is. And what is the goal of bad faith? To cause me to be what I am, in the mode of "not being what one is," or not to be what I am in the mode of "being what one is." We find here the same game of mirrors. In fact in order for me to have an intention of sincerity, I must at the outset simultaneously be and not be what I am. Sincerity does not assign me to a mode of being or a particular quality, but in relation to that quality it aims at making me pass from one mode of being to another mode of being. This second mode of being the ideal of sincerity, I am prevented by nature from attaining; and at the very moment when I struggle to attain it I have a vague prejudicative comprehension that I shall not attain it. But all the same, in order for me to be able to conceive an intention in bad faith, I must have such a nature that within my being I escape from my being. If I were sad or cowardly in the way in which this inkwell is an inkwell, the possibility of bad faith could not even be conceived. Not only should I be unable to escape from my being I could not even imagine that I could escape from it. But if bad faith is possible by virtue of a simple project, it is because so far as my being is concerned, there is no difference between being and non-being if I am cut off from my project.

Bad faith is possible only because sincerity is conscious of missing its goal inevitably, due to its very nature. I can try to apprehend myself as *"not being cowardly,"* when I *am* so, only on condition that the "being cowardly" is itself "in question" at the very moment when it exists, on condition that it is itself *one* question, that at the very moment when I wish to apprehend it, it escapes me on all sides and annihilates itself. The condition under which I can attempt an effort in bad faith is that in one sense, I *am not* this coward which I do not wish to be. But if I *were not* cowardly in the simple mode of not-being-what-one-is-not, I would be "in good faith" by declaring that I am not cowardly. Thus this inapprehensible coward is evanescent; in order for me not to be cowardly, I must in some way also be cowardly. That does not mean that I must be "a little" cowardly, in the sense that "a little" signifies "to a certain degree cowardly — and not cowardly to a certain degree." No. I must at once both be and not be totally and in all respects a coward. Thus in this case bad faith requires that I should not be what I am; that is, that there be an imponderable difference separating being from non-being in the mode of being of human reality.

But bad faith is not restricted to denying the qualities which I possess, to not seeing the being which I am. It attempts also to constitute myself as being what I am not. It apprehends me positively as courageous when I am not so. And that is possible, once again, only if I am what I am not; that is, if non-being in me does not have being even as non-being. Of course necessarily I *am not* courageous; otherwise bad faith would not be *bad* faith. But in addition my effort in bad faith must include the ontological comprehension that even in my usual being what I *am*. I am not it really and that there is no such difference between the being of "being-sad," for example — which I *am* in the mode of not being what I am — and the "non-being" of not-being-courageous which I wish to hide from myself. Moreover it is particularly requisite that the very negation of being should be itself the object of a perpetual nihilation, that the very meaning of "non-being" be perpetually in question in human reality. If I *were not* courageous in the way in which this inkwell is not a table; that is, if I were isolated in my cowardice, propped firmly against it, incapable of putting it in relation to its opposite, if I were not capable of *determining* myself as cowardly — that is, to deny courage to myself and thereby to escape my cowardice in the very moment that I posit it — if it were not on principle *impossible* for me to coincide with my *not-being-courageous* as well as with my being-courageous — then any project of bad faith would be prohibited me. Thus in order for bad faith to be possible, sincerity itself must be in bad faith. The condition of the possibility for bad faith is that human reality, in its most immediate being, in the intra-structure of the prereflective *cogito*, must be what it is not and not be what it is.

SIMONE DE BEAUVOIR

In the last two chapters of The Ethics of Ambuiguity, *de Beauvoir attempts to respond to some of the criticisms facing existentialism. She addresses in particular five specific objections:*

1. *that existentialists are inventing values;*
2. *that existentialists are overly pessimistic;*
3. *that existentialism would permit all forms of oppression;*
4. *that existentialism would allow one to do anything, and that everything is arbitrary, and*
5. *that existentialism would preclude the possibility of passing judgment on others' conduct.*

In response, she maintains that the absence of a priori values does not mean that the values that do emerge are capricious or oppressive. On the contrary, she claims, such values come from ourselves, and so we must take responsibility for those values as well as for the freedom of others, which also creates value. This is a philosophy of optimism, not pessimism, where we can decide for ourselves — without any "objective" external standards — who we will be.

The Ethics of Ambiguity

5. AMBIGUITY

The notion of ambiguity must not be confused with that of absurdity. To declare that existence is absurd is to deny that it can ever be given a meaning; to say that it is ambiguous is to assert that its meaning is never fixed, that it must be constantly won. Absurdity challenges every ethics; but also the finished rationalization of the real would leave no room for ethics; it is because man's condition is ambiguous that he seeks, through failure and outrageousness, to save his existence. Thus, to say that action has to be lived in its truth, that is, in the consciousness of the antinomies which it involves, does not mean that one has to renounce it. In *Plutarch Lied* Pierrefeu rightly says that in war there is no victory which can not be regarded as unsuccessful, for the objective which one aims at is the total

From *The Ethics of Ambiguity*, Simone de Beauvoir, pp. 129–38, 142–45, 148–50, 152–59. © The Philosophical Library, 1948.

annihilation of the enemy and this result is never attained; yet there are wars which are won and wars which are lost. So is it with any activity; failure and success are two aspects of reality which at the start are not perceptible. That is what makes criticism so easy and art so difficult: the critic is always in a good position to show the limits that every artist gives himself in choosing himself; painting is not given completely either in Giotto or Titian or Cezanne; it is sought through the centuries and is never finished; a painting in which all pictorial problems are resolved is really inconceivable; painting itself is this movement toward its own reality; it is not the vain displacement of a millstone turning in the void; it concretizes itself on each canvas as an absolute existence. Art and science do not establish themselves despite failure but through it; which does not prevent there being truths and errors, masterpieces and lemons, depending upon whether the discovery or the painting has or has not known how to win the adherence of human consciousnesses; this amounts to saying that failure, always ineluctable, is in certain cases spared and in others not.

It is interesting to pursue this comparison; not that we are likening action to a work of art or a scientific theory, but because in any case human transcendence must cope with the same problem: it has to found itself, though it is prohibited from ever fulfilling itself. Now, we know that neither science nor art ever leaves it up to the future to justify its present existence. In no age does art consider itself as something which is paving the way for Art: so-called archaic art prepares for classicism only in the eyes of archaeologists; the sculptor who fashioned the Korai of Athens rightfully thought that he was producing a finished work of art; in no age has science considered itself as partial and lacunary; without believing itself to be definitive, it has however, always wanted to be a total expression of the world, and it is in its totality that in each age it again raises the question of its own validity. There we have an example of how man must, in any event, assume his finiteness: not be treating his existence as transitory or relative but by reflecting the infinite within it, that is, by treating it as absolute. There is an art only because at every moment art has willed itself absolutely; likewise there is a liberation of man only if, in aiming at itself, freedom is achieved absolutely in the very fact of aiming at itself. This requires that each action be considered as a finished form whose different moments, instead of fleeing toward the future in order to find there their justification, reflect and confirm on another so well that there is no longer a sharp separation between present and future, between means and ends.

But if these moments constitute a unity, there must be no contradiction among them. Since the liberation aimed at is not a *thing* situated in an unfamiliar time, but a movement which realizes itself by tending to conquer, it can not attain itself if it denies itself at the start; action can not seek to fulfill itself by means which would destroy its very meaning. So much so that in certain situations there will be no other issue for man than rejection. In what is called political realism there is no room for rejection because the present is considered as transitory; there is rejection only if man lays claim in the present to his existence as an absolute value; then he must absolutely reject what would deny this value. Today, more or less consciously in the name of such an ethics, we condemn a magistrate who handed over a communist to save ten hostages and along with him all the Vichyites who were trying "to make the best of things:" it was not a matter of rationalizing the present such as it was imposed by the German occupation, but of rejecting it unconditionally. The resistance did not aspire to a positive effectiveness; it was a negation, a revolt, a martyrdom; and in this negative movement freedom was positively and absolutely confirmed.

In one sense the negative attitude is easy; the rejected object is given unequivocally and uneqivocally defines the revolt that one opposes to it; thus, all French anti-fascists were united during the occupation by their common resistance to a single oppressor. The return to the positive encounters many more obstacles, as we have well seen in France where divisions and hatreds were revived at the same time as were the parties. In the moment of rejection, the antinomy of action is removed, and means and end meet; freedom immediately sets itself up as its own goal and fulfills itself by so doing. But the antinomy reappears as soon as freedom again gives itself ends which are far off in the future; then, through the resistances of the given, divergent means offer themselves and certain ones come to be seen as contrary to their ends. It has often been observed that revolt alone is pure. Every construction implies the outrage of dictatorship, of violence. This is the theme, among others, of Koestler's *Gladiators*. Those who, like this symbolic *Spartacus*, do not want to retreat from the outrage and resign themselves to impotence, usually seek refuge in the values of seriousness. That is why, among individuals as well as collectivities, the negative moment is often the most genuine. Goethe, Barres, and Aragon, disdainful or rebellious in their romantic youth, shattered old conformisms and thereby proposed a real, though incomplete, liberation. But what happened later on? Goethe became a servant of the state, Barres of nationalism, and Aragon of Stalinist conformism. We know how the seriousness of the Catholic Church was substituted for the Christian spirit, which was a rejection of dead Law, a subjective rapport of the individual with God through faith and charity; the Reformation was a revolt of subjectivity, but Protestantism in turn changed into an objective moralism in which the seriousness of works replaced the restlessness of faith. As for revolutionary humanism, it accepts only rarely the tension of permanent liberation; it has created a Church where salvation is bought by membership in a party as it is bought elsewhere by baptism and indulgences. We have seen that this recourse to the serious is a lie; it entails the sacrifice of man to the Thing, of freedom to the Cause. In order for the return to the positive to be genuine it must involve negativity, it must not conceal the antinomies between means and end, present and future; they must be lived in a permanent tension; one must retreat from neither the outrage of violence nor deny it, or, which amounts to the same thing, assume it lightly. Kierkegaard has said that what distinguishes the pharisee from the genuinely moral man is that the former considers his anguish as a sure sign of his virtue; from the fact that he asks himself, "Am I Abraham?" he concludes, "I am Abraham;" but morality resides in the painfulness of an indefinite questioning. The problem which we are posing is not the same as that of Kierkegaard; the important thing to us is to know whether, in given conditions, Isaac must be killed or not. But we also think that what distinguishes the tyrant from the man of good will is that the first rests in the certainty of his aims, whereas the second keeps asking himself, "Am I really working for the liberation of men? Isn't this end contested by the sacrifices through which I aim at it?" In setting up its ends, freedom must put them in parentheses, confront them at each moment with that absolute end which in itself constitutes, and contest, in its own name, the means it uses to win itself.

It will be said that these considerations remain quite abstract. What must be done, practically? Which action is good? Which is bad? To ask such a question is also to fall into a naive abstraction. We don't ask the physicist, "Which hypotheses are true?" Nor the artist, "By what procedures does one produce a work whose beauty is guaranteed?" Ethics does not furnish recipes any more than do science and art. One can merely propose methods. Thus, in science the fundamental problem is to make the idea adequate to its content and the law adequate to the facts; the logician finds that in the case where the pressure of the given fact bursts the concept which serves to comprehend it, one is obliged to invent another concept; but he can not define *a priori* the moment of invention, still less foresee it. Analogously, one may say that in the case where the content of the action falsifies its meaning, one must modify not the meaning, which is here willed absolutely, but the content itself; however, it is impossible to determine this relationship between meaning and content abstractly and universally: there must be a trial and decision in each case. But likewise just as the physicist finds it profitable to reflect on the conditions of scientific invention and the artist on those of artistic creation without expecting any ready-made solutions to come from these reflections, it is useful for the man of action to find out under what conditions his undertakings are valid. We are going to see that on this basis new perspectives are disclosed.

In the first place, it seems to us that the individual as such is one of the ends at which our action must aim. Here we are at one with the point of view of Christian charity, the Epicurean cult of friendship, and Kantian moralism which treats each man as an end. He interests us not merely as a member of a class, a nation, or a collectivity, but as an individual man. This distinguishes us from the systematic politician who cares only about collective destinies; and probably a tramp enjoying his bottle of wine, or a child playing with a balloon, or a Neapolitan lazzarone loafing in the sun in no way helps in the liberation of man; that is why the abstract will of the revolutionary scorns the concrete benevolence which occupies itself in satisfying desires which have no morrow. However, it must not be forgotten that there is a concrete bond between freedom and existence; to will man free is to will there to *be* being, it is to will the the disclosure of being in the joy of existence; in order for the idea of liberation to have a concrete meaning, the joy of existence must be asserted in each one, at every instant; the movement toward freedom assumes its real, flesh and blood figure in the world by thickening into pleasure, into happiness. If the satisfaction of an old man drinking a glass of wine counts for nothing, then production and wealth are only hollow myths; they have meaning only if they are capable of being retrieved in individual and living joy. The saving of time and the conquest of leisure have no meaning if we are not moved by the laugh of a child at play. If we do not love life on our own account and through others, it is futile to seek to justify it in any way.

However, politics is right in rejecting benevolence to the extent that the latter thoughtlessly sacrifices the future to the present. The ambiguity of freedom, which very often is occupied only in fleeing from itself, introduces a difficult equivocation into relationships with each individual taken one by one. Just what is meant by the expression "to love others"? What is meant by taking them as ends? In any event, it is evident that we are not going to decide to fulfill the will of every man. There are cases where a man positively wants evil, that is, the enslavement of other men, and he must then be fought. It also happens that, without harming anyone, he flees from his own freedom, seeking passionately and alone to attain the being which constantly eludes him. If he asks for our help, are we to give it to him? We blame a man who helps a drug addict intoxicate himself or a desperate man commit suicide, for we think that rash behavior of this sort is an attempt of the individual against his own freedom; he must be made aware of his error and put it in the presence of the real demands of his freedom. Well and good. But what if he persists? Must we then use violence? There again the serious man busies himself dodging the problem; the values of life, of health, and of moral conformism being set up, one does not hesitate to impose them on others. But we know that this pharisaism can cause the worst disasters: lacking drugs, the addict may kill himself. It is no more necessary to serve an abstract ethics obstinately than to yield without due consideration to impulses of pity or generosity; violence is justified only if it opens concrete possibilities to the freedom which I am trying to save; by practising it I am willy-nilly assuming an engagement in relation to others and to myself; a man whom I snatch from the death which he had chosen has the right to come and ask me for means and reasons for living; the tyranny practised against an invalid can be justified only by his getting better; whatever the purity of the intention which animates me, any dictatorship is a fault for which I have to get myself pardoned. Besides, I am in no position to make decisions of this sort indiscriminately; the example of the unknown person who throws himself in to the Seine and whom I hesitate whether or not to fish out is quite abstract; in the absence of a concrete bond with this desperate person my choice will never be anything but a contingent facticity. If I find myself in a position to do violence to a child, or to a melancholic, sick, or distraught person the reason is that I also find myself charged with his upbringing, his happiness, and his health: I am a parent, a teacher, a nurse, a doctor, or a friend. . . . So, by a tacit agreement, by the very fact that I am solicited, the strictness of my decision is accepted or even desired; the more seriously I accept my responsibilities, the more justified it is. That is why love authorizes severities which are not granted to indifference. What makes the problem so complex is that, on the one hand, one must not make himself an accomplice of that flight from freedom that is found in heedlessness, caprice, mania, and passion, and that, on the other hand, it is the abortive movement of man toward being which is his very existence, it is through the failure which he has assumed that he asserts himself as a freedom. To want to prohibit a man from error is to forbid him to fulfill his own existence, it is to deprive him of life. At the beginning of Claudel's *The Satin Shoe,* the husband of Dona Prouheze, the Judge, the Just, as the author regards him, explains that every plant needs a gardener in order to grow and that he is the one whom heaven has destined for his young wife; beside the fact that we are shocked by the arrogance of such a thought (for how does he know that he is this enlightened gardener? Isn't he merely a jealous husband?) this likening of a soul to a plant is not acceptable; for, as Kant would say, the value of an act lies not in its *conformity* to an external model, but in its internal truth. We object to the inquisitors who want to create faith and virtue from without; we object to all forms of fascism which seek to fashion the happiness of man from without; and also the paternalism which thinks that it has done something for man by prohibiting him from certain possibilities of temptation, whereas what is necessary is to give him reasons for resisting it.

Thus, we can set up point number one: the good of an individual or a group of individuals requires that it be taken as an absolute end of our action; but we are not authorized to decide upon this end *a priori.* The fact is that no behavior is ever authorized to begin with, and one of the

concrete consequences of existentialist ethics is the rejection of all the
previous justifications which might be drawn from the civilization,
the age, and the culture; it is the rejection of every principle of authority.
To put it positively, the precept will be to treat the other (to the extent that
he is the only one concerned, which is the moment that we are considering at present) as a freedom so that his end may be freedom; in using
this conducting-wire one will have to incur the risk, in each case, of
inventing an original solution. Out of disappointment in love a young girl
takes an overdose of pheno-barbital; in the morning friends find her
dying, they call a doctor, she is saved; later on she becomes a happy
mother of a family; her friends were right in considering her suicide as a
hasty and heedless act and in putting her into a position to reject it or
return to it freely. But in asylums one sees melancholic patients who have
tried to commit suicide twenty times, who devote their freedom to seeking the means of escaping their jailers and of putting an end to their
intolerable anguish; the doctor who gives them a friendly pat on the
shoulder is their tyrant and their torturer. A friend who is intoxicated by
alcohol or drugs asks me for money so that he can go and buy the poison
that is necessary to him; I urge him to get cured, I take him to a doctor, I
try to help him live; insofar as there is a chance of my being successful, I
am acting correctly in refusing him the sum he asks for. But if circumstances prohibit me from doing anything to change the situation in which
he is struggling, all I can do is give in; a deprivation of a few hours will do
nothing but exasperate his torments uselessly; and he may have recourse
to extreme means to get what I do not give him. That is also the problem
touched on by Ibsen in *The Wild Duck*. An individual lives in a situation
of falsehood; the falsehood is violence, tyranny: shall I tell the truth in
order to free the victim? It would first be necessary to create a situation of
such a kind that the truth might be bearable and that, though losing his
illusions, the deluded individual might again find about him reasons for
hoping. What makes the problem more complex is that the freedom of one
man almost always concerns that of other individuals. Here is a married
couple who persist in living in a hovel; if one does not succeed in giving
them the desire to live in a more healthful dwelling, they must be allowed
to follow their preferences; but the situation changes if they have children; the freedom of the parents would be the ruin of their sons, and as
freedom and the future are on the side of the latter, these are the ones who
must first be taken into account. The Other is multiple, and on the basis of
this new questions arise.

One might first wonder for whom we are seeking freedom and
happiness. When raised in this way, the problem is abstract; the answer
will, therefore, be arbitrary, and the arbitrary always involves outrage. It
is not entirely the fault of the district social-worker if she is apt to be
odious; because, her money and time being limited, she hesitates before

distributing it to this one or that one, she appears to others as a pure externality, a blind facticity. Contrary to the formal strictness of Kantianism for whom the more abstract the act is the more virtuous it is, generosity seems to us to be better grounded and therefore more valid the less distinction there is between the other and ourself and the more we fulfill ourself in taking the other as an end. That is what happens if I am engaged in relation to others. The Stoics impugned the ties of family, friendship, and nationality so that they recognized only the universal form of man. But man is man only through situations whose particularity is precisely a universal fact. There are men who expect help from certain men and not from others, and these expectations define privileged lines of action. It is fitting that the negro fight for the negro, the Jew for the Jew, the proletarian for the proletarian, and the Spaniard in Spain. But the assertion of these particular solidarities must not contradict the will for universal solidarity and each finite undertaking must also be open on the totality of men.

But it is then that we find in concrete form the conflicts which we have described abstractly; for the cause of freedom can triumph only through particular sacrifices. And certainly there are hierarchies among the goods desired by men: one will not hesitate to sacrifice the comfort, luxury, and leisure of certain men to assure the liberation of certain others; but when it is a question of choosing among freedoms, how shall we decide?

Thus, we challenge every condemnation as well as every *a priori* justification of the violence practised with a view to a valid end. They must be legitimized concretely. A calm, mathematical calculation is here impossible. One must attempt to judge the chances of success that are involved in a certain sacrifice; but at the beginning this judgment will always be doubtful; besides, in the face of the immediate reality of the sacrifice, the notion of chance is difficult to think about. On the one hand, one can multiply a probability infinitely without ever reaching certainty; but yet, practically, it ends by merging with this asymptote; in our private life as in our collective life there is no other truth than a statistical one. On the other hand, the interests at stake do not allow themselves to be put into an equation; the suffering of one man, that of a million men, are incommensurable with the conquests realized by millions of others, present death is incommensurable with the life to come. It would be utopian to want to set up on the one hand the chances of success multiplied by the stake one is after, and on the other hand the weight of the immediate sacrifice. One finds himself back at the anguish of free decision. And that is why political choice is an ethical choice: it is a wager as well as a decision; one bets on the chances and risks of the measure under consideration; but whether chances and risks must be assumed or not in the given circumstances must be decided without help, and in so doing one sets up values. . . . [I]t is a matter of defining an end and realizing it, knowing that the choice of the means employed affects both the definition and the fulfillment.

Ordinarily, situations are so complex that a long analysis is necessary before being able to pose the ethical moment of the choice. We shall confine ourselves here to the consideration of a few simple examples which will enable us to make our attitude somewhat more precise. In an underground revolutionary movement when one discovers the presence of a stool-pigeon, one does not hesitate to beat him up; he is a present and future danger who has to be gotten rid of; but if a man is merely suspected of treason, the case is more ambiguous. We blame those northern peasants who in the war of 1914–18 massacred an innocent family which was suspected of signaling to the enemy; the reason is that not only were the presumptions vague, but the danger was uncertain; at any rate, it was enough to put the suspects into prison; while waiting for a serious inquiry it was easy to keep them from doing any harm. However, if a questionable individual holds the fate of other men in his hands, if, in order to avoid the risk of killing one innocent man, one runs the risk of letting ten innocent men die, it is reasonable to sacrifice him. We can merely ask that such decisions be not taken hastily and lightly, and that, all things considered, the evil that one inflicts be lesser than that which is being forestalled.

It is apparent that the method we are proposing, analogous in this respect to scientific or aesthetic methods, consists, in each case, of confronting the values realized with the values aimed at, and the meaning of the act with its content. The fact is that the politician, contrary to the scientist and the artist, and although the element of failure which he assumes is much more outrageous, is rarely concerned with making use of it. May it be that there is an irresistible dialectic of power wherein morality has no place? Is the ethical concern, even in its realistic and concrete form, detrimental to the interests of action? The objection will surely be made that hesitation and misgivings only impede victory. Since, in any case, there is an element of failure in all success, since the ambiguity, at any rate, must be surmounted, why not refuse to take notice of it? In the first number of the *Cahiers d' Action* a reader declared that once and for all we should regard the militant communist as "the permanent hero of our time" and should reject the exhausting tension demanded by existentialism; installed in the permanence of heroism, one will blindly direct himself toward an uncontested goal; but one then resembles Colonel de la Roque who unwaveringly went right straight ahead of him without knowing where he was going. Malaparte relates that the young Nazis, in order to become insensitive to the suffering of others, practised by plucking out the eyes of live cats; there is no more radical way of avoiding the pitfalls of ambiguity. But an action which wants to serve man ought to be careful not to forget him on the way; if it chooses to fulfill itself blindly, it will lose its meaning or will take on an unforeseen meaning; for the goal is not fixed once and for all; it is defined all along the road which leads to it. Vigilance alone can keep the validity of the goals and the genuine assertion of freedom. Moreover, ambiguity can not fail to appear on the scene; it is felt by the victim, and his revolt or his complaints also make it exist for his tyrant; the latter will then be tempted to put everything into question, to renounce, thus denying both himself and his ends; or, if he persists, he will continue to blind himself only by multiplying crimes and by perverting his original design more and more. The fact is that the man of action becomes a dictator not in respect to his ends but because these ends are necessarily set up through his will. Hegel, in his *Phenomenology*, has emphasized this inextricable confusion between objectivity and subjectivity. A man gives himself to a Cause only by making it *his* Cause; as he fulfills himself within it, it is also through him that it is expressed, and the will to power is not distinguished in such a case from generosity; when an individual or a party chooses to triumph, whatever the cost may be, it is their own triumph which they take for an end. If the fusion of the Commissar and the Yogi were realized, there would be a self-criticism in the man of action which would expose to him the ambiguity of his will, thus arresting the imperious drive of his subjectivity and, by the same token, contesting the unconditioned value of the goal. But the fact is that the politician follows the line of least resistance; it is easy to fall asleep over the unhappiness of others and to count it for very little; it is easier to throw a hundred men, ninety-seven of whom are innocent into prison, than to discover the three culprits who are hidden among them; it is easier to kill a man than to keep a close watch on him; all politics makes use of the police, which officially flaunts its radical contempt for the individual and which loves violence for its own sake. The thing that goes by the name of political necessity is in part the laziness and brutality of the police. That is why it is incumbent upon ethics not to follow the line of least resistance; an act which is not destined, but rather quite freely consented to; it must make itself effective so that what was at first facility may become difficult. For want of internal criticism, this is the role that an opposition must take upon itself. There are two types of opposition. The first is a rejection of the very ends set up by a regime: it is the opposition of anti-fascism to fascism, of fascism to socialism. In the second type, the oppositionist accepts the objective goal but criticizes the subjective movement which aims at it; he may not even wish for a change of power, but he deems it necessary to bring into play a contestation which will make the subjective appear as such. Thereby he exacts a perpetual contestation of the means by the end and of the end by the means. He must be careful himself not to ruin, by the means which he employs, the end he is aiming at, and above all not to pass into the service of the oppositionists of the first type. But, delicate as it may be, his role is, nevertheless, necessary. Indeed, on the one hand, it would be absurd to oppose a liberating action with the pretext that it implies crime and tyranny; for without crime and tyranny there could be no liberation of man; one can not escape that dialectic which goes from freedom to freedom through dictatorship and oppression. But, on the other hand, he would be guilty of allowing the liberating movement to harden into a moment which is acceptable only if it passes into its opposite; tyranny and crime must be kept from triumphantly establishing themselves in the world; the conquest of freedom is their only justification, and the assertion of freedom against them must therefore be kept alive.

CONCLUSION

Is this kind of ethics individualistic or not? Yes, if one means by that that it accords to the individual an absolute value and that it recognizes in him alone the power of laying the foundations of his own existence. It is individualism in the sense in which the wisdom of the ancients, the Christian ethics of salvation, and the Kantian ideal of virtue also merit this name; it is opposed to the totalitarian doctrines which raise up beyond man the mirage of Mankind. But it is not solipsistic, since the individual is defined only by his relationship to the world and to other individuals; he exists only by transcending himself, and his freedom can be achieved only through the freedom of others. He justifies his existence by a movement which, like freedom, springs from his heart but which leads outside of him.

This individualism does not lead to the anarchy of personal whim. Man is free; but he finds his law in his very freedom. First, he must assume his freedom and not flee it; he assumes it by a constructive movement: one does not exist without doing something; and also by a negative movement which rejects oppression for oneself and others. In construction, as in rejection, it is a matter of reconquering freedom on the contingent facticity of existence, that is, of taking the given, which, at the start, *is there* without any reason, as something willed by man. A conquest of this kind is never finished; the contingency remains, and, so that he may assert his will, man is even obliged to stir up in the world the outrage he does not want. But this element of failure is a very condition of his life; one can never dream of eliminating it without immediately dreaming of death. This does not mean that one should consent to failure, but rather one must consent to struggle against it without respite.

Yet, isn't this battle without victory pure gullibility? It will be argued that this is only a ruse of transcendance projecting before itself a goal which constantly recedes, running after itself on an endless treadmill; to exist for Mankind is to remain where one is, and it fools itself by calling this turbulent stagnation progress; our whole ethics does nothing but encourage it in this lying enterprise since we are asking each one to confirm existence as a value for all others; isn't it simply a matter of organizing among men a complicity which allows them to substitute a game of illusions for the given world?

We have already attempted to answer this objection. One can formulate it only by placing himself on the grounds of an inhuman and consequently false objectivity; within Mankind men may be fooled; the word "lie" has a meaning by opposition to the truth established by men themselves, but Mankind can not fool itself completely since it is precisely Mankind which creates the criteria of true and false. In Plato, art is mystification because there is the heaven of Ideas; but in the earthly domain all glorification of the earth is true as soon as it is realized. Let men attach value to words, forms, colors, mathematical theorems, physical laws, and athletic prowess; let them accord value to one another in love and friendship, and the objects, the events, and the men immediately *have* this value; they have it absolutely. It is possible he will prove this refusal and he will carry it out by suicide. If he lives, the reason is that, whatever he may say, there still remains in him some attachment to existence; his life will be commensurate with this attachment; it will justify itself to the extent that it genuinely justifies the world.

This justification, though open upon the entire universe through time and space, will always be finite. Whatever one may do, one never realizes anything but a limited work, like existence itself which tries to establish itself through that work and which death also limits. It is the assertion of our finiteness which doubtless gives the doctrine which we have just evoked its austerity and, in some eyes, its sadness. As soon as one considers a system abstractly and theoretically, one puts himself, in effect, on the plane of the universal, thus, of the infinite. That is why reading the Hegelian system is so comforting. I remember having experienced a great feeling of calm on reading Hegel in the impersonal framework of the Bibliotheque Nationale in August 1940. But once I got into the street again, into my life, out of the system, beneath a real sky, the system was no longer of any use to me: what it had offered me, under a show of the infinite, was the consolations of death; and I again wanted to live in the midst of living men. I think that, inversely, existentialism does not offer to the reader the consolations of an abstract evasion: existentialism proposed no evasion. On the contrary; its ethics is experienced in the truth of life, and it then appears as the only proposition of salvation which one can address to men. Taking on its own account Descartes' revolt against the evil genius, the pride of the thinking reed in the face of the universe which crushes him, it asserts that, despite his limits, through them, it is up to each one to fulfill his existence as an absolute. Regardless of the staggering dimensions of the world about us, the density of our ignorance, the risks of catastrophes to come, and our individual weakness within the immense collectivity, the fact remains that we are absolutely free today if we choose to will our existence in its finiteness, a finiteness which is open on the infinite. And in fact, any man who has known real loves, real revolts, real desires, and real will knows quite well that he has no need of any outside guarantee to be sure of his goals; their certitude comes from his own drive. There is a very old saying which goes: "Do what you must, come what may." That amounts to saying in a different way that the result is not external to the good will which fulfills itself in aiming at it. If it came to be that each man did what he must, existence would be saved in each one without there being any need of dreaming of a paradise where all would be reconciled in death.

Simone de Beauvoir's novel The Blood of Others *addresses some of the issues raised by an existential ethic. In particular, this work examines the nature of freedom and the obligations this freedom creates for ourselves as well as others. The novel concerns Jean Blomart, a patriot leader against the German forces of occupation, who has sent his lover Hélène on a mission that has led to her death. As he sits by her bedside waiting for her to die, he must consider his responsibility vis à vis her freedom and, more concretely, must decide whether to send others to the same fate.*

The Blood of Others

A ray of light filters through the venetian blinds. Five o'clock. The first doors are opening. The doctor and the midwife hasten to the bedside of the sick and of the expectant mother. The clandestine dance halls are emptying into the deserted streets. Round the railway stations, lights go up in some of the cafés. *They are putting them against the wall.* He thrust his hand into his pocket. Hard and cold. A toy. "One would never think that it could kill." It kills. He went up to the bed. She will not last the night. And the night is almost over. Shall I still be there to say: "I have killed her"? To say: "You must kill again." That voice . . . it speaks for me; for me it must be silent. What does it matter to them that my silence is still a voice? Nothing will save me. But I can go to sleep, sink myself in those guilty waters. Anguish rends and tears me; it tears me from myself. Let that tearing cease. . . .

"Jean."

He turned round. She had opened her eyes. She was looking at him. "Did Paul come?"

"Yes, he's here. All is well."

"Oh, I am glad," she said. That voice was weak, but clear. He sat down on the edge of the bed.

"How do you feel?"

"I'm comfortable." She took his hands between her own. "You know, don't be sad. I don't mind dying."

"You are not going to die."

"Do you think so?"

She looked at him; her same old look, suspicious, exacting. "What did the doctor say?"

This time he could not hesitate; he did not doubt; despite the sweat on her temples and her halting voice, this was no poor fleshly object; she saw, she was free; her last moments belonged only to her.

"He didn't give much hope."

"Ah," she said, "I thought so." She was silent for an instant. "I don't mind," she repeated.

He bent and his lips touched the mauve cheek.

"Hélène, you know I love you."

"Yes, now you love me," she said. She pressed his hand. "I'm happy that you are here; you'll think of me."

"My only love," he said. "You are here, and through my fault."

"Wherein lies the fault?" she said. "It was I who wanted to go."

"But I could have forbidden you."

She smiled. "You had no right to decide for me."

The same words. He looked at her. It is indeed her. She used to say: "It is for me to decide." Then her dull hair used to shine, her hollow cheeks were brilliant with life; it was still she. The same liberty. Then I have not betrayed anyone? Is it indeed you to whom I spoke, to you, and you only in the unique truth of your life? In that gasping breath, in those blue lids, do you still recognize your will?

"That is what you used to say; I let you choose, but did you know what you chose?"

"I chose you. I would make the same choice over again." She shook her head. "I would not have wished to have had any other life."

He did not yet dare to believe in these words which he heard; but the vice about his heart was loosened, and hope rose in the night.

"You hadn't chosen to meet me," he said. "You stumbled against me as you stumbled against a stone. And now — "

"Now," she said. "But what is there to regret? Was it really so necessary for me to grow old?"

The words scarcely passed her lips. But her eyes were watching. Living, present. It seemed suddenly that time had no more importance, all that time when she would be no more, since at this minute she existed, free and limitless.

"Is it true that you regret nothing?" he said.

"No. Why?"

"Why?" he repeated.

"And, above all, don't feel guilty," she said.

"I'll try."

"You mustn't feel guilty." She smiled weakly. "I did what I wanted. You were just a stone. Stones are necessary to make roads, otherwise how could one choose a way for oneself?"

"If it were true," he said.

"But it is true. I'm certain of it. What would I have been if nothing had ever happened to me?"

"Ah! I wish I could believe you," he said.

"Whom will you believe?"

"When I look at you, I believe you."

"Look at me." She closed her eyes. "I'm going to sleep for a little longer. I'm tired."

He was looking at her. "*It is well!*" Perhaps Paul was right to say "it is well." She was breathing softly and he was looking at her. It seemed to him that he could not have invented any other death, any other life for her. "I believe you, I must believe you. No harm came to you through me. Under your feet I was an innocent stone. As innocent as the stones, as that piece of steel that tore your lung. He did not kill you; it was not I who killed you, my dear love."

"Hélène!"

He choked back a cry. The veins are swollen and the mouth is half-open. She is sleeping; she has forgotten that she is going to die. A moment ago she knew it; now she is dying and she does not know it. "Do not sleep, wake up." He bent over her. He would have liked to take her by the shoulders to shake her, to implore her; by blowing with all his strength on a dying flame he could manage to revive it. But there is no passage from my mouth to her life; she alone could make herself flame up again toward the light. Hélène! She still has a name, can I no longer call her by it? Her breath is rising with effort from her lungs to her lips; it goes back, grinding from her lips to her lungs; life gasps and labors, and yet she is still complete; she will be complete until the last moment; won't you use it for some other purpose than to die? Each beat of her heart brings her nearer to death. Stop. Inexorably, her heart continues to beat; when it no longer beats, she will already be dead, it will be too late. Stop at once, stop dying.

She opened her eyes and he took her in his arms. Those open eyes no longer saw. Hélène! She no longer heard. Something remains that is not yet absent to itself, but is already absent from the earth, absent from me. Those eyes still have a look, a frozen look, a look that no longer sees anything. The breathing stops. She has said: "I am glad that you are here; but I am not here; I know that something is happening, but I cannot watch it; it is not happening here or elsewhere, but beyond all presence." She breathes once more, the eyes cloud over; the world detaches itself from her, it crumbles; and yet she does not slide out of the world; it is in the heart of the world that she becomes the dead woman that I hold in my arms. A spasm draws down the corner of her lips. Her eyes see no more. He closes the lids over the lifeless eyes. Dear face, dear body. This was your forehead, these were your lips. You have left me; but I can still cherish your absence; it keeps your features; it is there, present in that motionless form. Stay, stay with me. . . .

He raised his head again. He must have remained for a long time with his forehead resting against her silent heart. That flesh which was you. He looked with anguish at the motionless face. It had not changed, but already it was no longer she. A relic, an effigy, no longer anyone. Now her absence has lost its shape, now she has finally glided out of the world. And the world is as full as yesterday; nothing is missing: there is no flaw. It does not seem possible. As if she had been nothing on this earth.

As if I were nothing. Nothing and everything; present to all mankind throughout the entire world, yet separated from them forever; as guilty and innocent as the pebble on the road. So heavy and yet so light.

He started. Someone was knocking. He walked toward the door.

"What is it?"

"I want your answer," said Laurent. He took a step forward and looked at the bed.

"Yes," said Blomart. "It is over."

"Did she suffer much?"

"No."

He looked at the window. The day had dawned. The minutes were calling the minutes, chasing, driving one another forward, without end. Go on, go on. Decide. Once more the bell tolls, it will toll until my death.

"The time-bomb can be laid within an hour from now," said Laurent. "Do you agree or not?"

He looked at the bed. For you, only an innocent stone — you had chosen. Those who will be shot tomorrow have not chosen; I am the rock that crushes them; I shall not escape the curse; forever I shall be to them another being, forever I shall be to them the blind force of fate, forever separated from them. But if only I use myself to defend that supreme good which makes innocent and vain all the stones and all the rocks, that good which saves each man from all the others and from myself — Liberty — then my passion will not have been in vain. You have not given me peace; but why should I desire peace? You have given me the courage to accept forever the risk and the anguish, to bear my crimes and my guilt, which will rend me eternally. There is no other way.

"Don't you agree?" said Laurent.

"Yes," he said. "I agree."

Index